MW01268889

THE SHAPING OF FRENCH
NATIONAL IDENTITY

The Shaping of French National Identity casts new light on the intellectual origins of the dominant and 'official' French nineteenth-century national narrative. Focusing on the historical debates taking place throughout the eighteenth century and during the Restoration, Matthew D'Auria evokes a time when the nation's origins were being questioned and discussed and when they acquired the meaning later enshrined in the official rhetoric of the Third Republic. He examines how French writers and scholars reshaped the myths, symbols, and memories of pre-modern communities. Engaging with the myth of 'our ancestors the Gauls' and its ideological triumph over the competing myth of 'our ancestors the Franks', this study explores the ways in which the struggle developed, and the values that the two discourses consecrated, the collective actors they portrayed, and the memories they evoked. D'Auria draws attention to the continuity between ethnic discourses and national narratives and to the competition between various groups in their claims to represent the nation and to define their past as the 'true' history of France.

MATTHEW D'AURIA is a lecturer in Modern European History at the University of East Anglia. His main research interest lies in the relationship between images of the nation and discourses about Europe. Among his many publications on this topic are, with Mark Hewitson (eds.), *Europe in Crisis: Intellectuals and the European Idea, 1917–1957* (Berghahn, 2012) and, with Jan Vermeiren (eds.), *Visions and Ideas of Europe During the First World War* (Routledge, 2019). He is currently coediting, with Cathie Carmichael and Aviel Roshwald, *The Cambridge History of Nationhood and Nationalism* (Cambridge University Press, forthcoming).

NEW STUDIES IN EUROPEAN HISTORY

Edited by
PETER BALDWIN, University of California, Los Angeles
CHRISTOPHER CLARK, University of Cambridge
JAMES B. COLLINS, Georgetown University
MIA RODRÍGUEZ-SALGADO, London School of Economics
and Political Science
LYNDAL ROPER, University of Oxford
TIMOTHY SNYDER, Yale University

The aim of this series in early modern and modern European history is to publish outstanding works of research, addressed to important themes across a wide geographical range, from southern and central Europe, to Scandinavia and Russia, from the time of the Renaissance to the present. As it develops the series will comprise focused works of wide contextual range and intellectual ambition.

A full list of titles published in the series can be found at:
www.cambridge.org/newstudiesineuropeanhistory

THE SHAPING OF FRENCH NATIONAL IDENTITY

Narrating the Nation's Past, 1715–1830

MATTHEW D'AURIA

University of East Anglia

CAMBRIDGE
UNIVERSITY PRESS

CAMBRIDGE
UNIVERSITY PRESS

University Printing House, Cambridge CB2 8BS, United Kingdom

One Liberty Plaza, 20th Floor, New York, NY 10006, USA

477 Williamstown Road, Port Melbourne, VIC 3207, Australia

314–321, 3rd Floor, Plot 3, Splendor Forum, Jasola District Centre,
New Delhi – 110025, India

79 Anson Road, #06–04/06, Singapore 079906

Cambridge University Press is part of the University of Cambridge.

It furthers the University's mission by disseminating knowledge in the pursuit of
education, learning, and research at the highest international levels of excellence.

www.cambridge.org
Information on this title: www.cambridge.org/9781107128095
DOI: 10.1017/9781316423189

First published 2020

A catalogue record for this publication is available from the British Library.

Library of Congress Cataloging-in-Publication Data
NAMES: D'Auria, Matthew, author.
TITLE: The Shaping of French National Identity : Narrating the Nation's Past, 1715–1830 /
Matthew D'Auria, University of East Anglia.
OTHER TITLES: Narrating the nation's past, 1715–1830
DESCRIPTION: Cambridge, United Kingdom ; New York, NY : Cambridge University Press,
2021. | Series: New studies in European history | Includes bibliographical references and index.
IDENTIFIERS: LCCN 2020028715 (print) | LCCN 2020028716 (ebook) | ISBN 9781107128095
(hardback) | ISBN 9781316423189 (ebook)
SUBJECTS: LCSH: National characteristics, French. | Group identity – France – History. |
Nationalism – France. | France – History – 18th century. | France – History – 1789–1815.
CLASSIFICATION: LCC DC34 .D35 2021 (print) | LCC DC34 (ebook) | DDC 944/.034–dc23
LC record available at https://lccn.loc.gov/2020028715
LC ebook record available at https://lccn.loc.gov/2020028716

ISBN 978-1-107-12809-5 Hardback

To my parents
For their loving care and their unwavering support

Contents

Acknowledgements

My interest in the history of nationhood and nationalism dates from my undergraduate years at the University of Naples, L'Orientale. While there, I had the pleasure and privilege of meeting Biagio De Giovanni. An intellectual historian and a historian of political thought, his modules on the history and politics of European integration had a lasting impact on me. It was thanks to him that I first read two books that would, in effect, shape my research interests up until today: Federico Chabod's *Storia dell'idea d'Europa* (1961) and *L'idea di nazione* (1961), both originally delivered as lectures at the University of Milan under Fascist and Nazi occupation. De Giovanni's supervision of a dissertation on ideas of nationhood in France and Germany during the French Revolution did much to determine the direction of my future research, concerned as it still is today with the interaction between images of the nation and visions of Europe. After graduating, and inspired by his teaching, I began work on a PhD project that would eventually become the basis of the present book. The research and writing of my doctorate would prove to be an extremely rewarding and fulfilling experience, and this largely thanks to my supervisor, Mark Hewitson. From Mark I learned most of what I know on how to conduct careful and rigorous historical research as well as how to teach. His influence has been profound, and I could not have hoped for a better mentor. Not only is he a rigorous and highly knowledgeable scholar but, equally important, he is a wonderful person – and with a great sense of humour too! It has been a pleasure working with him and my debt of gratitude goes well beyond his supervision. He is and will remain an example for me to follow in all respects. While completing my PhD, I had the good fortune to meet another key figure in my academic, intellectual, and personal path. Vittorio Dini, at that time Head of the School of Sociology and Political Science at the University of Salerno, is as learned as he is kind. A true gentleman, his interests and expertise range from the works of Machiavelli and Baltasar Gracián to those by Slavoj

Žižek. His knowledge is encyclopaedic, and I have always enjoyed (and, whenever possible, still enjoy) our conversations as well as the wonderful hospitality of his equally remarkable wife, Luciana Vecchio. From Vittorio, I have learned much about the history of political ideas. But I have also learned a great deal on a personal level. He has been and still is to me a teacher and, what is more important, a model I hope to follow in the future. My fourth and last mentor is Cathie Carmichael, who was Head of School when I joined the University of East Anglia (UEA) in 2014. Her support and her help have been immense. Our discussions of nationalism, nationhood, and national identity have profoundly influenced my own work. But, again, I have learned much more from her on a personal as well as on a professional plane. And when in need or doubt, I always cherish her wisdom and advice.

During the past few years, I have been lucky enough to encounter a number of scholars from whom I have learned much. A special thanks goes to Jan Vermeiren, whom I first met at University College London (UCL), when we both started our PhD with Mark. Our fruitful, often lively, and even heated discussions regarding nationhood and nationalism have greatly influenced my own ideas. Jan was kind enough to read and comment on certain sections of this book – and I thank him for that. Since meeting him, I have come to appreciate his great intelligence and extraordinary kindness, and I am glad to say that I have cemented a splendid friendship with him. It is a cause for great pleasure that I can work with him at the School of History at UEA. As for the latter, it has indeed proved to be a wonderful place to work. Besides Cathie and Jan, in fairness I would have to mention most of my colleagues and thank them for all their kindness. But a special thanks goes, first, to Richard Deswarte, whose friendship dates from before I joined UEA and whose support has been precious. Like Jan, he also took the trouble to read and comment on parts of the present book. His useful suggestions on the one hand, and his exceedingly strong coffees on the other, have always been very useful – and both have taken away much sleep. My gratitude also goes to Francis King for his morning chats (and strong coffees) and to Jayne Gifford for our late afternoon conversations (and a bit of gossip). I would also like to thank the School of History and the Faculty of the Humanities of UEA for their generous travel grants allowing much-needed periods of research in France.

There are many other friends and colleagues, from institutions scattered throughout Europe and even across the Atlantic, whom I would like to thank for the time they devoted to reading and commenting on earlier drafts or sections of this book: Danilo Breschi, Cécile Laborde, Avi Lifschitz, Rolando Minuti, Richard Whatmore, and Rolf Petri. Their advice has been precious and has surely helped to make this a much better book. And so have the comments of the anonymous reviewers for Cambridge University Press, whose remarks were always fair and unfailingly accurate. I have tried, insofar as I am able, to address their queries. I would also like to thank many other friends with whom, throughout the years, I have discussed the ideas in this book and whose comments have contributed, in various ways, to improving it – in some cases, without them even knowing: Francesco Amoretti, Alessandro Campi, Giuseppe Foscari, Fernanda Gallo, Aviel Roshwald, Adriano Vinale, and Michael Wintle. While everyone mentioned here and above has helped to improve the form and content of the present work, any remaining faults, distortions, and omissions are my responsibility alone.

Like any other historian, I also owe an immense debt to many university and public libraries for their resources and for the shelter from the outside world they offer a researcher. In my case, most of them are in Paris and London: the Bibliothèque Nationale, the Bibliothèque de l'Arsenal, the Bibliothèque de Saint-Geneviève, the Sciences-Po library, the library of the Centre Pompidou, and the library of the Sorbonne; the University College London library, the Senate House Library of the University of London, the library of the Warburg Institute, the library of the Institute for Historical Research, and the library of the London School of Economics. Other libraries to which I am indebted are those of the University of Salerno and the University of Parma, the Biblioteca Nazionale of Naples, the Biblioteca Nazionale of Potenza, and the Biblioteca Palatina in Parma. A special thanks goes to the library staff of the UEA and to its interlibrary lending team and, in particular, to Alison Dyer for her patience with all my requests, however unreasonable.

I would also like to thank Maureen Galvin and Wendy Toole for having proofread earlier versions of this work with great patience and care. Maureen's encouragement and her contagious enthusiasm, especially in the earlier phase, surely the most difficult one, truly made a difference. But I owe an immense debt to Martin Thom, who has extensively revised and proofread the present version of this book and has offered precious suggestions on how to improve not only its form but, equally if not even more importantly, its content. I would also like to express my thanks to Michael Watson, Liz Friend-Smith, Atifa Jiwa, and Natasha Whelan of Cambridge University Press, as well as Gayathri Tamilselvan and Nancy de Rozario from Integra-PDY for their patience, help, and support. Working with them has been a genuine pleasure.

I should acknowledge that a different version of Chapter 8, much shorter but with a by and large similar argument, has been published as 'From Royal to Bourgeois: Augustin Thierry's National Narrative', in Carolina Armenteros et al. (eds.), *Historicising the French Revolution* (Cambridge: Cambridge Scholarly Press, 2008).

A very special thanks goes to my wife, Laura Anzano. I could never put into words how important she has been to me and to my work. She has always believed in and encouraged me with incredible patience, and over so many years. Being with her has made my work so much easier. In a way, I must also thank our two children, Francesca (now four and a half years old) and Alessandro (now two and a half), who have been so very patient with me – though not as much as I am with them – and whose forgiveness I ask for all the times that writing this book has made it impossible for me to be with them. When Francesca would ask me, very kindly, to stop working and play with her or when Alessandro, very abruptly, would shut my laptop – sometimes, I feared it might be for good – mumbling 'close it' or 'that's enough', they would be reminding me what the important things in life are. It is a reminder that has been immensely beneficial to my well-being and that has given me much joy. My brother, Anthony, although he might not fully realise it, has also been extremely helpful in many ways, especially in times of need. And I thank him for being there. Finally, my greatest debt is to my parents for their unshakeable faith in me. They have supported me all my life with loving care. No son could have asked for more. I hope I will be as capable, supportive, and understanding with my own children in the years to come. Without my parents, this book would never have been possible, and it is to my mother and to the memory of my late father that I dedicate it.

Parma, 25ᵗʰ March 2020   MATTHEW D'AURIA

Note on Sources

For all works cited, I have used the version in the original language of publication. For collected works, I refer to the most accessible and popular edition (e.g. the Pléiade) or the most complete. Where possible, I have tried to use as few collected editions of the same author as is feasible. In the case of individual works, I have used either the latest scholarly edition or the first edition. I have retained the original spelling for all titles.

Introduction
Narrating the Nation – From the Nineteenth to the Eighteenth Century

It must have been with a mixture of pride and awe that in the latter years of the nineteenth century French children learned from their textbooks about the Battle of Tolbiac; of how Clovis lifted his hands to Heaven, promising God that if he were granted victory he would accept baptism, and how, the divine pact having worked, the Alamanni fled. Had those children delved deeper into their *Première année d'histoire de France*, their delight would certainly have been compounded when they read about King Pepin and his beheading of a lion and a bull with a single blow of his sword – a deed that, it is easy to suppose, many of those eight- and nine-year-olds mimicked, impersonating their king. No doubt they would have been equally impressed to learn from their textbook that, as her body was burned at the stake, the soul of Joan of Arc was miraculously borne up to Heaven by a white dove – the just reward for the sacrifices she had made for France and the Church.[1] These anecdotes, assured Ernest Lavisse, were *récits*, stories in which 'the true and the false are muddled up'. As their author declared, their purpose was to capture and hold the attention of young readers, showing how memorable personages and events were once portrayed.[2] Although there is no reason to doubt that this was one of the intentions, another, no less important aim was also being pursued. In the wake of Sedan and amid the calls for *la haine sacrée* to restore lost honour, Lavisse like many others strove to muster a narrative of an extraordinary nation to which all would be proud to belong. The *récits* were a key to a particular reading of the French past and, though kept separate from the main narrative, they offered a frame, one explicitly meant to glorify and eulogise – rather than describe or explain. Coupled with this was the firm conviction that the purpose of teaching history, or at least the nation's

---

[1] Ernest Lavisse, *La première année d'histoire de France* (Paris: Armand Colin, 1876), 12, 22, 125. On Lavisse, see Pierre Nora, 'L'"Histoire de France" de Lavisse', in Nora (ed.), *Les lieux de mémoire* (Paris: Gallimard, 1997), i. 851–90.
[2] Lavisse, *La première année d'histoire de France*, 22.

history, was that of moulding good and heroic citizen-soldiers. As Lavisse made clear in the preface:

> [F]or centuries on French soil have lived men who, through their deeds and their ideas, have contributed to a specific work [*œuvre*], to which each generation has contributed. We are working on it today and those after us will do the same. A link binds us to those who have lived and to those who will live on our land. Our ancestors are us in the past; our descendants are us in the future. To know about the work of our ancestors, to be proud of their successes and sad at their setbacks, ... to devoutly honour their illustrious memories, to think of the great examples to follow and the mistakes to avoid, therein lies true patriotism, and it is the purpose of school to teach it to one and all.[3]

More than others, Lavisse, the 'nation's teacher', fully grasped the importance of history and memory in shaping the national imaginary and in forming devout citizens – a task that the Third Republic made the hallmark of its education projects.[4] It was an aim to be achieved by appealing to the most intimate feelings, reawakening an allegedly natural empathy between present, past, and future generations. The affective aspect was crucial: 'Do not let us teach history with the calm befitting the teaching of rules of participles. At stake is the flesh of our flesh, the blood of our blood.'[5]

Between 1876 and 1950 the *petit Lavisse* ran through fifty editions and was read and studied by millions. While a continuous creation on which its author worked during the best part of his life, the underlying message and the image of the nation that went with it remained unchanged. Moreover, by repeating the same narrative and presenting the same *récits* – often through a book passed down from father to son and, in certain cases, to grandchildren – it contributed to the creation of a community that was imagined historically, binding generations that read and memorised the same story. Playing at once a representational and a performative role, the *petit Lavisse* both told a particular 'national history' and contributed to shaping a specific 'national memory'. In doing so, it undertook the unlikely task of reconciling the Revolution with the Old Regime, the secularism of the *République* with the Catholicism of the *fille aînée de l'Eglise*, the inviolable nature of regional diversity with the sacredness of state unity,

---

[3] Ibid., 'Préface', n.p.

[4] See the classic by Eugen Weber, *Peasants into Frenchmen: The Modernization of Rural France, 1870–1914* (Stanford: Stanford University Press, 1976), 303–38; Mona Ozouf, *L'école de la France: Essais sur la Révolution, l'utopie et l'enseignement* (Paris: Gallimard, 1984), 185–213.

[5] Ernest Lavisse, *Questions d'enseignement national* (Paris: Armand Colin, 1885), 210.

the Classical with the Romantic soul of France, its traditionalist with its liberal passions. Lavisse's narrative was called upon to resolve, in other words, a series of insurmountable antinomies into a coherent national narrative where the stories of the *Gesta dei per francos*, the glories of the Crusades, and the accomplishments of the *Grande nation* were but different moments of a 'single history'. Surprisingly, in his search for a thread uniting the many pasts into a single story, the solution embraced by Lavisse was simple: 'Our country was once called Gaul.'[6] It was a straightforward statement, placed at the opening of Chapter 1 and it mirrored, importantly, an untold and unquestioned assumption shared by most French men and women – one burdened, however, with significant consequences. The belief in a shared ethnic origin and a common Gallic past marked in fact the onset, and constituted the frame, of the nation's history, holding together divisions and chasms within a single narration. In Lavisse's book, the 'blissful clarity' of a mythical ethnic unity was ultimately what turned an array of pasts into a 'French' history.[7]

By the late 1830s, the notion of a Gallic origin of France had been widely accepted.[8] When in Honoré de Balzac's *Le cabinet des antiques* (1838) the old Marquis d'Esgrignon despondently admitted 'the triumph of the Gauls', he was acknowledging a real-life matter of fact.[9] By then, the idea that the Gauls were the ancestors of the modern French had turned into a banal assumption, an unquestioned cliché upon which rested the unity of the nation's history. The most prominent historians of the second half of the century embraced it. Jules Michelet began his *Histoire de France* (1831–1867) with the Gauls, pushing into the background Romans, Iberians, and Franks.[10] In his influential *Histoire de la France populaire* (1867–1875) Henri Martin made the 'character of the Gauls' the thread of his narrative on the assumption that 'their blood has passed, from generation to generation, into our own veins'.[11] By 1926, when Camille Jullian published the last volume of his monumental *Histoire de la Gaule*

---

[6] Lavisse, *La première année d'histoire de France*, 3. On this, see Étienne Bourdon, *La forge gauloise de la nation: Ernest Lavisse et la fabrique des ancêtres* (Lyons: ENS éditions, 2017).

[7] The expression is borrowed from Roland Barthes, *Mythologies* (Paris: Seuil, 1957), 230–1.

[8] See Eugen Weber, *My France: Politics, Culture, Myth* (Cambridge, Mass: Harvard University Press, 1991), 21–39, and Paul Viallaneix and Jean Erhard (eds.), *Nos ancêtres les Gaulois* (Clermont-Ferrand: Publications de la Faculté des lettres de Clermont II, 1982).

[9] Honoré de Balzac, *Le cabinet des antiques* (Paris: Garnier, 1958), 238.

[10] See Christian Croisille, 'Michelet et les Gaulois, ou Les séductions de la patrie celtique', in Viallaneix and Erhard (eds.), *Nos ancêtres les Gaulois*, 211–19.

[11] Henri Martin, *Historie de France populaire depuis les temps les plus reculés jusqu'à nos jours* (Paris: Furne, 1867–1885), i. 5.

(1914–1926), it had become a truism.[12] The myth was also popularised in successful historical novels. Thus, Eugène Sue's best-selling *Les mystères du peuple* (1849–1856) told the story of a family of proletarians across the centuries on the basis of a straightforward continuity between Gallic and French history. One important consequence of the diffusion of such a narration was that the past and its memory became a powerful tool of integration, fed by and feeding in its turn a nationalist rhetoric that contributed to defusing and containing social and political conflicts. Dreyfusards and anti-Dreyfusards, Boulangists and anti-Boulangists, socialists and conservatives all came to view themselves as part of one and the same nation for they shared a common origin – though, of course, in bitter conflict as to how France should be ruled. That proletarians and bourgeois had a common origin and, hence, the same past as in Sue's novel, helped to contain class conflict within the bounds of nationhood. And, in this sense, the 'failure of alternative memories' to contest the narrative espoused by Martin, Lavisse, and Jullian might arguably be the most important ideological achievement of the Third Republic.[13]

That French nationalism, as a mass phenomenon, took root during the Third Republic thanks to obligatory mass conscription, compulsory education, and the development of a centralised administration and of communication and transport, is widely accepted in the current literature – and rightly so. More controversial, however, are the ways in which the official rhetoric came into existence, and the role of the state in its shaping. In fact, until recently it has often been claimed that late nineteenth-century public authorities cloaked with an eternal, natural, and mystical aura the very modern and very mundane phenomenon of the nation and that it was largely to their efforts that the latter owed its deceptive antiquity. However, as this book will argue, things are more complex. Although the role of state institutions in advancing nationalism is indeed undeniable, to assume that the nationalist narrative, in the way it was told, essentially stemmed from the minds of politicians and bureaucrats is a misconception. This book is based on the idea, spelled out shortly, that the official national narrative of the Third Republic was built on a specific past, one of several, that throughout the long eighteenth century had been reshaped into

[12] See, Société des Amis de Jacob Spon (eds.), *Camille Jullian, l'histoire de la Gaule et le nationalisme français* (Lyons: Presses Universitaires de Lyon, 1991); also Claude Nicolet, *La fabrique d'une nation: La France entre Rome et les Germains* (Paris: Perrin, 2003), 226–43.
[13] The expression is taken from Philippe Joutard, 'Une passion française: L'histoire', in André Burguière and Jacques Revel (eds.), *Histoire de la France: Choix culturels et mémoire* (Paris: Seuil, 2000), 355.

a coherent narrative as a result of an intellectual, ideological, and political struggle. Central to this book is the contention that the roots of that narrative, later inculcated in millions of French men and women, were deeper than is often supposed. The narrative in question seemed convincing to contemporaries precisely because it was tied to the antiquity of the Gallic symbols, memories, and myths which it evoked. As its bedrock, these elements influenced profoundly the dominant nineteenth-century narrative and helped it to convey the emotionally laden image of a past defined within clear boundaries. Understanding the relationship between ethnic past(s) and the national narrative is crucial in grasping the true nature of modern French nationalism, shedding light on the causes of its strength and comprehending how it defined boundaries and established hierarchies. From such a standpoint, if we are to grasp just why the official national narrative took on the actual form it did and if we are to uncover the reasons for its sheer tenacity, attention needs to be drawn to the pre-existing complex of myths, traditions, and cultural imaginaries.

Gaining such a perspective, a key concern becomes the ways in which one narrative came to organise so effective a superimposition of the many French pasts; how, in other words, so many historians came unthinkingly to assume that the Gallic origins were the only possible canvas on which to sketch the nation's history. In actual fact, the self-explanatory principle that Lavisse so nonchalantly placed as the logical and chronological beginning of his history, far from having always been an undeniable truth, was on the contrary the outcome of a drawn-out intellectual and ideological struggle, a struggle that is precisely the subject of the following pages. A main concern of this book is to cast light on the intellectual origins of the dominant nineteenth-century national narrative by looking at how French antiquaries, philosophes, and historians conceived their national past throughout the eighteenth century and during the Restoration – that is, when those origins were being questioned and debated and when they acquired the meaning later enshrined in the history books and textbooks of the Third Republic. The present work engages with the myth of 'our ancestors the Gauls' – championed in different ways by Sieyès, Thierry, and Guizot – and studies its triumph over the competing myth of 'our ancestors the Franks' – promoted by Boulainvilliers, Montesquieu, and Montlosier. It explores how the struggle developed and the values that the two discourses enshrined, the collective actors they portrayed, and the memories they conjured up. Comparing and dissecting the two myths, *The Shaping of French National Identity* is a genealogy of the nineteenth-century French national narrative, of the hierarchies it shaped, and the ways in which its mechanisms of inclusion and exclusion worked. Moreover, it is an attempt to assess how one of two ethnic discourses developed into a full-blown national narrative based on an ethos of work and sacrifice – beautifully captured in the above quotations from the *petit Lavisse* – and capable of imposing itself as a national memory so effectively overlapping with the national history.

The Nation and Its Past(s)

Since the early 1980s, one of the most widespread approaches to the study of nations and nationalism has been that referred to as 'modernism', proposed, among others, by Eric Hobsbawm, Tom Nairn, Paul Brass, Ernest Gellner, John Breuilly, and Benedict Anderson.[14] While the theories of these authors do differ in many respects, they all share the guiding assumption that nation and nationalism are modern phenomena or, rather, are a consequence of modernity itself. Taking hold during the last two centuries, the invention of the nation should be understood, the above authors argue, as a response directed and controlled by a political and economic elite to the problems caused by industrialisation, urbanisation, the emergence of the bureaucratic state, and by secularism. That before these developments the nation, as such, did not exist would prove it to be an invention. The faith in the nation is what actually creates it; like the Feuerbachian delusion about God, 'nationalism comes before the nation'.[15] All these authors stress the constructed as opposed to the essentialist nature

---

[14] Eric Hobsbawm, *Nations and Nationalism since 1780: Programme, Myth, Reality* (Cambridge: Cambridge University Press, 1990); Tom Nairn, *The Break-up of Britain: Crisis and Neo-nationalism* (London: Verso, 1981); Paul R. Brass, *Ethnicity and Nationalism: Theory and Comparison* (London: Sage, 1991); Ernest Gellner, *Nations and Nationalism* (Oxford: Blackwell, 1983); John Breuilly, *Nationalism and the State* (Manchester: Manchester University Press, 1982); Benedict Anderson, *Imagined Communities: Reflections on the Origins and Spread of Nationalism* (London: Verso, 1983). On more recent debates regarding nationalism: Paul Lawrence, *Nationalism: History and Theory* (Harlow: Pearson, 2005); Anthony D. Smith, *Nationalism: Theory, Ideology, History* (Cambridge: Polity Press, 2010); Umut Özkirimli, *Theories of Nationalism: A Critical Introduction* (Basingstoke: Palgrave Macmillan, 2017); John Coakley, '"Primordialism" in Nationalism Studies: Theory or Ideology?', *Nations and Nationalism*, 24 (2018), 327–47; Alessandro Campi, Stefano De Luca, and Francesco Tuccari (eds.), *Nazione e nazionalismi: Teorie, interpretazioni, sfide attuali* (Rome: Historica, 2018). More recently there has been a growing interest in so-called 'neo-perennialism'. See: Aviel Roshwald, *The Endurance of Nationalism: Ancient Roots and Modern Dilemmas* (Cambridge: Cambridge University Press, 2006); Caspar Hirschi, *The Origins of Nationalism: An Alternative History from Ancient Rome to Early Modern Germany* (Cambridge: Cambridge University Press, 2012); Azar Gat, *Nations: The Long History and Deep Roots of Political Ethnicity and Nationalism* (Cambridge: Cambridge University Press, 2013).

[15] Hobsbawm, *Nations and Nationalism*, 10.

of the nation which, however real in its consequences, is either 'imagined' or 'invented'. Consistently, they also maintain that the nation's past is constructed or, as Hobsbawm and Ranger argue, it is an 'invented tradition'.[16] This the two authors define as a set of practices of a ritual or symbolic nature 'which inculcate certain values and norms of behaviour by repetition, thereby automatically implying continuity with the past'.[17] It is to hide its novelty and to show itself as a permanent fact that the nation establishes an incontestable continuity with the past, making of history 'a legitimator of action and cement of group cohesion'.[18] Articulating a view that has long been widely accepted, Hobsbawm and Ranger's argument was in part a response – a legitimate one – to the perennialists' thesis regarding nationhood. For the latter had considered the nation to be a fixed entity, unchanging over the centuries except on the surface. Viewed from this angle, modernism indubitably represents a step forward in grasping the true nature of the nation, challenging those unproblematic histories from antiquity to the present day that were once so common.[19]

Despite its remarkable merits, however, the modernist approach has been criticised for several reasons. A first issue is the impossibility of defining a workable concept of modernity.[20] The difficulty in grasping its main traits or even understanding when modernity actually starts are problems overlooked by these authors, who consequently fail to explain why nationalism arises in deeply religious or in under-industrialised countries. A second limit derives from the underlying functionalist premises which lead authors like Gellner to explain nationalism through its effects on society, so that the consequences seemingly precede the causes. By such a token, the extraordinary strength of nationalism remains unaccounted for.[21] If the faith in the nation were the outcome of a manipulation intended to recreate an impossible *Gemeinschaft* now lost to modernity, this would not explain its success and why the nationalist delusion moves so many to sacrifice so much. Anderson's idea that a community is an

---

[16] Eric Hobsbawm and Terence Ranger, 'Introduction: Inventing Tradition', in Hobsbawm and Ranger (eds.), *The Invention of Tradition* (Cambridge: Cambridge University Press, 1983), 1–14.

[17] Ibid., 1.   [18] Ibid., 12. On the point, see Özkirimli, *Theories of Nationalism*, 116–20.

[19] See Colette Beaune, *Naissance de la nation France* (Paris: Gallimard, 1985), and Liah Greenfeld, *Nationalism: Five Roads to Modernity* (Cambridge, Mass: Harvard University Press, 1992), 89–188.

[20] See the arguments in Shmuel N. Eisenstadt (ed.), *Multiple Modernities* (New Brunswick: Transaction, 2002).

[21] On this point, Brendan O'Leary, 'On the nature of Nationalism: An Appraisal of Ernest Gellner's Writings on Nationalism', *British Journal of Political Science*, 27 (1997), 191–222.

'imagined' bond tying to one another individuals who have never met surely captures a fundamental aspect of what is at stake, and, in his study, he offers a useful list of the ways in which identification with the community takes place. Yet little is said of its strength. Imagining that two persons who have never met feel a special bond because they read the same newspaper, obey the same laws, or use the same currency cannot explain why the one might be willing to give his or her life for the other. Without clarifying this, modernism makes it difficult, if not altogether impossible, to tell the nation apart from other, no less imagined communities – an intellectual necessity that, it might be ventured, modernism itself creates.

Arguably, the strength of nationalism is its most salient aspect. Recently, Italian historian Alberto Mario Banti has tried to explain its success by building on the modernist approach and borrowing from and readapting the thesis of George Mosse. Banti claims that the capacity of nationalism to affect millions of individuals so deeply is connected to the fact that it appeals to what he calls 'deep images': basic, primeval emotions that belong to man as such. Analysing nationalistic rhetoric in nineteenth-century Italy, England, France, and Germany, Banti finds it constantly and invariably appealing to the same deep-seated affective constellations: honour, sacrifice, virility, the sanctity of the nation as a great family, a common ancestry and, most importantly for us, a common past. It is because of their nature that such appeals may move a person to sacrifice everything she or he has.[22] Focusing on novels, poetry, and plays as vehicles of nationalism, the merit of Banti's work lies in considering the emotional aspect central in grasping the causes of its strength. In part, *The Shaping of French National Identity* confirms the importance such images had in shaping French nationalist feelings as far back as the early years of the eighteenth century. Appeals to the family of the nation, to sacrifices made in the name of the *patrie*, to a common ancestry, and to a sacred past, all emerge time and time again in the discourses we will examine – if used in different ways by the various discursive and social groups. And yet, illuminating though it may be, Banti's use of 'deep images' remains problematic. In fact, by considering these the exclusive key for analysing nationalism and by defining a set

[22] Alberto Mario Banti, *La nazione del Risorgimento: Parentela, santità e onore alle origini dell'Italia unita* (Turin: Einaudi, 2000); Alberto Mario Banti, *L'onore della nazione: Identità sessuali e violenza nel nazionalismo europeo dal XVIII secolo alla Grande Guerra* (Turin: Einaudi, 2005); Alberto Mario Banti, *Sublime madre nostra: La nazione italiana dal Risorgimento al fascismo* (Rome: Laterza, 2011); Alberto Mario Banti, 'Conclusions: Performative Effects and "Deep Images" in National Discourse', in Laurence Cole (ed.), *Different Paths to the Nation: Regional and National Identities in Central Europe and Italy, 1830–1870* (London: Palgrave, 2007), 220–9.

of basic emotions common to all men in all ages, it becomes difficult to properly understand how national boundaries are conceived and how processes of inclusion and exclusion actually take place. Furthermore, one would be hard-pressed to explain how nations set themselves apart one from the other. In effect, Banti's is an ethnographic explanation of nationalism and, as such, it inevitably blurs the differences between various nationalist discourses.[23] Partly as a consequence of this, insisting on the constructed nature of national pasts, Banti, like other modernists, leaves unsolved the riddle of why a specific myth might appeal to some but not to others. Since at the centre of his study he places novels, operas, and plays – assuredly another great merit – the question is why, given that deep images are shared by all men and women, an empathic bond is established between the characters of a novel or a play and only some of its readership or audience – but not others.

One solution to the shortcomings of the modernist argument and to Banti's version of it might lie in Anthony D. Smith's ethno-symbolic approach, an approach usually overlooked by professional historians – with a few notable exceptions – in spite of the advantages it offers to the study of the history of nationhood and nationalism.[24] The ethno-symbolic point of departure is that the nation is a social phenomenon sustained and shaped by pre-existing myths, symbols, memories, and values shared by a pre-modern community. This is referred to as *ethnie*, a term that connotes a community with a 'proper collective name', a 'myth of common ancestry', 'shared collective memories', one or more 'differentiating elements of common culture', an association with a 'specific homeland', and, finally, a 'sense of solidarity for significant sectors of the population'.[25]

---

[23] On Banti's views, see Lucy Riall, 'Nation, "Deep Images" and the Problem of Emotions', *Nations and Nationalism*, 15 (2009), 402–9; Axel Körner, 'The Risorgimento's Literary Canon and the Aesthetics of Reception: Some Methodological Considerations', *Nations and Nationalism*, 15 (2009), 410–18; John Breuilly, 'Risorgimento Nationalism in the Light of General Debates about Nationalism', *Nations and Nationalism*, 15 (2009), 439–45; Matthew D'Auria, 'Risorgimento addio? Alcune riflessioni sulla "nazione italiana" di Alberto Mario Banti', *Rivista di politica*, 2 (2011), 17–30.

[24] Among the exceptions, for example, Adrian Hastings, *The Construction of Nationhood: Ethnicity, Religion and Nationalism* (Cambridge: Cambridge University Press, 1999); Colin Kidd makes a fleeting reference to ethno-symbolism in his *Subverting Scotland's Past: Scottish Whig Historians and the Creation of an Anglo-British Identity, 1689–c. 1830* (Cambridge: Cambridge University Press, 1993), 10.

[25] Anthony D. Smith, *The Ethnic Origins of Nations* (Oxford: Blackwell, 1986), 21–46; Anthony D. Smith, *National Identity* (Reno: University of Nevada Press, 1991), 19–42. Also see John Hutchinson, *Modern Nationalism* (London: Fontana Press, 1994); Anthony D. Smith, *The Cultural Foundations of Nations: Hierarchy, Covenant and Republic* (Malden: Blackwell, 2008); Anthony D. Smith, *Ethno-symbolism and Nationalism: A Cultural Approach* (London: Routledge,

The cultural nucleus of the *ethnie* is located in an articulation of myths, values, and symbols that the members of the group endeavour to preserve and pass on to succeeding generations. Like all cultural and social phenomena, the nation and the attachment to it are clearly constructed – and yet they are not constructed in a void. Shaped in response to external stimuli or internal struggles, national symbols and values are built, for Smith, around the *ethnie*. Accordingly, at play is a superimposition of several subsequent layers of social representations, the later ones readapting in complex, unpredictable, and often conflicting ways the previous ones. So, rather than a fixed entity, the nation should be viewed as a continuous process, a historical construction operating, however, within parameters set by 'culture and traditions'. It is for this reason that the nation can only be grasped in the *longue durée* since changes, gradual or sudden, take place within longer timespans than would be the case with other cultural phenomena, owing to the resistance offered by ethnic values, memories, and myths.[26] A sort of corrective to the constructivism of the modernists, the emphasis is here on the constraints and the limitations set by existing cultural beliefs and practices to elite understanding and strategies so that, as one pioneer of this approach, John Armstrong, has claimed, the formation of nations cannot be understood without giving due weight to their ethnic forebears.[27] Consistently with such a standpoint, ethno-symbolism assumes that nations are historical constructions in a dual sense. On the one hand, they are built up over long timespans, 'embedded in collective pasts' and embodying shared memories, hopes, and traditions. On the other, they emerge 'through specific historical processes' that end up influencing the previous understandings of the past.[28] Shared by *The Shaping of French National Identity*, the ethno-symbolists' postulate of

2009). For an appraisal of ethno-symbolism see Montserrat Guibernau and John Hutchinson (eds.), *History and National Destiny: Ethnosymbolism and its Critics* (Oxford: Blackwell, 2004). Also see Jonathan Hearn, 'Power, Culture, Identity, and the Work of Anthony Smith', *Nations and Nationalism*, 24 (2018), 286–91. Smith's notion of *ethnie* is clearly indebted to the vast anthropological literature on ethnicity. On the latter, see the seminal essays in Fredrik Barth (eds.), *Ethnic Groups and Boundaries: The Social Organization of Culture Difference* (Bergen: Universitetsforlaget, 1969). Also see T. H. Eriksen, *Ethnicity and Nationalism: Anthropological Perspectives* (London: Pluto Press, 2010), and Stephen Spencer, *Race and Ethnicity: Culture, Identity and Representation* (London: Routledge, 2006).

[26] Smith, *Nationalism*, 22–3.
[27] John A. Armstrong, *Nations before Nationalism* (Chapel Hill: University of North Carolina Press, 1982), 4; also see Hutchinson, *Modern Nationalism*, 7.
[28] Anthony D. Smith, *Myths and Memories of the Nation* (Oxford: Oxford University Press, 1999), 10. Also see: Anthony D. Smith, *The Nation in History: Historiographical Debates about Ethnicity and Nationalism* (Cambridge: Polity Press, 2000), 52–77; John A. Armstrong, 'Definitions, Periodization, and Prospects of the *longue durée*', in Guibernau and Hutchinson (eds.), *History*

a 'double historicity' brings into focus the complexity of the relationship between ethnic and national myths and memories, recognising their different roles and their different weights in shaping collective pasts.

Historians and the Making of National Narratives

The ethno-symbolists' emphasis on the idea of a 'double historicity' allows us to better appreciate the fundamental role played by historians, philosophers, and publicists in readapting and reshaping collective memories and brings to the fore their crucial role in creating a national narrative.[29] Central to this book, the latter notion is here taken to mean an intelligible concatenation of allegedly real events that chronologically follow one another and are tied together by virtue of some sort of causal relationship. Like all narratives, it has a clear beginning – for the nation, a mythical or even miraculous origin – a main body, and a conclusion, the latter being usually located, in the case of national narratives, in a luminous future. A continuous social and symbolic construction, a national narrative inevitably creates boundaries through the selection of what is admitted into it, a process that, at least from the ethno-symbolic perspective, is carried out on the corresponding complex of ethnic myths and memories. By setting such boundaries, a national narrative poses itself as a frame within which the meaning of the event itself is shaped and constitutes, at the same time, the *dramatis personae* moving within that frame.

One other fundamental element is necessary to our definition of national narrative. According to Hayden White, as a sense-making activity, narrating always has a moral purpose, and though this might not invariably be true, it surely is in the case of national narratives. It emerges clearly in

and National Destiny, 9–18; Walker Connor, 'The Timelessness of Nations', in Guibernau and Hutchinson (eds.), *History and National Destiny*, 35–47.

[29] The ensuing definition is based on a conflation of the ideas of various authors working on the relationship between history and narration. "For an overview on the concept of 'historical narrative'", see Alun Munslow, *Narrative and History* (Basingstoke: Palgrave, 2007). Also see Hayden White, *The Content of the Form: Narrative Discourse and Historical Representation* (Baltimore: Johns Hopkins University Press, 1990); David Carr, *Time, Narrative and History* (Bloomington: Indiana University Press, 1986); Sarah Maza, 'Stories in History: Cultural Narratives in Recent Works in European History', *The American Historical Review*, 101 (1996), 1493–515; Paul Ricœur, *La mémoire, l'histoire, l'oubli* (Paris: Seuil, 2000). On the idea of national narrative, see Homi Bhabha (ed.), *Nation and Narration* (London: Routledge, 1990). Also see the essays in Stefan Berger, Linas Eriksonas, and Andrew Mycock (eds.), *Narrating the Nation: Representations in History, Media, and the Arts* (New York: Berghahn, 2008), and Joep Leerssen, 'Setting the Scene for National History', in Stefan Berger and Chris Lorenz (eds.), *Nationalizing the Past: Historians as Nation Builders in Modern Europe* (Basingstoke: Palgrave Macmillan, 2010), 71–85.

the *petit Lavisse* where the discernible ethical purpose of telling the nation's story is to form good citizens and soldiers. Such a function is fulfilled by dint of the narrative's empathic strength, its capacity to forge a bond between the actors and the narrative's recipients – who consequently come to see themselves as part of a historical community. In the history books of the Third Republic – but the same holds true, as we shall see, for many eighteenth-century texts – the empathic bond derived its strength from Banti's deep images. References to the great family of the nation, to its sacredness, to its antiquity, and, most important of all, to past sacrifices made for the sake of the nation – including, that is, the narrative's recipients – served to cement an empathic bond between present and past generations by appealing to men's and women's deepest emotions. At the same time, the reference to ethnic pasts, myths, and memories in the defining of the boundaries of the narrative itself offers a key to how processes of inclusion and exclusion – who is moved by what – actually took place. In this respect, and in spite of their ostensible differences, the yoking together of Banti's thesis and Smith's approach would seem to be highly promising.

The above definition helps us to better grasp the peculiar nature of national narratives as a 'living past', as a narration, that is, midway between history and memory. The relationship between the latter two notions, relevant to this book, is also crucial to one of the most important works on French identity, itself an inevitable starting point for any understanding of national narratives. In the introduction to his monumental *Les lieux de mémoire*, Pierre Nora follows a distinction made by Maurice Halbwachs and draws a clear contrast between history, the learned construction and deconstruction of the past, and memory, the unreflective, mythical, emotional, and often patently wrong perception of a living past: 'Memory is life, borne by living societies founded in its name', a perpetual phenomenon 'tying us to the eternal present'. History, in contrast, is a 'representation of the past', separated by an unbridgeable distance from its observer. It is an 'intellectual and secular' construction, demanding unremitting, cold analysis and criticism. While memory, according to Nora, 'instils remembrance within the sacred, history, always prosaic, releases it again'.[30] Importantly, such an opposition appears to be a relatively recent phenomenon, dating back to the 1930s. In fact, according

---

[30] Pierre Nora, 'Entre mémoire et histoire: La problématique des lieux', in Nora (ed.), *Les lieux de mémoire*, i. 24–5. The English translation has been published as 'Between Memory and History: *Les lieux de mémoire*', *Representations*, 26 (1989), 7–24.

to the editor of *Les lieux de mémoire*, between Augustin Thierry's 1827 *Lettres sur l'histoire de France* and Charles Seignobos's *Histoire sincère de la nation française*, published in 1933, French history had been predominantly conceived as a means for remembrance and a way of making the past live once again in the present. During this timespan, a sort of 'tradition of memory' was fostered, so that between history, memory, and the nation there was a 'natural circularity', a 'symbiosis on all levels, scientific and pedagogic, theoretical and practical'.[31] Thanks to what became a sacred history, the memory of the French could rest on solid foundations. In the 1930s, the breaking up of this symbiosis led to a disenchanted national history incapable of educating, in the civic and patriotic sense, young French men and women – or so argues Nora. History had turned into a social science and memory into a private affair: 'The memory-nation was thus the last incarnation of the unification of history and memory,' Nora dejectedly admits. The eradication of the *milieux de mémoire* left behind those *lieux de mémoire* where historians now had perforce to seek the traces of a lost memory.[32]

Although the impact and the importance of *Les lieux de mémoire* can hardly be overstated, it has nonetheless received much criticism.[33] One of the main shortcomings is Nora's tacit but clear assumption of a single, unproblematic narrative not only indicating how the French past should be viewed, but also hinting at what the French future should be.[34] Nora is thus caught in the toils of that grand narrative whose demise he has himself announced, finally depicting the history of a seemingly timeless nation. In this respect, the parallel drawn by some critics between Nora and Lavisse – revealingly, one of his favourite authors – would seem only too apt.[35] If such a remark is useful insofar as it sheds light on Nora's standpoint, it does not detract from his other merits. There is, in particular, one aspect of

---

[31] Nora, 'Entre mémoire et histoire', 29.   [32] Ibid., 23.

[33] On *Les lieux de mémoire*, see Jean-Paul Willaime, 'De la sacralisation de la France: *Lieux de mémoire* et imaginaire national', *Archives des sciences sociales des religions*, 66 (1988), 125–45; Steven Englund, 'The Ghost of Nation Past', *The Journal of Modern History*, 64 (1992), 299–320; Marie-Claire Lavabre, 'Usages du passé, usages de la mémoire', *Revue française de science politique*, 44 (1994), 480–93; François Hartog, 'Temps et histoire: "Comment écrire l'histoire de France?"', *Annales: Histoire, sciences sociales*, 50 (1995), 1219–36; Ben Mercer, 'The Moral Rearmament of France: Pierre Nora, Memory, and the Crises of Republicanism', *French Politics, Culture and Society*, 31 (Summer 2013), 102–16. Also see François Dosse, *Pierre Nora: Homo historicus* (Paris: Perrin, 2011), 327–37 and 349–60.

[34] See Stefan Berger and Chris Lorenz, 'Introduction: National History Writing in Europe in a Global Age', in Berger and Lorenz (eds.), *The Contested Nation: Ethnicity, Class, Religion and Gender in National Histories* (Basingstoke: Palgrave Macmillan, 2008), 16.

[35] Englund, 'The Ghost of Nation Past', 301–2. See also Pierre Nora, 'Pourquoi lire Lavisse aujourd'hui?', in Nora, *Présent, nation, mémoire* (Paris: Gallimard, 2011), 193–204.

interest to our argument: the relationship between national memory and national history and the crucial role of historians in shaping it.[36] In his distinction between the two truth-claims embodied in memory and history, Nora contrasts, on the one hand, a past sacred, untouchable, appealing to the deepest emotions of men and women and nurturing the patriotic virtues necessary for a society to exist; and on the other, an idea of the past as an object of enquiry that must be explained, desacralised by the historian who can analyse the nation and the emotions attached to it only by stepping outside the nation-memory and unmasking its secrets, breaking the spell that confounds national history and national memory.

Of course, useful though Nora's distinction may be, we need to ask ourselves whether one way of representing the past can subsist without the other, if the two operate on distinct but related planes or even, as Paul Ricœur has suggested, whether memory inexorably remains the guardian of all ways of conceiving the relationship between present and past.[37] What is clear is that in his crucial role in shaping the nation's identity, a historian might, in different ways and to varying degrees, help to either sacralise or to desacralise the national past.[38] Like Lavisse and many other historians of the Third Republic, he might endlessly tell the story of a single nation, from its origins to the present, establishing a clear and unproblematic continuity – and an identity – of the present with the past. It would be a narrative in which the 'others' of the past are part of an imagined historical community: 'Our ancestors are us in the past; our descendants are us in the future', as Lavisse had it. So conceived, a national narrative might command 'the sacrifice of one's life' in the name of a 'legendary imaginary', working 'as an engine of integration, cohesion, and social promotion'.[39] Yet a historian might desacralise one version of the nation's past by exposing its secrets and proving it false. In the latter case he or she might offer his or her own version, which would have an impact not only on the way national history is understood but also on the way national memory is felt. He or she might, in other words, offer a counter-history contributing to an alternative image of the nation and its memory. Clearly,

---

[36] See Pierre Nora, 'Mémoire de l'histoire, mémoire de l'historien', in Nora, *Présent, nation, mémoire*, 306–23.

[37] Ricœur, *La mémoire, l'histoire, l'oubli*, 106; Roger Chartier, *Au bord de la falaise: L'histoire entre certitudes et inquiétude* (Paris: Albin Michel, 2009), 353–6.

[38] On this point, see also J. G. A. Pocock, 'The Politics of History: The Subaltern and the Subversive', in Pocock, *Political Thought and History: Essays on Theory and Method* (Cambridge: Cambridge University Press, 2009), 239–56.

[39] Pierre Nora, 'Introduction: Les trois pôles de la conscience historique contemporaine', in Nora, *Présent, nation, mémoire*, 20.

then, while in principle we might accept a distinction between two ways of representing the past – a national memory that creates an empathic bond with the past and a national history that might thin down that tie – it should be stressed not only that the two actually interact in complex and unpredictable ways but, moreover, that a different national memory might arise from a new understanding of the past. This book tries to bring to light the complex interaction between these two modes of representation, showing how out of the intellectual and ideological struggle over the nation's origins stemmed the symbiosis between memory and history Nora has argued for – and which, as we shall see, depended, to no small extent, on the 'Gallic triumph'.

Shaping a 'French' Past

It is consistently with the assumptions expounded above that the framework of *The Shaping of French National Identity* is set and its timespan established. Our starting point is the early eighteenth century, when the issue of the nation's origins acquired new significance. Several factors were in play, not least the greater political freedom of the French in the wake of the Regency and a growing intellectual liberty nurtured and nurturing public debate. The complex cultural, social, and intellectual changes this entailed – on which, following Jürgen Habermas's work on the bourgeois public sphere, much has been written – also and inevitably affected the way the past was imagined and scrutinised as well as its role in the ongoing political disputes.[40] Partly as a result, by the second half of the century historical arguments had turned into weapons in the ideological arsenal of politicians and pamphleteers.[41] Entwined with these transformations was the spread of a different understanding of what the study of the nation's history had been and what it should be. Authors such as Fréret,

[40] On the eighteenth-century emergence of a public sphere and public opinion, the literature is almost endless. Besides the classic works by Jürgen Habermas, *Strukturwandel der Öffentlichkeit: Untersuchungen zu einer Kategorie der bürgerlichen Gesellschaft* (Berlin: Luchterhand, 1962) and Reinhart Koselleck, *Kritik und Krise: Eine Studie zur Pathogenese der bürgerlichen Welt* (Freiburg: Alber, 1959). Also see: Mona Ozouf, '"Public Opinion" at the End of the Old Regime', *The Journal of Modern History* – *Supplement: Rethinking French Politics in 1788*, 60 (1988), S1–S21; Roger Chartier, *Les origines culturelles de la Révolution française* (Paris: Seuil, 1990), 32–52; Keith M. Baker, 'Public Opinion as Political Invention', in Baker, *Inventing the French Revolution* (Cambridge: Cambridge University Press, 1990), 167–99.
[41] On this, see for example Keith M. Baker, 'Memory and Practice: Politics and the Representation of the Past in Eighteenth-Century France', in Baker, *Inventing the French Revolution*, 31–85, and Stanley Mellon, *The Political Uses of History: A Study of Historians in the French Restoration* (Stanford: Stanford University Press, 1958).

Boulainvilliers, and, later on, Montesquieu, Voltaire, d'Alembert, and Mably complained about those all-monarchical histories that portrayed the nation's past as the illustrious deeds of kings and their entourages. The royalist paradigm, that 'structural constraint' of national historiography, became one of the main targets of the *histoires critiques* as well as the *histoires philosophiques*, many of them calling for a shift of focus on to the customs, usages, and traditions of the people and the overcoming of the political and legalistic paradigm by which the nation's narrative had been framed. It was largely as a consequence of their search for the deeper reasons underlying the history of laws and politics that many eighteenth-century philosophers and historians paved the way for a cultural and anthropological perspective in the study of history that brought to light the cultural and ethnic origins of the nation.[42]

Our timeframe ends with the 1830s, when the notion of the Gallic origins of France had become a tacit assumption and when, according to Nora, a substantial coincidence of national memory and national history was first experienced. There are of course many remarkable books on how, from the latter part of the nineteenth century onwards, the French imagined their past. Suzanne Citron's *Le mythe national* and the works by Christian Amalvi, Robert Gildea, and Claude Nicolet are admirable examples. Martin Thom, with his excellent *Republics, Nations and Tribes*, and Joep Leerssen even tackle directly the relationship with ethnicity.[43] However, indispensable as they are for shedding light on the nature of French identity, all of these works analyse how the national past was conceived at a time when the Gallic discourse had already developed into the dominant narrative; they focus, in other words, on an uncontested narration that presented itself as the only possible one – as Lavisse would

---

[42] Henri Duranton, 'Les contraintes structurales de l'histoire de France: Le cas Pharamond', *Synthesis*, 4 (1977), 153–64. On this aspect of the *histoires philosophiques*, see Hugh Trevor-Roper, 'The Historical Philosophy of the Enlightenment', in Trevor-Roper, *History and the Enlightenment* (New Haven: Yale University Press, 2010), 1–16; J. G. A. Pocock, *Barbarism and Religion. Volume 1: The Enlightenments of Edward Gibbon, 1737–1764* (Cambridge: Cambridge University Press, 1999), 167–207; J. G. A. Pocock, *Barbarism and Religion. Volume 2: Narratives of Civil Government* (Cambridge: Cambridge University Press, 1999), 7–25. The shift from the legalistic and political to the cultural and anthropological paradigm is also stressed by Michel Foucault who, however, misleadingly equates ethnicity with race: Michel Foucault, *Il faut défendre la société: Cours au Collège de France. 1976* (Paris: Seuil, 1997).

[43] Suzanne Citron, *Le mythe national: L'histoire de France rivisitée* (Paris: Les Éditions de l'Atelier, 2008); Christian Amalvi, *De l'art et de la manière d'accommoder les héros de l'histoire de France* (Paris: Albin Michel, 1988); Robert Gildea, *The Past in French History* (New Haven: Yale University Press, 1996); Nicolet, *La fabrique d'une nation*, passim; Martin Thom, *Republics, Nations and Tribes* (London: Verso, 1995); Joep Leerssen, 'Nation and Ethnicity', in Berger and Lorenz (eds.), *The Contested Nation*, 75–103.

have presumed when writing his textbooks. Inevitably, the crucial passage from competing ethnic discourses to a single national narrative is partly lost and its far-reaching consequences are overlooked. As this book will attempt to show, illuminating the political, intellectual, and symbolic struggle over the origins of the nation before then is instead crucial for grasping the nature of nineteenth- and twentieth-century French nationalism.

Compared to the many studies on nineteenth-century French national identity, there are as yet only a few books focusing on the eighteenth century – not least because of the still widely held view that the French attachment to the nation was essentially a by-product of the Revolution.[44] Among the latest works are the remarkably well-documented *Un nouveau patriotisme français, 1750–1770*, in which Edmond Dziembowski argues for an increasing attachment to the nation during the Seven Years War which, thanks to a growing reading public eager for news of battles at land and sea, cemented the feeling of unity of the French against the British. Building on Marcel Gauchet's 'disenchantment of the world', in his outstanding *The Cult of the Nation*, David Bell focuses instead on the importance of the distancing of the mundane from the extramundane and considers secularisation as the cornerstone of modern French nationalism. The latter, argues Bell, partly grew out of and in opposition to Catholicism, developing into a lay religion of modernity. For his part, Jay Smith has analysed the debates on the nature and role of the aristocracy taking place under the pressure from the rising bourgeoisie on the one hand and the growing self-criticism of the nobles on the other. Smith contends that this twofold movement finally led to radical disagreements on who represented the nation and its interests.[45]

[44] One such work is John Breuilly (ed.), *Oxford Handbook of the History of Nationalism* (Oxford: Oxford University Press, 2013); this volume has great virtues but the point of departure of almost every chapter is 1789. Another influential example is Otto Dann and John Dinwiddy (eds.), *Nationalism in the Age of the French Revolution* (London: Hambledon Press, 1988). More recent cases are Derek Hastings, *Nationalism in Modern Europe: Politics, Identity and Belonging since the French Revolution* (London: Bloomsbury Academic, 2017) and, this one limited to France, Chimène I. Keither, *The Paradoxes of Nationalism: The French Revolution and its Meaning for Contemporary Nation Building* (Albany: State University of New York Press, 2007). For an interesting discussion and a more nuanced stance, see David A. Bell, 'Revolutionary France and the Origins of Nationalism: An Old Problem Revisited', in Lotte Jensen (ed.), *The Roots of Nationalism: National Identity Formation in Early Modern Europe, 1600–1815* (Amsterdam: Amsterdam University Press, 2016), 67–83.
[45] Edmond Dziembowski, *Un nouveau patriotisme français, 1750–1770: La France face à la puissance anglaise à l'époque de la guerre de Sept Ans* (Oxford: Voltaire Foundation, 1998); David A. Bell, *The Cult of the Nation: Inventing Nationalism, 1680–1800* (Cambridge, Mass: Harvard University Press, 2001); Jay M. Smith, *Nobility Reimagined: The Patriotic Nation in Eighteenth-Century France* (Ithaca: Cornell University Press, 2005). Earlier works on eighteenth-century French national identity include Durand Echeverria, *The Maupeou Revolution: A Study in the History of Libertarianism* (Baton Rouge: Louisiana State University Press, 1985), and Peter Sahlins, *Boundaries: The Making of France and Spain in the Pyrenees* (Berkeley: University of California Press, 1989). For these and other earlier

Following Hobsbawm, Gellner, and Anderson, these authors concentrate on a specific feature of modernity – the emergence and consolidation of a wide reading public, disenchantment with religion, and the rise of the bourgeoisie – to explain French nationalist feelings before the Revolution. Espousing a modernist perspective, they tend to emphasise the radical rift with what came before. All such works deserve high praise and have indisputably contributed to a better understanding of the changing attitudes towards the nation before the Revolution – and we shall often refer to them throughout this book. Yet our standpoint is different. Rather than establishing a cause–effect relationship between a single social, economic or cultural shift and the advent and spread of nationalism, the present book recognises that changes tied to multifaceted processes of modernisation created the conditions for the proliferation of competing visions of the nation's past by freeing intellectual, cultural, and social energies. Rather than identifying a specific cause, the focus here is on the pre-existing symbols and myths and on how these influenced the reshaping of ethnic pasts into national narratives. We will examine in depth continuities and changes in alternative representations of the French past, focusing on the interaction between ethnic and national discourses. On the one hand, attention will be paid to the *continuity* between *ethnic groups* and national narratives; on the other hand, the focus will be on the *competition* between different *ethnic groups* in their claim to represent the nation and have a past that coincided with the 'true' history of France.

While adopting a different perspective than Dziembowski, Bell, and Jay Smith's, one questioning modernism and its assumptions, this book is essentially meant to integrate the content of their respective studies. In fact, it does not offer an overarching theory of the birth and origins of French nationalism as such. Rather, and in a more limited fashion, it seeks to shed new light on the way the French understood their national past and on the intellectual roots of the Third Republic's official narrative. It is almost inevitable for any study of national identity to hinge on either an external or an internal dimension. Focusing on the first means to consider how the attachment to a nation is influenced and shaped in contrast to representations and images of other political, social, or cultural entities – usually other nations. Focusing on the second requires instead assigning a more prominent role to the struggle between different groups to control state

works, see David A. Bell, 'Recent Works on Early Modern French National Identity', *The Journal of Modern History*, 68 (1996), 84–113.

and societal resources by claiming to represent the nation's interests. Evidently, the two dimensions are closely linked; and yet it is often useful to tackle them separately. The external dimension, so prominent in Dziembowski's work, will ostensibly play a limited role here. So, for example, the question of Anglophobia will only be considered fleetingly. This is not to say that it is unimportant to our overall understanding of French nationhood and nationalism but, rather, that it was of relatively limited importance in the historical debates over the nation's origins and, consequently, in the way the French understood their national past in the eighteenth, and early nineteenth century. The external dimension will emerge as part of that struggle for this was in some measure a contest of a transnational nature centring, as it did, on explaining the Germanic, Frankish, Gallic, or Roman elements forming the identity of the French people.

By contrast with Bell's fundamental book on feelings of nationhood and the rise of nationalism in the eighteenth century, the space devoted to religion will here be more limited. In part, this is because most of the discourses central to our work were couched in anti-absolutist terms and, in most cases, were built in tacit or explicit contrast to that identification of king and nation for which religion was so important. Many of our authors, combating the abuses of royal authority, accorded relatively little space to the story of Clovis's baptism or to the role of the *sacre* in cementing the nation.[46] After all, Boulainvilliers and Montesquieu, two of the most important authors in this book, were accused of Spinozism – which, at that time, amounted to irreligiosity. Perhaps surprisingly, even authors supporting the royalist cause, such as the abbé Dubos, did not insist on the sacred tie between the Christian God and the kings of France – as royalists, indeed, would have done in the previous century – but, rather, set forth legal reasonings merged with more modern social and cultural arguments. It would be rash to see in this a shift from Bossuet's world to Voltaire's, to use Eric Voegelin's famous wording. In truth, the eighteenth century remained deeply religious, even though differences between social groups and classes were noteworthy.[47] From

---

[46] The literature, on this, is almost endless. For a good overview, see René Rémond, 'La fille aînée de l'Eglise', in Nora (ed.), *Les lieux de mémoire*, iii. 4321–51. On the *sacre*, see Marina Valensise, 'Le sacre du roi: Stratégie symbolique et doctrine politique de la monarchie française', *Annales: Histoire, sciences sociales*, 41 (1986), 543–77.

[47] See Derek Beales, 'Religion and Culture', in Tim Blanning (ed.), *The Short Oxford History of Europe: The Eighteenth Century, Europe 1660–1815* (Oxford: Oxford University Press, 2000), 131–77, and, with a focus on the relationship between politics and religion, Michael Schaich, 'Introduction', in Schaich (ed.), *Monarchy and Religion: The Transformation of Royal Culture in Eighteenth-Century*

a different angle, as Dale Van Kley argued some time ago, in his now classic *The Religious Origins of the French Revolution*, the consequences of religious conflict tormenting early-modern France had profound political consequences.[48] Some religious movements even contributed to the rise of new ideas of the nation. The case of Jansenism is the most glaring.[49] However, if one were to take the works of its most important political exponent, Louis-Adrien Le Paige – and we will do so briefly in Chapter 6 – the arguments elaborated there would be found to be still essentially legalistic. They failed to highlight the connection between political practices and cultural beliefs that, as this book will show, was central to eighteenth- and early nineteenth-century debates over the nation's origins. Religion will instead feature prominently when discussing the rhetoric of sacrifice espoused by the nobility and the rising middle classes as a form of sacralisation of the nation.

In terms of content, it is perhaps with the book by Jay Smith that the present work has the greatest affinity. Although it focuses on the way the nation's past was interpreted and understood and accords far more space to the rise of the middle classes, it shares with Smith's study a concern with the claims to represent the nation made by the different and competing political and social groups. The latter, by no means a secondary point, brings us to the notion of representation, key to all political debates of the ancient regime and, consequently, also to this book. A protean concept, the term had at least three different meanings. It could indicate, following Roman law, the fact of being vested with authority by someone to express their will. It could, alternatively, refer to the act of making present, visible, what was absent, in the same way that a painting or a statue might represent a person.[50] Finally, stemming from Christian dogma, the term could also indicate an act through which a multitude became one, as the faithful became a single Church in the body of Christ. These three meanings were clearly related to one another and, as Keith Baker has pointed out, all of them were central to the ideology of royal absolutism. The idea that the king was the representative of God implied ruling over

---

Europe (Oxford: Oxford University Press, 2007), 1–11. See also Eric Voegelin, 'The Emergence of Secularized History: Bossuet and Voltaire', in Voegelin, *From Enlightenment to Revolution* (Durham, NC: Duke University Press, 1975), 11.

[48] Dale K. Van Kley, *The Religious Origins of the French Revolution: From Calvin to the Civil Constitution, 1560–1791* (New Haven: Yale University Press, 1996).

[49] Catherine Maire, *De la cause de Dieu à la cause de la nation: Le jansénisme XVIIIème siècle* (Paris: Gallimard, 1998), and Van Kley, *The Religious Origins of the French Revolution*, especially 249–302.

[50] Antoine Furetière, *Dictionnaire universel* (The Hague and Rotterdam: Arnout & Reinier Leers, 1690), s.v. 'représentation'.

the nation in His name. At the same time, by giving visibility to the nation, his person mystically united the multitude of his subjects. So, maintaining that the 'king represents the entire nation, and each individual represents but a single individual towards the king', Louis XIV was stating that the nation could not exist independently from his body for he was the only tie uniting a country divided by different customs, dialects, and by competing social and political groups pursuing their own interests.[51]

It is plausible to assume that because of the gradual erosion of monarchical legitimacy – referred to by some as the 'desacralisation of the monarchy' – this form of representation from above, somehow Hobbesian in nature, gradually subsided as the eighteenth century advanced, making it possible for other actors to contend for the role of representatives of the nation.[52] What is certain is that when the famous journalist and lawyer, Simon-Nicolas-Henri Linguet, complained in the 1770s that 'the king calls himself the nation; the parliaments call themselves the nation; the nobility calls itself the nation; only the nation is unable to say what it is, or even if it is', he was aptly describing the uncertainties caused by the many competing parties claiming to represent France.[53] What Linguet was less aware of was that such a fight was inexorably entangled with the one over who embodied the nation's history, of who represented its past. The point to take, here, is that the struggle for legitimacy was played out on grounds that were historiographical as much as political. In their claims to 'be', 'embody' or 'represent' the nation, social and political groups strove to redefine and reimagine their own past to make it stand for the nation's. Replacing the king as the representative of France also implied supplanting that royal genealogy standing as the nation's history. And, of course, the two main ethnic groups, the Gallic and the Frankish, with their myths and memories shaped by centuries of real legal and political divisions were, to many, the only credible contenders.

---

[51] Quoted in Pierre Édouard Lemontey, *Essai sur l'établissement monarchique de Louis XIV* (Paris: Déterville, 1818), 327.

[52] Keith M. Baker, 'Representation Redefined', in Baker, *Inventing the French Revolution*, 224–51. On the notion of 'desacralisation', Jeffrey Merrick, *The Desacralization of the French Monarchy in the Eighteenth Century* (Baton Rouge: Louisiana State University Press, 1990) and Chartier, *Les origines culturelles de la Révolution française*, 138–66. For a good theoretical overview, see Lucien Jaume, *Hobbes et l'État représentatif moderne* (Paris: Presses universitaires de France, 1986).

[53] Simon-Nicolas-Henri Linguet, 'Tableau de l'état politique actuel du globe', in *Mélanges de politique et de littérature* (Bouillon: n.p., 1778), 13.

Distinctions: Races, National Characters, and Classes

The Shaping of French National Identity is a work of intellectual history focusing on the scholars, historians, philosophers, and thinkers in whose workshops new ideas about the French nation and its past were forged. The purpose is to emphasise the importance of intellectual production as a crucial building block of national imaginaries, delving more deeply into the intellectual roots of nationalism. Of course, like any other approach, even this is partial. But the aim is not to offer an all-encompassing explanation of nineteenth-century French national narratives and even less so of French nationalism as such but, rather, to call attention to the complex relationship between the shaping of alternative versions of the French national past on the one hand, and claims to political legitimacy on the other.

The book is divided into three parts and nine chapters. With the aim of responding to the concerns laid out earlier, all parts mirror the same structure.

In the first chapter of each part – Chapters 1, 4, and 7 – a single concept is situated within the political, social, scientific or economic debates it was part of and analysed in relation to the way the nation's past was understood. The choice of the three notions – race, national character, and class – is, of course, not haphazard. All of them played a pivotal role in the way the French saw themselves on what many would now see as the threshold of modernity, and all were central to the struggle between the two ethnic discourses over who represented the nation. Attention will be drawn to the fact that both race and class were not construed as abstract political or social concepts. In most instances, on the contrary, their defining entwined with emotionally laden discourses, shaping the contours of historical actors endowed with an alleged identity, a memory, and a character of their own – then made to coincide with the nation's as a whole. When referring to social groups, the terms 'race' and 'class' were associated with myths and memories of sacrifices and examples of self-abnegation that were necessary to define their group identity and substantiate their claim to embody the nation while nourishing that empathic bond so central to national narratives. In this complex interplay of representations and identifications, the idea of national character became instrumental, connoting as it did the unvarying nature of a group deemed to carry the original traits of a now decaying or oppressed France. It provided, in this respect, a sort of guiding thread to a group's history that, importantly, was destined to become the frame of the nation's own narrative. Condensing several of the elements of the complex of symbols and memories of the descendants of the Franks or the descendants of the Gauls, national/group character thus became essential in the struggle over political legitimacy – a point often underplayed or neglected altogether. Consequently, the two ethnic discourses gradually ended up superimposing the claims of the 'heroic' nobles, who had cemented the nation with their blood, and of the 'industrious' bourgeoisie, who had built France with their toil and sacrifices.

The second chapter of each part – Chapters 2, 5, and 8 – investigates the contributions made by the Count de Boulainvilliers, the Baron de Montesquieu, and Augustin Thierry to the meaning of each notion. The selection of these authors is based on a twofold principle. On the one hand, each had a central role in defining our three notions, especially as regards the way the nation's history was understood. On the other, their ideas on race, national character, and class left a profound mark upon the debate over the origins of France, granting them a crucial role in the opposition between the Gallic and the Frankish theses. Of course, the political implications of their writings will be analysed in depth. However, since the study of the past – then just as today – was motivated by a myriad of considerations which were not only, or even mainly, political, it is necessary to also consider other motives. The daunting task of understanding where political concerns end and intellectual preoccupations start is by no means a matter of mere academic curiosity or of textual philology. Asking what authors 'did' with their texts in order to comprehend 'the relationship in which a writer stands to what he or she has written', as Quentin Skinner has constantly urged intellectual historians to do, helps to explain the responses to them and, consequently, sheds light on the way a specific discourse developed.[54] In this respect, political concerns cannot be separated from other motives unless at the risk of lapsing into old categorisations or, perhaps even worse, into the cliché of the 'use of the past'. This is particularly true in the cases of Boulainvilliers, Montesquieu, and Thierry, often and too simplistically made out to be an advocate of the *noblesse d'épée*, a supporter of the *noblesse de robe*, and a champion of the *bourgeoisie* respectively. On the contrary, as will be argued, intellectual and methodological concerns were central to their writings. Following in the footsteps of

[54] Quentin Skinner, 'Motives, Intentions and Interpretation', in Skinner, *Visions of Politics. 1: Regarding Method* (Cambridge: Cambridge University Press, 2002), 96. On these aspects of Skinner's ideas, see J. G. A. Pocock, 'Quentin Skinner: The History of Politics and the Politics of History', *Common Knowledge*, 10 (2004), 532–50, and Kari Palonen, *Quentin Skinner: History, Politics, Rhetoric* (Cambridge: Polity Press, 2003), 29–60.

Bayle, Fontenelle, and Simon, they all called for a more disenchanted, critical, and searching approach to the study of the past and all insisted, importantly for us, on the necessity of a shift from an outdated legalistic and political to a new anthropological and cultural paradigm in studying the nation's past.[55]

The last chapter of each part – Chapters 3, 6, and 9 – assesses the ways in which the works of Boulainvilliers, Montesquieu, and Thierry were used and reinterpreted by others in the debate on the origins of France.[56] Attention is paid to two specific aspects, both crucial for the eighteenth- and early nineteenth-century intellectual historian. The first is the importance of debates in shaping political and intellectual languages. These are taken to be the sites where discourses were shaped and crystallised and ideas were negotiated, rejected, appropriated, and distorted; but also where complex texts were made accessible, albeit often by misrepresentation, to a wider readership, entering larger discussions and influencing in intricate ways the reading public.[57] Precisely because of this, debates were also the setting for interactions and contests between established cultural beliefs and intellectual arguments supporting or, more often and intriguingly, challenging them. Therefore, by concentrating on the way debates developed it becomes possible to grasp the fluidity of viewpoints interacting and

[55] On eighteenth-century discussions over the need for a more critical approach to the study of the past, see Carlo Borghero, *La certezza e la storia: Cartesianesimo, pirronismo e conoscenza storica* (Milan: Franco Angeli, 1983); Phyllis K. Leffler, 'The "Histoire raisonnée", 1660–1720: A Pre-Enlightenment Genre', *Journal of the History of Ideas*, 37 (1976), 219–40; Mouza Raskolnikoff, *Histoire romaine et critique historique dans l'Europe des Lumières* (Rome: École française de Rome, 1992); Chantal Grell, *L'histoire entre érudition et philosophie: Étude sur la connaissance historique à l'âge des Lumières* (Paris: Presses universitaires de France, 1993).

[56] On the debate, Jacques Barzun, *The French Race: Theories of its Origins and their Social and Political Implications* (New York: Columbia University Press, 1932); Elie Carcassonne, *Montesquieu et le problème de la constitution française au XVIIIᵉ siècle* (Geneva: Slatkine, 1978); Catherine Volpilhac-Auger, *Tacite en France de Montesquieu à Chateaubriand* (Oxford: Voltaire Foundation, 1993); Nicolet, *La fabrique d'une nation*, passim; Krzysztof Pomian, 'Francs et Gaulois', in Nora (ed.), *Les lieux de mémoire*, ii. 2245–300; Jacques de Saint-Victor, *Les racines de la liberté: Le débat français oublié, 1689–1789* (Paris: Perrin, 2007).

[57] On the importance accorded to debates in the field of intellectual history, see Antoine Lilti, 'Querelles et controverses: Les formes du désaccord intellectuel à l'époque moderne', *Mil neuf cent: Revue d'histoire intellectuelle*, 25 (2007), 13–28, and Jean-Louis Fabiani, 'Disputes, polémiques et controverses dans les mondes intellectuels: Vers une sociologie historique des formes de débat agonistique', *Mil neuf cent: Revue d'histoire intellectuelle*, 25 (2007), 45–60; Jeanne-Marie Hostiou and Alain Viala (eds.), *Le temps des querelles*, special issue of *Littératures classiques*, 81 (2013/2); Alexis Tadié (ed.), *Theories of Quarrels*, special issue of *Paragraph*, 40 (2017); Jeanne-Marie Hostiou and Alexis Tadié (eds.), *Querelles et création en Europe à l'époque moderne* (Paris: Garnier, 2019). Also see Judith Schlanger, *L'enjeu et le débat: Les passés intellectuels* (Paris: Denoël-Gonthier, 1979), 7–17.

competing, bringing to light the discursive nature of 'essentially contested concepts' such as race, national character, and class.[58]

However, there is at least one other reason why debates are a privileged vantage point for historians and that is because, through them, certainties and dominant viewpoints lost their sacred aura – and this holds true whether these were refuted or supported by explanations and reasoning that, inevitably, demystified them. More specifically, in our case, the growing disenchantment with the royalist national narrative, encouraged by an 'historiographical operation' turned into a discursive practice, was partly a consequence of the increasing number of *gens de lettres*, historians, and pamphleteers taking part in the debate on the nation's most intimate secret, dissecting and scrutinising its origins.[59] This is all the more relevant since the debate we will concentrate on concerned nothing less than the 'true nature' of France, of its beginning and consequently – at least for the eighteenth-century frame of mind – of its entire history. In fact, as Antoine Furetière's famous dictionary confirms, the term 'origin' also meant at the time 'the cause of an effect' so that in it lay the explanation of everything that came after.[60] The origins of France were the place where the very reasons for its laws, customs, institutions, and character had to be sought. Because it carried within itself the history yet to come, properly understanding the founding moment of France was crucial.[61] Debating the nation's origins, understanding Gallic customs or the Frankish character or which Roman laws the Germans accepted as their own was in effect an inquiry into the nature of modern France, one that had a profound impact on the legitimacy of its institutions and on the way its identity was conceived. It was a debate that, ultimately, offered answers to the emotionally charged issue of where the collective 'us' came from and, in the mind of many, offered answers to what its future should be.

---

[58] On this point, see the famous essay by W. B. Gallie, 'Essentially Contested Concepts', *Proceedings of the Aristotelian Society*, 56 (1956), 167–98.

[59] The notion of 'historiographical operation' is borrowed and readapted from Michel de Certeau, *L'écriture de l'histoire* (Paris: Gallimard, 1975), 63–120.

[60] Furetière, *Dictionnaire universel*, s.v. 'origine'. On this ambiguity, Marc Bloch, *Apologie pour l'histoire, ou Le métier d'historien* (Paris: Armand Colin, 1997), 53–4.

[61] See Michel Foucault, *Les mots et les choses: Une archéologie des sciences humaines* (Paris: Gallimard, 1966), 339–40, and Bronisław Baczko, *Rousseau: Solitude et communauté* (Paris: Mouton, 1974), 60–70. Also see Chantal Grell and Christian Michel (eds.), *Primitivisme et mythe des origines dans la France des Lumières (1680–1820)* (Paris: Presses universitaires de la Sorbonne, 1989); Claudine Poulouin, *Le temps des origines: L'Eden, le Déluge et 'les temps reculés' de Pascal à L'Encyclopédie* (Paris: Honoré Champion, 1998); Christophe Martin (ed.), *Fictions de l'origine (1650–1800)* (Paris: Desjonquères, 2012). With an emphasis on French national narratives and myths of origin, see André Burguière, 'L'historiographie des origines de la France: Genèse d'un imaginaire national', *Annales: Histoire, sciences sociales*, 58 (2003), 41–62.

PART I

CHAPTER I

Race, Blood, and Lineage
The Nobility's National Narrative and the History of France

Eighteenth-Century Notions of Race

In April 1684, the traveller, diplomat, and essayist François Bernier (1625–1688) published anonymously in the *Journal des sçavans* his 'Nouvelle division de la terre, par les différentes espèces ou races d'hommes qui l'habitent'. He there made the case that although geographers had always divided the earth into countries and regions, thanks to his travels he now believed that another kind of mapping was possible:

> For although men are almost all different from one another as far as the external form of their bodies is concerned, especially their faces, according to the different areas of the world they live in, and while they differ so clearly that people who have travelled widely can thus often distinguish unerringly one nation from another, nevertheless I have observed that there are, in all, four or five types or races among men whose distinctive traits are so obvious that they can justifiably serve as the basis of a new division of the earth.[1]

In his judgement, Europeans, sub-Saharan Africans, Asians, and Sami were four separate and clearly differentiated races. Within these groups, minor physical differences, such as those usually supposed to be national traits, were deemed irrelevant. Bernier's categories were so broad that, for example, he saw the Indians as akin to the peoples of Europe: although they 'have something that makes them rather different from us', such as the

---

[1] [François Bernier], 'Nouvelle division de la terre, par les différentes espèces ou races d'hommes qui l'habitent, envoyée par un fameux voyageur à M. l'abbé de la *** à peu près en ces termes', *Le journal des sçavans*, 24 April 1684, 133–4. On Bernier, see Siep Stuurman, 'François Bernier and the Invention of Racial Classification', *History Workshop Journal*, 50 (2000), 1–21; Pierre H. Boulle, 'François Bernier and the Origins of the Modern Concept of Race', in Sue Peabody and Tyler Stovall (eds.), *The Color of Liberty: Histories of Race in France* (Durham, NC: Duke University Press, 2003), 11–27; Bruce David Baum, *The Rise and Fall of the Caucasian Race: A Political History of Racial Identity* (New York: New York University Press, 2006), 50–6; Nicholas Dew, *Orientalism in Louis XIV's France* (Oxford: Oxford University Press, 2009), 131–67, and Joan-Pau Rubiés, 'Race, Climate and Civilization in the Works of François Bernier', in Marie Fourcade and Ines G. Zupanov (eds.), *L'Inde des Lumières: Discours, histoire, savoirs (XVIIᵉ–XIXᵉ siècle)* (Paris: Purusartha, 2013), 13–38.

shape of their face or the colour of their skin, 'this does not seem enough to make of them a species apart', he noted. If differences such as these were taken into account when defining a race, then 'it would be necessary to make one also of the Spanish, another of the Germans, and so forth for several other peoples of Europe'.[2] Curiously, after making the point, Bernier embarked on a long discussion about the qualities of the women of each race, offering the reader abundant remarks on their beauty and devoting almost half of his essay to a topic that was seemingly beside the point.[3]

Notwithstanding the triviality and inconsistencies of some of the arguments, for several reasons Bernier's approach stood as a new way of classifying the peoples of the earth. That he used a few, very large groups marked a major difference with previous taxonomies. In his essay, one would not find the long and complex listings of the characteristics of national or tribal groups so common in the accounts of other European travellers. Bernier understood races to be the largest possible classes into which humanity could be divided. This being the case, each race would inevitably include peoples who differed from one another in many ways. One other important novelty was his decision wholly to detach his arguments from any religious concerns. The narrative elaborated by Bernier might even be considered an alternative to the biblical account that had all peoples descend from Noah and his sons and explained differences between races on such a basis.[4] Although Bernier did not openly contradict or contest such a notion – still widely accepted at the time – his taxonomy was not founded on the Scriptures. This lack of interest in pre-Adamite theories, whether to refute or confirm them, is striking, and indicative of a new attitude towards man, his world, and his relationship with God.[5] However, despite the importance of these elements, the originality of the

---

[2] [Bernier], 'Nouvelle division de la terre', 134–5. In passing, it is worth noting that Bernier's views were consistent with the increasingly influential thesis that saw central-south Asia as the mythical 'homeland' of the peoples of Europe, and which would eventually lead to Indo-European linguistic and Aryan race theories.

[3] An explanation is in Giuliano Gliozzi, *Adamo e il Nuovo Mondo: La nascita dell'antropologia come ideologia coloniale, dalle genealogie bibliche alle teorie razziali, 1500–1700* (Florence: La Nuova Italia, 1977), 603–4.

[4] Benjamin Braude, 'The Sons of Noah and the Construction of Ethnic and Geographical Identities in the Medieval and Early Modern Periods', *The William and Mary Quarterly*, 54 (1997), 103–42.

[5] See Stuurman, 'François Bernier and the Invention of Racial Classification', 11–12. On the relationship between early modern and modern views about race and the Scriptures, see Colin Kidd, *The Forging of Races: Race and Scripture in the Protestant Atlantic World, 1600–2000* (Cambridge: Cambridge University Press, 2006). Also see the classics by Léon Poliakov, *Le mythe aryen: Essai sur les sources du racisme et des nationalismes* (Paris: Calmann-Lévy, 1971), 125–9, and Gliozzi, *Adamo e il Nuovo Mondo*, passim.

'Nouvelle division de la terre' may in fact lie elsewhere. As Justin E. H. Smith has recently argued, Bernier's was in fact one of the first works in which physical characteristics were closely tied to races and these, in turn, to specific regions of the world.[6] It was an assumption built on two tenets. The first was that physical differences, rather than customs, mores, and languages, should be the sole criterion used to define a race. This was another radical break with previous taxonomies, Bernier having opted to define races by fixed and unalterable traits.[7] In fact, stating that races were not a matter of habits, mores, or religion, all of which a person might acquire or change throughout his life, denied the possibility of passing from one group to another. Here, races had far more rigid boundaries than ever before.[8] This was a crucial and dangerous innovation, but the second tenet was no less important. In the 'Nouvelle division de la terre', external characters were treated as a fact of nature and, as such, no actual explanation was offered for their formation. Climate or other geographical factors, which were still widely used in the eighteenth century to account for customs and institutions as well as physical differences, were of relatively limited importance.[9] Crucially, in Bernier's text, races seemed to be a fact to be observed, described, and classified. They simply were a fact of nature and, as such, they had no history.

The 'Nouvelle division de la terre' is usually thought of as one of the very first works in which the modern usage of 'race' features. Bernier's work is thus seen as having given rise to a long sequence of texts, books, and pamphlets dividing humanity through physical traits and culminating in modern racial theories.[10] While there is some truth in such a notion, it

[6] Justin E. H. Smith, *Nature, Human Nature, and Human Difference: Race in Early Modern Philosophy* (Princeton: Princeton University Press, 2015), 148.
[7] Margaret T. Hodgen, *Early Anthropology in the Sixteenth and Seventeenth Centuries* (Philadelphia: University of Pennsylvania Press, 1964), 213–14.
[8] Elsa Dorlin, *La matrice de la race: Généalogie sexuelle et coloniale de la nation française* (Paris: la Découverte, 2006), 215.
[9] We shall return to eighteenth-century debates regarding the effects of climate on a people's character and history in Chapter 5.
[10] See, for example, Paul Lester, 'L'anthropologie et la paléontologie humaine', in Maurice Daumas (ed.), *Histoire de la science* (Paris: Gallimard, 1957), 1354; Poliakov, *Le mythe aryen*, 138–9; Tzvetan Todorov, *Nous et les autres: La réflexion française sur la diversité humaine* (Paris: Seuil, 1989), 119; Boulle, 'François Bernier and the Origins of the Modern Concept of Race', passim; Stuurman, 'François Bernier and the Invention of Racial Classification', passim. Against such a view, see Thierry Hoquet, 'Biologization of Race and Racialization of the Human: Bernier, Buffon, Linnaeus', in Nicolas Bancel, Thomas David, and Dominic Thomas (eds.), *The Invention of Race: Scientific and Popular Representations* (New York: Routledge, 2014), 19–21, and Claude-Olivier Doron, *L'homme altéré: Races et dégénérescence, XVIIᵉ–XIXᵉ siècles* (Ceyzérieu: Champ Vallon, 2016), 429–33.

stands in need of qualification. As we have seen, Bernier did indeed believe
that races ought to be divided according to physical traits entirely determined by nature and, as such, unalterable. However, while this tenet
would later become the lynchpin of modern scientific racialism, differences
with nineteenth- and early twentieth-century conceptions of race are
noteworthy. For one, Bernier did not openly infer a hierarchy of races.
Although he lingered over the beauty of each race, he refrained from
explicitly declaring the superiority of one kind over another. Moreover,
and importantly, Bernier posited no correlation between physical characteristics and inner qualities, between physical traits and a person's intellectual or moral worth – something that others would soon do.[11] Considering
the content of his text, Bernier's contribution to the shaping of modern
racialism was in fact rather limited. The same might be said when considering its actual circulation. Although a slightly amended version was
republished in 1722, in eighteenth-century scholarly debates there were
few references to the 'Nouvelle division de la terre'.[12] It was only due to
fortuitous circumstances that it had an impact on *De generis humani
varietate nativa* (1775), the great work by Hans Blumenbach (1752–1840),
who may have mistakenly regarded a short text summarising Bernier's
views as containing the original insights of Gottfried Wilhelm Leibniz
(1646–1716).[13] The importance of the 'Nouvelle division de la terre' needs
to be sought elsewhere – not in its impact but, rather, in the fact that it
illustrates the emergence of a new attitude towards the study of man.
Indeed, Bernier's work testifies to an increasing preoccupation with understanding the world by means of new and more dispassionate approaches to
ordering and classifying its complexity. It is revealing of a taxonomic
compulsion that would take hold of the eighteenth century and shape
the nascent sciences of man in the mould of the natural sciences.[14] Driven

---

[11] See Claude Blanckaert, 'Les vicissitudes de l'angle facial et les débuts de la craniométrie (1765–1875)',
    Revue de synthèse, 108 (1987), 417–53, and David Bindman, *Ape to Apollo: Aesthetics and the Idea of
    Race in the Eighteenth Century* (London: Reaktion, 2002), especially 23–78.
[12] François Bernier, 'Nouvelle division de la terre, par les différentes espèces ou races d'hommes qui
    l'habitent, de la beauté des femmes, etc.', *Mercure de France*, December 1722, 62–70. This time,
    Bernier was cited as the author.
[13] This interesting claim is made by Smith, *Nature, Human Nature, and Human Difference*, 156–8. The
    text misconstrued by Blumenbach was Gottfried Wilhelm Leibniz's 'Pars altera, complectens
    meditationes, observationes et crises varias leibnitianas, gallico et latino sermone expressas, xvliii',
    in *Otium Hanoveranum, sive, Miscellanea, ex ore et schedis illustris viri, piæ memoriæ, Godofr. Gvileilmi
    Leibnitii* (Leipzig: Christiani Martini, 1718), 37–8.
[14] Foucault, *Les mots et les choses*, especially 137–76. Also see Edward Said, *Orientalism* (New York:
    Pantheon Books, 1978), 119–20, and Dorinda Outram, *The Enlightenment* (Cambridge: Cambridge
    University Press, 2005), 68–9. On the birth of the 'sciences of man' in the eighteenth century, see the
    classic by Georges Gusdorf, *L'avènement des sciences humaines au siècle des lumières* (Paris: Payot,

by such a passion, Voltaire (1694–1778), Denis Diderot (1713–1784), the Baron d'Holbach (1723–1789), and, more influentially, the Count de Buffon (1707–1788) and Jean-Baptiste de Lamarck (1744–1829) all divided men into races on the basis of external traits – and thus contributed to laying down the foundations of modern anthropology. In the German-speaking world, Immanuel Kant (1724–1804) and Blumenbach, and in England, Joseph Banks (1743–1820), all made important contributions.[15] Undeniably, theirs were momentous steps in man's understanding of his own world. However, it was often the case that entrenched prejudices about the Other and the new scientific – or pseudoscientific – frame of mind came to be tightly joined together. The consequences were deleterious since reason does not always dispel prejudice and may indeed serve to strengthen it. In this respect, there is an important difference between the comments made by Bernard Le Bovier de Fontenelle (1657–1757) when, in the late seventeenth century, he compared Africans to monkeys and those by Voltaire when, some years later, he made the same juxtaposition but adopted a more 'scientific' approach.[16]

Although the Age of Enlightenment has often been seen as the cradle of modern scientific racialism, the differences with later racial theories are in fact worthy of note.[17] Indeed, most eighteenth-century scholars were well

---

1973). Also see Sergio Moravia, *La scienza dell'uomo nel Settecento* (Bari: Laterza, 2000); Claude Blanckaert, 'La science de l'homme entre humanité et inhumanité', in Blanckaert (ed.), *Des sciences contre l'homme, Volume 1: Classer, hiérarchiser, exclure* (Paris: Autrement, 1993), 14–45; Christopher Fox, Roy Porter, and Robert Wokler (eds.), *Inventing Human Science: Eighteenth-Century Domains* (Berkeley: University of California Press, 1995); Anthony Pagden, *The Enlightenment and Why it Still Matters* (Oxford: Oxford University Press, 2013), 125–67.

[15] For an overview, see Larry Wolff and Marco Cipolloni (eds.), *The Anthropology of the Enlightenment* (Stanford: Stanford University Press, 2007). Also see Robert Wokler, 'Anthropology and Conjectural History in the Enlightenment', in Fox, Porter, and Wokler (eds.), *Inventing Human Science*, 31–52. For France, see the classic by Michèle Duchet, *Anthropologie et histoire au siècle des Lumières* (Paris: Albin Michel, 1995).

[16] Bernard de Fontenelle, 'Lettres galantes de M. le Chevalier d'Her***' (1683), in *Œuvres complètes* (Paris: Fayard, 1989–), i. 355; François-Marie Arouet Voltaire, 'Traité de métaphysique' (1734), in *Œuvres complètes* (Paris: Garnier, 1877–1885), xxii. 191 and 210.

[17] The claim was put forward, among others, by György Lukács, *Die Zerstörung der Vernunft: Der Weg des Irrationalismus von Schelling zu Hitler* (Berlin: Aufbau, 1955), 525–7. See also the classics by George L. Mosse, *Toward the Final Solution: A History of European Racism* (New York: Howard Fertig, 1997), 1–34, and Poliakov, *Le mythe aryen*, 151–81. For more recent examples, see Paul-Pierre Gossiaux, 'Anthropologie des Lumières ("Culture naturelle" et racisme rituel)', in Daniel Droixhe and Paul-Pierre Gossiaux (eds.), *L'homme des Lumières et la découverte de l'autre* (Brussels: Éditions de l'Université de Bruxelles, 1985), 49–69; Kenan Malik, *The Meaning of Race: Race, History and Culture in Western Society* (Basingstoke: Macmillan, 1996), 39–55; and Charles W. Mills, *The Racial Contract* (Ithaca: Cornell University Press, 1997), 53–81 and 122. At the time that Lukács was writing, Hannah Arendt expressed a more nuanced view in her 'Race-Thinking before Racism', *The Review of Politics*, 6 (1944), 36–73, later published as a chapter of her *The Burden of Our Time* (1951).

aware that races were their own ruse, nothing more than an instrument for apprehending the complexity of the worlds they were discovering. With a few notable exceptions, most of them firmly believed in the common origins of men and explained differences between races, even physical ones, through the environment.[18] Following an argument by the mathematician and philosopher Pierre-Louis Maupertuis (1698–1759), in the mid-eighteenth century Buffon made the case that all races shared the same origin and that variations were the consequence of a prolonged process of degeneration. Having spread throughout the world from an original nucleus, different peoples were, it was argued, subject to the effects of different physical environments. In time, the impact of external factors caused their degeneration. Only the white race, the archetype from which all other races had derived, retained unaltered its original physical characteristics.[19] Buffon's theory was immensely influential, and his views were often restated as needing no proof – as was the case, for example, in the *Encyclopédie* with the entry 'Humaine, espèce' penned by Diderot.[20] According to Buffon and the countless others who embraced his ideas, the notion that races had to be hierarchically ordered, and that external traits mirrored intellectual abilities and moral worth, was a truism. However, since differences were considered to be the result of environmental causes rather than a fact of nature, it was also assumed that over time they could be reversed.[21] Richard Popkin has written of a 'liberal racism' to define this way of conceiving races in non-essentialistic terms, arguing that such a view was dominant within eighteenth-century scientific discourses.[22] Of course, there were important exceptions that would prove

[18] See Ann Thomson, 'Issues at Stake in Eighteenth-Century Racial Classification', *Cromohs*, 8 (2003), 1–20. Also see Giuliano Gliozzi, 'Poligenismo e razzismo agli albori del secolo dei lumi', *Rivista di filosofia*, 70 (1979), 1–31.

[19] Pierre-Louis Moreau de Maupertuis, *Venus physique* (n.p., 1745), 160–5; Georges-Louis Leclerc Buffon, 'Variétés dans l'espèce humaine', in *Histoire naturelle, générale et particulière* (Paris: Imprimerie Royale, 1749–1789), iii. 529–30. See, on this, Doron, *L'homme altéré*, 419–504, and Andrew Curran, 'Rethinking Race History: The Role of the Albino in the French Enlightenment Life Sciences', *History and Theory*, 48 (2009), 151–79.

[20] Denis Diderot, 'Humaine, espèce', in Denis Diderot and Jean Le Rond d'Alembert (eds.), *Encyclopédie, ou Dictionnaire raisonné des sciences, des arts et des métiers* (Paris: Briasson, David l'aîné, Le Breton, Durand, 1751–1780), viii. 348.

[21] On this, with particular reference to Buffon, see Claude Blanckaert, 'Les conditions d'émergence de la science des races au début du XIXᵉ siècle', in Sarga Moussa (ed.), *L'idée de race dans les sciences humaines et la littérature (XVIIIᵉ–XIXᵉ siècles)* (Paris: L'Harmattan, 2003), 135–8.

[22] Richard H. Popkin, 'The Philosophical Bases of Modern Racism', in Popkin, *The High Road to Pyrrhonism* (San Diego: Austin Hill Press, 1980), 89. For a convincing examination of the connection between racialism and strands of liberal thought, see Domenico Losurdo, *Controstoria del liberalismo* (Rome: Laterza, 2005).

extremely influential, the Swedish botanist Carl Linnaeus (1707–1778) being the most obvious. In his monumental *Systema naturae* (1735), Linnaeus divided men into four 'varieties': the European, the American, the Asiatic, and the African. In his case, the divisions were rather more rigid. Interestingly, while Linnaeus used the word 'variety' for his taxonomy, Buffon preferred 'race', wishing as he did to convey the idea that human differences were constantly changing, mainly in response to the environment.

For our purposes, Buffon's choice of word is revealing, since it was consistent with contemporary usage.[23] The *Dictionnaire universel*, by the famous lexicographer Antoine Furetière (1619–1688), published just a few years after Bernier's text, offered its readers three meanings of the word 'race': 'Lineage, continuous generation from father to son; . . . in history, it is said of a long succession of kings of the same lineage; . . . it is also said of ancient, illustrious families.'[24] Race was thus first and foremost a synonym for offspring and referred to an alleged bond between generations based on the special relationship between father and son – particularly in noble families. The same definition could be found in the dictionary of the Académie: 'Line, lineage, extraction; all those who come from the same family.' But 'race' might also refer to 'domestic animals, dogs, horses, horned animals'. The dictionary mentioned the saying *Bons chiens chassent de race* to mean that children took after the 'habits and inclinations of their father'.[25] Definitions such as these, common to most late seventeenth-century dictionaries, clearly confirm that the common meaning of the word was close to the modern concepts of offspring or lineage. They also imply the handing down of personal qualities, moral principles, and modes of conduct from father to son. In short, it was assumed that a person's character was bequeathed to his or her offspring through some genealogical

---

[23] Nicholas Hudson, 'From "Nation" to "Race": The Origin of Racial Classification in Eighteenth-Century Thought', *Eighteenth-Century Studies*, 29 (1996), 253–4. On Buffon's definition of race in genealogical terms, see Claude-Olivier Doron, 'Race and Genealogy: Buffon and the Formation of the Concept of "Race"', *Humana.Mente: Journal of Philosophical Studies*, 22 (2012), 75–109. Also see Claude Blanckaert, 'Contre la méthode: Unité de l'homme et classification dans l'anthropologie des Lumières', in Claude Calame and Mondher Kilani (eds.), *La fabrication de l'humain dans les cultures et anthropologie* (Lausanne: Payot, 1999), 111–26.

[24] Furetière, *Dictionnaire universel*, s.v. 'race'.

[25] Académie française, *Dictionnaire de l'Académie française* (Paris: Coignard, 1694), ii. 364 (s.v. 'race'). For an overview, see Daniel Teysseire, 'De l'usage historico-politique de *race* entre 1680 et 1820 et de sa transformation', *Mots*, 33 (1992), 43–52, and, going beyond the French case, Antje Sommer and Werner Conze, 'Rasse', in Otto Brunner, Werner Conze, and Reinhart Koselleck (eds.), *Geschichtliche Grundbegriffe: Historisches Lexikon zur politisch-sozialen Sprache in Deutschland* (Stuttgart: Klett-Cotta, 1984–1992), v. 135–78.

principle expressed, albeit with many ambiguities and much vagueness, by the concept of race.[26] This meaning of the word persisted throughout the century. In the *Encyclopédie*, the prolific Louis de Jaucourt (1704–1779) continued to define race as 'a line of descendants of the same family', specifying, under the entry 'Naissance', that the families to which the notion applied were always noble.[27] The *Dictionnaire critique*, published in 1788, the year of Buffon's death, offered the same definition that Furetière had given his readers a century earlier. So too did the *Nouveau vocabulaire*, published the year of Lamarck's famous *Philosophie zoologique* (1809). A race was still a 'lineage; all those who come from the same family'.[28]

The relationship between the two meanings of race highlighted above is complex at best.[29] Undeniably, there was much interaction and reciprocal influence between the two, and the genealogical vision of Buffon is a case in point.[30] However, throughout the greater part of the eighteenth century, they belonged to separate discourses, shaped within two distinct fields of enquiry, and served different intellectual (and political) purposes. The scientific notion of race for its part developed in connection with colonial expansion and the need to understand a distant Other – and, for some, to justify their enslavement – on the basis of physical differences.[31] The notion of race as lineage, on the contrary, took on its meaning in connection with

[26] Arlette Jouanna, *L'idée de race en France au XVIᵉ siècle et au début du XVIIᵉ: 1498–1614* (Montpellier: Imprimerie de Recherche – Université Paul Valéry, 1981), i. 11–13 and ii. 723–7. Also see Diego Venturino, 'Race et histoire: Le paradigme nobiliaire de la distinction sociale au début du XVIIIᵉ siècle', in Moussa (ed.), *L'idée de race dans les sciences humaines et la littérature*, 19–38; Michel Nassiet, *La violence, une histoire sociale* (Paris: Champ Vallon, 2011), 210–14.

[27] Louis de Jaucourt, 'Race', in Diderot and d'Alembert (eds.), *Encyclopédie*, xiii. 740, and Louis de Jaucourt, 'Naissance', ibid., xi. 8.

[28] Jean-François Féraud, *Dictionnaire critique de la langue française* (Marseilles: Mossy, 1788), iii. 341; Jacques-Francis Rolland, *Nouveau vocabulaire* (Lyons: Rolland et Rivoire, 1809), 762.

[29] Doron, *L'homme altéré*, passim.

[30] See Guillaume Aubert, 'Kinship, Blood, and the Emergence of the Racial Nation in the French Atlantic World, 1600–1789', in Christopher H. Johnson et al. (eds.), *Blood and Kinship: Matter for Metaphor from Ancient Rome to the Present* (New York: Berghahn Books, 2013), 175–95.

[31] On debates over slavery and the idea of race in eighteenth-century France, see Carminella Biondi, *Mon frère, tu es mon esclave! Teorie schiaviste e dibattiti antropologico-razziali nel Settecento francese* (Pisa: Goliardica, 1973), 101–83; Louis Sala-Molins, *Les misères des Lumières: Sous la raison, l'outrage* (Paris: R. Laffont, 1992); Sue Peabody, *'There Are No Slaves in France': The Political Culture of Race and Slavery in the Ancien Régime* (Oxford: Oxford University Press, 1996); Guillaume Aubert, '"The Blood of France": Race and Purity of Blood in the French Atlantic World', *William and Mary Quarterly*, 61 (2004), 439–78; Saliha Belmessous, 'Assimilation and Racialism in Seventeenth- and Eighteenth-Century French Colonial Policy', *American Historical Review*, 110 (2005), 322–49; Dorlin, *La matrice de la race*, passim; Pierre H. Boulle, *Race et esclavage dans la France de l'Ancien régime* (Paris: Perrin, 2007); William Max Nelson, 'Making Men: Enlightenment Ideas of Racial Engineering', *The American Historical Review*, 115 (2010), 1364–94.

heraldry and genealogy and was meant to shape hierarchies within a more or less ethnically homogeneous society.[32] In this case, its main purpose was to separate the nobility from commoners and, within the nobility itself, establish ranks, functioning as it did within a society where physical differences were largely imperceptible and, therefore, inadequate in the marking of distinctions. Interestingly, there were instances in which the image of the French peasant, brutalised by hard work and a poor diet and degraded by ignorance, was closer to that of a savage from a distant colony rather than a well-bred Frenchman. The great moralist Jean de La Bruyère (1645–1696) and Voltaire – if with very different intentions – made comments of this sort.[33] But while both notions of race created boundaries and hierarchies, the ways these were visualised and the ways they operated were profoundly different.

While the alleged moral and intellectual superiority of the white race over the other races was manifested by the colour of the skin, in seventeenth- and eighteenth-century France establishing a relationship between a person's appearance and his inner qualities – a relationship that determined the place he or she should hold in society – required other means. Making visible those qualities was paramount in defining social boundaries. Indeed, noblemen's claims to moral superiority over commoners and bourgeois were based on a complex set of assumptions and preconceptions. As the libertine essayist and novelist Guez de Balzac (1595–1654) noted in the seventeenth century, their pretended nobility, something so 'precious' and yet so 'uncertain', only existed insofar as people believed in it: 'Beauty can be seen, wealth can be touched, but nobility is imagined and presumed,' he remarked.[34] Persuading others that by virtue of his birth a nobleman had an exceptional moral standing was crucial, as was persuading them of a 'nobility that only exists in the phantasy of men'.[35] One way of strengthening the illusion was by making that purported superiority visible,

---

[32] On the seemingly ethnic homogeneity of modern France, see Sue Peabody and Tyler Stovall, 'Introduction: Race, France, Histories', in Peabody and Stovall (eds.), *The Color of Liberty*, 2.

[33] Jean de La Bruyère, 'Les caractères ou les mœurs de ce siècle', in *Les caractères de Théophraste traduits du grec avec Les caractères ou Les mœurs de ce siècle* (1688) (Paris: Honoré Champion, 1999), 440–1, and François-Marie Arouet Voltaire, 'Essai sur les mœurs et l'esprit des nations' (1756), in *Œuvres*, xi. 19. On the relationship between images of the savage and representations of the peasant, see Amy S. Wyngaard, *From Savage to Citizen: The Invention of the Peasant in the French Enlightenment* (Newark: University of Delaware Press, 2004). The juxtaposition survived well into the nineteenth century; see Weber's classic *Peasants into Frenchmen*, 3–22.

[34] Jean-Louis Guez de Balzac, *Les entretiens* (1657 – published posthumously) (Paris: Marcel Didier, 1972), ii. 521.

[35] François de La Mothe Le Vayer, 'Petits traitez en forme de Lettres' (1648–1660), in *Œuvres* (Paris: Billaine, 1669), xii. 194.

embodied in external traits reflecting their inner qualities. In the sixteenth and early seventeenth centuries, Sumptuary Laws established norms of dress serving to display each person's moral worth and their station in society. But the sheer difficulty of enforcing such codes – a difficulty on which Michel de Montaigne (1533–1592) commented wryly – gradually made of good manners and refined fashions the new *marques de noblesse*, the sign of a moral superiority.[36] The entire issue was social and cultural as much as political, for politesse and good manners set up boundaries and, at one and the same time, suggested ways of straying across them. Obviously, royal courts played a crucial role in shaping mores and norms of politesse. To one observer, they were the true 'sources from which one might draw the art of becoming polite'.[37] There, extremely complex norms of etiquette, ritualistic in nature, established and bolstered equally complex distinctions, so nuanced that they might be imperceptible to the neophyte. Courts offered the onlooker an 'infinite gradation' of ranks and statuses so close to one another that 'important differences' could easily be overlooked. From the urgent need to avoid such unseemliness, 'politesse is born'.[38] The true nature of politesse and the sorts of distinctions it drew were a matter of debate from the late seventeenth century onwards. The Baron de Montesquieu (1689–1755) noted with some cynicism that the real function of good manners was to mark distinctions. As he saw it, politesse 'is born of the desire to distinguish oneself. It is because of pride that we are well-mannered.'[39] The famous *salonnière* Madame de Graffigny (1695–1758) believed instead that politeness could hide faults and vices under the surface of appearances and parade merits and virtues that, in truth, were wanting.[40]

[36] Michel de Montaigne, *Les essais* (1580) (Paris: Presses universitaires de France, 2004), 268–70 (book i. ch. 43).

[37] Anonymous, *Tablettes de l'homme du monde, ou Analyse des sept qualités essentielles à former le beau caractère d'homme du monde accompli* (The Hague: A. Le Catholique, 1715), 38. On the point: Orest Ranum, 'Courtesy, Absolutism, and the Rise of the French State, 1630–1660', *Journal of Modern History*, 52 (1980), 426–51. Also see the classics by Norbert Elias, *Die höfische Gesellschaft: Untersuchungen zur Soziologie des Königtums und der höfischen Aristokratie* (Neuwied: Luchterhand, 1969), and Erich Auerbach, 'La cour et la ville', in Auerbach, *Vier Untersuchungen zur Geschichte der französischen Bildung* (Bern: A. Francke Verlag, 1951), 12–50.

[38] Gabriel Sénac de Meilhan, *Considérations sur l'esprit et les mœurs* (London: n.p., 1787), 107.

[39] Charles-Louis Secondat de Montesquieu, 'De l'Esprit des lois' (1748), in *Œuvres complètes* (ed. Caillois) (Paris: Gallimard, 1949–1951), ii. 263 (book iv. ch. 2).

[40] See, for example, Françoise d'Issembourg d'Happoncourt de Graffigny, *Lettres d'une Péruvienne* (1747) (Paris: Garnier, 2014), 128. On this, see the remarks by Jean Starobinski, 'Le mot civilisation', in Starobinski, *Le remède dans le mal: Critique et légitimation de l'artifice à l'âge des Lumières* (Paris: Gallimard, 1989), 24–5. For a more detailed discussion, see Peter France, *Politeness and its Discontents: Problems in French Classical Culture* (Cambridge: Cambridge University Press, 1992), Emmanuel Bury, *Littérature et politesse: L'invention de l'honnête homme, 1580–1750* (Paris: Presses

Others were less critical. La Bruyère, for one, believed that although politesse was not always the product of kindness of the heart, it made 'man appear, from the outside, the way he should be on the inside'.[41] Others still genuinely believed that good manners reflected a nobility of soul. They were not merely a matter of appearances; far from it. According to the essayist Morvan de Bellegarde (1648–1734), politesse was but the outward display of inner virtues, of admirable qualities deeply rooted within a person's soul. The abbé Prévost (1697–1763), in a work on the art of conversation that declared politesse to be the 'most sacred of social ties', opined that a person's proper demeanour 'announced' to others the purity and generosity of his heart.[42] That a very close relationship existed between inner qualities and polished manners was reiterated by Voltaire in a much-quoted sonnet: 'Politeness is to the mind and the heart/what grace is to the face: it is the sweet image of the kindness of the heart/and it is this kindness that one cherishes.'[43]

Based on the straightforward assumption that the greater the nobility of someone's soul the more refined the etiquette he or she ought to follow, dividing people according to manners became the measure of all dignity and an obsession that the libertines were prepared to satirise. In the *Confessions du Comte de* *** (1741), the great novelist Charles-Pinot Duclos (1704–1772) wittily commented on how Parisian ladies were divided into classes, each with their own 'particular customs in company, and their particular tone and air'. Throughout *Les égarements du cœur et de l'esprit* (1736–1738), Crébillon *fils* (1707–1777) lampooned instead the obsession with rules of conduct by making his characters learn strange words, exotic fashions, and endless norms of etiquette to prove their noble origins. The playwright Jacques-Rochette De La Morlière (1719–1785) did the same in his *Angola* (1746), where aristocrats deplored bourgeois vulgarity and claimed bon-ton and quirks to be the signs of their moral superiority.[44] For their part, many members of the rising middle classes

universitaires de France, 1996), and Philippe Raynaud, *La politesse des Lumières: Les lois, les mœurs, les manières* (Paris: Gallimard, 2013).

[41] La Bruyère, 'Les caractères ou les mœurs de ce siècle', 257.

[42] Antoine François Prévost, *Elémens de politesse et de bienséance, ou La civilité qui se pratique parmi les honnêtes gens; avec un nouveau Traité sur l'art de plaire dans la conversation* (Strasbourg: Armand König, 1766), 233–4. The work was published posthumously.

[43] Jean Baptiste Morvan de Bellegarde, *Réflexions sur la politesse des mœurs, avec des maximes pour la societé civile: suite des Réflexions sur le ridicule* (Paris: Guignard, 1698), 1–2; François-Marie Arouet Voltaire, 'Stances ou quatrains, pour tenir lieu de ceux de Pibrac, qui ont un peu vieilli' (1772 or 1773), in *Œuvres*, viii. 545.

[44] [Charles Pinot Duclos], *Confessions du Comte de* *** (Amsterdam: n.p., 1741), i. 78; Claude-Prosper Jolyot de Crébillon, *Les égarements du cœur et de l'esprit* (Paris: Gallimard, 1990); Jacques-Rochette

much time and effort in acquiring the manners of the upper
believing that they would thereby be admitted to their ranks.[45] In
from the second half of the seventeenth century onwards, the
ving circulation of works disclosing to the neophyte the secrets of
litesse, of what was acceptable and what was deplorable in refined
society, testifies to an increasing urge to overcome the boundaries made
visible by etiquette.[46] Monsieur Jourdain, the central character of Molière's
(1622–1673) famous play *Le bourgeois gentilhomme* (1670), parodied a real-
life preoccupation. His delusion that, simply by studying the teachings of
his mentors and by reading manuals on *savoir-vivre*, he would be enabled
to rise in the social scale, while, in fact, he was only learning good manners,
was a source of great amusement.[47] And it was so for two reasons at least.
First, he was mistakenly equating good manners with nobility of the soul and
although such a mistake could easily be made, it was a serious fault nonetheless. In fact, true nobility implied a sense of selflessness and a commitment to
helping others that seemed of little or no concern to Monsieur Jourdain.
Such vulgarity would have seemed utterly (and outrageously) disgraceful to
most noblemen – who were, in the late seventeenth century, a large part of
Molière's audience. Second, Molière's character was wrongly – and
absurdly – assuming that true nobility could be rapidly acquired. This brings
us to another crucial aspect of race in late seventeenth- and eighteenth-
century France, namely, the fact that the distance separating noblemen from
bourgeois and commoners essentially pertained to the passage of time.[48] In
fact, most noblemen believed that even if good manners could indeed be
learned rapidly, what they represented, true virtue, could only be obtained
through sacrifice and, crucially, had to be confirmed and strengthened by its
transmission from one generation to another. Race as lineage was conceived
as a construction of time, as the conveying of social virtues, through proper
examples and teachings, to one's offspring. It was the outcome of a slow
process that could no doubt be influenced, shaped, and modified, but that

de la Morlière, *Angola: Histoire indienne* (Grenoble: Roissard, 1967). For an overview:
Warren Roberts, *Morality and Social Class in Eighteenth-Century French Literature and Painting*
(Toronto: University of Toronto Press, 1974), 25–43.

[45] See Daniel Roche, *La culture des apparences: Une histoire du vêtement, XVIIᵉ–XVIIIᵉ siècles* (Paris:
Fayard, 1989), especially 87–117.

[46] Christophe Losfeld, *Politesse, morale et construction sociale: Pour une histoire des traités de comportements (1670–1788)* (Paris: Honoré Champion, 2011).

[47] On Molière's views regarding the middle classes, see the classic by Paul Bénichou, *Morales du Grand
siècle* (Paris: Gallimard, 1948), 156–218.

[48] On this, see Roberto Moro, *Il tempo dei signori: Mentalità, ideologia, dottrine della nobiltà francese di
Antico regime* (Rome: Savelli, 1981), especially 179–217.

always required a great deal of time. Importantly, as we shall see shortly, the handing down of moral qualities and of the social status that was thought to underpin this notion of race was instrumental in shaping a narrative that allowed the nobility to claim that it embodied the entire nation.

The Royal Race and
the Duke de Saint-Simon's Nobility of Blood

Since in ancient regime France the word 'race' commonly referred to an eminent family, it was first and foremost associated with the most illustrious in the country: the royal family. As the readers of Furetière's dictionary learned, race was 'said of a long succession of kings of the same line. In France, one counts the kings of the first, second, and third race.' That the word could even stand as a synonym for the royal family as such was widely accepted. In his popular *L'art de bien parler françois* (1696), first published at the very end of the seventeenth century, the grammarian Pierre de La Touche (d. 1730) noted that 'one says, for example, *the three races of the kings of France* and would not say *the families of the kings of France*'. The same remark was still to be found in the 1760 edition.[49] Obviously, this was a recognition of the pre-eminence of the royal family. And yet, stating that the royal household was the most illustrious of noble families implied at once that there were other eminent families and that before the Capetians two other races had ruled the nation. Most importantly, it also meant that other families, the most ancient and noble, could aspire to the throne – remote though such a possibility might be. Like their counterparts across Europe, even the kings of France invested resources and energies in seeking to prove the antiquity of their lineage and the unity of the Merovingians, Carolingians, and Capetians. The *querelle de Childebrand*, dragging on between 1642 and 1659 and involving some of the greatest historians of the day, was only one among many episodes testifying to the political significance of genealogy. Against French genealogists who asserted the descent of the Capetians by the masculine line from Childebrand (678–751), Spanish scholars denied all relationships between the Carolingians and the Capetians. The stakes were high since the issue pertained to the legitimacy of Spanish claims to the French crown.[50] In this as in countless

---

[49] Pierre de La Touche, *L'art de bien parler françois, qui comprend tout ce qui regarde la grammaire et les façons de parler douteuses* (Amsterdam: H. Desbordes, 1696), ii. 320. Italics in the text. See also the 1760 edition, ii. 472.

[50] Louis-Alexandre Bergounioux, *L'esprit de polémique et les querelles savantes vers le milieu du XVIIe siècle: Marc Antoine Dominici (1605?–1650), un controversiste quercynois ami de Pascal* (Paris: Boivin,

other cases, the efforts made by the crown to prove its antiquity and the continuity of its lineage gave an extraordinary impulse to genealogy.[51] By the eighteenth century, such efforts had consolidated and rendered generally accepted the notion that the three royal races stemmed from a common origin. In an article published in 1720 on 'La noblesse de la race royale des François', the abbé de Camps (1643–1723), a numismatist and antiquary, claimed that the royal race was the most ancient and illustrious of France as well as the most eminent throughout the whole of Europe. Its three branches, he observed, could be traced back to the same origin, a fact that rendered it the most venerable dynasty on the continent.[52]

Interestingly, in his article the abbé de Camps reasserted another widely shared belief, identifying kings as the descendants of the heads of families that, over the centuries, had grown into nations.[53] The image of the nation as the union of the French with their king through a tie mirroring the one between a father and his sons would have been familiar to most readers. In the guise of a harmonious family, the nation lived by virtue of the obedience and respect of the subject-children and the protection and love of the king-father, a natural and unprompted sentiment.[54] For one, Jacques-Bénigne Bossuet (1627–1704), the celebrated Eagle of Meaux, made the case that obedience was due to kings for the same reason it was

---

1936), 455–89. Also see Alexandre Y. Haran, *Le lys et le globe: Messianisme dynastique et rêve impérial en France à l'aube des temps modernes* (Seyssel: Champ Vallon, 2000), 192–4.

[51] See Chantal Grell, 'L'histoire de France et le mythe de la monarchie à la fin du XVIIe siècle', in Yves-Marie Bercé and Philippe Contamine (eds.), *Histoires de France, historiens de la France* (Paris: Honoré Champion, 1994), 168–71.

[52] François de Camps, 'De la noblesse de la race royale des François', *Le nouveau Mercure*, July 1720, 11.

[53] De Camps, 'De la noblesse de la race royale des François', 3–5.

[54] For an overview: Jeffrey Merrick, 'Fathers and Kings: Patriarchalism and Absolutism in Eighteenth-Century French Politics', *Studies on Voltaire and the Eighteenth Century*, 308 (1993), 281–330, Sarah Hanley, 'Engendering the State: Family Formation and State Building in Early Modern France', *French Historical Studies*, 16 (1989), 4–27, and Ahmed Slimani, *La modernité du concept de nation au XVIIIe siècle* (Aix-en-Provence: Presses universitaires d'Aix-Marseille, 2004), 147–51. For some late seventeenth- and eighteenth-century examples: Eustache Le Noble, *L'école du monde, ou Instruction d'un père à un fils, touchant la manière dont il faut vivre dans le monde, divisée en entretiens* (Paris: Martin Jouvenel, 1702), iv. 186; Alexis Piron, 'L'école des pères, ou les fils ingrats' (1728), in *Œuvres complettes* (Paris: Imprimerie de M. Lambert, 1776), i. 7; Pierre Roques, *Les devoirs des sujets expliqués en quatre discours* (Basel: Thourneisen, 1737), 23; Pierre Barral, *Manuel des souverains* (n.p., 1754), 1–3; Joseph Marie Anne Gros de Besplas, *Des causes du bonheur public, ouvrage dédié à Monseigneur le Dauphin* (Paris: S. Jorry, 1768), 15, 189, 550, and 561; [Antoine-Fabio Sticotti], *Dictionnaire des gens du monde: Historique, littéraire, critique, moral, physique, militaire, politique, caractéristique et social* (Paris: J.-P. Costard, 1770), ii. 389; Puget de Saint-Pierre, *Dictionnaire des notions primitives, ou Abrégé raisonné et universel des éléments de toutes les connaissances humaines* (Paris: J.-P. Costard, 1773), iii. 135; Joseph Lanjuinais, *Le monarque accompli, ou Prodiges de bonté, de savoir et de sagesse qui font l'éloge de S. M. I. Joseph II* (Lausanne: J.P. Herbach, 1774), i. 1.

due to fathers: '[T]he name king is the name of a common father', love towards his subjects differing in no wise from love for his sons. It was this bond that turned a multitude into a nation.[55] The simile remained commonplace throughout the eighteenth century, and even during the Revolution it was used in arguments for the king's inviolability.[56] The author of an anonymous pamphlet written shortly before King Louis XVI's (1754–1793) execution insisted that kings derived their sacredness from sharing the source of the authority of all fathers. As fathers gave life to their sons, so kings gave life to their nations. Even the revolutionary Antoine-Adrien Lamourette (1742–1794) lent credence to such a thesis, arguing that a nation was a 'second and vast family, all members of which are bound by a sort of civic fraternity', the ruler being their father.[57] That the word 'patrie' derived from the Latin 'pater', as noted in the *Encyclopédie*, was not lost on many scholars – and some used it to bolster the patriarchal argument.[58] It was a point deployed by the author of the famous *Nouveau mémoire pour servir à l'histoire des Cacouacs* (1757), Jacob-Nicolas Moreau (1717–1803). In two articles written in 1760 defending the paternal authority of kings, Moreau made the claim that the word 'patrie' indicated in all languages the same bond, that 'between children and their father'. The very idea of nation was routinely associated with that of family on account of their 'common origin'. In fact, in the ancient world 'the first notions of society were confounded with that of a father governing his children'.[59] Moreau admitted that it might have been difficult to recognise

---

[55] Jacques-Bénigne Bossuet, *Politique tirée des propres paroles de l'Ecriture sainte* (published posthumously in 1709) (Geneva: Droz, 1967), 71; also see ibid., 46–50. Alse see La Bruyère, 'Les caractères ou les mœurs de ce siècle', 390.

[56] See, for example, François-Marie Arouet Voltaire, 'Supplément au Siècle de Louis XIV' (1753), in *Œuvres*, xv. 113. Montesquieu was among those who criticised such a notion: Montesquieu, 'De l'Esprit des lois', 237 (book i. ch. 3). For an overview of revolutionary debates, see Lynn Hunt, 'Discourses of *Patriarchalism* and anti-*Patriarchalism* in the French Revolution', in John Renwick (ed.), *Language and Rhetoric of the Revolution* (Edinburgh: Edinburgh University Press, 1990), 25–41, and Anne Verjus, 'Du patriarchalisme au paternalisme: Les modéles familiaux de l'autorité politique dans les républiques de France et d'Amérique', in Pierre Serna (ed.), *Républiques sœurs: Le Directoire et la révolution atlantique* (Rennes: Presses universitaires de Rennes, 2009), 35–51.

[57] Anonymous, *Réflexions sur l'inviolabilité des rois et sur la prétendue souveraineté des peuples* (n.p., n.d.), 2–4. Antoine-Adrien Lamourette, *Lettre pastorale de M. L'évêque du département de Rhône et Loire, métropolitain du Sud-Est* (Lyons: Imprimerie d'Amable le Roy, 1791), 13.

[58] Louis de Jaucourt, 'Patrie', in Diderot and d'Alembert (eds.), *Encyclopédie*, xii. 178.

[59] Jacob-Nicolas Moreau, 'De la monarchie en général et de son origine', *Le moniteur françois*, 1 (1760), 125–6, and Jacob-Nicolas Moreau, 'Réponses aux objections contre le pouvoir paternel', *Le moniteur françois*, 1 (1760), 152–9. For other examples: Jean-Baptiste-René Robinet et al., *Dictionnaire universel des sciences, morale, économique, politique et diplomatique, ou Bibliothèque de l'homme d'État et du citoyen* (London: Libraires Associés, 1777–1783), xxvi. 257; Gabriel-François Coyer, 'Dissertation sur le vieux mot *Patrie*', in Coyer, *Dissertations pour être lues: La première, sur le vieux mot de patrie, la seconde, sur la nature du peuple* (The Hague: Pierre Gosse, 1755), 14.

in present-day kings the descendants of the first fathers and in subjects the descendants of their children – but it could be inferred nonetheless, or so he believed. The same sort of conjectural genealogy was set out in de Camps's article, though there the inference was even stronger. The Jansenist jurist Jean Domat (1625–1696) had already made similar arguments, and the Chevalier de Ramsay (1686–1743) repeated them shortly after the publication of de Camps's article, in his collection of the manuscripts of his late friend and mentor, the great François La Mothe Fénelon (1651–1715).[60] Even the Genevan jurist Jean-Jacques Burlamaqui (1694–1784) framed the analogy between kingdom and family within a historical perspective: 'Humankind was originally divided solely into families and not into nations. Those families lived under the paternal government of the person who was their chief, such as their father or grandfather.' Burlamaqui also believed that fathers and grandfathers had once been rulers over their families and that modern-day kings were descended from them just as their subjects were descended from their children. The unity of each kingdom was produced by the perpetuation of those original ties.[61] In cases such as Burlamaqui's, of course, the juxtaposition between fathers and kings was predicated on something more than a simile. The fact that it could be logically inferred from history shifted the patriarchal argument on to more solid foundations – or so it might have seemed to its advocates.

Obviously, conceiving of the relationship between king and nation in such terms also meant that the genealogy of the royal household was the mainstay of the nation's history.[62] To an extent, in fact, this could be represented as a tree spreading out its branches to the whole of France – or, at least, to its most ancient and noble families. It is partly against this backdrop, and bearing the political significance of genealogy and the patriarchal paradigm in mind, that the fixation of noblemen with proving the antiquity of their lineage ought to be considered. Arguably, one of the

[60] Jean Domat, 'Le Droit public, suite des Lois civiles dans leur ordre naturel' (1697), in Œuvres complètes (Paris: Firmin-Didot, 1828–1830), iii. 4–5; Andrew Michael Ramsay, Essay philosophique sur le gouvernement civil, où l'on traite de la nécessité, de l'origine, des droits, des bornes et des différentes formes de la souveraineté selon les principes de feu M. François de Salignac de La Mothe-Fénelon (London: n.p., 1721), 50–1. Doubts may be raised over Ramsay's claim that he was repeating Fénelon's arguments. See Andrew Mansfield, 'Fénelon's Cuckoo: Andrew Michael Ramsay and Archbishop Fénelon', in Doohwan Ahn, Christoph Schmitt-Maaß, and Stefanie Stockhorst (eds.), Fénelon in the Enlightenment: Traditions, Adaptations, and Variations (Amsterdam: Rodopi 2014), 82–4.

[61] Jean-Jacques Burlamaqui, Principes du droit naturel (Geneva: Barrillot, 1747), 47.

[62] See Germain Butaud and Valérie Piétri, Les enjeux de la généalogie (XIIᵉ–XVIIIᵉ siècle): Pouvoir et identité (Paris: Autrement, 2006), 80–91.

most distinctive characteristics of the nobility had always been its preoccupation with a history in which individual, family, class, and national memories were inextricably intertwined. Obsessed with retracing their ancestral roots and enjoying a privileged vantage point from which to view the past, it was also thanks to the nobles that by the seventeenth century the study of genealogy had developed into a well-established discipline, at a meeting point of heraldry, diplomacy, erudition, and antiquarianism.[63] Indubitably, such interests and concerns were intellectual and social as much as political. As one scholar was still prepared to argue in 1780, '[i]f the study of genealogy is necessary to the *historian*, it is no less so for the *statesman* and the *gentleman* [*homme du monde*]. Both must resort to it to further the interests of princes, their rights, and the pretensions stemming from their kin and alliances.'[64] In most cases, genealogy was an instrument for ascertaining a family's antiquity and, on such a basis, establishing its place among other such families and vis-à-vis the court. With growing urgency, in the eighteenth century genealogy was also used to mount a resistance to the rise of the recently ennobled and the bourgeois who, lacking an illustrious past, were deemed unworthy of serving in the high – and highly lucrative – state offices.[65] From this angle, the struggle between the different groups of the nobility and between these and the bourgeoisie was often waged by means of genealogical treatises – whether authentic or not – so as to gain access to privileges rather than to abolish them.[66] However, genealogy was also a means for the nobles as a class to counter, by underscoring their antiquity and their services to the nation, what they experienced as an increasingly suffocating royal authority.[67] When in 1682 the king transferred the ministers and his court to Versailles, consolidating political power in his

---

[63] André Burguière, 'La généalogie', in Nora (ed.), *Les lieux de mémoire*, iii. 3879–907. On family histories and the study of the past in the seventeenth century, see Orest Ranum, *Artisans of Glory: Writers and Historical Thought in Seventeenth-Century France* (Chapel Hill: University of North Caroline Press, 1980), 3–17.

[64] Christophe-Guillaume Koch, *Tables généalogiques des maisons souveraines de l'Europe* (Strasbourg: Jean-Frédéric Stein, 1780), 1. Italics in the text.

[65] See Jay M. Smith, *The Culture of Merit: Nobility, Royal Service, and the Making of Absolute Monarchy in France: 1600–1789* (Ann Arbor: University of Michigan Press, 1996), 57–91.

[66] On the contribution of the bourgeoisie to genealogical research, see André Burguière, 'La mémoire familiale du bourgeois gentilhomme: Généalogies domestiques en France aux XVIIᵉ et XVIIIᵉ siècles', *Annales: Histoire, sciences sociales*, 46 (1991), 771–88.

[67] As late as 1815 the Vicomte de Bonald (1754–1840) insisted that the nobles deserved their rights because of their services to the state: '[T]he noble or the notables are the servants of the state . . .. They do not exercise a right; they fulfil a duty. They do not enjoy a prerogative; they deliver a public service': [Louis Gabriel Ambroise de Bonald], *Réflexions sur l'intérêt général de l'Europe, suivies de quelques considérations sur la noblesse* (Paris: Le Normant, 1815), 55; italics in the text.

own hands, the members of the second order were faced with a conundrum: they could remain in their châteaux in the provinces, maintaining their independence from the court but estranging themselves from politics, or they could move to Versailles, enhancing their authority at the price of losing a part of their freedom. Those who had the means or benefited from a royal pension moved to Versailles, while those who could not afford the costly life at court remained in their châteaux. There is still some truth in Hyppolite Taine's (1728–1893) masterful description: 'Many noble officers, finding that high grades are only for courtiers, abandon the service, and betake themselves with their discontent to their estates. Others, who have not left their domains, brood there in discomfort, idleness, and ennui, their ambition embittered by their powerlessness.'[68] Of course, the impoverishing of a large swathe of the nobility, on which many commented and about which some complained, was a cause and a sign of its weakness as a class. As the memoirist Edmond-Jean-François Barbier (1689–1771) wrote in 1751: 'The various provinces of the kingdom are filled with an infinity of poor noblemen, overburdened with children whose parents are unable to offer them a proper education, and much less to send them to court. The children of this nobility pass their youth amongst the peasants, in ignorance and rudeness, often working on their own farms, and only differ from the peasants in that they wear a sword and call themselves gentlemen.'[69] All they could then do was resort to marrying the children of wealthy bourgeois, giving them a noble name and sating their thirst for redress – an ambition on which Voltaire commented with typical sarcasm.[70]

It is unsurprising that, in casting their arguments to counter the power of kings and ministers, the model genealogical tree was for the nobility that of 'the only "maison", the only race, the only true genealogy, that of the sovereign'.[71] The royal race, the sacred lineage, was the one to imitate in the fullest degree since it was the most ancient and, hence, the most illustrious. One way sought by the nobles to reduce the social and political distance separating them from the monarch and, conversely, to increase the one dividing them from other classes was by making the case for a special

---

[68] Hippolyte Taine, *L'Ancien régime* (1876) (Paris: Éditions Complexe, 1991), 94. Of course, such a view was partial and has been contested. See, for example, Colin Jones, *The Great Nation: France from Louis XV to Napoleon* (London: Penguin, 2002), 13–18.

[69] Edmond-Jean-François Barbier, *Chronique de la régence et du règne de Louis XV (1718–1763), ou Journal de Barbier* (Paris: Charpentier, 1857–1866), v. 14–15 (January 1751).

[70] François-Marie Arouet Voltaire, 'Le droit du seigneur' (written in 1760 but first performed in 1762), in *Œuvres*, vi. 15–16.

[71] Georges Duby, *La société chevaleresque* (Paris: Flammarion, 1988), 174.

affinity with the royal lineage. The most straightforward way of doing so was perhaps to claim that in their veins ran the same blood as in the king's and that, therefore, they partook of the same dignity. In these arguments the use of blood – often a synonym for race – is particularly relevant.[72] As Michel Foucault has argued, ancient regime France was in several ways a 'society of blood', a place where familial ties played a fundamental role in shaping structures and systems of power: '[P]ower speaks *through* the blood; it is *a reality with a symbolic function*' deeply affecting the way power circulated, literally, within society.[73] Differences within the nobility and between the nobility and the royal household were often seen as depending on the purity of blood and, therefore, they were a matter of degree. The latter was a contention set forth by the nobility when contesting and readapting notions previously used by their opponents, the champions of royal authority. At the beginning of the seventeenth century, the doctor and royal counsellor Nicolas Abraham de La Framboisière (1560–1636) avowed that God had granted the Bourbons the privilege of issuing 'from the blood of Saint Louis, one of the wisest and most religious kings the earth has ever seen, who has led and driven to virtue his entire race'.[74] Like other physicians of his day, La Framboisière considered blood to be the conduit through which a person's character, qualities, vices, and virtues were transmitted to his offspring. But in the case of the royal family, blood was also the visible, physical sign of the king's immortal body. It was the unchanging substance representing the continuity of the monarchy throughout the ages and, by extension, the history of the nation at large.[75] It is interesting that more than half a century later, in 1687, the notion of royal blood was used in a somewhat different way by the Jesuit historian the père Ménestrier (1631–1705). Commenting on the late Prince de Condé's (1621–1686) request that after his death his heart be re-joined to

---

[72] See, for example, Furetière, *Dictionnaire universel*, s.v. 'consanguinité'.

[73] Michel Foucault, *Histoire de la sexualité: 1 – La volonté de savoir* (Paris: Gallimard, 1976), i. 194. Italics in the text. On the symbolic role of blood in ancient regime France, also see Pierre Giuliani, 'Le sang classique entre histoire et littérature: Hypothèses et propositions', *XVIIe Siècle*, 239 (2008), 223–42.

[74] Nicolas Abraham de La Framboisière, 'La suite de la principauté du petit monde, où la monarchie française est naïvement représentée', in *Œuvres* (Paris: n.p., 1624), 63. The dating of La Framboisière's 'La suite de la principauté' is uncertain. However, since it is not present in the previous edition of his works, dated 1613, we might assume it to have been written between then and 1624. On the relationship between medical sciences and political thought in early modern France, see Jacob Soll, 'Healing the Body Politic: French Royal Doctors, History, and the Birth of a Nation. 1560–1634', *Renaissance Quarterly*, 55 (2002), 1259–86.

[75] The reference, of course, is to Ernst H. Kantorowicz, *The King's Two Bodies: A study in Medieval Political Theology* (Princeton: Princeton University Press, 1997).

that of his great-uncle, King Henry IV (1553–1610), in the church of Saint Louis des Jesuites, the père noted with approval that the royal blood would thus return to its sacred source, the heart of Saint Louis.[76] Although Ménestrier, like La Framboisière, was essentially extolling the sacredness of the royal blood, by claiming it also ran in the veins of the Prince de Condé, he was diverging in an important way from his predecessor. Ménestrier was in fact introducing a sharp distinction between high and low nobility – the former, unlike the latter, sharing the royal blood – and placing an unbridgeable chasm between the two ranks.

An influential author who, in part at least, would have shared Ménestrier's arguments, being equally adamant about the mystical nature of the royal blood, was one of the eighteenth century's greatest memoirists. Louis de Rouvroy, Duke de Saint-Simon (1675–1755), firmly believed that the French constitution was founded on and shaped by the royal blood. Differences and distinctions of dignity within society and within the nobility itself, both crucial to the nation's safety and prosperity, were the consequence of the greater or lesser distance from the royal stock.[77] Consistently, Saint-Simon also argued that a person's role in the state should be decided following the principle that the closer that person was to the royal race, the purer the blood, and the more important the role. The failure to apply such a rule would lead to a degrading of the nation, endangering its security. When dwelling on the reasons behind the debasement of laws, customs, and morals, the duke invariably pointed in the most decided fashion to the incipient confusion of ranks and the downplaying of distinctions: 'It is through dignities and their gradations that all is preserved or all decays', he wrote in 1712.[78] On such premises, throughout his famous *Mémoires*, Saint-Simon criticised Louis XIV's (1638–1715) decision to recognise his illegitimate sons as heirs to the throne, placing them in the line of succession

---

[76] Claude-François Ménestrier, *La source glorieuse du sang de l'auguste maison de Bourbon dans le coeur de saint Louis* (Paris: Michallet, 1687), 1. On this, see Jean-Marie Apostolidès, *Le roi-machine: Spectacle et politique au temps de Louis XIV* (Paris: Éditions de Minuit, 1988), 14–15.

[77] On this, see Jean-Pierre Brancourt, *Le Duc de Saint-Simon et la monarchie* (Paris: Éditions Cujas, 1971), 171–209, and Emmanuel Le Roy Ladurie, *Saint-Simon, ou Le système de la Cour* (Paris: Fayard, 1997), 43–100. Also see François Formel, *Alliances et généalogie à la cour du Grand Roi: Le souci généalogique chez Saint-Simon* (Paris: Éditions Contrepoint, 1983–1984), 199–360. On Saint-Simon's political thought, see also Christophe Blanquie, *Saint-Simon, ou La politique des 'Mémoires'* (Paris: Garnier, 2014). On his life, see Marc Hersant, *Saint-Simon* (Paris: Gallimard, 2016).

[78] Louis de Rouvroy de Saint-Simon, 'Additions au journal de Dangeau' (1712), in *Mémoires* (Paris: Gallimard, 1982–1985), ii. 1012.

between the princes of the blood and the dukes.[79] In his view, the royal edict reversed 'all the most ancient and most sacred rules and laws of the kingdom', and denied the royal blood, the most 'illustrious of the universe', its due in the shaping of the legitimate order.[80] It was, he added, the outcome of 'countless usurpations, each one more monstrous than the other, that invert the order of the kingdom as well as all human and divine laws'.[81] Within a broader perspective, Saint-Simon considered the episode to be revealing of a growing tendency to curb the political role of the nobility. One of his greatest fears was that the levelling of distinctions sought by the court, 'disfiguring the state' and destroying all 'the advantages of the great and true nobility', would eventually cast 'everything into idleness, laziness, nothingness'.[82] The threats posed by absolutism, the pauperisation of the nobility, and the contempt for distinctions that the royal blood otherwise commanded would finally combine to remove all social divisions – a prospect that struck the duke as the 'vivid image of hell'.[83]

It is hardly surprising that Saint-Simon's insistence that society should revolve around the royal blood has led historians to brand him a forerunner of racialism.[84] In reality, the arguments he made throughout his *Mémoires* were more complex than they might seem on the surface. The intricacy – and perhaps even the convoluted nature – of his thought emerges when considering the distinctions he posited within the nobility. Saint-Simon divided the second order into three main classes. The 'royal blood', with its 'different degrees', included the king, the dauphin, the *fils* and *petits fils de France*, and the princes of the blood.[85] Its members were united by familial ties and distinctions dependent on their sharing, in physical terms, the king's blood. Immediately below was the nobility of the sword, the class

---

[79] On the Affair of the Princes: Matthew Gerber, *Bastards: Politics, Family, and Law in Early Modern France* (Oxford: Oxford University Press, 2012), 82–8. Also see, with reference to Saint-Simon's view of the affair, Saint-Victor, *Les racines de la liberté*, 80–5.

[80] Saint-Simon, *Mémoires* (1715), v. 593 and 591–2 respectively.   [81] Ibid. (1716), vi. 30.

[82] Ibid. (1718), vi. 648.

[83] Louis de Rouvroy de Saint-Simon, 'Projets de rétablissement du royaume de France' (1712), in *Écrits inédits* (Paris: Hachette, 1880–1893), iv. 199. On Saint-Simon's stance in relation to absolutism, see Jean-Marie Beyssade, 'L'idée de tyrannie dans les *Mémoires* du Duc de Saint-Simon: L'ordre et les degrés de l'usurpation', *Cahiers de philosophie politique et juridique de l'Université de Caen*, 6 (1984), 127–46, and Jay Caplan, *In the King's Wake: Post-Absolutist Culture in France* (Chicago: University of Chicago Press, 1999), 11–40.

[84] André Devyver, *Le sang épuré: Les préjugés de race chez les gentilshommes français de l'Ancien régime (1560–1720)* (Brussels: Éditions de l'Université de Bruxelles, 1973), 325–52.

[85] Louis de Rouvroy de Saint-Simon, 'Mémoire: Le sang Royal a ses degrés' (1753), in *Grimoires* (Paris: Klincksieck, 1975), 307–12.

whose members had ensured 'the safety of the country and the glory of the kings' through the 'spilling of their blood' and who had proven their unfaltering loyalty to the nation since the foundation of the monarchy.[86] The nobility of the sword was itself further divided into two distinct groups. First were the dukes and peers, whose dignity was 'the work of time and of kings' and that neither kings nor time could destroy.[87] Their prestige stemmed not from ties with the royal household but from the antiquity of their own lineages, dating back to the origins of France. The centuries of sacrifices made for the nation's sake granted them superiority over the lower nobility. Coming after dukes and peers were those noblemen who, thanks to their sacrifices, had deserved a title that was passed down to their descendants. Confirmed by time, the dignity of a family grew as the title passed from one generation to the next. On this point, it is worth noting that according to Saint-Simon, although just as in the case of dukes and peers time served to enhance its honour, a family of the lower nobility could never attain such heights since its lineage could never be as ancient. From his standpoint, therefore, dukes and peers deserved honours that other noblemen could never aspire to 'for the disproportion of birth between them'.[88] Saint-Simon even divided the First and the Third Estate. The one, consisting of the episcopate and the lesser ecclesiastical ranks; the other, of the bourgeoisie, the people, the men of law, and the parliamentarians. Both orders, he contended, ultimately owed their existence to the good will of the nobility. In fact, this had once been the only order 'representing and forming the state'.[89] Saint-Simon was here following in part the arguments in the *Histoire de la pairie de France et du Parlement de Paris*, a text originally drafted in the 1660s and circulating in manuscript form until it was published, in 1740.[90] This work, by the abbé Jean Le Laboureur (1623–1675), a 'very knowledgeable and thorough' scholar, had been commissioned in 1664 by several of the dukes of France, including

---

[86] Saint-Simon, *Mémoires* (1717), vi. 298.   [87] Ibid. (1711), iv. 175.   [88] Ibid. (1717), vi. 252.

[89] Louis de Rouvroy de Saint-Simon, 'Réfutation de l'idée du Parlement d'estre le premier corps de l'estat nouvellement prise et hasardée' (1716), in *Écrits inédits*, iii. 401–18. Quote is from page 402. On Saint-Simon's notion of representation, see Jean-Marie Goulemot, 'De la représentation dans la pensée politique du Duc de Saint-Simon', *Procès: Cahiers d'analyse politique et juridique*, 11–12 (1983), 41–9.

[90] That the manuscript was circulating is confirmed, for example, by a reference in a letter by Denis Dodart (1698–1775), Intendant of the generality of Bourges, to his friend, the Baron de Montesquieu: Denis Dodart to Charles-Louis Secondat de Montesquieu, 23 November 1723, in Charles-Louis Secondat de Montesquieu, *Œuvres* (ed. Masson) (Paris: Nagel, 1950–1955), iii. 753.

Saint-Simon's own father.[91] Le Laboureur lent credence to the old view of the Germanic origins of the French nobility. In the latter he saw the heirs of the Franks, a 'warlike nation' that, at the fall of the Roman Empire, had subdued the Gauls, the ancestors of modern-day commoners. The rights and privileges of the nobility stemmed from that original conquest.[92] Although Saint-Simon's view diverged from Le Laboureur's in several important respects, the duke espoused the abbé's Germanist thesis.[93] It is against such a backdrop that Saint-Simon's resentment at the humiliation and debasement of the French nobility, which, as he saw it, had been devised by Louis XIII (1615–1643) and pursued by Louis XIV, needs to be understood.[94] The duke was horrified at the thought of those plebeians, ministers, and secretaries, the descendants of a subjugated people, imposing their schemes on the greatest lords of the kingdom, against all notions of justice and order. The state built by the Mazarins and Colberts had finally produced a caste of officeholders, born into the lower classes and yet all-powerful – a 'monster' now devouring the nobility of France.[95]

In Saint-Simon's conception of French society, emphasis was firmly placed on the internal divisions and distinctions between various interdependent groups. Divisions, necessary to the existence of a well-ordered society, were either sharp or porous according to the different principles of inclusion and exclusion at play. In the case of the second order, the hierarchy depicted by Saint-Simon was open inasmuch as it allowed a commoner to become a noble or a member of the lower nobility to enhance his status; it was closed insofar as a dukedom or a peerage could never be attained. Exclusion from these ranks was not based on a biological

[91] The praise was due to Louis-Pierre Anquetil, *L'esprit de la Ligue, ou Histoire politique des troubles de France, pendant les XVIe et XVIIe siècles* (Paris: n.p., 1767), xlvi. On the commissioning of the work, see the copy, in Saint-Simon's own handwriting, of the 'Commission donnée en 1664 au sieur abbé Le Laboureur par Messieurs les Ducs et Pairs de France', in Saint-Simon, *Écrits inédits*, iii. 508. On Le Laboureur, see Anonymous, 'Jean Le Laboureur', in Louis-Mayeul Chaudon, Antoine-François Delandine, and Louis-Marie Prudhomme (eds.), *Dictionnaire universel, historique, critique et bibliographique* (Paris: Mame frères, 1810–1812), 413–4. For a discussion of Le Laboureur's views and a comparison with Saint-Simon's, Carcassonne, *Montesquieu et le problème de la constitution française au XVIIIe siècle*, 11–18.

[92] [Jean Le Laboureur], *Histoire de la pairie de France et du Parlement de Paris* (London: Harding, 1740), 87–8.

[93] See Louis de Rouvroy de Saint-Simon, 'Mémoire succinct sur les formalités desquelles nécessairement la renonciation du Roy d'Espagne tant pour luy que pour sa postérité doit estre revestue en France pour y estre justement et stablement validée' (1712), in *Écrits inédits*, ii. 191–3. Also see Saint-Simon, *Mémoires* (1714), v. 3–5.

[94] Saint-Simon, 'Réfutation de l'idée du Parlement d'estre le premier corps de l'estat', 404.

[95] Saint-Simon, *Mémoires* (1715), v. 299.

understanding of race – despite what André Devyver has argued.[96] On the
contrary, it was a question relating to a family's antiquity; in the main, it
was a matter of tradition. The passage of time was crucial to the way Saint-
Simon construed his hierarchy. Not only did the most significant difference between lower and higher nobility lie in the latter's longer history of
dedication to king and nation; but the fact that promotion from one rank
to another could only occur gradually, over several generations, also shows
the importance he accorded time in burnishing a family's dignity. From
a different angle, the passing of time was instrumental in shaping the
relationship between a family and the nation as a whole. In fact, according
to Saint-Simon, it was because the ancient nobility vaunted a longer
history of sacrifices that its affinity with the nation was deeper. From its
antiquity derived its capacity to 'communicate more intimately with the
génie of France and its institutions', as one modern-day commentator has
noted.[97] The identification of the nobility with the nation depended on its
putative antiquity. Saint-Simon's insistence on its devotion to the crown
was surely characteristic of the manner in which the second order imagined
itself.[98] On the one hand, as we shall see, this way of portraying the nobility
served to justify its identification with the nation and, on the other, it was
an alternative to the notion that the king embodied the nation. In this
respect, although Saint-Simon might still seem entrapped in the identification of France with its kings, he detached himself from it by ascribing to
the high nobility a crucial role in representing the nation and its history.[99]
His claim that because the peers had remained by succession the same
'since the foundation of things' they therefore shared 'legislative and
constitutive power with the kings' is revealing.[100] In line with his views

---

[96] Devyver, *Le sang épuré*, 325–52.
[97] Corrado Fatta, *Esprit de Saint-Simon: 1. La mort de Vatel* (Paris: Corrêa, 1954), 66. On Saint-Simon's views on history, Malina Stefanovska, *Saint-Simon, un historien dans les marges* (Paris: Honoré Champion, 1998). Also see Béatrice Guion, 'Savoir comment écrire l'histoire de son temps: Les *Mémoires* de Saint-Simon et l'*ars historica* à l'âge classique', in Marc Hersant (ed.), *La guerre civile des langues*: Mémoires *de Saint-Simon, année 1710, 'Intrigue du mariage de M. le Duc de Berry'* (Paris: Garnier, 2011), 41–63, and Sylvain Menant, 'La genèse des Mémoires de Saint-Simon et l'historiographie des Lumières', in Marc Hersant et al. (eds.), *Histoire, histoires: Nouvelles approches de Saint-Simon et des récits des XVIIᵉ–XVIIIᵉ siècles* (Arras: Artois presses université, 2011), 19–26.
[98] On this, see Nicolas Le Roux, 'Introduction: Aux âmes bien nées ... Les obligations du sang', in Nicolas Le Roux and Martin Wrede (eds.), *Noblesse oblige: Identités et engagements aristocratiques à l'époque moderne* (Rennes: Presses universitaires de Rennes, 2017), 7–23.
[99] That Saint-Simon still identified the king with the nation is a claim made in Stefanovska, *Saint-Simon*, 127–35.
[100] Louis de Rouvroy de Saint-Simon, 'Mémoire succinct sur les formalités desquelles nécessairement la renonciation du roy d'Espagne tant pour luy que pour sa postérité doit estre revestue en France' (1712), in *Ecrits inédits*, ii. 205.

about the importance of time in legitimating authority, Saint-Simon was in fact implying that the high nobility and the king, being both equally venerable, shared the same prerogatives and, consequently, it was in the combination of the two that the 'legislative and constitutive power [resided], and not in the king alone'.[101] It was the union of crown and high nobility, unchanged since its origins, that represented the immortal body of Saint-Simon's nation – rather than the king alone. In a sense, it might be argued that while the royal blood stood for an uninterrupted transmission of authority, uniting otherwise unrelated pasts, the insistence on the nobility's spilling of blood turned that past into an unquestionable narrative, a meaningful history cemented by its sacrifices. In line with these views and yet from a very different angle, commoners and bourgeois were absent from that meaningful history since they had never given proof of their dedication to the country – or so argued Saint-Simon. Contrary to the nobility's, their interests remained private, and the lack of a past worth telling, a past lived out for France and made meaningful through sacrifices, confirmed it.

Time, Education, and Sacrifice: From Noble Lineages to Bourgeois Ethnicities

The same rhetoric of sacrifice that underpinned Saint-Simon's writings also permeated the works of many other champions of the second order. In their writings, throughout the eighteenth century, an emphasis on the bravery and selflessness of the ancient nobility remained pervasive. And yet, as the century advanced, what noblemen considered a fair reward for the sacrifices of their ancestors was increasingly seen by others as an unjust privilege. One common argument was that since rights were inherited they were unwarranted concessions, divorced from the merits of those enjoying them. To counter such views, many noblemen argued that they received the offices and rights of their ancestors because they had also inherited their moral qualities. Obviously, at stake was the crucial relationship between nobility as a moral quality and nobility as a legal status.[102] In the ensuing debate, the connection

---

[101] Saint-Simon, 'Mémoire succinct sur les formalités desquelles nécessairement la renonciation du roy d'Espagne tant pour luy que pour sa postérité doit estre revestue en France', 197.

[102] Much has been written on this. An interesting discussion is in Robert Descimon, 'Chercher de nouvelles voies pour interpréter les phénomènes nobiliaires dans la France moderne: La noblesse, "essence" ou rapport social?', *Revue d'histoire moderne et contemporaine*, 46 (1999), 5–21. Also see Élie Haddad, 'The Question of the Imprescriptibility of Nobility in Early Modern France', in Charles Lipp and Matthew Romaniello (eds.), *Contested Spaces of Nobility in Early Modern Europe* (London: Routledge, 2011), 147–66.

between race and blood on the one hand and virtue and honour on the other became key to understanding how moral qualities were transmitted – and, consequently, whether or not the claims of the nobility had any foundation.[103] Within a broader frame, the relationship between race and honour became crucial to the way the nobility conceived of its ties with France, as well as its pretensions to representing the entire nation through being its worthiest part. On this point, Ellery Schalk has argued for a growing separation between nobility as a moral quality and nobility as a legal status taking place in seventeenth-century debates.[104] It was this drift that eventually forced the nobility of the sword to base its arguments solely on birth, as confirmed by its ever-growing insistence on the purity of blood and its obsession with genealogy.[105] Shedding light on competing discourses, Schalk has offered an important contribution to our understanding of the history of the second order. However, while it is undeniable that the ancient nobility increasingly insisted on birth in order to combat the growing influence of the robins, and while it became widely accepted that nobility as a status did not necessarily imply nobility of conduct, the conclusions drawn by Schalk may be misleading. In fact, arguing that seventeenth- and eighteenth-century authors accepted that virtue could be found outside of the second order does not mean they rejected each and every connection between social status and moral qualities. Elaborating upon Schalk's thesis and setting the debate within the vocabulary of the time, Jay Smith has reached different and more convincing conclusions.[106] According to Smith, in the seventeenth and early eighteenth centuries the words 'birth' and 'race' referred above all to a family's social status and to its capacity to give its children a proper upbringing. Belonging to a 'good race' or being of 'noble birth' meant that a person would in all likelihood be educated in the noble virtues since his or her upbringing would take place in a setting where – it was believed – these were highly praised.[107] Being born into a distinguished

---

[103] On honour, virtue, and nobility in modern Europe, Hervé Crévillon and Diego Venturino (eds.), *Penser et vivre l'honneur à l'époque moderne* (Rennes: Presses universitaires de Rennes, 2011); see also Marisa Linton, *The Politics of Virtue in Enlightenment France* (Basingstoke: Palgrave, 2001).

[104] Ellery Schalk, *From Valor to Pedigree: Ideas of Nobility in France in the Sixteenth and Seventeenth Centuries* (Princeton: Princeton University Press, 1986), 115–44. Interesting examples are Blaise Pascal, *Pensées* (1670 – posthumous) (Paris: Gallimard, 2004), 106 (§ 85), and Pierre Charron, *De la sagesse* (1601) (Geneva: Slatkine, 1968), i. 420–5.

[105] On this, see Élie Haddad, 'De la terre au sang: L'héritage de la noblesse (XVIe–XVIIIe siècle)', in François Dubet (ed.), *Léguer, hériter* (Paris: la Découverte, 2016), 19–32.

[106] Smith, *The Culture of Merit*, 57–91.

[107] On public virtue and patriotism in seventeenth- and early eighteenth-century France, see Jean Pierre Labatut, 'Patriotisme et noblesse sous le règne de Louis XIV', *Revue d'histoire moderne et contemporaine*, 29 (1982), 622–34.

family furnished a fertile 'soil in which seeds of virtue were sown'.[108] If it was then assumed that even a person born into a noble family could stray from the proper path, it was also believed that this would be less likely to occur than in the case of a commoner, since there was little likelihood of a commoner being educated in the civic virtues. Although there was no necessary and predefined relationship between virtue and nobility, a relationship did nonetheless exist, one based on the education that a young nobleman was expected to receive.

Predictably, the idea that education played an important part in inculcating noble values was often embraced by the robins. Already at the beginning of the seventeenth century the great jurist Charles Loyseau (1566–1672) claimed that if children's

> conduct should sometimes be found to tally with their fathers', this proceeds not from procreation, which contributes nothing to souls, but only from education. On this count, indeed, the children of the well-off are much more likely to be virtuous. They are given careful instruction; their fathers provide them with a continual and eloquent example; they are under an obligation neither to degenerate from nor to belie their lineage; and, finally, the memory of their ancestors secures standing and a good reputation for them.[109]

Loyseau saw no contradiction in contending, a few pages later, that nobility was transmitted 'to posterity through blood', then adding that 'the older the nobility, the more honourable' it was.[110] A plausible explanation of the seeming inconsistency is that for Loyseau blood had little to do with nature and referred instead to the circumstances of the family into which a person was born. In other writings of the period, blood, nobility, and education were likewise closely linked. At the end of the seventeenth century, the père Ménestrier opined that nobility was 'an advantage of birth' that 'seems to transmit by blood some inclinations superior to the inclinations of those born in a middling condition'. Importantly, he went on, the education offered to those born into more 'advantageous circumstances, contributes much to the generous sentiments that elevate their minds above those of commoners'. Like Loyseau, the Jesuit father also emphasised that the memory of illustrious predecessors and of their great deeds was key in the upbringing of the children of the nobility, preventing

[108] Smith, *The Culture of Merit*, 65. See also Mark Motley, *Becoming a French Aristocrat: The Education of the Court Nobility, 1580–1715* (Princeton: Princeton University Press, 1990), 18–67.
[109] Charles Loyseau, *Traité des ordres et simples dignitez* (Châteaudun: Abel L'Angelier, 1610), 37.
[110] Ibid., 45.

them from doing 'anything that might make them unworthy of the honour they have received by coming into the world from such a distinguished blood'.[111] A similar association of blood, lineage, and education could also be found in the well-known *L'honneste homme* (1630). Written by the statesman and poet Nicolas Faret (1596–1646), it was one of the most popular manuals on how to acquire the politesse needed to flourish in high society.[112] According to Faret, it was obvious that those born into a noble family 'naturally have good inclinations that others are wanting'. It was equally clear that in 'the blood flow seeds of good and evil which germinate through time in our souls and allow all the good and the bad qualities to be born'. Even in this case the examples of forefathers served to restrain noblemen from committing actions that would debase their lineage, spurring them to great deeds: '[A]s those who were born among the people do not think themselves obliged to improve on the ones they have come from, in the same way those from good families will believe themselves to be deserving of blame if they are not at least capable of earning the same admiration as their predecessors.' But Faret also believed that virtue had 'no status assigned' and that there were many examples of individuals who 'from a base birth have elevated themselves through heroic deeds and to illustrious greatness'.[113] In 1652, the jurist Daniel de Priezac (1590–1662) argued that birth in a noble family influenced the life a person would lead, since the recollection of the heroic deeds of one's ancestors would indicate the path to an honourable life: '[T]here is no greater way to persuade children to follow virtue than the example of the fathers who give them love with their blood.'[114] To an extent, genealogy was here the teaching of virtue through examples, all the more powerful because of the affinity a young nobleman would feel with his great ancestors.

In part, these arguments were accepted by the scholar and genealogist Alexandre de Belleguise. In his *Traité de la noblesse*, a popular work first published in 1669, he advanced the trenchant claim that 'nature does not make noble nor bourgeois'. The distinction simply depended, on the one hand, on the will of kings, who recognised and rewarded the merits of their subjects by granting them titles and honours. On the other, it depended on

---

[111] Claude-François Ménestrier, *Les diverses espèces de noblesse* (Paris: pour Thomas Amaulry, libraire à Lyon, 1681), 'Preface', n.p. On the idea that honour belonged to a family rather than to an individual, Michel Nassiet, 'L'honneur au XVIᵉ siècle: Un capital collectif', in Drévillon and Venturino (eds.), *Penser et vivre l'honneur à l'époque moderne*, 78–80.

[112] See Maurice Magendie, 'Introduction', in Nicolas Faret, *L'honneste homme, ou L'art de plaire à la court* (1630) (Geneva: Slatkine, 1970), i–lii.

[113] Faret, *L'honneste homme*, 10.

[114] Daniel de Priezac, *Discours politiques: Première partie* (Paris: P. Rocolet, 1652), 74.

the transmission of merits and virtue from one generation to the next, consolidated by and confirmed through time. On such a basis, Belleguise advanced a series of distinctions between the different sorts of nobility, the most important being that between nobility of race and what he named accidental nobility. In the case of the former, 'time, which consumes everything' had the 'opposite effect', so that the older a family the more illustrious it was.[115] Conversely, accidental nobility was acquired by an individual by dint of great or heroic deeds. Interestingly, Belleguise made the case that such a nobility, although 'less esteemed inasmuch as it presupposes bourgeois origins, is in effect most glorious since the title is a testament to virtue'. Obviously, Belleguise's was an assault on the rights and prerogatives of the ancient nobility, launched in a work commissioned by the crown and written by a robin. But, for us, what is interesting is the importance of time in shaping the two different sorts of nobility. On what blood and race stood for, and what their role was in the transmission of nobility, the genealogist André-Gilles de La Roque (1598–1686) took a different stance.[116] With its insistence that nobility could only be transmitted by birth – a principle of strict exclusion rarely expounded in other seventeenth-century writings – the *Traité de la noblesse et de ses différentes espèces* (1678) somehow stood at a mid-point between the pre-modern idea of lineage and modern conceptions of race. In an often-quoted passage from the first page of his work, La Roque maintained that: 'Nobility is a quality that renders a person bearing it generous and that secretly induces the soul to love honesty. The virtue of ancestors bestows this supreme mark of nobility. There is in the seed a force and a principle, the nature of which I ignore, that transmit the inclinations of the fathers to their descendants.' Prima facie, this might seem to be a quasi-biological vindication of race as lineage. However, matters are made more complex by the fact that a few lines later the readers were told that 'personal virtue is necessary to gentlemen to sustain their quality'. According to La Roque, in fact, the motivation for an honourable life was a nobleman's desire to emulate his forefathers. It was their memory that led him to proceed 'towards glory and good deeds'.[117] The older a family, 'the greater become its vigour and strength'

---

[115] Alexandre de Belleguise, *Traité de la noblesse suivant les préjugez rendus par les commissaires deputez pour la vérification des titres de noblesse en Provence* (n.p., 1669), 51. I was unable to find Belleguise's dates of birth and death.

[116] On de La Roque, see the laudatory remarks in [Pierre-Daniel Huet], *Les origines de la ville de Caen et des lieux circonvoisins* (Rouen: Maurry, 1702), 592–4. See also Dinah Ribard, 'Livres, pouvoir et théorie: Comptabilité et noblesse en France à la fin du XVIIᵉ siècle', *Revue de synthèse*, 128 (2007), 97–122, and especially 111–17.

[117] Gilles-André de la Roque, *Le traité de la noblesse et des différentes espèces* (1678) (Paris: Mémoire et documents, 1994), 23

since the shame of a nobleman would itself be all the greater should he prove unworthy of his name. The older the family, the 'deeper the chasm' into which his faults would make him fall.[118]

Despite differences, some of them important, all the above authors, including La Roque, seemed to agree on the importance of memorialising the forefathers' heroic deeds in the raising of the children of the nobility. Such a belief lived on well into the eighteenth century. A popular *Avis d'une mere à son fils et sa fille*, published in 1728, repeated the argument: 'The merits of your fathers', the author wrote, 'will enhance your glory and will be your shame if you degenerate; they shed light on your virtues and your faults.' Virtue was not inherited: 'Birth bestows less honour than it requires, and to vaunt one's own race is to praise the merit of others.'[119] This line of argument rested on the implicit assumption that an empathetic bond existed between the nobles and their ancestors and that memory allowed an identification of the two. It is a point already grasped by Alexis de Tocqueville (1805–1859) when, in his famous *De la démocratie en Amérique* (1835–1840), he contended that within noble families, 'all generations become, as it were, contemporaneous'. In them, each member

> almost always knows his forefathers and respects them. He thinks he already sees his remote descendants, and he loves them. He willingly imposes duties on himself towards the former and the latter; and he will frequently sacrifice his personal gratifications to those who went before and to those who will come after him.[120]

Indeed, a nobleman would have identified with his family's past, its name standing for a glory that transcended time.[121] But memory might play such a role only because it recalled heroic and selfless deeds; it recalled, that is, a sacrifice. By appealing to a person's innermost feelings and insisting that unworthy conduct would tarnish the lineage and demean the sacrifice of his or her forefathers, that memory could affect a person's conduct, establishing a connection between the merits of his or her ancestors and themselves. Race as lineage, defined by that same bond, forged a relationship that transcended time by virtue of a rhetoric of sacrifice that instilled in a person a sense of pride and belonging. Familial ties and

---

[118] Ibid., 56 and 23.
[119] Anne-Thérèse de Marguenat de Courcelles de Lambert, *Avis d'une mere à son fils et sa fille* (Paris: Ganeau, 1728), 11.
[120] Alexis de Tocqueville, *De la démocratie en Amérique* (Paris: Garnier-Flammarion, 1981), ii. 126.
[121] On this, Jean Starobinski, 'Sur Corneille', in Starobinski, *L'œil vivant* (Paris: Gallimard, 1961), 62–3.

the memory of sacrifices were then crucial to the political claims of the nobility and to the education of their children.

Since the cornerstone of the nobility's discourse on rights was the notion that sacrifices had always been made for the sake of France, most if not all of those who perpetuated it celebrated time and again that spirit of self-denial in order to present the privileges of the second order as legitimate. As one nobleman stated in the late sixteenth century, their special relationship with the nation stemmed from the fact that they had 'cemented with their own blood the building' of the French state.[122] At the Estates General of 1614, the last before 1789, even the king was reminded that the distinctive feature of his nobles was their courage and that their 'quality is called nobility of blood' because their 'predecessors have generously spilt it in the furious combats and the bloody battles taking place over centuries within and without the kingdom'.[123] Blood was a mark of courage and self-denial. In some cases, references such as these even allowed a mystical identification of the nobility with the king and the nation at large. In a work on the duties of men at arms by the essayist Nicolas Rémond des Cours (1639?–1716), it was claimed that anguish at the loss of a father or a son would be assuaged by the glory of their having died for the nation:

> It seems that it is with joy that one remembers these precious losses in the victories won by the king, and each person secretly reads in a genealogy the death of a son or a nephew as the most beautiful passage, illuminating the rest. The virtue of the dead is considered the soul of a family's nobility, so it is glorious to partake of the sovereign's plans even in dying and, I would venture to say, if it is not a kind of sacrilege, that in these moments the king's glory becomes our own, common to all of us. We shall feel a part of him by contributing with our losses to the greatness of the state.[124]

It is a passage reminiscent of the words uttered by the old Horatius, in Pierre Corneille's (1606–1684) eponymous tragedy, when he resorts to killing his own son after he had fled the battlefield: 'He owes his country every drop of blood/and every drop saved has tarnished his fame.'[125]

---

[122] Pierre d'Origny, 'Le Hérault de la noblesse de France' (1578), *Revue historique, nobiliaire et biographique*, 12 (1875), 334.

[123] Henri de Bauffremont de Sennecey, 'Harangue de M. de Sennecey, président de la chambre de la noblesse, à la clôture des états et présentation des cahiers' (1614), in Jean Charlemagne Lalourcé and Jean-Jacques Duval d'Eprémesnil (eds.), *Recueil de pièces originales et authentiques, concernant la tenue des États généraux* (Paris: Barrois l'aîné, 1789), viii. 244.

[124] Nicolas Rémond des Cours, *Les véritables devoirs de l'homme d'épée* (Amsterdam: Adrian Braakman, 1697), 174.

[125] Pierre Corneille, 'Horace' (1639), in *Théâtre complet* (Paris: Gallimard, 1957), i. 878 (act iii, scene 6).

Emphasis on sacrifices remained strong throughout the eighteenth
century, despite – or, rather, because of – the increasing attacks on the
nobility's privileges. Moreover, they were now directly and variously
associated with ideas of usefulness and notions of public welfare. In 1763,
the abbé Poncelet (1720?–1780), after reminding his readers that it was
every nobleman's duty to educate his children to be 'virtuous citizens by
burning into their souls the principles of true honour', remarked that
noblemen should have 'no other aim but to be useful to the public'.[126]
When explaining what virtue actually stood for, the abbé referred to the
original traits of their Frankish ancestors, reminding his readers that in the
French constitution, 'fully martial from its origins', and in the spirit of
the ancient Franks one should 'seek the honour that has stamped on the
nation its character'.[127] According to Poncelet, noblemen were generous
souls affected 'more by the glory of the state than by their own interest',
who 'would sacrifice their fortune, spill their blood, [and] risk their lives to
do their duty'.[128] A few years later, an anonymous text rehearsed the same
arguments. It called for a regeneration of the nation against the debasing of
the 'patriarchal virtues', the 'simple *mœurs*', and the 'venerable honour'
that distinguished the French from other European peoples. To do so,
members of the second order should prove themselves the deserving
descendants of 'those worthy knights who have cemented the French
monarchy with their own blood'.[129]

As might be expected, given its importance for the claims of the nobility,
one of the targets of anti-aristocratic feelings was precisely the notion that
nobles alone had given up their lives for France. Fuelled by the rising
bourgeoisie and the nobility of the robe, arguments against privileges increasingly pointed out that other classes had shown their attachment to the nation
over the centuries. If nobility consisted in giving up one's life for it, then many
bourgeois and – though this was argued with less conviction – many commoners did indeed deserve its titles. It was a blow struck at the very heart of
nobility since it questioned the validity of the distinction between nobles and
non-nobles. But it was also an important tessera in the mosaic of what Jay
Smith has considered to be the self-ennobling of the lower classes.[130] A good

---

[126] [Polycarpe Poncelet], *Principes généraux pour servir à l'éducation des enfans, particulièrement de la
noblesse françoise* (Paris: P.G. Mercier, 1763), iii. 66–7, and 73–4.
[127] Ibid., iii. 74.   [128] Ibid., iii. 75–6.
[129] [Reboul], *Essai sur les mœurs du temps* (Paris: Vincent, 1768), 286–9.
[130] Smith, *Nobility Reimagined*, 182–221; see also Diego Venturino, 'Ni dieu ni roi: Avatars de
l'honneur dans la France moderne', in Drévillon and Venturino (eds.), *Penser et vivre l'honneur à
l'époque moderne*, 91–107.

example of how the nobility's claims to moral superiority were contested, in
the second half of the eighteenth century, is offered by the *Siège de Calais*
(1765), a work by the dramatist Pierre-Laurent Buirette de Belloy (1727–1775).
Performed for the first time in the wake of the Seven Years War, it was one of
the most popular plays of the century. It was a retelling of the story of the six
burghers that Auguste Rodin (1840–1917) would later immortalise in one of
his great sculptures.[131] The action takes place in 1374, during Edward III's
(1312–1377) siege of Calais. After a long-drawn-out resistance and after refusing
to accept Edward III as its king, the city finally surrenders. In retaliation for
the resistance it had offered until then, the English order the execution of six
citizens. Many, all of non-noble origin, volunteer to give up their lives to save
their fellow citizens. At the end of a complex plot furnished with romantic
affairs, political betrayals, and signal acts of bravery, Edward III relents and
abandons his campaign, disheartened by the patriotism of the citizens of
Calais. The burghers are hailed as the 'martyrs of the country'[132] – though, in
fact, Edward III finally decides to spare their lives. Whether the *Siège* was
a hymn to the monarchical feelings of the bourgeoisie, as Dziembowski and
Bell maintain, or a veiled critique of royal absolutism, as Eric Annandale
argues, it indubitably was a paean to bourgeois heroism and a disparagement
of the nobility – since, in the play, the Calaisian noblemen take to their
heels.[133] By recounting the story of the six burghers in the way he did, Belloy
was reminding the French that noblemen were not the only ones capable of
great, heroic deeds and that throughout history burghers and commoners
alike had sacrificed their lives for the nation. On the one hand, the play was
clearly intended as a refutation of the supposed patriotic selflessness of the
nobility; on the other, it was also a lesson to all non-nobles. In fact, as one

---

[131] On the political meanings and the patriotic message of the play, see: Carminella Biondi, 'Le siège de Calais di Dormont de Belloy: Ragioni di un successo', in Corrado Rosso (ed.), *Intorno a Montesquieu* (Pisa: Goliardica, 1970), 5–20; Dziembowski, *Un Nouveau Patriotisme français*, 472–86; Eric Annandale, 'Patriotism in de Belloy's Theatre: The Hidden Message', *Studies on Voltaire and the Eighteenth Century*, 304 (1992), 1225–8; John Dunkley, 'Medieval Heroes in Enlightenment Disguises: Figures from Voltaire and Belloy', in Peter Damian-Grint (ed.), *Medievalism and* manière gothique *in Enlightenment France* (Oxford: Voltaire Foundation, 2006), especially 164–76. For an assessment of the play, see Logan J. Connors, 'Introduction', in Pierre-Laurent Buirette de Belloy, *Le siège de Calais* (London: Modern Humanities Research Association, 2014), 1–59. On the place of the siege in the national imaginary, see Jean-Marie Moeglin, *Les bourgeois de Calais: Essai sur un mythe historique* (Paris: Albin Michel, 2002), 105–326. Also see, on Rodin's masterpiece and nineteenth-century nationalism, Richard Swedberg, 'Auguste Rodin's *The Burghers of Calais*: The Career of a Sculpture and its Appeal to Civic Heroism', *Theory, Culture and Society*, 22 (2005), 45–67.

[132] Belloy, *Le Siège de Calais*, 121 (act iv, scene 6).

[133] Dziembowski, *Un Nouveau Patriotisme français*, 474; Bell, *The Cult of the Nation*, 63–5; Annandale, 'Patriotism in de Belloy's theatre', 1226.

spectator remarked, the *Siège* did not offer examples of the *Grands* that were 'impossible to follow' but showed, on the contrary, ordinary citizens ready to sacrifice their lives for France.[134] Thus, Belloy's 'masterpiece of patriotism' made it possible for its (bourgeois) audience to empathise with the heroes of his play, being no longer constrained to look up to a nobility whose deeds it could not emulate because of its humble origins.[135]

The self-ennobling of the lower classes reflected in Belloy's play needs to be considered against the increasingly widespread conception that, as the Marquis de Vauban (1633–1707) wrote in the late seventeenth century, 'all men are born commoners'.[136] A noteworthy aspect of the mounting disaffection towards the privileges of the upper orders was the fact that while the bourgeois clearly rejected many of the pre-existing rules and beliefs concerning birthright, virtue, and honour, the wording they used was remarkably similar to that employed by those who outranked them. Moreover, the feelings to which they appealed were often the same. References to sacrifice were in fact a constant feature in the arguments of both parties. In his eulogy for the navy's lieutenant-general René Duguay-Trouin (1673–1736), the poet and academician Antoine Léonard Thomas (1732–1785) thus recalled that his hero, 'obliterating the obscurity' of his birth thanks to his undaunted courage, had been educated in the merchant navy with those values that marked out the path to glory.[137] Going as far as to undermine the belief that those born into a noble family were more inclined to heroic deeds, Thomas wrote that nature had granted Duguay-Trouin 'the fortune of being born without ancestors'. True nobility, he insisted, 'comes from serving the state: blood spilt for the country is always noble'.[138] In his influential *Le soldat citoyen* (1780), the historian Joseph Servan (1741–1808) went even further. Complaining that in monarchies 'a man without illustrious blood cannot serve his country without infinite trouble', he also lamented that the love for the nation, so typical of the ancestors of the French, had now faded away.[139] After urging his readers

---

[134] [Manson], *Examen impartial du Siège de Calais* (Calais: n.p., 1765), 5.

[135] The expression is due to Emmanuel de Croÿ-Solre, *Journal inédit (1718–1784)* (Paris: Flammarion, 1906–1921), ii. 187 (1765).

[136] Sébastien Le Prestre de Vauban, 'Des moyens à tenir pour faire une excellente noblesse par les services', in *Les oisivetés de monsieur de Vauban* (Paris: Champ Vallon, 2007), 254. The short text might have been written around 1691. For the dating, see Michel Nassiet, 'Idée d'une excellente noblesse', ibid., 237–8.

[137] Antoine Léonard Thomas, *Eloge de René Duguay-Trouin* (Paris: Bernard Brunet, 1761), 26.

[138] Ibid., 7.

[139] [Joseph Servan], *Le soldat citoyen, ou Vues patriotiques sur la manière la plus avantageuse de pourvoir à la défense du Royaume* (Neuchâtel: n.p., 1780), 429.

to follow their example, he went on to claim: 'We are still Frenchmen like our fathers and the germ of their *virtues* was transmitted to us along with the *blood* that runs through our veins.'[140] Blood, and the virtues and values it stood for, was the cement that allowed a community to transcend time. The lawyer Rossel, a scholar and editor of the *Bibliothèque du Nord*, made similar arguments in his six-volume *Histoire du patriotisme françois* (1769).[141] He maintained that, just like any nobleman, every upstanding citizen was capable of 'sacrificing himself', thinking 'only of the glory of his king or the honour and advantages of his nation'.[142] Making of patriotism the key to the history of France, Rossel argued that it was on the 'unfaltering love of the people for its kings and of the kings for its people', on this 'reciprocal attachment, finally, this patriotism', that the monarchy rested.[143] However, he remarked, the history of patriotism was not only that of 'a king sacrificing himself for his people nor of his people immolating themselves for their king'. Distancing himself from Thomas and Servan and, most importantly, from the arguments of the nobility as such, Rossel contended that 'one can be a great patriot without spilling any blood', contributing to the greatness of the nation by fostering its culture or augmenting its riches.[144] Even those who contributed in such ways to the greatness of the nation deserved a place in the history of French patriotism.[145] At the end of the eighteenth century, the abbé de Saint-Martin (1733–1819) took the argument still further, suggesting a rather curious comparison between the nobility of the sword and the robins and maintaining that both, though in different ways, gave up their lives for the nation. The 'great edifice of the republic', he argued, rested on two classes of noblemen:

> The one, consisting of a warrior nobility, eager to risk its life in the defence of its country and to earn the laurels watered by its blood, counting as nothing death when it is won on the fields of glory. . . . The other, formed of grave and virtuous magistrates, charged with the most sublime function of

[140] Servan, *Le soldat citoyen*, 51. Emphasis added.
[141] Unfortunately, information on Rossel is extremely scarce. Even his actual name is in doubt. That he was the editor of the *Bibliothèque du Nord*, is noted by an anonymous author in the *Journal des sçavans*, August 1778, 1713. See 'Rossel', in Joseph-Marie Quérard, *La France littéraire ou Dictionnaire bibliographique des savants, historiens et gens de lettres de la France* (Paris: Firmin Didot père et fils, 1827–1839), viii. 158.
[142] Rossel, *Histoire du patriotisme françois, ou Nouvelle historie de la France* (Paris: Lacombe, 1769), i. p. vi.
[143] Ibid., i. 15–16.   [144] We shall return to this point in Chapter 4.
[145] Rossel, *Histoire du patriotisme françois*, i. 52–3.

royalty, to dispense justice, to keep the peace, to safeguard custom, to ensure order in all ranks of society; endeavouring to emulate the first class through toil, virtue and services rendered; persuaded that, if blood spilt for the country is always noble, the glory of consuming one's own life through a long and slow sacrifice, is certainly worth as much, in the eyes of honour itself, as the honour of spilling it in an instant.[146]

The abbé de Saint-Martin's attempt to liken sacrifices on the battlefield to those made in libraries and archives might seem bizarre. Yet the importance he attached to notions of selfless dedication and sacrifice for the country's sake remains nonetheless revealing. Patriotic selflessness was surely a way of proving that personal interests and those of the nation were one and the same. And on this basis a group could set forth more effectively its own political claims.

The trope of sacrifice was thus instrumental in establishing an identification of one social group – be it the nobility of the sword, the nobility of the robe, or the bourgeoisie – with the entire nation. Indeed, in different ways, René Girard and Jean-Paul Roux have both argued that for a multitude to represent itself as a community the sacrifice of some of its members is often required.[147] Nowhere is this more in evidence than in the case of the nation, a community unfailingly built, in rhetorical terms, on that deepest source of integration, namely, the giving up of one's own life for one's fellow members. In fact, the adamantine strength of the nation rests in large measure on the bond it creates between those who surrender their lives and those whose lives are thereby saved. It is a crucial element that contributes to turning the 'imagined community' of the nation into a 'sacred' and living union so powerful that, appealing as it does to the memory of the dead, it can exact the lives of the living. Arguably, the insistence on past and present sacrifices came to perform this very function

---

[146] Louis-Pierre de Saint-Martin, 'Panégyrique de Saint Louis, prononcé dans la Chapelle du Louvre, le 25 Août 1784', in de Saint-Martin, *Les établissemens de Saint Louis, roi de France suivant le texte original, et rendus dans le langage actuel avec des notes; suivis du Panégyrique de S. Louis* (Paris: Nyon l'aîné, 1786), 552–3.

[147] René Girard, *La violence et le sacré* (Paris: B. Grasset, 1972), 13–62; Jean-Paul Roux, *Le sang: Mythes, symboles et réalités* (Paris: Fayard, 1988), 235–54. On the role of sacrifice in building social integration, see the classic study by Henri Hubert and Marcel Mauss, *Essai sur la nature et la fonction du sacrifice* (1898) (Paris: Presses universitaires de France, 2016). See also Roberto Esposito, *Communitas* (Turin: Einaudi, 1998); Philip Spencer and Howard Wollman, 'Blood and Sacrifice: Politics versus Culture in the Construction of Nationalism', in Kevin J. Brehony and Naz Rassool (eds.), *Nationalisms Old and New* (Basingstoke: Macmillan Press, 1999), 87–124; Ivan Strenski, *Contesting Sacrifice: Religion, Nationalism, and Social Thought in France* (Chicago: University of Chicago Press, 2002), 1–51; Jesse Goldhammer, *The Headless Republic: Sacrificial Violence in Modern French Thought* (Ithaca: Cornell University Press, 2005); Marcel Detienne, *L'identité nationale, une énigme* (Paris: Gallimard, 2010), 49–70.

within the discourses of eighteenth-century noblemen and bourgeois alike – often independently of their specific political ambitions. From the viewpoint of patriots and nationalists, sacrifices and the constant recalling of them could clearly fulfil an important pedagogical role. In this respect, the statements of the nobility of the sword and of a Servan present more similarities than differences. Even the manner in which noblemen and bourgeois sacralised the past, consolidating an unquestionable narrative with which its recipients may well have empathised, are comparable. But the differences are equally worthy of note. A crucial distinction concerns the relationship between the way groups imagined their history and their connection with the nation's past. While in fact seventeenth- and early eighteenth-century aristocratic discourses were centred on single families and their lineages, the bourgeois tended to evoke a history in which a particular class of industrious townsmen, anonymous yet culturally compact, claimed to embody the nation's history. The difference was between a narrative hinging on a genealogical conception of race and one implying a cultural, ethnic notion. To the bourgeois narrative we shall return in the third part of this book. What interests us, here, is the fact that from the 1730s onwards aristocratic discourse manifested a greater concern with the allegedly Frankish roots of the nobility. Poncelet's reference to the martial character of its Frankish ancestors in the quotation above was by that date far from unusual. Courage, honour, and selflessness were ever more closely tied to the values and memories of a group that was, in cultural terms, purportedly homogeneous – just as industriousness was starting to be associated with the bourgeoisie and its ancestors. There was, in other words, a crucial shift from a genealogical to an ethnic conception of the nobility's portrayal of itself. One author in particular would come to exert a profound influence over such changes, offering a history that depicted noblemen as an ethnic group embodying the nation; his ideas and works, as well as the cultural and intellectual shift they precipitated and informed, are the subject of the chapters that follow.

CHAPTER 2

History and Race
The Subject of Boulainvilliers's National Narrative

Boulainvilliers's Seditious Historiography

On 8 September 1722, Mathieu Marais (1665–1737), a lawyer in the *Parlement* of Paris, confided to his diary how much he had been struck by a text prefacing Antoine Aubery's (1616–1695) *Journal de l'histoire de Saint-Louis*. At the head of the *Journal*, Marais wrote, was:

> [A] *preface* among the most curious that may be read, and which is a rare piece of our history, where he [the author] deals with the most important subjects, as the succession to the crown, the part borne in it by the lords of the great fiefs, the regency of the queens, the private wars waged against the kings; [he deals] with justice, summons, and appeals, and all with a liberty and a candour, and a striking style that are nowhere else to be found. . . . Nothing is stronger and more daring than such reasonings, nothing more refined. And though they do not appear to be much used nowadays, it seems that the authorities should take action nonetheless, preventing the circulation of these manuscripts which teach things so curious and so contrary to sovereignty that it is almost a crime even to read them.[1]

The author of the subversive text was Henri de Boulainvilliers, Count de Saint-Saire (1658–1722).[2] The head of a well-known family of the ancient nobility and possibly descended from Stephen IV, King of Hungary (c. 1133–1165),[3]

---

[1] Mathieu Marais, *Journal et Mémoires (1715–1737)* (Paris: Firmin-Didot, 1863–1868), ii. 348–9. Italics in the text.

[2] The most complete biography of the Count de Boulainvilliers is Renée Simon's *Henry de Boulainviller: Historien, politique, philosophe, astrologue, 1658–1722* (Paris: Boivin, 1942). Also see Harold Ellis, *Boulainvilliers and the French Monarchy* (Ithaca: Cornell University Press, 1988); Diego Venturino, *Le ragioni della tradizione: Nobiltà e mondo moderno in Boulainvilliers (1658–1722)* (Turin: Le lettere, 1993); Olivier Tholozan, *Henri de Boulainvilliers: L'anti-absolutisme aristocratique légitimé par l'histoire* (Aix-en Provence: Presses universitaires d'Aix-Marseille, 1999). Although 'Boulainviller' is the correct spelling, we will use the form most common from the eighteenth century onwards. See, on the latter: Mathieu Marais to Jean Bouhier, 2 January 1726, in *Journal et Mémoires*, iii. 384.

[3] Henri de Boulainvilliers, 'Généalogie de la maison de Boulainvilliers' (Paris: Bibliothèque nationale de France, MS fonds français 32948), fol. 25.

during his youth Boulainvilliers followed a path common to those of his rank, going through the Collège and then serving as a royal musketeer. At the age of thirty, he retired from the army after a dispute with his father that worsened his economic circumstances and forced him to re-establish the household's fortunes. While the task must have consumed much of his time, he was still able to dedicate himself to his many intellectual interests, and after the unfortunate, premature death of two of his four children in 1709, he immersed himself completely in his studies. A member of the Burgundy circle together with Saint-Simon, Fénelon, the Dukes of Beauvilliers (1648–1714) and Chevreuse (1646–1712),[4] he was also a close friend of the Duke de Noailles (1650–1708).[5] It was perhaps at the gatherings organised by the duke, where politics and religion were freely discussed, that he made the acquaintance of Nicolas Fréret (1688–1749).[6] Sharing many intellectual concerns, not least an intense passion for history, the two struck up a warm friendship that would later inspire Voltaire's *Dîner du Comte de Boulainvilliers* (1767) – that 'very amusing and very impious' work.[7] According to Robert Shackleton and Renée Simon, Boulainvilliers even came into contact with Montesquieu, Bayle (1647–1706), and the young Voltaire – whom the count wrongly predicted would die at the age of thirty-two.[8] Although during his lifetime only the *Memoire pour la noblesse de France contre les ducs et les pairs* (1717) was published, many of his writings circulated in France well before his death in 1722.[9] Denis Dodart (1698–1775), the celebrated botanist and naturalist, wrote in 1723 to his friend the Baron de Montesquieu informing him that many possessed copies of

[4] Ellis, *Boulainvilliers and the French Monarchy*, 57–64. On the Burgundy Circle, see Andrew Mansfield, 'The Burgundy Circle's Plans to Undermine Louis XIV's "Absolute" State through Polysynody and the High Nobility', *Intellectual History Review*, 27 (2016), 223–45. Mansfield has noted Boulainvilliers's 'tenuous' connection with the Burgundy Circle: ibid., 223, n. 1.
[5] Saint-Simon, *Mémoires* (1715), v. 222.
[6] See Ira O. Wade, *The Clandestine Organization and Diffusion of Philosophic Ideas in France* (Princeton: Princeton University Press, 1938), 98. Also see Francesco Colonna d'Istria, 'Introduction', in Baruch Spinoza, *Éthique* (Paris: Armand Colin, 1907), xiv.
[7] The phrase is in Louis Petit de Bachaumont, Mathieu-François Pidansat de Mairobert, and Mouffle d'Angerville, *Mémoires secrets pour servir à l'histoire de la république des lettres en France depuis 1762 jusqu'à nos jours* (London: Adamson, 1783–1789), iii. 281 (10 January 1768). On the friendship between the two: M.-H. Guervin, 'Deux amis: Nicolas Fréret (1688–1749), Henry de Boulainviller (1658–1722)', *XVIIᵉ Siècle*, 7–8 (1950–1951), 197–204. The article contains a 'Lettre de M. Fréret écrite à M***, au sujet de la personne et des ouvrages de M. le Comte de Boulainvilliers' where his affection for the count emerges clearly.
[8] Robert Shackleton, *Montesquieu: A Critical Biography* (Oxford: Oxford University Press, 1961), 12; Simon, *Henry de Boulainviller*, 36 and 47. On Boulainvilliers's prediction, see François-Marie Arouet Voltaire, 'Dictionnaire philosophique' (1764), in *Œuvres*, xvii. 448.
[9] The attribution of the *Memoire pour la noblesse de France* to Boulainvilliers, accepted by Venturino and Seguin, is disputed by Tholozan. See: Venturino, *Le ragioni della tradizione*, 348; Maria Susana Seguin, 'Boulainvilliers, de l'inédit au clandestin', *La lettre clandestine*, 11 (2002), 21; Tholozan, *Henri de Boulainvilliers*, 26–7.

Boulainvilliers's manuscripts, including himself, and stating that, because of their content, they would 'never be printed, except in times of war and in a foreign country'.[10] Dodart was right in one respect, for in the latter half of the 1720s the count's works were indeed published in Amsterdam and London and smuggled into France. It was then that Boulainvilliers became 'à la mode'.[11] In the preface to the 1727 *Mémoires présentez a monseigneur le Duc d'Orléans*, the publishers even claimed that they were preparing an edition of 'all the works of this interesting and learned historian', a scholar who was 'truly well known in *France*' but whose writings had never been published 'notwithstanding the voracious appetite that the *French* have shown and continue to show for manuscript copies'.[12]

A polymath, Boulainvilliers was a celebrated philosopher, a translator of and commentator on Spinoza's (1632–1677) writings, an astrologer and astronomer, a theologian, and an erudite genealogist. But he was above all a learned, provocative, and widely read historian, a scholar whose works attracted the attention of readers through their elegant explanations of French history as well as their political implications.[13] According to Saint-Simon, Boulainvilliers 'had an excellent command of history, especially that of France'. Voltaire went so far as to describe him as 'the kingdom's most learned gentleman in history', a scholar who, 'had he not been so systematic', would have been 'the most capable of writing that of France'.[14] He touched on issues ranging from the origins of the monarchy to the history of noble families, and of the laws and institutions of the kingdom. His *État de la France* (1727), the *Histoire de l'ancien gouvernement de la France* (1727), the *Essais sur la noblesse de France* (1732), and the *Lettres sur les anciens Parlements de France* (1737) were all widely read, discussed, and even plagiarised throughout the century.[15] Somewhat less known were those texts in which he expounded his ideas on how history should be studied, understood, and written. The manuscript that had struck Marais so vividly was precisely one of three writings in which

[10] Dodart to Montesquieu, 23 November 1723, 753.
[11] Bernard Faÿ, *La Franc-maçonnerie et la révolution intellectuelle du XVIIIe siècle* (Paris: la Librairie française, 1961), 41.
[12] Pierre Gosse and Jean Néaulme, 'Avis des libraires', in Henri de Boulainvilliers, *Mémoires présentez à Monseigneur le Duc d'Orléans* (The Hague: aux dépens de la Compagnie, 1727), i. n.p. Italics in the text.
[13] Ellis, *Boulainvilliers and the French Monarchy*, 2–4.
[14] Saint-Simon, *Mémoires* (1715), v. 222; François-Marie Arouet Voltaire, 'Catalogue de la plupart des écrivains français qui ont paru dans le siècle de Louis XIV' (1756), in *Œuvres*, xiv. 45.
[15] On the dissemination of Boulainvilliers's works, see Tholozan, *Henri de Boulainvilliers*, 347–432.

the count distilled his ideas about the study of the past.[16] In all likelihood written between 1707 and 1714, the 'Préface critique au Journal de Saint Louis' was a plea for a national history 'free from lies and free from the impediments posed by political power'.[17] The other two texts, written in 1707 and 1708 respectively, are a letter 'Sur l'histoire et sa méthode' addressed to a Mademoiselle Cousinot – presumably from the prominent Parisian family of doctors – and the first of his *Lettres sur les Parlements ou États généraux*.[18]

The best starting point for appreciating Boulainvilliers's approach to the study of the past might be the 'Préface critique'. In it, after praising the erudition of André Duchesne (1584–1640), Pierre Pithou (1539–1596), and of the Jesuit and the Benedictine historians, the count argued that to write with discernment about the French past a scholar would not only need the freedom 'to think and to speak the truth' but should also be able to access 'the treasures of the Palace, of the Charters as well as those of the Parliament, of the Chamber of the Court of Account' and other similar bodies.[19] Direct access to sources, free from the authorities' scrutiny, was a necessary condition for writing a truthful and impartial history. From his standpoint, the immense mass of edicts, manuscripts, and private journals collected by kings, peers, and dukes for centuries were heedlessly hidden away in the king's libraries and in state archives, abandoned to the ravages of time. So, lamented the count:

> [I]t is impossible to have access to them without permission, which is only granted with great precautions and difficulties – besides the money it costs – since these treasures, which are not accessible otherwise than by reason of a vile interest, are guarded by ignorant people unable to care for them. Consequently, a great part of what would make the glory of the nation must perish each year in dust and be consumed by worms.[20]

Rather than let the French monuments perish in misery, the care of learned and concerned scholars should restore them to their deserved greatness,

---

[16] Henri de Boulainvilliers, 'Préface critique au Journal de Saint Louis', in Renée Simon, *Un révolté du Grand siècle: Henry de Boulainviller* (Garche: Éditions du nouvel humanisme, 1948), 85–131. See also Tholozan, *Henri de Boulainvilliers*, 447, and Gian Carlo Corada, 'La concezione della storia nel pensiero di Henry de Boulainviller', *A.C.M.E.: Annali della Facoltà di lettere e filosofia dell'Università degli studi di Milano*, 28 (1975), 324.

[17] Georges Benrekassa, 'Savoir politique et connaissance historique à l'aube des Lumières', *Studies on Voltaire and the Eighteenth Century*, 151 (1976), 265.

[18] The *Lettres sur les Parlements ou États généraux* contained fourteen letters written between 1708 and 1721. They were published posthumously as *Lettres sur les anciens Parlements de France*.

[19] Boulainvilliers, 'Préface critique au Journal de Saint Louis', 87.   [20] Ibid., 90.

finally arresting the debasement of the nation's history – in a literal as well as in a figurative sense.

Intent upon being in the best possible position in which to write about the history of France, Boulainvilliers's plea was in line with a new attitude towards the study of the past. References to the need for convincing proof and original sources were in fact increasingly present in the works published between the end of the seventeenth and the first half of the eighteenth century. Writing in 1694, the Jesuit father Ménestrier noted with delight how important the use of 'proof' had become in sustaining any historical narrative. It was a turn in scholarship that, he claimed, was 'characteristic of this century which, loving the truth as much as ingenious inventions, has found a way of uniting the two'. Evidence gathered from charters, chronicles, and memoirs was now being merged into 'reasonable narratives' for the benefit of readers and scholars. Ménestrier made a point of noting that such a change had only become possible by virtue of the antiquaries' meticulous compilation of sources. Their patient labours had made available to historians an unprecedented amount 'of material that awaits to be shaped' into a history.[21] It was an important recognition of the role of antiquaries in advancing historical knowledge, and an equally significant appreciation of the importance of primary sources in the study of the past. But while some authors, including Boulainvilliers, would have agreed with the Jesuit scholar, others did not. The abbé Vertot (1665–1735), for one, did not hesitate to declare that for his *Histoire de la conjuration du Portugal* (1689) he had refused to use the 'rare manuscripts' and 'the precious original' documents made available to him. Indeed, he deemed it safer to base his work on 'the most well-known books' on the history of Portugal. Others noted the increasing use of primary sources but by the same token deplored it. The lawyer and philosopher Géraud de Cordemoy (1626–1684) even complained that references to original sources were now so widespread that they had become 'very unpleasant', interrupting, as they did, the narrative: too 'much evidence' was being offered to the reader and 'our histories are now full of it'. A growing number of authors, such as the Benedictine scholars praised by Boulainvilliers in the 'Préface critique', did in fact pride themselves on their extensive use of original sources. The great Dom

---

[21] Claude-François Ménestrier, *Les divers caractères des ouvrages historiques, avec le plan d'une nouvelle histoire de la ville de Lyon* (Paris: J. Collombat, 1694), 59–60, and 69. On the notion of 'proof' in eighteenth-century historical scholarship, see Carlo Borghero, 'La prova: Problemi comuni e prestiti disciplinari nel Settecento', in Carlo Borghero and Rosamaria Loretelli (eds.), *Le metamorfosi dei linguaggi nel Settecento* (Rome: Edizioni di storia e letteratura, 2011), 3–21.

Mabillon (1632–1707) insisted on the need to offer the reader the original sources so as to 'firmly support' the narrative, while Bernard de Montfaucon (1655–1741) took care to stress that his *Monuments de la monarchie française* (1729–1733) was based on evidence 'taken from the originals of the time' and that, therefore, it would teach 'many things hitherto unknown'. The need to use primary sources eventually came to be felt even outside of the antiquaries' circles. That the père Gabriel Daniel (1649–1728), while working on his *Histoire de France* (1713), disregarded the manuscripts held in the king's library, those 'useless papers', might be a myth. But the fact that by 1734 Lenglet Du Fresnoy (1674–1755) mentioned the episode with contempt, testifies to the growing importance of primary sources for the scholarship of the time.[22] On the whole, such a turn was part of that complex, uncertain, and even contradictory merging of narrative history and erudition on which the Marquis de Condorcet (1743–1794) commented in the late eighteenth century and which paved the path to works such as Edward Gibbon's (1737–1794) monumental *History of the Decline and Fall of the Roman Empire* (1776–1789).[23] It was a path that would finally lead to a new understanding of historical scholarship as such and, on that path, Boulainvilliers himself stood.

Against the backdrop of early eighteenth-century debates over the respective worth of original and secondary sources, Boulainvilliers's call for an unhindered access to the nation's monuments might seem unoriginal. In truth, the count's plea to be granted access to royal libraries and state archives had significant implications for the ways in which the relationship between politics and the study of the past was imagined. While its arguments were in line with a widespread scholarly concern,

---

[22] René Aubert de Vertot, *Histoire de la conjuration du Portugal* (Amsterdam: H. Desbordes, 1689), 'Avertissement', n.p.; Géraud de Cordemoy, 'Observations sur l'histoire d'Hérodote', in de Cordemoy, *Divers traitez de métaphysique, d'histoire et de politique* (Paris: Veuve de J.-B. Coignard, 1691), 35; Jean Mabillon, *Brèves réflexions sur quelques règles de l'histoire* (1677) (Paris: P. O.L., 1990), 105. For the dating of Mabillon's manuscript: Blandine Barret-Kriegel, 'Jean Mabillon et la science de l'histoire', ibid., 18. Bernard de Montfaucon, *Les monumens de la monarchie françoise* (Paris: Gandouin et Giffart, 1729–1733), i. p. ii; the text was published posthumously; Nicolas Lenglet Du Fresnoy [C. Gordon de Percel], *De l'usage des romans, où l'on fait voir leur utilité et leurs différens caractères* (Amsterdam: Veuve de Poilras, 1734), i. 110, n.

[23] Jean-Antoine-Nicolas de Condorcet, 'Esquisse d'un tableau historique des progrès de l'esprit humain' (1793–1794), in *Œuvres* (Paris: Firmin Didot, 1847–1849), vi. 229–30. See, on the point, the classic essay by Arnaldo Momigliano, 'Ancient History and the Antiquarian', *Journal of the Warburg and Courtauld Institutes*, 13 (1950), 285–315. Also see Arnaldo Momigliano, 'Gibbon's Contribution to Historical Method', *Historia: Zeitschrift für Alte Geschichte*, 4 (1954), 450–63, and Chantal Grell, 'Les philosophes et l'histoire en France au dix-huitième siècle', in Sonja Asal and Johannes Rohbeck (eds.), *Aufklärung und Aufklärungskritik in Frankreich: Selbstdeutungen des 18. Jahrhunderts im Spiegel der Zeitgenossen* (Berlin: Berliner Wissenschafts-Verlag, 2003), 149–53.

the 'Préface' stressed in fact the need to access, without intermediaries, documents that until then had been available only to the king's historians. Boulainvilliers's was a plea for a history no longer written by the *Historiographes du Roi* or the *Historiographes de France* but rather by independent scholars offering their own interpretation of the sources and recounting their version of the French past. It would thus be possible for them to penetrate the secrets of the cabinet – without which, as an observer noted at the time, '[o]ne narrates but does not teach; one is a compiler but not a historian'.[24] Crucially for us, the end of the control of the king's historians over the 'truth' of the nation's history sought by Boulainvilliers would have produced a series of inherently anti-monarchical counter-narratives – narratives, that is, independent of the king and his ministers. Indeed, from such an angle, the count's was a reaction to the seventeenth-century distorting of national history into royalist propaganda. It was a response to a historiography subservient to royal power, one that, as Richelieu (1585–1642), Mazarin (1602–1661), and Colbert (1619–1683) conceived of it, was essentially designed to celebrate the king and, through him, the French nation at large.[25] Interestingly, well into the second half of the eighteenth century, public authorities were assiduously engaged in a study of the past that was plainly intended to arrest the weakening of royal absolutism. To such an end, in 1759 Jacob-Nicholas Moreau was commissioned to gather all those sources that could assist the authorities in their duties. As a sort of 'minister of history', Moreau's duty was to defend the throne and help 'prepare the ways of legislation' by leading public opinion.[26] His privileged access to the nation's monuments was precisely the sort that Boulainvilliers had castigated half a century earlier.

---

[24] Anonymous, review of [Charles Sevin Mis de Quincy], *Maximes et instructions sur l'art militaire par M***, officier général des armées du roy*, in *Journal de Trévoux, ou Mémoires pour servir à l'histoire des sciences et des arts*, October 1724, 1798.

[25] See the classic by Ranum, *Artisans of Glory*, passim. Also see Michel Tyvaert, 'L'image du roi: Légitimité et moralité royales dans les histoires de France au XVIIᵉ siècle', *Revue d'histoire moderne et contemporaine*, 21 (1974), 521–46, Christian Jouhaud, *Les pouvoirs de la littérature: Histoire d'un paradoxe* (Paris: Gallimard, 2000), 151–250, and Chantal Grell, 'Histoire et pouvoir dans la France du XVIIᵉ siècle', in Chantal Grell and Benoît Pellistrandi (eds.), *Les cours d'Espagne et de France au XVIIᵉ siècle* (Madrid: Casa de Velázquez, 2007), 279–305. On the offices of *Historiographe du Roi* and *Historiographe de France*, see Chantal Grell, 'Les historiographes en France XVIᵉ–XVIIIᵉ siècles', in Grell (ed.), *Les historiographes en Europe de la fin du Moyen Âge à la Révolution* (Paris: Presses de l'Université Paris-Sorbonne, 2006), 127–56.

[26] Jacob-Nicholas Moreau, *Mes souvenirs* (Paris: Plon, 1898), i. 79. On the point, Keith M. Baker, 'Controlling French History: The Ideological Arsenal of Jacob-Nicolas Moreau', in Baker, *Inventing the French Revolution*, 59–85, and Dieter Gembicki, *Histoire et politique à la fin de l'Ancien régime: Jacob-Nicolas Moreau (1717–1803)* (Paris: Nizet, 1979), especially 235–339. The expression 'minister of

In his pursuit of a more impartial and critical approach to the study of the past, Boulainvilliers attached immense importance to the plausibility of historical accounts – or to their 'vraisemblance', to use a notion central to eighteenth-century debates.[27] It was a concern that emerged in the majority of his writings, where he scrutinised and questioned some of the most common assumptions about the French past, disputing ancient and modern authors alike regardless of their reputation. Whether influenced by Richard Simon's (1638–1712) teachings at the Collège de Juilly,[28] or by his Spinozist readings,[29] or even by the ideas of Jean Le Clerc (1657–1736),[30] Boulainvilliers probed many received historical truths and rejected all implausible accounts. In his *Abrégé de l'histoire universelle*, he even went so far as to treat the Bible as a historical source like any other – though he refrained from judging the moral worth of its teachings. Highlighting the implausibility of many of its stories, first and foremost that of Adam and Eve, the count stressed its utter unreliability as a historical document – still a subversive notion at that time.[31] A similar attitude underpins his works on the French past. In his *Mémoires sur l'histoire du gouvernement de France*, he dismissed as unfounded the existence of Pharamond and the 'simple and naïve narration of Gregory of Tours' on the mythical king.[32] Even the legend of the Trojan origins of France was a target of his criticism: 'One is

---

history' is used by Carcassonne, *Montesquieu et le problème de la constitution française au XVIIIᵉ siècle*, 518, as well as Foucault, *Il faut défendre la société*, 120.

[27] See Nathalie Kremer, *Vraisemblance et représentation au XVIIIᵉ siècle* (Paris: Honoré Champion, 2011). On the notion of 'vraisemblance' in eighteenth-century historiography: Carlo Borghero, 'Les philosophes face à l'histoire: Quelques discussions sur la connaissance historique aux XVIIᵉ et XVIIIᵉ siècles', in Chantal Grell and Jean-Michel Dufays (eds.), *Pratiques et concepts de l'histoire en Europe, XVIᵉ–XVIIIᵉ siècles* (Paris: Presses de l'Université Paris-Sorbonne, 1990), 73–83.

[28] Simon, *Henry de Boulainviller*, 25, n. 48; Tholozan, *Henri de Boulainvilliers*, 18–19.

[29] See Paul Vernière, *Spinoza et la pensée française avant la Révolution* (Paris: Presses universitaires de France, 1954), i. 306–22. Also see Miguel Benítez, 'Un spinozisme suspect: A propos du Dieu de Boulainvilliers', *Dix-huitième siècle*, 24 (1992), 17–28, Stefano Brogi, *Il cerchio dell'universo: Libertinismo, spinozismo e filosofia della natura in Boulainvilliers* (Florence: Olschki, 1993), 137–214, and Lorenzo Rustighi, 'Pour une théologie politique du contemporain: La perspective de Boulainvilliers', *Dix-huitième siècle*, 48 (2016), 369–85.

[30] See Maria G. Zaccone Sina, 'L'interpretazione della *Genesi* in Henry de Boulainvilliers. Fonti: Jean Le Clerc e Thomas Burnet', *Rivista di filosofia neo-scolastica*, 72 (1980), 494–532, and Brogi, *Il cerchio dell'universo*, 32–9.

[31] Henri de Boulainvilliers, 'Abrégé de l'histoire universelle' (Paris: Bibliothèque nationale de France, MS fonds français 6363), i. p. ii. The work, unpublished, was probably written between 1700 and 1707. For the dating: Renée Simon, *A la recherche d'un homme et d'un auteur: Essai de bibliographie des ouvrages du Comte de Boulainviller* (Paris: Boivin, 1941), 15 and 18.

[32] Henri de Boulainvilliers, 'Mémoires sur l'histoire du gouvernement de France', in Boulainvilliers, *État de la France* (London: Palmer, 1727), i. 4. Boulainvilliers worked on the *État de la France* between 1699 and 1712, while the 'Mémoires' were written between 1710 and 1712. For the dating, Simon, *A la recherche d'un homme et d'un auteur*, 18.

absolutely struck, reading our early authors, to find them taking for granted a chimera so vain as the one that looks for the origins of the French nation in Phrygia and in the ruins of Troy without being able to provide any credible evidence.'[33]

According to Boulainvilliers, the implausibility of myths such as these would have been apparent if only historians had considered the reasons behind the events told in their stories. But, with regret, he lamented that people often halted at the surface of things and that most scholars focused only on 'events, with no attention to their causes'.[34] As he saw it, the purpose of history was not that of adding details to existing accounts, as the antiquaries endlessly did, 'ignoring the real usefulness of history'.[35] While collecting primary sources and verifying facts and dates was crucial, there was much more to the study of the past. In his letter to Mademoiselle Cousinot, Boulainvilliers suggested that a young person need not cram his or her memory with as many historical facts as he or she might learn. Conversely, he 'should untangle as much as he can the causes of the events of which this history [French history] does not speak from those same facts with which it dazzles us'.[36] Embellishing and adding details to existing narratives might have been praiseworthy, but it was only one aspect of the study of the past. Much more important, for Boulainvilliers, was understanding and explaining its causes. At that date, such a view was far from commonplace. The 1727 edition of Furetière's dictionary, echoing the seventeenth-century definition by the Jesuit scholar Le Moyne (1602–1671), still considered history to be 'an artful narrative; a description, an unrelenting, continuous, and truthful narration of the most memorable facts and the most famous deeds'. The need to understand causes or engage with original sources was not mentioned. For his part, Cordemoy suggested that historians should use their time to 'arrange the facts of history rather than research them'.[37] But, once again, Boulainvilliers's ideas were in line with those of the most innovative scholars of his day. Indeed, as early as 1671 the abbé Saint-Réal (1643–1692) had ceased to believe that the study of the past should be a mere narration of events and insisted that

[33] Henri de Boulainvilliers, 'Préface', in Boulainvilliers, État de la France, i. p. xxvii. The 'Préface' was probably written between 1710 and 1712.
[34] Henri de Boulainvilliers, 'Lettre à Mademoiselle Cousinot sur l'histoire et sa méthode', in Simon, Un révolté du Grand siècle, 72.
[35] Boulainvilliers, 'Lettre à Mademoiselle Cousinot sur l'histoire et sa méthode', 74.   [36] Ibid., 75.
[37] Antoine Furetière, Dictionnaire universel (The Hague: P. Husson, 1727), ii. s.v. 'histoire'. See also Pierre Le Moyne, De l'histoire (Paris: A. Billaine, 1670), 76–7. Géraud de Cordemoy, 'Ce qu'on doit observer en écrivant l'histoire', in Divers traitez de métaphysique, d'histoire et de politique, 68–9.

knowing history meant 'knowing facts through their causes'. The Jesuit scholar René Rapin (1661–1725) was adamant that historians should seek 'the true knot of each affair' and, by doing so, shed light on it. For his part, the Protestant scholar, Henri-Philippe de Limiers (16??–1728), remarked that only if and when history were to be 'used to teach the causes of events' would it be of any use. It was a view shared by Saint-Simon, and even Fénelon insisted that historians should not only describe but also 'discover the causes of events'.[38]

Firmly believing that a scholar should always buttress his arguments with sound evidence, Boulainvilliers sought the merging of antiquarian erudition, narrative history, and 'histoire critique'.[39] His aim was to forge a historiography based on a vast collection of original sources, relating verified facts, and seeking the causes of events.[40] Obviously, the count's works were far from the 'histoires philosophiques' of later eighteenth-century scholars. But, in some respects, they were a step in that direction.[41] His views were consistent with a changing understanding of the past and the usefulness of history, one intertwined with the momentous – if ambiguous and uncertain – victory of the *Modernes* over the *Anciens*.[42] One element that would have placed Boulainvilliers firmly in

---

[38] César de Saint-Réal, *De l'usage de l'histoire* (Paris: Barbin, 1671), 4; René Rapin, *Instructions pour l'histoire* (Paris: Mabre-Cramoist, 1677), 121; Henri-Philippe de Limiers, *Annales de la monarchie françoise, depuis son établissement jusques à présent* (Amsterdam: l'Honoré, 1724), 'Préface', i. n.p.; Louis de Rouvroy de Saint-Simon, 'Savoir s'il est permis d'écrire et de lire l'histoire, singulièrement celle de son temps' (July 1743), in *Mémoires*, i. 6; François de Salignac de La Mothe Fénelon, *Lettre à l'Académie française* (read out at the Académie in 1714, but published posthumously in 1716) (Geneva: Droz, 1970), 108.

[39] Henri de Boulainvilliers, *Lettres sur les anciens Parlemens de France que l'on nomme États-généraux* (London: T. Wood and S. Palmer, 1753), i. 6.

[40] Diego Venturino, 'Metodologia della ricerca e determinismo astrologico nella concezione storica di Henry de Boulainvilliers', *Rivista storica italiana*, 95 (1983), 393. On the eighteenth-century idea of 'histoire critique': Eugenio Garin, 'La storia "critica" della filosofia nel Settecento', *Giornale critico della filosofia italiana*, 49 (1970), 37–69.

[41] On the notion of 'histoire philosophique', see Trevor-Roper, 'The Historical Philosophy of the Enlightenment', passim. Also see Pocock, *Barbarism and Religion: Volume 2*, 7–25. An interesting overview is: Dario Perinetti, 'Philosophical Reflection on History', in Knud Haakonssen (ed.), *The Cambridge History of Eighteenth-Century Philosophy* (Cambridge: Cambridge University Press, 2006), 1107–40.

[42] See, for example, Jean Le Clerc, *'Parrhasiana', ou Pensées diverses sur des matières de critique, d'histoire, de morale et de politique* (Amsterdam: Héritiers d'Antoine Schelte, 1699–1701), i. 130–223. The relevant section of Le Clerc's book is tellingly entitled: 'De l'histoire et de la différence des historiens modernes et des anciens'. On the famous *Querelle*, see: Dan Edelstein, *The Enlightenment: A Genealogy* (Chicago: University of Chicago Press, 2010), especially 21–43; Paddy Bullard and Alexis Tadié (eds.), *Ancients and Moderns in Europe: Comparative Perspectives* (Oxford: Voltaire Foundation, 2016). An original perspective is in Marc Fumaroli, *Le sablier renversé: Des modernes aux anciens* (Paris: Gallimard, 2013). On its consequences for the study of the past, see Joseph M. Levine, *The Battle of the Books: History and Literature in the Augustan Age* (Ithaca: Cornell University Press,

the former camp was his rejection of all received historical truths and his
determination to assess the merits and faults of previous scholars on the
basis of primary sources alone. In line with the growing emphasis on
original documents, he conceived of the past as 'a bundle of facts that are
independent of one another, the truthfulness of which is doubtful until they
have been confirmed by evidence'.[43] It was the historian's task to find the
thread and connect events to their causes. Importantly, this aspiration to
forge a more analytical history also implied a shift from history as
a description to history as an explanation of the past. It was a turn that
certainly enabled the historian to preside over his sources, thereby shifting
the focus of his work from narration to discussion.[44] This more critical
approach, calling for a historian-interpreter to take the place of or work
alongside the historian-narrator, inevitably made of history an increasingly
controversial matter. When, in 1763, Adam Smith (1723–1790) noted that
modern historians were ever more litigious, he was making precisely this
point.[45] Interestingly, of these consequences Boulainvilliers himself was well
aware: '[I]n writing a work, every person will use his own method and his
own ideas, which, in a way, make its character independent of the subject.'
For such a reason, in the preface to his *État de la France* he stressed that his
views had not been influenced by the works of earlier scholars, nor indeed by
the père Daniel's forthcoming history of France: '[A]lthough we all seek the
truth of history and of the same subject, our points of view are so different
that we shall meet but rarely in the way we portray the same facts.'[46] Given
such an assumption, it is unsurprising to find that Boulainvilliers's works
contributed to rendering the historiography of France a fiercely contested
domain, and this to an unprecedented degree.

'Boulainvilliers's Transformation': Anti-histories, Politics, and Anthropology

An unhindered access to the monuments of the nation and an unbiased
critical spirit, 'animated by no passion, and without seeking any other
objective than attaining to the truth', were then for Boulainvilliers the

1991), and Chantal Grell, *Le dix-huitième siècle et l'antiquité en France: 1680–1789* (Oxford: Voltaire
    Foundation, 1995), 415–29.
[43] Boulainvilliers, *Lettres sur les anciens Parlemens*, i. 15.
[44] On this, see Krzysztof Pomian, *L'ordre du temps* (Paris: Gallimard, 1984), 21.
[45] Adam Smith, *Lectures on Rhetoric and Belles Lettres* (7 January 1763) (Oxford: Clarendon Press, 1983),
    101–2.
[46] Boulainvilliers, 'Préface', in Boulainvilliers, *État de la France*, i. p. xix.

essential tools of any serious scholar.[47] However, he knew well that the authorities' curbs on sources and a widespread lack of critical thinking made it difficult to find historians truly capable of explaining the nation's history. So, when asked by Mademoiselle Cousinot which authors one should read to learn about the French past, he declared himself 'remarkably dissatisfied'. And his disappointment was partly due to the lack of critical spirit among his fellow scholars. There was, however, another equally important reason for his discontent. Particularly discomforting was the persistent identification of the nation with the king, the only subject of most national histories:

> In truth, mademoiselle, do you believe we have gone very far if we know the dates of some events, the names of kings, of their ministers, and of their generals or their mistresses, if we ignore the reasons for their actions and for their rule, if we do not learn about the spirit [*génie*] of each century, the opinions, the *mœurs*, the dominant ideas or, to say it all, the passions that guide men? I would hardly take an interest in kings and I would not even bother with them if the misery of the human condition did not make peoples' happiness depend on them – or, rather, on their caprices.[48]

Lamenting the fact that French scholars only spoke 'of the kings or of their favourites, a few battles, treaties and, at most, a few rare characters', Boulainvilliers called for a history focusing on the actual lives of the French people. It was a plea against those many stories 'recounting only the deeds of kings'.[49] Even the histories of other countries were told in the same disappointing manner, a shortcoming that prompted the count to write an *Abrégé de l'histoire universelle* for his children, a work teaching 'the history of the *mœurs*, opinions, and religions of the different peoples of the earth', portraying 'as much as possible, the origins of the arts, ceremonies, and *mœurs*' of each nation.[50] Importantly, his aversion towards those 'entirely monarchical histories' was shared by many other scholars who, throughout the century, denounced the identification of royal biographies with national histories.[51] For one, Fénelon stressed that a historian's greatest merit lay in knowing a nation's forms of government and the details of its customs and morals. For the author of the *Aventures de Télémaque* (1699), in the writing of history a 'portrait that ignores what is called *il*

---

[47] Boulainvilliers, 'Préface critique au Journal de Saint Louis', 87–8.
[48] Boulainvilliers, 'Lettre à Mademoiselle Cousinot sur l'histoire et sa méthode', 72.
[49] Ibid., 73–4. [50] Boulainvilliers, 'Abrégé de l'histoire universelle', i. 2.
[51] The expression is from Boulainvilliers, 'Lettre à Mademoiselle Cousinot sur l'histoire et sa méthode', 74.

costume, does not really depict anything'.[52] Much later on, with a passion that recalled Boulainvilliers's, Voltaire complained that in reading most histories 'it seems that the earth was made for a few sovereigns and for those who have served their desires; everything else is ignored. By doing so, historians mimic those tyrants they speak of. They sacrifice humanity to a single man.'[53] The abbé Velly (1690–1759) also criticised his predecessors, for in their works he saw nothing 'but long descriptions of battles and sieges – no mentioning of the *mœurs* and the mind [*esprit*] of the nation'. Even Anne-Robert-Jacques Turgot (1727–1781) and Condorcet expressed their distaste for those histories that purported to represent the nation's past, but which merely told of the lives of its kings.[54] In the second half of the eighteenth century, the scholars still faithful to the royalist canon themselves became the target of mounting criticism. Such was the case with the père Daniel and his influential *Histoire de France* (1713), a work that, some maintained, ignored the usages of the people and focused entirely on the throne. It was a fault pointed out by the abbé Mably (1709–1785), for whom the Jesuit father, 'by seeing the monarchy wherever he finds the name of the king, never speaks of the customs, more or less rude, which form the only public law of the nation'. The same reproach was levelled by the novelist and essayist Nicolas Bricaire de la Dixmerie (1731–1791) when he complained that Daniel had 'written the history of the French kings rather than that of the French nation'. In his book, there was nothing 'on the *mœurs* and the usages; nothing that might show the national mind [*génie*] and character'.[55]

---

[52] Fénelon, *Lettre à l'Académie française*, 113. Italics in the text. The Italian word 'costume' would have been translated at the time by the French 'mœurs': Antoine Oudin and Lorenzo Ferretti, *Dictionnaire italien et françois* (Paris: n.p., 1681), i. 238.

[53] François-Marie Arouet Voltaire, 'Introduction de l'Abrégé de l'histoire universelle' (1753), in *Œuvres*, xxiv. 51–2. François-Marie Arouet Voltaire to Jacob Vernet, 1 June 1744, in *Œuvres*, xxxvi. 300. Also see François-Marie Arouet Voltaire, 'Nouvelles considérations sur l'histoire' (1744), in *Œuvres*, xvi. 140. On the importance given by Voltaire to a people's customs, see Myrtille Méricam-Bourdet, *Voltaire et l'écriture de l'histoire: Un enjeu politique* (Oxford: Voltaire Foundation, 2012), 141–65. It was an aspect already noted by Condorcet: Jean-Antoine-Nicolas de Condorcet, 'Vie de Voltaire' (1789), in *Œuvres*, iv. 94.

[54] Paul-François Velly, *Histoire de France depuis l'établissement de la monarchie jusqu'au règne de Louis XIV* (Paris: Desaint & Saillant, 1755–1786), i. pp. x–xi. Velly's *Histoire* was later continued by Jean-Jacques Garnier (1729–1805) and Claude Villaret (1715?–1766); Anne-Robert-Jacques Turgot, 'Second discours, sur les progrès successifs de l'esprit humain' (1750), in *Œuvres* (ed. Daire) (Osnabrück: Zeller, 1966), ii. 597–611; Condorcet, 'Esquisse d'un tableau historique des progrès de l'esprit humain', 232–5.

[55] Gabriel Bonnot de Mably, 'De la manière d'écrire l'histoire' (1783), in *Œuvres* (Darmstadt: Scientia Verlag Aalen, 1977), xii. 428; Nicolas Bricaire de la Dixmerie, *Les deux âges du goût et du génie français, sous Louis XIV et sous Louis XV* (Paris: Lacombe, 1769), 376. We shall return to the père Daniel and his work in the next chapter.

The growing tendency to disparage Daniel's book in the second half of the century, whether justified or not, is in many ways revealing. His *Histoire* was increasingly seen as part of a longstanding tradition of national narratives articulated through a succession of battles, royal marriages, and diplomatic treaties all decided and directed by the king and his closest ministers. It was a tradition that had crystallised long before, establishing itself in the seventeenth century as part of official state doctrine.[56] As the historiographical counterpart of the theory of the king's two bodies, the idea that the history of France and that of the royal family were essentially one and the same was a view largely shaped by the royal historiographers and the historiographers of France – and, of course, by the many who aspired to such posts.[57] Among others, it was an assumption accepted by the famous novelist and historiographer of France Charles Sorel (1602–1674). As he made clear in his *Advertissement sur l'histoire de la monarchie françoise* (1628): 'The most beautiful history of a kingdom is the one that speaks of the king's actions, since from these depends everything remarkable that is achieved by his subjects.'[58] The poet and critic Nicolas Boileau (1636–1711), himself royal historiographer since 1677, concurred.[59] Jean Racine (1639–1699), the great dramatist and playwright, appointed royal historiographer alongside Boileau, perfectly expressed such a viewpoint in a speech at the Académie: 'In the history of the king everything is alive, everything moves, everything is in action. It suffices to follow him, if one can, and study closely him alone. It is a continuous sequence of marvellous facts, which he alone starts, which he alone completes, as clear, as intelligible once they are executed as they were impenetrable before the execution.'[60] All decisions were made by the sovereign and communicated

[56] Ranum, *Artisans of Glory*, passim. Also see Louis Marin, *Le portrait du Roi* (Paris: Éditions de Minuit, 1981), 49–107.

[57] Many historians have used Ernst Kantorowicz's famous theory to shed light on the nature of French absolutism. See, for example, Ralph Giesey, *Cérémonial et puissance souveraine: France, XVe–XVIIe siècles* (Paris: Armand Colin, 1987); Apostolidès, *Le roi-machine*, passim; Marin, *Le portrait du Roi*, passim.

[58] Charles Sorel, *Advertissement sur l'histoire de la monarchie françoise* (Paris: C. Morlot, 1628), 53. On this, Jean-Marie Apostolidès, 'The Problem of History in Seventeenth-Century France', *Diacritics*, 12 (1982), 60–1. On Sorel's ideas concerning the nation's history, see Michèle Rosellini, 'Écrire l'histoire de France au service de la patrie: Le projet singulier de Charles Sorel', *Dix-septième siècle*, 246 (2010), 69–95.

[59] Nicolas Boileau, 'Epistre I: Au roy' (1669), in *Œuvres* (Paris: Gallimard, 1966), 103–7. Also see, Marc Fumaroli, 'Les abeilles et les araignées', in Fumaroli (ed.), *La Querelle des Anciens et des Modernes: XVIIe–XVIIIe siècles* (Paris: Gallimard, 2001), 129–63, and Ranum, *Artisans of Glory*, 297–302.

[60] Jean Racine, 'Discours prononcé à l'Académie française à la réception de MM. de Corneille et de Bergeret' (speech delivered in 1685), in *Œuvres* (Paris: Gallimard, 1950–1966), ii. 350. On Racine's

to his subjects, so that by studying his deeds alone a scholar could write a complete history of the nation.[61]

The consequences of the special tie between the king and his historians were deleterious in many respects. In the nineteenth century, Abel François Villemain (1790–1870) went so far as to complain that 'under Louis XIV, history had definitely degenerated from the greatness that the sixteenth century had bestowed on it'. Surviving only in unpublished journals and memoirs, during his reign history 'was official and untruthful, even when dealing with the most ancient past'.[62] Villemain's verdict might be somewhat harsh, but there is little doubt that throughout the seventeenth century historical scholarship suffered deeply from the stifling control of state authorities. And, indeed, most versions of the nation's past differing from the official state doctrine were marginalised. But the identification of the history of France with the history of its kings proved a resilient view even for scholarly reasons and, in particular, for the way historical writing itself was conceived of at the time. In fact, as late as the first half of the eighteenth century it was commonly assumed that historians should present the works of their worthiest predecessors, simply amending or adding details, embellishing the narrative according to the taste of the day.[63] As the bibliophile Jacques Le Long (1665–1721) noted in the late 1710s, historians only rarely offered 'solid evidence', and usually did 'nothing but copy one another endlessly'.[64] As late as 1784 one commentator – who, incidentally, credited Boulainvilliers with being the first to have plunged into 'the deep night of the origins of France' – remarked how the greatest historians of France, 'Le Gendre, Mézeray, Daniel', simply 'copy the chronicles or copy one another', thus repeating the same story over and over again. The main cause for this, he contended, was their difficulty in gaining access to the nation's monuments, which had only 'very recently been gathered'.[65]

---

views about history: Marie-Claude Canova-Green and Alain Viala (eds.), *Racine et l'histoire* (Tübingen: G. Narr, 2004).

[61] See Louis Marin, *Le récit est un piège* (Paris: Éditions de Minuit, 1973), 67–115; Richard Lockwood, 'Subject and Ceremony: Racine's Royalist Rhetoric', *MLN*, 100 (1985), 789–802; Pierre Zoberman, 'Représentation de l'homme, représentation du roi', in Gilles Declercq and Michèle Rosellini (eds.), *Jean Racine: 1699–1999* (Paris: Presses universitaires de France, 2003), 211–29.

[62] Abel François Villemain, *Cours de littérature française: Tableau du dix-huitième siècle* (Paris: Didier, 1838), ii. 140.

[63] Philippe Ariès, 'L'attitude devant l'histoire: Le XVIIe siècle', in Ariès, *Le temps de l'histoire* (Monaco: Éditions du Rocher, 1954), 160–2.

[64] Jacques Le Long, *Bibliothèque historique de la France, contenant le catalogue de tous les ouvrages tant imprimez que manuscrits qui traitent de l'histoire de ce roïaume* (Paris: G. Martin, 1719), preface, n.p.

[65] Dominique-Joseph Garat, review of Pierre Chabrit, *De la monarchie françoise, ou Ses loix*, in *Mercure de France*, 6 March 1784, 12–13.

Clearly, if old historiographical canons were inherently difficult to overcome, this was all the truer of the one identifying king and nation.

Despite the best efforts of state authorities to control the past, sparks of the sixteenth-century critical mind smouldered beneath the ashes, reignited at the end of the seventeenth century.[66] As we have already seen, Boulainvilliers's case is particularly instructive. Adamant that a historian's sole obligation was towards the truth, he insisted on the need to found history on original sources, looking for the causes of events rather than merely describing them. Most importantly, he advocated shifting the historian's gaze from the king and his ministers to the nation and its *mœurs*. This recommendation was crucial because of its political implications but also because it dovetailed with the other tenets of Boulainvilliers's historiography. First of all, the shift from a history centred on political conflicts and decisions to one that covered all aspects of society and culture required studying and dissecting sources that had been neglected until then and which the labours of antiquaries had now, if only in part, made available.[67] Second, the idea that direct knowledge about the nation could be produced independently of, and beyond the state, also meant rejecting the principle that only the king and his entourage knew the nation's history. Finally, the call for unhindered access to primary sources also implied a greater independence from the works of previous scholars and, therefore, from the canonical identification of king and nation. Freed from the king's sway, historians would also be free from the spell cast by those who had preceded them.

In his assessment of Boulainvilliers's historiography, Guy Chaussinand-Nogaret has focused on his calls for a history built around the customs and way of life of a people and, highlighting the originality of such an approach, he has gone so far as to make of him the '[i]nventor of cultural anthropology'.[68] While this is an overstatement, it is undeniable that the count's work was driven by the desire to set aside those monarchical narratives that pretended to tell the history of France and to embark instead upon a study of the arts, laws, institutions, religion, and *mœurs* of its people. The importance of this aspect of Boulainvilliers's thought was

---

[66] See Jacob Soll, 'Empirical History and the Transformation of Political Criticism in France from Bodin to Bayle', *Journal of the History of Ideas*, 64 (2003), 297–316.

[67] On this point, T. J. Cornell, 'Ancient History and the Antiquarian Revisited: Some Thoughts on Reading Momigliano's *Classical Foundations*', in M. H. Crawford and C. R. Ligota (eds.), *Ancient History and the Antiquarian: Essays in Memory of Arnaldo Momigliano* (London: The Warburg Institute, 1995), 8.

[68] Guy Chaussinand-Nogaret, *Le citoyen des Lumières* (Brussels: Éditions complexe, 1994), 27.

also stressed in the late 1970s by Mona Ozouf and François Furet in a well-known and much-quoted article. The two scholars made a compelling case for interpreting the count's *plan historique* as an attempt to discard the old royalist lens through which the nation's history was viewed.[69] Boulainvilliers's sorrow at the debasement of the aristocracy, coupled with his dissatisfaction with absolutist historiography, prompted him to reject the old identification of king and nation and find in the descendants of the Franks the actor embodying the nation. Crucially, these were a group of equals; of individuals with the same rights in the face of a monarch who, moreover, was reduced to a primus inter pares. Here, in this form of 'aristocratic liberalism', some have recently seen an important stage in the development of a specific French idea of freedom.[70] From a different angle, others, pondering this aspect of Boulainvilliers's thought, have instead made him out to be a 'classical republican, in all but name'.[71] Importantly for us, these two distinct views are both consistent with Furet and Ozouf's ideas. Emerging from their reading is in fact the subversive nature of a history that was radically anti-absolutist inasmuch as it denied the all-encompassing representational identification of the king with the people of France. Part of their contention was that the turn ventured by the count paved the path to new narratives stemming from the conceptual separation of king and nation. From such an angle, the comparison made by Furet and Ozouf between two authors as different as Boulainvilliers and the abbé Mably, highlighting the similarities of their claims and relegating their obvious political divergences to the background, becomes plausible.[72]

Perhaps even more useful for grasping the nature of Boulainvilliers's turn are certain references – marginal to his own endeavour, but central to our arguments – put forward by Claude Lévi-Strauss in the chapter on dialectics and history from his influential *La pensée sauvage*. The starting point of Lévi-Strauss's reasoning is that, just like any other form of knowledge, history also requires an encoding and a classification of its

[69] François Furet and Mona Ozouf, 'Deux légitimations historiques de la société française au XVIIIe siècle: Mably et Boulainvilliers', in Furet, *L'atelier de l'histoire* (Paris: Flammarion, 2007), 165–83. The essay was originally published in *Annales: Économies, sociétés, civilisations*, 34 (1979), 438–50.
[70] Annelien Dijn, *French Political Thought from Montesquieu to Tocqueville: Liberty in a Levelled Society?* (Cambridge: Cambridge University Press, 2008), 14–20; Saint Victor, *Les racines de la liberté*, 110–39.
[71] Johnson Kent Wright, 'The Idea of a Republican Constitution in Old Régime France', in Martin van Gelderen and Quentin Skinner (eds.), *Republicanism: A Shared European Heritage* (Cambridge: Cambridge University Press, 2002), i. 292.
[72] The similarities between the republicanism of the abbé and aristocratic liberalism have also been highlighted by Dijn, *French Political Thought from Montesquieu to Tocqueville*, 19–20.

object of enquiry. Yet since an event or a date never repeats itself, historical classifications may only be created by grouping a series of dates into a class in which each event 'has meaning [only] insofar as it relates to other dates in a complex relationship of correlation and opposition'.[73] Every class is defined by a specific frequency and represents a unique historical domain. The passage of a date or an event from one domain to another is impossible since these derive their meaning from the relationship with the other dates and events belonging to the same domain. A similar relationship is held to exist by Lévi-Strauss between different domains of history. Each class receives its meaning from its relationship to other classes of the same level or – which is the same – from the higher class to which it belongs. Just as in the case of dates and events, even historical classes lack an intelligibility of their own, deriving their meaning from a wider class within which they are necessarily inscribed. Because they are part of a strict hierarchy, to different classes correspond histories of 'unequal strength', depending on their capacity to explain or to describe reality. According to Lévi-Strauss, biographical or anecdotal narratives would then be the 'weakest' histories, which, while containing the greatest possible amount of information, are only capable of grasping and explaining a fairly limited portion of social and historical reality. The further an observer moves away from biographical and anecdotal history, the greater his or her capacity to apprehend a vast historical reality while, conversely, the weaker becomes his or her capacity to accurately describe it.[74]

The broader implications of Lévi-Strauss's arguments, as well as the debate over the faults and merits of structuralism that prompted them, are of secondary importance here. Instead, what is relevant is that on these grounds Lévi-Strauss went on to define an 'anti-history' as a narrative that, when inscribed in a given class or domain of analysis, contrasts with other accounts of that same class. It is a narrative that tries to describe and explain through different tools the same reality already described and explained by existing narratives belonging to the same domain. Of fundamental importance, since it introduces into political discourses a strong element of confrontation, the creation of an anti-history was explained by Lévi-Strauss by changes in the means through which knowledge is produced. In his own words: '[The] progress of knowledge and the creation of new sciences take place through the creation of anti-histories, showing that a certain order which is possible only on one plane ceases to be so on

[73] Claude Lévi-Strauss, *La pensée sauvage* (Paris: Plon, 1962), 343–4.   [74] Ibid., 346.

another.' The passage from one historiographical plane to another to explain the same facts is referred to by Lévi-Strauss – tellingly, for us – as 'Boulainvilliers's transformation'.[75] Although Lévi-Strauss only mentioned the count in an ambiguous remark on the Count de Gobineau (1816–1882), the nature of the shift he was referring to may easily be inferred from the overall argument. Obviously, through his work Boulainvilliers sought a displacement of the plane of interpretation of French history, passing from the time of politics to the time of anthropology. His anti-history did not merely entail a shift of focus from king to nation or from state to society. On the contrary, by changing the lens through which the nation was understood, he was changing the means through which it was represented: from king to nobles, from state to 'race'. Rather than the king's body, 'race' was now the medium giving unity to the nation.[76]

By stressing the shift from a fundamentally political to an essentially anthropological history of France, the arguments of Furet and Ozouf and those advanced by Lévi-Strauss are particularly helpful in understanding Boulainvilliers's interpretation of the French past. His nation was not an imagined unity produced by the subjects' obedience to the will of a king, nor was it the union created by his symbolic and immortal body. By inscribing it within a sort of anthropological *longue durée*, the nation's history no longer received its meaning from a single and everlasting royal lineage but, rather, from a series of seemingly immutable and clearly discernible anthropological features. Furet and Ozouf and Lévi-Strauss's interpretations have the great merit of highlighting in different ways the consequences of Boulainvilliers's resolute anti-absolutism for his national narrative. However, despite their merits, these interpretations fail to illuminate the manner in which Boulainvilliers conceived the new historical actor representing the nation. This is by no means a secondary detail. It is a point rightly grasped by Foucault who, in his lectures at the Collège de France on the relationship between race and politics, gave considerable space to Boulainvilliers's anti-history and his 'war of races'.[77] As he saw it, the kernel of the count's historiographical turn could be understood by considering two distinct aims.[78] The first, just as Furet and Ozouf argued, had been to discard the identification of king and nation and thus to

---

[75] Lévi-Strauss, *La pensée sauvage*, 346 n.

[76] As to what the count meant by the word 'race', we shall return to this topic shortly.

[77] For a comparison of the concept of anti-history in *La pensée sauvage* and *Il faut défendre la société*, see Jean-Claude Monod, 'Structure, spatialisation et archéologie, ou: "L'époque de l'histoire" peut-elle finir?', in Jocelyn Benoist and Fabio Merlini (eds.), *Historicité et spatialité* (Paris: Vrin, 2001), 55–76.

[78] Foucault, *Il faut défendre la société*, 125–48.

sunder the relationship between royalist knowledge and royal power, a relationship based on a 'circular knowledge which derives knowledge from knowledge' and stemming from the king's encounter 'with the image of his own absolutism'.[79] Pursuing such an aim and disrupting the identification of the king with the nation, Boulainvilliers began writing the 'history of subjects, or, in other words, to look at power from the other side'. For Foucault, the most important consequence of this shift was that the nation's history was no longer interpreted and depicted in juridical and legalistic terms. Instead, it was conceived as a political struggle between the monarchy and the nobility, and as the history of an unjust domination of the former over the latter.[80] From such an angle, Boulainvilliers's anti-history drove a wedge between the actor invested with political authority and what he perceived as the real subject of the nation's history.

According to Foucault, if Boulainvilliers's first objective was deeply anti-monarchical – or, more correctly, anti-absolutist – his second was anti-egalitarian. In fact, in the historical field he depicted, the nobility was but 'one nation among others circulating within the state', competing for access to social, economic, and political resources.[81] War between groups was central to a history that was no longer that of a state pacified by one uncontested and always just royal authority. In Boulainvilliers's scheme, argued Foucault, though the state might temper conflicts between groups, it could never eliminate them. This latent and at times even manifest struggle was not between individuals, contrary to the classical contractarian schemes. It was a war between social groups, identified by Boulainvilliers with the races composed of the descendants of the conquering Franks and the conquered Gauls. These were the real actors on the political stage, and the struggle between the race of the nobles and that of the commoners was the key to explaining the nation's history.[82] Boulainvilliers's interpretation of the relationship between the nobility and the nation did therefore contain two distinct elements. On the one hand, the nobility sought its independence from the monarch by rejecting the absolutist identification of king and nation. On the other, it asserted its rights over and against the commoners on the basis of the original conquest. On both sides was a highly antagonistic relationship that political authority could only temporarily muffle.

---

[79] Ibid., 114.   [80] Ibid., 149–50.   [81] Ibid., 117.   [82] Ibid., 144–6.

In line with the aims of his lecture course, Foucault also considered the form of Boulainvilliers's nation. He did so by insisting on the permanent and unrelenting conflict between the two races and on the authority of the one over the other. Placing such a conflict within his own biopolitical paradigm, he turned the concept of race into an instrument accounting for political antagonism as well as political pacification.[83] However, by so doing, and by assuming the existence of an unproblematic contiguity between nation and race in the count's writings, Foucault downplayed their semantic and conceptual complexity. The result was, so to speak, an exceedingly Foucauldian reading of Boulainvilliers's works. In fact, the interpretation of his scheme as the conquest of one race over another that legitimised the rule of the descendants of the conquerors over the descendants of the conquered loses strength when confronted with the complexity of Boulainvilliers's concept of nation – a complexity initially acknowledged but then downplayed by Foucault.[84] Indeed, Foucault correctly stressed that the eighteenth-century idea of nation often identified any group of individuals who believed that a special tie existed among them. The nobles were therefore a nation since they enjoyed immemorial rights over the commoners, just as the commoners were a nation since all were under the yoke of the nobility.[85] While Boulainvilliers himself would have accepted such a definition, he would have added that the French, nobles and commoners together, were also a single nation.[86] One crucial problem in grasping Boulainvilliers's theory is precisely the fact that the tie uniting commons and nobles has often been overlooked or misinterpreted. As we will see shortly, far from being merely a philological problem, this lies at

---

[83] Foucault's *Il faut défendre la société* has attracted more and more scholarly attention in recent years. See, for example: Ann Laura Stoler, *Race and the Education of Desire: Foucault's History of Sexuality and the Colonial Order of Things* (Durham, NC: Duke University Press, 1995), 55–94; John Marks, 'Foucault, Franks, Gauls. *Il faut défendre la société*: The 1976 Lectures at the Collège de France', *Theory, Culture and Society*, 17 (2000), 127–47; Stuart Elden, 'The War of Races and the Constitution of the State: Foucault's "*Il faut défendre la société*" and the Politics of Calculation', *Boundary 2* (2002), 125–51; Andrew W. Neal, 'Cutting Off the King's Head: Foucault's *Society Must Be Defended* and the Problem of Sovereignty', *Alternatives: Global, Local, Political*, 29 (2004), 373–98; Kim Su Rasmussen, 'Foucault's Genealogy of Racism', *Theory, Culture and Society*, 28 (2011), 34–51; Richard Groulx, *Michel Foucault, la politique comme guerre continuée: De la guerre des races au racisme d'État* (Paris: L'Harmattan, 2015); Florence Hulak, 'La guerre et la société: Le problème du "savoir historico-politique" chez Michel Foucault', *Philosophie*, 138 (2018), 61–75.

[84] See, for example, Foucault, *Il faut défendre la société*, 117 and 126.   [85] Ibid., 125–48.

[86] On the semantic complexity of the word 'nation' in eighteenth-century France, see Elisabeth Fehrenbach, 'Nation', in Rolf Reichardt and Hans-Jürgen Lüsebrink (eds.), *Handbuch politisch-sozialer Grundbegriffe in Frankreich: 1680–1820* (Munich: R. Oldenbourg, 1986), vii. 75–107; also Jacques Godechot, 'Nation, patrie et patriotisme en France au 18ᵉᵐᵉ siècle', *Annales historiques de la Révolution française*, 43 (1971), 481–501.

the very heart of the relationship between nation and race in the count's historical and political views.

The Nation and Hierarchical Opposition

In a well-known and much-quoted passage from the *Mémoires sur l'histoire du gouvernement de France*, the count made the trenchant claim that the conquest 'is the foundation of the French state in which we live'. It was there that the 'nation's political order' had its origin.[87] The form of rule existing before then was of little relevance; nor was the fact that the Franks were barbarians of greater significance: '[I]t was enough that they were conquerors. The antiquity of origin lost relevance in the face of the greater force of conquest – with reason. In a word, the Gauls became *subjects* while the others were *masters* and independent.'[88] Boulainvilliers reiterated the argument in the *Lettres sur les anciens Parlements*, where he explained that having conquered the Gallic lands under Clovis, the Franks 'established there their government as completely separate from the subdued nation, . . . which was always seen as having to work and cultivate the land'.[89] While there were many reasons why contemporaries might have found Boulainvilliers's views unappealing, paramount among them perhaps was the importance he apparently gave to the Frankish conquest. Not only his opponents, like Voltaire, the Président Hénault (1685–1770), the historian Jean-Jacques Garnier (1729–1805), and the abbé de Gourcy (1719–1805), but even Montesquieu and the Viscount d'Alès de Corbet (1715–1770?), whose views were in some respects closer to Boulainvilliers's, rejected the idea that a legitimate order could rest on an act of violence. In this, they were following a tradition running through from Pascal (1623–1662) to Rousseau (1712–1778), at the very least.[90] For these scholars, such

---

[87] Boulainvilliers, 'Mémoires sur l'histoire du gouvernement de France', 15.
[88] Ibid., 18. Our italics.   [89] Boulainvilliers, *Lettres sur les anciens Parlemens*, i. 62.
[90] Voltaire, 'Essai sur les mœurs et l'esprit des nations', xii. 129; Charles-Jean-François Hénault, *Histoire critique de l'établissement des Français dans les Gaules* (Paris: Buisson, 1801), i. 235, published posthumously; Jean-Jacques Garnier, *Traité de l'origine du gouvernement français* (Paris: Vente, 1765), 111–2; François-Antoine-Étienne de Gourcy, *Quel fut l'état des personnes en France sous la seconde race de nos rois?* (Paris: Desaint, 1769), 20; Augustin-Pierre Damiens de Gomicourt, 'Dissertation historique et critique pour servir à l'histoire des premiers temps de la monarchie française' (1754), in Carl Leber (ed.), *Collection des meilleurs dissertations relatifs à l'histoire de France* (Paris: J.-G. Dentu, 1838–), v. 40–112; Montesquieu, 'De l'Esprit des lois', 890–5 (book xxx. chaps. 10 and 11); Pierre-Alexandre d'Alès de Corbet [Le Vicomte D*****], *Origine de la noblesse françoise depuis l'établissement de la monarchie* (Paris: G. Desprez, 1766), 79–80; Pascal, *Pensées*, 110 (§ 94); Jean-Jacques Rousseau, 'Du contrat social' (1762), in *Œuvres* (Paris: Gallimard, 1959–), iii. 354–9.

considerations alone were reason enough to question Boulainvilliers's theories. Others, for their part, highlighted the practical impossibility of
grounding authority solely on brute force. Discussing the count's
Mémoires sur l'histoire du gouvernement de France, the abbé Proyart (1743–
1808), a celebrated essayist, pointed out the drawback:

> An army of Franks has defeated the Gauls. In such a way, all the Frankish
> soldiers have become nobles and all the Gauls have become slaves; and *this is
> right*, concludes the author. Nonetheless, by following such a new principle
> of justice, who might now prevent the Gauls from telling the Franks, that is,
> the commoners [telling] the nobles: 'Messieurs Franks, we are one thousand
> to one. We have long since been your vassals, now you [must] become ours.
> It pleases us to regain the patrimony of our fathers.'? As soon as such
> a decision were taken, all commoners would become nobles, and
> Monsieur de Boulainvilliers, turned into a commoner himself along with
> all the Frankish nobles, would be obliged to say, if he were consistent: *this is
> right.*[91]

Almost to the letter, the abbé Proyart was anticipating the arguments
famously made a few years later by the abbé Sieyès (1748–1836).[92] There
were thus moral as well as practical reasons that led many to reject the
notion that violence could be a basis of legitimacy. However, it would be
wrong to assume that Boulainvilliers himself did not share such concerns.
In truth, in the eyes of his commentators the conquest would in the end
assume a greater importance than it had for the count himself. The latter
point is confirmed by two elements emerging from a close study of his
writings. The first is that the separation between conquerors and conquered is actually somewhat blurred. Redescribed in the course of his
various works, it would seem to portray a far more complex legal, economic, and social situation. In fact, in his *Dissertation sur la noblesse
françoise* Boulainvilliers maintained that although they had lost their
freedom, 'the Gallo-Romans were not expropriated' nor did they entirely
lose their goods since, for practical reasons, the Franks seized only the lands
of the Romans, leaving to the Gauls almost all their properties.
Furthermore, the land was divided into 'servile *mas* and *mansions* which
were the legacies of the Gauls; into free goods or freeholds which were
hereditarily and freely possessed by single Frenchmen . . .; and into fiscal

---

[91] Liévin-Bonaventure Proyart, 'Vie du Dauphin père de Louis XV, écrite sur les mémoires de la cour,
enrichie des écrits du même Prince' (1777), in *Œuvres* (Paris: Méquignon fils aîné, 1819), vii. 275–6.
Italics in the text.
[92] Emmanuel-Joseph Sieyès, *Qu'est-ce que le tiers-état?* (1789) (Paris: Flammarion, 1988), 44–6. To
Sieyès's view we shall return in Chapter 7.

goods divided into royal domains and into benefits'.[93] To such a multifaceted diversification of landed property corresponded an equally complex social hierarchy. According to Boulainvilliers, below the nobles of Frankish origin, who were at the summit of the pyramid, were the 'ingenus', a class of free men that included part of the Franks but also some descendants of the Gallo-Romans who owned property and goods and who took part in the 'general contribution that the entire subdued nation owed to the public treasury'. Beneath the 'ingenus' were the 'lides', semi-free men who could own property and money but who were legally and financially subject to noble masters.[94] At the base of the pyramid were the serfs, who had no rights and could not own land. Obviously, in and of itself, such a scheme contradicts the idea of a neat separation between conquered and conquerors, or slaves and masters.

But there is another element that forces us to reconsider the place of the conquest in Boulainvilliers's thought. The complex system of property rights, obligations, and loyalties he depicted was in fact tied to a momentous historical change in French society. As Diego Venturino has pointed out, the historical and political system described by the count cannot be entirely understood by referring exclusively to, or even by simply concentrating on, the single act of the conquest – important though it was.[95] The conquest was a single historical moment which Boulainvilliers coupled with another turning point, that is, the rise of feudalism. Starting with Hugh Capet's (c. 934–996) usurpation and ending with the reign of Philip the Fair (1268–1314), feudalism was seen by Boulainvilliers not only as a fundamental phase for understanding legal and historical rights.[96] Importantly, it also had a broader cultural meaning relating to a specific vision of society and to the values and hierarchies shaping it. It was because of the principles that such a system enshrined and the order it established that Boulainvilliers famously referred to feudalism as 'the masterpiece of the human mind' – another claim that greatly displeased many of his contemporaries.[97] According to the count, the merits of feudalism were clear:

---

[93] Henri de Boulainvilliers, 'Dissertation sur la noblesse françoise', in Devyver, *Le sang épuré*, 514. Italics in the text. The 'Dissertation' was probably written around 1700; see Simon, *A la recherche d'un homme et d'un auteur*, 13.

[94] Boulainvilliers, 'Mémoires sur l'histoire du gouvernement de France', 32.

[95] Venturino, *Le ragioni della tradizione*, 229–43.

[96] Boulainvilliers, *Lettres sur les anciens Parlemens*, i. 171.

[97] Ibid., i. 127. For a detailed analysis of Boulainvilliers's views on feudalism, Diego Venturino, 'Feudalismo e monarchia nel pensiero di Henri de Boulainvilliers', *Annali della fondazione Luigi Einaudi*, 18 (1984), 215–41. On the censure of eighteenth-century authors, see, for example, Voltaire,

> [N]othing is better and more convenient than the order of the fiefs, which establishes a fixed revenue and yet, if necessary, is subject to increase; a levy of troops always ready when necessary, which may also be increased in number depending on needs. Furthermore, this order, by making men owners of their goods, leads them to favour the conservation of the whole [social order] and uses for such a purpose the liveliest passions of nature: the love for oneself and for one's own well-being and the love for one's own family.[98]

Here, the notion of the original conquest as the founding moment of legitimate rule and the belief in the natural subjugation of the commoners by the nobles ceases to be so central to Boulainvilliers's theory. This is a point that becomes even clearer further on in the *Mémoires sur l'histoire du gouvernement de France* when, trying to prove that the rights over the lands of the nobles were not a king's concession since they were not within his domain, Boulainvilliers claimed that the nobles need not insist on conquest, for

> our best title is not that, since feudality, which has convention as its principle and reciprocal trust as its guarantee, places our kings in an obligation towards us as it places us in an obligation towards them, the only difference being force, which is on their side.[99]

Venturino holds this to be a crucial passage, since it represents the 'definitive dismissal of all references to the original conquest as the true foundation of rights'.[100] Though this may be an overstatement, it nonetheless remains the case that another principle, encapsulated in the notion of feudalism, is here coupled with the right of conquest. It is a point that

---

'Catalogue de la plupart des écrivains français', 45; René-Louis de Voyer de Paulmy d'Argenson, *Considérations sur le gouvernement ancien et présent de la France* (Amsterdam: Marc Michel Rey, 1764), 126–7; Nicolas Bergasse, *Observations sur les préjugés de la noblesse héréditaire* (n.p., 1789), 8–14; Antoine Sabatier de Castres, *Les trois siècles de notre littérature, ou Tableau de l'esprit de nos écrivains depuis François Ier jusqu'en 1772* (Amsterdam: Gueffier, 1772), i. 157; Robinet et al., *Dictionnaire universel des sciences morale, économique, politique et diplomatique*, ix. 188. For an overview of the debates surrounding the idea of feudalism in eighteenth-century France, see the classic studies by John Q. C. Mackrell, *The Attack upon Feudalism in Eighteenth-Century France* (London: Routledge and Kegan Paul, 1973), and Lionel Gossman, *Medievalism and the Ideologies of the Enlightenment: The World and Work of La Curne de Sainte-Palaye* (Baltimore: Johns Hopkins Press, 1968). Also see: J. H. M. Salmon, 'Renaissance Jurists and "Enlightened" Magistrates: Perspectives on Feudalism in Eighteenth-Century France', *French History*, 8 (1994), 387–402; Ian Wood, *The Modern Origins of the Early Middle Ages* (Oxford: Oxford University Press, 2013); Alicia C. Montoya, *Medievalist Enlightenment: From Charles Perrault to Jean-Jacques Rousseau* (Cambridge: D.S. Brewer, 2013).
[98] Boulainvilliers, 'Mémoires sur l'histoire du gouvernement de France', 152.   [99] Ibid., 180.
[100] Venturino, *Le ragioni della tradizione*, 239.

renders any reading of Boulainvilliers's works more complex since the history of a violent conquest resulting in the rule of conquerors over conquered is combined with an almost consensual relationship between the two parts. If feudalism is another key turning point in French history, then the importance of the dichotomy opposing conquerors to conquered needs to be re-thought since the relationship between nobles and commoners is no longer based solely on the subjugation of the Gauls and their descendants. In fact, feudalism introduced a complex system of social, political, and juridical relationships ultimately resting on the reciprocal trust of all members of the body politic united in a single – if not entirely peaceful – system. As Boulainvilliers saw it, feudalism 'supposed inviolable rules for the superiors and the inferiors, based on equity, faith, and agreement; so that the master of the fief could not vex nor oppress his vassals, nor treat them arbitrarily . . . if not at the cost of losing his right; in the same way the vassals could not fail to serve and to be loyal without losing their property'.[101] Within such a frame of reference, the relationship between noblemen and commoners slowly but radically changed:

> [A]t the accession of Hugh Capet, the two peoples were confounded under one and the same law, even though the distinction of the Salic lands was as great as ever and the slavery of the inhabitants of the country subsisted for a long time to come in relation to the rights of the lords, but not in relation to the difference between the nations.[102]

According to Boulainvilliers, during the Feudal Age the relationship between the two nations, conqueror and conquered, underwent a momentous change. A legacy of the initial subjugation, the rights of the nobles were now coupled with a series of duties towards their vassals. The original racial antagonism had been replaced by a legal opposition. The contrast slowly became internal to one single community. Even cultural distinctions, which had played a crucial role in the aftermath of the conquest, had faded away because of the merging of the two groups. Far from merely being the imposition of the heirs of the conquerors upon the heirs of the conquered, feudal law was instead a rule 'accepted by the kings and by the people, if not by solemn deliberation, at least by public usage'.[103] Rejecting the notion that a violent conquest could, in and of itself, lead to a legitimate form of rule, Boulainvilliers believed that authority should be based on some sort of recognition by all parties. Contrary to

---

[101] Boulainvilliers, *Lettres sur les anciens Parlemens de France*, i. 127–8. Italics in the text.
[102] Boulainvilliers, 'Dissertation sur la noblesse françoise', 515.
[103] Boulainvilliers, 'Mémoires sur l'histoire du gouvernement de France', 180.

contractarian theories, however, the consensus was expressed in this case by the succeeding generations of Frenchmen, voicing their single will by shaping and by accepting tradition. Legitimacy did not lie in the original conquest *per se*, nor was feudalism legitimate because it derived from the conquest. The two created a rightful order only because a lasting order emerged from them: '[T]rue authority is not that which requires all that it wants at certain moments and which ceases as soon as one opposes it, but that which is equally solid and befitting those upon whom it is exerted, following the axiom that *whatever is violent cannot endure*.'[104] An act of violence could be a source of legitimacy only if it created an order that withstood the test of time.

Within Boulainvilliers's scheme, the overcoming of the opposition between Franks and Gauls led to a new distinction between noblemen and commoners which, in turn, came to forge a new relationship between each group within the nation as a whole. In the count's writings, in fact, following the feudal period, the nobles were by turns said to be *a* nation, to be a *part* of the French nation, and, most importantly, to be *the* French nation. In the first case, they were simply defined as a group bound by a specific tie and, in this sense, even the commoners were a nation. In the second case the nobles were a part of the nation with a specific social role and, again, the same could be said of the commoners. In the third and final instance, on the contrary, the nobles were said to be the French nation as a whole since they represented it – a prospect clearly denied the commoners. But considering the last two meanings inevitably begs the question of how the nobles could tell themselves apart from the commoners and, at the same time, represent them. One explanation might be ventured with the help of Louis Dumont's studies of Indian caste societies and his notion of 'hierarchical opposition'.[105] In his well-known *Homo Hierarchicus*, Dumont made the case that what he defined as 'traditional societies' are usually structured around the antagonism between a lower and an upper pole. Since this is inscribed within a series of values accepted by all, the opposition does not necessarily erupt into open confrontation. Moreover, the two poles are not mutually exclusive, since the upper can include the lower one by representing the whole of society. According to Dumont, this is made possible by the fact that the upper pole enjoys its dominant position because it allegedly embodies the values on which

---

[104] Boulainvilliers, *Lettres sur les anciens Parlemens de France*, i. 128–9; italics in the text.
[105] Louis Dumont, *Homo hierarchicus: Le système des castes et ses implications* (Paris: Gallimard, 1979). For a detailed analysis of Dumont's theory, Robert Parkin, *Louis Dumont and Hierarchical Opposition* (New York: Berghahn, 2003).

society is founded.[106] It is on such a basis that the upper pole can imagine – and the lower pole may accept – a schema for a coherent society in spite of the obvious antagonism. Although Dumont's thesis derives from the study of caste societies, the extent to which it applies to Boulainvilliers's own system is striking. In fact, according to the count, the nobles dominated the commoners but also encompassed them since they embodied those values identifying the French nation as such: courage, selflessness, and an enduring willingness to serve the community. Their alleged self-abnegation for the common good and their belonging to families that had served the state at the cost of great sacrifices were values that many non-nobles would also have recognised as fundamental. Only on such a basis could Boulainvilliers posit a clear distinction between commoners and nobles while at the same time claiming that the latter deservedly represented the French as a whole.

Like his seventeenth-century predecessors, Boulainvilliers then imagined a unique relationship between the nobles and the nation, a relationship based on their sacrifices and their lineage. Indeed, his works abound in references to blood. For this reason, György Lukács saw him as a forerunner of modern racism, while Marc Bloch labelled him a 'prototype Gobineau with less enthusiasm and more learning'.[107] More recently, scholars have contested such a reading, emphasising the distance between Boulainvilliers's conception of 'race' and the modern meaning.[108] Tellingly, it was a point already made by Gobineau himself when he remarked that Boulainvilliers 'did not have the faintest notion of race'.[109] Doubtless his ideas, which were in line with the discourses of the nobility in the seventeenth and early eighteenth centuries, readily lent themselves to distortion by modern racialist thinkers.[110] But, crucially, according to the count virtue was not an inherited quality biologically passed down from father to son. It was on the contrary a good upbringing that rendered 'certain virtues hereditary'.[111] This would be more likely to occur in noble families, not only because of the greater social and economic means they

---

[106] Dumont, *Homo hierarchicus*, 396–403.
[107] Lukács, *Die Zerstörung der Vernunft*, 526; Marc Bloch, *La société féodale* (Paris: Albin Michel, 1989), 12. Also see: Devyver, *Le sang épuré*, passim, and Gerhard Gerhardi, 'L'idéologie du sang chez Boulainvilliers et sa réception au 18e siècle', *Études sur le XVIIIe siècle*, 11 (1984), 11–20.
[108] Venturino, *Le ragioni della tradizione*, passim; Tholozan, *Henri de Boulainvilliers*, passim.
[109] Quoted in Ludwig Schemann, *Gobineaus Rassenwerk: Aktenstücke und Betrachtungen zur Geschichte und Kritik des* Essai sur l'inégalité des races humaines (Stuttgart: F. Frommann, 1910), 476.
[110] It was a point hinted at by Arendt in her 'Race-Thinking before Racism', 44–5.
[111] Henri de Boulainvilliers, 'Idée d'un système général d'éducation' (1700), in *Œuvres philosophiques* (The Hague: M. Nijhoff, 1973–1975), ii. 135.

enjoyed, but also because the stirring deeds of ancestors could be portrayed as compelling examples to follow.[112] In this sense he could claim virtue to be 'more common in good races than in others'.[113] That the worth of nobility was proven only in services to the nation was an assumption Boulainvilliers shared with some of the seventeenth-century and early eighteenth-century moralists considered in the previous chapter:

> That the great actions of a man of war, that the judiciousness, the equity, the virtues of a magistrate or of a minister raise him, if you wish, above the ancient nobility, this distinction remains personal. It is not passed down to the children unless they are as virtuous and as fortunate as he is. For it is right that they [the members of the ancient nobility] should always have the privilege of a rank to which a long succession of ancestors, illustrious because of their fidelity and their services to the country, assures the title of a true and ancient nobility. ... It is surprising how some believe today that it [nobility] depends on the absolute power of the king without listening to the testimony of thirteen centuries during which one can see that the kingdom, after being established, has only survived thanks to the blood, the exploits and the sacrifices of the ancient nobility. It is therefore certain that it [nobility] is the foundation and the most solid support of royalty and, consequently, it does not owe to it its establishing nor its rights.[114]

In this passage are distilled the main tenets of the nobility's discourse discussed in the previous chapter. It was patriotic virtues that made possible the identification of the nobles with the nation at large, enabling anyone to tell them apart from the commoners. Their sacrifices had not only saved France from its enemies but had also cemented the nation's unity, endowing it with a sacred aura. The outcome was a hierarchical nation, one where the fundamental equality of all members of the nobility was the counterweight to their pre-eminence over the commoners as a group. Like his precursors, Boulainvilliers also believed that a family's dignity depended on its genealogy and that nobility emerged only when a person's qualities were passed down to his offspring. True nobility, he wrote, 'consists in a tradition of virtue, glory, honour, the sentiment of dignity and good'.[115] It was virtue confirmed by time. But while the count

---

[112] See Harold Ellis, 'Genealogy, History, and Aristocratic Reaction in Early Eighteenth-Century France: The Case of Henri de Boulainvilliers', *Journal of Modern History*, 58 (1986), 434–5.

[113] Henri de Boulainvilliers, *Essais sur la noblesse de France, contenant une dissertation sur son origine et abaissement* (Amsterdam: n.p., 1732), 7.

[114] Boulainvilliers, 'Dissertation sur la noblesse françoise', 506. On this, see Linton, *The Politics of Virtue in Enlightenment France*, 36–7.

[115] Boulainvilliers, 'Dissertation sur la noblesse françoise', 545.

built his arguments on the ideas of seventeenth-century authors, he shaped them into a coherent narrative, depicting the history of a well-defined actor embodying the French nation. Crucially, this implied a shift in the arguments about the nobility's rights from the plane of individuals, their families, and their lineages, to that of a social group with its own specific character. That these were no longer the qualities only of the Frankish tribes – fierce, brave, and free warriors – was another important change. Because of the merging of Franks and Gauls over the centuries, such qualities could now be seen in all Frenchmen, if in varying degrees, and might be taught and learned through time and handed down from fathers to sons. The genealogies of the French noble families were thus woven by Boulainvilliers into a single narrative outlining the nation's true history. No longer built around the king's immortal body, it told the story of a group that had sacrificed itself for France over the centuries. In it, the commoners were passive subjects since they were without a story worth telling. Their past lacked the unremitting bravery, abnegation, and selflessness necessary to shape a multitude into a community – in rhetorical as well as in real terms. They were a nameless extension of the nobility, represented as the ones protected and defended, the unnamed part of the nation's history.

CHAPTER 3

Debating the Nation's History
From Royal(ist) to Ethnic Origins

Nicolas Fréret, the Père Daniel,
and the Contested Origins of the French Nation

On the evening of 26 December 1714, Nicolas Fréret, at that time a young and little-known historian, was arrested and taken to the Bastille, where he would spend the next three months of his life. Earlier that same year he had been elected *élève* at the Académie des inscriptions et des belles-lettres, thanks to Jean-François Félibien (1658–1733), Charles Rollin (1661–1741), and the members of the circle of the Duke de Noailles.[1] Although he had yet to publish any major works, in his inaugural lecture he lived up to the expectations of his patrons with an essay on 'L'origine des Français et de leur établissement dans les Gaules'. Antoine Galland (1646–1715), the orientalist and translator of the *Arabian Nights*, attended the session. In his own words, Fréret's dissertation treated the origins of France 'in a very different and much more plausible way than our historians have done hitherto'. If we are to believe Galland, the essay was followed 'with great attention' and won the new *élève* 'general applause'.[2] In the ensuing sessions, on 11 and 14 December, Fréret resumed his reading

---

[1] Léo Joubert, 'Fréret', in Ferdinand Hoefer (ed.), *Nouvelle biographie générale, depuis les temps les plus reculés jusqu'à nos jours* (Paris: Firmin Didot, 1852–1866), xviii. 807–18. On Fréret, see: Renée Simon, *Nicolas Fréret: Académicien* (Geneva: Institut et musée Voltaire, 1961); Chantal Grell and Catherine Volpilhac-Auger (eds.), *Nicolas Fréret: Légende et vérité* (Oxford: Voltaire Foundation, 1994); Blandine Barret-Kriegel, *Les historiens et la monarchie: 1. Jean Mabillon* (Paris: Presses universitaires de France, 1988), 163–209. Throughout the eighteenth century, Fréret enjoyed a brilliant reputation. See, for example: Guillaume-Thomas Raynal, 'Nouvelles littéraires' (1747–1755), in Friedrich Melchior Grimm et al., *Correspondance littéraire* (Paris: Garnier, 1877–1882), i. 108 (nouvelle ix), and i. 238 (nouvelle xxxv); Jean Jacques Barthélemy to Paolo Maria Paciaudi, 18 December 1758, in, Anne Claude Philippe de Caylus et al., *Correspondance inédite du Comte de Caylus, avec le P. Paciaudi, théatin (1757–1765), suivie de celles de l'abbé Barthélemy et de P. Mariette avec le même* (Paris: Imprimerie nationale, 1877), ii. 235; François-Marie Arouet Voltaire, 'Lettres à S. A. Monseigneur le Prince de*****, sur Rabelais, et sur d'autres auteurs qui ont mal parlé de la religion chrétienne' (1767), in *Œuvres*, xxvi. 506.

[2] Antoine Galland, *Le journal: La période parisienne* (Louvain: Peeters, 2011–), iv. 189 (13 November 1714).

but now met with severe censure from the abbé Vertot, who challenged many of the young scholar's ideas and even accused him of plagiarising the work of the historian Adrien Jourdan (1617–1692).[3] Vertot's interruptions began a dispute that ended only when, late in the evening, the members of the Academy decided to adjourn, granting the abbé the right to read a response in the following days.[4] Vertot offered his refutation on 18 December, causing another stir and, according to the official proceedings, prompting Fréret to draft a new version of his text.[5] However, the newly appointed *élève* never had a chance to reply, for his *embastillement* came only a few days later. Many were surprised by the arrest. The editor of the *Journal de Trévoux*, the père Tournemine (1661–1739), who had been following Fréret's progress, wrote to the lieutenant-general of police, the Marquis d'Argenson (1652–1721), to protest his innocence and testify to his 'candour' and 'probity'.[6] Although the reasons for the arrest were unknown at the time, many assumed – and would continue to assume long afterwards – that Fréret had been denounced to the authorities by a resentful Vertot intent upon presenting his essay as seditious.[7] The notion that the abbé was in any way to blame is in fact speculation at best.[8] But the fact that the authorities strongly disapproved of Fréret's essay was confirmed when the *lettre de cachet* was finally made public, in the 1820s. In the warrant, Fréret was accused of having written pamphlets against the bull *Unigenitus*, of being a member of the 'Jansenist party', and, interestingly, of working on a book to be pitted 'against the père Daniel's *Histoire de France*'.[9] In truth, there are no indications that Fréret had authored any subversive pamphlets attacking the *Bulle*, while it is possible that the Jansenism of his mentor Rollin had some part in the arrest. But the reference

[3] Académie Royale des inscriptions et médailles, 'Registre journal des assemblées et délibérations pendant l'année 1714' (Paris: Bibliothèque nationale de France, MS fonds français 9415), 185 and 187.

[4] Ibid., 187.   [5] Ibid., 189.

[6] René-Joseph de Tournemine, 'Lettre à M. d'Argenson au sujet de l'emprisonnement de Nicolas Fréret' (Paris: Manuscrits de la bibliothèque interuniversitaire de la Sorbonne, MS 1638), 199.

[7] See Raoul Rochette, 'Fréret', in Louis-Gabriel Michaud (ed.), *Biographie universelle ancienne et moderne* (Paris: A.T. Desplaces, 1843–1865), xvi. 29, and Gabriel Peignot, *Dictionnaire critique, littéraire, et bibliographique des principaux livres condamnés au feu, supprimés ou censurés* (Paris: Renouard, 1806), i. 147. Also see Christian Cheminade, 'La querelle Fréret-Vertot (1714) et le débat sur les origines de la monarchie française', in Jacqueline Hoareau-Dodinau and Pascal Texier (eds.), *Mélanges Pierre Braun, anthropologies juridiques* (Limoges: Presses universitaires de Limoges, 1998), 161–4.

[8] See Charles-Athanase Walckenaer, *Rapport à l'Académie des inscriptions et belles-lettres au sujet des manuscrits inédits de Fréret* (Paris: Imprimerie nationale, 1850), 52–3 and 60.

[9] The letter is in Joseph Delort, *Histoire de la détention des philosophes et des gens de lettres à la Bastille et à Vincennes* (Paris: Didot père et fils, 1829), ii. 10–11.

to Daniel's book is telling. For the appointment of the père as royal historiographer only the previous year meant that his *Histoire* had become a sort of
official narrative of the nation's history.

Close scrutiny of Fréret's essay would reveal that its content was hardly
seditious.[10] Following the analysis made much later by Augustin Thierry
(1795–1856), 'L'origine des Français' might be seen as hinging on three
main axes. First of all, it argued that the Franks were a confederation of
peoples arising in the third century and comprising several tribes living in
the southern regions of Germany and roughly corresponding to the
Sicambrian league. Second, it maintained that it was impossible to trace
the descendants of the Franks since these latter were not a race separate
from the other Germanic tribes. Finally, it contended that the name 'franc'
did not mean 'free', but 'fierce, intrepid, proud, cruel'.[11] Arguments such as
these were hardly a threat to the state's stability; nor did they diminish the
prestige of the monarchy; and surely they were not more subversive than
others circulating at the time. The notion, espoused by Fréret, that Franks
and Gauls were not two different ethnic groups was actually used by the
defenders of the monarchy in their struggle against the *thèse nobiliaire*.
Compared to other works, not least some by Vertot himself, Fréret's essay
stayed well within the bounds of politically appropriate scholarship.[12] As
for the charge of belonging to the Jansenist party, this was almost invariably levelled at those whose writings had political implications. Finally, the
allegation of plagiarism, which was effectively dismissed by Fréret immediately and on the spot, would hardly have led to a punishment as severe as
that meted out to the young scholar.[13] The true reasons for the *embastillement* are therefore still obscure. However, as one historian suggested long
ago, a possible explanation might be that the arrest was intended as
a warning to the entire Académie, whose members at the time 'made the
mistake' of dwelling 'too much on French modern and contemporary
history'. In fact, according to Charles-Athanase Walckenaer, in the years
immediately preceding Louis XIV's death all inquiries about the origins

[10] Nicolas Fréret, 'De l'origine des Français, et de leur établissement dans la Gaule', in *Œuvres
complètes* (Paris: Dandré, 1796), v. 155–367, and vi. 1–227.
[11] See Augustin Thierry, 'Considérations sur l'histoire de France' (1840), in Thierry, *Récits des
temps mérovingiens précédés des Considérations sur l'histoire de France* (Paris: Tessier, 1840), i. 39–41.
On the content of the essay, also see Barret-Kriegel, *Les historiens et la monarchie: 1. Jean Mabillon*,
201–9.
[12] See Catherine Volpilhac-Auger, '*Mon siège est fait*, ou La méthode historique de l'abbé de Vertot',
Cromohs, 2 (1997), 1–14.
[13] See Académie Royale des inscriptions et médailles, 'Registre journal des assemblées et délibérations
pendant l'année 1714', 187.

of the French monarchy, the rights of the legitimate or legitimised heirs, of the princes of the blood, of the peers of France, and of the *Parlements* assumed huge political importance, so much so that 'it was necessary to pay great attention to everything that was written on the history of France'.[14] Bearing in mind the nature of Fréret's essay and the fact that he was a novice, it might be plausible to suggest that he had in fact paid for his own intellectual curiosity as well as for that of the other academicians. From this angle, his arrest would speak volumes as to just how vexed the issue of the origins of the French nation was in political terms. The fact remains that after his release, on 31 March 1715, Fréret decided to concentrate on less controversial questions. Although he revised 'L'origine des Français', he never published it and he only returned twice to the origins of France, at a time when greater freedom of thought was allowed.[15]

However, even accepting the idea that Fréret's *embastillement* was a message from the authorities to the entire Académie, the reference in the warrant to Daniel's *Histoire* still deserves some attention. In fact, it was Fréret himself, when asked to choose a topic for his lecture, who suggested a work on 'the history of the origins of the French people, one very different from those of Mézeray and the père Daniel'.[16] It was an audacious statement, not only because the works of the two historians were at the time – and would remain until the second half of the century – extremely popular, but also because the former had been and the latter still was official historiographer of France.[17] One of the most popular French history books of the eighteenth century, the first volume of Daniel's *Histoire* was published in 1696. A complete edition in three quarto volumes appeared in 1713 and was reprinted in 1722, 1729, and 1742. A new edition was published in 1755–1757, reprinted in 1757–1758, and then edited and expanded between 1755 and 1760 by the Jesuit scholar Henri Griffet (1698–1771). Soon to be translated into English, Italian, and German, the

---

[14] Walckenaer, *Rapport à l'Académie des inscriptions et belles-lettres au sujet des manuscrits inédits de Fréret*, 60–61.

[15] The other two texts were an essay read at the Académie in 1747, the 'Observations sur la religion des Gaulois et sur celle des Germains', *Mémoires de littérature, tirés des registres de l'Académie royale des inscriptions et belles lettres*, 24 (1756), 389–431, and the 'Mémoire sur les États-généraux'. On these two works, see Jean-Jacques Tatin-Gourier, 'Les recherches de Fréret sur l'origine de la nation française', in Grell and Volpilhac-Auger (eds.), *Nicolas Fréret*, 73–87.

[16] Académie Royale des inscriptions et médailles, 'Registre journal des assemblées et délibérations pendant l'année 1714', 43 verso.

[17] On their popularity: Antoine-René de Voyer d'Argenson and André-Guillaume Constant d'Orville, *Bibliothèque historique à l'usage des dames* (Paris: Moutard, 1779), 85–6.

Histoire could be found in the libraries of learned men and women across Europe. The *Abrégé*, completed in 1723, enjoyed an even wider circulation.[18] The Duke de Saint-Simon, who strongly disapproved of Daniel's *Histoire*, could not deny that it was appreciated in the highest circles of society. It was, he wrote, 'the only history book of which the king and Madame de Maintenon have ever spoken' – a fact that made it immediately popular at court.'[19] However, although it enjoyed a remarkable circulation, it met with a highly varied reception. The President Hénault praised its merits and subsequently, in the nineteenth century, so too did Stendhal (1783–1842), Augustin Thierry, Charles Augustin Sainte-Beuve (1804–1869), and Gabriel Monod (1844–1912). Some commentators were particularly enthusiastic. Griffet even claimed, very generously, that Daniel's *Histoire* was the finest history of France, 'and many years, or maybe even centuries, will pass before there is a better one'.[20] On the other side were the bitter comments of the Marquis de Lezay-Marnézia (1735–1810), who went so far as to write that it would be 'cruel to suggest to a young lady' that she read Daniel's work. Many of Voltaire's books and pamphlets likewise contained invectives against the *Histoire* of the 'Jesuit Daniel', a work that was, he proclaimed, an insult to its readers as much as to truth itself.[21] Even Fréret's friend and mentor Boulainvilliers did not mince words when judging the book of the Jesuit father. Adamant that a man of the cloth could never write an unbiased history of the nation, he considered this even truer of a Jesuit who enjoyed a royal pension. He condemned Daniel out of hand, declaring that he had

---

[18] On the diffusion of Daniel's *Histoire*, see Bernard Grosperrin, *La représentation de l'histoire de France dans l'historiographie des Lumières* (Lille: Atelier national de reproduction des thèses, 1982), i. 79–84.

[19] Saint-Simon, *Mémoires* (1713), iv. 657–8. Françoise d'Aubigné, Marquise de Maintenon (1635–1719) was, of course, Louis XIV's famous 'secret wife'.

[20] [Charles-Jean-Louis-François Hénault], *Nouvel abrégé chronologique de l'histoire de France* (Paris: Prault père, 1744), 413; Marie Henry Beyle Stendhal to Adolphe de Mareste, 20 October 1820, in *Correspondance générale* (Paris: Honoré Champion, 1997–1999), iii. 307; Augustin Thierry, 'Sur les Histoires de France de Mézeray, Daniel et Anquetil' (1820), in Thierry, *Lettres sur l'histoire de France* (Paris: Sautelet, 1827), 32–6; Charles-Augustin Sainte-Beuve, 'Mézeray' (1853), in *Causeries du lundi* (Paris: Garnier frères, 1852–1876), viii. 188; Gabriel Monod, 'Du progrès des études historiques en France depuis le XVIe siècle', *Revue historique*, 1 (1876), 18; Henri Griffet, *Traité des différentes sortes de preuves qui servent à établir la vérité de l'histoire* (Liège: J.F. Bassompierre, 1769), 373.

[21] Claude-François-Adrien Lezay-Marnézia, *Plan de lecture pour une jeune dame* (Paris: Prault, 1784), 24; Voltaire, 'Essai sur les mœurs et l'esprit des nations', xii. 547. For other Voltairian examples: Voltaire, 'Catalogue de la plupart des écrivains français qui ont paru dans le siècle de Louis XIV', 61; Voltaire, 'Supplément au siècle de Louis XIV', 105; Voltaire, 'Dictionnaire philosophique', xix. 365; François-Marie Arouet Voltaire, 'Remarques autographes de Voltaire en marge d'un livre anonyme du père Daniel' (1775), in *Œuvres*, xxix. 413.

only 'learnt about the history of France while writing it', and censuring his famous book for the 'ten thousand mistakes' in it.[22]

The count's idea of a twofold allegiance preventing the Jesuit father from placing historical truth above altar and throne was a point well made. Interestingly, it helps to explain some of the differences between Fréret's and Daniel's accounts of the nation's origins. Through their works, both authors were trying to establish precisely when the history of France could be conceived in truly national terms – and both, inevitably, felt obliged to come to terms with founding myths and legends. Tellingly, Fréret's essay began by applauding the fact that the story of the Trojan origins of France, which had played an important role in shaping national narratives in the sixteenth and seventeenth centuries, had finally 'been abandoned by everyone'.[23] But while this was a welcome turn, according to Fréret such a rejection had led to a dismissal of all examinations of the age preceding the foundation of the monarchy. The Trojan myth had been replaced by a narrative void. And this was a particularly apt observation where Daniel's book was concerned. In fact, according to the père, the centuries prior to the institution of the monarchy were shrouded in an obscurity that could never be dispelled. All attempts to understand them simply led to new legends and myths. Since the nation's 'origin could not be found any-where', scholars had been forced to 'go to the sources of the legends' and accept them as true – regardless of their implausibility. While ancient scholars wrote about mythical episodes of antiquity 'plainly and in earnest', modern historians lavished a 'few words' only on the first ages of the French people. But, noted Daniel, 'they are not to be blamed' for their silence.[24] In the preface to two dissertations intended to pave the way to the publication of his *Histoire*, Daniel thus made the forthright claim that 'the history of France must start with Clovis since he was the first king'.[25] It was

---

[22] Boulainvilliers, *Lettres sur les anciens Parlemens*, iii. 197–9. But also see ibid., i. 16, as well as Boulainvilliers, 'Préface critique au Journal de Saint Louis', 93. Voltaire, who was familiar with Boulainvilliers's writings, recalled the count's harsh comments in his 'Catalogue de la plupart des écrivains français qui ont paru dans le siècle de Louis XIV', 61.

[23] Fréret, 'De l'origine des Français', v. 155. On the importance of the Trojan myth in shaping French national discourses before the eighteenth century, see George Huppert, 'The Trojan Franks and their Critics', *Studies in the Renaissance*, 12 (1965), 227–41, and Beaune, *Naissance de la nation France*, 19–54. On the myth's dismissal, see Elizabeth A. R. Brown, 'Myths Chasing Myths: The Legend of the Trojan Origin of the French and its Dismantling', in Balázs Nagy and Marcell Sebők (eds.), *The Man of Many Devices, Who Wandered Full Many Ways: Festschrift in Honour of János M. Bak* (Budapest: Central European University Press, 1999), 613–33.

[24] Gabriel Daniel, *Histoire de France, depuis l'établissement de la monarchie françoise dans les Gaules* (Paris: Simon Benard, 1696), 'Préface', n.p.

[25] Gabriel Daniel, *Deux dissertations préliminaires pour une nouvelle histoire de France depuis l'établissement de la monarchie dans les Gaules* (Paris: Simon Benard, 1696), 17. The two dissertations,

a controversial statement that went against the commonly held view that Pharamond had been the first monarch.[26] Daniel's claim earned him the censure of several scholars, including the Baron de Montesquieu, for having 'retrenched our first kings' from the nation's history. One commentator even wrote that Daniel had 'dishonoured the history of his country'.[27] Fréret himself may have been referring to the père and his work when he attacked those authors for whom 'the history and the antiquities of our nation do not deserve any credibility before Clovis.'[28]

The relationship conceived by Daniel between the nation and its monarchy was far from straightforward. From his standpoint, these were two separate though closely linked entities: 'We must consider in our history two kinds of beginning, that of the French nation and that of the French monarchy,' he wrote.[29] However, he was adamant that any attempt to grasp the nation's history before the institution of its monarchy, that is, before the creation of an effective political authority, was futile. No coherent narrative could be forged since there was no stable connection between the French people, the French lands, and a political authority holding sway over the two. In this regard, the fact that 'no king before Clovis has retained possession of any part of what today we call the French Kingdom' allowed the père to dismiss as irrelevant everything that came before his reign. The lack of a permanent authority simply deprived the nation of a canvas upon which its history could be portrayed. It is in this sense that Daniel could claim that the subject matter of a nation's history 'is the state and the king, who is like the centre towards which everything tends and [to which it] must be related. Individuals have a part in it only inasmuch as they have a relationship to the one or the other.'[30] From his viewpoint, the king was the link that conferred unity upon the countless

---

in a much revised form, would become part of the 1713 edition of Daniel's *Histoire*. A few years later, President Hénault also argued that the history of France should start with Clovis since so little was known of the previous kings: [Hénault], *Nouvel abrégé chronologique de l'histoire de France*, i.

[26] See Duranton, 'Les contraintes structurales de l'histoire de France', passim. Also see John Rogister, 'The Frankish Tradition and New Perceptions of the Monarchy: Louis XV – The New Pharamond?', *History and Anthropology*, 15 (2004), 207–17.

[27] Charles-Louis Secondat de Montesquieu, 'Mes pensées', in *Œuvres* (ed. Caillois), i. 1344 (§ 1458); Ignace Hyacinthe Amat de Graveson, 'Copie d'une lettre écrite à M. l'abbé de Camps', *Le nouveau Mercure*, August 1720, 48. Also see Mathieu Marais to Jean Bouhier, 12 March 1734, in Jean Bouhier, *Correspondance littéraire du Président Bouhier* (Saint-Étienne: Université de Saint-Étienne, 1974–), xiii. 73, and François de Camps, 'Réponse de M. l'abbé de Camps, du 1 Mai 1720, à la réfutation du père Daniel', *Le nouveau Mercure*, Juin 1720, 7.

[28] Fréret, 'De l'origine des Français', v. 159.

[29] Gabriel Daniel, *Histoire de France, depuis l'établissement de la monarchie françoise dans les Gaules* (Paris: J.-B. Delespine, 1713), 'Preface', n.p.

[30] Daniel, *Histoire de France* (ed. 1713), 'Preface', n.p.

individual wills, interests, and passions that, in reality, formed a nation and shaped its history. It was a representation of the past in which only the sovereignty embodied by the monarch and enshrined in the state could lend a discernible order to events, a vision still attached to the old idea that sovereign authority imposed order on everything. Here, as in the works of a Bossuet, the king was the only 'public person' of the kingdom and, as such, the story of his life subsumed those of his subjects.[31] The differences with Fréret's views are at once striking and revealing. In his essay, the monarchy had by no means the same importance as in Daniel's narrative. There were only a few meaningful references to the role of kings in 'L'origine des Français'. In one such passage, Fréret recognised that although 'the body of the nation was only re-united at the time of Clovis', at his death 'it was divided again among his sons'. It was a wording that suggested that the continuity and the unity of the nation could not be represented by the royal lineage.[32]

An equally important aspect of Daniel's narrative, one that Boulainvilliers would have accounted for by referring to the père's duties towards the Church, was that by assuming Clovis to have been the first king he was reasserting the bond between Christianity and the nation – for, of course, it was the conversion of Clovis that had made of France the *Fille aînée de l'Eglise.*[33] In truth, this argument was far from original, others having made the same point in the seventeenth century. In his *Les heureux commencements de la France chrétienne sous l'apôtre de nos rois S. Remy* (1633), the Jesuit René de Ceriziers (1603–1662) assumed that Clovis had to have been the first king for the simple reason that a non-Christian French ruler was unimaginable. The abbé de Marolles (1600–1681), glossing over the 'still pagan' Pharamond and Mérovech, both unworthy of his readers' attention, insisted that Clovis deserved the title of true founder of the nation for having shown the French the light of Christianity. The Capuchin Balthazar de Riez (1599–1678) made the same point in his *L'incomparable piété des très-chrestiens rois de France* (1672–1674).[34] Yet throughout the eighteenth century many scholars retained the

---

[31] See Bossuet, *Politique tirée des propres paroles de l'Ecriture sainte,* 177–8.
[32] Fréret, 'De l'origine des Français', v. 166–7.
[33] On the point, Rémond, 'La fille aînée de l'Eglise', passim.
[34] René de Ceriziers, *Les heureux commencements de la France chrétienne sous l'apôtre de nos rois S. Remy* (Paris: Angot, 1633); Michel de Marolles, *Histoire des rois de France* (Paris: Pierre le petit, 1663), 5–15; Balthazar-Honoré de Caseneuve de Riez, *L'incomparable piété des tres-chrestiens rois de France* (Paris: Gilles Alliot, 1672–1674), i. 4–5.

mythical Pharamond as their first king while praising Clovis for his conversion.[35] Importantly, in Daniel's narrative the intelligibility of the nation's past offered by Clovis's effective monarchical authority was reinforced by the sacred aura stemming from his baptism and spreading out to the whole nation. In the père's *Histoire*, the political origin of the French was thus as religious and mystical as it was political. It is against such a backdrop and by considering the role of religion in the moulding of French identity that seventeenth- and eighteenth-century debates over Clovis and Pharamond need to be set.[36] Returning to Fréret's essay, there was no significant treatment there of the role of Christianity in the nation's past – throughout his career he maintained a clear separation between his historical and his religious preoccupations, concerned as he was to turn religion into a profane object of study.[37] The baptism of Clovis was treated without the grandiloquence – nor even the attention – that most scholars thought it deserved.[38]

While Fréret and Daniel both conceived of the nation's origin as a fundamental and irreducible object of enquiry, that is, as the beginning and end of their research, the differences between their respective narratives were indeed remarkable. If the one portrayed by Daniel was an essentially monarchical and religious origin, Fréret, by claiming that the history of France had begun in a Frankish league and by retrenching the symbolic role of the monarchy, offered his readers a cultural and ethnic origin of the nation. His investigation started and ended at the Frankish tribes, which were the main characters in his story. Importantly, the fact that the Franks were seen by Fréret as a cohesive community, sharing the same values and way of life, and that from them were descended modern Frenchmen was a truism that seemed to require no proof – just as for other scholars the existence of Pharamond or the miraculous anointing of Clovis were indisputable facts. Viewed from this angle, Fréret was actually replacing the royalist and Christian myth of origins with the 'blissful clarity' of the unity of the Franks and their historical continuity with

[35] See, for example, Jacques-Bénigne Bossuet, 'Abrégé de l'histoire de France' (written between 1675 and 1679, but first published in 1767), in *Œuvres complètes* (Besançon: Outhenin-Chalandre fils, 1836), v. 1–4.
[36] Chantal Grell, 'Clovis: Du Grand siècle aux Lumières', *Bibliothèque de l'École des chartes*, 154 (1996), 193–5. Also see Myriam Yardeni, 'La genèse de l'État et la naissance de la nation dans les "Histoires de France" du XVIIᵉ siècle', in Yardeni, *Enquêtes sur l'identité de la 'nation France': De la Renaissance aux Lumières* (Seyssel: Champ Vallon, 2005), 92–5.
[37] See Grell, *L'histoire entre érudition et philosophie*, 91–2.
[38] Fréret, 'De l'origine des Français', v. 213–7.

that of the French.[39] Of course, it is not of secondary importance that in so doing he was trying to eradicate myth – as he understood it – from the nation's past by means of a thorough analysis of primary sources. He was adamant that 'great nations have their chimaeras just like great families' and that it was the historian's task to unmask them.[40] It was a point he was to make abundantly clear in his 'Réflexions sur les études des anciennes histoires, et sur le degré de certitude de leurs preuves', an essay read out at the Académie in 1724.[41] There was much truth in the comment made by Jean-Pierre de Bougainville (1722–1763), the brother of the famous explorer, that Fréret's greatest merit was his constant striving to 'break through the veil of mysteries, to explain legends' and thus to 'bring daylight into that obscure heap of traditions and lies' that so often obscured the origins of nations.[42]

And yet the père Daniel was doing precisely the same thing – or so at least he claimed in the preface to the 1713 edition of his *Histoire*. In effect, there is an important distinction to be made between the introductions to the two editions of his famous book. As has been noted, the version of 1696 was primarily concerned with questions of narrative style and still interpreted the past in a manner consonant with the old *Ars historica*. Conversely, the 1713 introduction insisted on the need to seek out the causes of events, focused on the issue of the author's impartiality, and emphasised the importance of original sources. The differences between the two introductions are remarkable. That they might be explained by Daniel's reading of Pierre Bayle's works, as Carlo Borghero has suggested, is as fascinating as it is debatable – not least because of the père's deference towards altar and throne.[43] But a shift did take place, one compatible with the increasingly critical attitude towards the study of the past shared by many scholars of the day.[44] Crucially for us, in the 1713 text there also transpires an abiding concern with the nation's *mœurs* and usages. It is

---

[39] The expression is taken from Barthes, *Mythologies*, 230–1.

[40] Fréret, 'De l'origine des Français', v. 155–6.

[41] Nicolas Fréret, 'Réflexions sur les études des anciennes histoires, et sur le dégrée de certitude de leurs preuves' (published in 1729), in *Œuvres*, i. 55–156. Also see his 'Réflexions sur les prodiges rapportés dans les anciens' (1723), ibid., i. 157–214.

[42] Jean-Pierre de Bougainville, 'Eloge de Fréret', *Histoire de l'Académie royale des inscriptions et belles-lettres*, 23 (1756), 330. On Fréret's critical approach to the study of the past, see Carlo Borghero, 'Méthode historique et philosophie chez Fréret', *Corpus: Revue de philosophie*, 29 (1995), 19–38, and Chantal Grell, 'Nicolas Fréret, la critique et l'histoire ancienne', in Grell and Volpilhac-Auger (eds.), *Nicolas Fréret*, 51–71.

[43] Borghero, *La certezza e la storia*, 303–4, n. 26. See Daniel, *Histoire de France* (ed. 1713), 'Preface', n.p.

[44] See Leffler, 'The "Histoire raisonnée", 1660–1720', passim. Also see the arguments in Chapter 2.

there, Daniel explained to his readers, that 'the historian's knowledge emerges through the remarks on the *mœurs* of the people that he disseminates in his narration'.[45] In his other great historical work, the *Histoire de la milice françoise* (1721), published a few years later, he even claimed that a history of France ought to teach about 'the customs and usages of the nation'.[46] Whether the père actually pursued such an intent, as the clergyman Daniel Lombard (1678–1746) claimed in 1723, or whether his works were essentially the biographies of the French kings, or, finally, whether the royal figures he portrayed were crucial to grasping the lives of the French people, is a matter of dispute.[47] But what is noteworthy, is that these intentions were shared by Fréret. In fact, if Daniel insisted that the 'shape and the language of each age' should be 'scrupulously reproduced', so too did the young academician.[48] Indeed, in his 'L'origine des Français', Fréret lamented that while the greatest historians of antiquity had made of customs and usages their principal object of inquiry, modern scholars 'have neglected to follow their path'.[49] Doing precisely this, shedding light on the *mœurs* and on the ways of life of ancient peoples, would become the central aim of his research. Of course, a focus on the language, customs, and ways of life of the Franks and Gauls with a view to unmasking the origins of France would produce a narrative at variance with those histories that placed at their heart court politics and the designs of kings. It might well be that the importance that Daniel gave to customs anticipated the works of a Boulainvilliers or a Dubos.[50] But Fréret belonged to the same intellectual climate. As Augustin Thierry wrote much later on, Fréret was part of that 'revolution in the way of understanding and writing history' that hastened the birth of the 'science of our social origins'.[51]

---

[45] Daniel, *Histoire de France* (ed. 1713), 'Preface', n.p.

[46] Gabriel Daniel, *Histoire de la milice françoise* (Paris: Coignard, 1721), i. p. ii.

[47] Daniel Lombard, *Comparaison des deux histoires de M. de Mézeray et du P. Daniel, en deux dissertations, avec une dissertation préliminaire sur l'utilité de l'histoire* (Amsterdam: aux dépens de la Compagnie, 1723), 84. For the detractors, see Chapter 2 of this book.

[48] It was a point made by Thierry, in his 'Sur les Histoires de France de Mézeray, Daniel et Anquetil', 32–3.

[49] Quoted in Thierry, 'Considérations sur l'histoire de France', 42–3. Thierry claimed he was quoting from the 1714 manuscript. The sentence is not in the 1796 text; nor is it in the manuscript copy held at the Bibliothèque de l'Arsenal. Two other copies are held by the Archives of the Institut de France, but I was unable to consult them.

[50] Borghero, *La certezza e la storia*, 303–4, n. 26.

[51] Thierry, 'Considérations sur l'histoire de France', 73.

Rethinking the Past: The 'Science of Our Social Origins'

Fréret's 'L'origine des Français' was not published until 1796, more than eighty years after the famous session at the Académie. Notwithstanding this, it was known long before then, circulating clandestinely as a manuscript.[52] In his 1753 preface to Samuel von Pufendorf's (1632–1694) *Introduction à l'histoire moderne, générale et politique de l'univers*, Thomas-François de Grace (1713–1798), agronomist, historian, and one of Fréret's protégés, not only mentioned having read the essay, but also described it as a 'seminal source' on which he had drawn heavily for his own research. He reproduced large sections of it in the introduction and in the footnotes scattered throughout Pufendorf's book. Montesquieu, who was personally acquainted with Fréret, summarised 'L'origine des Français' in a fragment of his *Spicilège* dating from the late 1730s. A manuscript copy was even held by the library of the Parisian Order of Lawyers, where the historian and bibliophile Fevret de Fontette (1710–1772) consulted it in the late 1760s.[53] Importantly, 'L'origine des Français' was one of a growing number of works on the origins of France. It was but one tessera in an ever-expanding mosaic of writings and part of a wide-ranging debate that had as its main forum, significantly enough, Colbert's Académie.[54] Fréret himself remarked that an increasing number of books were being devoted to the nation's origins and that 'even a simple list of them would be too long' – then caustically adding that 'an entire volume' would be needed to discuss their faults.[55] The intensifying interest in the nation's origins was also noted by Du Fresnoy, who in 1729 lamented that '[m]atters concerning the origins of the French have been examined by a great number of authors who have immersed themselves [in them], displaying an embarrassing and pompous erudition'.[56] Even the Count de Boulainvilliers complained about the 'many different

---

[52] Volpilhac-Auger, *Tacite en France*, 313.

[53] Thomas-François de Grace, 'Avertissement de l'éditeur', in Samuel Pufendorf, *Introduction à l'histoire moderne, générale et politique de l'univers* (Paris: Merigot, 1753–1759), i. n.p. Charles-Louis Secondat de Montesquieu, 'Spicilège', in *Œuvres* (ed. Caillois), ii. 1375–7. For the dating of the fragment, see the footnote by Salvatore Rotta in Charles-Louis Secondat de Montesquieu, 'Spicilège', in *Œuvres complètes* (Oxford: Société Montesquieu and Voltaire Foundation, 1998–), xiii. 512, n.; Jacques Le Long and Charles-Marie Fevret de Fontette, *Bibliothèque historique de France* (Paris: Herissant, 1768–1778), ii. 18. Fréret and Montesquieu first met between 1713 and 1716. On this: Miguel Benítez, 'Montesquieu, Fréret et les remarques tirées des entretiens avec Hoangh', in Montesquieu, *Œuvres* (ed. Société Montesquieu), xvi. 420, and Charles-Louis Secondat de Montesquieu to Pierre-Nicolas Desmolets, 19 April 1716, in *Œuvres* (ed. Société Montesquieu), xviii. 6. On their intellectual relationship: Lorenzo Bianchi, 'Montesquieu et Fréret: Quelques notes', *Corpus: Revue de philosophie*, 29 (1995), 105–28.

[54] See Goulemot, *Le règne de l'histoire*, 172–80.   [55] Fréret, 'De l'origine des Français', v. 161.

[56] Nicolas Lenglet Du Fresnoy, *Méthode pour étudier l'histoire* (Paris: Gandouin, 1729), ii. 245. Tellingly, the remark is not to be found in the 1713 edition of Du Fresnoy's work. With regard to the growing interest in the origins of the French nation, one figure is striking. Under the heading

opinions of those authors who have written on the origins of the French' –
though overlooking the fact that his own work had led to a further proliferation of interpretations.[57]

Of course, the origins of the French people had been studied long before
Fréret, Daniel, and Boulainvilliers. Authors with views and aims as different as Étienne Pasquier (1529–1615), Jean Bodin (1529–1596),
François Hotman (1524–1590), Charles Sorel, and Mézeray had all written
about the birth of the nation.[58] In 1676, in a book claiming that the origins
of modern France were Gallic, the historian and clergyman Pierre Audigier
(1659–1744) discussed at length the many different theories and interpretations on the origins of France, which in his view amounted to some
fourteen in number.[59] But the works Audigier referred to were very different from those that came later. As in any other field of knowledge, the
'crisis of the European mind' produced a radical break even in the study of
the nation's history. The most obvious change was that enquiries over its
origins were now informed by a more critical attitude towards the past.
They would be increasingly shaped by the emergence and the merging, to
use Ménestrier's distinctions, of 'histoire raisonnée' (focusing on causes),
'histoire autorisée' (based on primary sources), and 'histoire critique'
(questioning other scholars).[60] Writing at the turn of the seventeenth
century, Mézeray could claim that Pharamond had given the French
people the Salic Laws since 'it is so gratifying to convince ourselves' of
this, that 'one need not give credence' to scholars who argued to the
contrary.[61] As late as the 1710s some authors still believed that historical
traditions provided a solid ground for national narratives. In a work
written around 1717 for the young Louis XV, the Cardinal de Fleury
(1653–1743) could contend that in an 'obscurity as great as that of the
earliest times of the French monarchy, one should keep to the most

---

'Tracts on the origins of the French' the *Bibliothèque historique de la France* only lists three writings
between 1700 and 1714 – including the dissertations read out by Fréret and Vertot at the Académie –
and four times as many for the period between 1715 and 1730. Although the criteria used for this
classification might be contentious, the discrepancy is nevertheless remarkable: Le Long and Fevret
de Fontette, *Bibliothèque historique de France*, ii. 3–20.

[57] Henri de Boulainvilliers, *Histoire de l'ancien gouvernement de la France* (The Hague: aux dépens de la
Compagnie, 1727), i. 1.

[58] For the views of these authors: Barzun, *The French Race*, 59–113.

[59] Pierre Audigier, *De l'origine des François et de leur empire* (Paris: Barbin, 1676). For a summary and
commentary, see Anonymous, review of Pierre Audigier, *De l'origine des François et de leur empire*, in
Le journal des sçavans, 29 March 1677, 73–4.

[60] Ménestrier, *Les divers caractères des ouvrages historiques*, 56–71. On this, see Chapter 2.

[61] François Eudes de Mézeray, *Histoire de France depuis Pharamond jusqu'à maintenant* (Paris: Mathieu
Guillemot, 1643–1651), i. 6.

universally received traditions; such is the one that makes of Pharamond the first of our kings'.[62] But by that date many had rejected such an idea, considering it their duty to tell apart history from myth – or 'fable', to use the word current at the time – through sound arguments and verified facts.[63] In 1714, Fontenelle made of such principles the lynchpin of his *L'origine des fables*, insisting that all received truths be scrutinised to discover if they stood the test of reason, and this regardless of their antiquity.[64] But no other scholar did more than Pierre Bayle to promote the questioning of received truths and established intellectual traditions.[65] As he made clear in his *Pensées diverses sur la comète* (1680), the main objective of his work was to discredit 'those opinions that are only based on the great number' of believers.[66] Nor, for the Huguenot thinker, could the antiquity of a story ever be 'a sign of its truthfulness'.[67] He reiterated these views with even greater conviction in that great precursor of the *Encyclopédie* (1751–1772), the *Dictionnaire historique et critique* (1697). Firmly opposed to the ideas encapsulated in the words of Cardinal de Fleury quoted earlier, Bayle's works profoundly affected the attitudes of many of the foremost thinkers and historians of the eighteenth century – not least Fréret himself.[68]

The rejection of tradition as a source of truth, whether historical or religious, had a remarkable impact on the notion of origin, since the two were closely intertwined.[69] The latter notion, in the eighteenth century,

---

[62] André-Hercule de Fleury, *L''Abrégé de l'histoire de France' écrit pour le jeune Louis XV* (Montigny-le-Bretonneux: Archives départementales des Yvelines, 2004), 125. For the dating, Chantal Grell, 'L'éducation de l'enfant-roi', ibid., 35.

[63] See, on this, Jean Starobinski, 'Le mythe au XVIIIᵉ siècle', *Critique: Revue générale des publications français et étrangères*, 366 (1977), 975–97.

[64] Bernard Le Bovier de Fontenelle, 'De l'origine des fables' (1714), in *Œuvres*, iii. 187–202, and especially 199–200. On the dating, see Shozo Akagi, *'Suite des Œuvres diverses de Mr de F**** de 1714: La première édition de l'*Origine des Fables* et de deux autres discours de Fontenelle', *Études de langue et littérature françaises*, 50 (1987), 18–31. On Fontenelle's views on history: Isabelle Mullet, 'Fontenelle et l'histoire: Du fixisme des passions aux progrès de l'esprit humain', *Dix-huitième siècle*, 44 (2012), 335–47.

[65] See Isabelle Delpla and Philippe de Robert (eds.), *La raison corrosive: Études sur la pensée critique de Pierre Bayle* (Paris: Honoré Champion, 2003).

[66] Pierre Bayle, *Pensées diverses sur la comète* (Paris: Nizet, 1984), i. 81. Also see ibid., i. 134.

[67] Bayle, *Pensées diverses sur la comète*, i. 271–3; also see i. 35–8. On Bayle's historical thought: Ruth Whelan, *The Anatomy of Superstition: A Study of the Historical Theory and Practice of Pierre Bayle* (Oxford: Oxford Foundation, 1989).

[68] See Antony McKenna, *Études sur Pierre Bayle* (Paris: Honoré Champion, 2015), 139–70. On Bayle's influence on Fréret, ibid., 168–70. A broader perspective is offered by Anton M. Matytsin, *The Specter of Skepticism in the Age of Enlightenment* (Baltimore: Johns Hopkins University Press, 2016), 233–63. Bayle is discussed by Matytsin on pages 236–9.

[69] Nicolas Piqué, *De la tradition à l'histoire: Éléments pour une généalogie du concept d'histoire à partir des controverses religieuses en France, 1669–1704* (Paris: Honoré Champion, 2009).

referred to an absolute beginning that determined the course of things to
come, a locus usually devoid of all contradiction, contrast, or struggle.
There, the chronological was also the logical beginning of the history to
come.[70] In such a light, tradition preserved, reasserted, and incessantly
reproduced that original and fundamental truth. The works of a Sorel or
a Mézeray, retelling and repeating the stories of previous scholars, were
essentially memorialising an unproblematic origin, reiterating
a foundation that encapsulated an unquestionable truth. From such an
angle, the eighteenth century's increasing urge to scrutinise the nation's
origins partly testifies to a loss of faith in tradition and a growing confi-
dence in the historian's individual abilities. However, the rejection of
Pharamond's coronation or of Clovis's baptism as founding myths – stories
of lawgivers shaping a barbarous multitude into a single, sacred people –
required the setting up of another origin, one that could be grounded in
verifiable sources and that would stand to reason. Importantly, from the
early eighteenth century many authors moved the birth of the nation back
to an age preceding the creation of the monarchy. They did so on the
assumption that it was impossible to understand a people's history if its
distant past were shrouded in mystery. As Bougainville wrote in his eulogy
of Fréret: 'Knowledge about the origins of nations weighs heavily upon the
rest of their history. One may not gain a truthful idea of them if they are
partly concealed, if the chain of facts, rather than being firmly attached to
a fixed point, floats at its [furthest] extremity in an obscure and inchoate
space.'[71] Giving a form to distant origins might have appeased what the
great Giambattista Vico (1668–1744) called the 'arrogance of nations' – the
presumption that one's own country was the most ancient and that,
therefore, it should enjoy some sort of pre-eminence.[72] But, even more
important, investigating the pre-monarchical past of France served to turn
the nation into a seemingly natural fact. In spite of the proliferating
references to culture and language, throughout the seventeenth century
the nation had still been essentially conceived in political terms, as the
product of the will and deeds of its kings and ministers.[73] But now, looking
at an ancient past lacking an effective political order, the unity of the

---

[70] See, on this, Michel Foucault, 'Nietzsche, la généalogie, l'histoire', in *Dits et écrits: 1954–1988* (Paris:
Gallimard, 1994), ii. 237–40, and Foucault, *Les mots et les choses*, 339–40. Also see Louis Marin, 'De
l'*Utopia* de More à la Scandza de Cassiodore-Jordanès', *Annales: Économies, sociétés, civilisations*, 26
(1971), 306–27.
[71] Bougainville, 'Eloge de Fréret', 321.
[72] Giambattista Vico, *La scienza nuova (ed. 1730)* (Rome: Edizioni di storia e letteratura, 2013), 92.
[73] Yardeni, 'La genèse de l'État et la naissance de la nation dans les "Histoire de France" du XVIIe
siècle', 100.

ancestors of the modern French had to be sought elsewhere, in their usages, character, *mœurs*, and language. It was a radical departure from those seventeenth-century histories centred around king and state. And it was a turn fraught with challenges. Precisely at that time, the possibility of writing reliable histories of the remote past was being fiercely debated. The dispute between the philosopher Levesque de Pouilly (1691–1751) and the philologist the abbé Sallier (1685–1761) over the origins of Rome, and the debate occasioned by the *Dissertations sur l'incertitude des cinq premières siècles de l'histoire romaine* (1738), written by the Huguenot scholar Louis de Beaufort (1703–1795), testify to the difficulties faced by antiquaries and historians when dealing with ancient history.[74] Yet when addressing these challenges, Boulainvilliers, Fréret, and many others resorted to new methods, combining their critical historiography with classical philology and according customs, rituals, and language a central place in their works.[75]

It was partly on account of concerns such as these that in 1710 Gottfried Wilhelm Leibniz presented at the Prussian Academy of Sciences an essay on the ancient history of the peoples of Europe and on the place of languages in understanding their past.[76] His main contention was that spoken languages were the oldest monuments of nations, more so than customs, the arts, religion, and the written word and, as such, they enshrined the secret of the origins of nations. Consistently, Leibniz made the case that they could offer insights when other sources were wanting: '[W]hen the origins of ancient nations transcend time, language performs the duty of ancient monuments.'[77] Based on the assumption that proper names, such as those of forests, rivers, and mountains, had initially been appellatives, the Saxon polymath contended that their ever-changing pronunciation had finally led to the emergence of distinct dialects and new languages. When coupled with more traditional historical research, semantics could then help scholars to grasp the original meaning of those words and shed light on the origins of

---

[74] On this, see: Chantal Grell, 'Les origines de Rome: Mythe et critique. Essai sur l'histoire aux XVIIᵉ et XVIIIᵉ siècles', *Histoire, économie et société*, 2 (1983),255–80, and Raskolnikoff, *Histoire romaine et critique historique dans l'Europe des Lumières*, passim.

[75] See Poulouin, *Le temps des origines*, 493–546.

[76] Gottfried Wilhelm Leibniz, 'Brevis designatio meditationum de Originibus Gentium, ductis potissimum ex indicio linguarum' (1710), in *Opera Omnia* (Geneva: Fratres de Tournes, 1768), iv. part 2, 186–98. For an analysis: Toon Van Hal, 'Sprachen, die Geschichte schreiben: Zu Leibniz' sprachhistorischem Forschungsprogramm und dessen Nachwirkung', in Wenchao Li (ed.), *Einheit der Vernunft und Vielfalt der Sprachen – Beiträge zu Leibnizens Sprachforschung und Zeichentheorie* (Stuttgart: Franz Steiner Verlag, 2014), 177–206.

[77] Leibniz, 'Brevis designatio meditationum de Originibus Gentium', 186.

nations. Dissecting, comparing, and contrasting ancient and modern languages, Leibniz went on to devise a complex classification of most of the
known peoples of Africa, Asia, and Europe, examining their migrations in
ancient times. Indeed, the essay was as original as it was ambitious. As one
commentator put it, Leibniz's essay was built around 'intriguing research'
and offered many convincing arguments.[78] And yet, captivating as the work
may have been, the methods used and the underlying principles were not
entirely new. Not only had Leibniz already discussed them in the *Nouveau
essai sur l'entendement humain* as well as in a previous work on the origins of
the Germanic peoples but, importantly, the same ideas were being debated at
the time across Europe.[79] In his *Histoire critique du Vieux Testament* (1678),
for example, Richard Simon had considered how the comparison of living
and dead languages might help to shed light on the most ancient pasts of
nations. Other French authors followed suit.[80] But despite the growing
interest in such issues and methods, it was Leibniz himself who turned
semantics into a crucial element in the debate over the origins of France.
He did so with his 'Essai sur l'origine des François', a work that first appeared
in 1715 in Latin and then, soon after Leibniz's death, was translated into
French and circulated in manuscript form in Paris before finally being
published, in 1720.[81] A detailed summary even appeared in the *Journal de
Trévoux* as early as 1716.[82] In its opening pages, the famous philosopher
dismissed with scorn the myth of the Trojan founding of France as well as
the legend that saw in the Greek hero Priam its first ruler. Importantly, he
did so with the aid of semantics and by discussing primary sources when
searching for plausible explanations.[83] Using these principles and methods,

---

[78] Anonymous, review of *Miscellanea Berolinensia ad incrementum scientiarum ex scriptis*, in *Le journal des sçavans*, 8 December 1710, 646.

[79] Gottfried Wilhelm Leibniz, 'Nouveau essai sur l'entendement humain' (written in 1703 but first published in 1765), in *Sämtliche Schriften und Briefe: Reihe 6, Philosophische Schriften* (Berlin: Akademie-Verlag, 1962), vi. 285; Gottfried Wilhelm Leibniz, 'Dissertatio de origine Germanorum' (1696), in *Opera Omnia*, iv. part 2, 198–205. Also see Gottfried Wilhelm Leibniz, 'Nouvelles ouvertures' (1686), in *Opuscules et fragments inédits* (Paris: Alcan, 1903), 225. On the diffusion of such ideas, see the classic by Daniel Droixhe, *La linguistique et l'appel de l'histoire (1600–1800): Rationalisme et révolutions positivistes* (Geneva: Droz, 1978), 118–59.

[80] See Droixhe, *La linguistique et l'appel de l'histoire*, 160–4.

[81] See Louis de Jaucourt [Louis de Neufville], *Histoire de la vie et des ouvrages de Leibnitz* (Amsterdam: François Changuion, 1734), 112–3.

[82] Anonymous, review of Gottfried Wilhelm Leibniz, *De origine francorum disquisitio*, in *Journal de Trévoux, ou Mémoires pour servir à l'histoire des sciences et des arts*, January 1710, 1–10. For an analysis of the essay, see Frédéric de Buzon, 'Leibniz, étymologie et origine des nations', *Revue française d'histoire des idées politiques*, 36 (2012), 394–7.

[83] Gottfried Wilhelm Leibniz, 'Essai sur l'origine des François', in Pierre Desmaiseaux (ed.), *Recueil de diverses pièces sur la philosophie, la religion naturelle, l'histoire, les mathématiques, etc.* (Amsterdam:

Leibniz criticised as equally groundless the so-called Gallo-Frankish theories of Bodin, Audigier, and of the classical scholar the abbé Lacarry (1605–1684), all of whom believed, 'for the glory of their country', that it would be more honourable 'to have the modern inhabitants of Gaul be descended from the Gauls themselves'.[84] Leaning on the works of classical historians and geographers, Leibniz tried to prove that the French were originally a Teutonic people related to the Angles, the Saxons, and the Cambrians. Originating in a region between the Baltic Sea and the River Elbe, the Franks had migrated to the lands between the Weser and the Rhine, finally settling in Gaul and giving birth to modern France.

Although Leibniz's notion of a Germanic origin of the Gauls was not new, in the seventeenth century it had been almost entirely absent from scholarly debates – not least for political reasons.[85] Unsurprisingly, the reception of the 'Essai sur l'origine des François' was mixed. In Leibniz's own words, the idea that the French were born of the Germans 'seemed a paradox'.[86] While some scholars, such as Le Long, embraced the notion, others, including Fréret, were fiercely critical.[87] But the most detailed and coherent response came from the père Tournemine, who had perhaps been encouraged by the Duke d'Orléans (1674–1723) to revive the thesis of the Gallic origins of France.[88] Following Bodin and Lacarry's 'simple and yet convincing' arguments, in a short article published in January 1716 Tournemine made the case that, in the sixth century BC, Gallic tribes had left their lands of their own free will in order to cross the Rhine.[89] Later, at

H. Du Sauzet, 1740), ii. 288–91. The text was originally published as *De origine francorum disquisitio* (Hanover: Nicol Foerster, 1715).

[84] Leibniz, 'Essai sur l'origine des François', 294. For Gilles Lacarry's ideas, see his *Historia Coloniarum a Gallis in exteras nationes missarum, tum exterarum nationum Coloniae in Gallias deductae* (Clermont: Jacquard, 1677), 242–3.

[85] Anna Maria Battista, *La 'Germania' di Tacito nella Francia illuminista* (Urbino: Quattro Venti, 1999), 26–7.

[86] Leibniz, 'Essai sur l'origine des François', 287. On the debate stirred up by the essay, see Julien Marie Lehuërou, *Histoire des institutions mérovingiennes et du gouvernement des Mérovingiens* (Paris: Joubert, 1842), 86–7.

[87] Jacques Le Long to Gottfried Wilhelm Leibniz, 29 February 1712, quoted in Louis Davillé, *Leibniz historien: Essai sur l'activité et la méthode historique de Leibniz* (Paris: Alcan, 1909), 296, n. 6; Fréret, 'De l'origine des Français', v. 196–8. Fréret might have read Leibniz's text in the late 1720s. See: Géry De Cafmeyer, 'Un manuscrit de Nicolas Fréret: *Mémoire sur le mot dunum* (1745)', in Daniel Droixhe and Chantal Grell (eds.), *La linguistique entre mythe et histoire* (Munster: Nodus Publikationen, 1993), 152–5.

[88] It is a conjecture made by Leibniz himself in a letter to the abbé de Saint-Pierre: Gottfried Wilhelm Leibniz to Charles-Irénée Castel de Saint-Pierre, 2 October 1716, in Leibniz and Saint-Pierre, *Correspondance* (Paris: Paris II: Centre de philosophie du droit, 1995), 72.

[89] René-Joseph de Tournemine, 'Réflexions sur la dissertation de M. Leibnits, touchant l'origine des François', *Journal de Trévoux, ou Mémoires pour servir à l'histoire des sciences et des arts*, January 1716, 16. On the père's work and life, see Charles Weiss, 'Tournemine', in Michaud (ed.), *Biographie universelle ancienne et moderne*, xlvi. 369–71.

the time of Gallien's (circa 218–268 CE) rule over the Empire, they took on the name of 'French' to celebrate their ancient freedom – a name that gave them, according to Tournemine, the strength to fight for their independence.[90] The French were then originally Gauls, and this was seemingly confirmed by Tournemine's own semantic research, which showed that 'Allemands' and 'Français' were simply two sub-groups of the same Teutonic race with very similar languages. On such a basis, the père could then conclude, with a syllogism, that: '[T]he French are the Germans; the Germans are the Gauls who crossed the Rhine under Sigovese; consequently, the origin of the French is entirely Gallic.'[91] Tournemine's essay soon prompted Leibniz to write a response in which, using once again philology and semantics, he reiterated his view that 'the Gauls are descended from the Germans and the Germans from the Scythians'.[92] But the debate lingered on.

In 1722, the Benedictine historian Dom Vaissette (1685–1756) intervened in the debate with his *Dissertation sur l'origine des Français*, contesting the racial unity of modern France and attempting to discredit Tournemine's views.[93] As he saw it, there was scant proof that the French were descendants of the ancient Gauls who had settled across the Rhine. Tournemine's was 'nothing more than a *convincing reasoning* which is not founded on any sound argument'.[94] However, rather than offer an explanation of the nation's origins, the Benedictine scholar limited himself to showing that France's racial unity was pure sophistry. It was a limit promptly noted by a critic writing in the *Journal des sçavans*.[95] However, while the *Dissertation* did not add much to what was already known about the nation's origins, it definitively discredited the idea of the Gallic origins of France – or so it might have seemed. Dom Vaissette ended the discussion started by Leibniz, which was, in the words of Augustin Thierry, the last one 'between sensible and learned men' on the 'patriotic theory of the unity of race'.[96] Although the thesis did re-emerge time and again throughout the century, the assumption of a common racial origin so cherished by many sixteenth-

[90] Tournemine, 'Réflexions sur la dissertation de M. Leibnits', 16–19.   [91] Ibid., 20.
[92] Gottfried Wilhelm Leibniz, 'Réponse aux objections du père de Tournemine contre la Dissertation sur l'origine des François' (1716), in Desmaiseaux (ed.), *Recueil de diverses pièces sur la philosophie, la religion naturelle, l'histoire, les mathématiques, etc.*, ii. 274.
[93] Joseph Vaissette, 'Dissertation sur l'origine des français', in Leber (ed.), *Collection des meilleurs dissertations relatifs à l'histoire de France*, i. 133–77.
[94] Vaissette, 'Dissertation sur l'origine des français', 177. Italics in the original.
[95] Anonymous, review of Joseph Vaissette, *Dissertation sur l'origine des Français*, in *Le journal des sçavans*, 4 January 1723, 9.
[96] Thierry, 'Considérations sur l'histoire de France', 39.

and seventeenth-century historians became in due course little more than a myth.[97] But what is noteworthy is the fact that, in making his argument, Dom Vaissette interspersed his essay with semantic arguments and comments about the ancient names of rivers, mountains, and kings.[98] Language had clearly become a key element in the discussions over the origins of France. From an essentially institutional framework focusing on the monarchy, the debate was gradually but surely moving on to a cultural plane, concentrating on customs, *mœurs*, language, and social practices. In the writings of Leibniz, the père Tournemine, and Dom Vaissette there was remarkably little space for Clovis and Pharamond.

Contesting Boulainvilliers: The Abbé Trianon, Foncemagne, and Dubos

The dismissal of the theory of the nation's racial unity left a void that had somehow to be filled. The increasing circulation of Boulainvilliers's works, shortly after the publication of Dom Vaissette's *Dissertation*, offered the nobility of the sword and its advocates an explanation that was sound in a scholarly sense but also politically convenient. It was then that the count's thesis of the two races inaugurated a new phase in the dispute over the nation's origins, one that would last up to the revolution and beyond. A first reaction to Boulainvilliers's thesis – though rather simplistic and misguided – was in the anonymous 'Lettre d'un conseiller du Parlement de Rouen au sujet d'un écrit du Comte de Boulainvilliers'. Possibly by one abbé Trianon, the short tract was published in 1730 after circulating for some time as a manuscript.[99] According to its author, Boulainvilliers's history of the French was entirely based on the clear-cut division between two orders, 'the nobility and the slaves', stemming from the subjugation of

---

[97] On the persistence of such views, see Henri Duranton, '"Nos ancêtres les Gaulois": Genèse et avatars d'un cliché historique', *Cahiers d'histoire*, 16 (1969), 343–7.

[98] See, for example, Vaissette 'Dissertation sur l'origine des Français', 141, 145, 147, and 153–4.

[99] [Trianon], 'Lettre d'un conseiller du Parlement de Rouen au sujet d'un écrit du Comte de Boulainvilliers', in Pierre-Nicolas Desmolets (ed.), *Continuation des Mémoires de littérature et d'histoire de M. de Sallengre* (Paris: Simart, 1726–1732), ix. 107–244 and 247–311. On the tract, see Thierry, 'Considérations sur l'histoire de France', 62–5. On authorship, see Claude-Pierre Goujet, *Supplément au Grand dictionnaire historique, généalogique, géographique de M. Louis Moreri* (Paris: Lemercier, 1735), i. 171. The only other relevant reference I have found on one abbé de Trianon, 'a man who had entirely devoted himself to learning', is in Pierre-François Guyot Desfontaines and François Granet, *Observations sur les écrits modernes* (Paris: Chaubert, 1735–1743), viii. 140. In this case, he might be Henri de La Grange-Trianon, the brother of the well-known Charles-Sébastien de La Grange-Trianon (1650?–1733). A different hypothesis is in Tholozan, *Henri de Boulainvilliers*, 348, n. 1428.

the Gauls by the Franks. Since all distinctions derived from the initial conquest, and since ennobling was contrary to law, Boulainvilliers allegedly considered the magistrates to be the descendants of the 'slave secretaries of the ancient nobles'. Against such a hateful system, 'love for truth' moved the abbé to expose its faults.[100] Although he certainly agreed that social distinctions were necessary, he claimed that these had to be based on personal merit alone. Following the arguments of seventeenth-century moralists, he refused to accept that a person's character depended on birth and, addressing the nobles, he reminded them: '[Y]our ancestors have placed you on the path to nobility and in the obligation of being noble; but they have not given you true nobility, which is an attribute of virtue, nor the glory that accompanies it.'[101] Arguing that even noblemen had to show they deserved their privileges could imply, conversely, that even a member of the Third Estate might rise to the nobility through his services to the state. But this was only possible because, according to the abbé, the division between orders was not a consequence of conquest.

To prove the last point, which was central to his refutation of Boulainvilliers's ideas, the abbé Trianon advanced an original thesis. Part of his contention was that, well before the invasion of Gaul, the Franks had become divided into two separate groups. On the one hand were the rich landowners who did not work and who could train for war and buy their armour, swords, and spears; on the other were the destitute who were obliged to work. After invading the lands of Gaul, where each worked for himself, wealthy Franks started to claim rights to which they were not entitled. Moreover, since the defence of the country was the main occupation of this wealthy class, they soon earned the king's gratitude and were rewarded with titles and fiefs.[102] So, even though the Franks had not enslaved the Gauls, a clear distinction was nonetheless established.[103] Remarkably, such a viewpoint implied that the Franks were warriors not because they were braver than the Gauls, nor were these latter more industrious because naturally inclined to work. The division of society was merely a consequence of the fact that the wealthy had the possibility of fighting and displaying their courage, earning glory and respect. Rather than wealth and rights being a reward for bravery, bravery could only be proven thanks to these. There was no inherent, natural distinction between Franks and Gauls. Nor was the antiquity of a family a mark of its nobility

---

[100] [Trianon], 'Lettre d'un conseiller du Parlement de Rouen', 109–10.   [101] Ibid., 118–19.
[102] Ibid., 122–9   [103] Ibid., 188.

since, as the author of the 'Lettre' noted, only a very few could trace their lineage back more than five centuries. Once again addressing the nobles, he reminded them that their ancestors might once have been peasants, artisans or, at best, honest and hardworking bourgeois.[104] As for the latter, the bourgeois whom 'the Count de Boulainvilliers has so outrageously debased', had always dutifully served his country: '[H]is education, his bravery in defending the nation, his wealth, his generosity, have earned' him the highest esteem. There were many ways of serving the nation, and trade and hard work, not at all incompatible with courage and honour, were among these. Therein lay what the abbé called the 'nobility of the bourgeois'.[105]

Another refutation of Boulainvilliers's thesis, this one more refined and erudite, was by the Oratorian and academician Étienne Lauréault de Foncemagne (1694–1779) – a man who, according to Melchior Grimm (1723–1807), 'knew the history of France better than anyone else'.[106] It was contained in the *Examen critique d'une opinion de M. le Comte de Boulainvilliers*, a dissertation first read out at the Académie des inscriptions in 1732 and then published a few years later. As Foncemagne made clear, it was because he feared that Boulainvilliers's reputation might 'lend great weight to the feelings he embraces' that he decided to defend the monarchy against the notion that its authority was not absolute. To do so, he tried to disprove two of the count's main assumptions. The first one, stemming from Boulainvilliers's own reading of Tacitus's *Germania* (circa 98 CE), was that the Franks chose the head of their army and that this need not be their king. Boulainvilliers had in fact contended that it was only through election that Clovis had reunited in his person both royalty and the command of the army. The second assumption was that the *Maires du Palais*, freely chosen by the nation, 'were *by such a charge generals of the army*', independently of the king's will.[107] With regard to the first claim, Foncemagne believed it was a mistake to assume that when Tacitus spoke of the Germans, he was describing the Franks. On the contrary, he argued, the Roman historian had posited a clear distinction between the two, seeing in the Franks a 'new people, under a new form of government',

---

[104] Ibid., 168–9.   [105] Ibid., 232–3.

[106] Grimm et al., *Correspondance littéraire*, xii. 363 (January 1780). On his life and work, see Charles Cuissard, 'Les Laureault de Boiscommun et Laureault de Foncemagne', *Annales de la Société historique et archéologique du Gâtinais*, 10 (1892), 345–67.

[107] Étienne Lauréault de Foncemagne, 'Examen critique d'une opinion de M. le Comte de Boulainvilliers', *Mémoires de littérature tirés des registres de l'Académie royale des inscriptions et belles-lettres*, 10 (1736), 526. Italics in the text.

a league uniting several Germanic tribes.[108] If this were true, and if the 'beginning of the history of the Franks' coincided with the creation of such a confederation, then Tacitus's arguments could not be used to describe the Frankish constitution. Consequently, the count's claim that the king of the Germans was also the head of the army was irrelevant. Quoting a passage from Gregory of Tours (538–594) in which *reges* and *duces* were used as synonyms, Foncemagne went on to show that the head of the Frankish army and the Frankish king were one and the same. But for the Oratorian scholar this was hardly surprising since in a 'nation entirely made up of soldiers' the two roles 'were inevitably confounded in the same person'.[109] Going on to refute Boulainvilliers's second assumption, Foncemagne granted that general assemblies did meet in March to elect the mayors, but he denied these the importance ascribed to them by Boulainvilliers. They were simply officers whose duty it was to rule in the name of an underage monarch should the need arise. Contrary to what the count believed, the fact that their power had grown during the rule of the Carolingian kings was a usurpation and, as such, could never constitute a legal right.[110]

The explanation offered by Foncemagne was surely an erudite and convincing vindication of the absolute authority of the French monarchy. Years later, such views would account for his involvement in Moreau's plans to provide the king's ministers with the historical arguments for their political disputations and campaigns.[111] For us, two aspects of the *Examen critique* are noteworthy. First, the dissertation hardly touched on the relationship between the descendants of the Franks and those of the Gauls. In fact, from Foncemagne's perspective, the crucial struggle was between the legitimate authority of the crown and the claims of a few seditious noblemen. As for other royalist advocates, the existence of an opposition between two races within the French nation did not have much importance for Foncemagne, and in this respect he followed the path of most of his seventeenth-century royalist predecessors. The second element is the emphasis he placed on the cultural traits of the Franks and on their alleged natural inclinations, such as their innate bravery. Combined with a marked interest in semantic issues, this emphasis is indicative of a strong preoccupation with the cultural traits of the French people and their

---

[108] Ibid., 527.   [109] Ibid., 528.   [110] Ibid., 532–4.
[111] See Baker, 'Controlling French History', 77–80, and Gembicki, *Histoire et politique à la fin de l'Ancien régime*, 93–7.

ancestors – which inevitably diverted attention from its kings and the royal house. Importantly, this is an aspect at odds with the more institutional appreciation of the French past shown by earlier champions of absolute rule and, to an extent, is revealing of the difficulties of defending absolutist prerogatives on the ground occupied by their opponents.

The most important and the best-known refutation of Boulainvilliers's thesis was by the abbé Dubos (1670–1742), a polymath who had become famous thanks to his *Réflexions critiques sur la poésie et sur la peinture* (1719) and who enjoyed the esteem, among others, of d'Alembert (1717–1783), Fénelon, and Voltaire.[112] In 1734, the publication of his *Histoire critique de l'établissement de la monarchie française* furthered his celebrity, provoking, as one scholar has written, a 'universal clamour' for its 'audacity'.[113] President Hénault went as far as to claim that the book had given rise to a 'revolution' in the study of the past comparable to the one caused by Descartes (1596–1650) in philosophy. In a letter to the President of the *Parlement* of Bourgogne, Jean de Bouhier (1673–1746), Marais praised the *Histoire critique* for effectively challenging the ideas of the père Daniel as well as those of the Count de Boulainvilliers – a comment that the President repeated word for word a few days later in a letter to the Marquis de Caumont (1688–1745). For his part, the abbé Prévost expressed his undisguised admiration for Dubos's achievement in having 'utterly destroyed' Boulainvilliers's theory. Up until then, argued Prévost, the notion that the Franks had conquered Gaul had been so widely accepted simply because no 'author has ever argued to the contrary'. Dubos's efforts had to be applauded.[114] François-René de Chateaubriand (1768–1848) later defended the *Histoire critique* from the jibes of Montesquieu, while in the late nineteenth century Camille Jullian (1859–1933) still held it to be one of the 'most penetrating' works

[112] Jean Baptiste le Rond d'Alembert, 'Eloge de Dubos', in *Œuvres* (Paris: Belin, 1821–1822), iii. 203; François de Salignac de La Mothe Fénelon to Jean-Baptiste Dubos, 20 November 1713, in Paul Denis (ed.), *Lettres autographes de la collection de Troussures* (Beauvais: Imprimerie départementale de l'Oise, 1912), 199; François-Marie Arouet Voltaire to Jean-Baptiste Dubos, 30 October 1738, in *Œuvres*, xxxv. 29, and François-Marie Arouet Voltaire to Nicolas Claude Thieriot, 13 April 1739, in *Œuvres*, xxxv. 244. The best intellectual biography of Dubos is still Alfred Lombard, *L'abbé Du Bos: Un initiateur de la pensée moderne* (Paris: Hachette, 1913). The abbé's name is sometimes spelt 'Du Bos' and even 'du Bos'. I have decided to use 'Dubos' since it was prevalent in the eighteenth century.
[113] Alfred Maury, *L'ancienne Académie des inscriptions et belles-lettres* (Paris: Didier et Cie, 1864), 161.
[114] Marais to Bouhier, 12 March 1734, 73; Jean Bouhier to Joseph de Seytres, Marquis de Caumont, 17 March 1734, in *Correspondance littéraire du Président Bouhier*, vi. 50; Antoine François Prévost et al., *Le pour et le contre: Ouvrage périodique d'un goût nouveau* (Paris: Didot, 1733–1740), iii. 37–8 and also 26–7.

on the origins of France.[115] Interestingly, while the *Histoire critique* may have been the most convincing rebuttal of the theory of the Frankish conquest, the abbé Dubos continued to accept it until at least 1719, even believing it to be a legitimate source of the rights of the nobility. Only in the 1720s did he radically change his stance and set out to refute what he now saw as a dangerously misleading notion.[116]

Obviously, there were many crucial differences between the thesis of Dubos and those of Boulainvilliers. However, when considering their approach to the study of the past, it is the resemblances that stand out. The two shared in fact a strikingly similar determination to forge a critical and well-founded history. In this regard, the preface to the *Histoire critique* is revealing. For the abbé there expounded the principles of a history based on the thorough analysis of primary sources, texts, and works written by authors who had witnessed the events they chronicled. Faithful to such a principle, his own work was particularly well-documented – for some, even to a fault. Montesquieu, who was highly critical of Dubos's views, wrote of his 'endless erudition', which had given birth to the 'three deadly volumes' of the *Histoire critique*. Mably was deeply annoyed by Dubos's long-winded discussions regarding the validity of each and every one of his sources. Du Fresnoy concurred, believing that the abbé could have condensed his work to one fourth of its actual length. In a letter addressed to Dubos himself, Voltaire might have been thinking of the abbé's pedantry when he wrote that details were the 'vermin that kill great works'.[117] While some saw Dubos's constant references to sources and their thorough discussion as a novelty to be applauded, the abbé himself felt the urge to clarify and qualify his approach.[118] As he made clear in the 'Discours préliminaire', his book was meant to 'destroy an entrenched system and

---

[115] Hénault, *Histoire critique de l'établissement des Français dans les Gaules*, i. 1; François-René de Chateaubriand, 'Préface – Études historiques' (1831), in *Œuvres complètes* (Paris: Pourrat Frères, 1836–1839), iv. 36; Camille Jullian, 'Introduction', in Charles-Louis Secondat de Montesquieu, *Considérations sur les causes de la grandeur des Romains et de leur décadence* (1734) (Paris: Hachette, 1896), ix.

[116] See Lombard, *L'abbé Du Bos*, 420–3.

[117] Montesquieu, 'De l'Esprit des lois', 926 (book xxx. ch. 23); Montesquieu's analysis of Dubos's work is discussed in Chapter 5. Mably, 'De la manière d'écrire l'histoire', 525–6; Nicolas Lenglet Du Fresnoy, *Tablettes chronologiques de l'histoire universelle sacrée et prophane depuis la création du monde jusqu'à l'an 1743* (Paris: De Bure l'aîné, 1744), i. p. lvi; Voltaire to Dubos, 30 October 1738, 30. Also see: Jean Bouhier to Mathieu Marais, 30 March 1734, in *Correspondance littéraire du Président Bouhier*, xiii. 79; Jean-Baptiste-François Née de La Rochelle, *Le guide de l'histoire, à l'usage de la jeunesse, et des personnes qui veulent la lire avec fruit, ou L'écrire avec succès* (Paris: Bidault, 1803), iii. 102.

[118] See for example, the positive comments in Anonymous, review of Jean-Baptiste Dubos, *Histoire critique de l'établissement de la monarchie française*, in *Le journal des sçavans*, May 1734, 279.

establish a new' one. The narration itself was of secondary importance and, Dubos maintained, it could be interrupted whenever necessary to discuss the authority of sources, to explain the reasons for siding with one historian in particular, or even to clarify the interpretation of a text by a modern scholar. He was well aware that 'such discussions often weary the reader', but the pursuit of a more critical historiography required them. Having taken it upon himself to refute the notion of a Frankish conquest of Gaul, he had merely chosen the 'kind of writing the most suited to convince, though the one least likely to please'.[119]

One of the main reasons that had led Dubos to ground his work so firmly on the documents collected by the antiquaries was his determination to avoid the faults of those historians who, relying on secondary sources alone, endlessly repeated the mistakes of their predecessors.[120] It was his conviction that received truths accepted on account of a historiographical tradition were to be rejected when the examination of primary sources belied them. His critical approach to the study of the past was in line with that of the most forward-thinking scholars of the day, many of whom he had read and some of whom he knew personally. When Marais speculated that while writing the *Histoire critique* the abbé possibly 'profited from the reading of Bayle', he was right – although he was not aware that Dubos and the great Huguenot scholar were friends.[121] Importantly for us, emerging from the private correspondence between the two is a shared concern with the current state of historical studies, especially in France. In 1697, in a letter to Bayle, Dubos declared himself profoundly dissatisfied with how the past was studied, lamenting that his fellow countrymen were only interested in 'stories, novellas, and petty histories [*historiettes*]'. Bayle agreed with the abbé: '[T]here is nothing more correct than your thoughts on the sins committed in France against history.'[122] There were many causes for their discontent, but one was the clear-cut division between historical scholarship and philosophy which, as they saw it, made of history

[119] Jean-Baptiste Dubos, *Histoire critique de l'établissement de la monarchie française* (Paris: Osmont, 1734), i. 55. See, on this, Anonymous, review of Jean-Baptiste Dubos, *Histoire critique de l'établissement de la monarchie française*, in *Bibliothèque raisonnée des ouvrages des savans de l'Europe*, October–December 1734, 402.
[120] Dubos, *Histoire critique de l'établissement de la monarchie française*, i. 47–8.
[121] Mathieu Marais to Jean Bouhier, 22 March 1734, in Bouhier, *Correspondance littéraire du Président Bouhier*, xiii. 77. On the friendship between Bayle and Dubos: Lombard, *L'abbé Du Bos*, 53–68.
[122] Jean-Baptiste Dubos to Pierre Bayle, 1 March 1697, in Bayle et al., *Correspondance* (Oxford: Voltaire Foundation, 1999–), x. 439; Pierre Bayle to Jean-Baptiste Dubos, 2 May 1697, in Bayle et al., *Correspondance*, x. 517. Bayle's remarks may be in response to a letter by Dubos now lost. See the comments by the editors of Bayle's correspondence: ibid., x. 518, n. 5.

a description of great deeds with little attention paid to their causes. So, as Dubos remarked while commenting on Daniel's *Histoire* – and referring to views already expressed by Bayle – it was a 'pleasant metamorphosis that of a philosopher into a historian', one that might prove to be seminal.[123]

It is possibly because of the importance Dubos accorded to original sources and his declared search for impartiality that one nineteenth-century admirer resolutely insisted that the *Histoire critique* was devoid of 'any political objective' and that 'no feeling of hostility towards any one of the nation's classes' could be discerned in it.[124] In truth, as has been pointed out, Dubos's scholarly concerns were not irreconcilable with his political aims – or, rather, they could hardly be told apart.[125] The main purpose of Dubos's work was to refute the thesis of a violent Frankish conquest severing the history of Rome from that of France. His theoretical point of departure was the contention that the condition of Gaul under Clovis and his immediate successors was 'more or less the same as that under the last emperors'.[126] Having centred his thesis around Roman laws and institutions, the abbé could argue for a continuity between the absolute rule of the Roman emperors and the absolute rule of the French kings. But, crucially, his arguments even had a bearing on the relationships between the Gauls, the Romans, and the Franks. In fact, according to Dubos, by the end of the fourth century the Gauls and the Romans were perfectly integrated: 'There was no longer any real difference between the inhabitants of Gaul and the inhabitants of Italy', he claimed.[127] In his description of the Gallo-Romans, he recognised four different social groups: the slaves, who already existed in significant numbers well before the settling of the Franks; the clergy; the patricians; and, finally, 'the good bourgeois', who were mainly property owners or artisans. The latter class enjoyed the particular privileges attached to their cities and its members sat in the local assemblies.[128] Passing on to the Germanic tribes, the abbé had to admit that their history was extremely uncertain since they often mingled with other peoples and frequently moved from place to place. But what was clear to him – and here he adopted Fréret and Foncemagne's

---

[123] Jean Baptise Dubos to Pierre Bayle, 27 April 1696, in Bayle et al., *Correspondance*, x. 32.

[124] François Jules de Pétigny, *Études sur l'histoire, les lois et les institutions de l'époque mérovingienne* (Paris: Brockhaus et Avenarius, 1843–1851), ii. 599–600, n. 1. Against such views, see the harsh comment made by Montesquieu, 'Mes pensées', 1249 (§ 915).

[125] Thomas E. Kaiser, 'Rhetoric in the Service of the King: The abbé Dubos and the Concept of Public Judgment', *Eighteenth-Century Studies*, 23 (1989–1990), 194–8.

[126] Dubos, *Histoire critique de l'établissement de la monarchie française*, i. 54.   [127] Ibid., i. 2.

[128] Ibid., i. 14–28. Quote is on page 22.

viewpoint – was that they were an association of tribes living in the fifth century on the right bank of the Rhine and known as the Armorican league. Central to Dubos's argument was the idea of an alliance between such a confederation and the Romans who, he contended, trusted them because they were different from the other Germanic peoples. Dismissing out of hand the idea of savages only seeking glory through war, pillaging, and destruction, he claimed on the contrary that the Franks were 'the most civilised among the barbaric peoples'.[129] Such a notion – which was later espoused by the antiquary Dom Martin Bouquet (1685–1754), challenged by Dubos's friend, the historian Johann Wilhelm Hoffmann (1710–1739), and then again reaffirmed by Dubos in response to Hoffmann – was the basis of his argument that the Franks had lost no time in absolving the Romans of their military duties, receiving in turn protection and gratitude from the emperor.[130] It was within such a framework that Dubos could describe the fusion of the Gallo-Romans with the Franks, claiming that, through the widening and the strengthening of the alliance on the one hand, and the falling apart of the Roman Empire on the other, Clovis had finally acquired his supremacy. What turned him into an unchallenged king was that following his accession to the throne he 'was invested with the dignity of the empire'. After his conversion to Christianity, the Armorican league yielded to Clovis and the Roman troops pledged their loyalty. The final step was taken when 'Anastasius, the Eastern Emperor, granted him civil power through the title of consul'.[131] Importantly, since the shift from the Roman Empire to the kingdom of Clovis had been peaceful and sealed by treaties, Dubos denied that the Franks had intro-duced any formal distinction between themselves and the Gauls. No laws granted specific privileges to their families, nor was a distinct order of subjects ever created.[132] In fact, the abbé went on, the Franks had gone so far as to adopt the language, manners, and customs of the Romans as well as their laws.[133] Even the supposed superior fighting skills of the Franks were denied. Soldiers came from every group making up the nation, and, in

---

[129] Ibid., i. 204.
[130] See: Martin Bouquet, *Recueil des historiens de la France* (Paris: Libraires Associés, 1739), ii. pp. xxxiii–xxxvi; Johann Wilhelm Hoffmann, 'Foedera quae imperatores Romani cum Francis ante tempora Clodovei fecerunt', *Bibliothèque germanique ou Histoire littéraire de l'Allemagne*, 42 (1738), 190–208; Johann Wilhelm Hoffmann and Jean-Baptiste Dubos, 'Lettres de Mrs. Hoffmann et Du Bos sur l'article précédent', *Bibliothèque germanique ou Histoire littéraire de l'Allemagne*, 42 (1738), 208–15.
[131] Dubos, *Histoire critique de l'établissement de la monarchie française*, i. 10.   [132] Ibid., iii. 317.
[133] Ibid., iii. 525–9 and 339.

turn, the Franks could become members of the clergy and were admitted to all professions.[134]

Dubos's *Histoire critique* soon became a work with which all scholars interested in the origins of France had to reckon. Yet, with the notable exception of Voltaire, few of the great eighteenth-century thinkers defended its precepts. Montesquieu bitterly criticised the *Histoire critique*, and even d'Alembert, his admiration for Dubos notwithstanding, decided to side with the baron. As one commentator noted, even the learned journals of the time were critical. One detractor, writing in the *Journal littéraire*, went as far as to state that the true aim of the *Histoire critique* was to 'erase from the French the memory itself of freedom'.[135] As always, political concerns clouded scholarly judgement. But the fact that, much later on, Fustel de Coulanges (1830–1889) adopted and readapted Dubos's ideas testifies to their worth.[136] If were many merits to the *Histoire critique*, a crucial one, duly highlighted by Thomas Kaiser, is that it was centred on the character of the Franks, on their *mœurs*, and on those of the Gallo-Romans.[137] In fact, the abbé's attention to usages and ways of life had already emerged in earlier works. Commenting on the *Ligue de Cambray* (1709), Voltaire noted how it revealed 'the usages and the *mœurs* of the age', standing as 'a model in such a genre'.[138] The originality of the *Histoire critique* was that *mœurs* and the values they stood for were now used to explain the ancient constitution of France. To refute the notion of a violent conquest, Dubos depicted a people that, far from being barbaric and indomitable, were willing to accept the Romans as their allies and equals and even to adopt their laws and ways of living. The abbé was going well beyond the classical jurisprudential arguments on the historical legitimacy of institutions. He was calling into question the nature of a people and explaining, through it, their history. Crucially for us, such a method was akin to Boulainvilliers's. Like the count, in fact, Dubos believed that to judge the legitimacy of modern

---

[134] Ibid., iii. 329–30.

[135] Voltaire, 'Dictionnaire philosophique', xx. 11–13; Montesquieu, 'De l'Esprit des lois', 795 (book xxviii. ch. 3), and 926–37 (book xxx. chaps. 23, 24 and 25); D'Alembert, 'Eloge de Dubos', 208; Jean Lebeuf to Jean-Basile-Pascal Fenel de Dargny, 17 August 1734, in *Lettres* (Auxerre: G. Perriquet, 1866–1868), ii. 159; Anonymous, review of Jean-Baptiste Dubos, *Histoire critique de l'établissement de la monarchie française*, in *Journal littéraire*, 22 (1734), 133.

[136] Numa Denis Fustel de Coulanges, *Histoire des institutions politiques de l'ancienne France* (Paris: Hachette, 1875–1889). See François Hartog, *Le XIXme siècle et l'histoire: Le cas Fustel de Coulanges* (Paris: Presses universitaires de France, 1988), 87–8.

[137] Thomas E. Kaiser, 'The abbé Dubos and the Historical Defence of Monarchy in Early Eighteenth-Century France', *Studies on Voltaire and the Eighteenth Century*, 267 (1989), 96.

[138] Voltaire, 'Catalogue de la plupart des écrivains français qui ont paru dans le siècle de Louis XIV', 66.

political institutions it was necessary to apprehend and comprehend a people's values and manners and how these had changed over the centuries. Both scholars were part of a broader discourse that was producing a gradual yet momentous shift of emphasis from a history essentially focused on the decisions of rulers and political elites, to one based on a people's customs, beliefs, character, and *mœurs*. The authors we have considered, notwithstanding the different and even contrasting political implications of their work, could enter into a dialogue because they shared the same point of departure – having denied the conceptual identity of king and nation, it was now necessary to grasp a nation's character if they were to understand its history and, through it, the legitimacy of its laws and institutions. As we shall see in the next part of this book, the relationship between the nation's character, its history, and its constitution became the leading preoccupation of an increasing number of scholars throughout the eighteenth century.

PART II

CHAPTER 4

Thinking the Nation's Character
At the Crossroads of Literature, Anthropology, and History

Defining a Caractère and Telling Its Story

In 1751, in his popular *Considérations sur les mœurs de ce siècle*, Duclos observed that 'the examination of the different characters of nations and the physical or moral causes of such differences' would make a particularly interesting subject. However, aware of the difficulties and fearing that, were he to undertake such a task, he would be 'suspected of partisanship', the secretary of the Académie française decided to concentrate on the manners and *mœurs* of the French alone.[1] After all, he noted, the study of the 'men with whom we must live is what is truly useful to us'.[2] Many scholars, however, would not have shared Duclos's reticence. Some even claimed that knowing about other countries could shed light on one's own, indicating possible improvements in its *mœurs*, manners, and even its literary and artistic taste.[3] Of course, there were many plausible reasons for comparing the character of the French with that of other nations, not least the enjoyment to be derived from learning about close yet exotic worlds – or from disparaging neighbouring countries. With different intentions and with greater or lesser sobriety, studying national characters, manners, and *mœurs* became a practice in which many would indulge.[4]

---

[1] The semantic complexity of *mœurs* is captured in a quote by the père Daniel: 'With this word, *mœurs*, one does not only mean a nation's mind [*génie*], but also the customs, usages, laws, the jurisprudence, the ways of the military and civil government, and other similar things, along with the changes taking place throughout time': Daniel, *Histoire de France* (ed. 1713), 'Preface', n.p. Given its semantic complexity, *mœurs* may not be translated into English by a single word and, for this reason, the French word will be used throughout.

[2] Charles Pinot Duclos, *Considérations sur les mœurs de ce siècle* (Paris: Honoré Champion, 2005), 100. On the *Considérations*, see Carole Dornier, 'Introduction', ibid., 7–64.

[3] See, for example, Anonymous, 'Lettre à un ami sur le *Spectateur françois*, qui s'imprime en Hollande', *Bibliothèque françoise, ou Histoire littéraire de la France*, 4 (1724), 44; Anonymous, *Valentine ou Lettres et mémoires interessants d'une famille anglaise* (Lausanne: n.p., 1786), 20; Anonymous, review of *Journal étrangère, ouvrage périodique*, in *Mercure de France*, February 1755, 84.

[4] There has been a growing interest in the history of national stereotyping, not least because of the increasing academic importance of imagology. For a theoretical overview: Joep Leerssen, 'The

129

According to one contributor to the *Bibliothèque des sciences et des beaux-arts*, writing in 1757, never before had so many scholars devoted so much energy to 'study[ing] the heart of man and investigat[ing] in depth the character of nations'. For his part, the Piedmontese linguist and literary critic Giuseppe Baretti (1719–1789) remarked that those depicting the character of modern nations were a 'species that has prodigiously multiplied during this century throughout Europe'.[5] Yet the fact that in their ranks could be found some of the greatest minds of the day is telling. Vico's *Principi di una scienza nuova d'intorno alla natura delle nazioni* (1725–1744), David Hume's (1711–1776) essay 'Of National Characters' (1748), Montesquieu's *Esprit des lois* (1748), and Kant's 'Von den Nationalcharaktern' (1764) all testify to an abiding preoccupation with the idea of national character. While by mid-century its study had become a subject of scientific enquiry in its own right, not all were agreed as to its merits. Adam Ferguson (1723–1816), for one, was strongly critical, believing it was misleading to derive the 'notion of a people from the example of one or a few of its members'. A few years earlier, the great rationalist philosopher Nicolas Malebranche (1638–1715) had expressed similar doubts and, a few years later, the abbé Coyer (1707–1782) and the abbé Guénée (1717–1803) would follow suit. In his literary masterpiece, the *Lettres persanes* (1721), Montesquieu satirised the absurdity of national stereotypes by

Rhetoric of National Character: A Programmatic Survey', *Poetics Today*, 21 (2000), 267–92; Manfred Beller and Joep Leerssen (eds.), *Imagology: The Cultural Construction and Literary Representation of National Characters* (Amsterdam: Rodopi, 2007). On national stereotyping in the eighteenth century: John G. Hayman, 'Notions on National Characters in the Eighteenth Century', *Huntington Library Quarterly*, 35 (1971), 1–17; Marc Crépon, *Les géographies de l'esprit: Enquête sur la caractérisation des peuples de Leibniz à Hegel* (Paris: Payot, 1996); Alain Montandon (ed.), *L'Europe des politesses et le caractère des nations: Regards croisés* (Paris: Anthropos, 1997); Jean-François Dubost, 'Les stéréotypes nationaux à l'époque moderne (vers 1500 – vers 1800)', *Mélanges de l'École française de Rome*, 11 (1999), 667–82. With a focus on eighteenth-century France: Ann Rigney, 'Narrative Representation and National Identity: On the "Frenchness" of the Revolution', *Yearbook of European Studies*, 2 (1989), 53–69; Isabel Herrero and Lydia Vasquez, 'Types nationaux européens dans des œuvres de fiction françaises (1750–1789)', *Dix-huitième siècle*, 25 (1993), 115–27; Roberto Romani, *National Character and Public Spirit in Britain and France, 1750–1914* (Cambridge: Cambridge University Press, 2002), 19–62; David A. Bell, 'Le caractère national et l'imaginaire républicain au XVIIIᵉ siècle', *Annales: Histoire, sciences sociales*, 57 (2002), 867–88; Pauline Kra, 'The Concept of National Character in Eighteenth-Century France', *Cromohs*, 7 (2002), 1–6; Jocelyn Huchette, *La gaieté, caractère français?: Représenter la nation au siècle des Lumières (1715–1789)* (Paris: Classiques Garnier, 2015).

[5] Anonymous, review of Adam Fitz-Adam, *Le monde, ou Feuilles périodiques sur les mœurs du tems*, and of [Roger Urbain], *Le traducteur, ou Traduction de diverses feuilles choisies, tirées des papiers périodiques Anglois*, in *Bibliothèque des sciences et des beaux-arts*, January–March 1757, 214; Giuseppe Baretti, 'Viaggio da Londra a Genova passando per l'Inghilterra occidentale, il Portogallo, la Spagna e la Francia' (1770), in *Opere scelte* (Turin: UTET, 1975), ii. 411. The note was written on 10 October 1760. Baretti spent most of life in England and was also known as Joseph Baretti.

listing a series of bizarre prejudices purportedly held by a French traveller describing the Spaniards and Portuguese. Hume, however, believed that such generalisations, although not always precise, usually contained a kernel of truth and could serve to enhance one's knowledge of other countries.[6] It was perhaps inevitable that even those who decried national stereotypes used them in their works. In his *Voyage de Hollande* (1780–1782), Diderot expressed the opinion that when travelling one of the most common mistakes was to take 'particular cases and turn them into general ones, and to write ... in a hundred different ways: In Orléans all innkeepers are bad-tempered and have red hair.'[7] Yet, despite the note of caution, commonplaces and national stereotypes abounded in his travelogue, and a number of his readers were surely confirmed in their belief that all Dutchmen were inclined to trade.[8]

Many of the reasons why national stereotypes were (and still are) so difficult to overcome relate to the fact that they render the social world more readily intelligible. They draw distinctions and divisions which simplify a complex and unpredictable reality. In his famous *Dictionnaire françois* (1680), the lexicographer Pierre Richelet (1626–1698) defined a character as a sign that 'distinguishes a person or a thing from another'.[9] Where nations are concerned, a character impresses on it a quality, a vice or a virtue that makes it essentially different from any other. Searching for such a trait may prove to be an interesting and rewarding practice. Diderot was one of those who thought as much: 'The observer takes pleasure in grasping the particular trait that characterises each people and disentangles it from the many general characters accompanying it.'[10] Behind this

---

[6] Adam Ferguson, *An Essay on the History of Civil Society* (1767) (Cambridge: Cambridge University Press, 1995), 183; Nicolas Malebranche, *Recherche de la vérité* (1674–1675) (Paris: Galerie de la Sorbonne, 1991), 458; Gabriel-François Coyer, *Voyages d'Italie et de Hollande* (Paris: Veuve Duchesne, 1775), ii. 175; Antoine Guénée, *Lettres de quelques juifs portugais et allemands à M. de Voltaire, avec des réflexions critiques* (Paris: Prault, 1769), 8–10; Charles-Louis Secondat de Montesquieu, 'Lettres persanes', in *Œuvres* (ed. Caillois), i. 248–51 (letter 78); David Hume, 'Of National Characters', in *Selected Essays* (Oxford: Oxford University Press, 1998), 113.

[7] Denis Diderot, 'Voyage de Hollande', in *Œuvres complètes* (ed. Dieckmann et al.) (Paris: Hermann, 1975–2004), xxiv, 46. The *Voyage* was first published in instalments in the *Correspondance littéraire*.

[8] See, for example, Diderot, 'Voyage de Hollande', 112, 117, and 137.

[9] Pierre Richelet, *Dictionnaire françois* (Geneva: Widerhold, 1680), i. 110. On the definition of 'character' in the late seventeenth century, see Louis Van Delft, *Littérature et anthropologie: Nature humaine et caractère à l'âge classique* (Paris: Presses universitaires de France, 1993), 19–40.

[10] Guillaume-Thomas Raynal, *Histoire philosophique et politique des établissements et du commerce des Européens dans les deux Indes* (1770, and 1780 in a revised edition) (Geneva: Pellet, 1780), i. 571. The passage has been attributed to Diderot by Gianluigi Goggi, 'Les contributions de Diderot aux livres i–v', in Guillaume-Thomas Raynal, *Histoire philosophique et politique des établissements et du commerce des Européens dans les deux Indes* (Ferney-Voltaire: Centre international d'étude du XVIIIe siècle, 2010–), i. 763.

gratifying and seemingly harmless pursuit, the associating of a given trait with a specific country implied two contradictory processes, one of generalisation and one of differentiation. First, it was necessary that a trait of an individual be considered common to all his fellow countrymen. Second, such a trait needed also to be seen as prominent within or even unique to the nation in question. To some scholars, the underlying inconsistencies were patent. As the abbé Guénée pointed out in his famous rejoinder to Voltaire's *Traité sur la tolérance* (1763), when trying to grasp a nation's character, differences between classes, regions, towns, and cities were unduly overlooked. Moreover, he asked, since no two men are ever the same, 'how could one make the moral portrait of a whole nation with a single stroke?'[11] Many others were aware that national stereotyping was founded on a logical fallacy. Among them was the traveller, essayist, and contributor to the *Encyclopédie* Pierre-Jean Grosley (1718–1785): 'When a person has a system or an abiding prejudice, he tries to justify it, collecting whatever he finds. He takes a joke for a fact, a wisecrack for an opinion. He generalises everything; from the particular he deduces the general, and thus he grounds his hypothesis . . . . Are there no popular ideas, no tales about Mother Goose? To infer the national character from such is surely to be guilty of a facetious judgement.'[12]

It was, therefore, crucial for an observer to already have a firm idea of what a people were like so that, when considering its manners, way of life, and morals he or she would easily adapt the truth to fit his or her preconceived image. Through this selective perception, facts were conveniently and readily arranged. That national stereotypes were 'like proverbs' meant precisely that they were widely known, would be uncritically accepted, and, importantly, when contradicted they would still be held to be generally true.[13] In point of fact, because such stereotypes were based on prejudice, solid evidence was of little use when trying to refute them. The absence of a distinctive trait or the failure of a member of a nation to display a typical behaviour was often downplayed or even wholly ignored. That 'such a disposition is not met with in all the members of the nation', as Jaucourt had noted in the *Encyclopédie*, did not seem to detract from nor

---

[11] Guénée, *Lettres de quelques juifs portugais et allemands*, 9. For an interesting and very different view, see Anonymous, 'Réflexions oubliées par quelques voyageurs', *Nouveau Mercure*, 1775, ii. 91–2.

[12] Pierre-Jean Grosley, *Londres: Ouvrage d'un françois, augmenté dans cette édition des notes d'un Anglois* (Neuchâtel: aux dépens de la Société typographique, 1770), ii. 16, footnote.

[13] The expression is in Louis de Jaucourt, 'Nation', in Diderot and d'Alembert (eds.), *Encyclopédie*, xi. 36. On this point, see Elizabeth Rechniewski, 'References to "national character" in the *Encyclopédie*', *Studies on Voltaire and the Eighteenth Century*, 2003:12 (2003), 228.

disprove the worth of a stereotype.[14] It was the proverbial exception that proved the rule. The misrepresentations produced by such preconceptions were deemed acceptable even by those who understood their tendency to distort. They were the price for a knowledge that required little effort and allowed the overcoming of important geographical, social, political, and economic distinctions. From this angle, it was precisely the assumption that national characters were usually truthful – if not always true – and a kind of 'unphilosophical probability' that rendered them acceptable to many enlightened minds throughout the seventeenth and eighteenth centuries.[15]

Importantly, the twofold process of distinguishing and generalising not only offered convenient portraits of other nations but, implicitly at least, also defined one's own. Declaring that the Italians were jealous, the Spaniards serious, the English wicked, the Scots proud, the Germans drunken, the Irish lazy, and the Greek duplicitous – all eighteenth-century commonplaces listed in the *Encyclopédie* – implied, conversely and if only to some degree, that the French were trusting, carefree, good-hearted, sober, energetic, and honest.[16] Not only were differences between countries exaggerated and distinctions within them overlooked but, importantly, hidden in plain view was a hierarchy set out and shaped by the observer standing within his or her (more or less national) cultural context.[17] National stereotyping was clearly a self-referential process, so that the vices attributed to other nations might have been such only for the observer – or, at least, their gravity might have been judged differently by the observed. But what should be noted is that while stereotyping shaped a moral hierarchy, its form varied depending on political, social, and historical circumstance. Therefore, although comparing the character of one's own to another nation usually resulted in a positive verdict for the latter, the opposite could indeed occur. And yet if such were the case, it would be accompanied by more or less explicit calls to reform or regenerate its morals and character.

As Duclos very judiciously remarked in the *Considérations*, 'men do not need proof to adopt an opinion; their mind simply needs to be familiar with it'.[18] This clearly applied to the case of national stereotypes. Evidence

[14] Louis de Jaucourt, 'Caractère des nations', in Diderot and d'Alembert (eds.), *Encyclopédie*, ii. 666.

[15] The expression is from David Hume, *A Treatise of Human Nature* (1738–1740) (Oxford: Clarendon Press, 2007), i. 99–100.

[16] These stereotypes are all listed in Jaucourt, 'Nation', 36.

[17] Daniel-Henri Pageaux, 'De l'imagerie culturelle à l'imaginaire', in Pierre Brunel and Yves Chevrel (eds.), *Précis de littérature comparée* (Paris: Presses universitaires de France, 1989), 140.

[18] Duclos, *Considérations sur les mœurs de ce siècle*, 112.

was of secondary importance in defining a nation's character, not least because such a practice was based on 'poetical rather than empirical principles'.[19] Therefore, it is unsurprising that especially privileged sites for the forging and dissemination of national stereotypes were novels and plays. Admittedly, only there could one find the Englishman, the Italian, and the Spaniard, ideal types or caricatures serving to amuse and entertain. But, interestingly, some scholars were convinced that novels could be exceptionally useful in apprehending a given people's way of life and values. The writer and dramatist Louis-Sébastien Mercier (1740–1814) thus claimed that novels offered 'the most faithful history of the *mœurs* and usages of a nation'. He believed they had the great merit of focusing on the actual lives of people, in contrast to the works of the historian, who 'fixes his arrogant gaze only on kings, on their particular deeds, and on their vast and dark political machinations'. More than elsewhere, it was in novels that one could grasp how a nation's character had changed over the centuries.[20] In effect, the claim that novels might help to understand a people's true nature was not entirely new and would often be repeated.[21] But what Mercier's words bring to the fore is, on the one hand, the relationship between history and literature and, on the other, that between truth and truthfulness. It is an issue best understood by considering a specific genre, one that represented a privileged vantage point for describing the character of nations. By the late seventeenth century, travel literature had indeed become a respected and popular literary form.[22] If we are to believe one eighteenth-century commentator, 'the mere presence of the word *travel* in a title is enough to excite the

[19] Joep Leerssen, 'L'effet de typique', in Alain Montandon (ed.), *Mœurs et images: Études d'imagologie européenne* (Clermont-Ferrand: Université Blaise Pascal, 1997), 134.

[20] Louis-Sébastien Mercier, 'Mon bonnet de nuit' (1784), in *Mon bonnet de nuit, suivi de Du théâtre* (Paris: Mercure de France, 1999), 514.

[21] See, for example, Du Fresnoy, *De l'usage des romans*, i. 53–133; Denis Diderot, 'Eloge de Richardson' (1762), in *Œuvres* (ed. Dieckmann et al.), xiii. 201–2. For an interesting discussion, see Tzvetan Todorov, *Les morales de l'histoire* (Paris: Grasset, 1991), 129–59.

[22] See the comments by Jean Chapelain to Jacques Carrel de Sainte-Garde, 15 December 1663, in *Lettres* (Paris: Imprimerie nationale, 1880–1883), ii. 340–1, and Jean Thévenot, *Relation d'un voyage fait au Levant* (Paris: L. Bilaine, 1664), 1. Countless works analyse French late seventeenth- and eighteenth-century travel literature. Some classic, and a few more recent texts are: René Pomeau, 'Voyages et Lumières dans la littérature française du dix-huitième siècle', *Studies on Voltaire and the Eighteenth Century*, 57 (1967), 1269–89; Friedrich Wolfzettel, *Le discours du voyageur: Pour une histoire littéraire du récit de voyage en France, du Moyen Age au XVIIIe siècle* (Paris: Presses universitaires de France, 1996), 231–311; Daniel Roche, *Humeurs vagabondes: De la circulation des hommes et de l'utilité des voyages* (Paris: Fayard, 2003); Gilles Bertrand, *Le Grand tour revisité: Pour une archéologie du tourisme. Le voyage des Français en Italie, milieu XVIIIe siècle – début XIXe siècle* (Rome: École française de Rome, 2008); Ellen R. Welch, *A Taste for the Foreign: Worldly Knowledge and Literary Pleasure in Early Modern French Fiction* (Newark: University of Delaware Press, 2011);

curiosity of readers'.[23] The genre's popularity partly stemmed from the fact that travelogues might amuse and instruct at one and the same time. Readers would find in them curious anecdotes and descriptions of bizarre habits, as well as scholarly dissertations on the customs of other nations. The *récits de voyages* were indeed at the crossroads of literature, geography, history, and the fashionable study of *mœurs*.[24] Significantly, by the end of the seventeenth century and in connection with the 'crisis of the novel', stories of journeys that had never taken place started to feature many details drawn from accounts of real voyages with the aim of convincing readers of their authenticity.[25] The abbé Prévost's fabricated *Voyages du Capitaine Robert Lade* (1744) is an especially persuasive example. Telling the story of a Captain Lade, it was written as a logbook, in the first person, and reported many carefully researched facts about the real places and the real peoples it described. There were even narrative lacunae left by Lade, ostensibly to protect his trading interests and serving thus to confirm the genuineness of the account – or so the abbé contended. In fact, 'it would have been easy to fill such a void with imaginary suppositions', but 'respect for truth' simply prevented it.[26] As the author of an essay on the life and works of the abbé Prévost pointed out, in the *Voyages* 'everything concerning the geography is noted with greater precision than would befit a fanciful book'. If certain episodes seemed implausible, this was because the places described were unfamiliar.[27] Prévost succeeded in his intent. The account was so plausible that even Buffon deemed it authentic, using it in his dissertations as a reliable source.[28] But the abbé's was only one of many pseudo-travels circulating at the time, and this made it increasingly

Gabor Gelléri, 'Absences et présences de l'art du voyage dans la France du XVIIIᵉ siècle', *Lumen: Selected Proceedings from the Canadian Society for Eighteenth-Century Studies*, 34 (2015), 55–69.

[23] Jean Le Clerc, review of [Maximilien Misson], *Nouveau voyage d'Italie, fait en l'année 1688*, in *Bibliothèque universelle et historique*, September 1691, 160. Italics in the text.

[24] Paul Hazard, *La crise de la conscience européenne (1680–1715)* (Paris: Boivin, 1935), 3–37.

[25] On this, Jean-Michel Racault, *Nulle part et ses environs: Voyage aux confins de l'utopie littéraire classique (1657–1802)* (Paris: Presses de l'Université de Paris-Sorbonne, 2003), 119–29. On the late seventeenth-century crisis of the novel, see Franco Piva, 'Crise du roman, roman de la crise: Aspects du roman français à la fin du XVIIᵉ siècle', in Dipartimento di lingue e letterature straniere moderne dell'Università di Pavia (ed.), *Perspectives de la recherche sur le genre narratif français du XVIIᵉ siècle* (Geneva: Slatkine, 2000), 281–303.

[26] Antoine François Prévost, 'Préface', in Prévost, *Voyages du Capitaine Lade en différentes parties de l'Afrique, de l'Asie et de l'Amérique* (Paris: Didot, 1744), i. p. xvi.

[27] Pierre Bernard d'Héry, 'Essai sur la vie et sur les ouvrages de l'abbé Prévost', in Antoine François Prévost, *Œuvres choisies* (Amsterdam: n.p., 1783–1785), i. 53.

[28] See, for example, Buffon, *Histoire naturelle, générale et particulière*, i. 371–2 and xxiv. 63, footnote. On this point: Federico Italiano, *Translation and Geography* (London: Routledge, 2016), 73–92.

difficult to tell real and imaginary journeys apart.[29] Eighteenth-century scholars had good reason to complain that only a small number of travellers' accounts were reliable.[30]

Long after such doubts had first been raised, many readers still assumed that travelogues described the real customs and *mœurs* of other nations – if with greater or lesser accuracy. Bearing in mind their pedagogic worth, Furetière was therefore adamant that nothing was 'more instructive than reading about travels'.[31] Others argued that meeting peoples from different countries or even only reading about those encounters were the surest means of overcoming national prejudice.[32] In effect, describing the manners and characters of nations was a crucial aspect of travel literature, so much so that, by the mid-eighteenth century, it would have been practically '[i]mpossible to open a book of travels without finding some description of the characters and *mœurs* of other nations'.[33] The 'literary anthropology' emerging from the plethora of travel accounts, real or imaginary as the case may be but usually truthful, had profound consequences for the nascent sciences of man as well as for the study of the past.[34] According to the essayist the abbé Gros de Besplas (1734–1783), travels were crucial to understanding the history of civilised and savage nations alike: 'It is for the science of the history of nations that I see, most importantly, the usefulness of travels.'[35] It is at once interesting and telling that authors sometimes compared the duty of the traveller-narrator to that of the historian. In effect, both were expected to tell an instructive, entertaining, and well-written story. Moreover, many travellers made of the description of the past of the countries they visited an important part of their accounts so that, in some instances, the term

---

[29] See the classic by Percy Guy Adams, *Travelers and Travel Liars, 1660–1800* (Berkeley: University of California Press, 1962).

[30] See, for example, [Cornélius De Pauw], *Défense des recherches philosophiques sur les Américains* (Berlin: George Jacques Decker, 1770), 198–9.

[31] Furetière, *Dictionnaire universel* (ed. 1690), s.v. 'voyage'.

[32] Louis de Jaucourt, 'Voyage', in Diderot and d'Alembert (eds.), *Encyclopédie*, xvii. 477; Jean-Jacques Rousseau, 'Émile, ou de l'éducation' (1762), in *Œuvres*, iv. 855; Joseph Marie Anne Gros de Besplas, *De l'utilité des voyages relativement aux sciences et aux mœurs* (Paris: Berthier, 1763), 31–4; Louis-Sébastien Mercier, *Eloge de René Descartes* (Geneva: Veuve Pierres, 1765), 59. An interesting exception is Béat Louis de Muralt, *Lettres sur les Anglois et les François et sur les voiages* (1728) (Paris: Honoré Champion, 1933), 284–7.

[33] Jean-Jacques Rousseau, 'Discours sur l'origine et les fondements de l'inégalité parmi les hommes' (1755), in *Œuvres*, iii. 143, n. 10. The quote is on page 212.

[34] The expression is taken from van Delft, *Littérature et anthropologie*, 97.

[35] Gros de Besplas, *De l'utilité des voyages relativement aux sciences et aux mœurs*, 3–13. Quote is from page 3.

'historian-traveller' was used.[36] But it is of still greater importance to note that both traveller and historian were increasingly asked to write accounts that were as truthful as possible. Both should 'wish to say nothing false' and to 'dare to tell the whole truth'.[37] To pursue such an aim, if historians increasingly relied on primary sources, for their part the authors of travel narratives described with ever greater accuracy and in ever greater detail the places where a people's history unfolded. Crucially, associating a real space with a behaviour that could be ascribed to a whole nation increased the truthfulness of the account and reinforced national stereotypes. It was a way of imposing order on the world, but also of populating it with actors endowed with a character that rendered their deeds comprehensible. Dividing, placing, and characterising were tightly intertwined practices intended to make the world comprehensible.[38] If travelogues contributed to the drawing of a global map of human diversity, associating one behaviour with one place, this was a practice to which even historians resorted, forging in their turn a number of similar tools that they used, often misguidedly, in their own works.

Individual and National Character

In 1701, the anonymous reviewer of a work condemning La Bruyère's famous *Les caractères* (1688) marvelled at the increasing number of books on the topic: the 'world of letters has been flooded with *caractères*', he claimed. The outpouring of such texts was also noted a few months later by the theologian, translator, and printer Pierre Coste (1668–1747) in his *Défense de M. de La Bruyère et de ses Caractères*: over the past few years, it seemed as if only 'works are being printed that bear the name of *Caractères*, or something similar meaning more or less the same thing. . . . Bookshops are inundated by them'.[39] Undeniably, since the publication of La

---

[36] See, for example, Guillot de Marcilly, *Relation historique et théologique d'un voyage en Hollande et autres provinces des Pays-Bas* (Paris: J. Estienne, 1719), 99.

[37] Jean Benjamin de La Borde, *Tableaux topographiques, pittoresques, physiques, historiques, moraux, politiques, littéraires de la Suisse* (Paris: Lamy, 1780–1786), ii. 162. Also see Charles-Georges-Thomas Garnier, 'Avertissement de l'éditeur', in Daniel Defoe, *La vie et les aventures surprenantes de Robinson Crusoé* (Amsterdam: n.p., 1787), i. 1.

[38] Van Delft, *Littérature et anthropologie*, 41–63.

[39] Anonymous, review of [Bonaventure d'Argonne], *Sentimens critiques sur Les caractères de Monsieur de La Bruyère*, in *Mémoires pour l'histoire des sciences et des beaux-arts*, March–April 1701, 77; Pierre Coste, *Défense de M. de La Bruyère et de ses Caractères contre les accusations et les objections de M. de Vigneul-Marville* (Amsterdam: Lombrail, 1702), 156–7. On this intellectual vogue, in late seventeenth-century France, see: J. W. Smeed, *The Theophrastan 'Character': The History of a Literary Genre* (Oxford: Clarendon Press, 1985), 47–63.

Bruyère's masterpiece, there had been a growing interest in the study of the character of individuals and peoples alike and in the various ways of classifying and making sense of them. It was an interest shared by scholars and readers that was partly tied to a new attitude towards morals and the relationship between man and God. This preoccupation was reflected in a heightened awareness of the complexity of human nature, a theme on which, from the second half of the seventeenth century onwards, many scholars elaborated. The Duke de La Rochefoucauld's (1613–1680) musings over the possibility of knowing oneself and his search for a morality detached from religion were illustrative of this tendency. The concerns of the Protestant theologian Jacques Abbadie (1654–1727) and the Benedictine monk the abbé François Lamy (1636–1711) that prompted them to investigate the fate of man's soul in a society that was changing so rapidly had much in common with the duke's anxieties – though they differed radically in their premises and their conclusions.[40] Like many others, even the père Rapin was aware of the difficulties of understanding a person's character: 'Men's heart is an abyss of such depths that its end cannot be reached. It is a mystery impenetrable even to the most enlightened [of men]. No matter how skilled one is, one always misreads it.' He believed that the only solution was 'to speak about *mœurs* in accordance with public opinion', which, in turn, he saw as the yardstick for 'truthfulness'.[41] Eventually, in the eighteenth century, such perplexities led to many attempts to found a 'science of *mœurs*' – Duclos's among them.[42]

The questioning of man's place in society and the increasing interest in *mœurs* had momentous consequences for notions of individual and national character, and these may be grasped by considering the distance between Duclos's and La Bruyère's views. In effect, La Bruyère had sought to establish a typology of essentially fixed, static classes, unchanging over time. His concern to adhere to the classical canon was confirmed by the fact that his work on modern France was preceded by his translation of Theophrastus's (371–287 BC) *Characters*. Like most classical typologies,

---

[40] See, for example, François de La Rochefoucauld, 'Maximes' (ed. 1664), in *Œuvres complètes* (Paris: Gallimard, 1964), 318–20 (§ 105); Jacques Abbadie, *L'art de se connaître soi-même* (1692) (Paris: Fayard, 2003), 21–5; François Lamy, *De la connaissance de soi-même* (Paris: Pralard, 1694–1698), i. preface. On La Rochefoucauld's concerns see, in particular, C. F. Danielou, 'La Rochefoucauld, ou L'impossible connaissance de soi', *Papers on French Seventeenth Century Literature*, 23 (1996), 635–49.

[41] René Rapin, *Les réflexions sur la poétique et sur les ouvrages des poètes anciens et modernes* (1684) (Paris: Honoré Champion, 2011), 425 and 412.

[42] The expression is from Duclos, *Considérations sur les mœurs de ce siècle*, 94.

imbued with a strong dose of Aristotelianism, La Bruyère's was meant to make sense of the ways people acted by reducing the complexity of their nature and by personifying specific attitudes, vices, and passions. His classes were construed as impermeable to one another and the focus was on unchanging inclinations and ways of being. As he put it: 'The hearts and passions of men have hardly changed'; they were still the same as 'those described by Theophrastus'.[43] It was this fixity that La Bruyère sought to grasp, for he was among those who assumed that the immobility of things 'shows their truth'.[44] Of course, in his study of manners, *mœurs*, and characters he considered changes over time and looked for inconsistencies in a people's actions. But his main aim was to simplify the intricacies of society rather than dwell upon its complexity.[45] The abstractions and generalisations this led to were remarkably distant from the reality they were meant to grasp, but the purpose was, in a way, to attain the ideal in the form of the individual. Other moralists, like Montaigne and La Rochefoucauld, fascinated as they were by the many facets of human nature, would have found it difficult to imagine a similar typology – and refrained from producing one.

However, alongside La Bruyère's rather static notion of character, so important in the contemporary entanglement of literature with nascent anthropology, by the 1720s a different understanding had begun to emerge, one that would lead to Duclos's *Considérations*. It was a notion indebted to some of the greatest moralists of the seventeenth century, and to their assumption that the human subject was constantly changing, 'day by day, minute by minute'.[46] The acknowledgement of an 'incessant engendering of passions' and of a continuous shift of individual emotions and volitions was a principle underlying the *Considérations*.[47] From such a perspective, when Madame de Graffigny labelled Duclos's book 'a La Bruyère', she was discounting his contribution to the emergence of the new understanding of character and underplaying the distance separating him from the great seventeenth-century moralist. Conversely, by comparing the ideas of the secretary of the Académie to La Bruyère's, though judging the former's to be more 'philosophical' than the latter's, Montesquieu

---

[43] Jean de La Bruyère, 'Discours sur Théophraste', in *Les caractères de Théophraste traduit du grec avec Les caractères ou les mœurs de ce siècle*, 95.

[44] Roland Barthes, 'La Bruyère', in *Essais critiques* (Paris: Seuil, 1981), 239.

[45] La Bruyère, 'Les caractères ou les mœurs de ce siècle', 447. For a useful discussion, see van Delft, *Littérature et anthropologie*, 137–48.

[46] Montaigne, *Les essais*, 805 (book iii. ch. 2).

[47] The expression is from François de La Rochefoucauld, 'Maximes' (ed. 1678), in *Œuvres*, 404 (§ 10).

might have been hinting at just such a difference.[48] In fact, Duclos rejected the idea that a person's character could be fixed and unchanging. As he wrote in his *Histoire de Louis XI* (1745), published only a few years before the *Considérations*: 'The main error into which one may fall when depicting men is to assume they have a fixed character, while their lives are but a tissue of contradictions. The more one studies them, the less one dares to define them.'[49] He even believed that a person might radically change his or her character as a consequence of the vicissitudes of life – as was the case with his fictitious Madame de Luz.[50] In effect, as has been noted, in Duclos's works the character was not only, nor merely, a person's distinctive mark; it was 'a positive attribute, the energy through which an individual asserts himself in his world.'[51]

This new understanding of the idea of character, with all its ambiguities and uncertainties, emerged even more clearly in plays and novels and especially in works about the proper ways of narrating a story. In 1639, in his *Poétique*, the physician and dramatist Jules de la Mesnardière (1610–1663) offered his readers a detailed list of several types and characters that playwrights should use in their works.[52] The principle underlying his classification was that, in a tragedy, the way characters acted had to be consistent with their social condition, age, sex, and, importantly, their nationality. Hence, according to la Mesnardière, a tragedy should never present a 'brave' or 'knowledgeable lady', nor 'a wise valet' since this would have made it untruthful.[53] For the same reason, an author should refrain from introducing into his plot a valiant Asian warrior, a loyal African, an impious Persian, a modest Spaniard, or an uncivilised Frenchman.[54] To avoid such mistakes, la Mesnardière even listed a long series of national

---

[48] Françoise d'Issembourg d'Happoncourt de Graffigny to François-Antoine Devaux, 29 September 1750, in *Correspondance* (Oxford: Voltaire Foundation, 1985–), xi. 1608; Charles-Louis Secondat de Montesquieu to Charles Pinot Duclos, 4 March 1751, in *Œuvres* (ed. Masson), iii. 1368.

[49] Charles Pinot Duclos, *Histoire de Louis XI* (Paris: Frères Guerin, 1745), iii. 466.

[50] Charles Pinot Duclos, *Histoire de Madame de Luz* (1740) (Saint-Brieuc: Presses universitaires de Bretagne, 1972), 72.

[51] Henri Coulet, 'La notion de caractère dans l'œuvre de Duclos, moraliste et romancier', in Claire Blanche-Benveniste, André Chervel, and Maurice Gross (eds.), *Grammaire et histoire de la grammaire: Hommage à la mémoire de Jean Stéfanini* (Aix-en-Provence: Université de Provence, 1988), 167.

[52] On the *Poétique*: Helen Reese Reese, *La Mesnardière's* Poétique *(1639): Sources and Dramatic Theories* (Baltimore: Johns Hopkins University Press, 1937), and Jean-Marc Civardi, 'Introduction', in Hippolyte Jules Pilet de la Mesnardière, *La poétique* (Paris: Honoré Champion, 2015), 7–72. For an analysis of la Mesnardière's work in relation to national character, see Joep Leerssen, *National Thought in Europe: A Cultural History* (Amsterdam: Amsterdam University Press, 2006), 58–60.

[53] La Mesnardière, *La poétique*, 266.   [54] Ibid., 258.

types to which authors were to remain faithful.[55] Of course, in tragedies truthfulness was of the utmost importance since their cathartic function largely depended on it. In tragedies, stated la Mesnardière, evil actions should always be punished and virtuous deeds somehow or other rewarded.[56] A person's character determined his fate – a principle challenged by Diderot and then radically overturned by the Marquis de Sade (1740–1818).[57] The point to note, true for all plays and novels that followed the canons of seventeenth-century poetics, was that by tying the nature of his fictional characters to an abstract and stereotyped disposition, an author allowed his audience to understand, follow, and, to an extent, predict the way the plot would unfold. Obviously, different rules applied to tragedies and comedies, but in either case a character was presumed to be an essential nature influencing, if not determining, an individual's decisions. It was a fundamental inclination that motivated the way a person acted and shaped the narrative he or she was a part of.[58] Interestingly, the same arguments could still be found much later, in the *Encyclopédie*, at the entry 'Caractére dans les personnages' written by the abbé Mallet (1713–1755). In a play, a character was 'the inclination or the dominant passion that shows at every step and in every speech of these characters and that is the principle and the first aim of their actions'.[59] A character was marked by an identifiable predisposition which was the main cause of his deeds and which rendered these intelligible to the audience. It was a key to explaining his or her story. And yet, by that date, the assumption that there was a dominant inclination implied that a struggle with other less prominent dispositions might occur, making a character's decisions less predictable – and, all in all, a play more interesting.

The new and more complex meaning of the notion of character had already emerged in the works of the great dramatist and novelist Pierre de Marivaux (1688–1763). Hailed as the 'modern Theophrastus' and likened to La Bruyère, Marivaux rejected the comparison not least because of his dislike for all systems and classifications.[60] His works showed a subtler

[55] Ibid., 255–7.   [56] Ibid., 173.
[57] Denis Diderot, 'Entretien sur le fils naturel' (1757), in *Œuvres* (ed. Dieckmann et al.), x. 144. Of course, the reference is to the marquis's *Justine, ou Les malheurs de la vertu* (1791) and his *Histoire de Juliette, ou Les prospérités du vice* (1797).
[58] Leerssen, 'The Rhetoric of National Character', 272.
[59] Edmé-François Mallet, 'Caractère dans les personnages', in Diderot and d'Alembert (eds.), *Encyclopédie*, ii. 667. See Patrick Coleman, 'The Idea of Character in the *Encyclopédie*', *Eighteenth-Century Studies*, 13 (1979), 29–33.
[60] See Pierre-François Buchet, note in *Le nouveau Mercure*, October 1717, 20; Jean-Joseph Languet de Gergy, 'Réponse de l'Archevêque de Sens' (1743), in Pierre de Marivaux, *Journaux et œuvres diverses*

reading of the human nature emerging through the lengthy analysis he offered of the reasonings, ideas, and feelings of his characters – something that led to the coining of the pejorative 'marivaudage'.[61] Observers even objected that the complex and drawn-out discussions of feelings and emotions interrupted the narrative, making the viewing of his plays or the reading of his novels particularly irksome.[62] By the mid-1740s, the increasing number of novels and plays featuring complex and unpredictable characters led some to complain about the portraits of heroes endowed 'with opposed qualities', at once greedy and generous, proud and humble, reasonable and bereft of common sense. Lacking any real 'support', their actions seemed utterly incomprehensible.[63] Others, however, sought to emulate Marivaux. The celebrated polymath Pierre-Augustin Caron de Beaumarchais (1732–1799) went to great lengths to depict ever more complex and unpredictable characters. Whereas in the classical canon each character's conduct was somehow consistent with his own status, Beaumarchais insisted on creating a disparity: '[T]o heighten the turmoil and the interest, I seek to have the situation of all the characters be always at odds with their desires and inclinations.'[64] The fact that he endeavoured to carry 'social inconsistency to the highest possible level' surely did much to make his works stand out – and Figaro's famous monologue, in this respect, is emblematic.[65] Henri Colet has gone so far as to claim that Beaumarchais's heroes embodied the 'energy of the bourgeois individual

(Paris: Garnier frères, 1969), 453–4; Pierre de Marivaux, 'Lettre écrite par M. De Marivaux à l'auteur du *Mercure*' (October 1717), in *Journaux et œuvres diverses*, 22. On this: Henri Coulet, *Marivaux romancier: Essai sur l'esprit et le cœur dans les romans de Marivaux* (Paris: Armand Colin, 1975), 264.

[61] Among those who criticised his style: Grimm et al., *Correspondance littéraire*, v. 236 (February 1763), and Jean-François Marmontel, *Éléments de littérature* (1787) (Paris: Desjonquères, 2005), 109–10. On the importance he gave to the ever-changing nature of emotions and the fluidity of characters: Coulet, *Marivaux romancier*, 129–54; Daniel Acke, 'La notion de caractère dans les *Journaux*', in Frank Salaün (ed.), *Marivaux subversif?* (Paris: Desjonquères, 2003), 213–4; Sarah Benharrech, *Marivaux et la science du caractère* (Oxford: Voltaire Foundation, 2013).

[62] See, for example, Prévost et al., *Le pour et le contre*, 1 (1733), 246. Interestingly, it is a criticism resembling that levelled against the champions of the *histoire critique* for their excessive use of evidence and explanations disrupting the narrative flow. See, on this, Chapters 2 and 3.

[63] [Jean-Baptiste Jourdan], *Le guerrier philosophe, ou Mémoires de M. le Duc de ** * (Amsterdam: aux dépens de la Compagnie, 1744), i. p. xii–xiii. Also see Jean-Baptiste de Boyer d'Argens, *Lettres juives* (1736–1737) (Paris: Honoré Champion, 2013), i. 431–2.

[64] Pierre-Augustin Caron de Beaumarchais, 'Essai sur le genre dramatique sérieux' (1767), in *Œuvres* (Paris: Gallimard, 1988), 135.

[65] Pierre-Augustin Caron de Beaumarchais, 'Le Mariage de Figaro' (1778), in *Œuvres*, 358 (preface). On the debate over the subversive nature of his famous trilogy, see Virginie Yvernault, 'La trilogie, une œuvre révolutionnaire?', in Sophie Lefay (ed.), *Nouveaux regards sur la trilogie de Beaumarchais* (Paris: Garnier, 2015), 25–37. For Figaro's monologue: Beaumarchais, 'Le Mariage de Figaro', 469–71.

revolting against a closed and hierarchical society'.[66] Although this may be an overstatement, the fact remains that the great playwright depicted most of his heroes in opposition to their social milieu, often fighting against injustices to better their condition. Interestingly, in late eighteenth-century plays and novels, it would have been easier to find the rejection of class conventions than dissonances between an individual's actions and the alleged character of his nation. In effect, while Marivaux and Beaumarchais wrote about their desire to amaze and amuse the public by having their heroes stepping out of their social condition, they stopped short of having them abandon their nationality. But this might have been the limit to truthfulness beyond which the public was unwilling to venture.

If the notion of character might serve to explain or at least clarify the reasons for a person's deeds, it also fulfilled another no less important function. In fact, the classification of characters always implied, to a greater or lesser degree, some sort of moral judgement. In his *livre de mœurs*, which he wrote to denounce the 'vices of the heart and the mind' of the French people, La Bruyère made clear as much.[67] Giving a detailed account of the *mœurs* of his own time, he was handing his readers a mirror in which they might recognise their faults. La Bruyère's characterology was a study in morality.[68] Indeed, that *mœurs* and character, whether individual or national, were notions tightly entwined was widely acknowledged throughout the seventeenth and the eighteenth centuries. In many cases, the two were even treated as synonyms. In the first edition of the *Dictionnaire de Trévoux* (1704), for example, *mœurs* referred to a '[n]atural or acquired habit, for good or bad, through which peoples or individuals lead their lives'. It could also indicate 'good or bad predispositions; the character, the inclination, the temper of the persona on the stage'.[69] But

[66] Henri Coulet, 'La notion de caractère dans l'œuvre de Beaumarchais', *Revue de l'Université de Moncton*, 1–3 (1978), 27.

[67] Jean de La Bruyère, 'Préface: Discours de réception à l'Académie française' (speech delivered in 1693), in Académie française (ed.), *Recueil des harangues prononcées par Messieurs de l'Académie françoise, dans leurs receptions, et en d'autres occasions différentes* (Amsterdam: aux dépens de la Compagnie, 1709), ii. 268.

[68] Françoise Berlan, 'Le mot "caractère" dans *Les caractères* de La Bruyère', *Champ du signe*, 1 (1991), 126.

[69] Vv. Aa., *Dictionnaire universel françois et latin, vulgairement appelé Dictionnaire de Trévoux* (Paris: Compagnie des libraires associés, 1704), ii. s.v. 'mœurs'. On the notion, see Georges Benrekassa, 'Mœurs comme "concept politique": 1680–1820', in Benrekassa, *Le langage des Lumières: Concepts et savoir de la langue* (Paris: Presses universitaires de France, 1995), 47–97, and Franck Salaün, *L'ordre des mœurs: Essai sur la place du matérialisme dans la société française du XVIIIᵉ siècle (1734–1784)* (Paris: Éditions Kimé, 1996). Also see J. G. A. Pocock, 'Virtue, Rights, and Manners: A Model for Historians of Political Thought', in Pocock, *Virtue, Commerce, and History: Essays on Political Thought and History* (Cambridge: Cambridge University Press, 1985), 37–50.

differences between the two notions were also noteworthy. For example, while both served to describe the inclinations of men and nations, *mœurs* referred more explicitly to the set of ethical principles by which those inclinations were judged. It was a contrast – between the descriptive and prescriptive functions of *mœurs* – that emerged in some eighteenth-century treatises on morality. One such was *Les mœurs* (1748), a 'dangerous book' banned on the grounds of impiety – and, as often in these cases and for this very reason, much sought after. Its author, the lawyer and writer François-Vincent Toussaint (1715–1772), used *mœurs* in two related yet distinct senses.[70] In the first, the word identified the habitual conduct of individuals, groups, or nations. In the second, it denoted a set of universal moral principles and rules. It was in the latter that Toussaint was truly interested, since his intention was to write a book for all men, aside from or beyond any national or religious divisions.[71] Obviously, the relationship between the normative and historical dimension of *mœurs*, in Toussaint's as well as in the works of many others writing at that time, was problematic at best. But, here, what is truly noteworthy is that throughout the eighteenth century there was a progressive historicising of the notion and an increasing tendency to discard its moral aspects – a shift, that is, from the one to the other meaning highlighted above. It was a change in emphasis already discernible in the work of the Jesuit scholar Jean-François Lafitau (1681–1746). In fact, in his influential *Mœurs des sauvages amériquains comparées aux mœurs des premiers temps* (1724), perhaps the first work of modern ethnography, he treated *mœurs* from an essentially historical perspective, looking at a people's modes of conduct, beliefs, and customs and how these had changed throughout the centuries. Moral concerns, though present, were relegated to the background.[72] The increasing use of *mœurs* as an object of historical enquiry rather than ethical speculation eventually produced a radical alteration in the study of the past, paving the way to masterpieces such as Voltaire's *Essai sur les mœurs et l'esprit des nations*.[73]

The ambiguities regarding the notion were largely a consequence of the fact that, through it, scholars sought to grasp the equally complex relationship between an individual's conduct, the social conventions shaping the

---

[70] On the diffusion of *Les mœurs*, see the comments by Barbier, *Chronique de la régence et du règne de Louis XV*, iv. 300–8 (May 1748). Quote is on page 308. Also see: Thomas J. Barling, 'Toussaint's *Les mœurs*', *French Studies*, 12 (1958), 14–20.

[71] François-Vincent Toussaint, *Les mœurs* (n.p., 1748), foreword, n.p.

[72] Andreas Motsch, *Lafitau et l'émergence du discours ethnographique* (Paris: Presses de l'Université de Paris-Sorbonne, 2001), 15–88.

[73] On the gradual historicising of the idea of *mœurs* in the eighteenth century, see Benrekassa, 'Mœurs comme "concept politique"', 62–72.

nation he or she belonged to, and a set of universally valid moral precepts. But the historicising of *mœurs* in the second half of the century contributed to a growing preoccupation with the ways in which they could best serve the interests of society.[74] So, writing at the turn of the century, de Sade offered a definition of *mœurs* devoid of all references to morality. Good *mœurs*, he contended, were simply those modes of conduct that ensured happiness for the individual and the welfare of society.[75] Of course, the marquis's was an extreme case; and yet it is revealing of a subtler and more widespread change in the notion since, as the century advanced, greater emphasis was indeed placed on the impact of *mœurs* on society. For one, Duclos considered man's interest and passions as commendable or reprehensible depending upon 'the effects they produce' on a nation's ways of thinking and its feelings rather than in terms of some ethical and universal principle.[76] Consistently, his *Considérations* were intended to shed light on the ways in which French society might strive to instil in its members a strong feeling of citizenship and love for their country.[77] He saw this as an urgent task, for the 'corrupting of *mœurs*' was a threat to French society.[78] That the danger was grave and impending could be seen in the excessively refined manners of the French, the mask of a frivolous and hypocritical world, dominating the court and Parisian society. Appearances seemed to count far more than a person's actions, ideas, and feelings. According to Duclos, unpretentious manners, which were the emblem of integrity, virtuousness, and selflessness, could only be found in those nations that praised 'reason and moderation' above all else.[79] Famously, a few years later, Rousseau was yet more caustic: '[P]olitesse incessantly demands, propriety issues orders, and people ceaselessly follow customary usages and never their own inclinations.'[80] The citizen of Geneva contended that, on the one hand, excessively refined manners, sanctioning form over substance, weakened social ties since men only knew the true intentions and

---

[74] See Daniel Gordon, *Citizens Without Sovereignty: Equality and Sociability in French Thought, 1670–1789* (Princeton: Princeton University Press, 1994).

[75] Donatien Alphonse François de Sade, 'Histoire de Juliette' (1797–1801), in *Œuvres* (Paris: Gallimard, 1990–1998), iii. 235.

[76] Duclos, *Considérations sur les mœurs de ce siècle*, 97. It was a view shared by Paul-Pierre Lemercier de la Rivière in his *De l'instruction publique* (Paris: Didot l'ainé, 1775), 72.

[77] Duclos, *Considérations sur les mœurs de ce siècle*, 108.

[78] Ibid., 132–3. On ideas of social virtue in Duclos's writings, see Jacques Brengues, *Charles Duclos (1704–1772): Ou l'obsession de la vertu* (Saint-Brieuc: Presses universitaires de Bretagne, 1970).

[79] Duclos, *Considérations sur les mœurs de ce siècle*, 100.

[80] Jean-Jacques Rousseau, 'Discours sur les sciences et les arts' (1750), in *Œuvres*, iii. 8.

feelings of others through great effort. Conversely, the increasing uniformity of manners meant that people simply renounced their individuality to follow rules of conduct decided by others. Rousseau lamented the loss of the 'rustic yet natural habits' of an age when, 'although men were not naturally better', differences in behaviour 'announced at the first glance differences in character'.[81]

Duclos did not venture as far as the author of the *Contrat social*. In fact, while censuring the excessive frivolity of manners dominating French high society, he believed nonetheless that it was uncivilised nations that committed the most detestable injustices and hideous crimes.[82] He assumed that only by attaining a sort of midpoint between the two extremes, between the excesses of the court and Parisian high society on the one hand, and the coarse usages of savages and barbarous peoples on the other, could a society pursue the greater good. Duclos was not the only one to have formed such an opinion. The idea that politesse might be a symptom of moral shallowness had preoccupied Montesquieu since his juvenile 'Eloge de la sincérité', possibly written as early as 1717 and, of course, since his literary masterpiece, the *Lettres persanes*.[83] In particular, the baron was adamant that politesse, though a fundamental social quality, could bring about corruption and decadence if it became too refined, sophisticated, and frivolous. A balance was hard to strike and, importantly, it could deeply affect the history of nations. As Montesquieu noted in his *Pensées*, '[A]lmost all the nations of the world unfold in this circle: first they are barbarous; they conquer and they become civilised nations; civilisation makes them great, and they become polite nations; politeness weakens them, they are conquered in turn and become once again barbarous. Testimonies of this are the Greeks and the Romans.'[84] The undeclared target here was plainly modern-day France. In fact, while Montesquieu could not but praise the great artistic and cultural achievements of European civilisation, he was also concerned about the 'corruption of modern times' and wrote with alarm about the debasing of *mœurs* in his own country.[85] Although he admitted that 'the desire to

---

[81] Rousseau, 'Discours sur les sciences et les arts', 8.

[82] Duclos, *Considérations sur les mœurs de ce siècle*, 100.

[83] Charles-Louis Secondat de Montesquieu, 'Eloge de la sincérité', in *Œuvres* (ed. Caillois), i. 101; Montesquieu, 'Lettres persanes', 140–1 (letter 8). See, on this, Céline Spector, *Montesquieu, les 'Lettres persanes': De l'anthropologie à la politique* (Paris: Presses universitaires de France, 1997), 11–44.

[84] Charles-Louis Secondat de Montesquieu, 'Dossier de l'Esprit des lois', in *Œuvres* (ed. Caillois), ii. 1048 (§ 236). The dating is uncertain; the dossier was compiled by Henri Barkhausen through the collection of manuscripts that did not find their way into the final version of the *Esprit des lois*.

[85] Montesquieu, 'De l'Esprit des lois', 268 (book iv. ch. 6); Montesquieu, 'Mes pensées', 1146 (§ 621) and 1316 (§ 1299).

please' evident in good manners was what held a society together, rendering it 'unshakeable', he thought that the French had 'attained a highly regrettable refinement' and this, in turn, he saw as a symptom of their corruption.[86] Pursuing the proper balance between uncouthness and superficiality was therefore the key to a sound, healthy society, and moderation, here as elsewhere in the writings of the baron, a crucial concern.

It is worthy of note that this dichotomy between coarseness and frivolity has been seen by Jean Ehrard as mirroring the contrast between the alleged ignorance and vulgarity of the lower classes on the one hand, and what was assumed to be the refined corruption of the higher classes on the other. Implicitly, the search for the midpoint between the two might then be interpreted as praise of the moderation, sobriety, and virtues of the middle classes.[87] The great historian, writer, and *Encyclopédiste* Jean-François Marmontel (1723–1799) seems to have suggested as much in his *Éléments de litterature* (1787). A poet-philosopher, he contended,

> will take notions of nobility and decency from the world of the refined and the learned. But what about the passions of the human heart? It is with the ignorant that he should live if he wishes to see them in nature. Eloquence is more real, feeling more unsophisticated, passion more energetic, and the soul, lastly, is freer and more sincere in the people than at court. This does not mean that men are not always men, but politesse is a deceit that erases one's natural inclinations. High society is but a masked ball.[88]

By commending the merging of the dignity of honourable feelings and the energy of passions, Marmontel might have been praising the meeting point of the nobility and the people and their respective qualities, distilled in the image that the modern bourgeoisie was then forming of itself.[89]

Importantly, the complex search for the proper balance between these two extremes can be tied to what was seen, throughout the eighteenth century, as the key character of French men and women, that is, their

---

[86] Montesquieu, 'Mes pensées', 1274 (§ 1042) and 1249 (§ 916).

[87] Jean Ehrard, *L'idée de nature en France dans la première moitié du XVIIIᵉ siècle* (Paris: Albin Michel, 1994), 782. Ehrard's classic was first published in 1963. See, with regard to this, the interesting praise of the middle class made by Daniel Defoe (1660–1731) in his *Robinson Crusoe* (1719) (London: Penguin, 2003), 6.

[88] Marmontel, *Éléments de littérature*, 724–5.

[89] On the semantic complexity and the ideological pitfalls of the term *bourgeoisie*, see Michel Vovelle and Daniel Roche, 'Bourgeois, rentiers, propriétaires: Éléments pour la définition d'une catégorie sociale à la fin du XVIIIᵉ siècle', *Actes du 77ᵉ congrès des sociétés savantes*, 84 (1959), 419–52, and Sarah Maza, 'Bourgeoisie', in William Doyle (ed.), *The Oxford Handbook of the Ancien Régime* (Oxford: Oxford University Press, 2011), 127–40. For an overview of representations of and discourses about the bourgeoisie between the eighteenth and nineteenth century, see Sarah Maza, *The Myth of the French Bourgeoisie* (Cambridge, Mass: Harvard University Press, 2003).

unpredictability and unsteadiness – their *légèreté*. In effect, according to Furetière, to be 'light as a Frenchman' was a proverbial expression. Mercier, in his *Tableau de Paris* (1781–1788), wrote of a '*légèreté* that belongs to the French alone'. The Peruvian princess of Madame de Graffigny's famous epistolary novel thought that their *légèreté* often made the French unreasonable. For his part, in 1786, the essayist Jean-François Sobry (1743–1820) remarked that 'in spite of its apparent *légèreté*', the French nation was 'deeply coherent and solid' – alas, Sobry refrained from elaborating upon the contradiction.[90] Some even believed that the lightness of the French had been the cause of their wretchedness and political decadence and that the Revolution had brought their deplorable condition to an end. So, during the trial of Louis XVI, the journalist and revolutionary Jean-Louis Carra (1742–1793) made the case that the *légèreté* of the French had ended when they decided to cast off the yoke of their tyrants: 'Enslaved nations are inconstant and unsteady, for they have no will of their own. But a free people has a character, and a great character is not unsteady. Therefore, let us no longer speak of the *légèreté* of the French.'[91]

In many cases, *légèreté* was used as a pejorative or disparaging term, often associated with frivolity, superficiality, and other faults imputed to most French men or women.[92] But it could also be used as a synonym of 'mutability'.[93] Precisely with the latter meaning, in the second half of the eighteenth century, *légèreté* came to define a trait that, in given historical circumstances, could lead to outcomes at odds with the frivolousness ordinarily expected of the French. In 1757, in the *Encyclopédie*, Voltaire surmised that the character of the French had not changed since the times of Julius Caesar (100–44 BC): '[P]rompt to resolve, ardent to [engage in] combat, impetuous in attack, and easily discouraged.' It was because of their inconsistency and, in this sense, their *légèreté*, that the French might be valiant soldiers or worthless deserters. Because of their nature, they could follow either path. But Voltaire went further. As he saw it, the 'fury',

---

[90] Antoine Furetière, *Dictionnaire universel* (The Hague and Rotterdam: Arnout & Reinier Leers, 1701), s.v. 'nation'; Louis Sébastien Mercier, *Tableau de Paris* (Paris: Mercure de France, 1994), ii. 204; Graffigny, *Lettres d'une Péruvienne*, 165; Jean-François Sobry, *Le mode françois, ou Discours sur les principaux usages de la nation française* (London: n.p., 1786), 59–60. For an interesting overview, see Marine Ganofsky and Jean-Alexandre Perras (eds.), *Le siècle de la légèreté: Emergences d'un paradigme du XVIIIᵉ siècle français* (Liverpool: Liverpool University Press, 2019).

[91] Jean-Louis Carra, *Discours contre la défense de Louis Capet, dernier roi des Français, par le citoyen Carra, député de Saône et Loire, prononcé à la séance du 3 janvier 1793* (Paris: Imprimerie nationale, 1793), 9. Also see [Adrien Cyprien Duquesnoy], *L'ami des patriotes, ou Le défenseur de la Révolution*, 16 (12 March 1791), 464–5.

[92] Bell, 'Le caractère national et l'imaginaire républicain au XVIIIᵉ siècle', 872–3.

[93] Académie française, *Dictionnaire de l'Académie française*, i. 367 (s.v. 'légèreté').

which had been such a distinctive feature of the French throughout their history, now manifested itself through that 'vivacity' devoted to seeking the 'pleasures of society' and shaping that 'easiness of *mœurs* that the whole of Europe cherishes'.[94] French *légèreté* could then take on different forms, depending on historical circumstances. Writing in 1780, Servan followed the great *philosophe* almost to the letter. From his viewpoint, the French nation was as 'impetuous in its pleasures as it once was in its *furore*, the foundations of its character having always remained the same'. Whether considering their impetuosity on the battlefield or their exuberance in the salons, Servan believed he could always recognise in the French a remarkable vigour and an extraordinary energy.[95] The nation's *légèreté*, as the one truly unchanging trait of the French people, was here the thread running through their history, allowing historians to see beyond a surface of fleeting events. Duclos might well have endorsed such arguments. As he noted in the *Considérations*, 'of all the different peoples, the French is the one whose character has experienced the fewest changes. This nation has always been lively, light-hearted, generous, courageous, sincere, arrogant, inconstant, and inconsiderate.' He argued that the nation's 'good qualities correct or balance the bad ones' and this, in turn, contributed to 'make of the French the most sociable of men'.[96] That changeableness was the key to understanding the nation's character and, with it, its history was a point also made by Chateaubriand at the turn of the century.[97] In a similar vein, though much later on, Tocqueville tried to explain the course of the French Revolution by insisting on the nation's constant inconstancy:

> Was there ever on earth another nation so fertile in contrasts, so extreme in its acts; more under the dominion of feeling, less ruled by principle; always better or worse than was expected; now below the level of humanity, now far above; a people so unchangeable in its leading characteristics that it may be recognised by portraits drawn two or three thousand years ago, and yet so fickle in its daily opinions and tastes that it becomes, at last, a mystery to itself; and is as much astonished as strangers at the sight of what it has done.[98]

Framing the nation's character in such terms offered a convenient explanation for the loftiest accomplishments and the most wretched

---

[94] François-Marie Arouet Voltaire, 'François, ou Français', in Diderot and d'Alembert (eds.), *Encyclopédie*, vii. 285.
[95] Servan, *Le soldat citoyen*, 16. [96] Duclos, *Considérations sur les mœurs de ce siècle*, 161.
[97] François-René de Chateaubriand, 'Essai historique sur les révolutions' (1797), in *Œuvres*, i. 76–8.
[98] Alexis de Tocqueville, *L'Ancien régime et la Révolution* (Paris: Gallimard, 1952–1953), i. 249.

failures of the French people – and, therefore, one that might be of little use to historians. However, from the second half of the eighteenth century, increasing attention had been paid to its actual complexity – something that partly mirrored the concerns of late eighteenth-century playwrights and novelists with the characters in their works. Exploring and highlighting the complexity of national character while considering *légèreté* as the essence of the French people had important consequences for the way the nation was imagined since it suggested the possibility of channelling its capacities, strength, and energy towards specific political aims. Seeing the nation's variability as its essential characteristic made changing its ways of acting, thinking, and feeling much more plausible.

By the second half of the eighteenth century, a growing awareness of the complexity of national character came to be dovetailed with an increasing sense of the intricacy of its relationship with individual character. Several authors tackled the issue, so much so that when, in 1796, in her *De l'influence des passions sur le bonheur des individus et des nations*, Madame de Staël (1766–1817) tried to grasp the effects of passions on individual freedom and on social ties, her argument rested on sound foundations. De Staël's aim was to shed light, on the one hand, on 'man's relationship with himself', focusing on his 'passions, desires, and character', and, on the other, to consider how feelings influenced the relationship among individuals as part of a national community. The two aims she saw as tightly intertwined, not least because, she believed, 'a nation presents the character of a man', so much so that 'the force of government must act on it as the power of reason of an individual must act on himself'.[99] These important observations, as well as the reasoning she developed throughout her book, bring to the fore two issues that are crucial to the history of the idea of national character. The first is related to the fact that the analogy made by de Staël was widely accepted throughout the eighteenth century. Voltaire, for one, believed that 'each people has its own character, just as every man [does], and this general character is composed of all the similarities that

---

[99] Anne-Louise-Germaine de Staël, 'De l'influence des passions sur le bonheur des individus et des nations', in de Staël, *De l'influence des passions sur le bonheur des individus et des nations, suivi de Réflexions sur le suicide* (Paris: Payot et Rivage, 2000), 31. Also see Anne-Louise-Germaine de Staël, *De la littérature considérée dans ses rapports avec les institutions sociales* (1800) (Geneva: Droz, 1959), i. 181. On de Staël's ideas on national character, see Romani, *National Character and Public Spirit in Britain and France*, 63–92. To what extent de Staël's book succeeded in its intent is a matter of debate. See, on this, Biancamaria Fontana, *Germaine de Staël: A Political Portrait* (Princeton: Princeton University Press, 2016), 132–57.

nature and habits have placed amidst the inhabitants of a specific country'. Many others agreed.[100] When explaining his views about national character, the abbé Mably even compared the life of the individual to the history of a nation.[101] All in all, the parallel served many purposes, but the most interesting is precisely the one Mably referred to. In fact, just as for a character in a play, historians could imagine the nation as an actor moving through history, endowed with clear intentions and influenced by natural inclinations that deserved to be observed and studied. This was even truer for those scholars who were trying to break away from the royalist narratives, where the intentions of the king-state were so central in explaining the nation's history. The impersonal, anthropomorphic image of the nation, existing side by side if not yet replacing the one identifying the king with his people, became the ground for that plethora of bodily metaphors flourishing around the time of the Revolution.[102] Crucially, historians would no longer seek the causes of the nation's history solely, nor indeed primarily, in the motives of its kings and their ministers. They would devote increasingly close attention to the nation's character, assessing its present and past virtues and vices and deciding whether or not these had remained unchanged. In effect, the analogy between nation and individual offered the image of a coherent community endowed with a readily identifiable character influencing its will and motives – both of which, of course, were now crucial to the judge-historian in his study of the past.[103] Yet the fact that motives and aims, in turn, were intelligible partly because of the supposed accuracy of national stereotypes was lost on many observers.[104]

In her approach to national character, Madame de Staël also hinted at the crucial relationship between individual and national character. That the relationship was twofold was clear to many; the extent and the modes

---

[100] Voltaire, 'Dictionnaire philosophique', xix. 179. For other examples: Honoré Lacombe de Prezel, *Dictionnaire d'anecdotes, de traits singuliers et caractéristiques, historiettes, bons mots, naïvetés, saillies, réparties ingénieuses* (Paris: La Combe, 1766), 516; Charles Remi, *Considérations philosophiques sur les mœurs, les plaisirs et les préjugés de la capitale* (Paris: Leroy, 1787), 331; Louis-Félix Guinement Keralio, 'Géneral', in Louis-Félix Guinement Keralio, Jean-Girard Lacuée, and Joseph Servan (eds.), *Encyclopédie méthodique: Art militaire* (Paris: Panckoucke, 1784–1797), ii. 549.

[101] Gabriel Bonnot de Mably, 'Du cours et de la marche des passions dans la société' (1784), in *Œuvres*, xv. 160.

[102] See, on this, Antoine de Baecque, *Le corps de l'histoire: Métaphores et politique (1770–1800)* (Paris: Calmann-Lévy, 1993).

[103] On the point, Carlo Ginzburg, 'Checking the Evidence: The Judge and the Historian', *Critical Inquiry*, 18 (1991), 79–92.

[104] On the relationship between narration, motives, and truthfulness, see Gérard Genette, 'Vraisemblance et motivation', in Genette, *Figures II* (Paris: Seuil, 1969), 71–99.

through which the one influenced the other remained, however, a matter of debate throughout the eighteenth century. Mably addressed the issue and did so in one of his most important works on the study of the past, *De la manière d'écrire l'histoire*: 'The character of each man – he wrote – is always subordinated to national character, both because he arrives at it through education and because he is forced to comply with it to succeed in his own projects.'[105] A few years later, accepting and restating the analogy between individual and national character, one commentator noted how often for 'nations, just like individuals, a series of circumstances changes their character and gives them a new shape'. He then asked his readers whether a capable king might not change the character of his people.[106] In effect, the idea that the nation's character could – and, in some cases, ought to – be changed was being increasingly discussed. Maintaining that '*men are made*' and that 'it is more or less possible to give them the shape one wishes' meant that education could then be seen as a crucial instrument in the hands of rulers for shaping their people's *mœurs* and modes of conduct.[107] In 1757, the diplomat and scholar Antoine Pecquet (1704–1762), in a work ambitiously intended to complement Montesquieu's *Esprit des lois*, pondered the issue. Pecquet made the case that a ruler might change a nation's 'natural *génie*' by educating his people to follow new precepts. However, he warned against departing from the natural disposition of the nation, for only by following its tastes and inclinations could 'superior men' be formed. Taking any other path would lead to mediocre results at best.[108] Like several other authors, Rousseau insisted on the importance of education in changing a nation's *mœurs* and ways of life. Adamant that 'no people will ever be but what the nature of its government will cause it to be', he famously declared that all 'have or should have a national character and if this were missing, it would be necessary to start by giving it one'.[109] As he saw it, education had a crucial role since it 'must

---

[105] Mably, 'De la manière d'écrire l'histoire', 507.

[106] [Turlin], *Extrait des discours qui ont concouru pour le prix que l'académie des sciences, belles-lettres et arts de la ville de Lyon a adjugé à M. Turlin sur cette question: Les voyages peuvent-ils être considérés comme un moyen de perfectionner l'éducation?* (Lyons: Aimé de la Roche, 1788), 71.

[107] Charles-Georges Le Roy, 'Homme (morale)', in Diderot and d'Alembert (eds.), *Encyclopédie*, viii. 278. Italics in the text.

[108] Antoine Pecquet, *L'esprit des maximes politiques, pour servir de suite à l'Esprit des lois, du Président de Montesquieu* (Paris: Prault, 1757), 145.

[109] Jean-Jacques Rousseau, 'Les confessions' (completed in 1762 but published in 1782), in *Œuvres*, i. 404; Jean-Jacques Rousseau, 'Projet de constitution pour la Corse' (written in 1765 but first published in 1825), in *Œuvres*, iii. 913. On this, Pauline Kra, 'Rousseau et la politique du caractère national', in Robert Thiéry (ed.), *Jean-Jacques Rousseau, politique et nation* (Paris: Honoré Champion, 2001), 813–22.

give to minds the national strength and direct their opinions and their tastes to such an extent that they become patriots by inclination, by passion, by necessity. A child, opening his eyes, must see the country, and up to his death must only see that.'[110] He understood national character to be a construction of time shaped by education and as the outcome, more or less intended and more or less successful, of the decisions of its rulers. Others made similar arguments. In his *De l'esprit* (1758), Claude-Adrien Helvétius (1715–1771) discussed at length the importance of education in shaping a nation's *mœurs* and influencing the character of its people. Years later, in *De l'homme* (1773 – posthumous), he elaborated further on the nature of the relationship: 'In each country there are some objects which education offers in the same way to all, and the uniform impression of these objects produces in the citizens the resemblance of ideas and feelings which are called national mind and character.'[111] Arising out of these convictions a great many projects for the education of citizens were forged by the jurist Louis-René de la Chalotais (1701–1785), the historian Jean-Jacques Garnier, the abbé Coyer, the economists Turgot and Paul-Pierre Lemercier de la Rivière (1719–1801), Diderot, and Condorcet.[112] One and all insisted on inculcating in children respect for civic values and love for their country. For some, education was mainly about teaching citizens the skills necessary to fulfil their role in society.[113] But it could also be a means for changing their character, their deep-seated inclinations, and their passions – even against their own innermost nature. The idea that 'it is nature which decides everything', wrote de La Chalotais in his

[110] Jean-Jacques Rousseau, 'Considérations sur le gouvernement de Pologne' (completed in 1772, but published posthumously in 1782), in *Œuvres*, iii. 966.

[111] Claude-Adrien Helvétius, *De l'esprit* (Paris: Fayard, 1988), 553–63; Claude-Adrien Helvétius, *De l'homme* (Paris: Fayard, 1989), i. 451.

[112] Louis-René de la Chalotais, *Essai d'éducation nationale ou plan d'études pour la jeunesse* (n.p., 1763); Jean-Jacques Garnier, *De l'éducation civile* (Paris: Vente, 1765); Gabriel-François Coyer, *Plan d'éducation publique* (Paris: Duchesne, 1770); Anne-Robert-Jacques Turgot, 'De la manière de préparer les individus et les familles à bien entrer dans une bonne constitution de société' (1775), in *Œuvres* (ed. Daire), ii. 506–9; Lemercier de la Rivière, *De l'instruction publique*, passim; Denis Diderot, 'Plan d'une université pour le gouvernement de Russie ou d'une éducation publique dans toutes les sciences' (1776), in *Œuvres complètes* (ed. Lewinter) (Paris: le Club français du livre, 1969–), xi. 725–34; Jean-Antoine-Nicolas de Condorcet, 'Sur l'instruction publique' (1791–1792), in *Œuvres*, vii. 167–573. For an overview of 'national education' in the second half of the eighteenth century, see Marcel Grandière, *L'idéal pédagogique en France au dix-huitième siècle* (Oxford: Voltaire Foundation, 1998), 213–400. On pedagogic concerns and discussions on the ways of educating the lower classes, see Rotraud von Kulessa (ed.), *Démocratisation et diversification: Les littératures d'éducation au siècle des Lumières* (Paris: Garnier, 2015). On projects of national education during the Revolution, see Bronisław Baczko, 'Introduction', in Baczko (ed.), *Une éducation pour la démocratie: Textes et projets de l'époque révolutionnaire* (Paris: Garnier frères, 1982), 9–58.

[113] Louis-Bernard Guyton De Morveau, *Mémoire sur l'éducation publique* (n.p., 1764), 66–80.

influential *Essai sur l'éducation nationale* (1763), 'is a pernicious principle that sustains the nonchalance of fine minds and increases the dejection of the mediocre'. Given the right circumstances, in the space of a few short years education 'could change the *mœurs* of an entire nation'.[114] Yet what de La Chalotais had failed to fathom was that this left unresolved the issue of which changes in particular were to be pursued. And as the victims of the Revolution would soon realise, the project of pursuing a wholesale transformation of a nation's *mœurs* would prove to be founded upon a harmful precept.

Social Distinctions: Embodying the Nation's Character

In 1766, the historian and playwright Germain-François Poullain de Saint-Foix (1698–1776) published the fourth edition of his *Essais historiques sur Paris*. In the final pages, he added a note to defend his work against the charge of relating many facts that had little to do with the city of Paris. In truth, he claimed, the aim of his book was

> to offer a historical picture of the character, inclination, *mœurs*, usages, and customs of my nation, and let them be known through facts. Now, it is beyond doubt that the capital of a monarchy, the ordinary residence of the sovereign and of the most prominent people within a state, is the seat of the nation's *mœurs* and that its provinces, more or less, take from it the mind, the way of thinking, the fashions, customs, and manners. So, I thought that by calling my work *Essais historiques sur Paris* it was as if I had written *Essais historiques sur les Français*.[115]

In many ways it was a questionable statement, and the opposite case could easily be made. Rousseau himself was in fact adamant that large cities and capitals invariably corrupted and degraded a people's *mœurs*. To grasp a nation's character, its truest nature, one ought to consider instead the ways of life prevailing in its most 'remote provinces, where the inhabitants have maintained their natural inclinations. ... All that they have in common, and which other peoples do not share, would form the national mind [*génie*].'[116] While some scholars repeated the argument a few years

[114] La Chalotais, *Essai d'éducation nationale*, 8–9.
[115] Germain-François Poullain de Saint-Foix, *Essais historiques sur Paris* (Paris: Veuve Duchesne, 1766), v. 238–9.
[116] Jean-Jacques Rousseau, 'La nouvelle Héloïse' (1761), in *Œuvres*, ii. 242; also see Rousseau, 'Émile', 850, and Rousseau, 'Projet de constitution pour la Corse', 911–2. The abbé Coyer made similar remarks with reference to England: [Gabriel-François Coyer], *Nouvelles observations sur l'Angleterre* (Paris: Veuve Duchesne, 1779), 258.

later, others, though not venturing as far as Saint-Foix, recognised the importance of Paris in shaping the nation's character and *mœurs* – for good or ill.[117] According to Montesquieu, it was 'especially the capital that makes the *mœurs* of a nation', so much so that, 'without Paris, Normandy, Franche-Comté, and Picardy would be more German than the Germans'.[118] Whether this was intended to be a positive judgement is, however, unclear for, as he had it, in large cities *mœurs* were always corrupt.[119]

The idea that capitals and large cities could affect profoundly a nation's character and even corrupt its *mœurs* was far from original.[120] More interesting is that the entire issue related to the social group allegedly embodying the nation's character. Once again, the *Considérations* are illuminating. Duclos, in fact, was sure that '[i]t is in Paris that a Frenchman must be considered, because there he is more French than anywhere else'. Mindful of the differences between the provinces and the capital in *mœurs* and manners, he also assumed that every class had its own character and that all of them deserved the reader's attention. However, Duclos believed that the key to grasping the nation's character was to find the group that represented it the most, and then to focus on it alone: 'My considerations do not concern those who, devoted to private and burdensome occupations, are only aware of their own situation and needs.' Instead, he would 'mainly consider those to whom wealth and idleness suggest a variety of ideas, bizarre opinions, inconstant feelings, and affections that give their character a full scope'.[121] Espousing the idea that vivacity and *légèreté* were the distinctive traits of the French, Duclos's decision to focus on the higher ranks of French society alone might have occasioned some perplexity at the time. It surely did so later on, after the Revolution. One commentator, writing in 1808, lambasted Duclos for supposing that the nation's *mœurs* had to be sought 'in the class of

---

[117] Among those who shared Rousseau's views was, for example, [Petiot], *De l'opinion et des mœurs, ou De l'influence des lettres sur les mœurs* (Paris: Moureau, 1770), 234–5.

[118] Montesquieu, 'Mes pensées', 1332 (§ 1409) and 1333 (§ 1410). On the influence of the capital and the court on the nation's character, also see, Montesquieu, 'Mes pensées', 1327 (§ 1381).

[119] Montesquieu, 'Dossier de l'Esprit des lois', 1073 (§ 311).

[120] See, for example, François de Salignac de La Mothe Fénelon, *Les aventures de Télémaque* (1699) (Paris: Gallimard, 1995), 367–8. For an overview of the 'Indictment of Paris and civilisation' in the eighteenth century, see Simon Davies, *Paris and the Provinces in Eighteenth-Century Prose Fiction* (Oxford: Voltaire Foundation, 1982), 67–78.

[121] Duclos, *Considérations sur les mœurs de ce siècle*, 99–101.

men that fortune shelters from needs, *and who might freely abandon themselves to their fancies and the natural gait of their character*.[122]

Admittedly, assuming, as Diderot did, that it was by the 'greatest part of a nation that one ought to judge its *mœurs*' might well have seemed the best course to follow.[123] And yet it would have been an impractical solution. In fact, as in the case of any other nation, French society offered a spectacle of breath-taking complexity that could be grasped, in its entirety, only with great difficulty.[124] The challenge was to make sense of such a variety without impoverishing it. According to some eighteenth-century observers, one plausible point of departure was to consider the *mœurs* and ways of life of the nation's different classes. Throughout the eighteenth century, the idea that each class of citizen had its own specific character and *mœurs* was widely accepted. Marmontel, for example, praised the variety of *mœurs* in evidence in the various classes: '[E]ach condition has their own, the nobility, the bourgeoisie, the man-at-arms, the man of the robe, the artisan, and the financier.' All of these classes formed a living and variegated painting of the nation. Their different *mœurs* were its 'thousands upon thousands of different colours'.[125] A few years earlier, the scholar and advocate of the royalist cause the abbé Sabatier de Castres (1742–1817) had listed in his *Dictionnaire de littérature* (1770) the different classes forming the nation and divided them by their character and *mœurs*.[126] Most of such listings and classifications – and Sabatier de Castres's was no exception – described the nobility, dividing it between sword and robe, and depicted the middle classes, dividing it between financiers, merchants, scholars, and, in a few cases, artisans. However, the lower classes, farmers, and labourers were excluded. What might seem today a glaring omission was at that time more or less to be expected. In effect, the issue of defining the lower classes, of grasping the nature of what seemed to many but a shapeless multitude, remained unsolved throughout the century. The largest and yet 'the less

[122] Jacques J. Lemoine, *Discours qui a remporté le prix sur cette question proposée en 1808 par l'Académie des sciences, arts et belles-lettres de Dijon: La nation française mérite-t-elle le reproche de légèreté que lui font les nations étrangères?* (Paris: Giguet et Michaud, 1809), 13. Italics in the text.
[123] Denis Diderot, 'Essai sur les règnes de Claude et de Néron et sur les mœurs et les écrits de Sénèque' (1778–1782), in *Œuvres* (ed. Dieckmann et al.), xxv. 44.
[124] See the expression used in Charles Dufresny, *Amusements sérieux et comiques* (1699) (Paris: Bossard, 1921), 61.
[125] Marmontel, *Éléments de littérature*, 726.
[126] Antoine Sabatier de Castres, *Dictionnaire de littérature, dans lequel on traite de tout ce qui a rapport à l'éloquence, à la poësie et aux belles-lettres, et dans lequel on enseigne la marche et les règles qu'on doit observer dans tous les ouvrages d'esprit* (Paris: Vincent, 1770), ii. 585–90.

significant' part of the nation, it was almost invariably defined in 'opposition to those who are noble, wealthy or enlightened'.[127] The notoriously disparaging judgement of many of the greatest thinkers of the day – though, in truth, a judgement more complex than latter-day scholarship has tended to assume – exacerbated the difficulty of representing and defining the people.[128] In most cases, the image crystallising in the works of eighteenth-century philosophers, scholars, novelists, and journalists was of an ignorant and mercurial mob or rabble, following its passions with no restraint, extremely unpredictable and unstable. During the Revolution, Jean-Paul Marat (1743–1793) bitterly complained that the '*légèreté*, frivolity, and volatility of the people's character' was such that should it grant him the crown in the morning, it might well hang him by the evening.[129] The proverbial *légèreté* of the French, when embodied in the lower classes, led to extreme volatility, chaos, and anarchy – an image that, in the minds of the middle and upper classes, was reinforced during the Revolution. It is then unsurprising that many held that the character of the lower classes did not represent that of the nation at large. As one commentator wrote in the *Correspondance littéraire*, the people in the streets of 'Les Halles and Place Maubert', so absorbed in their daily labours, 'clearly have their own well-defined *mœurs*. But these are not the *mœurs* of the nation. Therefore, they do not deserve to be portrayed.'[130]

The difficulty in representing the lower classes and grasping their character ought to be considered against the backdrop of a complex process through which the people's upper echelons gradually distanced themselves from the multitude. It was a development already noted by Coyer in a short essay published in 1755. In his 'Dissertation sur la nature du peuple', in fact, the abbé remarked that the people, the lower classes, were no longer considered the most useful, virtuous, and respectable part of the nation.

---

[127] Académie française, *Dictionnaire de l'Académie française*, ii. 228 (s.v. 'peuple'); Vv. Aa., *Dictionnaire de Trévoux*, iii. s.v. 'peuple'.

[128] See, for example, Montesquieu, 'De l'Esprit des lois', 241 (book ii. ch. 2); François-Marie Arouet Voltaire to Jean Tabareau, 3 February 1769, in *Œuvres*, xlvi. 254; Jean-Jacques Rousseau, 'Lettres écrites de la montagne' (1764), in *Œuvres*, iii. 729 and 889. For an overview, see Centre aixois d'études et de recherches sur le XVIIIe siècle, *Images du peuple au dix-huitième siècle* (Paris: Armand Colin, 1973), and Gérard Fritz, *L'idée de peuple en France du XVIIe au XIXe siècle* (Strasbourg: Presses universitaires de Strasbourg, 1988). On the revolutionary period, see Pierre Rosanvallon, *Le peuple introuvable: Histoire de la représentation démocratique en France* (Paris: Gallimard, 1998), 33–55. On the relationship between *peuple* and *nation* in the eighteenth century, see Slimani, *La modernité du concept de nation au XVIIIe siècle*, 47–52.

[129] Jean-Paul Marat, 'Le publiciste de la République française', 19 June 1793, in *Œuvres politiques* (Brussels: Pôle Nord, 1989–1995), x. 6538.

[130] Anonymous, in Grimm et al., *Correspondance littéraire*, ii. 269 (1 August 1753).

He imputed such a regrettable change to the fact that men of letters, financiers, lawyers, magistrates, and even shopkeepers, all of whom belonged to the people, had deserted it, now considering themselves above the rest. Only farmers, domestics, and menial artisans were still within the ranks of the people.[131] In his short pamphlet, imbued with an uncommon sympathy for the lower classes, Coyer was making a valid point, describing a process by which the wealthier and the more educated workers had acquired the manners, tastes, and even the *mœurs* of the nobility.[132] Already in 1748, one commentator remarked with sarcasm that the 'bourgeois was the courtesan's monkey', incessantly trying to mimic the ways of high society – also noting that, in turn, the people constantly strove to imitate the bourgeoisie.[133] Crucially, these attempts to draw a dividing line between the middle and the lower classes proceeded in parallel with the dissemination of a new understanding of the nature of work and the ways it affected men and women. From the late seventeenth century onwards, the idea that work could ennoble a person started to gain currency, so much so, that by the mid-eighteenth century, many thinkers would have argued that a worker's daily endeavours were something more than a painful necessity.[134] Helvétius, for one, praised the effects that work had on men and censured those wealthy noblemen who spent their lives in idleness. Work averted the dangers of ennui and, 'when it is moderate, it is the most agreeable way of employing our time'.[135] Interestingly, Helvétius made no distinction between the work of the magistrate, the blacksmith, the errand boy, and the poet. From his standpoint – that of a wealthy *fermier-général* – work would always have a valued impact upon a person's way of life and character. However, on this, many disagreed. In fact, professions that required specific intellectual or artistic skills were usually considered in a different light to menial and repetitive tasks. Loyseau had already made the distinction at the beginning of the seventeenth century, arguing that activities relying more on the exertions of the body were the vilest, while those depending upon a person's intellect were honourable

---

[131] Gabriel-François Coyer, 'Dissertation sur la nature du peuple', in Coyer, *Dissertations pour être lues*, 44–6. See, on this, Harvey Chisick, *The Limits of Reform in the Enlightenment: Attitudes to the Education of the Lower Classes in France, 1762–1789* (Princeton: Princeton University Press, 1981), 52–5.

[132] On this, see also Tocqueville, *L'Ancien régime et la Révolution*, i. 146.

[133] Étienne-André Philippe de Prétot, *Les amusemens du cœur et de l'esprit* (Paris: Veuve Pissot, 1748–1749), i. 412.

[134] An interesting discussion is in Alain Rey, 'Dire le travail: Une histoire d'idées', in Rey, *Des pensées et des mots* (Paris: Hermann, 2013), 197–214.

[135] See Helvétius, *De l'homme*, ii. 661–4. Quote is on page 663.

and admirable. De La Roque, sharing similar views, contended that the barrier between the body and the mind somehow corresponded to that between commoners and noblemen.[136] Years later, for their part, Diderot and D'Alembert, while praising the mechanical arts as the most useful to society, still maintained a similar distinction.[137] In effect, in the *Encyclopédie*, this emerged in the contrast between the artist and the artisan. The first 'excelled in those mechanical arts that presuppose great intelligence', while the latter practised those 'mechanical arts that require the least intelligence'. They admitted that the distinction was not clear-cut – nor could it be. In fact, 'one says of a good shoemaker, that he is a good *artisan*, and of a clever watchmaker, that he is a great *artist*'.[138] The uncertainties about the distinction, relevant because it defined the boundaries between the people and the lower echelons of the nascent bourgeoisie, are revealing. The difficulties were also noted by the abbé Coyer, who confessed to being at a loss when having to classify artisans. The hands of the skilled artisan, which 'paint a carriage divinely, perfectly mount a diamond, excellently mend a dress, no longer resemble those of the people'.[139] It was a porous boundary and a person's place, on either side of it, largely depended on his or her capacities. Work could then ennoble or degrade, depending on its nature and the intellectual and artistic skills it required. But it was widely assumed that it always had a profound impact on the worker and, in turn, on the *mœurs*, values, ideas, and character of his or her class.

It is important to emphasise that, throughout the eighteenth century, there was no strong feeling or deep awareness of belonging to the bourgeoisie.[140] Partly, this might have been due to the fact that, as one

---

[136] Loyseau, *Traité des ordres et simples dignitez*, 102–3. De La Roque, *Le traité de la noblesse et des différentes espèces*, 530–1. Also see, on this, Mathieu Marraud, 'Dérogeance et commerce: Violence des constructions socio-politiques sous l'Ancien régime', *Genèses*, 95 (2014), 7–9.

[137] On their praise for the mechanical arts, see: Jean Baptiste le Rond d'Alembert, 'Discours préliminaire des éditeurs' (1751), in *Discours préliminaire de 'L'Encyclopédie' et articles de 'L'Encyclopédie'* (Paris: Honoré Champion, 2011), 97, and Denis Diderot, 'Art', in Diderot and d'Alembert (eds.), *Encyclopédie*, i. 714. Also see Georges Friedmann, 'L'Encyclopédie et le travail humain', *Annales: Économies, sociétés, civilisations*, 8 (1953), 53–61.

[138] [Denis Diderot – uncertain attribution], 'Artiste', in Diderot and d'Alembert (eds.), *Encyclopédie*, i. 745; [Denis Diderot – uncertain attribution], 'Artisan', in Diderot and d'Alembert (eds.), *Encyclopédie*, i. 745. Italics in the text. On the point, see, William H. Sewell Jr., *Work and Revolution in France: The Language of Labor from the Old Regime to 1848* (Cambridge: Cambridge University Press, 1980), 23–5. Also see Maria Teresa Zanola, *Arts et métiers au XVIIIᵉ siècle: Études de terminologie diachronique* (Paris: L'Harmattan, 2014), 41–56.

[139] Coyer, 'Dissertation sur la nature du peuple', 46.

[140] See Sarah Maza, 'Luxury, Morality, and Social Change: Why There Was No Middle-Class Consciousness in Prerevolutionary France', *The Journal of Modern History*, 69 (1997), 199–229.

foreign observer noted as late as 1771, in France '*bourgeois* is a term of reproach', usually used to remind those who aspired to join the upper classes of their actual status.[141] Nor were the character and *mœurs* of the bourgeoisie clearly identifiable. In an article published anonymously in the *Nouveau Mercure* in September 1717, Marivaux, after mentioning with scorn the bourgeoisie, 'that crossbred animal that takes after the lord and the people', denied it had any *mœurs* of its own. The bourgeois simply and grotesquely mimicked the manners of the higher classes: 'Noble by imitation and plebeian by character', he commented with contempt.[142] However, throughout the eighteenth century and especially from the 1770s onwards, many attempts were made to give precise contours to that increasingly influential class poised between the nobility and the populace. By 1776, the chemist and novelist Geneviève Thiroux d'Arconville (1720–1805) had no difficulty in clearly locating the bourgeoisie and defining its character. She wrote of its members as forming a 'people apart', almost immune to the influences of other classes: 'Its principles, prejudices, *mœurs*, usages, and conduct make of it a unique class.' Its traits seemed to her unchanging, being 'today as they had been a thousand years ago'. Political institutions, manners, and even religions changed, but the bourgeoisie remained 'unwavering in the midst of this universal variableness'. According to Thiroux d'Arconville, its members despised luxuries and scorned frivolity, while duties and hard work filled the lives of 'these happy inhabitants of the world'. It was in this class of citizens, at a 'midpoint between splendour and misery', that one 'mainly finds these honest men who have no vices'.[143] Remarkable though the cosmopolitanism of Thiroux d'Arconville's bourgeoisie was, still more startling was the fact that the moderation and restraint it embodied were set in stark contrast to the frivolity of the nobility on the one hand and the volatility of the people on the other. It was an implicit yet clear condemnation of the two extreme manifestations of French *légèreté*. Another author, writing in 1783, also praised the bourgeoisie for its moderation, a virtue that stemmed from its being at an ideal midpoint between the lower and upper classes: 'If shallowness disheartens the soul, opulence corrupts the *mœurs*. It is always in the bourgeoisie, and especially among

---

[141] Anonymous, 'An Essay on the National Sincerity of the French, in Opposition to the General Belief', *The London Magazine*, August 1771, 405. Italics in the text.

[142] Pierre Marivaux, 'Lettres sur les habitants de Paris', in *Journaux et œuvres diverses*, 14.

[143] [Marie-Geneviève-Charlotte Thiroux d'Arconville], *De l'amitié* (Amsterdam: Desaint & Saillant, 1761), 115–9. The book, which appeared anonymously, at the time, was erroneously attributed to Diderot: Roland Mortier, *Diderot en Allemagne (1750–1850)* (Geneva: Slatkine, 1986), 352–3.

tradesmen, that one might find the example of domestic virtues.'[144] The reference to tradesmen and merchants, to be found even in Thiroux d'Arconville's book, was precisely meant to recall the good sense, the self-imposed discipline, and even the sociability so important to a profession that, moreover, required little menial labour. Curiously, by the 1780s, the bourgeoisie's seriousness and moderation seemed to Mercier to have spread out even to Parisian society. The Marquis de Caraccioli (1719–1803) also noted the turn, predicting, however, that the change would not last – after all, the French were inconsistent by nature.[145]

As the century advanced, the urge to define the character of the bour-geoisie came to be tied to its mounting political demands. Such claims were often vindicated by demonstrating its worth and usefulness, as a class, to the entire nation. The perception of a decaying nobility, more con-cerned with its appearance than its duties to the state, played a fundamental role and troubled several essayists – many of whom were noblemen themselves.[146] Concerns over such issues had already been expressed, among others, by La Rochefoucauld, La Bruyère, Fénelon, and Boulainvilliers.[147] However, these concerns acquired a new political hue from the 1730s onwards, when the worth and merits of merchants, craftsmen, and artisans, contributing to the greatness of their nation through work, came to be explicitly contrasted with the hollowness of the nobility. Already in his *Lettres philosophiques* (1734), Voltaire con-tended that the safety of a state increasingly depended upon its commerce and industry, and even compared the English merchants to the citizens of ancient Rome for their attachment to their country. As he saw it, the usefulness of the working middle classes was even greater than that of the warring noblemen – assuming, that is, that noblemen still fought. Partly sharing such views, the abbé de Saint-Pierre (1658–1743) suggested that the French nobility, following the example of the English, should practise commerce for its own as well the nation's sake. A few years later, the

---

[144] Alexandre-Balthazar-Laurent Grimod de La Reynière, *Réflexions philosophiques sur le plaisir, par un célibataire* (Neuchâtel: Veuve Duchesne, 1783), 58.

[145] Mercier, *Tableau de Paris*, i. 58–9; [Louis-Antoine Caraccioli], *L'Europe françoise* (Paris: Veuve Duchesne, 1776), 245 and 214. On this, see Jocelyn Huchette, 'La "gaieté française" ou la question du caractère national dans la définition du rire, de *L'Esprit des lois* à *De la littérature*', *Dix-huitième siècle*, 32 (2000), 106–7.

[146] Renato Galliani, *Rousseau, le luxe et l'idéologie nobiliaire: Étude socio-historique* (Oxford: Voltaire Foundation, 1989), and Chad Denton, *Decadence, Radicalism, and the Early Modern French Nobility: The Enlightened and Depraved* (Lanham: Lexington Books, 2017).

[147] François de La Rochefoucauld, 'Maximes supprimées', in *Œuvres*, 496 (§ 629); La Bruyère, 'Les caractères ou les mœurs de ce siècle', 353–72; Fénelon, *Les aventures de Télémaque*, 210 and 252–3; Boulainvilliers, *Essais sur la noblesse de France*, 297–8.

economist Nicolas Dutot (1684–1741) reiterated the argument in his popular *Réflexions politiques sur les finances et le commerce* (1738). Reflecting on the political situation of the Old Continent and the changing nature of power relationships, the famous economist Vincent de Gournay (1712–1759) remarked that since Europe was now 'becoming commercial, its rulers need tradesmen' more than soldiers and generals.[148]

But such views did not go unchallenged. Montesquieu, for one, argued against a trading nobility, at least in France, since he believed this to be contrary to the nature of monarchical rule.[149] In a short essay possibly written around 1736 but published in 1754, the Marquis de Lassay (1652–1738), an army officer and member of the Club de l'Entresol, also opposed the idea of a trading nobility, but did so on different grounds, contending that to allow noblemen to grow rich would undermine their 'warring spirit'.[150] Since the nobility was the sole bulwark against foreign enemies and ensured the nation's safety, to degrade and demean it would endanger the French state. Discussions over the nobility's role in a modern state and in modern warfare continued and intensified during the Seven Years War. In early 1756, possibly prompted by his friend Gournay and responding to de Lassay's arguments, the abbé Coyer published a widely read and controversial book adopting a new stance over the issue of a trading nobility. In his *La noblesse commerçante* – a book that, noted Voltaire with misplaced sarcasm, 'wanted to put into shops the Montmorencys and Châtillons' of France – the abbé listed all the advantages that would accrue to the nation if noblemen tried their hand at commerce. These included an increase in the nation's wealth, the improvement of cultivation and navigation, and a growth in population.[151] While strengthening the nation, the nobleman would also avoid falling into a 'contemptible idleness

---

[148] François-Marie Arouet Voltaire, 'Lettres philosophiques', in *Œuvres*, xxii. 110–1. The *Lettres* had already been published in 1733 as *Letters Concerning the English Nation*. Charles-Irénée Castel Saint-Pierre, 'Projet pour perfectioner le comerse de France' (1733), in *Ouvrajes de politique* (Rotterdam: Beman, 1733–1740), v. 216–7 and 219–20; Nicolas Dutot, *Réflexions politiques sur les finances et le commerce* (The Hague: Frères Vaillant et N. Prevost, 1738), ii. 313–7; Jacques Claude Marie Vincent de Gournay to Daniel-Charles Trudaine, 10 April 1754, in *Mémoires et lettres* (Paris: Institut Coppet, 2017), 219.

[149] Montesquieu, 'De l'Esprit des lois', 598 (book xx. ch. 21).

[150] Armand-Léon de Madaillan de Lesparre de Lassay, 'Réflexions de M. le Marquis de Lasse', *Mercure de France*, December 1754, ii. 87. The dating of the drafting is suggested by Gabriel-François Coyer, *La noblesse commerçante* (Paris: Duchesne, 1765), 6. Since de Lassay in fact spent the last two years of his life writing about a variety of subjects, the dating might be plausible. See Max de Marande, 'Un Don Juan du Grand siècle et de la Régence: Le Marquis de Lassay', *Revue de France*, July–August 1936, 492–3.

[151] Coyer, *La noblesse commerçante*, 54–94. For Voltaire's remark: François-Marie Arouet Voltaire to Michel de Servan, April 1766, in *Œuvres*, xliv. 276.

and a lethargy as harmful to himself as to the state'.[152] Dismissing de
Lassay's concerns as groundless, Coyer insisted that commerce would
'not ruin the blood', nor lessen the dignity of those who engaged in it as
long as they were virtuous, hard-working, and spent their earnings
wisely.[153] Most importantly, it would not corrupt the 'military spirit of
France'.[154] As for the nobles' insistence that they could not engage in
commerce since their forefathers had not done so, the abbé bitterly
remarked that it was for such a reason that they were 'so useless to the
country'.[155] Coyer's arguments were linked to the realisation that in the
waging of war wealth had become more important than bravery, war itself
having turned into the 'spending of money rather than human beings'.[156]
Considering how political questions were decided and wars fought, Coyer
concluded that 'the balance of commerce and the balance of power are one
and the same'.[157]

The book sparked an intense debate and many replies followed.[158] The
reception was mixed. Grimm was indignant at the prospect of a trading
nobility but had to admit that Coyer's work contained a number of good
ideas and enjoyed 'some success'. The *Journal de Trévoux* was more
flattering, praising the abbé's book for the 'wonderful and very noble'
cause it espoused. Another favourable review appeared in January 1756 in
the *Année littéraire*. Possibly written by the Marquis d'Argenson (1694–
1757), it presented a closely argued comparison between de Lassay's and
Coyer's arguments, praising the latter for his work, 'remarkable, above all,
for its views on the common good'. It is perhaps surprising that two

---

[152] Coyer, *La noblesse commerçante*, 139.   [153] Ibid., 176.   [154] Ibid., 26–9.   [155] Ibid., 207.
[156] Ibid., 151.   [157] Ibid., 158–9.
[158] See Edgard Depitre, 'Le système et la querelle de la *noblesse commerçante* (1756–1759)', *Revue
d'histoire économique et sociale*, 6 (1913), 137–76; Leonard Adams, *Coyer and the Enlightenment*
(Oxford: Voltaire Foundation, 1974), 45–103; Kiyoji Kisaki, 'Controversy on the *Noblesse
commerçante* between abbé Coyer and Chevalier d'Arcq', *The University of Kyoto Economic
Review*, 49 (1979), 48–79; Frank E. Sutcliffe, 'The Abbé Coyer and the Chevalier d'Arc', *Bulletin
of the John Rylands Library*, 65 (1982), 235–45; Catherine Larrère, *L'invention de l'économie au XVIIIe
siècle: Du droit naturel à la physiocratie* (Paris: Presses universitaires de France, 1992), 150–61; Jay
M. Smith, 'Social Categories, the Language of Patriotism, and the Origins of the French
Revolution: The Debate over *noblesse commerçante*', *The Journal of Modern History*, 72 (2000),
339–74; John Shovlin, *The Political Economy of Virtue: Luxury, Patriotism and the Origins of the
French Revolution* (Ithaca: Cornell University Press, 2006), 58–65; Ulrich Adam, 'Nobility and
Modern Monarchy – J. H. G. Justi and the French Debate on Commercial Nobility at the
Beginning of the Seven Years War', *History of European Ideas*, 29 (2003), 141–57. On the expression
'noblesse commerçante' and how it affected the perception of the nation, see Marie-France Piguet,
'Noblesse *commerçante* / Nation *commerçante*: Genèse d'un adjectif', in Loïc Charles,
Frédéric Lefebvre, and Christine Théré (eds.), *Le cercle de Vincent de Gournay: Savoirs
économiques et pratiques administratives en France au milieu du XVIIIe siècle* (Paris: INED, 2011),
161–78.

months later, in the same journal, its editor, Élie Fréron (1718–1776), commended a refutation of the *Noblesse commerçante* in a work 'bringing back everything to its true perspective, saving the French nobility from the debasing' that Coyer's ideas would surely bring about.[159] The work referred to by Fréron was the most famous reply to the abbé's thesis. The author of *La noblesse militaire* (1756), the Chevalier d'Arcq (1721–1795), a man of arms and letters, made the case that although commerce could be of crucial importance for a state, this actually depended on its location, the character of its people, and, finally, its form of government.[160] It was by looking at the latter two elements that d'Arcq argued that allowing the nobility to engage in commerce would be detrimental to France. In fact, on the one hand the French were a bellicose nation and had been so since their origins.[161] On the other, their constitution did not favour commerce since monarchies had a tendency to expand and the 'spirit of conquest, is not always harmonious with the great establishment of commerce'.[162] But d'Arcq went further. Considering division into classes and the rights of each group, he related these to a nation's character. As he saw it, should the latter be commercial, as in almost all the insular states, 'the people of the Third Estate must be favoured' since they were the most valuable class. Conversely, if the *génie* of a people was essentially warlike – and the French surely was – privileges and honours ought to be reserved for the nobility alone.[163] Following this general principle, d'Arcq concluded that support-ing the involvement of the nobility in commerce would not only weaken France and leave it a prey to its enemies but, moreover, would sap the character of the French as a whole, diminishing the prestige of its worthiest class. Addressing himself to those noblemen who had died for the nation, he imagined their contempt at learning of Coyer's work: 'Illustrious manes, whose blood has cemented the glorious name of France, you, whom we still revere in the names of your descendants, whom we constantly admire, and whose virtues we strive to imitate, what

---

[159] Grimm et al., *Correspondance littéraire*, iii. 176 and 170–3 respectively (February 1756); Anonymous, review of Gabriel-François Coyer, *La noblesse commerçante*, in *Journal de Trévoux, ou Mémoires pour servir à l'histoire des sciences et des arts*, March 1756, 727; [René-Louis de Voyer de Paulmy d'Argenson – uncertain attribution], review of Gabriel-François Coyer, *La noblesse commerçante*, in *L'année littéraire*, 1756, i. 55. On the issue of authorship, see: René-Louis de Voyer de Paulmy d'Argenson, *Mémoires et journal inédit* (Nendeln: Kraus reprint, 1979), v. 135; Élie Fréron, review of Philippe-Auguste de Sainte-Foix d'Arcq, *La noblesse militaire*, in *L'année littéraire*, 1756, ii. 31–2.

[160] [Philippe-Auguste de Sainte-Foix d'Arcq], *La noblesse militaire, ou Le patriote françois* ([Paris: Michel Lambert], 1756), 7–10. On his thought, see Jean-Pierre Brancourt, 'Un théoricien de la société au XVIIIe siècle: Le Chevalier d'Arcq', *Revue historique*, 250 (1973), 337–62.

[161] [D'Arcq], *La noblesse militaire*, 124.   [162] Ibid., 14.   [163] Ibid., 47–9.

would you say if you saw the title of this work? What! A *trading nobility* in a bellicose state!'[164]

Importantly, in his refutation of Coyer's work, d'Arcq insisted on the identification of nation and the nobility on account of the latter's selflessness, emphasising the greediness of the bourgeois, who incessantly pursued his own petty benefit. He made a point of stressing that while the 'purpose of commerce is interest', by the very nature of their stance the nobles have 'no other interest' but that of the state.[165] In a nation as bellicose as the French, surrounded by many enemies, the nobleman, so ready 'to run [headlong] to his death, if his death may be useful to the country', had the most important of public functions. His role was to sustain 'the glory and the interests of king and nation, to shed all his blood to defend those whose daily labour contributes to his sustenance and well-being'.[166] D'Arcq's pamphlet was followed by such a quantity of tracts and articles that, by August 1756, Grimm was hoping that 'this trading and non-trading nobility will finally leave us in peace'.[167] Yet the debate continued, so much so that the abbé Coyer even felt impelled to write a *Développement et défense du système de la noblesse commerçante*. The respective contribution of the middle classes and the nobility to the state's strength remained a matter of dispute. But, indubitably, the image of the bourgeoisie was changing. And, within the latter, the representation of traders and merchants seemed particularly affected. A work first published in 1779 and then reprinted in 1784, allegedly by a merchant named Bedos and tellingly entitled *Le négociant patriote*, insisted that merchants were the nation's most useful class of citizens.[168] On the one hand, the author was reaffirming Coyer's thesis that, by accruing personal wealth, merchants were also strengthening the entire nation. On the other, he claimed that 'good faith, assiduous work, and patriotism' were the distinctive marks of French merchants and that the 'healthy philosophy, work, and moderate desires' practised by them would lead to a virtuous serenity.[169] In passing, it is worth noting that all these were once again correctives to the most extreme and most deleterious forms of a proverbial French *légèreté*.

---

[164] Ibid., 3. Italics in the text.   [165] Ibid., 60.   [166] Ibid., 198 and 37–8.
[167] Grimm et al., *Correspondance littéraire*, iii. 269 (15 August 1756); On the discussion following d'Arcq's work, see Depitre, 'Le système et la querelle de la *noblesse commerçante*', 138–42.
[168] [Bedos], *Le négociant patriote, contenant un tableau qui réunit les avantages du commerce, la connoissance des spéculations de chaque nation* (Brussels: n.p., 1779), 1–3.
[169] Ibid., 250 and 206 respectively. On the idea that 'bourgeois happiness' might derive from hard work, see Robert Mauzi, *L'idée du bonheur dans la littérature et la pensée françaises au XVIIIᵉ siècle* (Geneva: Slatkine, 1979), 269–89.

It is significant that the works extolling the role of merchants and the working middle classes often accepted and restated Bernard Mandeville's (1670–1733) famous thesis, so often discussed at the time, on private vices and public virtue.[170] It surely was the case with Coyer's *Noblesse commerçante*.[171] But the author of the *Négociant patriote* went even further, emphasising the bourgeoisie's hard work and moderation as the source of those domestic virtues that made of a merchant a good father and a worthy citizen. Such ideas slowly gained currency and from the 1770s onwards were used to support various political arguments.[172] In 1783, for example, Mably claimed that 'domestic virtues', which included temperance, love of work, love of glory, and respect for religion, were constitutive of the social tie and even 'determined the public *mœurs*'.[173] These virtues could serve as a remedy to the risks of moral corruption posed by the accumulation of wealth. Similar arguments were also made by the Prince Luigi Gonzaga di Castiglione (1745–1819) in a work first published in Italian in 1776 and translated into French the following year. Partly contesting Mandeville's thesis, Gonzaga di Castiglione argued that the pursuit of individual interests did not necessarily have positive consequences for the state. For such to be the case, it was necessary to place fetters on people's greed, and these lay precisely in domestic virtues. Consistently, he went on to claim that it was the duty of rulers to foster and encourage through education love for family and hard work.[174] Others, writing later on, during the Revolution, were adamant that private interest alone could not instil in citizens a genuine attachment to the nation and that domestic virtues were the sole corrective. As one revolutionary had it: 'True patriotism, this exclusive and deep-seated attachment towards the country in which one is born, towards the

---

[170] On the reception of Mandeville's thesis in France, see: Elena Muceni, 'Mandeville and France: The Reception of the Fable of the Bees in France and its Influence on the French Enlightenment', *French Studies*, 69 (2015), 449–61. On Mandeville's ideas, Edward M. Hundert, *The Enlightenment's Fable: Bernard Mandeville and the Discovery of Society* (Cambridge: Cambridge University Press, 2005).

[171] Smith, 'Social Categories, the Language of Patriotism, and the Origins of the French Revolution', 353.

[172] See, for example, Joseph Lanjuinais, *Manuel des jeunes orateurs, ou Tableau historique et méthodique de l'éloquence* (Moudon: Société typographique, 1777), ii. 437; Robinet et al., *Dictionnaire universel des sciences morale, économique, politique et diplomatique*, xxv. 218; Jean-Xavier Bureaux de Pusy, *Opinion de M. Bureaux de Pusy, député du bailliage d'Amont, dans la séance du mercredi 16 décembre 1789* (Paris: Imprimerie nationale, 1789), 9; Jean-Marie Chassaignon, *Le tiers-état rétabli pour jamais dans tous ses droits, par la résurrection des bons rois et la mort éternelle des tyrans* (Langres: n.p., 1789), 277; Louis Mathieu Langlès, *Adresse de la Convention nationale au peuple français, décrétée dans la séance du 13 vendémiaire an III* (n.p., 1794), unpaginated.

[173] Gabriel Bonnot de Mably, 'De l'étude de l'histoire, à Monseigneur le Prince de Parme' (1783), in *Œuvres*, xii. 350.

[174] Luigi Gonzaga di Castiglione, *L'homme de lettres, bon citoyen* (Geneva: n.p., 1777), 101.

government under which one lives, this sentiment that brings to mind feelings that are so noble and tender. Patriotism is made up of all the domestic virtues. One may not be a good citizen if one is a bad son, husband or father, for he is failing with regard to the first of social ties.'[175] The old idea of family, here centred around the figure of the father-worker, had been brought back into political language in a new garb.

Within a broader perspective, attention towards the effects that work and education had on the character of an individual – and, by extension, on his or her class and the nation at large – was becoming increasingly important in debates about the public welfare. From the 1750s onwards, for example, several authors campaigned for an improvement in the conditions of the farmers in order to strengthen the state and to counter the nation's moral debasement.[176] Partly intending to combat the arguments of Coyer and his followers, they shared with these an emphasis on hard work and discipline but argued that better farming conditions would strengthen the state by increasing its population. Knowledge and learning, as well as the development of the arts and the (moderate) refinement of manners, all envisaged in works such as the *Négociant patriote* and considered crucial in forming the good father-citizen-worker, were less relevant. The contrast was between 'rustic' and 'domestic virtues'.[177] The key difference between the 'commercialist' and the 'agrarian' thesis was that the latter referred to social and political models that mirrored an idealised past – usually Republican Rome – while the former was inspired by the belief in an endless progress prompted by the accumulation of wealth and the affirmation of individual freedom – and, here, the model often was England. Two different political models and two different forms of republicanism. Two different claims regarding the usefulness of a class, its moral superiority, and its right to represent the nation. Two different views that shared, however, the notion that hard work and the virtues it fostered would be instrumental in restoring to the French their lost vigour and would help to regenerate the nation's character.[178]

---

[175] Adrien Duquesnoy, *L'ami des patriotes ou le Défenseur de la Révolution* (Paris: Demonville, 1790–1792), iii. 505.

[176] See Shovlin, *The Political Economy of Virtue*, 51–8.

[177] On the idea of 'rustic virtues', see Robert M. Schwarz, 'Le paysan comme héro: Rousseau, Restif de la Bretonne et la représentation des vertus rustiques', in Jean-Jacques Clère, Françoise Fortunet, and Philippe Jobert (eds.), *Le bonheur est une idée neuve: Hommage à Jean Bart* (Dijon: Centre Georges Chevrier, 2000), 385–408.

[178] The reference, of course, is to Mona Ozouf, 'La Révolution française et la formation de l'homme nouveau', in Ozouf, *L'homme régénéré: Essais sur la Révolution française* (Paris: Gallimard, 1989), 116–57. Also see Lucien Jaume, *Le religieux et le politique dans la Révolution française: L'idée de régénération* (Paris: Presses universitaires de France, 2015).

CHAPTER 5

Moral and Physical Causes
Montesquieu's History of Nations

National Character and Moral and Physical Causes:
Montesquieu and (a Few of) His Predecessors

On 3 February 1770, an unsigned letter was sent to Élie Fréron, the editor of the *Année littéraire*. In it, the author accused the scholar and encyclopaedist Jean-Louis Castilhon (1720–1798?) of plagiarising a book published anonymously in 1743, the *Essai sur le génie et les caractères des nations*, a work later revised in 1752 as *L'esprit des nations*. The letter's author was adamant that Castilhon's *Considérations sur les causes physiques et morales de la diversité du génie, des mœurs et du gouvernement des nations* (1769) were little else than a replica of the *Essai sur le génie* which, inelegantly rephrasing a few sentences of the original, had simply served to reduce the clarity of the argument. Love for the truth had compelled the anonymous accuser to unmask the offender and teach treacherous 'authors that their larcenies cannot be concealed for long'.[1] In fact, in the subtitle of the *Considérations*, Castilhon had alerted the reader that his book was 'partly drawn' from the *Esprit des nations*. He also acknowledged the debt in the introduction, explaining that the *Esprit* contained 'excellent things, wise observations, and sound research' and that, without it, he would never have been able to write his own book.[2] According to one reviewer, writing in the *Journal encyclopédique*, the 'honesty of this acknowledgement' was laudable and surely testified to the many merits of the *Considérations*.[3] A few months after the publication of the accusatory letter, the *Journal encyclopédique*

---

[1] Anonymous [François-Ignace d'Espiard de la Borde – uncertain attribution], 'Lettre à l'auteur de ces feuilles au sujet d'un livre intitulé, *Considérations sur la diversité du génie des nations, etc.*', *Année littéraire*, 1770, i. 348.

[2] Jean-Louis Castilhon, *Considérations sur les causes physiques et morales de la diversité du génie, des mœurs et du gouvernement des nations* (Bouillon: aux dépens de la Société typographique, 1769), x–xi.

[3] Anonymous, review of Jean-Louis Castilhon, *Considérations sur les causes physiques et morales de la diversité du génie, des mœurs et du gouvernement des nations*, in *Journal encyclopédique*, 1 July 1769, 148.

168

published a flattering review of the *Considérations*. Its anonymous author explicitly stressed the many differences with the *Esprit*, even arguing that the two books reached very different conclusions about the causes shaping national character.[4] The quarrel dragged on, however, so much so that the *Correspondance littéraire* commented with bitter sarcasm on the whole affair.[5] The letter that sparked the dispute may have been written by the author of the *Esprit* itself, the abbé François-Ignace d'Espiard de la Borde (1707–1777), advisory clerk to the *Parlement* of Bourgogne and member of the Société Physique et Littéraire of Dijon.[6] A learned and passionate scholar, the abbé only published two works in his lifetime, the *Essai sur le génie et les caractères des nations*, and the *Esprit des nations*, the latter being a revised and extended version of the former. As for their circulation, the case is far from clear. In a letter to her friend François-Antoine Devaux (1712–1796), Madame de Graffigny declared herself pleased that he was enjoying the *Esprit*, the book of a 'little-known abbé' whose works had 'never enjoyed much success'.[7] To a degree de Graffigny's observation was unjust. Admittedly, the circulation of the *Essai* was limited, not least because the copies that d'Espiard attempted to smuggle in from the Low Countries were seized by the French authorities.[8] And yet the *Esprit* enjoyed a measure of success – if short-lived. A second edition was published in 1753 and translations into English and German appeared in 1753 and 1754 respectively.

---

[4] Anonymous, review of Jean-Louis Castilhon, *Considérations sur les causes physiques et morales de la diversité du génie, des mœurs et du gouvernement des nations*, in *Journal encyclopédique*, 1 August 1770, 332. It might be worth noting that Castilhon himself was a key contributor to the *Journal encyclopédique*. On Castilhon, see Maurice Caillet, 'Un ami des Lumières: Jean Castilhon', in Etienne Dennery (ed.), *Humanisme actif: Mélanges d'art et de littérature offerts à Julien Cain* (Paris: Herrmann, 1968), ii. 21–35.

[5] Grimm et al., *Correspondance littéraire*, ix. 182–3 (December 1770).

[6] On the abbé's character and his personal qualities, see the opinion of the president of the audit chamber of Dijon, Gilles-Germain Richard de Ruffey (1706–1794), in his *Histoire secrète de l'Académie de Dijon (de 1741 à 1770)* (Paris: Hachette, 1909), 114. For d'Espiard's ideas about national character, see: Ira O. Wade, *The Structure and Form of the French Enlightenment* (Princeton: Princeton University Press, 1977), i. 448–53; Bell, *The Cult of the Nation in France*, 140–9, and Huchette, *La gaieté, caractère français?*, especially 93–5. Interestingly, the *Esprit* was plagiarised by the Irish novelist, poet, and essayist Oliver Goldsmith (1730–1774): Michael Griffin, 'Oliver Goldsmith and François-Ignace Espiard de la Borde: An Instance of Plagiarism', *The Review of English Studies*, 50 (1999), 59–63.

[7] Françoise d'Issembourg d'Happoncourt de Graffigny to François-Antoine Devaux, 27 April 1753, in *Correspondance*, xiii. 265.

[8] Jean-Baptiste Bonardy to Jean Bouhier, 11 January 1743, in Bouhier, *Correspondance littéraire du Président Bouhier*, v. 88. Also see, Archives de la Chambre syndicale de la Librairie et Imprimerie de Paris, 'Registre des livres arrêtés dans les visites faites par les syndics et adjoints, 1742–1771' (Paris: Bibliothèque nationale de France, MS manuscrits français, 21932), 3.

The abbé's main argument was straightforward. As he saw it, the key factor shaping a nation's character was its climate. This was 'the most universal, most intimate physical cause' that scholars should consider when seeking the causes of a people's habits, attitudes, and beliefs.[9] Consistently, he claimed that Rome owed its greatness to its mild climate, that France, sharing that climate, could boast the same fortune, or that the northern peoples, because of their harsh and inclement weather, were better suited to war.[10] To an extent, d'Espiard's book might seem to be a vast and well-informed comparison of usages, customs, and histories of nations from all over the world – and, at times, of common national stereotypes – explained through climatic differences. Associating the *Esprit* with a form of determinism might be simple enough. Yet, at a second glance, things are more complex. One first element worthy of note was that the abbé believed that to gain an exact knowledge of a nation's climate, it was necessary to know the surface and fertility of its lands, the temperature of the air, the kind of vegetables and fruits its lands produced, the minerals and resources it possessed, the direction and strength of the winds, the quality of waters, and even which goods were imported from other countries.[11] Cleary, it was a particularly broad understanding of climate, referring to the morphology of a nation rather than to its weather in the narrow sense. A second element, which also brings out the complexity of d'Espiard's ideas, is his curious statement that 'climates are not always immutable: sometimes they are altered by changes in nature itself or by dint of human industry'. Indeed, he argued, immense forests had been cleared in France and Germany, thus providing vast territories for cultivation, and in China, Persia, and throughout Europe canals had been built and so, thanks to man's ingenuity, barren soil had been turned into fertile fields. In these as in countless other examples, the lives of thousands of men and women had been radically improved and the character of their nation had thereby been changed.[12] If one were to fail to take the volitions and deeds of man into account, the abbé went on, it would be impossible to explain, for example, how the English, with their notoriously bad weather, could ever have developed their commerce, their great political institutions, how they could possibly have built such a vast empire and, most remarkably, how they

---

[9] François-Ignace d'Espiard de la Borde, *L'esprit des nations* (The Hague: Beauregard, 1752), i. 4. It might be useful to note that, throughout the eighteenth century, 'climate' usually referred to 'a stretch of the globe placed between two parallels': Académie française, *Dictionnaire de l'Académie française*, i. 198 (s.v. 'climat'). Writing in the late 1780s, the lexicographer Jean-François Féraud (1725–1807) stated that 'climate' usually meant 'a region, a country': Féraud, *Dictionaire critique de la langue française*, ii. 461.

[10] D'Espiard de la Borde, *L'esprit des nations*, i. 44–6, and ii. 25.   [11] Ibid., i. 22–3.

[12] Ibid., i. 26–8.

could indulge in the pastime of philosophy, which is normally the preserve of peoples enjoying a mild climate.[13] Clearly, then, d'Espiard's theory implied a complex relationship between moral and physical causes, neither of which, taken individually, would serve to account for a nation's character.

In 1753, a flattering review of the *Esprit des nations* praised its author for his knowledge of the past, a quality that made of his work a 'fascinating' piece of scholarship. The review was by none other than the young Gotthold Ephraim Lessing (1729–1781). One of the reasons for Lessing's favourable appraisal was that he believed that a nation's character was essentially the product of its climate: 'There are nothing but physical causes for national differences in passions, talents, and physical skills, since what are called moral causes are nothing but the consequences of physical ones.' In reality, Lessing's praise rested on a misguided and simplistic reading of d'Espiard's work, a reading in which the importance of physical causes was overstated at best. But another blemish in Lessing's review was the conviction that so detailed a description of the nations and their characters, based on historical facts as well as personal experiences, had 'never been attempted before'.[14] Although one might agree that the *Espirit* was highly informative and rich in historical and geographical detail, Lessing's praise for the originality of the work, made out to be the first consistent attempt to explain national differences through climate, went too far. If we look beyond d'Espiard's method in treating the subject and his recognition of the complexity of the relationship between geographical factors, *mœurs*, and politics, then many of his arguments were far from new. That the nature of a people as well as its institutions were strongly influenced by climate had been an important claim in the history of Western thought from Hippocrates (c. 460–c. 370 BC) and Aristotle (384–322 BC) onwards.[15]

In France, in the sixteenth and seventeenth century, Bodin expounded a popular theory of the influence of climate on the customs and usages of a nation, and Montaigne, Pascal, Boileau, La Bruyère, and Fontenelle all commented on its effects on a people's character.[16] The idea was still so widespread in the latter part of the seventeenth century that, in 1685, the

---

[13] Ibid., ii. 164–5.

[14] Gotthold Ephraim Lessing, review of [François-Ignace d'Espiard de la Borde], *L'esprit des nations* (1753), in *Werke und Briefe* (Frankfurt: Deutscher Klassiker, 1985–), ii. 475.

[15] For a history of climate theory, see Mario Pinna, *La teoria dei climi: Una falsa dottrina che non muta da Ippocrate a Hegel* (Rome: Società Geografica Italiana, 1988).

[16] Jean Bodin, *Les six livres de la république* (1576) (Paris: Fayard, 1986), v. 7–57; Nicolas Boileau, 'Art Poétique' (1674), in *Œuvres*, 171; Montaigne, *Les essais*, 575 (book ii. ch. 12); Pascal, *Pensées*, 94 (§ 56); La Bruyère, 'Les caractères ou les mœurs de ce siècle', 240; Bernard de Fontenelle, 'Digressions sur les anciens et les modernes' (1688), in *Œuvres*, ii. 141–6.

critic Adrien Baillet (1649–1706) remarked in his monumental *Jugements des Savants* (1685–1686) on the resilience of such a misconception, taking it upon himself to show how the effects of climate upon a nation's *génie* were overstated.[17] Yet, notwithstanding Baillet's best efforts, the assumption continued to inform the works of many eighteenth-century French authors.[18] So, in his important study of Persia, the Near East, and the Muslim world, the traveller Jean Chardin (1643–1713) used climate to explain the differences between the East and the European world, holding it in large part responsible for the alleged despotism of the Orient.[19] A few years later, the philologist Jean-Baptiste Bullet (1699–1775) made of climate, along with migrations, one of the main reasons for differences between languages and dialects.[20] The abbé de Saint-Pierre, the abbé Prévost, and Maupertuis, if in different ways and with various intentions, all believed that climate played a central role in the shaping of a people's character and ways of life.[21] In 1787, Marmontel likewise argued that differences in climate helped to explain differences in the characters of nations.[22] In an unusual book published in 1748, *La psycantropie, ou Nouvelle théorie de l'homme*, the ex-Jesuit Camille Falconnet de la Bellonie (1720?–1750?) went further than most scholars. Trying to prove the moral superiority of the French, he argued that virtue changed according to the weather and the winds, almost 'increasing or

[17] Adrien Baillet, *Jugemens des savans sur les principaux ouvrages des auteurs* (Hildesheim: G. Olms, 1971), i. 76–8. See Raymond Naves, 'Un adversaire de la théorie des climats au XVIIᵉ siècle: Adrien Baillet', *Revue d'histoire littéraire de la France*, 43 (1936), 430–3.

[18] On the theory of climate in the eighteenth century, Roger Mercier, 'La théorie des climats des "Réflexions critiques" à "L'Esprit des lois"', *Revue d'histoire littéraire de la France*, 53 (1953), 17–37 and 159–75; Ehrard, *L'idée de nature en France dans la première moitié du XVIIIᵉ siècle*, 691–717; Clarence J. Glacken, *Traces on the Rhodian Shore: Nature and Culture in Western Thought from Ancient Times to the End of the Eighteenth Century* (Berkeley: University of California Press, 1967), 551–622; Pinna, *La teoria dei climi*, passim; Gonthier-Louis Fink 'De Bouhours à Herder: La théorie française des climats et sa réception Outre-Rhin', *Recherches germaniques*, 15 (1985), 3–62; Giuliano Gliozzi, 'L'insormontabile natura: Clima, razza, progresso', in Gliozzi, *Differenze e uguaglianza nella cultura europea moderna: Scritti, 1966–1991* (Naples: Vivarium, 1993), 307–40. Also see, Jean-François Staszak and Marie-Dominique Couzinet, 'À quoi sert la 'théorie des climats'? Éléments d'une histoire du déterminisme environnemental', *Corpus: Revue de philosophie*, 34 (1998), 9–43.

[19] Jean Chardin, *Voyages de Monsieur le Chevalier Chardin en Perse et autres lieux de l'Orient* (Amsterdam: J.-L. de Lorme, 1711), iv. 116.

[20] Jean-Baptiste Bullet, *Mémoires sur la langue celtique* (Besançon: Daclin, 1754–1760), i. 6–7.

[21] Saint-Pierre, 'Projet pour perfectioner le comerse de France', 209, and Charles-Irénée Castel de Saint-Pierre, 'Discours contre le Mahométisme' (1733), in *Ouvrajes de politique*, v. 113; Prévost et al., *Le pour et le contre*, 3 (1734), 159–61; Pierre-Louis Moreau de Maupertuis, 'Relation d'un voyage fait dans la Laponie septentrionale, pour trouver un ancien monument' (1747), in Osmo Pekonen and Anouchka Vasak (eds.), *Maupertuis en Laponie: A la recherche de la figure de la Terre* (Paris: Hermann, 2014), 201.

[22] Marmontel, *Éléments de littérature*, 723–4.

diminishing like a thermometer'.[23] Of course, such views did not go unchallenged, especially in the eighteenth century. And while in England Hume raised doubts, but admitted that he was unsure, in Spain, the great scholar and philosopher Friar Benito Feijóo (1676–1764) denounced in no uncertain terms the idea that climate determined a people's character. In France, among others, Rollin and the abbé Desfontaines (1685–1745) also rejected the notion.[24] However, in the 1740s the belief was still so widespread that the *Journal de Trévoux* declared that the 'overall thesis cannot be contested' – though it admitted that as regards the ways it was used 'not all will agree'.[25]

Importantly for us, climatic theories also entered debates over the origins of France. In fact, a key figure in the confrontation between Romanists and Germanists was also one of the most ardent and controversial advocates of the importance of climate in the shaping of a nation's *mœurs*. In his highly praised *Réflexions critiques sur la poésie et la peinture* (1719), reiterating the platitude that 'each people, just as each single individual, has its character', the abbé Dubos made the claim that the explanation for the differences between national characters, passions, inclinations, and taste had to be sought in differences of climate, air, and soil. He was adamant that therein lay the root of a person's as well as a people's ways of life. Indeed, 'our spirit marks the present state of the air with an exactitude close to that of our barometers and thermometers'.[26] Therefore, to understand why, in the space of a few generations, settlers came to resemble those who had inhabited a country before them and with whom they had no genealogical tie, it was to climate, which he defined in rather broad terms, that one had to turn.[27] Neither race nor blood were responsible for the different traits: '[C]limate is more powerful than blood and origin', insisted the abbé.[28] To make his point, Dubos even considered

---

[23] Camille Falconnet de la Bellonie, *La psycantropie, ou Nouvelle théorie de l'homme* (Avignon: Chambeau, 1748), iii. 14.

[24] Hume, 'Of National Characters', 115 and 119–20; Benito Jerónimo Feijóo, 'Mapa intelectual y cotejo de naciones' (1728), in Feijóo, *Teatro crítico universal o Discursos varios en todo género de materias para desengaño de errores comunes* (Madrid: Castalia, 1986), 192–3 (book ii, § 9); Charles Rollin, *De la manière d'enseigner et d'étudier les belles-lettres* (Paris: Estienne, 1726–1728), i. p. vi–vii; [Pierre-François Guyot Desfontaines], review of Jean-George Le Franc de Pompignan, *Essai critique sur l'état présent de la République des lettres*, in *Jugemens sur quelques ouvrages nouveaux*, 2 (1744), 122–3.

[25] Anonymous, review of Claude-Marie Guyon, *Histoire des Amazones anciennes et modernes*, in *Journal de Trévoux, ou Mémoires pour servir à l'histoire des sciences et des arts*, April 1741, 681.

[26] Jean-Baptiste Dubos, *Réflexions critiques sur la poésie et la peinture* (Paris: Beaux-arts de Paris éditions, 2015), 387. For an overview of Dubos's theory of climate, see Lombard, *L'abbé Du Bos*, 248–54, and Armin Hajman Koller, *The Abbé du Bos: His Advocacy of the Theory of Climate. A Precursor of Johann Gottfried Herder* (Champaign, Ill: Garrard Press, 1937).

[27] Dubos, *Réflexions critiques sur la poésie et la peinture*, 384–402.   [28] Ibid., 398.

the history of ancient France. He claimed that although most Frenchmen who had settled in Gaul were descended from the Germanic tribes, their inclinations and character resembled those of the Gauls – and this for the simple reason that they had been moulded by the Gallic and French climate. A people's origins seemed of secondary importance. Dubos found proof of his claim in the accounts of Caesar and Livy (c. 59 BC – c. 17 CE), and by comparing the characters of ancient Gauls and the modern French. In fact, both possessed a 'surprising industriousness', which enabled the Gauls to imitate the most complex war machines of the Roman army; both shared an 'insurmountable propensity to gaiety'; and both had a remarkably warlike demeanour.[29] Obviously, such a scheme suffered from the deep-seated contradiction between the weight given to climate and context on the one hand, and the need to explain the rise of extraordinary artists and great geniuses on the other, a central preoccupation of the *Réflexions*.[30] But, still more remarkably, the importance Dubos ascribed to climate clashed with any sort of genealogical approach to history. It clashed, in short, with any notion of race and blood. In fact, the abbé saw the Gallo-Romans and the French as the same people not because of common origins; nor because, through blood, the former had passed on to the latter their character and inclinations; but simply because they lived under the same unvarying climate.

Crucially – and perhaps surprisingly – another key figure in the debates over the nation's origins, and the fiercest advocate of the Germanist thesis, pondered the impact of climate on a people's *génie*. In a work that may have been written in 1711, the *Astrologie mondiale*, the Count de Boulainvilliers argued for a rather curious blending of climatic and astrological determinism, explaining that the character of some civilisations was influenced by longitude as well as the stars.[31] This was an original view at variance with more traditional climatic theories. A few years later, in his famous *La vie de Mahomet*, possibly written between 1718 and 1721, the count made a fleeting and yet significant remark on the alleged fanaticism of the Islamic religion, claiming it to be a product of the harsh climate and the consequent aridity of the soil and scarcity of food.[32] Even more interesting are the remarks in his

[29] Ibid., 395–7.

[30] The contradiction was noted, with heavy sarcasm, by Helvétius, *De l'esprit*, 412.

[31] Henri de Boulainvilliers, *Astrologie mondiale, histoire du mouvement de l'apogée du soleil ou Pratique des règles d'astrologie pour juger des événements généraux* (written in 1711) (Garches: Éditions du nouvel humanisme, 1949), 191–3.

[32] Henri de Boulainvilliers, *La vie de Mahomet* (London: n.p., 1730), 149. For the dating: Diego Venturino, 'Un prophète "philosophe"? Une *Vie de Mahomet* à l'aube des Lumières', *Dix-huitième siècle*, 24 (1992), 321, n. 1.

État de la France, where Boulainvilliers mused about the different climates of the regions of France. As he saw it, the climate of Champagne was 'rather mild and the character of the people, which is normally a consequence, is equally temperate, pleasant, polite, and obedient'.[33] The weather of Bourbonnais was also mild and the character of its people likewise gentle and placid. In contrast, noted Boulainvilliers, since Nivernais was particularly cold, its 'people are more hard-hearted, prouder, and less accommodating'.[34] Here, the weight of context was seemingly at odds with the count's genealogical explanation of a people's character.

Discussions regarding the relationship between climate and a nation's character, in the first half of the eighteenth century, were so commonplace that they could be plucked out of studies almost at will. It is perhaps more interesting to note that the mid-century witnessed a turn in the way the relationship was conceived. Not only were the arguments more sophisticated – and, in this, d'Espiard was surely a forerunner. But, moreover, increasing attention was paid to how politics might favour or counter the effects of climate in the shaping of a nation's *mœurs*. Such a shift at once prompted and, in turn, was influenced by one of the greatest masterpieces of Enlightenment thought, a work that, furthermore, was key to the debates over the origins of the French nation. According to Robert Shackleton, with the sole exception of Montesquieu's theory on the separation of powers, no other doctrine was more influential or attracted more attention than his theory of climate.[35] Indeed, right from the start the latter was central to the quarrel over the *Esprit des lois*. In 1749, the Jansenist

[33] Boulainvilliers, *État de la France*, i. 190. On Boulainvilliers's views about the effects of climate on the peoples inhabiting the different parts of France, see Simon, *Henry de Boulainviller*, 218–26.
[34] Boulainvilliers, *État de la France*, ii. 218.
[35] Robert Shackleton, 'The Evolution of Montesquieu's Theory of Climate', *Revue internationale de philosophie*, 9 (1955), 317. On the baron's theory of climate, also see, Georges Benrekassa, *La politique et sa mémoire* (Paris: Payot, 1983), 205–56; Salvatore Rotta, 'Quattro temi dell'*Esprit des lois*', *Miscellanea storica ligure*, 20 (1988), 1347–407; Jean-Patrice Courtois, 'Le physique et le moral dans la théorie du climat de Montesquieu', in Caroline Jacot-Grapa et al. (eds.), *Le travail des Lumières: Pour Georges Benrekassa* (Paris: Honoré Champion, 2002), 139–56; Carlo Borghero, 'Libertà e necessità: Clima ed "Esprit général" nell'*Esprit des lois*', in Domenico Felice (ed.), *Libertà, necessità e storia: Percorsi dell'*Esprit des lois *di Montesquieu* (Naples: Bibliopolis, 2003), 137–201; John C. O'Neal, 'Pour une mappemonde de l'âme: Les effets du climat sur la culture d'une nation dans *L'Esprit des lois* de Montesquieu', in Jean Dagen et al. (eds.), *Morales et politique* (Paris: Honoré Champion, 2005), 247–69; Denis de Casabianca, *Montesquieu: De l'étude des sciences à l'Esprit des lois* (Paris: Honoré Champion, 2008), especially 445–90; Catherine Larrère, 'Montesquieu et l'espace', in Thierry Paquot and Chris Younès (eds.), *Espace et lieu dans la pensée occidentale: De Platon à Nietzsche* (Paris: la Découverte, 2012), 147–69; Richard Spavin, *Les climats du pouvoir: Rhétorique et politique chez Bodin, Montesquieu et Rousseau* (Oxford: Voltaire Foundation, 2018), especially 117–68; Rolando Minuti, *Studies on Montesquieu – Mapping Political Diversity* (Cham: Springer, 2018), 1–20.

periodical the *Nouvelles ecclésiastiques*, complaining in two articles over the book's lack of religious sentiment, accused it of Spinozist subversion because everything was held to derive from climate rather than God's will. A similar rebuke was to be found in the *Journal de Trévoux*.[36] The wit Gimat de Bonneval (1711–1783), in his satirical *L'esprit de l'Esprit des lois*, sardonically insisted that Montesquieu explained politics, religion, and *mœurs* entirely through climate: 'It is possible, in the century we are in / by the sole inclination of the sun / to estimate the value of men .... Climate is the only judge / of gods and governments.' The poet, dramatist, and critic the abbé de la Porte (1714–1779) also lamented that in *L'Esprit des lois* 'it is climate that produces everything, that decides everything'.[37] Even some central figures of the Enlightenment accused Montesquieu of having fallen prey to climatic determinism. In discussing the relationship between climate and legislation, the Count Algarotti (1712–1764) commented that: 'Nobody was a greater advocate of the physical cause than the famous Montesquieu, according to whom the empire of climate is the greatest of all empires. It is the hinge around which states turn. ... As it was said that Malebranche saw everything in God, so Montesquieu saw everything in climate.' For the Marquis d'Argenson, there was no possible justification for Montesquieu's 'obstinacy over climate'. It was a 'folly to believe that climate influences the *mœurs* of men'.[38] Also Voltaire, who particularly enjoyed contradicting the baron, condemned him for having pushed the climate theory 'further than Dubos, Chardin, and Bodin'.[39] Ridiculing the conclusions that Montesquieu had reached from observing the changes in a sheep's tongue occasioned by changes in temperature,

[36] Anonymous, review of Charles-Louis Secondat de Montesquieu, *De l'Esprit des lois*, in *Nouvelles ecclésiastiques*, 9 October 1749, 163 and 16 October 1749, 166. [Pierre Joseph Plesse], 'Lettre au P. B. J. sur le livre intitulé *L'Esprit des lois*', *Journal de Trévoux, ou Mémoires pour servir à l'histoire des sciences et des arts*, April 1749, 723–4 and 728–9. On the criticism levelled against the *Esprit des lois*, see the texts in: Catherine Volpilhac-Auger (ed.), *Montesquieu: Mémoire de la critique* (Paris: Presses de l'Université de Paris-Sorbonne, 2003).

[37] Jean-Baptiste Gimat de Bonneval, 'L'esprit de *L'Esprit des lois*', in Volpilhac-Auger (ed.), *Montesquieu*, 103–4; [Joseph de la Porte], *Observations sur l'Esprit des loix, ou L'art de lire ce livre, de l'entendre et d'en juger* (Amsterdam: Pierre Mortier, 1751), 81.

[38] Francesco Algarotti, 'Saggio sopra la questione se le qualità varie de' popoli originate siano dallo influsso del clima, ovveramente dalla virtù della legislazione' (1762), in *Saggi* (Bari: Laterza, 1963), 371–2. The comparison with Malebranche had already been made, though with a laudatory intent, by Pierre-Jean Grosley, a fervent admirer of Montesquieu, in his *De l'influence des loix sur les mœurs, mémoire présenté à la Société royale de Nancy* (Nancy: Hæner, 1757), 6; René-Louis de Voyer de Paulmy d'Argenson, 'Apologie de l'*Esprit des lois*, ou réponse aux observations de l'abbé Delaporte' (1751), in *Mémoires et journal inédit*, v. 118.

[39] Voltaire, 'Dictionnaire philosophique', xviii. 199. On Voltaire's criticism, see Domenico Felice, 'Voltaire lettore e critico dell'"Esprit des lois"', in Felice (ed.), *Montesquieu e i suoi interpreti* (Pisa: ETS, 2005), i. 177–81.

Voltaire remarked that such an experiment could never explain 'why the quarrel between the empire and the priesthood scandalised and stained Europe with blood for over six hundred years'.[40] Turgot regretted that Montesquieu, 'one of the greatest minds of our century', had embraced such a theory. A few years later, the Count de Volney (1757–1820) sarcastically asked what, in the baron's opinion, would be the precise temperature that would make a country free.[41] More articulate were the arguments that the philosopher Antoine Destutt de Tracy (1754–1836) later formulated in his *Commentaire sur* L'Esprit des lois (1819). According to the eminent *idéologue*, Montesquieu's theory had several flaws. The first was that the definition of climate, since it referred only to the latitude and temperature of a region, omitted important elements of 'a country's physical constitution'.[42] The second, more pertinent flaw was that Montesquieu had underestimated the degree to which men could adapt to their environment. Skill, will, and capacity might free them from physical wants, creating new moral and intellectual needs. In other words, argued Destutt de Tracy, 'the more civilised a man is, the weaker becomes the sway of climate'.[43] Although Destutt de Tracy judged Montesquieu to have exaggerated the effects of climate, he did also himself believe that physical factors played an important role in the life of a nation, so much so that he had to 'agree with Montesquieu, that *bad legislators are those who favour the vices of climate, while good ones are those who oppose them*'.[44]

However, things were more complex than the great *idéologue* had supposed. The views expressed in the *Esprit des lois* regarding the effects of climate upon a nation's religion, arts, commerce, institutions, laws, and character were the outcome of a long period of intellectual gestation – one, in fact that stretched throughout Montesquieu's entire scholarly life. It was an interest that had already emerged in his 'Sur la différence des génies',

---

[40] François-Marie Arouet de Voltaire, 'Commentaire sur l'*Esprit des lois*' (1777), in *Œuvres*, xxx, 456–7. The experiment is described in Montesquieu, 'De l'Esprit des lois', 474–7 (book xiv. ch. 2). On this, see Renato Giuseppe Mazzolini, 'Dallo "spirito nerveo" allo "spirito delle leggi": Un commento alle osservazioni di Montesquieu su una lingua di pecora', in Giles Barber and C. P. Courtney (eds.), *Enlightenment Essays in Memory of Robert Shackleton* (Oxford: Voltaire Foundation, 1988), 205–21.

[41] Anne-Robert-Jacques Turgot, 'Recherches sur les causes des progrès et de la décadence des sciences et des arts' (1748), in *Œuvres* (ed. Schelle), i. 140. Constantin-François Volney, *Voyage en Syrie et en Égypte* (1787) (Paris: Fayard, 1998), 598.

[42] Antoine-Louis-Claude Destutt de Tracy, *Commentaire sur l'*Esprit des lois *de Montesquieu* (Paris: Vrin, 2016), 205. On Destutt de Tracy's remarks, see Borghero, 'Libertà e necessità', 143–5.

[43] Destutt de Tracy, *Commentaire sur l'*Esprit des lois *de Montesquieu*, 205.

[44] Ibid., 206; italics in the text. The reference was to Montesquieu, 'De l'Esprit des lois', 479–80 (book xiv. ch. 5).

a paper read to the Académie of Bordeaux on 25 August 1717. Although it remained unpublished and although the Académie did not keep written records, excerpts can be found in Montesquieu's *Pensées*.[45] Moreover, parts were inserted into another work, the *Essai sur les causes qui peuvent affecter les esprits et les caractères*, possibly written between 1734 and 1736 and, which, in turn, served as a quarry when Montesquieu returned to the topic in the *Esprit des lois*.[46] In the *Essai sur les causes*, he began by setting out a distinction between the moral and the physical causes shaping the character of men and nations. It was a point already hinted at in the *Lettres persanes* and in the *Considérations sur les causes de la grandeur des Romains* (1734), and yet only explained in the *Essai sur les causes*.[47] The essay was divided into two parts. The first one dealt with the physical causes, which included the climate, the nature and temperature of the air, the quality of the soil, the strength of the winds, the height of mountains, and so forth. According to Montesquieu, the influence of these elements on men and women was transmitted through fibres that, acting on the internal organs, provoked a response to the external impulses of the air. The baron made the case that all ideas, perceptions, and memories were the product of sensations that external objects transmitted to the soul through nerve fibres. The condition of these, their greater or lesser flexibility, their consistency, and quality influenced perceptions. To make his point, Montesquieu used a striking metaphor:

> The soul is, in our body, like a spider in its web. It cannot move without shaking one of the threads that are extended at a distance, and similarly, none of these threads can be stirred without moving the spider. It may not touch one of these threads without moving another, which responds to this action. The more these threads are extended, the better the spider is warned. If there are some slack threads, the communication will be less good from

---

[45] See, for example, Montesquieu, 'Mes pensées', 1013–4 (§ 181 and § 182). See Catherine Volpilhac-Auger, 'La dissertation *Sur la différence des génies*: Essai de reconstitution', *Revue Montesquieu*, 4 (2000), 226–37.

[46] The *Essai* was first published in 1892. On its dating and content, see Guillaume Barrera, 'Introduction: *Essai sur les causes qui peuvent affecter les esprits et les caractères*', in *Œuvres* (ed. Société Montesquieu), ix. 205–17. Also see, Melvin Richter, 'An Introduction to Montesquieu's "An Essay on the Causes that May Affect Men's Minds and Characters"', *Political Theory*, 4 (1976), 132–8, and Domenico Felice, 'Introduzione', in Charles-Louis Secondat de Montesquieu, *Saggio sulle cause che possono agire sugli spiriti e sui caratteri* (Pisa: ETS, 2004), 1–33. Shackleton went as far as to claim that the *Essai* served as a 'storehouse of ideas' later used in the *Esprit*: Shackleton, *Montesquieu*, 314–5.

[47] Montesquieu, 'Lettres persanes', 299 (letter 113), and Charles-Louis Secondat de Montesquieu, 'Considérations sur les causes de la grandeur des Romains et de leur décadence', in *Œuvres* (ed. Caillois), ii. 173.

this thread to the spider, or from this thread to another thread and the spider's system will be reduced to almost nothing.[48]

The condition of the nerve fibres, Montesquieu went on to argue, was deeply affected by the environment, so that if in colder regions these were more contracted and less sensitive, the opposite was true in warmer regions. It was on such a reasoning that the Baron de la Brède argued that differences in the physical condition of men – which, in turn, were affected by their environment – shaped their different characters and attitudes. In effect, the metaphor used by Montesquieu, rooted in Stoic thought and popular at that time, was meant to show that the outside world could only be reached through a web of sensations that allowed a person to gain awareness of himself and form his own consciousness.[49] This connection of the external world with the centre, of the physical environment with the soul, through fibres and nerves, so seemingly mechanistic in nature, was based on the Cartesian distinction between *res extensa* and *res cogitans* interacting with a sensist and materialist representation of man's place in his world.[50] Such a reading allowed physical causes and their effects to be almost quantified and understood scientifically, relating, as it did, the environment to a person's mind in medical terms. In this respect, as has been noted, the *Essai sur les causes* may well be the 'connecting link' between Montesquieu's science of the physical world and his science of society.[51] Indebted to the writings of the Spanish physician Juan Huarte (1592–1588) and the Scottish physician John Arbuthnot (1667–1735), through this description, apparently 'more medical than geographical', Montesquieu sought to offer a tool for explaining the extraordinary variety of national characters.[52] In effect, the baron was arguing that since the same

---

[48] Charles-Louis Secondat de Montesquieu, 'Essai sur les causes qui peuvent affecter les esprits et les caractères', in *Œuvres* (ed. Caillois), ii. 49. On this, see Felice, 'Introduzione', 16–23.

[49] Catherine Glyn Davies, *Conscience as Consciousness: The Idea of Self-awareness in French Philosophical Writing from Descartes to Diderot* (Oxford: Voltaire Foundation, 1990), 126. On the meaning of this metaphor in eighteenth-century thought, see Georges Poulet, *Les métamorphoses du cercle* (Paris: Plon, 1961), 78–82. Also see, Isabelle Moreau, 'L'araignée dans sa toile: Mise en images de l'âme du monde de François Bernier et Pierre Bayle à l'*Encyclopédie*', in Moreau (ed.), *Les Lumières en mouvement: La circulation des idées au XVIIIᵉ siècle* (Lyons: ENS éditions, 2009), 199–228. Unfortunately, Moreau does not mention Montesquieu.

[50] The point is made by Minuti, *Studies on Montesquieu*, 8. Denis de Casabianca has argued, in his reading of Montesquieu's *Essai*, for a radical overcoming of the Cartesian dichotomy: Casabianca, *Montesquieu*, 756–7 and 780–1.

[51] Sergio Cotta, *Montesquieu e la scienza della società* (Turin: Ramella, 1953), 94.

[52] Catherine Larrère, 'Galiani, lecteur de Montesquieu', in Jean-Louis Jam (ed.), *Éclectisme et cohérences des Lumières* (Paris: Nizet, 1992), 101–2; also see, Judith N. Shklar, *Montesquieu* (Oxford: Oxford University Press, 1987), 94–5. On the debt towards the two scholars, Shackleton, *Montesquieu*, 306–7.

physical causes acted on all members of a nation, they would end up having a similar physical constitution and, by the same token, many common traits in their ways of thinking and acting. Indeed, Montesquieu was among the many who believed that every nation possessed its own character and that this was the product of physical causes, 'which depend on climate', and moral causes. To the latter he would devote the second part of the *Essai*.[53]

According to the baron, moral causes included laws, politics, religion, customs, traditions, and, not least, education. And the latter played a central role in shaping a person's being. As he phrased it, insofar as education 'increases the emotions of the soul, refines our faculties, allows us to find those slight and delicate differences which are imperceptible to those unluckily born or educated'. Teachers and educators, those 'builders of ideas', were clearly instrumental in providing 'us with new ways of being and of perceiving'. Education allowed the 'perfect unity' of mind and body which was commonly found, according to Montesquieu, in civilised societies.[54] Indeed, the definition of education he offered was so broad as to include a person's acquaintances as well as his readings, experiences acquired through travel, the judgements of others, and even the desire to maintain a good reputation.[55] These elements pertained to what Montesquieu called 'private education' and, of course, differed for each single individual. 'Public education', as he understood it, was, however, the same for all members of a nation and concerned its *mœurs*, shared traditions, and religion. To these, the baron also added 'that certain emanation of the way of thinking, the atmosphere, and the foolishness of the court and of the capital, which spreads itself far and wide'.[56] The two forms of education, private and public, interacted in complex and unpredictable ways. But while the former, through its very nature, encouraged differences between individuals, the latter had the opposite effect. In fact, since it was common to all members of a community, it encouraged those shared feelings and ways of being that formed the nation's character. Therefore, Montesquieu saw education as a twofold and even contradictory process of differentiation and generalisation.[57]

---

[53] Montesquieu, 'Essai sur les causes', 58.

[54] Ibid., 54. On the place of education in Montesquieu's works, especially the *Esprit*, see Diana J. Schaub, 'The Regime and Montesquieu's Principles of Education', in David W. Carrithers and Patrick Coleman (eds.), *Montesquieu and the Spirit of Modernity* (Oxford: Voltaire Foundation, 2002), 77–100.

[55] Montesquieu, 'Essai sur les causes', 62–3.   [56] Ibid., 58.

[57] Similar claims regarding the effects of education upon a nation's character were made a few years later by Montesquieu's friend and admirer Helvétius: Helvétius, *De l'esprit*, 389–92, and Helvétius, *De l'homme*, i. 451–2.

As for the relationship between moral and physical causes, Montesquieu, while recognising the enormous 'complexity of causes shaping the general character of a people', peremptorily stated that: 'Moral causes form the general character of a nation and decide more of the quality of its mind than physical causes.'[58] It was a straightforward claim. And one that, interestingly, seemed to contradict the arguments the baron made elsewhere in his works. In the *Lettres persanes*, for example, Montesquieu wrote of the tyranny of the body over the soul.[59] The idea was reiterated throughout the *Esprit* and especially in Book XIV: 'It is the different needs in the different climates that have shaped the different ways of living, and it is these ways of living that have shaped the different kinds of laws.'[60] From such an angle, there might seem to be a discrepancy between the reasonings in the *Essai sur les causes* and those laid out by Montesquieu in his other, later works, above all the *Esprit*. Indeed, according to Ehrard, there might have been a simplification, from the *Essai* to the *Esprit*, of the arguments over climate and its influence on nations. Similarly, Georges Benrekassa has suggested that Montesquieu's ideas on the importance of physical causes grew increasingly rigid, then going on to stress the dangers this implied. But the case might prove to be more nuanced. So, for example, in his dissertation on the character of the people of Rome, the baron noticed that the force and vigour of the ancient Romans starkly contrasted with the indolence of the city's present-day inhabitants. Such a difference was explained by Montesquieu partly by the fact that the ancients took frequent baths to ward off the baleful effects of the oppressive heat. By so doing, they gave back to the nerve fibres their strength and thus countered the indolence caused by the hot weather. Habits could then correct the vices caused by climate. However, in the *Esprit*, the baron made it clear that should the ancient or natural laws be subverted by physical causes, then the good legislator ought to 'force the nature of climate' to restore the rightful order.[61] Indeed, there might be some truth in Villemain's claim that Montesquieu 'always corrects with some new truth a previous thought which seemed excessive' and that such was surely the case with his reasonings about climate.[62] But the point remains as to whether the baron's own defence of the *Esprit* as 'a perpetual triumph of the

---

[58] Montesquieu, 'Essai sur les causes', 59–60. On the relationship between moral and physical causes, see Paul A. Rahe, *Montesquieu and the Logic of Liberty: War, Religion, Commerce, Climate, Terrain, Technology, Uneasiness of Mind, the Spirit of Political Vigilance, and the Foundation of the Modern Republic* (New Haven: Yale University Press, 2009), especially 150–69.

[59] Montesquieu, 'Lettres persanes', 179 (letter 33).

[60] Montesquieu, 'De l'Esprit des lois', 483–4 (book xiv. ch. 10).   [61] Ibid., 518 (book xvi. ch. 12).

[62] Abel François Villemain, *Eloge de Montesquieu* (Paris: Didot, 1816), 31.

moral over the climate or, rather, in general, over physical causes', was simply an expedient.[63] And, perhaps even more importantly, whether Montesquieu rejected any pre-eminence of one sort of cause over the other.[64]

Montesquieu on Freedom: History and the Nation's *Moeurs*

In his 'L'influence des climats sur la civilisation', a short text possibly written between 1749 and 1754, Jean-Jacques Rousseau reflected on the role of the historian and the elements that influenced the deeds and the ideas of the men and nations that were the object of his or her studies. In his musings, the Genevan scholar attributed a crucial place to physical factors. As he put it:

> [M]an is influenced by everything that surrounds him. He depends on everything, and he becomes what this everything, from which he depends, forces him to be. The climate, soil, air, water, the produce of the land and the sea form his disposition, his character, determine his tastes, passions, ventures, and his actions of all sorts. If this is not exactly true for individuals, it is incontestably so for peoples.[65]

The short text might have been inspired by a reading of the *Esprit des lois*. Admittedly, the relationship between physical factors and national character remained a concern throughout Rousseau's later works. As he wrote in the *Contrat social*: 'Since freedom is not a fruit of all climates, it is therefore not within the reach of all peoples. The more one meditates on this principle established by Montesquieu, the more one sees its truth. The more it is criticised, the more chances are offered to confirm it by new proofs.'[66] Similar arguments were also to be found in the *Essai sur l'origine des langues*, where differences in the characters of southern and northern peoples were related to differences of climate.[67] And yet, although

---

[63] Charles-Louis Secondat de Montesquieu, 'Réponses et explications données à la faculté de théologie' (1752–1754), in *Œuvres* (ed. Caillois), ii. 1173. Montesquieu praised Hume for having granted moral causes a much greater role in the shaping of national character than physical ones: Charles-Louis Secondat de Montesquieu to David Hume, 19 May 1749, in *Œuvres* (ed. Masson), iii. 1230.

[64] Ehrard, *L'idée de nature en France dans la première moitié du XVIIIᵉ siècle*, 719–21; Georges Benrekassa, *Montesquieu: La liberté et l'histoire* (Paris: Librairie générale française, 1987), 155. Also see the arguments in Jean-Patrice Courtois, *Inflexions de la rationalité dans 'L'Esprit des lois'* (Paris: Presses universitaires de France, 1999), 5–6.

[65] Jean-Jacques Rousseau, 'L'influence des climats sur la civilisation', in *Œuvres*, iii. 530.

[66] Rousseau, 'Du contrat social', 414. That the 'Influence' might have been inspired by Montesquieu's *Esprit des lois*, is a claim made by Robert Derathé, in Rousseau, 'L'influence des climats sur la civilisation', ibid., 1533, n. 1. On Rousseau's ideas about the effects of climate on a nation's character, see Spavin, *Les climats du pouvoir*, 169–228.

[67] Jean-Jacques Rousseau, 'Essai sur l'origine des langues' (written in 1755 but published posthumously in 1781), in *Œuvres*, v. 407–10.

Rousseau recognised in his most important political treatises the weight of physical factors in shaping a people's character, in other writings there seemed to be statements contradicting such pronouncements, and a central role was given to politics instead. In his *Confessions*, for example, Rousseau argued that 'everything depended on politics and that, from whatever angle one looks at it, a people would never be more than that which the nature of the government made them'. And the best government was the one most capable of shaping a multitude into a wise, virtuous, loyal, and enlightened people. In his *Discours sur l'économie politique* (1755), Rousseau repeated the argument almost verbatim, while in *Émile*, reasoning on the differences between natural and civil man, he went so far as to claim that 'good social institutions are those that better know how to disfigure man [*dénaturer l'homme*]'. These ideas were also expounded in his *Considérations sur le gouvernement de la Pologne* and in the *Projet de constitution pour la Corse*. In the latter, he famously wrote that all 'peoples have or should have a national character and if this were missing, it would be necessary to start by giving it one', then adding that this could only be achieved through 'public education', which had the capacity to turn men into good citizens.[68] To the two seemingly contrasting viewpoints – the first one seeing in nature the main factor in shaping a people's character, the other claiming such a role for politics – another element that further complicated Rousseau's stance needs to be considered. In fact, in a long note in the *Discours sur l'origine et les fondements de l'inégalité* (1755), the Genevan scholar argued that 'cultures differ because of the powerful effects of the diversity of climates, air, food, ways of life, general habits, and, above all, the astonishing strength of the same causes acting continuously over a long succession of generations'.[69] It is the latter element that is particularly significant, for it differs radically from the others. Indeed, as David Bell has aptly pointed out when commenting on this passage, for Rousseau history was the third crucial category that, alongside politics and nature, shaped a nation's character.[70]

---

[68] Rousseau, 'Les confessions', 404–5; Jean-Jacques Rousseau, 'Discours sur l'économie politique', in *Œuvres*, iii. 251; Rousseau, 'Émile', 249; Rousseau, 'Considérations sur le gouvernement de Pologne', 960; Rousseau, 'Projet de constitution pour la Corse', 913. On this, see Kra, 'Rousseau et la politique du caractère national', passim. On Rousseau's views on the nation and national character, see also the other essays in the volume edited by Thiéry and the book by Anne Marie Cohler, *Rousseau and Nationalism* (New York: Basic Books, 1970).

[69] Jean-Jacques Rousseau, 'Discours sur l'origine et les fondements de l'inégalité parmi les hommes', 208.

[70] Bell, 'Le caractère national et l'imaginaire républicain au XVIIIᵉ siècle', 871.

Like most authors writing in the second half of the eighteenth century, Rousseau was a careful reader of the works of the Baron de La Brède, and though his ideas differed in many respects from those of his famous predecessor, there are noteworthy analogies between their views on the effects of climate on national character.[71] While a first similarity lies in the apparent tendency to oscillate between physical and moral factors, it is of yet greater interest to note that both scholars attributed to the passing of time a crucial role in the interaction of the two different kinds of causes. It is a point that the baron made even more clearly than Rousseau. In fact, in a well-known passage from Book XIX of the *Esprit*, readers were informed that

> Several things govern men: climate, religion, laws, the maxims of government, the examples of past things, *mœurs*, manners; from this, arises a general mind [*esprit général*]. To the degree that, in each nation, one of the causes acts with greater force, the other gives way to it correspondingly. Nature and climate dominate almost entirely the savages; manners govern the Chinese; laws tyrannise Japan; *mœurs* once set the tone in Sparta; the maxims of government and ancient *mœurs* set it in Rome.[72]

Commenting on this passage, Robert Shackleton has written that, according to Montesquieu, the greater the distance of a society from the moment of its origins, the 'more important are the non-physical factors in defining the general mind [*esprit*]'.[73] It might therefore be argued that when Montesquieu claimed that 'climate is the first of all empires' – one of the propositions that earned him a severe rebuke from the *Nouvelles ecclésiastiques* and from many other commentators – he was considering climate to be the first cause in a historical sense rather than the most important.[74] In truth, such a reading of the baron's work had already been suggested by Villemain when he noted that, according to Montesquieu, '[n]ature and climate dominate almost entirely savage people' while 'civilised people obey moral influences'.[75] In this understanding of the

---

[71] For a useful comparison, see Jean-Patrice Courtois, 'Le climat chez Montesquieu et Rousseau', in Emmanuel Le Roy Ladurie, Jacques Berchtold, and Jean-Paul Sermain (eds.), *L'événement climatique et ses représentations (XVIIᵉ–XIXᵉ)* (Paris: Desjonquères, 2007), 157–80. On their different views about politics in general, see Jean Ehrard, 'Rousseau et Montesquieu: Le mauvais fils réconcilié', *Annales de la société Jean-Jacques Rousseau*, 41 (1997), 57–77.

[72] Montesquieu, 'De l'Esprit des lois', 558 (book xix. ch. 4).

[73] Shackleton, *Montesquieu*, 318. Also see, on this, Domenico Felice, *Per una scienza universale dei sistemi politico-sociali: Dispotismo, autonomia della giustizia e carattere delle nazioni nell'Esprit des lois di Montesquieu* (Florence: Olschki, 2005), 141–3.

[74] Montesquieu, 'De l'Esprit des lois', 565 (book xix. ch. 14).

[75] Villemain, *Eloge de Montesquieu*, 31.

relationship between physical and moral causes, savages, who had the least control over their environment, and civilised people, who were influenced the least by physical causes, stood at either end of a continuum in which the importance of physical causes lessened as a society became more civilised.[76] Such views, vesting history and the passage of time with a crucial role, were already adumbrated in Montesquieu's *Essai sur les causes*, where he had noted that if climate contributed to the forging of a nation's character, 'the effect is not immediate and a long succession of generations is necessary to produce it'.[77] Such views also partly emerged in his *De la politique*, a short pamphlet written in 1725, where Montesquieu contended that every nation 'acquires a way of thinking which is the effect of a chain of infinite causes that multiply and combine with one another throughout the centuries'.[78] National character was then the outcome of the complex interaction of physical and moral factors and, crucially, the product of time. On the one hand, physical and moral causes always combined to influence a nation's character, so much so that neither could ever be found acting alone, in its 'pure condition'.[79] On the other hand, if a hierarchy between the two kinds of causes existed, it was not fixed or predetermined, but depended on the turns in a nation's history.

Studying the entanglement of physical and moral causes within a historical framework, preserving its complexity while making sense of it, was crucial to Montesquieu's attempts to grasp those 'necessary relationships deriving from the nature of things' – that is, the laws governing the social and historical world.[80] Book XVIII of the *Esprit*, devoted to the effects of nature on a nation's forms of rule and laws, is one of the places where the merits (and faults) of this line of thought emerge with greater clarity. One at once revealing and exemplary argument, expounded by Montesquieu in Chapter 1, was that in any country the fertility of lands 'naturally establishes subjection and dependence'. In fact, as he saw it, farmers and husbandmen were usually not particularly 'jealous of their liberty', too 'busy and too intent on their own private affairs', and more fearful of losing their wealth to pillage and war than their freedom. The

---

[76] On the image of the 'savage' in works by Montesquieu, see Catherine Larrère, 'Montesquieu et les sauvages', *Les colloques ethnologiques de Bordeaux*, 1 (1994), 59–68. On the savage as a myth and an object of inquiry in seventeenth- and eighteenth-century thought, see the classic, recently revised and republished, by Sergio Landucci, *I filosofi e i selvaggi: 1580–1780* (Turin: Einaudi, 2014).

[77] Montesquieu, 'Essai sur les causes qui peuvent affecter les esprits et les caractères', 44.

[78] Charles-Louis Secondat de Montesquieu, 'De la politique', in *Œuvres* (ed. Caillois), i. 114.

[79] Céline Spector, *Le vocabulaire de Montesquieu* (Paris: Ellipses, 2001), 6. For an example, see Montesquieu, 'De l'Esprit des lois', 574–5 (book xix. ch. 27).

[80] Ibid., 232 (book i. ch. 1).

opposite was often the case in poorer countries, with less fertile soil, where people took a keener interest in politics.[81] Following such a line of thought, in the ensuing chapter he went on to make the case that since flat and fertile lands were more prone to fall prey to covetous neighbours, and since, once people were conquered 'the spirit of liberty cannot return', there freedom was destined to dissolve. The wealth of the subdued people would serve as 'a pledge of their fidelity' and, usually, as long as they kept their goods they willingly renounced their independence. On the other hand, Montesquieu observed that peoples living in mountainous regions, 'less liable to be conquered' and more covetous of the little they possessed, would often be more anxious to 'preserve what they have' and would fight their enemies with greater conviction. The freedom they enjoyed was 'the only blessing worthy of their defence'. It was for this reason that liberty was more often found in mountainous regions – or so thought Montesquieu.[82] It is noteworthy that the baron made similar comments with regard to those peoples that, living on islands, 'relished freedom' more than those living on the mainland. Islands were usually 'of small extent' and were separated and protected by the sea from great and tyrannical empires – the reference, obviously, was to England.[83]

In all these instances, Montesquieu considered the impact of physical factors on a nation's forms of rule – and, if indirectly, on the values, beliefs, and way of life of its people. But he even went so far as to offer his readers several examples in which physical factors directly influenced a nation's character. Of particular importance was his idea that the 'barrenness of the earth renders men industrious, sober, inured to hardship, courageous, and fit for war'. Men living in countries poor in resources and with an infertile soil were in fact forced to 'procure by labour what the earth refuses to bestow spontaneously'. The condition in those lands where nature almost spontaneously offered its people all sorts of goods was very different. There, fertility and a warm or mild climate gave people, along with the gifts of nature, 'ease, effeminacy, and a certain fondness for the preservation of life'.[84] According to Montesquieu, idleness usually led to apathy and a lack of interest in politics. Love of freedom, on the contrary, he

[81] Ibid., 531 (book xviii. ch. 1). On these issues, see Thomas Casadei and Domenico Felice, 'Modi di sussistenza, leggi, costumi', in Domenico Felice (ed.), *Leggere* Lo Spirito delle Leggi *di Montesquieu* (Milan: Mimesis, 2010), i. 315–20. Also see, Jean Goldzink, *La solitude de Montesquieu: Le chef-d'œuvre introuvable du libéralisme* (Paris: Fayard, 2011), 109–10.
[82] Montesquieu, 'De l'Esprit des lois', 531–2 (book xviii. chaps. 1 and 2).
[83] Ibid., 534 (book xviii. ch. 5). Also see, Montesquieu, 'Mes pensées', 1433 (§ 1808).
[84] Montesquieu, 'De l'Esprit des lois', 533 (book xviii. ch. 4).

linked to hard work and industriousness which, in turn, were a response to the constraints imposed by nature: 'Countries are not cultivated in proportion to their fertility, but to their liberty', noted Montesquieu.[85] Partly, this was a point he had already made in the *Lettres persanes*, when arguing that 'Switzerland and Holland', surely two nations worthy of admiration for their political, economic, and cultural achievements, were the 'worst countries of Europe' if one were to consider the fertility of their soil.[86] In truth, throughout Montesquieu's writings there emerges an undisguised admiration for all those peoples that had overcome the challenges posed by nature, and an emphasis upon the positive effects that the struggle against the constraints of the environment had on individual as much as on national character. This transpires, for example, in a remarkable chapter from Book XX on the history of commerce, where Montesquieu praised the people of Marseilles who, in the face of a 'tempestuous sea' and the 'sterility of the surrounding country', living amid barbarians, had grown rich thanks to their hard work and trade. The same tone of admiration was reserved for 'Tyre, Venice, and the cities of Holland', all founded by refugees compelled by the hostile conditions of their surroundings to draw their 'subsistence from all parts of the world'.[87] Contrary to the views of many of its critics, the *Esprit* might thus be judged to be a hymn of praise to human freedom over all forms of determinism and, indeed, as the monument to the 'perpetual triumph of the moral over the climate' that Montesquieu took his masterpiece to be.[88]

A crucial issue raised by Montesquieu when reflecting upon the complex entanglement of moral with physical causes was the place of men's decisions in shaping their worlds. Since the *Esprit* was indeed 'a book of politics', understanding the modes of interaction of the political with the physical as well as with other moral causes in forming the nation's character is crucial.[89] The issue may be conveniently tackled by considering the differences that Montesquieu posited within moral causes. In fact, throughout the *Esprit*, the baron assigned a specific and distinct role to positive laws as the conscious and direct expression of the will of legislators

---

[85] Ibid., 532 (book xviii. ch. 3).   [86] Montesquieu, 'Lettres persanes', 313 (letter 122).

[87] Montesquieu, 'De l'Esprit des lois', 588–9 (book xx. ch. 5). On this, see Pierre Manent, *La cité de l'homme* (Paris: Fayard, 1994), 57–9.

[88] Montesquieu, 'Réponse et explications données à la faculté de théologie', 1173. See Ana J. Samuel, 'The Design of Montesquieu's *The Spirit of the Laws*: The Triumph of Freedom over Determinism', *American Political Science Review*, 103 (2009), 305–21.

[89] The expression is in Charles-Louis Secondat de Montesquieu to Ottaviano di Guasco, 8 August 1752, in *Œuvres* (ed. Masson), iii. 1435. Also see, Montesquieu, 'De l'Esprit des lois', 714 (book xxiv. ch. 1), and 744 (book xxv. ch. 9).

and governments. These alone had an intentional scope that made it possible to interpret their meaning by considering the aims of their authors. As the conscious and direct expression of the will of governments, they differed from all other moral causes since only through these was an intended change in the interaction of the other causes possible.[90] Of the capacity of politics to change nature Montesquieu was already fully aware in one of his early writings, the 'Projet d'histoire physique de la terre', first published in the *Nouveau Mercure* in 1719. In it, he praised the merits of those 'men who have given a new face to the earth' with canals, irrigation systems, mining, and the ploughing of lands. The same commendation was later made in the *Esprit*, where Montesquieu remarked that 'men, through good care and good laws, have made the earth more fitting to be their home'.[91] Yet when considering the possibility of intervening to influence moral causes or counter their effects, Montesquieu was far more cautious.[92] So, for example, pondering the gaiety and politesse of the French and partly imputing these to the place of women in society, the baron conceded that 'laws could be enacted to correct their *mœurs*', but he then raised doubts as to the consequences for the nation as a whole.[93] Indeed, Montesquieu was adamant that governments should always be fully aware of the many limits circumscribing any actions they might take. In the *Lettres persanes*, Usbek had famously claimed that in the few cases in which it might be necessary to change a law and counter its pernicious effects, this 'should only be done with trembling hands'.[94] From this angle, governments were far from being masters of the people they ruled and laws were 'not a pure act of power'. If changes were necessary, then the greatest 'spirit of moderation' ought to guide the hand of rulers.[95] Behind such

---

[90] See Catherine Larrère, 'Le législateur chez Montesquieu', *Il pensiero politico*, 40 (2007), 307–8.

[91] Charles-Louis Secondat de Montesquieu, 'Projet d'une histoire physique de la terre ancienne et moderne', in *Œuvres* (ed. Caillois), i. 21; Montesquieu, 'De l'Esprit des lois', 535 (book xviii. ch. 7).

[92] See Benrekassa, *Montesquieu*, 160–70.

[93] Montesquieu, 'De l'Esprit des lois', 559 (book xix. ch. 5).

[94] Montesquieu, 'Lettres persanes', 323 (letter 129); also see, Montesquieu, 'Mes pensées', 1485 (§ 1969), and Montesquieu, 'De l'Esprit des lois', 775 (book xxvi. ch. 23).

[95] Montesquieu, 'De l'Esprit des lois', 565 (book xix. ch. 14), and 865 (book xxix. ch. 1). On Montesquieu's idea of moderation, see Georges Benrekassa, 'Modéré, modération, modérantisme: Le concept de modération de l'âge classique à l'âge bourgeois', in Benrekassa, *Le langage des Lumières*, 134–40. Also see, Robert Derathé, 'La philosophie des Lumières en France: Raison et modération selon Montesquieu', *Revue internationale de philosophie*, 21 (1952), 275–93; Céline Spector, 'Montesquieu et l'histoire: Théorie et pratique de la modération', in Bertrand Binoche and Franck Tinland (eds.), *Sens du devenir et pensée de l'histoire au temps des Lumières* (Seyssel: Champ Vallon, 2000), 53–75, and Paul Carrese, *Democracy in Moderation: Montesquieu, Tocqueville, and Sustainable Liberalism* (Cambridge: Cambridge University Press, 2016), 22–49. Also see, Dennis C. Rasmussen, *The Pragmatic Enlightenment: Recovering the*

concerns was the belief that changes always entailed vast, unintended, and unanticipated consequences for, in society just as in nature, 'everything is linked and everything holds together'.[96] A great deal of knowledge and moderation were then necessary, and only the few who could penetrate at a 'single glance the state's constitution' should attempt the daunting task of changing it.[97]

Dovetailing with these concerns was a crucial aspect of Montesquieu's typology of forms of rule and his distinction between monarchy and despotism. A key element of his definition of monarchy, in fact, was that authority was always based on and restricted by a set of fundamental laws that were fixed and known by all.[98] These could not be altered without subverting the whole constitution. If, according to Montesquieu, the nature itself of monarchy as a form of rule depended on the delicate balance between the rights of the king, the nobility, and the other bodies forming the nation, the fundamental laws were, in their very immutability, the historical crystallisation of that balance – and, as such, were another crucial counterbalance to royal authority. Conversely, in the case of despotism, not only was all power in the hands of a single person but, furthermore, all laws were but 'the king's momentary will', fleeting phantasies of 'his own mind' and, as such, 'constantly changing'.[99] There was thus a clear antithesis between fixity and fluidity, between a history enshrined in the nation's fundamental laws on the one hand and the rejection of the past mirrored in the despot's volatile will on the other. But this divide, political in nature, was entwined in Montesquieu's reasoning with another distinction, at once historical and geographical.[100] In fact, the baron was convinced that modern monarchies were a consequence of the barbarian invasions that had ended the Roman Empire, rendered obsolete the republics of antiquity, and replaced virtuous citizens with free individuals pursuing their own interests. To this chasm opposing, in fact, antiquity to

Liberalism of Hume, Smith, Montesquieu, and Voltaire (Cambridge: Cambridge University Press, 2014), especially 252–8.

[96] Montesquieu, 'Mes pensées', 1057 (§ 542).

[97] Montesquieu, 'De l'Esprit des lois', 230 ('Preface'). On the 'single glance' necessary to grasp the 'whole', see Jean Starobinski, *Montesquieu* (Paris: Seuil, 1994), 27–34.

[98] On this, see Felice, *Per una scienza universale dei sistemi politico-sociali*, 7–10. On Montesquieu's interpretation of the notion of fundamental law, see Jean Ehrard, 'La notion de "loi(s) fondamentale(s)" dans l'œuvre et la pensée de Montesquieu', in Catherine Volpilhac-Auger (ed.), *Montesquieu en 2005* (Oxford: Voltaire Foundation, 2005), 267–78.

[99] Montesquieu, 'De l'Esprit des lois', 300 (book v. ch. 16); Charles-Louis Secondat de Montesquieu, 'Réflexions sur la monarchie universelle en Europe' (written in 1734 or shortly before), in *Œuvres* (ed. Caillois), ii. 24.

[100] Goldzink, *La solitude de Montesquieu*, 104–8.

modernity, Montesquieu added the geographical contrast between Asia, the place of despotism, and Europe, the home of that freedom that had originated in 'the forests' of the north.[101] Once again, climatic factors were key, for Montesquieu built this divide around the idea that warm weather made men wary and cowards – 'almost always made them slaves' – while bravery and strength were usually the product of cold weather.[102] And, he went on to argue, since in Asia there were 'no temperate zones' and very cold areas 'immediately touch upon those that are exceedingly hot', then it was inevitable that 'the strong nations are opposed to the weak; the warlike, brave, and active, people touch immediately on those that are indolent, effeminate, and timorous; the one must, therefore, conquer, and the other be conquered'. Of course, things were different in Europe, since, according to Montesquieu, here differences in climate were gradual and, therefore, 'strong nations are opposed to strong' nations and neighbouring countries 'have nearly the same courage'. This, in turn, made it difficult for one nation to subdue its neighbours. Therein, according to the baron, lay the main reason '[for] the liberty of Europe and [for] the slavery of Asia'.[103] It is perhaps worth noting that such ideas were Montesquieu's personal contribution to that liberal discourse regarding Europe that, from Machiavelli (1469–1527) onwards, would prevail – and, in the second half of the twentieth century, would be so harshly criticised.[104]

In elaborating his comparison between Europe and Asia, Montesquieu also argued for another crucial divide which, in a way, was a consequence of the above distinction. In fact, consistently with his views about climate, Montesquieu made the case that the hot weather imposed an 'indolence of the mind' upon the peoples of China, Korea, Japan, and India. This, in turn, caused laws, *mœurs*, and manners to remain unchanged over the centuries, so that these were 'today in the Orient as they were a thousand

---

[101] Montesquieu, 'De l'Esprit des lois', 407 (book, xi. ch. 6). On Montesquieu's idea of Europe, see Alberto Postigliola and Maria Grazia Bottaro Palumbo (eds.), *L'Europe de Montesquieu* (Naples: Liguori, 1995).

[102] Montesquieu, 'De l'Esprit des lois', 523 (book xvii. ch. 2).   [103] Ibid., 525–6 (book xvii. ch. 3).

[104] Niccolò Machiavelli, *Il principe* (1513) (Milan: Feltrinelli, 2004), 92–3, and Niccolò Machiavelli, 'L'arte della guerra' (1521), in Machiavelli, *L'arte della guerra; Scritti politici minori* (Rome: Salerno Editrice, 2001), 119–23. The authors contrasting Europe with Asia as the lands of freedom and slavery respectively were, of course, a target of Said's famous *Orientalism*. Said's views have been challenged by Jürgen Osterhammel in his *Die Entzauberung Asiens: Europa und die asiatischen Reiche im 18. Jahrhundert* (Munich: C.H. Beck, 1998). Montesquieu's ideas are discussed throughout Osterhammel's book. For a treatment of Montesquieu's ideas regarding the cause of cultural and political differentiations within Europe, see Pierre Bourdieu, 'Le Nord et le Midi: Contribution à une analyse de l'effet Montesquieu', *Actes de la recherche en sciences sociales*, 35 (1980), 21–5, and Roberto Dainotto, *Europe (in Theory)* (Durham, NC: Duke University Press, 2007), 52–86.

years ago'.[105] If Montesquieu saw Asia as a place of stagnant immobility and fixity, he considered things to be very different in Europe. The latter he viewed as a place of unremitting change, of the unfolding of history and, crucially, the home of freedom, however fragile.[106] In effect, the baron believed that any of the European monarchies could suffer a corruption of its 'principle', to use his own term. Each one of them could undergo a profound alteration and turn into a republic – a form that Montesquieu deemed unsuited to the modern world – or even into some form of despotic rule.[107] The fear that in some European countries political freedom was in jeopardy was present throughout the *Esprit*.[108] With regard to France, such a concern had already been expressed in many of his *Lettres persanes*, where Montesquieu made clear his concerns over the present state of his country. He did so in his remarks on the king's scorn for the ancient laws of the kingdom during the *affaire des princes légitimes* or in the capricious way he distributed pensions and titles, on a whim rather than on merit.[109] It was a point also made by Usbeck in his comments on Louis XIV's admiration for the rule of sultans.[110] Strikingly, in Montesquieu's literary masterpiece there was a clear awareness that the king's vices could hardly exist without those of his people. If Louis XIV enjoyed a power greater than that granted by the ancient constitution, it was because of the 'inexhaustible' vanity and the meekness of his subjects, always ready to follow his ever-changing tastes.[111] If he could turn into 'a great magician', making everybody believe that 'one crown is worth two' or that he could

---

[105] Montesquieu, 'De l'Esprit des lois', 479 (book xiv. ch. 4).

[106] See Montesquieu, 'Lettres persanes', 335–6 (letter 136).

[107] Montesquieu offered his famous definitions of 'principle' and 'nature' of government in 'De l'Esprit des lois', 250–1 (book iii. ch. 1). On his concerns over republics in the age of modernity, a concern that partly stemmed from his interpretation of the changing nature of commerce, see the remarks in 'De l'Esprit des lois', 252 (book iii. ch. 3). On history and corruption see Jean-Patrice Courtois, 'Temps, corruption et histoire dans *L'Esprit des lois*', in Michel Porret and Catherine Volpilhac-Auger (eds.), *Le temps de Montesquieu* (Geneva: Droz, 2002), 305–17.

[108] See, for example, Montesquieu, 'De l'Esprit des lois', 247–9 (book ii. ch. 4), 354–5 (book viii. ch. 6), and 356 (book viii. ch. 8). On the point, see Domenico Felice, 'Francia, Spagna e Portogallo: Le monarchie europee "qui vont au despotisme" secondo Montesquieu', in Postigliola and Bottaro Palumbo (eds.), *L'Europe de Montesquieu*, 283–305. Also see, Vickie B. Sullivan, *Montesquieu and the Despotic Ideas of Europe: An interpretation of* The Spirit of the Laws (Chicago: University of Chicago Press, 2017).

[109] Montesquieu, 'Lettres persanes', 267–8 (letter 92), 184 (letter 37), and 263 (letter 88). According to Roland Bonnel the *Lettres persanes* were 'a little treatise on despotism': Roland G. Bonnel, 'Le despotisme dans *Les lettres persanes*', *Studies on Voltaire and the Eighteenth Century*, 278 (1990), 89. Also see, Rolando Minuti, 'La geografia del dispotismo nelle *Lettres persanes* di Montesquieu', in Lea Campos Boralevi and Sara Lagi (eds.), *Viaggio e politica* (Florence: Firenze University Press, 2009), 135–47.

[110] Montesquieu, 'Lettres persanes', 184 (letter 37).   [111] Ibid., 165 (letter 24), and 278 (letter 99).

cure diseases through his touch, the fault lay with the French and their
naïveté.[112] Indeed, while Montesquieu summoned Louis XIV's absolutism
to appear before the tribunal of his readership, his castigation of the French
for those faults that tolerated and even nurtured his detested rule was no
less severe.[113] The important aspect, here, was that a nation's politics and
history could not be understood by looking only, or even essentially, at its
rulers. Montesquieu argued as much in his 'Réflexions sur le caractère de
quelques princes', a text possibly written in the early 1730s, implicitly but
clearly criticising all attempts to understand a nation's history by looking at
the character, inclinations, and deeds of its rulers.[114] Of course, in the
Considérations sur les Romains and the *Esprit* the baron insisted on the need
to explain history not only by taking into account the intentions, interests,
and actions of rulers but, more importantly, by considering a variety of
complex social, political, and economic causes.[115] At heart, Montesquieu
despised the idea of a single person holding sovereign power. He assumed
that insofar as a nation had rejected despotism, it would by the same token
have a history to be told and understood in terms of many different causes,
such a multiplicity of factors being taken to be a preserver of freedom.
From this angle, there was a circular relationship between Montesquieu's
ideas on history and freedom and, in turn, a close connection between
these and his rejection of all teleological readings of the past.[116]

A deeper understanding of the relationship between freedom and history, as conceived of by Montesquieu, might be reached by considering

---

[112] Ibid., 166 (letter 24). It seems that this letter infuriated Cardinal de Fleury and posed an obstacle to
Montesquieu's election to the Académie. See: Pierre-Joseph Thoulier, abbé d'Olivet to Jean
Bouhier, 11 December 1727, in Bouhier, *Correspondance littéraire du Président Bouhier*, iii. 116.

[113] See, on this Spector, *Montesquieu, les 'Lettres persanes'*, 96–112.

[114] Charles-Louis Secondat de Montesquieu, 'Réflexions sur le caractère de quelques princes et sur
quelques événements de leur vie' (circa 1730–1733), in *Œuvres* (ed. Caillois), i. 519–31. On the text,
the dating, and its content, see Sheila Mason and Catherine Volpilach-Auger, 'Introduction:
Réflexions sur le caractère de quelques princes et sur quelques événements de leur vie', in
Montesquieu, *Œuvres* (ed. Société Montesquieu), ix. 45–9, and David Carrithers, 'Montesquieu's
Philosophy of History', *Journal of the History of Ideas*, 47 (1986), 72–7. On this, also see the fleeting
remark already made in 1725 by the baron: Montesquieu, 'De la politique', 114.

[115] See Guillaume Barrera, *Les lois du monde: Enquête sur le dessein politique de Montesquieu* (Paris:
Gallimard, 2009), 29–37.

[116] See, on Montesquieu's rejection of any teleological interpretation of history, Jean-Marie Goulemot,
'Vision du devenir historique et formes de la révolution dans les *Lettres persanes*', *Dix-huitième siècle*,
21 (1989), 13–22; Carrithers, 'Montesquieu's Philosophy of History', 79–80; Bertrand Binoche,
'Montesquieu et la crise de la rationalité historique', *Revue germanique internationale*, 3 (1995), 41–2;
Casadei and Felice, 'Modi di sussistenza, leggi, costumi', 346–51. Paul Rahe, on the contrary, has
emphasised the presence of evolutionistic elements in Montesquieu's historical thought: Paul
A. Rahe, 'Was Montesquieu a Philosopher of History?', in Lorenzo Bianchi and Rolando Minuti
(eds.), *Montesquieu et les philosophies de l'histoire au XVIIIᵉ siècle* (Naples: Liguori, 2013), 71–86.

another notion that had a prominent place throughout the *Esprit*, namely, the idea of *mœurs*.[117] A first definition was offered to readers in Book XIX where, after contrasting *mœurs* and manners and drawing out the difference between the two notions, the baron noted that while the former pertained to 'inner conduct', the latter related instead to 'outward' behaviour.[118] The relationship between the two, both of which were listed as moral causes by Montesquieu, was far from straightforward. On the one hand, like other scholars of his day, the baron considered manners to be a manifestation of a nation's deep-seated dispositions.[119] On the other, he believed they were an important means for channelling, taming, and controlling a people's passions, inclinations, and *mœurs*.[120] And here, another distinction, that between *mœurs* and laws, becomes central to his argument. As he saw it, while the latter were clearly the decisions of a nation's rulers, pursuing their own political objectives, *mœurs* were instead 'habits that laws have not established' because rulers were 'unable or unwilling to establish' them. Moreover, Montesquieu went on to argue, while 'laws regulate more the actions of citizens … *mœurs* regulate more the actions of men'.[121] The distinction between men and citizens, here only hinted at, is surely intriguing and would seem to suggest a division between state and society somehow reminiscent of the classical liberal tradition.[122] And yet, again, things might be more complex. In effect Montesquieu was adamant that for laws to be effective they should work in accordance with the nation's *mœurs* since these sprung from society itself. That 'a people

[117] On this, see: Bertrand Binoche, *Introduction à* De l'esprit des lois *de Montesquieu* (Paris: Publications de la Sorbonne, 2015), 187–205; Catherine Larrère, 'Droit et mœurs chez Montesquieu', in Céline Spector and Thierry Hoquet (eds.), *Lectures de l'Esprit des lois* (Pessac: Presses universitaires de Bordeaux, 2004), 233–46; Céline Spector, *Montesquieu: Liberté, droit et histoire* (Paris: Michalon, 2010), 230–7; Raynaud, *La politesse des Lumières*, 75–80; Brian C. J. Singer, *Montesquieu and the Discovery of the Social* (Basingstoke: Palgrave Macmillan, 2013), 159–69; Céline Spector, 'L'équivoque du concept de "mœurs": La lecture althussérienne de Montesquieu', in Francesco Toto, Laetitia Simonetta, and Giorgio Bottini (eds.), *Entre nature et histoire: Mœurs et coutumes dans la philosophie moderne* (Paris: Classiques Garnier, 2017), 191–203.

[118] Montesquieu, 'De l'Esprit des lois', 566 (book xix. ch. 16). Tocqueville, writing much later, maintained the same distinction: Tocqueville, *L'Ancien régime et la Révolution*, i. 146.

[119] See the definition of manners in the *Encyclopédie*: [Denis Diderot – uncertain attribution], 'Manières, façons', in Diderot and d'Alembert (eds.), *Encyclopédie*, x. 36.

[120] Montesquieu, 'De l'Esprit des lois', 566–7 (book xix. ch. 16). On this, see Larrère, 'Droit et mœurs chez Montesquieu', 236–41.

[121] Montesquieu, 'De l'Esprit des lois', 566 (book xix. ch. 16). Also see, Montesquieu, 'De l'Esprit des lois', 564 (book xix. ch. 14).

[122] On Montesquieu's distinction between state and civil society, see Céline Spector, *Montesquieu: Pouvoirs, richesses et sociétés* (Paris: Presses universitaires de France, 2004), 166–77, and Melvin Richter, 'Montesquieu and the Concept of Civil Society', *The European Legacy*, 3 (1998), 33–41.

knows, loves, and always defends more its *mœurs* than its laws' was self-evident – or so he thought.[123] Indeed, in certain circumstances, rulers could be forced to counter the effects of *mœurs*, but such cases were rare and, moreover, when they occurred, rather than forcibly change the way people acted through laws it would be preferable to encourage them to change their conduct and habits of their own accord. Hence, should a prince act to change the *mœurs* and manners of his nation, he should do so not through laws, for this would seem 'too tyrannical', but 'through other *mœurs* and manners'.[124] The reason was that the two acted on, and belonged to, distinct planes, laws being 'established' while *mœurs* were 'inspired', noted Montesquieu.[125]

Examining the history of the concept of *mœurs* in the eighteenth century, Benrekassa has emphasised the remarkable contribution that Montesquieu made to historicising its meaning.[126] As we have seen, Fénelon, Daniel, Boulainvilliers, Fréret, Lafitau, and Dubos were among the many who, between the late seventeenth and the first half of the eighteenth century, insisted that scrutiny of a nation's *mœurs* was the key to deciphering its history.[127] In 1734, in the *Lettres philosophiques*, Voltaire offered his own original contribution, depicting the *génie* of the English by deducing it from their sciences, arts, laws, manners, and *mœurs* and, by so doing, paved the way to a new kind of history.[128] A few years later, in his *Discours sur les sciences et les arts*, Rousseau went even further, arguing that a nation's morals had to be judged by comparing its past to its present *mœurs*.[129] And yet, according to Benrekassa, it is Montesquieu who should be credited with being 'the true theoriser of the historical dimension of *mœurs*, in France, before Tocqueville'.[130] In effect, there are many reasons that might justify such a claim. Already in the *Considérations sur les Romains*, published the same year as Voltaire's *Lettres*, the baron had penned a history in which usages, manners, and *mœurs* played a fundamental role in explaining the greatness and the decline of Rome. But it was in the *Esprit* that he gave a new meaning to the notion, doing so on two different but related planes. First, *mœurs* were an essential component in defining the 'principle' of government, what made it possible for

---

[123] Montesquieu, 'De l'Esprit des lois', 385 (book x. ch.11).   [124] Ibid., 564 (book xix. ch. 14).
[125] Ibid., 563 (book xix. ch. 12).   [126] Benrekassa, 'Mœurs comme concept politique', passim.
[127] See Chapters 2 and 4.
[128] See the classic by Ira O. Wade, *The Intellectual Development of Voltaire* (Princeton: Princeton University Press, 1969), 451–510. Also see, Méricam-Bourdet, *Voltaire et l'écriture de l'histoire*, 141–53.
[129] Rousseau, 'Discours sur les sciences et les arts', 8–9.
[130] Benrekassa, 'Mœurs comme concept politique', 59.

a state to function, the 'human passions that make it move'. Consistently, any change in a nation's *mœurs* would corrupt the nature of government, its 'particular structure'.[131] Since the principles of monarchy, republic, and despotism were respectively honour, virtue, and fear, any changes in the way these were conceived, perceived, understood, or experienced would have momentous repercussions for the nature of a government, possibly leading to its dissolution. From this perspective, a nation's beliefs, way of life, and *mœurs* were the engine of history, even more important than the decisions of rulers and kings. Here was an important shift of focus from previous scholars who, by contrast, had fixed their gaze on the sovereign and his power to grasp the causes of historical changes.[132]

But Montesquieu also considered the *mœurs* of a nation, as an object of enquiry, from another perspective. In fact, in one of his *Pensées*, he made the remark that changing a government would be impossible 'without changing the manners and *mœurs*' of its people, then going on to confess that he could not 'see how, given the extreme brevity of life, it would be useful for men to change in all respects the inclination they have acquired'.[133] In fact, only through much time and effort could *mœurs* be modified, for the obvious reason that these were the product of time. Their endurance made them so valuable to social stability and endowed them with the respectability that, according to the Baron de la Brède, all 'established things' deserved.[134] Therefore, there was usually 'much to gain, in matters of *mœurs*', in maintaining those that already existed.[135] Far from being a social element to be changed at will through laws and public education, Montesquieu saw a nation's *mœurs* as an important curb upon the decisions and the actions of rulers, a crucial one since they were, by their own nature, deeply embedded in a nation's social fabric. Time turned them into seemingly natural habits, inclinations, and beliefs, and they therefore represented an element of 'social inertia' that limited power and averted the ever-present risk that the monarchies of Europe might turn to despotism.[136] On this point, it might be useful to note that

---

[131] Montesquieu, 'De l'Esprit des lois', 250–1 (book iii. ch. 1).

[132] On Montesquieu's views about sovereignty, see Jean Ehrard, 'La souveraineté', in Ehrard, *L'esprit des mots: Montesquieu en lui-même et parmi les siens* (Geneva: Droz, 1990), 147–57, and Catherine Larrère, 'Montesquieu: L'éclipse de la souveraineté', in Gian Mario Cazzaniga and Yves Charles Zarka (eds.), *Penser la souveraineté à l'époque moderne et contemporaine* (Paris: Vrin, 2002), i. 199–214.

[133] Montesquieu, 'Mes pensées', 1153 (§ 632).   [134] Ibid., 1460 (§ 1916).

[135] Montesquieu, 'De l'Esprit des lois', 281 (book v. ch. 7).

[136] Benrekassa, 'Mœurs comme concept politique', 74.

a similar reasoning also seemed to apply to laws themselves, should these become customary. As Montesquieu wrote in a fragment, in 1742:

> Monarchies do not have only one day [of life]. They are the work of centuries. Laws are their structure and foundations. It is the work of each monarch, and the laws of one monarchy are the wills of all the monarchs who have ruled. One will cannot destroy all others, but each will is the completion of all. It is necessary that each monarch adds to such work, for this is never complete. Perfect today, tomorrow it is imperfect because it is subject to time as other things in the universe; because they are subject to circumstances as [are] all other things of the universe; because each society of men is an action, made up by the actions of all minds. The world of the intellect, which is in motion as the physical one, changes as the physical world does.[137]

Montesquieu's moral causes, including customary laws yet excluding positive laws, owed their strength to the past they stood for, setting limits to politics because of that complex entanglement of habits, beliefs, inclinations, ways of life, and *mœurs* that formed, in the baron's judgement, a nation's character. The somewhat conservative implications of Montesquieu's reasoning seem obvious. Indeed, to the inattentive reader of his day it might seem that institutions and laws were always legitimate because deeply rooted social reasons for their existence might always be found.[138] The baron's stance, in effect, prompted the criticisms of authors as diverse as Hume, Rousseau, the Neapolitan jurist Gaetano Filangieri (1753–1788), and the Viscount de Bonald, all of whom accused Montesquieu of explaining how things were rather than discussing how they ought to be.[139] In truth, Montesquieu intended his theory to be descriptive rather than prescriptive: 'I write not to censure anything established in any country whatsoever. Every nation will here find the reasons on which its maxims are founded,' he explained in the preface to the

---

[137] Charles-Louis Secondat de Montesquieu, 'Mes pensées: Appendice (b)', in *Œuvres* (ed. Masson), ii. 676–7 (§ 2266).

[138] On Montesquieu's alleged conservatism, Louis Althusser, *Montesquieu: La politique et l'histoire* (Paris: Presses universitaires de France, 2003), 109–22. The book was first published in 1959. On Althusser's controversial reading of Montesquieu, see Alessandro Ceccarelli, 'Il momento montesquieuiano di Louis Althusser', in Domenico Felice (ed.), *Montesquieu e i suoi interpreti* (Pisa: ETS, 2005), ii. 775–804.

[139] David Hume, *An Enquiry Concerning the Principles of Morals* (1751) (Oxford: Oxford University Press, 2009), 59, n.; Rousseau, 'Émile', 836; Gaetano Filangieri, *La scienza della legislazione* (1780–1791; the last volume of this masterpiece was published posthumously and incomplete) (Naples: Procaccini, 1995), i. 81; Louis Gabriel Ambroise de Bonald, 'Théorie du pouvoir politique et religieux dans la société civile' (1796), in *Œuvres* (Geneva: Slatkine, 1982), xiii. 12. According to Althusser, Montesquieu 'refuses to judge what is by what ought to be': Althusser, *Montesquieu*, 27.

Esprit.[140] It is then unsurprising that both Émile Durkheim and Raymond Aron saw in him one of the founding fathers of sociology. However, this does not mean he was unconcerned with the issue of political legitimacy – to the contrary, this was central to his views. The point neglected by his critics was that Montesquieu expressed his views from a historicist perspective. In effect, he assumed the existence of an inevitable discrepancy between the changing needs of society on the one hand and state institutions on the other, and in this difference, between the 'principle' and the 'nature' of government, he identified the cause of historical change. As Louis Althusser pointed out, the dialectic between the two was precisely what made it possible to explain history but, equally important, it also offered a yardstick for judging the legitimacy of existing political institutions. This, Montesquieu would have contended, was not to be sought in the past as such – for he saw change as inevitable – but in history itself, seen as a slow and incessant development that encompassed the present too.[141] What he called the 'corruption' of a government was simply its progression towards a new form of rule and a response or a reaction to the changes in a nation's *mœurs* and character. Seen from this perspective, the legitimacy of a government was then always in the making rather than in the alleged rightness of the existing – or of a desirable – state.[142]

The latter point leads to one further aspect that might be useful in grasping the relationship between a nation's character and its history and the legitimacy of its institutions. This lies in the use of 'law' made by Montesquieu, an unusual use of the word, at least for the eighteenth century. As he famously wrote in Book I of the *Esprit*: '[I]n the broadest sense, laws are the necessary relationships deriving from the nature of things.'[143] He intended laws, hence, not as an order or a command – be it from God or the sovereign – but as a relationship between historical, social or political facts that the enlightened observer was called to somehow

---

[140] Sergio Cotta, *Il pensiero politico di Montesquieu* (Rome-Bari: Laterza, 1995), 21. Émile Durkheim made the claim in his dissertation on Montesquieu: *Quid Secundatus politicae scientiae instituendae contulerit* (1892). The text was first translated into French as 'Montesquieu, sa part dans la fondation des sciences politiques et de la science des sociétés', *Revue d'histoire politique et constitutionnelle*, 1 (1937), 405–63; Raymond Aron, *Les étapes de la pensée sociologique: Montesquieu, Comte, Marx, Tocqueville, Durkheim, Pareto, Weber* (Paris: Gallimard, 1967), 53–61. Auguste Comte himself had already grasped the baron's crucial role in the birth of sociology: Auguste Comte, *Cours de philosophie positive: Leçons 46–51* (Paris: Hermann, 2012), 122–6 (lecture 47). For the quote: Montesquieu, 'De l'Esprit des lois', 230 ('Preface').

[141] Althusser, *Montesquieu*, 43–64.

[142] On this aspect of Montesquieu's thought see the classic by Friedrich Meinecke, *Die Entstehung des Historismus* (Munich: Oldenbourg, 1965), 116–67. Meinecke's book was first published in 1936.

[143] Montesquieu, 'De l'Esprit des lois', 232 (book i. ch. 1).

decipher. Indeed, such a definition had already been put forward by Nicolas Malebranche and Samuel Clarke (1675–1729).[144] Yet no other author had stated them in clearer terms than Montesquieu – a daring that lent credence to the allegations of Spinozism levelled against him.[145] As he saw them, positive laws were an imperfect reflection of the 'nature of things' and had to be evaluated not on the basis of universal and abstract principles but through the physical and moral factors forging the unique character of a people.[146] The readers of the *Esprit* were clearly being offered original notions of legitimacy and justice.[147] In fact, the idea that 'the government most conformable to nature is the one which best agrees with the humour and the disposition of a people in whose favour it is established' would have been unfamiliar to many readers.[148] And the same would have been true of Montesquieu's argument that no positive law could suit two different peoples or, for that matter, one nation at two different moments in its history.[149] Once more, it might seem easy to grasp why Montesquieu's views have been seen as inherently relativistic. However, the baron was convinced that by observing real societies and their history, by focusing on 'the particulars', he could discover the ever-valid rules through which national differences might be understood, those principles of which 'the histories of all nations are but consequences'.[150] If this might seem to be a denial of universal values, it was in truth simply a way of imagining a universally valid instrument – the 'spirit of laws' – for appraising the suitability of a law to a nation at a given moment in its history. The conformity of norms to a nation's character was the measure

---

[144] See Shackleton, *Montesquieu*, 245–6.

[145] Charles-Louis Secondat de Montesquieu, 'Défense de l'Esprit des lois' (1750), in *Œuvres* (ed. Caillois), ii. 1122–5.

[146] Spector, *Le vocabulaire de Montesquieu*, 37–9.

[147] Céline Spector, 'Quelle justice? Quelle rationalité? La mesure du droit dans *L'Esprit des lois*', in Catherine Volpilhac-Auger (ed.), *Montesquieu en 2005* (Oxford: Voltaire Foundation, 2005), 219–42.

[148] Montesquieu, 'De l'Esprit des lois', 237 (book i. ch. 3). The same argument had already been made by the Italian jurisconsult Gian Vincenzo Gravina (1664–1718) in his *Originum juris civilis libri tres* (1713) (Naples: Liguori, 2004), i. 271. On the latter point, see Joseph Dedieu, *Montesquieu* (Paris: Alcan, 1913), 48–50.

[149] Montesquieu, 'De l'Esprit des lois', 237 (book i. ch. 3), and ii. 770 (book xxvi. ch. 16). Already in his *Considérations sur les Romains*, Montesquieu remarked that it was folly for a conqueror to impose his laws upon another people: 'Considérations sur les causes de la grandeur des Romains et de leur décadence', 108. On his belief that legitimacy changed over the centuries, see Montesquieu, 'De l'Esprit des lois', 902 (book xxx. ch. 14); also see, Céline Spector, '"Il faut éclairer l'histoire par les lois et les lois par l'histoire": Statut de la romanité et rationalité des coutumes dans l'*Esprit des lois* de Montesquieu', in Mikhail Xifaras (ed.), *Généalogie des savoirs juridiques: Le carrefour des Lumières* (Brussels: Bruylant, 2007), 21.

[150] Montesquieu, 'De l'Esprit des lois', 229 ('Preface').

of 'rationality itself'.[151] On this, when observing that since Montesquieu had never spoken of the justice of the laws he was discussing, he had failed to offer his readers any principle to distinguish legitimate from illegitimate laws, Condorcet was mistaken.[152] On the contrary, according to the baron, the suitability of a law to a people was a sort of universal benchmark, always and everywhere valid, for appraising its justice. Justice was simply a relationship. It was, as he had already written years before, in the *Lettres persanes*, 'a relation of suitability that exists between two things'.[153] It was on the basis of the discrepancy or the correspondence between the principle and the nature of government that it ought to be decided which laws were 'most agreeable to reason' and to a nation.[154]

Montesquieu, the Franks, and the Gallo-Romans

On 28 March 1748, in a letter to his friend Monsignor Gaspare Cerati (1690–1769), superintendent of the University of Pisa, Montesquieu confessed that his studies had all but exhausted him. He was now working on the final section of the *Esprit* but still needed 'to complete two books on the feudal laws'. Should he be able to rest and recover his strength, he would surely finish them but, he added, if this were not possible then the 'book would do without'.[155] In effect, the last two books of the *Esprit*, devoted to the history of the French laws, seem almost to be an afterthought or an addendum. When comparing them to the other twenty-nine books, one is assuredly tempted to doubt their place in the baron's masterpiece.[156] However, the uncertainty in Montesquieu's letter notwithstanding, the examination of the history of the French constitution contained in them is perfectly consistent with the premises expounded in the previous sections of the *Esprit*.[157] For such a reason, they were far from being a legal history of France – contrary to what they might

---

[151] Spector, '"Il faut éclairer l'histoire par les lois et les lois par l"histoire"', 37. On the concept of rationality in Montesquieu see, Courtois, *Inflexions de la rationalité dans 'L'Esprit des lois'*, passim.

[152] Jean-Antoine-Nicolas de Condorcet, 'Observations sur le vingt-neuvième livre de l'Esprit des lois' (written in 1780 but published posthumously in 1819), in *Œuvres*, i. 365.

[153] Montesquieu, 'Lettres persanes', 256 (letter 83).

[154] Montesquieu, 'De l'Esprit des lois', 872 (book xxix. ch. 11).

[155] Charles-Louis Secondat de Montesquieu to Gaspare Cerati, 28 March 1748, in *Œuvres* (ed. Masson), iii. 1116–7.

[156] On this, see Iris Cox, *Montesquieu and the History of French Laws* (Oxford: Voltaire Foundation, 1983), 3–4. In this respect, the full title of the *Esprit* might be misleading: *The Spirit of the Laws; or of the Relation that Laws Ought to Have with the Constitution of Each Government, Manners, Climate, Religion, Commerce, etc ... to which the Author has Added some new Studies on Roman laws of Succession, on French laws, and feudal laws.*

[157] See Montesquieu, 'Dossier de l'Esprit des lois', 1103 (§ 399).

seem on the surface.[158] Obviously, while Montesquieu saw the usefulness of
the many existing histories of the French constitution, those 'cold, dry,
insipid, and crude writings', his intentions were altogether different. His
main concern was the relationship between the laws of France and
the *mœurs* and character of its people throughout the centuries.[159] It was not
enough to consider how a law had changed. On the contrary, Montesquieu
saw it as necessary to 'follow each law in the spirit of each age', considering its
changes in relation to political, economic, and social transformations.[160] The
purpose was to grasp its origins and causes, firmly placing it within, and
considering the interaction with, its larger context. Indeed, the subject matter
of his studies was 'not the laws, but the spirit of the laws'.[161] To do so in the
case of France – as in that of many other European nations – he relied heavily
on the works of Caesar and especially Tacitus describing the *mœurs* of the
Germanic tribes: 'These two authors agree so perfectly with the codes still
extant of the laws of the barbarians, that reading Caesar and Tacitus we
imagine we are perusing these codes and, perusing these codes, we fancy we
are reading Caesar and Tacitus.' Studying in conjunction the *mœurs* of the
ancient Franks and their codes, allowing Montesquieu to find his way through
the 'labyrinth' of the feudal laws, was key to comprehending the *esprit* of their
laws and, hence, the origins of the French monarchy.[162] In turn, on a different
and yet related plane, this also meant offering the reader a yardstick for
judging the validity and legitimacy of a nation's laws and institutions since
these had to be compatible with the *mœurs* of its people. From this angle,
although Montesquieu's concerns were essentially scholarly, their political
implications were obviously momentous.

It was in Books XXX and XXXI that Montesquieu took his stand in the
debate over the origins of the nation and in the dispute between Romanists
and Germanists.[163] His point of departure was a castigation of the ideas of

---

[158] According to Mercier, the *Esprit* was initially 'consigned, so to speak, to the books on jurisprudence': Mercier, 'Mon bonnet de nuit', 499.

[159] The quote is from Montesquieu, 'De l'Esprit des lois', 895 (book xxx. ch. 11).

[160] Montesquieu, 'Dossier de l'Esprit des lois', 1103 (§ 399).   [161] Ibid., 1103 (§ 398).

[162] Montesquieu, 'De l'Esprit des lois', 884 (book xxx. ch. 2). See also Montesquieu, 'Dossier de l'Esprit
des lois', 1112 (§ 416), where, however, the reference to Caesar is dropped. On the crucial role played
by Tacitus's *Germania* in Montesquieu's *Esprit*, see Catherine Volpilhac-Auger, *Tacite et
Montesquieu* (Oxford: Voltaire Foundation, 1985).

[163] The reference text is still Carcassonne, *Montesquieu et le problème de la constitution française au
XVIIIe siècle*, passim. Also see, Cox, *Montesquieu and the History of French Laws*, passim; Volpilhac-
Auger, *Tacite en France de Montesquieu à Chateaubriand*, passim; Battista, *La 'Germania' di Tacito
nella Francia illuminista*, 33–41; Dieter Gembicki, 'Le Moyen Âge de Montesquieu', in
Michel Porret and Catherine Volpilhac-Auger (eds.), *Le temps de Montesquieu* (Geneva: Droz,
2002), 363–76; Saint Victor, *Les racines de la liberté*, 141–74; Massimiliano Bravi, 'Montesquieu, le
invasioni barbariche e le ripercussioni del diritto germanico sulla storia giuridica della monarchia

both Boulainvilliers and Dubos. In his own words: 'The Count de Boulainvilliers and the abbé Dubos have formed two different systems, the one seems a conspiracy against the commons and the other one against the nobility.' Referring to Ovid's *Metamorphoses* and the myth of Phaeton, to whom the sun had granted the right to ascend into the sky so long as he flew neither too high nor too low, Montesquieu assured his readers he would 'keep to the middle' of the paths laid down by the count and the abbé.[164] Whether he did so, however, is debatable. In fact, some scholars have argued – with good reason – that the baron's views were closer to Boulainvilliers's and this was reflected in a more measured criticism of the latter's works.[165] Admittedly, Montesquieu criticised the count above all for failing to prove that the Franks, following the conquest, had issued a 'general regulation to reduce the Romans into a kind of servitude'.[166] It was a critical issue, especially with regard to the rights of and the relationship between the descendants of the Franks and the Gallo-Romans. The conclusions reached by Montesquieu on the latter point had important consequences for the way in which he conceived of the relationship between conquerors and conquered. First, Montesquieu contended that since the Franks 'only made regulations between themselves', this meant that their relationship with the Gallo-Romans could not but be the outcome of a slow process of negotiation and a series of partial agreements.[167] Furthermore, it was difficult to imagine that the Franks, soon after the conquest, had suddenly abandoned the characteristic habits of a pastoral and nomadic people to start managing vast estates and

---

francese', in Domenico Felice (ed.), *Studi di storia della cultura:* Sibi suis amicisque (Bologna: CLUEB, 2012), 197–243; Alicia C. Montoya, 'Montesquieu's Aristocratic Medievalism', in Bianchi and Minuti (eds.), *Montesquieu et les philosophies de l'histoire au XVIIIe siècle*, 31–45. With an emphasis on Montesquieu, Dubos, and Boulainvilliers's understanding of history, see the dated yet still useful article by Friedrich Meinecke, 'Montesquieu, Boulainvilliers, Dubos', *Historische Zeitschrift*, 145 (1932), 53–69. Also see, with particular reference to the notion of origins in Montesquieu's views regarding the Frankish conquest, Claude Gautier, 'À propos du "commencement" ou de l'"établissement": Quelques remarques sur l'histoire', in Louis Desgraves (ed.), *Actes du colloque international de Bordeaux pour le 250e anniversaire de L'Esprit des lois* (Bordeaux: Académie de Bordeaux, 1999), 353–69.

[164] Montesquieu, 'De l'Esprit des lois', 891–2 (book xxx. ch. 10).

[165] See, for example, Nicolet, *La fabrique d'une nation*, 89–90, and Saint Victor, *Les racines de la liberté*, 14. Also see, Spector, *Montesquieu: Liberté, droit et histoire*, 260.

[166] Montesquieu, 'De l'Esprit des lois', 891 (book xxx. ch. 10). It is worth noting that in this as in many other cases Montesquieu used 'Romans' to stand for 'Gallo-Romans'.

[167] Montesquieu, 'De l'Esprit des lois', 888 (book xxx. ch. 7). I am here relying on Binoche, *Introduction à De l'esprit des lois de Montesquieu*, 351–6. For a comparison of Montesquieu and Boulainvilliers's ideas, see Diego Venturino, 'Boulainvilliers et Montesquieu, ou De la modération nobiliaire', in Postigliola and Bottaro Palumbo (eds.), *L'Europe de Montesquieu*, 103–12. Also see, Tholozan, *Henri de Boulainvilliers*, 373–87.

hundreds of serfs. In fact, according to Montesquieu the Franks acted with remarkable moderation and restraint, and 'did not strip the Romans [of everything] wherever they extended their conquests. . . . They took what suited them and left the rest.'[168] That moderation had been a principle guiding the conduct of the Franks was due to their awareness of the 'mutual needs of the two peoples that were to inhabit the same land'.[169] If servitude increased between the fifth and the tenth century, this was not a consequence of the conquest but, rather, an outcome of the ensuing revolutions and internecine struggles tearing the nation apart. As he wrote:

> The conquest was not immediately productive of servitude; it arose nevertheless from the law of nations that subsisted after the conquest. Opposition, revolts, and the taking of towns were followed by the enslaving of the inhabitants. And, not to mention the wars that the conquering nations waged against one another, as there was this particularity among the Franks, that the different partitions of the monarchy gave rise continually to civil wars between brothers or nephews, in which this law of nations was constantly practised, servitudes of course became more general in France than in other countries.[170]

His own counterargument to Boulainvilliers's ideas led Montesquieu to the conclusion that the division between the Franks and the Gallo-Romans, in the centuries following the conquest, could not have been clear-cut.[171] Indeed, it was an important contention. And yet it did not entirely invalidate the count's arguments, but simply mitigated them. Furthermore, and interestingly, Montesquieu believed that since Boulainvilliers 'speaks with the simplicity, frankness, and candour of that ancient nobility from whence he descends, everyone is capable of judging of the fine things he says and of the errors into which he has fallen'. Oddly enough, Montesquieu then thought he could dispense with the task of assessing his ideas any further.[172]

When considering the tone and the tenor that the Baron de la Brède used in his refutation of Dubos's theories, one is immediately struck by a severity that is not to be found in his analysis of Boulainvilliers's. In truth, with the exception of the *Histoire critique de l'établissement de la monarchie française*, the baron thought highly of Dubos's works and he invited his readers to judge him on the merits of these alone.[173] He then saw the abbé's

---

[168] Montesquieu, 'De l'Esprit des lois', 889 (book xxx. ch. 8).   [169] Ibid. (book xxx. ch. 9).
[170] Ibid., 893 (book xxx. ch. 11).
[171] As we have already seen in Chapter 2, Boulainvilliers's ideas were, in truth, more complex.
[172] Montesquieu, 'De l'Esprit des lois', 891 (book xxx. ch. 10).   [173] Ibid., 936 (book xxx. ch. 25).

scheme as particularly insidious not only for its faults, but also because '[n]othing is a greater obstacle to the progress of knowledge, than a bad performance by a celebrated author'.[174] According to Montesquieu, the shortcomings and errors in Dubos's work on the origins of the monarchy were partly a consequence of the fact that 'he had more in view the Count de Boulainvilliers's work than his own subject'.[175] And, in so doing, Montesquieu believed Dubos was pursuing an overtly political aim, working in the interests of the king and influenced by the designs of his ministers. As he noted in private and very acerbically in one of his *Pensées*: 'In his work on the beginnings of our monarchy, the abbé Dubos reads only to seek the authority of kings and the dependence of the ancient French and the right they had of fleecing the lords. That man never saw anything in that history but a pension.'[176] Needless to say, this was a serious allegation and aspersion. Furthermore, Montesquieu saw his own ideas as 'perpetually contrary' to the abbé's and this, implicitly at least, must have meant that disproving his views would have been tantamount to proving his own.[177] Trying to undermine the scholarly credibility of his opponent to combat what he perceived as a political threat, Montesquieu criticised his pedantry and verbosity, remarking that should Dubos's ideas have been 'well grounded, he would not have been obliged to write three tedious volumes to prove them'. He censured his choice of sources, deeming that references to 'poets and orators' were 'improper foundations for building systems'. He even criticised some of the abbé's translations of the works of Gregory of Tours, identifying in them faults and mistakes for which, he wrote, 'any grammarian would have been ashamed'.[178]

In truth, most of these reproaches were unfair. More interesting were the analyses of the actual content of the abbé's work. These clearly reflected Montesquieu's own concerns with the rights of the nobility encroached upon by the royal authority whose standard-bearer – or so he believed – Dubos was.[179] A first point of contention was represented by the fiscal

---

[174] Ibid., 905 (book xxx. ch. 15). Montesquieu was acquainted with Dubos and the two were certainly on speaking terms: Montesquieu, 'Mes pensées', 1089 (§ 594), and Montesquieu, 'Spicilège', 1403 and 1405. It is possible that the two had first met at Madame de Lambert's (1647–1733) famous gatherings: Shackleton, *Montesquieu*, 55–61. On Madame de Lambert and her role in Parisian intellectual life, see Roger Marchal, *Madame de Lambert et son milieu* (Oxford: Voltaire Foundation, 1991).
[175] Montesquieu, 'De l'Esprit des lois', 937 (book xxx. ch. 25).
[176] Montesquieu, 'Mes pensées', 1249 (§ 915).
[177] Montesquieu, 'De l'Esprit des lois', 926 (book xxx. ch. 23).
[178] Ibid., 926 (book xxx. ch. 23), 795 (book xxviii. Chapter. 3), 896 (book xxx. ch. 12).
[179] See Dubos, *Histoire critique de l'établissement de la monarchie française*, iii. 505–16.

rights of the nobility and their roots in the history of the ancient Germanic tribes. The latter he saw as a 'simple, poor, free, and martial people, who lived without any other industry than that of tending their flocks', consisting of men who followed 'their chiefs for the sake of booty and not as a way of paying or levying taxes'.[180] Following the conquest, taxes were neither levied nor paid by the Franks, who hardly had any notion of tolls. On the contrary, they were decided by the ecclesiastics, all of whom were Gallo-Romans, and imposed upon the inhabitants of towns, who were likewise Gallo-Romans. But soon taxes were paid only by the serfs, through the yield from their labour. Free men did not pay any tribute. After disputing Dubos's translation of a passage from Gregory of Tours and his misleading interpretation of the Latin word *ingenui*, Montesquieu went on to accuse him of misusing capitularies, laws, and the works of other historians so that, 'when he wants the Franks to pay taxes, he applies to freemen what can be understood only of bondmen'.[181] All freemen fought but were exempted from taxation, while all serfs paid tribute.[182] The point Montesquieu was trying to make was twofold. On the one hand, he sought to show that no system of taxation from the Roman Empire had survived in France after the conquest. On the other, he wished to prove that the nobility's exemption from taxes, far from being a usurpation, stemmed from Germanic usages and had developed in accordance with the creation of fiefs. Believing himself to have thus settled the issue of the nobility's fiscal rights, the baron went on to examine another crucial matter, namely, the role of the nobility in justice and civil jurisdiction. According to Dubos, the administration of justice was initially in the hands of the king alone and only at the end of the Carolingian dynasty did the vassals, who until then had simply administered justice in the name of the king, begin to claim a sort of patrimonial right.[183] Once again, though this time without naming the abbé, Montesquieu set out to refute his arguments.[184] He did so by emphasising the indissoluble relationship between civil jurisdiction and military leadership in the Frankish world. In fact, the obligation of any vassal was to bear arms for his lord and to judge his peers in court. The reason the judicial right and that of leading troops into battle were so closely linked was that 'rendering justice among those rude and

---

[180] Montesquieu, 'De l'Esprit des lois', 895 (book xxx. ch. 12).
[181] Ibid., 896 (book xxx. ch. 12), and 898 (book xxx. ch. 12). See Dubos, *Histoire critique de l'établissement de la monarchie française*, iii. 516.
[182] Montesquieu, 'De l'Esprit des lois', 902–5 (book xxx. ch.15).
[183] See Dubos, *Histoire critique de l'établissement de la monarchie française*, iii. 549–51.
[184] Montesquieu, 'De l'Esprit des lois', 923 (book xxx. ch. 22).

unpolished nations' amounted to little else than 'granting to the person who had committed an offence protection against the prosecution of the party offended' and forcing 'the latter to accept the satisfaction due to him'.[185] It was only logical, therefore, that those capable of enforcing justice should also decide about it. Interestingly, Montesquieu remarked that the concentration of military, civil, and even fiscal authority in the hands of one and the same lord might have seemed a 'distinguishing mark of despotism' – and this according to the principles expounded by Montesquieu himself in the previous books of the *Esprit*. However, he reassured his readers, such was not the case since, among the Franks, whoever held jurisdiction, be it the king, the counts, the lords, or the clergy, 'never tried causes alone'. Such a usage, which was designed to preserve justice and assure impartiality, 'derived its origin from the forests of Germany, and was still continued even after the fief, if in a new form'.[186]

Obviously, Montesquieu was seeking to prove, through the careful reading of capitularies, laws, and collections of customs, that immediately after the conquest the ancient Franks enjoyed tax exemption and judicial rights and that, therefore, in the ensuing centuries, there had been no usurpation on their part. However, the baron also had to disprove a further two corollaries, even more significant ones, to definitively dismiss the abbé Dubos's theories. The first was the latter's contention that the Franks knew no distinction of ranks and that, therefore, they lacked the very notion of nobility. As one might expect, Montesquieu considered this to be an assertion 'injurious to the noble blood of our principal families' and that the claim was 'equally offensive to the three great houses which successively governed this kingdom'.[187] As he saw it, Dubos had reached his conclusion by way of a misleading interpretation of the Salic Laws. In effect, the abbé had contended that in case of murder, these laws allowed the perpetrator to offer a compensation of two hundred sous for the killing of any Frank while, among the Gallo-Romans, they distinguished 'the king's guest, for whose death it allowed three hundred sous', the 'proprietor, to whom it granted a hundred', and, finally the 'tributary, to whom it gave only a composition of forty-five'. Since no distinction was made for the killing of a Frank and while such was the case for the Gallo-Romans, Dubos assumed that Frankish customs posited no distinction between orders, though things were different for the Gallo-Romans.[188] From Montesquieu's viewpoint, such an argument

---

[185] Ibid., 917 (book xxx. ch. 20).
[186] Ibid., 911–2 (book xxx. ch. 18). Also see, Ibid., 917 (book xxx. ch. 20).
[187] Ibid., 930 (book xxx. ch. 25).   [188] Ibid., 931 (book xxx. ch. 25).

had manifold shortcomings. First, it went against the grain since 'it would have been truly extraordinary if the Roman nobility, who lived under the domination of the Franks, had had a larger compensation, as people of much greater importance than the most illustrious among the Franks and their greatest generals'. Second, Montesquieu pointed out that the abbé himself had recognised in his work the existence of a nobility in the case of other Germanic tribes but had made no real or convincing attempt to account for the Frankish anomaly. In order to demonstrate the underlying inconsistency, Montesquieu undertook a detailed and scrupulous analysis of the original sources.[189] He deemed the effort to be worthwhile, since he believed that, by denying the existence of a Frankish nobility, Dubos 'carries us to Turkey'.[190] In fact, Montesquieu was adamant that without a nobility limiting the king's authority and curbing his ambitions, he would inevitably turn into a despot. As he expressed it in one of the strongest of all vindications of the aristocratic idea of freedom: 'The most natural intermediate and subordinate power is that of the nobility. This, in some measure, seems to be essential to a monarchy, whose fundamental maxim is, *No monarch, no nobility; no nobility, no monarch:* but there may be a despotic prince.'[191] This contention was central to Montesquieu's definition of monarchy and would later be restated in various ways by others, including Chateaubriand, Bonald, and Joseph de Maistre (1753–1821).[192]

It was in Chapter 24 of Book XXX that Montesquieu attacked directly that 'immense colossus with feet of clay', the kernel of Dubos's thesis, namely, the denial of the conquest.[193] In his reading of the *Histoire critique*, a work endeavouring 'by every means to explode the opinion that the Franks made the conquest of Gaul', Montesquieu was bewildered and dismayed by the idea that 'our kings were invited by the people, and only substituted themselves in the place, and succeeded to the rights, of the Roman emperors'.[194] As he saw it, the claim of continuity between the rule of the Roman emperors and the first kings of France was but a vindication

---

[189] Ibid., 931–6 (book xxx. ch. 25). Also see, Montesquieu, 'Dossier de l'Esprit des lois', 1034–5 ('Histoire de droit').

[190] Montesquieu, 'De l'Esprit des lois', 936 (book xxx. ch. 25).

[191] Ibid., 247 (book ii. ch. 4); italics in the text.

[192] François-René de Chateaubriand, *De la monarchie selon la charte* (Brussels: A. Wahlen, 1816), 118–9; [Bonald], *Réflexions sur l'intérêt général de l'Europe, suivies de quelques considérations sur la noblesse*, 53; Joseph de Maistre, 'Étude sur la souveraineté' (1794), in *Œuvres complètes* (Geneva: Slatkine, 1979), i. 430–1.

[193] The quote is from Montesquieu, 'De l'Esprit des lois', 926 (book xxx. ch. 23).

[194] Montesquieu, 'De l'Esprit des lois', 927 (book xxx. ch. 24).

of absolute rule, a notion so perfidious that Montesquieu thought it necessary to ridicule it:

> The Franks then the best friends of the Romans, they who did, and they who suffered from, the Romans such an infinite deal of mischief! The Franks, the friends of the Romans, they who, after subduing them by their arms, oppressed them in cold blood by their laws! They were as much the friends of the Romans, as the Tartars, who conquered China, were the friends of the Chinese.[195]

Refuting this claim, the key to Dubos's own system, was obviously crucial. First, noted Montesquieu, such a reasoning could not be applied to the time when Clovis, entering Gaul, plundered the Roman towns, nor when he defeated the Gallo-Roman commander, Syagrius (430–486 or 487), at the Battle of Soissons (486). The only occasion upon which the claim might be judged to have some pertinence was when Clovis, 'already master of a great part of Gaul by open force, was called by the choice and affection of the people to the sovereignty over the rest'. But then the abbé would have to demonstrate that the Gallo-Romans 'chose' to live under Frankish rule rather than that of the Empire. In truth, argued the baron, Dubos had failed to 'produce any convincing proof' that the Gallo-Romans, still subject to the Empire, had called Clovis into Gaul as their sovereign. The consequence of such a fault in interpreting the origins of the French monarchy ought to have been clear: 'For when we behold a conqueror entering a country and subduing a great part of it through force and violence and soon after we find the whole country subdued, without any mention in history of the manner of its being effected, we have sufficient reason to believe that the affair ended as it began.' Having found that Dubos was mistaken on this count, added Montesquieu, 'it is easy to see that his whole system falls to the ground'.[196]

Montesquieu's rejection of Dubos's thesis, undertaken in order to safeguard the rights of the nobility against royalist encroachments, also implied a displacement of the Roman intellectual and cultural heritage – or, more specifically, of the imperial Roman order – within the nation's history and within the set of its most fundamental political values. In fact, to sustain his views, it was crucial for Montesquieu to demonstrate that the Franks had carried with them the seeds of modern freedom.[197] Such an idea had already been stated in the *Lettres persanes*, where Rhedi wrote to Rica

---

[195] Ibid., 795 (book xxviii. ch. 3).   [196] Ibid., 928 (book xxx. ch. 24).
[197] On this, see the excellent essay by Umberto Roberto, 'Montesquieu, i germani e l'identità politica europea', in Felice (ed.), *Libertà, necessità e storia*, 277–322.

about an 'infinity of unknown nations pouring like torrents into the Roman provinces. ... These peoples were free, and they put such restrictions on the authority of their kings, that they were properly only chiefs or generals. Thus, these kingdoms, although founded by force, never endured the yoke of the conqueror.' The power of their kings was limited 'in a thousand different ways' and 'laws were made in national assemblies'. Therein lay the 'fundamental principles of all those states that were formed from the ruins of the Roman Empire'.[198] The contrast, in political terms, between the Romans and the Franks, depicted later in greater detail by Montesquieu in the *Considérations*, is striking: 'No two systems in the world were so antithetical', he wrote. As he saw it, '[T]he former was the work of strength, the latter of weakness; in one, subjection was extreme, in the other, independence'. In the lands conquered by the Germans, 'power was in the hands of the vassals and the only legal authority was in the hands of the prince. The exact opposite was true with the Romans.'[199] However, once conquered and following the 'first devastation', and after entering 'into an agreement with the inhabitants', they 'left them all their political and civil rights. This was the law of nations in those days; they plundered everything in time of war, and granted everything in time of peace.'[200] Partly contradicting the views expressed by Boulainvilliers on this point, Montesquieu contended that through marriages, laws, the birth of new usages and customs, and through a certain 'conformity of mind [*esprit*]', all modes of subjection ended thanks to the good will of 'our fathers', the Franks. As he phrased it: 'The draconian laws they made in the [first] flush of victory were gradually softened and rendered impartial', and the Franks made 'Romans and barbarians their fellow-citizens'.[201] Love for freedom as well as the spirit of restraint and moderation in times of peace were the main traits of Frankish *mœurs*, so much so that they were barely able to hold in subjection the vanquished Gallo-Romans. Placed within such a frame, modern monarchies were seen as a creation of the Germanic tribes and a consequence of conquests. In fact, these same tribes had in earlier times lived in small groups and could easily assemble to discuss and take decisions but, following the conquest, and having dispersed throughout

---

[198] Montesquieu, 'Lettres persanes', 329 (letter 131).

[199] Montesquieu, 'Considérations sur les causes de la grandeur des Romains et de leur décadence', 108. On Montesquieu's ideas concerning the Romans, see Vanessa de Senarclens, *Montesquieu, historien de Rome: Un tournant pour la réflexion sur le statut de l'histoire au XVIIIe siècle* (Geneva: Droz, 2003), and Patrick Andrivet, *'Rome enfin que je hais'? Une étude sur les différentes vues de Montesquieu concernant les anciens Romains* (Orléans: Paradigme, 2012).

[200] Montesquieu, 'De l'Esprit des lois', 892 (book xxx. ch. 11).

[201] Ibid., 379–80 (book x. ch. 3), and Montesquieu, 'De l'Esprit des lois', 892–3 (book xxx. ch. 11).

France, this was no longer possible. However, according to Montesquieu, since 'it was necessary that the nation should deliberate on public affairs and faithful to their usual method before the conquest', the Franks 'had recourse to representatives'. At first, such a form of rule was a combination of 'aristocracy and monarchy', which, however, had the 'inconveniency, that the common people were bondsmen'. But usages and *mœurs* slowly changed, letters of enfranchisement were granted with greater frequency, and soon there followed 'so perfect a harmony between the civil liberty of the people, the privileges of the nobility and clergy, and the prince's prerogative'. It was a new form of rule in which the power of the different components of the nation, with different interests and aims, balanced one another in such a way that, to Montesquieu's eye, 'there never was in the world a government so well tempered as that of each part of Europe so long as it lasted'. By the same token, the 'corruption of the government of a conquering nation' gave birth to 'the best sort of constitution that could possibly be imagined by man'.[202]

In part, with hindsight Montesquieu bestowed on the Germanic tribes, and especially the Franks, a sort of historical mission. As he wrote somewhat loftily in Book XVII, the book on the effects of climate upon national character, the north of Europe was the 'forge where the weapons that broke the chains of the southern nations were framed'. There 'were formed those valiant people who sallied forth and deserted their countries to destroy tyrants and slaves, and to teach men that, nature having made them equal, reason could not render them dependent, except where it was necessary to their happiness'.[203] As might be expected, the reasons for this were partly climatic. But there was more to it, and Montesquieu's comparison between the Germanic tribes and the northern barbarians of Asia, the Tartars, the most 'singular people in the universe' – as he wrote – may prove instructive.[204] The distinction he posed between the two was in fact sharp. Both nomadic peoples and both from northern and cold regions, hence, both inclined to love freedom, their histories did nonetheless differ radically. In fact, the Germanic tribes had conquered Europe 'as a free people' while the Tartars had subjugated Asia 'as slaves, and subdued

---

[202] Montesquieu, 'De l'Esprit des lois', 409 (book xi. ch. 8).   [203] Ibid., 528 (book xvii. ch. 5).

[204] Ibid., 541 (book xviii. ch. 19). That Montesquieu was fascinated by the Tartars and their history was also noted by his friend, the Jesuit mathematician and journalist Louis Bertrand Castel (1688–1757): *L'homme moral opposé à l'homme physique de M. R***: Lettres philosophiques, où l'on réfute le déisme du jour* (Toulouse: n.p., 1756), 125–6. On this, see Rolando Minuti, *Oriente barbarico e storiografia settecentesca: Rappresentazioni della storia dei Tartari nella cultura francese del XVIII secolo* (Venice: Marsilio, 1994), 63–93.

others only to gratify the ambition of a master'.[205] The contradictory predicament of the Tartars, a northern people ruled by a despot, might be explained by the fact that since ancient times, the conquests of the Tartars had been at the expense of a despotic empire, that of the Chinese:

> The people of Tartary, the natural conquerors of Asia, are themselves enslaved. They are incessantly making conquests in the South of Asia, where they form empires; but that part of the nation which continues [to live] in the country finds that it is subject to a great master, who, being despotic in the south, will likewise be so in the north, and, exercising an arbitrary power over the vanquished subjects, pretends to do the same over the conquerors.[206]

In his reading of the *Esprit*, Rolando Minuti has argued that, because of the nature itself of Chinese despotism, the alleged liberating force of the barbarians of Asia had been arrested and the Tartars' way of life corrupted by those peoples they had subdued, losing therefore, in time, their own love of freedom. Between the servile *mœurs* of the Chinese and the unyielding *mœurs* of the Tartars, the former had prevailed.[207] This, reasoned Montesquieu, was in the main a consequence of the fact that in China, 'manners, *mœurs*, laws, and religion, being one and the same, cannot change all at once'. Since 'either the conqueror or the conquered must change' and since 'in China it has always been the conqueror', it was then more likely, in Montesquieu's judgement, that the Tartars would adapt to the way of life and values of the vanquished.[208] Things in France and in Europe were altogether different. First, Roman rule had not always been despotic. Indeed, noted Montesquieu, 'Caesar destroyed the Roman Republic and subjected it to arbitrary power', so that for a long time it 'groaned under the violence of a military

[205] Montesquieu, 'De l'Esprit des lois', 527 (book xvii. ch. 5). The contrast had been laid out in the *Lettres persanes*: Montesquieu, 'Lettres persanes', 329 (letter 131).
[206] Montesquieu, 'De l'Esprit des lois', 527 (book xvii. ch. 5).
[207] Minuti, *Oriente barbarico e storiografia settecentesca*, 73–5.
[208] Montesquieu, 'De l'Esprit des lois', 568 (book xix. ch.18). The passage was also in Charles-Louis Secondat de Montesquieu, 'Geographica', in *Œuvres* (ed. Société Montesquieu), xvi. 405–6. The texts, part of Montesquieu's notes, and the marginalia to the *Lettres édifiantes et curieuses, écrites des missions étrangères par quelque missionnaires de la Compagnie de Jésus* (1702–1776) were written in 1739. Regarding Montesquieu's views on China, see Louis Desgraves, 'Notes de Montesquieu sur la Chine', in Desgraves, *Montesquieu: L'œuvre et la vie* (Bordeaux: L'esprit du temps, 1995), 157–83, and Jacques Pereira, *Montesquieu et la Chine* (Paris: L'Harmattan, 2008). With a particular emphasis on Montesquieu's ideas concerning Chinese despotism, see Antonio Lenarda, 'La concezione del dispotismo cinese in Montesquieu', *Annali dell'Istituto di Filosofia dell'Università di Firenze*, 1 (1979), 261–90, and Joan-Pau Rubiés, 'Oriental Despotism and European Orientalism: Botero to Montesquieu', *Journal of Early Modern History*, 9 (2005), 109–80.

government'.[209] However, until then, and while still a republic, Rome had embodied the spirit of freedom in the ancient world and its virtues were assuredly to be praised and admired. Later, having become an empire and expanded beyond Italy, its increasing power and wealth gradually brought about its decadence.[210] But to explain the contrasting effects of the Germanic tribes and the Tartar hordes on Europe and Asia respectively, Montesquieu also considered physical factors. A crucial contention was that the invasions from the north had brought freedom also because of the natural boundaries that divided Europe into many different regions. Asia was instead the land of 'great plains' and such a condition was favourable to the rise of despotism. In Europe, natural

> division forms many nations of a moderate extent, in which rule by laws is not incompatible with the maintenance of the state. On the contrary, it is so favourable to it that, without this, the state would fall into decay and become a prey to its neighbours. It is this which has formed a genius for liberty, that renders every part extremely difficult to be subdued and subjected to a foreign power.[211]

In turn, the various Germanic tribes, with their different *mœurs*, gave rise to the many monarchies and the many states of Europe, all of a moderate size and as such favouring freedom.[212]

Within the writings of the Baron de la Brède, the relationship between the Franks and the Gauls is complex at best.[213] In a text read out at the *Parlement* of Bordeaux in September 1725, Montesquieu expressed the view that:

> At the beginning of our monarchy, our fathers, poor and shepherds rather than workers, soldiers rather than citizens, had but few interests to regulate. A few laws on the sharing of loot, on provender or the theft of cattle, regulated the entire republic. Everyone was capable of being a magistrate

---

[209] Montesquieu, 'Lettres persanes', 328–9 (letter 131).

[210] Montesquieu, 'De l'Esprit des lois', 428–9 (book xi. ch. 19). Montesquieu even suggested a comparison between the 'first Romans', still uncorrupted, and the Germans: Montesquieu, 'Dossier de l'Esprit des lois', 1092 (§362).

[211] Montesquieu, 'De l'Esprit des lois', 529 (book xvii. ch. 6). Also see, Montesquieu, 'Réflexions sur la monarchie universelle en Europe', 23–4.

[212] Throughout the *Esprit*, Montesquieu did draw important differences, in terms of *mœurs* and institutions, between the Franks and the other Germanic tribes: Montesquieu, 'De l'Esprit des lois', 380 (book x. ch. 3), 790–3 (book xxviii. ch. 1), 487–8 (book xiv. ch. 14). Also see, Montesquieu, 'Mes pensées', 1384 (§ 1588). See, on this, Roberto, 'Montesquieu, i germani e l'identità politica europea', 283–8.

[213] See Jean Ehrard, 'Etonnants Gaulois!', in Ehrard, *L'esprit des mots*, 67–79.

among a people which, in its *mœurs*, followed the simplicity of nature . . . .
Yet since we have abandoned our savage *mœurs*, since, conquerors over the
Gauls, we have adopted the Gallic policy, the military code has yielded to
the civil code. Moreover, since the laws of the fiefs were no longer the only
laws and nobility the only body of the state, and since by the latter change,
commerce and tillage were encouraged, the wealth of single individuals and
their greed have grown . . .; good faith is left to few businesses of little
importance, while trick and fraud are now used in contracts; our codes have
increased and it has been necessary to blend together foreign and national
laws.[214]

Here, clearly seeing in himself a descendant of the Franks, Montesquieu's
views might seem to be reminiscent of those set out by Boulainvilliers a few
years earlier. The Gauls, one might say, corrupted the Franks by under-
mining their military valour and hindering their devotion towards the
nation. However, Montesquieu's stance would apparently undergo change
in ensuing works. Only a few years later, in his *Considérations*, he made the
claim that the courage and the military valour of the Gauls were 'equal' to
those of their Roman enemies: 'The love of glory, the contempt for death,
and the stubborn will to conquer were the same in the two peoples.' Yet the
weapons of the Romans were far superior, and this made all the difference
in battle.[215] It was an important concession. In effect, although
Montesquieu refrained from explaining the origins of the Gauls themselves, he did believe them to be a Germanic people and, as such, before
suffering the Roman yoke, a warring nation cherishing freedom above all
else. But, this granted, the paramount issue became that of explaining the
reasons behind Frankish domination at the fall of the Empire:

No states are in greater need of taxes than those which are growing weaker,
so that burdens must be increased in proportion as the ability to pay
decreases. Soon, in the Roman provinces, taxes became unbearable. It is
necessary to read, in Salvian, of the horrible exactions imposed on the
population. Harried by tax farmers, the citizens could do nothing but seek
refuge among the barbarians or surrender their liberty to the first person
who wanted to take it. This will explain, in our French history, the patience
shown by the Gauls in enduring the revolution which was to establish so
overwhelming a difference between a nation of nobles and a nation of
commoners. In making so many citizens serfs – that is, slaves of the field

---

[214] Charles-Louis Secondat de Montesquieu, 'Discours prononcé à la rentrée du Parlement de
Bordeaux' (1725), in *Œuvre* (ed. Caillois), i. 45. The speech is now also known as 'Discours sur
l'équité'.
[215] Montesquieu, 'Considérations sur les causes de la grandeur des Romains et de leur décadence', 83.

to which they were attached – the barbarians scarcely introduced anything which had not been more cruelly practised before them.[216]

Such a condition soon ended under the Franks, and the Gallo-Romans, although they at first had continued to pay, were exempted from taxes and started to serve in the army.[217] Montesquieu's description of a seemingly unproblematic process might seem somewhat naïve. In reality, as has been noted, the baron was rather 'discreetly' restoring to the Gauls their allegedly natural warring spirit and, with it, their inborn love for freedom.[218] In actual fact, implied here was the idea that under the Roman yoke the Gauls had never wholly renounced their nature and, after the crossing of the Rhine by the Franks, they regained not only their lost freedom but they also rekindled their true character. That such had not been erased was a point partly confirmed by considering their political institutions. Indeed, according to Montesquieu, under the rule of the Romans and the first Merovingian kings, there existed a municipal auton-omy that was typical of the Gallic world and that would later contribute to that 'gothic government' so much praised by the baron.[219] In this, as Ehrard has rightly noted, Montesquieu's views might have been closer to Dubos's than to Boulainvilliers's.[220] But, notwithstanding the seeming incongruity, the point to take is that once again Montesquieu was preoccupied with tying together – and, hence, explaining – a people's character, its political institutions, and its political beliefs. And this was especially true with regard to the notion of freedom.

---

[216] Ibid., 175–6.   [217] Montesquieu, 'De l'Esprit des lois', 898 (book xxx. ch. 13).
[218] Ehrard, 'Etonnants Gaulois!', 76–7.
[219] Montesquieu, 'De l'Esprit des lois', 892 (book xxx. ch. 11). Also see, ibid., 409 (book xi. ch. 8).
[220] Ehrard, 'Etonnants Gaulois!', 77.

CHAPTER 6

Debating the Nation's History
Franks, Gauls, and the French Character

The Franks, Their Character, and Their Freedom

In his *Decline and Fall of the Roman Empire*, Gibbon pondered the study of the origins of France and its eighteenth-century developments:

> At length, the eye of criticism and philosophy was directed to the antiquities of France but even philosophers have been tainted by the contagion of prejudice and passion. The most extreme and exclusive systems, of the personal servitude of the Gauls, or of their voluntary and equal alliance with the Franks, have been rashly conceived, and obstinately defended; and the intemperate disputants have accused each other of conspiring against the prerogative of the crown, the dignity of the nobles, or the freedom of the people. Yet the sharp conflict has usefully exercised the adverse powers of learning and genius; and each antagonist, alternately vanquished and victorious, has extirpated some ancient errors, and established some interesting truths.

In a footnote, Gibbon went on to praise the 'free spirit of the Count de Boulainvilliers', the 'learned ingenuity of the abbé Dubos', the 'comprehensive genius of the President de Montesquieu', and the 'good sense and diligence of the abbé de Mably'. It was because of their efforts that in 'the space of [about] thirty years', new light had been shed upon 'this interesting subject'.[1] The great English historian had many reasons to eulogise the four scholars, highlighting their different merits and contributions. In part, his words testify to the affinity between their approach and the new kind of historiography that Gibbon himself was pursuing at the time.[2] In fact, notwithstanding their many intellectual and political differences, one crucial element common to all was the importance they attributed to the relationship between *mœurs* and national character, howsoever defined,

---

[1] Edward Gibbon, *The Decline and Fall of the Roman Empire* (London: David Campbell, 1993), iv. 74 and footnote 2.

[2] See Pocock, *Barbarism and Religion. Volume 2*, passim.

and the form of a nation's 'fundamental laws'.[3] That these were tightly intertwined and that the latter somehow depended on the former became a truism in the second half of the century.

In different ways and with contrasting aims, Boulainvilliers and Dubos had both tied the character of the Franks – and the modern French – to their form of rule, claiming that the legitimacy of the latter needed to be judged in terms of the former. It was a point that arose time and again throughout their works. It was the case, for example, with their readings of the famous story of the vase of Soissons, a crucial episode of which, as the abbé Velly noted, 'all historians spoke'.[4] According to the myth, told for the first time by Gregory of Tours, during the pillage of the Gallo-Roman town of Soissons in 486, a sacred vase was stolen from a church together with many other relics and precious objects. After the sacking, the bishop of Rheims asked the Franks to return the vase, and Clovis, as an act of good will, claimed it as part of his booty with the intention of giving it back. Yet one of his soldiers, seeing this as an act of high-handedness and claiming it for himself, smashed the vase. The following year, during a parade, Clovis asked the same soldier to show him his weapon and accused him of not taking due care of his axe. After throwing the axe to the ground, Clovis killed the soldier in cold blood in front of the entire army, reminding those present of the soldier's insolence the previous year. It is a matter of debate whether the episode ever took place, given that Gregory of Tours wrote about it a century after the alleged episode. Instead, it is of relevance, as the diplomat and historian Louis-Philippe de Ségur (1753–1830) noted, that the incident served some scholars as 'proof of the authority of our first kings and to the others of the excesses of their despotism'.[5] All placed emphasis on the relationship between Clovis and his men, its significance with regard to the nature of the French monarchy at the time of its origins, and, most importantly for us, on the character of the ancestors of the modern French. According to Boulainvilliers, the act of the Frankish

---

[3] On the notion of fundamental laws, see André Lemaire, *Les lois fondamentales de la monarchie française d'après les théoriciens de l'Ancien régime* (Geneva: Slatkine, 1975). Although the work was first published in 1907, it is still highly informative. Also see, Gabrielle Radica, 'Trois interprétations de la notion de "lois fondamentales" au XVIIIᵉ siècle', in Moreau (ed.), *Les Lumières en mouvement*, 229–53.

[4] Velly, *Histoire de France*, i. 46.

[5] Louis-Philippe de Ségur, 'Histoire de France', in *Œuvres complètes* (Paris: Eymery, 1824–1830), xxi. 11; the work was partly published posthumously. See also [Louis-Joseph-Charles-Amable d'Albert de Luynes], *L'histoire, le cérémonial et les droits des États généraux du royaume de France* (n.p., 1789), ii. 64. On the episode and its importance for eighteenth-century French historical scholarship, see Henri Duranton, 'Le vase de Soissons et les historiens du XVIIIᵉ siècle', *Revue de synthèse*, 79–80 (1975), 283–316.

warrior was 'an example of the ancient liberty of the Franks'.[6] As he saw it, while it was true that the Franks obeyed their king blindly, this only held on the battlefield, and for military reasons alone; their rights reverted to them once hostilities were over. Afterwards, the elected king was once again a *primus inter pares*. Dubos's counterargument to Boulainvilliers's thesis was based on the answer that several warriors gave Clovis when he asked for the vase – as told by Gregory of Tours: 'Great prince, you are the master of all that can be seen here and even of ourselves. Are we not your subjects? Use them at your discretion since nobody has the right to oppose your will.'[7]

No two readings of the episode could be further apart, and the implications of the two versions are clear as regards the relationship between Clovis and the Frankish warrior. One crucial difference between these two interpretations lies in the character of the Franks themselves. The one suggested by Boulainvilliers was of a fierce and proud tribe of warriors who could bear to give up their freedom only for a short time, for a specific purpose, and to a general they themselves had chosen. In contrast, the character of the Franks implied by Dubos was that of faithful and loyal soldiers submitting to the king's authority. Their fierceness on the battlefield did not seem to contradict their deference towards Clovis. Crucially, Boulainvilliers fostered the idea that alongside the Franks' warlike character there existed a yearning for independence, as if the one quality complemented the other. This was not an entirely new notion. Others had made a similar argument long before, tying the fierceness of northern peoples to their love of freedom. As early as 1576, in the *Six livres de la République*, Bodin explained the relationship:

> [N]orthern races, or those that live in mountainous regions, are proud and warlike, relying on their physical prowess, and so they prefer popular states, or at any rate elective monarchies, and will not endure being ruled by overweening braggarts. All their kings are elective, and they expel them the moment they turn tyrant . . . . This is not a consequence of confidence born of the natural impregnability of their country but comes from their naturally savage nature which cannot be easily tamed.[8]

Boulainvilliers himself believed that love of freedom, prowess in battle, and physical strength were closely intertwined. It was from such a standpoint

---

[6] Boulainvilliers, *Essais sur la noblesse de France*, 34.

[7] Dubos, *Histoire critique de l'établissement de la monarchie française*, ii. 339. Montesquieu, reflecting on the episode, inclined towards Boulainvilliers's view: Montesquieu, 'Mes pensées', 1384 (§ 1589).

[8] Bodin, *Les six livres de la république*, v. 47–8.

that he could argue that grasping the reasons for the debasement of the present-day nobility, its degrading from the ancient martial race it had once been, would shed light on the political servitude of the modern French, their subservience to a despotic monarch. According to the count, the crux of the matter was to understand how the valiant Frankish warriors had become the weak nobility that stood before him. It was a political as much as a social – or even anthropological – question. Consistently, the dominant role of Clovis in Frankish society was explained not in legal or political terms but as being directly related to the character of the Franks themselves, a people 'whose mind [*génie*] was wholly martial' and who, consequently, were prone to confer upon their most important general an especially prominent role.[9]

Several authors assumed that the search for the character of the ancestors of the French required discerning the origins of their name. As Fréret pointed out in his famous speech at the Académie: 'Nations take on or receive their name to differentiate themselves from the others, and such names communicate certain specific qualities belonging to these nations or, at least, that they can assign to themselves to a far greater degree than others.'[10] Finding the origins of the name of the ancient Franks was key in understanding their character and, hence, in shedding light on that of the modern French. In most cases, the name was associated with various – and often unclear – notions of freedom. Accepting an opinion generally shared at the time, Boulainvilliers endorsed the idea that the Franks owed their name to the fact that they were free and, therefore, exempt from all levies and taxes.[11] For his part, the abbé Dubos argued that since they were a confederation of Germanic tribes, created 'to safeguard their own freedom', it was only natural that they would call themselves Franks – which, the abbé took for granted, meant free.[12] That the ancient Frankish peoples cherished freedom above all else, and that their name derived from their love of liberty, was an opinion still widely accepted many years later. In 1767, the abbé Bertoux (1723–1810) made the case that the Franks were a community of various Germanic nations that had merged into a federation to defend their freedom. It was this noble cause that had made a single people of them. They took on the name of Franks because it

[9] Boulainvilliers, 'Préface', in Boulainvilliers, *État de France*, i. p. xx. On the concept of *génie* in Boulainvilliers's writings, see Diego Venturino, 'Parlement e génie nel linguaggio storico di Henry de Boulainvilliers', in Caterina Cicala (ed.), *Lo storico e il suo lessico* (Naples: Società degli Storici Italiani, 1985), 90–1.

[10] Fréret, 'De l'origine des Français', v. 201.   [11] Boulainvilliers, *Essais sur la noblesse*, 148.

[12] Dubos, *Histoire critique de l'établissement de la monarchie françoise*, i. 245.

'represented what they were fighting for', the word, in Old High German, meaning 'free'. The abbé Bertoux went on to note that 'bravery and nobility of feelings were the foundation of the character of the Franks'.[13] For their part, in their famous *L'art de vérifier les dates* (1750), the Benedictine historians of Saint-Maur considered the words 'Franks' and 'free, independent', almost as synonyms. The playwright and historian Louis-Gabriel Du Buat-Nançay (1732–1787), a staunch champion of the Germanist thesis, agreed.[14] Even Louis-Sébastien Mercier argued along much the same lines. The Franks, Mercier maintained, had chosen their name after forming a federation to protect their freedom against the Roman threat. Others, such as the historian Louis-Pierre Anquetil (1723–1806), reiterated the notion that the name 'Frank' was due to their 'love for freedom'.[15] The academician, Joseph-Balthasar Gibert (1711–1771), who participated in the dispute between Germanists and Romanists with his *Mémoires pour servir à l'histoire des Gaules et de la France* (1744), advanced a different interpretation: 'Frank' came from 'fram', which was 'the name of their main weapon', a kind of spear that they also used in public deliberations to express their consent.[16] Once again, though in a novel and original way, their name was said to be related in some fashion or other to war, which clearly was of central importance to their lives, and their political freedom. In the eighteenth century few participants in the debate contested the notion of a close link between the name of the Franks and their love of freedom – howsoever understood. But one scholar who did challenge the connection was Fréret. He was adamant that there was no proof of the claim that the name came from the Franks' readiness 'to take

[13] Guillaume Bertoux, *Anecdotes françoises, depuis l'établissement de la monarchie jusqu'au règne de Louis XV* (Paris: Vincent, 1767), 2. The comment is in an unnumbered footnote running across several pages.
[14] Maur Dantine, Ursin Durand, and Charles Clémencet, *L'art de vérifier les dates des faits historiques, des chartes, des chroniques, et autres anciens monumens depuis la naissance de Notre Seigneur* (Paris: Guillaume Desprez and Pierre-Guillaume Cavelier, 1750), ii. 466; Louis-Gabriel Du Buat-Nançay, *Les origines ou L'ancien gouvernement de la France, de l'Allemagne et de l'Italie* (Paris: Didot, 1757), i. 4. Also see, for a later example: Jean-Marie Viallon, *Clovis-le-Grand, premier roi chrétien, fondateur de la monarchie française* (Paris: Méquignon l'aîné, 1788), 14.
[15] Louis-Sébastien Mercier, *Portraits des rois de France* (Neuchâtel: Imprimerie de la Société typographique, 1783), i. 3; Louis-Pierre Anquetil, *Précis de l'histoire universelle, ou Tableau historique présentant les vicissitudes des nations* (Paris: Lesguilliez frères, 1799), v. 557–8. For another example: Pierre Fresneau, *Petit abrégé chronologique et historique des rois de France, orné de leurs médaillons* (Paris: Veuve Hérissant, 1784), 3.
[16] Joseph-Balthasar Gibert, *Mémoires pour servir à l'histoire des Gaules et de la France* (Paris: Brunet fils, 1744), 213–4. On Gibert's work, see Lelong and de Fontette, *Bibliothèque historique de la France*, i. 223.

up arms to defend their freedom'.[17] Pointing out that the name had often been misused by Roman panegyrists to accuse the Franks of barbarous ferocity by associating them with the Latin 'ferox', Fréret concluded that the word actually 'was a highly honourable name meant to express their courage and their intrepidity in combat'.[18] It was therefore neither intended to designate a people who loved freedom more than others, nor to describe a most barbarous Germanic clan. It was simply used to define a particularly brave and daring tribe.

The matter was not simply one of academic interest. As Jean-Baptiste Bullet pointed out, because of its illustriousness, discovering the origin of the name 'Franks' was 'a sort of duty' for every single Frenchman.[19] National pride was important, but even more so were the underlying political implications. Shedding light on the history of their name and, hence, the original character of the French people, also meant establishing a yardstick for the legitimacy of their past and present institutions. The conviction that understanding the Franks and their way of life was tantamount to grasping the nature of the French constitution was shared, along with many others, by the historian and academician the abbé de La Bléterie (1696–1772). In an essay prefacing his own translation of a collection of Tacitus's works dedicated to d'Argenson, the abbé contended that since the 'Germanic blood and government pervades' most of modern Europe, all 'the nations formed by the mixing of conquerors and conquered' ought therefore to consider the history of the ancient Germans as the 'archives' of their laws and constitution. Among the works he had translated was Tacitus's *Germania*, the short pamphlet on the customs and character of the ancient Germanic peoples, a text that was gaining a notable reputation. According to Jaucourt, by the mid-eighteenth century it was 'in everyone's hands'.[20] One reason for its popularity was the increasingly widespread notion, sanctioned by the *Esprit des lois*, that it was 'impossible to gain any insight into our political laws unless we are intimately acquainted with

[17] Fréret, 'De l'origine des Français', v. 200.   [18] Ibid., v. 206–7.
[19] Jean-Baptiste Bullet, *Dissertations sur différens sujets de l'histoire de France* (Besançon: Charmet, 1759), 179–80.
[20] Jean-Philippe-René de La Bléterie, 'Vie de Tacite, pour servir de préface à ses ouvrages', in Tacite, *Traduction de quelques ouvrages* (Paris: Duchesne, 1755), i. pp. li–lii; Louis de Jaucourt, 'Germanie', in Diderot and d'Alembert (eds.), *Encyclopédie*, vii. 645. On the importance of Tacitus's *Germania* in eighteenth-century France, especially in connection with the debate between Romanists and Germanists, see Volpilhac-Auger, *Tacite en France de Montesquieu à Chateaubriand*, 291–401, and Battista, *La 'Germania' di Tacito nella Francia illuminista*, passim. On the impact of Tacitus's works on scholarly and political debates in early modern Europe, see Alexandra Merle and Alicia Oïffer-Bomsel (eds.), *Tacite et le tacitisme en Europe à l'époque moderne* (Paris: Honoré Champion, 2017).

the laws and manners of the German nations'.[21] Of course, some did contest the soundness of Tacitus's work or, indeed, the very idea that the foundations of the French constitution ought to be sought in the laws and customs of the Franks.[22] But since Montesquieu had made of this the cornerstone of his understanding of French history, from the mid-eighteenth century onwards many scholars accepted such an assumption. While the rediscovery of Tacitus's work through a Montesquieuan lens was an important innovation, the idea that grasping the character of the Franks could help in judging the legitimacy of French institutions was far from new. As early as 1689, in a famous and vitriolic Huguenot pamphlet *Les soupirs de la France esclave*, the debasement of political freedom was considered in conjunction with the character of the Franks. As the author unhesitatingly stated, the fact that 'now, finally, the king is everything and the state is nothing' was the result of a degeneration of the ancient Frankish nature.[23] As he saw it, since the Franks were a nomadic and warring people, their king could not have been more than a captain, the bravest and most valiant of their soldiers. They would never have granted him absolute authority since doing so would have contradicted their character and customs. Reminding his readers that 'Frank' meant 'free', he went on to make the case that Pharamond had decreed two fundamental laws: the first was that 'the people will be the masters in the election of the king'; the second, that the 'authority of the king will be limited by the will of the people'.[24] An important corollary was that the 'general assembly of the nation', which would later evolve into the Estates General, was the holder of sovereign power.[25] It was a radical thesis and, of course, it was a complete distortion of the French past given that the Estates General, even at the time of its greatest influence, had never held sovereignty. Unsurprisingly, given the subversive nature of such ideas, the pamphlet soon became extremely rare. The

---

[21] Montesquieu, 'De l'Esprit des lois', 912 (book xxx. ch. 19).

[22] See, for example, [Pierre Bouquet], *Lettres provinciales, ou Examen impartial de l'origine, de la constitution et des révolutions de la monarchie française* (The Hague: Le Neutre, 1772), 57–8.

[23] Anonymous, *Les soupirs de la France esclave, qui aspire après la liberté* (n.p., 1689), 82–3. The pamphlet is often believed to be the work of the protestant theologian and writer Pierre Jurieu (1637–1713) or of the former French Oratorian and Calvinist convert, Michel le Vassor (1648–1718). On the uncertainties concerning authorship: Antony McKenna, '*Les Soupirs de la France esclave, qui aspire après la liberté*: La question de l'attribution', in Pierre Bonnet (ed.), *Littérature de contestation: Pamphlets et polémiques du règne de Louis XIV aux Lumières* (Paris: Éditions le Manuscrit, 2011), 229–68.

[24] Anonymous, *Les soupirs de la France esclave*, 83.

[25] Ibid., 102. On this: McKenna, '*Les Soupirs de la France esclave, qui aspire après la liberté*', 258–61.

authorities went to great lengths to confiscate all copies, paying exorbitant sums to buy them from the libraries of wealthy noblemen.[26]

The pamphlet was republished almost in its entirety with a new title in 1788, possibly thanks to the Protestant clergyman and future revolutionary – and one of the countless victims of the Terror – Jean-Paul Rabaut de Saint-Étienne (1743–1793). In his introduction, the author deplored how little had changed since the times of Louis XIV, so very little, indeed, that the reader might even be misled into believing that the pamphlet in his hands was the work 'of a contemporary who has set it back one hundred years to disorient the curious or the malicious'.[27] Certainly, between the first publication of the *Les soupirs de la France esclave* and the Revolution, concerns about a royal authority seen, whether with reason or not, as curtailing the rights of the French people remained unchanged. During those one hundred years, interest in the *mœurs* of the ancient Franks extended well beyond scholarly circles, partly thanks to the *Esprit des lois*.[28] It was an intellectual development that had crucial political consequences when coupled with the increasingly intense struggle opposing the *Parlements* to the crown. The quarrel over the *Refus de sacrements* and the Maupeou coup were only the best-known episodes of the confrontation. Within this, the relationship between the ancient Frankish assemblies on the one hand, and the *Parlement* of Paris, the various *Parlements* scattered across France, and the Estates General on the other, became central in defining the limits of royal authority and establishing which institutions could rightfully claim to represent the nation.[29]

---

[26] Santé A. Viselli, '*Les Soupirs de la France esclave* (1689) et la pensée pré-révolutionnaire', *Romance Quarterly*, 37 (1990), 280–1.

[27] Anonymous, 'Avertissement de l'éditeur', in Anonymous, *Les vœux d'un patriote* (Amsterdam: n.p., 1788), x. That the publication was due to Rabaut de Saint-Étienne's initiative is a claim made, among others, by Émile Kappler, *Bibliographie critique de l'œuvre imprimée de Pierre Jurieu, 1637–1713* (Paris: Honoré Champion, 2002), 424.

[28] On the importance of Montesquieu's work in the debates concerning the *Parlements*, the Estates General, and their role, see Carcassonne, *Montesquieu et le problème de la constitution française au XVIIIᵉ siècle*, 261–96.

[29] The literature on this is almost limitless. Among the most useful works are: Roger Bickart, *Les Parlements et la notion de souveraineté nationale au XVIIIᵉ siècle* (Paris: Alcan, 1932); William Doyle, 'The Parlements of France and the Breakdown of the Old Regime, 1771–1788', *French Historical Studies*, 6 (1970), 415–58; Jean Egret, *Louis XV et l'opposition parlementaire, 1715–1774* (Paris: Armand Colin, 1970); Paolo Alatri, *Parlamenti e lotta politica nella Francia del Settecento* (Bari: Laterza, 1977); J. H. Shennan, 'The Political Vocabulary of the Parlement of Paris in the Eighteenth Century', in Società italiana di storia del diritto (ed.), *Diritto e potere nella storia europea: Atti in onore di Bruno Paradisi* (Florence: Olschki, 1982), 951–64; John Rogister, *Louis XV and the 'Parlement' of Paris, 1737–1755* (Cambridge: Cambridge University Press, 1995); Julian Swann, *Politics and the Parlement of Paris under Louis XV, 1754–1774* (Cambridge: Cambridge University Press, 1995); Arnaud Vergne, *La notion de constitution d'après les cours et assemblées à la fin de l'Ancien régime, 1750–1789* (Paris: De

One author who made a massive contribution to the debate was Louis-Adrien Le Paige (1712–1802), a leader of the Jansenist party and a prominent member of the *Parlement* of Paris.[30] According to Mably, Le Paige's most important work, the *Lettres historiques sur les fonctions essentielles du Parlement* (1753), was so much in fashion that its author had become a 'sort of oracle' for the advocates of the rights of the *Parlement*.[31] Another commentator went as far as to claim that thanks to his work 'everyone' was now aware of the fact that the *Parlement* 'represents the assemblies of the Franks, first called *Champs de Mars* and afterwards *Champs de Maï*'.[32] The main assumption behind the *Lettres historiques* was that the Frankish constitution contained the principles of a just and well-ordered monarchy. In it, one could find the fundamental laws of the modern state.[33] Partly basing his views on those of Tacitus, Le Paige argued that the *Parlement* and the monarchy, 'born at the same moment', constituted the two pillars on which the French state rested. Both equally important to the well-being of the nation, the two had different roles and functions, the king being the sole legislator and the *Parlement* the depositary of the fundamental laws.[34] Endorsing the idea that the various *Parlements* scattered throughout France were but one single institution, Le Paige campaigned for the restoration of its ancient role, that of verifying the validity of the royal edicts and turning them into legitimate laws. Of course, within such a scheme, the *Parlement* was heir to the *Champs de*

Boccard, 2006). For a good historiographical overview: Julian Swann, 'Repenser les parlements au XVIIIᵉ siècle: Du concept de "l'opposition parlementaire" à celui de "culture juridique des conflits politiques"', in Alain J. Lemaître (ed.), *Le monde parlementaire au XVIIIᵉ siècle: L'invention d'un discours politique* (Rennes: Presses universitaires de Rennes, 2010), 17–38. On the consequences of the debates over the nature and rights of the *Parlements* for conceptions of the nation, see Slimani, *La modernité du concept de nation au XVIIIᵉᵐᵉ siècle*, passim.

[30] On Le Paige's ideas: John Rogister, 'Louis-Adrien Lepaige and the Attack on *De l'Esprit* and the *Encyclopédie* in 1759', *The English Historical Review*, 92 (1977), 522–39; Catherine Maire, 'Louis-Adrien Le Paige entre Saint-Simon et Montesquieu', *Cahiers Saint-Simon*, 27 (1999), 37–47; Maire, *De la cause de Dieu à la cause de la nation*, passim.; Francesco Di Donato, 'Le concept de représentation dans la doctrine juridico-politique de Louis-Adrien Le Paige', in Centre d'études et de recherches d'histoire des idées et des institutions politiques (ed.), *Le concept de représentation dans la pensée politique* (Aix-en-Provence: Presses universitaires d'Aix-Marseille, 2003), 53–73.

[31] Gabriel Bonnot de Mably, 'Observations sur l'histoire de France' (1765–1788), in *Œuvres*, iii. 357. The third and last volume of the *Observations* was published posthumously.

[32] Barthélemy-Gabriel Rolland d'Erceville, *Lettre à M. l'abbé Velly, sur les tomes III et IV de son histoire de France: Au sujet de l'autorité des États, et du droit du Parlement de vérifier les édits, déclarations, etc.* (n.p., 1756), 3.

[33] Louis-Adrien Le Paige, *Lettres historiques sur les fonctions essentielles du Parlement, sur le droit des pairs et sur les loix fondamentales du royaume* (Amsterdam: aux dépens de la Compagnie, 1753), i. 5.

[34] Le Paige, *Lettres historiques sur les fonctions essentielles du Parlement*, i. 123. References to Tacitus may be found throughout the two volumes. See, for example, ibid., i. 8, 10, 14, 19, 22, 90, 274 and ii. 5.

Mars. The only difference was in the number of its members. While originally the entire nation made up this assembly, now it was restricted to 'the grandees, the princes, peers, and its first senators'.[35] Importantly, while in Le Paige's scheme the king alone held legislative power, the fact that the *Parlement*'s magistrates were the heirs of those sitting in the Frankish assemblies turned them into the custodians of the fundamental laws. Consequently, their role in perfecting any edict was essential. From such an angle, if they were the nation's representatives, meaning that they (re)presented to the king the grievances of his people, their exceptional knowledge of the ancient constitution reflected their unique relationship with the French past.[36] Arguably, while some of the ideas in the *Lettres historiques* were aimed at limiting the royal authority, the views expressed were, all in all, far from subversive. As Baker has pointed out, Le Paige accepted the old royalist national narrative 'as a kind of subtext to the work itself, one constituted by an assumed collective memory of shared national existence'.[37] The intrinsic merits of Le Paige's work lay in his attempts, through the study of the past, to discover arguments serving to limit the absolute power of the kings, which he saw as a debasement of the ancient constitution. But it was an attempt destined to fail, and this for several reasons. One crucial shortcoming of the *Lettres historiques* was its failure to tie the nature, morals, and customs of the Franks to their own laws or the French constitution. In fact, in the opening pages, the reader was told of a ferocious and warlike people with many faults and vices offset by a 'purity of *mœurs*' now lost.[38] However, not much was made of this. The connection between the Frankish passion for war and their love of freedom remained unexplored; and so too did the relationship between the debasing of the constitution and the corruption of the French character. Importantly, as we shall see shortly, it was a concern to which others would return in the second half of the eighteenth century.

[35] [Louis-Adrien Le Paige], *Lettre dans laquelle on examine s'il est vrai que la doctrine de l'État contenue dans les dernières remontrances du Parlement, au sujet du grand conseil, porte aucune atteinte à l'autorité souveraine du roi et à son caractère sacré de seul législateur dans son royaume* (n.p., n.d.), 43 and 47. The pamphlet might have been written in 1756. For dating and attribution: Maire, *De la cause de Dieu à la cause de la nation*, 687.

[36] See, on this, Di Donato, 'Le concept de représentation dans la doctrine juridico-politique de Louis-Adrien le Paige', 57–63.

[37] On the point, Baker, 'Memory and Practice', 42.

[38] Le Paige, *Lettres historiques sur les fonctions essentielles du Parlement*, 7–8.

Germanic Freedom(s) and Myths of Regeneration:
Mably and Lézardière

According to the scholar Pierre-Charles Levesque (1736–1812), the abbé de Mably deserved a place of honour among historians. The principal aim of Mably's works, he noted, was to understand 'the character of those nations of which he outlines the history; to find in the facts he chooses [to examine] the corruption or the goodness of their legislation or their regime; the influence of the government on the peoples, and that of the peoples' manners and mind on the endurance or the decadence of states; finally, to instruct the present times and posterity through the picture of the vices and virtues of the past'.[39] Obviously, given its nature and aims, the text is highly deferential. However, Levesque's eulogy grasped certain aspects of the abbé's approach to the study of the past.[40] One was the firm belief that history 'must be a school of morals and politics'.[41] From the publication of his *Parallèle des Romains et des François par rapport au gouvernement* (1740) onwards, the abbé had insisted time and time again that only through the study of the past could rulers and statesmen learn to govern with fairness and justice their people, and these, in their turn, might learn to be good and loyal citizens.[42] As for the historian, he should 'feel the most profound respect' for his nation's usages, *mœurs*, and customs and should strive to unmask the vices and extoll the virtues of his countrymen.[43] Mably tied this moral and civic duty to the historian's main intellectual objective, that of grasping the causes of events by focusing on the relationship between customs and laws which, in turn, he saw as the engine of historical change.[44] The influence of Montesquieu, whom

---

[39] Pierre-Charles Levesque, *Eloge historique de M. l'abbé de Mably* (Paris: Guillot, 1787), 33–4.

[40] On Mably's ideas about history and its relationship to politics: Luciano Guerci, 'Note sulla storiografia di Mably: Il problema dei Franchi nelle *Observations sur l'histoire de France*', in Istituto italiano per gli studi storici (ed.), *Saggi e ricerche sul Settecento* (Naples: Istituto italiano per gli studi storici, 1963), 453–512; Johnson K. Wright, *A Classical Republican in Eighteenth-Century France: The Political Thought of Mably* (Stanford: Stanford University Press, 1997), 125–61. Another well-researched intellectual biography of Mably, besides Wright's, is: Peter Friedemann, *Die politische Philosophie des Gabriel Bonnot de Mably (1709–1785): Eine Studie zur Geschichte des republikanischen und des sozialen Freiheitsbegriffs* (Berlin: LIT, 2014).

[41] Mably, 'De l'étude de l'histoire', 1. The quote is the title of the first chapter of Mably's work.

[42] Mably, 'De la manière d'écrire l'histoire', 397. See also Gabriel Bonnot de Mably, *Parallèle des Romains et des François par rapport au gouvernement* (Paris: Didot, 1740), i. p. ii–iv. On the study of the past and its role in educating rulers, see also Gabriel Bonnot de Mably, 'Observations sur l'histoire de la Grèce' (1764), in *Œuvres*, iv, p. iv, and Mably, 'De l'étude de l'histoire', 352–64.

[43] Mably, 'De la manière d'écrire l'histoire', 398.

[44] On this, see Guerci, 'Note sulla storiografia di Mably', 465–8. On Mably's historical thought, see Luciana Alocco-Bianco, 'L'abbé de Mably et sa conception de l'histoire', in Centre aixois d'études et de recherches sur le XVIIIᵉ siècle (ed.), *L'histoire au dix-huitième siècle* (Aix-en-Provence: La Calade, 1980), 223–32.

Mably profoundly admired, is patent: 'If I am not instructed on the *mœurs* and the laws that form the political constitution, in vain will you offer me a series of events that deserve to be known. I fail to unravel the causes, and I attribute the success accompanying them to those who are in command.'[45] Considering the influence of *mœurs* and ways of life on a nation's constitution seemed to Mably all the more important in the case of the Germanic tribes, those 'barbarians who laid the foundations of our modern states'. These he saw as even worthier of the historian's attention than the Romans who, after all, had lived to witness the destruction of their empire. The ancient Germanic tribes, having founded many states that were still in existence, had offered the 'world a model for the most perfect code of politics'. And if the few historians who had written about the ancient Germans failed to attract the attention of their readers, it was because they neglected their *mœurs* and customs. It was a fault that made it impossible to grasp their history and condemned the reader 'to follow in the track of a historian who does not know the paths along which he wanders'. Instead, argued Mably, it would suffice to consider 'the character of the army under Clovis, the spirit of liberty which they brought from Germany, and the acceptance of slavery they found on the part of the Gauls', to properly understand the whole history of France.[46]

It was in his *Observations sur l'histoire de France*, a work that one observer deemed 'the most precious monument ever built on the debris of our history', that Mably made of the Frankish character the lynchpin of the political institutions of ancient France.[47] Another eulogy of the abbé, this one by a lawyer in the *Parlement* of Paris, Gabriel Brizard (1744–1793), summarised the main thesis of the *Observations*:

> [It] gives us a picture of a Frankish republic which, regardless of what others have said, is not at all imaginary. One can see freedom emerging with them from the forests of Germany and releasing the Gauls from the Roman oppression and yoke. Clovis is only the general and the first magistrate of the liberating people; and it is, so to speak, on a republican constitution that Mably places the cradle of the monarchy.[48]

---

[45] Mably, 'De la manière d'écrire l'histoire', 408–9. On Mably's appreciation of Montesquieu, see, for example: Gabriel Bonnot de Mably, 'Observations sur les Romains' (1751), in *Œuvres*, iv, 571, n. 1. The influence of Montesquieu on Mably had already been noted by Voltaire: François-Marie Arouet Voltaire to Charles-Jean-François Hénault, 2 March 1740, in *Œuvres*, xxxv. 392.

[46] Mably, 'De la manière d'écrire l'histoire', 411–2.

[47] Anonymous, review of Gabriel Bonnot de Mably, *Observations sur l'histoire de France*, in Grimm et al., *Correspondance littéraire*, xv. 359 (December 1788). On the popularity of Mably's *Observations* and his other works in the second half of the eighteenth century and during the Revolution, see: Éphraïm Harpaz, 'Mably et ses contemporains', *Revue des sciences humaines*, 82 (1955), 351–66.

[48] Gabriel Brizard, 'Eloge historique de l'abbé Mably' (1787), in Mably, *Œuvres*, i. 23.

In effect, Brizard's own political stance might have clouded his judgement and led him to offer an excessively republican reading of the *Observations*.[49] And yet he rightly emphasised Mably's conviction that the political institutions of the Franks, created to preserve and protect their freedom, ought to be considered against the backdrop of their character and customs. In fact, Mably's Franks – whom he rather confusingly called French, *François* – were:

> A proud, brutal people, without a country, without laws, in which each soldier lived only for loot, [a people] that did not want to be troubled with any chastisements and did not punish with death [anything] but treason, or murder, or laziness, [that] had to have a captain and not a monarch. The French could tolerate, from their chief, even atrocious acts of violence, since these were part of their public *mœurs*, but an authority accepted, supported by reason was impracticable. . . . As a prince, the king had no subjects, since, as a general, he commanded soldiers who fought for their own interest.[50]

Once again, Clovis was depicted as nothing more than a general ruling over an army; and, once again, the ferocity and the martial nature of the Franks was used to explain their love for freedom. Proceeding then to consider the relationship between the Gauls and the Franks, Mably contended that, following the invasion, the former were no longer slaves, since the 'French only knew the idea of freedom'. The notion itself of tyranny seemed to imply views and principles that were alien to them.[51] However, and notwithstanding Brizard's keenness on the point, Mably never believed that the Gauls were instantly exempted from all burdens, and, certainly, he never thought they were immediately permitted to take part in the public assemblies. On the contrary, their political emancipation was a slow process that began long after the Franks had settled in Gaul and was completed only much later, thanks to Charlemagne (748–814), the true 'legislator of the French'.[52] Interestingly, and importantly, a swifter change was experienced on the side of the conquerors. In fact, no sooner had the Franks invaded than the wealth and luxuries acquired through the conquest transformed their character: '[A]s soon as they established themselves in Gaul – wrote Mably – their love for freedom was no longer their first passion. Their conquests loosened the spring of their government. New needs and new circumstances, instilling in them ideas different to those

[49] On Gabriel Brizard, see René-Jean Durdent, 'Brizard', in Michaud (ed.), *Biographie universelle ancienne et moderne*, v. 632–3.

[50] Mably, 'Observations sur l'histoire de France', i. 133–4.   [51] Ibid., i. 144.

[52] Ibid., i. 248. See, on this, Guerci, 'La storiografia di Mably', 484–5.

they had brought with them from Germany, foolishly severed them from their ancient political principles.'[53] The first consequence of this moral corrupting and political debasing – the former being the cause of the latter – was that the principles of popular government were soon forgotten. Power was seized by the king and a few noblemen who, against the interests and the welfare of France, began a long-lasting struggle to gain absolute power.[54] If the Franks had once been 'absolutely free', their new lust for riches brought about the end of their freedom. Here the abbé's reasoning seemed to be borne out by comparing the histories of England and France, an apt comparison since, in both countries, the constitution had been forged from that of the ancient Germans – or so Mably contended. According to the abbé, while the English always fought and opposed royal authority and 'always maintained their character', the opposite was true of the French. Vexed though they were by their kings' abuses and injustices, their irritation was invariably but 'a passing effervescence', their habits always leading 'them back under the yoke of the monarchy'.[55] To see the truth of this, it sufficed to examine:

> [T]he character of the French nation and to judge the resistance it might oppose to the government. The faults of laxity, luxury, avarice, and a servile impulse that have so debased the French since the kingdom of Louis XIII, have degraded their souls to such a degree that having still enough reasons for fearing despotism, they have no more courage to love freedom.[56]

It was by considering this demeaning of the ancient freedom that the abbé, if only in passing, offered an explanation of the Maupeou coup, an episode that had proven that fear of disorder in the French was stronger than their fear of despotism. The conclusion he reached was bitter: 'The more such fear is vain and puerile, the more it is certain that our character is in accordance with our government and that we do not have, deep within us, any principle of revolution.'[57] The only possible solution lay in educating the nation to the virtues of patriotism, reviving in all citizens their love for freedom.

Of course, Mably shared Montesquieu's belief that the Franks were 'warriors and freemen' and the baron's notion that these two qualities were somehow inseparable. As he saw it, the Frankish nation was 'savage, poor, free, and warring'.[58] Here, the abbé's reference to their frugality is revealing

---

[53] Mably, 'Observations sur l'histoire de France', i. 155.   [54] Ibid., i. 152.   [55] Ibid., ii. 250.
[56] Ibid., iii. 305.
[57] Ibid., iii. 306; see Wright, *A Classical Republican in Eighteenth-Century France*, 153.
[58] Montesquieu, 'De l'Esprit des lois', 329 (book vi. ch. 18); Mably, 'Observations sur l'histoire de France', ii. 508.

since it tied in with eighteenth-century debates over luxury and decadence and the idea, espoused by all those who chastised the opulence and self-indulgence tainting the French nation, that virtues could only 'grow and flourish' out of poverty.[59] Famously, in his *Discours sur les sciences et les arts*, Rousseau insisted on the contrast between wealth, the arts and sciences, and decadence on the one hand, and frugality, the warring spirit, and the flourishing of patriotic virtues on the other. Although the Spartans, those 'demi-gods', were his unsurpassable model, he did mention other peoples, including the Franks, who had subdued the Gauls by dint of their 'courage and poverty' alone.[60] The idea that frugality and martial spirit were often to be found together was not new. Velly had contended that the Franks, a 'more warlike than civilised' people, were 'more jealous of their freedom than desirous of those possessions that procure the delights of life'. They were even unaware of the very existence of gold and silver. Despising all those 'abominations that [had] dishonoured Greece and Italy', they were 'zealous citizens, always ready to sacrifice their lives for the nation'. Vertot had made similar arguments long before, when he contended that even in their looting and pillage the Franks never sought gold or silver out of pure greed: 'Like most of the Germans, they were blithely unaware of the value and uses of such useful and dangerous metals', cherishing above all else 'strength, courage, and freedom'.[61]

The relationship between the Franks' love of freedom and their lust for war or readiness to sacrifice themselves for the nation underscoring such views is complex, to say the least. While the beliefs described above clearly related to debates over the respective merits of the fighting and the trading nobility, they also entailed or required a reassessment of the place of Rome in French history.[62] It was a controversial topic, not least because it

---

[59] The expression is from Helvétius, *De l'esprit*, 369. On this point, see: Galliani, *Rousseau, le luxe et l'idéologie nobiliaire*, passim, and Istvan Hont, 'The Early Enlightenment Debate on Commerce and Luxury', in Mark Goldie and Robert Wokler (eds.), *The Cambridge History of Eighteenth-Century Political Thought* (Cambridge: Cambridge University Press, 2006), 379–418.

[60] Rousseau, 'Discours sur les sciences et les arts', 20. The reference to the Spartans is on page 12. On the point, see Alexis Philonenko, *Jean-Jacques Rousseau et la pensée du malheur* (Paris: Vrin, 1984), i. 85–8. Also see, Carlo Borghero, 'Sparta tra storia e utopia: Il significato e la funzione del mito di Sparta nel pensiero di Jean-Jacques Rousseau', in Giovanni Solinas (ed.), *Saggi sull'Illuminismo* (Cagliari: Pubblicazioni dell'Istituto di Filosofia, 1973), 253–318.

[61] Velly, *Histoire de France*, i. p. 5; René Aubert de Vertot, 'Dissertation dans laquelle on tâche de démêler la véritable origine des Français, par un parallèle de leurs mœurs avec celles des Germains' (published in 1717 but written between 1710 and 1711), in Leber (ed.), *Collection des meilleurs dissertations relatifs à l'histoire de France*, i. 62.

[62] On the debate over fighting and trading nobility, see Chapter 4. On the place of Rome in the historiography of France, see: Grell, *Le dix-huitième siècle et l'antiquité en France*, passim; de Senarclens, *Montesquieu, historien de Rome*, passim; Nicolet, *La fabrique d'une nation*, passim.

touched upon the part played by Roman cultural heritage in modern France, in a society still wholly captivated by the classical world. In his *Parallèle des Romains et des François*, Mably favourably compared the Roman Empire to the kingdom of Louis XIV, claiming that both had achieved political and cultural perfection and that the two shared a unique role in world history.[63] Portraying the French monarchy as the most perfect polity, even superior to that of ancient Rome, the *Parallèle* was welcomed by royalist authors as a vindication of the crown's authority and as the promising debut of a talented scholar.[64] But Mably would soon recant, even coming to despise the *Parallèle*.[65] In an anecdote told by Brizard, Mably once saw a copy in the library of a friend, picked it up, and, without a word, tore it to pieces.[66] By the time of the publication of his *Observations sur les Romains*, in 1751, the abbé had turned into a firm advocate of a kind of classical republicanism that many revolutionaries would themselves later espouse. The Roman cult of civic virtues, the unremitting struggle between patricians and plebeians, the partition of authority between different institutions, and the love of each and every class for the common good all struck Mably as key elements in a faultless polity. It was following the creation of the tribunate, when the 'people took possession of sovereignty' and an equitable balance between the different classes had been established, that Rome became the 'perfect republic'.[67] Contained in the *Observations* was a veiled and yet clear disparagement of the claim of the French kings to absolute authority. Yet Mably's *Des droits et des devoirs du citoyen*, published posthumously in 1789 but already circulating in manuscript form, went even further.[68] One conservative critic, the abbé de Gourcy, appalled by the audacity of the *Des droits et des devoirs*, discerned in its pages a 'fanaticism for liberty' that went beyond

---

[63] See, on the point, Edward G. Andrew, *Imperial Republics: Revolution, War, and Territorial Expansion from the English Civil War to the French Revolution* (Toronto: University of Toronto Press, 2011), 127.

[64] Anonymous, review of [Gabriel Bonnot de Mably], *Parallèle des Romains et des François par rapport au gouvernement*, in *Journal de Trévoux, ou Mémoires pour servir à l'histoire des sciences et des arts*, February 1741, 323–5. On Mably's 'royalist debut': Wright, *A Classical Republican in Eighteenth-Century France*, 22–38.

[65] Mably, 'Observations sur les Romains', 253–4, and Mably, 'Observations sur l'histoire de France', i. 121–2.

[66] Brizard, 'Eloge historique de l'abbé Mably', 98.

[67] Mably, 'Observations sur les Romains', 280.

[68] On *Des droits et des devoirs du citoyen* and on Mably's republicanism, Keith M. Baker, 'A Script for a French Revolution: The Political Consciousness of the abbé Mably', in Baker, *Inventing the French Revolution*, 86–106.

all acceptable limits.[69] The expression used by de Gourcy is remarkable since, in some respects, it adumbrated the criticism formulated a few years later by Benjamin Constant (1767–1830). In his famous 'La liberté des anciens comparée à celle des modernes' (1819), the great liberal thinker accused Mably of bearing even greater responsibility than Rousseau for endorsing a notion of freedom that could have no place in the world of the *modernes*.[70] His republicanism, argued Constant, had inspired the Jacobins and their cult for ancient republics, leading to their dismal and deleterious attempt to transpose the ancient idea of freedom into the modern world. Famously, Constant defined the freedom of the ancients, whose existence was so centred on war and conquest, as the greatest possible participation in the exercise of power. Conversely, the kernel of the liberty of the moderns, so much inclined to commerce and trade, was in the sets of rules and principles guaranteeing the independence of citizens from the authority of the state.[71] It was a distinction that informed a state's institutions and modes of rule as much as a people's customs and manners. Crucially, according to Constant, it was the absence of clear constraints upon the action of rulers that made Mably's and Rousseau's ideas so dangerous.

In truth, the abbé's understanding of freedom(s) was more complex than Constant contended and, indeed, Mably had never argued that the forms of rule of ancient republics were applicable to modern-day France. The fact

---

[69] François-Antoine-Étienne de Gourcy, *Des droits et des devoirs du citoyen dans les circonstances présentes, avec un jugement impartial sur l'ouvrage de M. l'abbé de Mably* (n.p., 1789), 9.

[70] Benjamin Constant, 'De la liberté des anciens comparée à celle des modernes', in *Écrits politiques* (Paris: Gallimard, 1997), 605. The speech was delivered in 1819 at the Paris Athénée Royal. Partly, this argument was already in Benjamin Constant, *Principes de politique (1806)* (Geneva: Droz, 1980), ii. 420–44. For an overview of Constant's distinction between ancient and modern freedom, see Biancamaria Fontana, *Benjamin Constant and the Post-Revolutionary Mind* (New Haven: Yale University Press, 1991), 48–67, and Jeremy Jennings, 'Constant's Idea of Modern Liberty', in Helena Rosenblatt (ed.), *The Cambridge Companion to Constant* (Cambridge: Cambridge University Press, 2009), 69–91. On previous distinctions between ancient and modern notions of freedom, see: Luciano Guerci, *Libertà degli antichi e libertà dei moderni: Sparta, Atene e i philosophes nella Francia del Settecento* (Naples: Guida, 1979), and François Hartog, 'Liberté des anciens, liberté des modernes: La Révolution française et l'antiquité', in Roger-Pol Droit (ed.), *Les Grecs, les Romains et nous: L'antiquité est-elle moderne?* (Paris: Le Monde, 1991), 119–38. Interestingly, Constant's dear companion Madame de Staël had already made the distinction, in 1795, in her *Réflexions sur la paix intérieure*, and in her *Des circonstances actuelles qui peuvent terminer la Révolution et des principes qui doivent fonder la République en France*, written around 1798. On this, see John Claiborne Isbell, 'Le contrat social selon Benjamin Constant et Mme de Staël, ou La liberté a-t-elle un sexe?', *Cahiers de l'Association internationale des études françaises*, 48 (1996), 439–56.

[71] Constant, 'De la liberté des anciens comparée à celle des modernes', 595. In passing, it is perhaps worth noting that Constant was overlooking the fact that between 1792 and 1793, it was the *moderate* Girondins who promoted the war against Austria, Great Britain, and the Dutch Republic, while the *radical* Jacobins opposed it.

that during the Revolution his works became popular among royalists, advocates of the rights of the nobility, supporters of the bourgeoisie, and – if to a lesser degree and thus partly refuting Constant's argument – Jacobin enthusiasts is revealing of the malleability of his ideas and hints at the complexity of his thought.[72] How Mably's republicanism stood in relation to the ideas of freedom of the *anciens* and the *modernes* is a matter of debate.[73] But what is interesting, here, is the underlying relationship between the Roman heritage and the character of the Franks – and, by extension, the French. Throughout the eighteenth century, a good number of scholars accepted the view that the fall of Rome could be imputed to its moral decadence, to the growing thirst for wealth of its citizens, and their rejecting of their ancestors' *mos maiorum*. Many accepted Montesquieu's argument, set out in his *Considérations sur les Romains*, that the turning point lay in the passage from republican to imperial Rome, a shift that was political as much as cultural.[74] However, in Mably's scheme this change affected even the Franks, their values, and their way of life. According to the abbé, it was because of their contact with the Roman Empire at the time of its moral debasement and corruption, but also at the acme of its wealth and power, that the Franks became possessed by an 'insatiable avidity' for gold and turned to the pleasures of life.[75] It was an interesting way of depicting the relationship between Rome, responsible for the degrading of the Frankish character, and French civilisation at large. The point was developed at length in an anonymous pamphlet inspired by the works of Mably, possibly published in 1790. According to the author, 'our fathers the Germans' enjoyed the most liberal of governments until they crossed the Rhine. Then, 'once they had settled in Gaul, they exchanged their virile energy for the corrupted mores of the Romans. The king knew how to take advantage' of the new state of affairs.[76] Decadence, the craving for wealth, and loss of freedom, the author implied, were all caused by

[72] On the popularity of Mably's works during the Revolution, see the comment in [Jean-Baptiste Isoard de Lisle], 'Discours préliminaire', in Gabriel Bonnot de Mably, *Des droits et des devoirs du citoyen, édition augmentée d'un Discours préliminaire par l'auteur de La philosophie de la nature* (Paris: Louis, 1793), i. 2. Also see, Thomas Schleich, *Aufklärung und Revolution: Die Wirkungsgeschichte Gabriel Bonnot de Mablys in Frankreich (1740–1914)* (Stuttgart: Klett-Cotta, 1981), 155–61, and Thomas Schleich, 'Presupposti, forme e conseguenze della risonanza politica di Mably nel periodo della Rivoluzione francese', *Rivista di storia della filosofia*, 39 (1984), 687–719.
[73] See, on this, Stéphanie Roza, 'L'abbé de Mably, entre modérantisme et radicalité', *Tangence*, 106 (2014), 29–50. Also see, Jean-Fabien Spitz, 'Droit et vertu chez Mably', *Corpus: Revue de philosophie*, 14–15 (1990), 61–95.
[74] On this, Senarclens, *Montesquieu, historien de Rome*, 21–60.
[75] Mably, 'Observations sur l'histoire de France', i. 143.
[76] Anonymous, *Réflexions d'un ami de la liberté ou Principes de M. l'abbé de Mably* (n.p., 1790), 4.

contamination from the decadent Roman Empire. It was a process precipitated from outside of the Frankish – and, by extension, the French – nation.
Yet returning to the *Observations*, it becomes clear that Mably's own image
of the Franks, even before the invasion of Gaul, was far from entirely
positive. In fact, while he was adamant that the Franks originally cherished
freedom above all else, he also added that they were 'brutal, without
fatherland [*patrie*], lawless', and that each 'citizen soldier', living only 'off
his own plunder', fought for his own interest.[77] A gulf clearly separated the
inchoate and precarious freedom of the Frankish tribes and the republicanism praised by Mably in his *Des droits et des devoirs du citoyen*.

As Augustin Thierry noted in the late 1830s, Mably's *Observations*
posited a 'divorce' between French history and the Roman heritage. The
same was true of the *Théorie des lois politiques de la monarchie française*.[78]
Written by Marie-Charlotte-Pauline Robert Lézardière (1754–1835),
a member of the Vendean aristocracy with a passion for history, it was
a work of remarkable erudition and scholarship, the product of twenty-five
years of tireless research.[79] Its main aim was to offer its readers a theory of
the French constitution and a historical account of the nation's political
institutions, from their origins to the eighteenth century. The approach
was that of a committed Germanist, cherishing the notion of a moderate
monarchy limited by the authority of its aristocracy. Published by Nyon
aîné et fils in 1792, it was secretly subsidised by the king in a last unavailing
effort to persuade public opinion to accept his rule as legitimate.[80]
Unsurprisingly, its circulation ended immediately because of the radical
turn taken by the Revolution, when theories of constitutional monarchy
had become unpopular in France. The *Théorie* was only published posthumously, in its entirety and with a section added and edited by Lézardière's

---

[77] Mably, 'Observations sur l'histoire de France', i. 133.

[78] Thierry, 'Considérations sur l'histoire de France', 129.

[79] On de Lézardière's life and ideas, see: Carcassonne, *Montesquieu et le problème de la constitution*,
478–512; Elie Carcassonne, 'Introduction', in Marie-Charlotte-Pauline Robert de Lézardière, *Écrits
inédits* (Paris: Presses universitaires de France, 1927), 2–38; Christine Fauré, 'Mademoiselle de
Lézardière entre Jeanne d'Arc et Montesquieu', in Marie-France Brive (ed.), *Les femmes et la
Révolution française* (Toulouse: Presses universitaires du Mirail, 1989–1991), i. 183–90;
Brigitte Carmaux, 'Mlle de Lézardière: Une certaine idée de la monarchie française', *Annales de
Bretagne et des pays de l'Ouest*, 102 (1995), 67–74; Jean-François Jacouty, 'Une contribution à la
pensée aristocratique des Lumières: La *Théorie des lois politiques de la monarchie française* de Pauline
de Lézardière', *Revue française d'histoire des idées politiques*, 17 (2003), 3–47; Carolina Armenteros,
'Royalist Medievalism in the Age of Revolution: From Robert de Lézardière to Chateaubriand,
1792–1831', *RELIEF*, 8 (2014), 20–47.

[80] Carla Hesse, 'French Women in Print, 1750–1800: An Essay in Historical Bibliography', in Haydn
T. Mason (ed.), *The Darnton Debate: Books and Revolution in the Eighteenth Century* (Oxford:
Voltaire Foundation, 1998), 77.

brother, in 1844, thanks to the support of Villemain and François Guizot (1787–1874), at the time Minister of Education and Minister of Foreign Affairs respectively.[81] Although the circulation of the *Théorie* was limited, both Guizot and the great jurist and historian Friedrich Carl von Savigny (1779–1861) praised Lézardière's scholarship and erudition.[82]

Ambitiously conceived as an attempt to complement and thus to perfect the *Esprit des lois*, Lézardière's *Théorie* made the case that the Frankish invasion of Gaul had been a war against the Romans rather than an act of conquest.[83] While this was a thesis she shared with Mably, Lézardière, unlike the abbé, did not argue for a blending of the Franks and the Gauls, not even in the long run. On the contrary, she maintained that they continued to be politically distinct throughout history. In her judgement, when the Germanic tribes invaded France, the Gauls remained passive spectators since centuries of serfdom had led them 'into a purely passive condition', a torpor they seemed unable to shake off.[84] Their character, debased and degraded by a long and humiliating servitude, prevented them from fighting against the Romans first and the Franks afterwards to regain their liberty. Moreover, while most peoples of Europe had endured the Roman yoke, the 'savage peoples of Germany' retained their independence and fought back until they finally destroyed the Empire. One had to seek in the 'original character' of the Franks 'the precious germ which was destined to reproduce liberty on earth'.[85] Their bravery, their 'passion for war, for liberty and equality and hatred of luxury' were the main characteristics of the German tribes.[86] These she saw as 'warriors, free, indomitable, ignorant, barbarians' who, nonetheless – or, possibly, for these very reasons – having a clear idea of their political interests, cherished 'freedom and independence' as their 'supreme good'. This made all the difference with the submissive Gauls.[87] As free men, the Franks alone had the right to bear

[81] Eutrope-Charles-Athanase-Benjamin Robert de Lézardière, 'Avertissement', in Marie-Charlotte-Pauline Robert de Lézardière, *Théorie des lois politiques de la monarchie française* (Paris: Comptoir des imprimeurs-unis, 1844), i. p. ix.

[82] François Guizot, *Histoire générale de la civilisation en Europe* (Paris: Pichon et Didier, 1828), 14 (lecture 1); Friedrich Carl von Savigny, *Geschichte des römischen Rechts im Mittelalter* (Heidelberg: Mohr and Zimmer, 1815–1831), i. pp. xxvi–xxvii.

[83] On the author's ambitious intent: Marie-Charlotte-Pauline Robert de Lézardière, 'Mes adieux ou Mon dernier mot' (1829), unpublished manuscript quoted in Jacouty, 'Une contribution à la pensée aristocratique des Lumières', 7, n. 9. On the point, see also the fleeting remark in Thierry, 'Considérations sur l'histoire de France', 118.

[84] Lézardière, *Théorie des lois politiques de la monarchie française*, i. 54.   [85] Ibid., i. 57.

[86] Ibid., i. 60.

[87] Marie-Charlotte-Pauline Robert de Lézardière, 'Tableau des droits réels et respectifs du monarque et des sujets depuis le fondement de la monarchie française jusqu'à nos jours' (1774), in *Ecrits inédits*, 55.

arms and defend the nation and, consequently, they alone had the right to meet in the general assemblies, where they 'deliberated on all major questions'. In this rather narrow sense, Lézardière could claim that the Frankish government 'was essentially democratic'.[88] The division between free men and slaves, between nobles and commoners, subsisted, corresponding as it did to the one between fighters and farmers; in a way, between those who had loved freedom to the point of risking their lives, and those who had accepted the rule of the Romans. In time, of course, that distinction acquired a new meaning, but its consequences for the French constitution remained unaltered. In the France of her day, it was in fact the duty of the nobility to defend freedom and to resist the excesses of royal authority. In many ways, Lézardière's *Théorie* encapsulated the main tenets of the Germanist approach, echoing some of Boulainvilliers's arguments. That during the Revolution her work could be used to support the idea of a moderate monarchy and its nobility for one last, desperate attempt to save the crown is unsurprising. What is remarkable is that she had adhered strictly to the scheme that contrasted Roman decadence with Germanic regeneration, reiterating the divorce between Roman heritage and French history in Mably's works.[89]

On Romans, Celts, and Gauls

The downplaying of the role of Rome in the nation's past by the Germanist scholars had important ideological consequences and significant political implications. The myth of Rome, so cherished by the Humanist tradition, was often associated with those notions of progress and civilisation that somehow stood at the centre of the Enlightenment. These were pitted against the brutal and obscurantist centuries following the fall of Rome at the hands of barbaric hordes that knew no law, philosophy, sciences, nor arts. Many scholars who praised the splendour of Roman civilisation celebrated the Empire – whether with reason or not – for having carried throughout Europe and to the shores of the Mediterranean justice and order, and for the social and material progress it brought to its peoples. Gibbon and William Robertson (1721–1793) were, of course, among them.[90] Yet so too was Voltaire. In many of his works the great *philosophe*, denying the Germanic tribes their role as bearers of modern freedom, saw

---

[88] De Lézardière, *Théorie des lois politiques*, 61.

[89] See Jacouty, 'Une contribution à la pensée aristocratique des Lumières', 9–14.

[90] See, for example, Gibbon, *The Decline and Fall of the Roman Empire*, iii. 246–328; William Robertson, *The History of the Reign of the Emperor Charles V: With a View of the Progress*

them as mere savages who had destroyed one of the greatest civilisations in history, bringing to an end the classical world he so admired: 'To pass from the history of the Roman Empire to that of the peoples that tore it apart in the East, is to resemble a traveller who, leaving a proud city, finds himself in deserts covered with brambles.'[91] Tacitus's book had misled scholars and historians into believing the Germans to be a valorous, free, and indomitable people. Extolling the so-called Germanic virtues was merely Tacitus's way of scorning and criticising the Roman Emperors and their courts. In truth, argued Voltaire, the Germans were barbarians who 'lived by rapine rather than the ploughing of the land, and who after having plundered their neighbours returned home to enjoy their booty. Today, this is the life of cut-purses and highwaymen, whom we punish on the wheel and by hanging.'[92] As he declared in his *Traité sur la tolérance* (1763), the human sacrifices perpetrated by the Germans confirmed that they were bloodthirsty savages, slaves to absurd myths and horrendous superstitions.[93] Even when considering their political institutions, Voltaire was no less severe. As he saw it, the assemblies of the ancient Germans were places where 'almost all the great questions were decided with the sword'. Tellingly, he added, 'one had to admit that these ancient assemblies of wild warriors and our courts of justice share nothing but the name'.[94] Voltaire's overall judgement of the ancient Germans may well have been, in truth, more nuanced.[95] But what is important, here, is that all attempts to tie their warring spirit and barbaric nature to any notion of freedom would have struck the great *philosophe* as wholly absurd.

of Society in Europe, from the Subversion of the Roman Empire to the Beginning of the Sixteenth Century (London: W. Strahan, 1769), i. 1–192.

[91] Voltaire, 'Essai sur les mœurs et l'esprit des nations', xi. 246.

[92] Ibid., xi. 161–2. On Voltaire's dislike of Tacitus as a historian, see François-Marie Arouet Voltaire to Marie Anne de Vichy-Chamrond, Marquise du Deffand, 30 July 1768, in *Œuvres*, xlvi. 88.

[93] François-Marie Arouet Voltaire, 'Traité sur la tolérance, à l'occasion de la mort de Jean Calas', in *Œuvres*, xxv. 72, n. 2. It was a point also made by the great philosopher and brother of Mably, Condillac (1714–1780): Étienne Bonnot de Condillac, *Cours d'études pour l'instruction du prince de Parme* (written between 1767 and 1773 and first published in 1775) (Deux-Ponts: n.p., 1782), v. 445.

[94] François-Marie Arouet Voltaire, 'Histoire du Parlement de Paris' (1769), in *Œuvres*, xv. 447. That here, as elsewhere, Voltaire referred to the *Parlements* simply as courts of justice is telling. On his judgement of the *Parlements*, see James Hanrahan, *Voltaire and the* Parlements *of France* (Oxford: Voltaire Foundation, 2009). On Voltaire's struggle against the *Parlements*, see Diego Venturino, 'Histoire et politique: Quelques réflexions autour de l'*Histoire du Parlement de Paris*', in Ulla Kölving and Christiane Mervaud (eds.), *Voltaire et ses combats* (Oxford: Voltaire Foundation, 1997), ii. 1371–8.

[95] See Peter Raedts, 'Representations of the Middle Ages in Enlightenment Historiography', *The Medieval History Journal*, 5 (2002), 7–11.

Others shared Voltaire's perplexities over the nature of Germanic freedom. The Count de Mirabeau (1749–1791), the son of the famous economist Victor de Riqueti, Marquis de Mirabeau (1715–1789), and later
a leading figure in the National Assembly, published in 1782 a long
pamphlet, *Des lettres de cachet et des prisons d'État*, denouncing the tyrannical power of the crown. He made the case that the system of the *lettres de
cachet*, of which he himself had been a victim, was both morally despicable
and legally unconstitutional. Interestingly, in the same work he commented at some length on the alleged freedom of the ancient Franks. His
judgement was lapidary. He invited his readers to be wary of any notion of
a Germanic freedom. In fact, 'our fathers enjoyed a tumultuous independence rather than a true freedom'.[96] The ancient Germans had no real
understanding of freedom since their customs – or so argued Mirabeau –
allowed them to cede to others their own rights. The Germans' love of
'independence was a vague sentiment, almost as close to slavery as it was to
licentiousness for, in the circle of human things, the extremes touch one
another, and order only exists in the centre'.[97] Their lust for war merely led
to abuses, violence, and despotism. Other scholars agreed. Condorcet,
writing of the 'feudal anarchy' of the Middle Ages, yet seeing there the
'germs of freedom', seemed to follow Mirabeau, criticising the Germanic
tribes for 'mistaking independence for freedom'.[98] Here was a distinction
and contrast between an unbridled independence, in itself little else than
the rule of the stronger, and a just and steady freedom based on individual
rights. The latter, argued Mirabeau, could never have been attained by
a 'barbarous and ignorant' people. On the contrary, it needed 'the most
profound reflection' and knowledge. It demanded a complex balance of
powers between state institutions. It required that individual rights counter
the authority of the crown.[99] But the Franks had founded their power on
force rather than reason and this, in turn, could never have led to a fair and
just form of rule. Importantly, Mirabeau and Condorcet's remarks regarding Germanic freedom were propounded from a liberal perspective and, for
this reason, the judgement was not entirely negative. But a wholly critical
assessment was indeed formulated by the conservative champions of royal
authority. Jacob-Nicolas Moreau, for one, in his struggle against the
Germanists to defend the crown, was adamant that the Franks were

[96] Honoré-Gabriel Riqueti de Mirabeau, 'Des lettres de cachet et des prisons d'État', in *Œuvres* (Paris: Lecointe et Pougin, 1834–1835), vii. 470–1.
[97] Ibid., 473–4.
[98] Condorcet, 'Esquisse d'un tableau historique des progrès de l'esprit humain', 114–6.
[99] Mirabeau, 'Des lettres de cachet et des prisons d'État', 473–4.

barbarians whose natural inclinations were irreconcilable with true freedom. The Franks, he argued, 'took with them into Gaul barbarous vices, abuses, and usages' that profoundly contrasted with the values and government of the Romans, which 'the conquerors had themselves felt compelled to admire. But those barbarous vices, abuses, and usages, far from favouring freedom, were on the contrary the most terrible instruments of tyranny.'[100] Depicting the Franks before crossing the Rhine in a condition of war of all against all, individuals and families alike, he rhetorically asked his readers whether they had ever been free: 'Yes, gentlemen, if man's freedom is that of tigers and bears,' he answered. Revenge rather than justice had been the norm. Undoubtedly, this was not the sort of freedom that God had granted the French people.[101] Wisely, the French kings had retained some of the Roman principles and laws and, sensibly, 'the Franks themselves sacrificed part of their fierce freedom' to gain peace and justice.[102] As Moreau noted in 1789 with irony, 'it was not in the swamps nor the forests of Germany that the French constitution had been shaped'. Its roots had to be sought in the ideas and principles on which Rome had been founded.[103]

One point that deserves attention is that, in his works, Moreau essentially referred to the Gallo-Romans who, having merged with the Franks, he saw as the ancestors of the modern French. On the side of the Romanists, the idea that the nation's origins had to be sought in the union of Gauls and Romans was largely undisputed. And yet throughout the eighteenth century there was an increasing attention to the Gauls as a nation in their own right, distinct from the Romans.[104] The notion of the Gallic origins of France had first started to gain currency within learned circles in the sixteenth century. Largely, this was thanks to the *Recherches de la France* (1560), by Pasquier, and the controversial *Francogallia* (1573), by Hotman.[105] However, as an eighteenth-century

---

[100] Jacob-Nicolas Moreau, *Principes de morale, de politique et de droit public puisés dans l'histoire de notre monarchie, ou Discours sur l'histoire de France* (Paris: Imprimerie royale, 1777–1789), iii. 21–2.

[101] Ibid., ii. 6–8.   [102] Ibid., v. 261.

[103] Jacob Nicolas Moreau, *Exposition et défense de notre constitution monarchique françoise, précédé de l'historique de toutes nos assemblées nationales, dans deux mémoires* (Paris: Moutard, 1789), i. 10.

[104] Raymond Mas, 'Recherches sur les Gaulois et sentiment national en France au XVIIIᵉ siècle', in Chantal Grell and Jean-Michel Dufays (eds.), *Pratiques et concepts de l'histoire en Europe: XVIᵉ– XVIIIᵉ siècles* (Paris: Presses de l'Université de Paris-Sorbonne, 1990), 161–221.

[105] Corrado Vivanti, 'Les *Recherches de la France* d'Étienne Pasquier: L'invention des Gaulois', in Nora (ed.), *Les lieux de mémoire*, i. 759–86. Donald R. Kelley, *François Hotman: A Revolutionary's Ordeal* (Princeton: Princeton University Press, 1973). For an overview, see Claude-Gilbert Dubois, *Celtes et Gaulois au XVIᵉ siècle: Le développement littéraire d'un mythe nationaliste* (Paris: Vrin, 1972).

observer noted, such works had failed to dispel the old and deep-rooted prejudice: 'Our ancestors are treated as barbarians and adventurers; as people with no faith, *mœurs*, nor religion.' In part, he claimed, this was a consequence of the fact that a critical approach to the study of the past was not sufficiently widespread at that date.[106] But by the early eighteenth century the development of linguistics and philology and the changes in historical scholarship lent the notion new impetus. In 1703, the Breton monk, theologian, and historian Paul-Yves Pézron (1640–1706) published his *Antiquité de la nation et de la langue des Celtes, autrement appelés Gaulois*. In what was a widely read and influential work, aimed at demonstrating that the Celts had populated most of Europe and that the Greeks, Romans, and Gauls were their direct descendants, he also claimed that Celts and Gauls were names 'referring to the same thing, meaning powerful and courageous men'.[107] He substantiated his claims through semantics and philology, advancing the thesis that the Gauls were the closest people, linguistically and culturally, to the Celts. Some if not most of Pézron's views were questionable, but the *Antiquités* did have the great merit of reviving interest in the Gauls. Discussions on their origins even entered the Académie des inscriptions et des belles-lettres, partly thanks to the works of Fréret and Duclos.[108] In a famous dissertation on the druidic origins of the Gauls, Duclos was particularly prone to defending their civilisation, disputing the degree of barbarism usually imputed to them.[109] It was a view he had already set forth a few years earlier, when he claimed that, after all, it had been the Romans who had corrupted the Gauls. Fréret, a more cautious scholar, rejected such views.[110]

---

[106] Anonymous, review of Jacques Martin, *Histoire des Gaules, et des conquêtes des Gaulois, depuis leur origine jusqu'à la fondation de la monarchie françoise*, in *Le journal des sçavans*, June 1752, 349.

[107] Paul-Yves Pézron, *Antiquité de la nation et de la langue des Celtes, autrement appelés Gaulois* (Paris: Marchand, 1703), 'Préface', n.p.

[108] Catherine Volpilhac, 'Les Gaulois à l'Académie des inscriptions et belles-lettres de 1701 à 1793', in Viallaneix and Erhard (eds.), *Nos ancêtres les Gaulois*, 77–83.

[109] Charles Pinot Duclos, 'Mémoire sur les Druides', *Histoire de l'Académie royale des inscriptions et belles-lettres*, 19 (1753), 483–94. The paper was read at the Académie on 4 February 1746.

[110] Charles Pinot Duclos, 'Mémoire sur les épreuves par le duel et par les élémens, communément appellées Jugemens de Dieu par nos anciens François', *Mémoires de littérature tirés des registres de l'Académie royale des inscriptions et belles-lettres*, 15 (1743), 618–9. The paper was read at the Académie on 13 November 1739; Nicolas Fréret, 'Sur l'usage des sacrifices humains, établi chez les différentes nations et particulièrement chez les Gaulois', *Mémoires de littérature tirés des registres de l'Académie royale des inscriptions et belles-lettres*, 18 (1753), 178–81. The text is a summary of a paper read by Fréret at the Académie in 1746.

The works of the Maurist antiquary Dom Jacques Martin (1684–1715), the first modern 'historian of the Gauls', were particularly influential.[111] In his *Histoire des Gaules et des conquêtes des Gaulois* (1752–1754), a 'well-known work, worthy of its fame', he insisted on the need to seek in the Gallic world the true beginning of the nation's history.[112] As he stated succinctly in the introduction: 'The history of France, without that of the Gauls, is like a great and magnificent building severed from its foundations.' From his standpoint, those scholars, antiquaries, and historians who continued to hold apart the history of the French from that of their Gallic ancestors were committing a 'gross mistake', one that, unfortunately, was 'extremely widespread'.[113] Relying on ancient Greek and Roman chronicles, Dom Martin offered his readers the story of the slow partition of mankind into different races settling in various countries and continents. The Indians, he contended, had peopled Asia, the Ethiopians Africa, the Scythians the northern regions of the world, and the Celts Western Europe. All had been created by God and, from Palestine, had dispersed throughout the world. Within Martin's scheme, the Gauls were the most prominent branch of the Celts and had maintained almost intact – and surely to a greater degree than any other people – the language and customs of their forbears. Because of this, the ancient Greeks and Romans considered the Celts and the Gauls to be one and the same people.[114] These arguments allowed Martin to contend that even the Franks, like most of the peoples of Europe, were of Gallic or Celtic origin and to deny the original Frankish conquest and the idea of two distinct races inhabiting France.[115] The notion was far from new.[116] But Martin made the point with greater conviction, consistency, and erudition than previous scholars. Crucially, he meticulously tried to demonstrate that the customs, morals, and virtues of the Gauls were those that the Germanists attributed to the Franks. So, argued Martin, the Gauls despised all luxuries and even mistrusted any changes that might improve their lives for fear of corrupting and weakening them. This was reflected in their cities, which, in contrast to

---

[111] The expression is from Raymond Mas, 'Dom Jacques Martin, historien des Gaulois (1684–1751)', in Viallaneix and Erhard (eds.), *Nos ancêtres les Gaulois*, 41–50. On Martin's life and works, see René Prosper Tassin, *Histoire littéraire de la congrégation de Saint-Maur, ordre de Saint-Benoît* (Brussels: Humblot, 1770), 683–90.

[112] Anonymous, 'Nouvelles littéraires: France', *Journal encyclopédique*, 15 May 1780, 167.

[113] Jacques Martin, *Histoire des Gaules, et des conquêtes des Gaulois, depuis leur origine jusqu'à la fondation de la monarchie françoise* (Paris: Imprimerie de Le Breton, 1752–1754), i. p. ii. The second volume appeared posthumously, edited and completed by Martin's nephew and colleague Dom Jean-François De Brézillac (1710–1780).

[114] Martin, *Histoire des Gaules*, i. 68.   [115] Ibid., i. p. ii.   [116] On this, see Chapter 3.

Greek and Roman settlements, had no magnificent palaces and edifices, no monuments or places for public amusement. They were built only for the 'safety and the glory of the nation'.[117] Coupled with their frugality was their bravery. Martin saw in the Gauls daring and impetuous soldiers, always ready to give their lives for the nation. Their victories over the Roman legions testified to their martial spirit.[118] But Martin went further, even offering a new reading of the relationship between the Gauls and the Romans. In fact, from his Gallocentric viewpoint, he argued that at the time of their settlement in modern-day France, the Gauls even invaded Italy and there they gave birth to one of the greatest civilisations of antiquity: 'The Gauls are the sole founders of the Roman Republic, of this monstrous power that eclipsed all others.'[119] Of course, it was an original way of considering the place of Rome in French history, overturning the more common and straightforward understanding. But it was also a way of replacing the traditional analogy between Roman and French greatness with a genealogy that was, at its core, essentially ethnic.

By the mid-eighteenth century, an increasing number of authors were writing of 'our ancestors the Gauls', discerning a close connection between the Celtic tribes and the modern French. In the *Encyclopédie*, Voltaire argued that the French nation was 'mainly made up of Gallic families, and the character of the ancient Gauls has survived intact'. In the main, the character of 'the French is today the same as the one that Caesar ascribed to the Gauls: ready to take action, ardent when fighting, impetuous when attacking, and easily discouraged'.[120] Mercier concurred. Noting that '[t]he Gaul or Celts, howsoever merged with the Franks, are our fathers', he argued that when looking at their 'bellicose character' and customs, their 'liveliness', one could easily see many traits still surviving in modern-day Frenchmen. Indeed, this he considered to be proof that 'we are their true descendants'.[121] The historian and rhetorician the abbé Millot (1726–1785) took a similar view. A learned and respected scholar and, from 1777, also a member of the Académie, according to d'Alembert he had the 'merit of having written history in a philosophical manner' – and, no less important, of forgetting 'he was a Jesuit and a priest'.[122] In the 1770 edition of

---

[117] Martin, *Histoire des Gaules*, ii. 34 and 38–9. See also Jacques Martin, *La religion des Gaulois, tirée des plus pures sources de l'antiquité* (Paris: Saugrain Fils, 1727), i. 82.
[118] Martin, *Histoire des Gaules*, i. p. xxix–xxx.   [119] Ibid., i. 150.
[120] Voltaire, 'François, ou Français', 285.   [121] Mercier, *Portraits des Rois de France*, i. 3–4.
[122] Jean Baptiste le Rond d'Alembert to François-Marie Arouet Voltaire, 27 December 1777, in Voltaire, *Œuvres*, v. 246. On Millot, see Charles Weiss, 'Millot', in Michaud (ed.), *Biographie universelle ancienne et moderne*, xxix. 50–3. Also see, Claude-François-Xavier Millot, 'Mémoires', *Nouvelle revue rétrospective*, 8 (January–June 1898), 73–120, 145–92, and 217–35. The text, edited by

his *Élémens de l'histoire de France*, after equating the Gauls with the Celts, Millot claimed without hesitation that the former, merging with the Franks, had given birth to the French nation and that therefore they 'are our fathers'. He sought confirmation in the resemblance between the Gallic and French character. In fact, the Gauls displayed in their conduct that 'bravery, vivacity, and hospitality that might so easily be recognised in their descendants'.[123] Their martial spirit was particularly striking, so much so, he claimed, that the 'Gauls seem to live only for war'. Their bravery was so well known that they struck fear even in the hearts of the Roman legionaries. Had it not been for their 'lack of discipline and had military science regulated their bravery, most likely they would have subdued that ambitious republic'.[124] They despised all activities other than fighting and preparing for war. Ploughing the land, tending fields, working, and prac- tising arts and sciences, deemed by them unworthy of a martial people, they left to 'slaves and women'. However, once the Gauls had been defeated and subdued by the Romans, their craving for wealth and the satisfaction of material needs intensified: 'Needs spurred on their love of work. Industriousness banished idleness.' The belief that all activities other than war were dishonourable 'no longer fettered the body of the nation'.[125] According to Millot, the Romans had corrupted the martial character of the Gauls, creating new needs for them. Even a passion for the arts and literature, brought by their conquerors, made them 'weaker and softened their character'. And yet, they constantly fought to shake off the Roman yoke, which they always saw as a hateful infamy.[126] As we have seen, the censure of Rome and the idea that the conquest was the seed of the moral decadence of the Gallic nation were not new. The Germanists had made similar criticisms and advanced similar claims. Where Millot took a radically different view from theirs was in arguing that the Gauls valued freedom above all else. Although he was forced to admit that they tolerated slavery, 'despite this, the nation, in general, cherished freedom even more than life itself. ... This love for freedom emerged even in their form of government.' The most important political matters were always discussed in general assemblies. Just like the ancient Greeks, even the Gauls were

---

Léonce Pingaud, includes letters between Millot and Turgot, d'Alembert, Moreau, and other prominent scholars. On his approach to the study of the past, see Olga Penke, 'L'abbé Millot et l'historiographie des Lumières françaises', *Acta Romanica Szegediensis*, 7 (1982), 339–87.

[123] Claude-François-Xavier Millot, *Élémens de l'histoire de France, depuis Clovis jusqu'à Louis XV* (Paris: Durand neveu, 1770), i. 2–3. The first edition was published in 1768, but it did not contain the introduction from which these quotes are taken.

[124] Millot, *Élémens de l'histoire de France*, i. 3.   [125] Ibid., i. 5.   [126] Ibid., i. 13.

united in a federation of free peoples. But internal discord made them weak and the Romans took advantage of their divisions to subdue them.[127]

In the thirty years preceding the Revolution, others wrote of the martial spirit of the Gauls and of their love for freedom.[128] Some even spoke of the decadence occasioned by the Roman yoke and the debasing of a free, proud, and bellicose people.[129] However, in such writings there was no real, explicit, or articulated ideological vision or substantial political argument. References were made to the greatness of the ancient Gauls, the ancestors of the modern French, and in so stirring a tone that a feeling of pride at belonging to a nation that had peopled Europe, defeated the Romans, and sacked their capital is evident. But in vain would one look for a republicanism of a Gallic kind. Even during the Revolution, the main arguments against the Germanists' thesis and the (aristocratic) idea of freedom it enshrined were based on the unification of the Gauls and Romans.[130] However, it is undeniable that from 1789 onwards there was a growing interest in the place of the Gauls in the history of France.[131] From a scholarly concern, of interest only to antiquaries, linguists, and historians, it turned into a political preoccupation, leading to discussions and debates in which notions of an alleged Gallic freedom were prominent. In a pamphlet published in 1793, one de Lagrange (17??–18??), commander of the battalion of the Capuchins du Marais, and the well-known Baron Étienne Dupin (1767–1828), called for the nation's true name to be restored. Signing themselves as 'Republican Gauls', they inveighed against the nobility, the descendants of the ancient Franks, and asked why, the constitution of 1793 having given back to the people all its rights, the nation still called itself France: 'Magnanimous people, regaining your liberty, take back your glorious name. You are *Gallic*.' A fierce and proliferating people,

---

[127] Ibid., i. 11–12.

[128] See, for example, Pierre Chiniac de La Bastide, Dedicatory letter to 'Monsieur le Dauphin', in Simon Pelloutier, *Histoire des Celtes, et particulièrement des Gaulois et des Germains* (Paris: Quillaud, 1771), i. n.p.

[129] François Sabbathier, *Les mœurs, coutumes et usages des anciens peuples* (Châlons-sur-Marne: Imprimerie de Bouchard, 1770), i. 230; Guillaume Germain Guyot, *Histoire de France, représentée par figures accompagnées de discours* (Paris: David, 1787–1791), i. 5. [Bourdon de Sigrais], *Considérations sur l'esprit militaire des Gaulois, pour servir d'éclaircissements préliminaires aux mêmes recherches sur les Français, et d'introductions à l'histoire de France* (Paris: Veuve Desaint, 1774), 615–6.

[130] We shall return to this question in Part III.

[131] See Jean-Yves Guiomar, 'La Révolution française et les origines celtiques de la France', *Annales historiques de la Révolution française*, 64 (1992), 63–85; Annie Jourdan, 'The Image of Gaul during the French Revolution: Between Charlemagne and Ossian', in Terence Brown (ed.), *Celticism* (Amsterdam: Rodopi, 1996), 183–206; Xavier Martin, 'L'image du Gaulois (et celle de la femme) dans le miroir du français révolutionnaire', *Revue d'histoire du droit*, 77 (1999), 463–89.

the Gauls made Rome 'tremble' and peopled the whole of Europe, from Spain to Germany, from Britain to Italy. Crucially, the authors also claimed that the Gallic nation, 'at length celebrated for its liberty and its other virtues', would never have known the meaning itself of tyranny if it had not learned it from foreign peoples. The two authors also contended that the ancient Gauls had been a federation of free peoples 'united by their love for freedom', that they were ignorant of the very notion of elective rights, cherished the principle of 'popular sovereignty', and even ruled through national assemblies.[132] However, the underlying Gallocentric argument was not taken to its logical conclusion. According to the authors, the consequence of defeat by Caesar's legions was less a conquest than a union, so that 'today, Roman blood runs in our veins as does that of the Gauls'. But with the Empire came the decadence of the Romans as well as the Gauls.[133]

The issue of the Gallic origins of France was brought up time and again during the Revolution. The aims were as disparate as could be. Some, for example, even speculated that the origins of the name *Sans-culottes* had to be sought in ancient Gaul.[134] In cases such as these, there was a striking lack of scholarly rigour. All in all, the issue of the Gallic origins of France acquired an overtly political hue. In his popular *Origines gauloises* (1796), an officer in the Napoleonic army and an antiquary Théophile Malo de La Tour d'Auvergne (1743–1800) argued for a continuity of the moral and physical character of the Celts, 'our ancestors', and the French. One crucial aim of his work was to 'restore to the list of nations the Gauls, this famous people that would seem to have been erased from it'.[135] He insisted on their bravery, frugality, and love of freedom: 'Glory and the love for their country, the sublime enthusiasm for liberty, these feelings, so appropriate

[132] Claude-François-Étienne Dupin and [. . .] de Lagrange, *Pétition pour rendre à la France son véritable nom, par Dupin et Lagrange, républicains gaulois* (n.p., 1793), 2–3. Another interesting call to restore to the French their true name, made during the Convention, was [Ducalle], 'Les Gaulois et les Francs', *Revue rétrospective: Seconde série*, 1 (1835), 145–7. Signed by a 'Ducalle, fellow citizen', its precise dating is uncertain.

[133] Dupin and de Lagrange, *Pétition pour rendre à la France son véritable nom*, 4–5.

[134] See Philippe-François-Nazaire Fabre d'Églantine, *Rapport fait à la Convention nationale dans la séance du 3 du second mois de la seconde année de la République française, au nom de la Commission chargée de la confection du calendrier* (Paris: Imprimerie nationale, 1793), 14–15. On this, Bronisław Baczko, 'Le calendrier Républicain', in Nora (ed.), *Les lieux de mémoire*, i. 83–4, and Michael Sonenscher, *Sans-culottes: An Eighteenth-Century Emblem in the French Revolution* (Princeton: Princeton University Press, 2008), 14 and 16.

[135] Théophile Malo de La Tour d'Auvergne, *Origines gauloises, celles des plus anciens peuples de l'Europe, puisées dans leur vraie source* (Paris: Quillau, 1796), vii–viii. On this, Jean Balcou, 'La Tour d'Auvergne, théoricien breton du mythe gaulois', in Viallaneix and Erhard (eds.), *Nos ancêtres les Gaulois*, 107–13.

for heightening courage, often placed arms in their hands to decide whether they should live as free men or languish like slaves.' Although the power and strength of Rome had been able, for some time, 'to bend their proud heads under the yoke', the Gauls never became accustomed to such a state: 'Their character always remained indomitable.'[136] Admittedly, words such as these would have been in tune with the rhetoric of the Revolutionary and Napoleonic armies. And they would also have been shared by most members of the Académie celtique, a society of scholars and of amateur philologists, historians, and archaeologists created in 1804 and dedicated to shedding light on the Gallic origins of France.[137] As one of its members explained, the Académie was a 'truly national institution', pursuing an eminently patriotic aim. It was born 'to illustrate our cradle by finding once again our ancestors, and restore to them everything that a credulous admiration attributes to the Romans who defeated them'.[138] Among its most prominent members were the archaeologist and historian Jacques-Joseph Champollion-Figeac (1778–1867), the Piedmontese historian Carlo Denina (1731–1813), the philologist Éloi Johanneau (1770–1851), the Breton writer Jacques Cambry (1749–1807), and the Count de Volney.[139] The great linguist and mythologist Jacob Grimm (1785–1863) was a corresponding fellow, and was influenced by the work of the Académie in his studies of Germanic folklore.[140] The Académie's most famous initiative was a questionnaire issued in 1807 to all the *departments* to improve the understanding of the regional customs of the French. It was the first attempt at an ethnographic mapping of France.[141]

---

[136] La Tour d'Auvergne, *Origines gauloises*, 109–12.

[137] On the Académie celtique, see: Nicole Belmont, 'L'Académie celtique et George Sand: Les débuts des recherches folkloriques en France', *Romantisme*, 9 (1975), 29–38; Henry Senn, 'Folklore Beginnings in France: The Académie Celtique, 1804–1813', *Journal of the Folklore Institute*, 18 (1981), 23–31; Nicole Belmont, 'Introduction', in Belmont (ed.), *Aux sources de l'ethnologie française: L'Académie celtique* (Paris: Éditions du CTHS, 1995), 9–21. Also see, on the Académie's precursor, the Société des observateurs de l'homme, Jean-Luc Chappey, *La Société des observateurs de l'homme, 1799–1804: Des anthropologues au temps de Bonaparte* (Paris: Société des études robespierristes, 2002).

[138] Jean-Marie Pardessus, 'Notice sur les voyages d'antiquités celtiques et druidiques de M. É. Johanneau', *Mémoires de l'Académie celtique*, 1 (1807), 382–3.

[139] For a complete list of its members, see: Académie celtique, 'Liste des membres et associés correspondans', *Mémoires de l'Académie celtique*, 1 (1807), 1–20.

[140] Bärbel Plötner, 'Langue, littérature et identité nationales et régionales: Jacob Grimm entre l'Allemagne et la France: Le cas breton', in Michel Espagne and Michel Werner (eds.), *Philologiques 3: Qu'est-ce que c'est une littérature nationale?* (Paris: Éditions de la Maison des sciences de l'homme, 1994), 224–34.

[141] Mona Ozouf, 'L'invention de l'ethnographie française: Le questionnaire de l'Académie celtique', *Annales: Histoire, sciences sociales*, 36 (1981), 210–30. Van Gennep's account of the *questionnaire* was particularly laudatory: Arnold van Gennep, 'Rôle de l'Académie celtique et de la Société des

Despite the very real merits of the questionnaire and notwithstanding some interesting attempts to use in new ways philology and etymology in the study of the French past, the Académie failed in its intent. As one observer commented in 1810, the Académie had not 'received great consideration in the learned and literary world', adding that 'newspapers have taken up the habit of mentioning such an Academy only to amuse themselves at its expense'.[142] The reasons for its failure and shortcomings are revealing. Scholarly causes entwined with political ones. First, the excessive passion and enthusiasm of the members of the Académie, many of whom were amateurs, often clouded their judgement, attracting the criticism of more rigorous scholars. Moreover, their Celtomania and their Gallocentrism informed a pursuit that devalued or even denied altogether the Roman heritage in the creation of a French identity. And this was a difficult stance to adopt since, as Ozouf has pointed out, the Gauls were a 'scholarly invention and, therefore, could only blossom in a culture nourished by Graeco-Roman history'.[143] Almost inevitably, the more rigorous historical research refrained from downplaying the nation's Roman past in favour of its Gallic one. The point might also be made with reference to the field of politics where, likewise, the Roman heritage could not easily be dismissed. The fact that the veneration of ancient Rome was shared by many leaders of the Revolution and that Napoleon himself (1769–1821) made of the cult of Rome a pillar of his rhetoric, comparing himself to Caesar and calling upon his armies to follow the example of its legions, clearly posed an obstacle to the expunging of Rome from the French past.[144] Even when considering the patriotic aim of the Académie, that of extolling and glorifying the Gallic past, the endeavour appears arduous. In fact, as one of its members asked his readers, 'how can one revive the memory of a people whose splendour does not exist?'[145] Although the question was meant to be rhetorical, it pointed to the crux of the matter. There was no substantial tradition of heroic Gallic deeds, nor was the notion that the

Antiquaires de France', in van Gennep, *Textes inédits sur le folklore français contemporain* (Paris: Maisonneuve et Larose, 1975), 22–5.

[142] Conrad Malte-Brun, 'Mémoires de l'Académie celtique: Cahiers I – XIV', *Journal de l'Empire*, 26 April 1810, 3.

[143] Mona Ozouf, 'Les Gaulois à Clermont-Ferrand', in Ozouf, *L'école de la France*, 347.

[144] On the importance of Rome in the Revolution and under Napoleon, the literature is immense. Two useful texts are Mouza Raskolnikoff, 'L'"adoration" des Romains sous la Révolution française et la réaction de Volney et des idéologues', in Raskolnikoff, *Des anciens et des modernes* (Paris: Publications de la Sorbonne, 1990), 199–213, and Daniela Gallo, 'Pouvoirs de l'antiquité', in Jean-Claude Bonnet (ed.), *L'empire des muses: Napoléon, les arts et les lettres* (Paris: Belin, 2004), 317–29.

[145] Alexandre Lenoir, 'Discours préliminaire', *Mémoires de l'Académie celtique*, 1 (1807), 6.

Gauls were proud warriors widely accepted. Surprisingly, to convince the French that their Celtic ancestors had once 'conquered the world', as Chateaubriand wrote emphatically in 1806, would take much time and work.[146] Overcoming the cumbersome weight of Romanisation would require the efforts of scholars such as Amédée Thierry (1797–1873) and Camille Jullian – and, much later on and in a very different way, the cartoonists René Goscinny (1926–1977) and Albert Uderzo (1927–2020). And yet the intellectual premises for the Gallic triumph had now been formulated.

---

[146] François-René de Chateaubriand, 'Sur les mémoires de Louis XIV' (1806), in Œuvres, viii. 228.

PART III

CHAPTER 7

Classifying the Nation
The Past(s) of 'Social Classes' before and after the Revolution

Thinking about Classes before 1789

In 1718, in his popular *Dictionnaire comique*, Philibert-Joseph Le Roux (16??–17??) observed that 'class' had become 'a very fashionable word, accepted by the greatest minds of France'.[1] Indeed, it is clear enough that men of letters and scholars were using the term and were classifying the object of their studies. 'Class' was constantly employed by the grammarian César Dumarsais (1676–1756) to group verbs, nouns, and adjectives, while the abbé Dubos, in his famous *Réflexions critiques sur la poésie et la peinture*, used various systems of classification to arrange and order paintings and poems. Even more interestingly, the abbé de Condillac expounded on epistemology through his classifications of human perceptions and their relationship to words and ideas.[2] All three scholars were aware that classes – as they used them – were ruses, mental tools intended to advance their own and their reader's knowledge. So, according to Dumarsais, if a noun or a verb did not fit into any of the existing classes, he saw no problem in 'making a new class'. For his part, Condillac insisted that the observer was

---

[1] Philibert-Joseph Le Roux, *Dictionnaire comique, satyrique, critique, burlesque, libre et proverbial* (Amsterdam: M.C. Le Cène, 1718), s.v. 'classe'. On the famous *Dictionnaire* and on its mysterious author, see Yves Giraud, 'Le "Dictionnaire comique" de Le Roux', *Cahiers de l'association internationale des études françaises*, 35 (1983), 69–86. On the notion of 'class' in the second half of the eighteenth century and during the Restoration, see Marie-France Piguet, *Classe: Histoire et genèse du concept des physiocrates aux historiens de la Restauration* (Lyons: Presses universitaires de Lyon, 1996). See also Tullio De Mauro, 'Storia e analisi semantica di classe', in De Mauro, *Senso e significato: Studi di semantica teorica e storica* (Bari: Laterza, 1971), 163–227, and Otto Gerhard Oexle, Werner Conze, and Rudolf Walther, 'Stand, Klasse', in Brunner, Conze, and Koselleck (eds.), *Geschichtliche Grundbegriffe*, vi. 155–284.

[2] César Dumarsais, *Des tropes ou des diférens sens dans lesquels on peut prendre un même mot dans une même langue* (Paris: Veuve de J.B. Brocas, 1730), 188, 202, 265, 269; Dubos, *Réflexions critiques sur la poésie et sur la peinture*, 92, 143, 343, 379, 454, 457, 463, 515; Étienne Bonnot de Condillac, 'Essai sur l'origine des connaissances humaines' (1746), in *Œuvres philosophiques* (Paris: Presses universitaires de France, 1947–1951), i. 17, 24, 31, 38, 87.

clearly the one placing ideas or sensations into a given group, while for Dubos the decision as to which painter or *comédien* belonged to a given class was either at the discretion of critics or, as was increasingly the case, the general public.[3] If it was clear that classes were tailored to the needs of those who created them, whether there existed a hierarchical relationship between the different groupings was less so. Though absent from Dumarsais's text, such a relationship did emerge in Dubos's work, in the form of a distinction between 'superior' and 'inferior' authors and painters according to criteria that he himself stipulated – and which, of course, he considered to be self-evident. More interesting is Condillac's stance. Based on the assertion that 'different sorts of perceptions determine different classes of beings', Condillac argued that beings developed their own self-awareness through stages in which their bodies and minds underwent specific changes. It was through the realisation of a potential inherent in every being that self-awareness was made possible, allowing it to rise 'to a superior condition'.[4] Importantly, due to such an ascent, a hierarchy expressed in terms of inferiority or superiority was at least implied. Classes thereby became something more real than Condillac had implied elsewhere, since beings, by virtue of the development of their inner qualities, changed class independently of the observer. Interestingly, introducing and coupling with class ideas of progress and development would seem to vest the former with a greater reality, independently of the person classifying.

The idea that a classification implied some sort of hierarchy emerged more strongly in the everyday use of the word. From the 1690 edition of Furetière's *Dictionnaire*, readers learned in fact that a class was a 'distinction of people or objects arranged depending on their merit, value or nature'. Similarly, the 1694 edition of the *Dictionnaire de l'Académie* stated that a class 'is an order in which people of the same profession are placed in accordance with their merit or capacities'. While the two definitions confirm that class was something artificial and that people were 'placed in them', both insisted upon merit as the main criterion for classification. References to merit and social esteem also featured in the definition given in the 1680 edition of Richelet's *Dictionnaire*, although the use of the word was limited to authors and their works. Here, class meant a rank, the 'order in which public esteem

---

[3] Dumarsais, *Des tropes*, 269; Dubos, *Réflexions critiques sur la poésie et la peinture*, 475–6; Condillac, 'Essai sur l'origine des connaissances humaines', 24, 31, 38.
[4] Étienne Bonnot de Condillac, 'Traité des systêmes' (1749), in *Œuvres philosophiques*, i. 158–9.

places the works of certain authors'. It is interesting that the same dictionary, in the edition of 1709, while retaining this definition, added another,
attesting to the diffusion of the scientific meaning of the word: class, in
fact, now also indicated 'the rank in which different things, between which
distinctions are made, are placed. One arranges natural bodies in different
classes of metals, minerals, vegetables, animals etc. It is also said of
persons.'[5] The juxtaposition of scientific taxonomies with the classification
of individuals might well be an example of the passage of a scientific
definition of a term into the ordinary language.[6]

Another important meaning of the word, widespread during the reign of
Louis XIV, referred instead to the classification of people according to the
distribution of wealth.[7] In his popular *Le roman bourgeois* (1666), Furetière
depicted with irony the rising bourgeoisie, with its many faults, not least its
pettiness, and divided its members into classes according to levels of
income – then making the wry remark that an advantageous marriage
and a conspicuous dowry could easily elevate a bourgeois into the higher
class.[8] In *Télémaque*, Fénelon imagined an ideal society of 'seven classes',
each of which would receive plots of land according to the number of its
members. Overturning, in a sense, the world described by Furetière,
Fénelon's classes were defined and the redistribution of wealth was made
according to the needs of their members.[9] Another, closely related use of
class referred to the division of the tax burden among the different
members of society. It was a meaning dating back to the Roman world –
as eighteenth-century scholars were well aware.[10] This specific legal and
fiscal usage was revived in the late seventeenth century and used to establish
a system for the collection of the *taille*. To finance the wars waged by
France, in 1695 the Controller-General of Finances, Louis Phélypeaux,
soon to become Count de Pontchartrain (1643–1727), introduced a poll
tax, the 'capitation', dividing the French people, from the Dauphin and

---

[5] Furetière, *Dictionnaire universel* (ed. 1690), s.v. 'class'; Académie française, *Dictionnaire de l'Académie française*, i. 197 (s.v. 'classe'); Richelet, *Dictionnaire françois*, i. 142 (s.v. 'classe'); Pierre Richelet, *Dictionnaire françois* (Amsterdam: Jean Elzevir, 1709), i. 253 (s.v. 'classe').

[6] For a different view, Giampietro Gobo, 'Class: Stories of Concepts. From Ordinary Language to Scientific Language', *Social Science Information*, 32 (1993), 467–89.

[7] Dallas L. Clouatre, 'The Concept of Class in French Culture prior to the Revolution', *Journal of the History of Ideas*, 45 (1984), 230–1.

[8] Antoine Furetière, *Le roman bourgeois* (Paris: Gallimard, 1981), 47–9.

[9] Fénelon, *Les aventures de Télémaque*, 226.

[10] See, for example, René Aubert de Vertot, *Histoire des révolutions arrivées dans le gouvernement de la république romaine* (Paris: F. Barois, 1719), i. 34; Montesquieu, 'De l'Esprit des lois', 241 (book ii. ch. 2); Mably, 'Observations sur les Romains', 264; Rousseau, 'Du contrat social', 447; Condillac, *Cours d'études pour l'instruction du prince de Parme*, vi. 247–9.

princes of the blood down to servants and shepherds, into twenty-two classes of taxpayers according to wealth and income.[11] In that same year, in a work on the condition of France and the means to increase its wealth, Pierre Le Pesant de Boisguilbert (1646–1714), one of the great protoliberal economists, used 'class' in this sense. He suggested the adoption of a tax system where workers would be divided into classes following 'their degree and rank', or 'the classes made in the repartition of the contribution of arts and crafts'. He also proposed that to each rank should correspond a specific part of the overall tax burden, thus 'dividing it equally among those of the same profession' who, Boisguilbert assumed, earned comparable incomes.[12] The division of society according to wealth and the allocation of tax burden according to income became an important element in the development of the concept of class. Importantly, in the history of political and economic thought this relationship between class, wealth, and the needs of the state would remain close.[13]

A fundamental shift in the meaning of class was prompted by the *économistes* – later known as the physiocrats.[14] It being their guiding

---

[11] See Sara E. Chapman, *Private Ambition and Political Alliances: The Phélypeaux de Pontchartrain Family and Louis XIV's Government, 1650–1715* (Rochester, NY: University of Rochester Press, 2004), 105–13.

[12] [Pierre le Pesant de Boisguilbert], *Le détail de la France, la cause de la diminution de ses biens et la facilité du remède, en fournissant en un mois tout l'argent dont le Roi a besoin, et enrichissant tout le monde* (n.p., 1695), 145; also see ibid., 234–6. When the book was published in 1707 as *Le détail de la France sous le règne présent*, Boisguilbert was widely recognised as its author.

[13] Marie-France Piguet, 'Réduire en classes / être divisés en ordres: Les sources françaises du mot "classe" au 18ᵉᵐᵉ siècle', *Mots*, 17 (1988), 58.

[14] The word 'physiocratie' was first used, in a published work, by Nicolas Baudeau in a review of Claude François-Joseph d'Auxiron, *Principes de tout gouvernement, ou Examen des causes de la splendeur ou de la foiblesse de tout État considéré en lui-même, et indépendamment des mœurs*, in *Éphémérides du citoyen*, April 1767, 121–2. It was popularised by Pierre-Samuel Dupont de Nemours in a collection of texts by François Quesnay published a few months later, the *Physiocratie, ou Constitution naturelle du gouvernement le plus avantageux au genre humain* (Paris: Merlin, 1767–1768). On the physiocrats, see the classics by Georges Weulersse, *Le mouvement physiocratique en France (de 1756 à 1770)* (Paris: Alcan, 1910), and Elizabeth Fox-Genovese, *The Origins of Physiocracy: Economic Revolution and Social Order in Eighteenth-Century France* (Ithaca: Cornell University Press, 1976). For more recent works: Simone Meyssonnier, *La balance et l'horloge: La genèse de la pensée libérale en France au XVIIIᵉ siècle* (Montreuil: Éditions de la passion, 1989), 279–92; Yves Citton, *Portrait de l'économiste en physiocrate: Critique littéraire de l'économie politique* (Paris: L'Harmattan, 2000); Michael Sonenscher, 'Physiocracy as Theodicy', *History of Political Thought*, 23 (2002), 326–39; Reinhard Bach, 'Les physiocrates et la science politique de leur temps', *Revue française d'histoire des idées politiques*, 20 (2004), 5–35; Michael Sonenscher, *Before the Deluge: Public Debt, Inequality and the Intellectual Origins of the French Revolution* (Princeton: Princeton University Press, 2007), 189–239; Christine Théré and Loïc Charles, 'The Writing Workshop of François Quesnay and the Making of Physiocracy', *History of Political Economy*, 40 (2008), 1–42; Anthony Mergey, *L'état des physiocrates: Autorité et décentralisation* (Aix-en-Provence: Presses universitaires d'Aix-Marseille, 2010); Liana Vardi, *The Physiocrats and the World of the Enlightenment* (Cambridge: Cambridge University Press, 2012). Also see Loïc Charles and Christine Théré, 'Jeux de

assumption that nature was the sole real source of revenue, the members of this influential coterie were adamant that natural rules governed the economy through laws that could be discovered by following the methods of the natural sciences. Between the 1760s and the 1770s, partly as a reaction against mercantilism and inspired by the *Essai sur la nature du commerce en général* (1755), the work of the great economist Richard Cantillon (168?–1734), the physiocrats recast many of the notions previously used in political economy.[15] The ideas of class and nation were among those most deeply affected by their theories. Seeing themselves as the heralds of 'an exact science' that could be 'proven in all its claims', the physiocrats forged a new language to emphasise their break with the past and underscore the originality of their ideas.[16] Tellingly, their insistence on a new idiom was strongly and repeatedly criticised by their opponents, one going as far as to scorn their 'mysterious language' which, concealing the poverty of their ideas, was 'as useful as the books of our alchemists'.[17] Because of the cryptic nature of their prose, their absolute faith – of a Malebranchian nature – in the notion of evidence, their zeal and their uncompromising rebuttal of their critics, many adversaries accused them of being a 'sect'.[18] François Quesnay (1694–1774), a well-known surgeon and,

mots, Narrative and Economic Writing: The Rhetoric of Anti-physiocracy in French Economic Periodicals (1764–1769)', *The European Journal of the History of Economic Thought*, 22 (2015), 359–82. Also see the chapters on physiocracy in Steven Kaplan and Sophus Reinert (eds.), *The Economic Turn: Recasting Political Economy in Enlightenment Europe* (London: Anthem Press, 2019). On the relationship between economic and political thought in eighteenth-century France, see Larrère, *L'invention de l'économie au XVIIIe siècle*, passim, and Arnault Skornicki, *L'économiste, la cour et la patrie: L'économie politique dans la France des Lumières* (Paris: CNRS Éditions, 2011).

[15] The *Essai* circulated widely in manuscript form before 1755 and was known to many of the physiocrats. On Cantillon's influence on the physiocrats, see Anthony Brewer, *Richard Cantillon: Pioneer of Economic Theory* (London: Routledge, 1992), 159–75.

[16] The expression is from Pierre-Samuel Dupont de Nemours, 'Analyse du Tableau économique: Avis aux lecteurs' (1766), in François Quesnay, *Œuvres économiques et philosophiques* (Frankfurt: J. Baer, 1888), 442. For a discussion on the shaping of a new language by the physiocrats, see Marie-France Piguet, 'Quesnay, le langage et le "langage de la science économique"', *Histoire, épistémologie, langage*, 21 (1999), 123–47.

[17] Anonymous, 'Principes et observations économiques, par M. de Forbonnais: Second extrait', *Journal de l'agriculture, du commerce et des finances*, May 1767, 9–10. Despite the title, this was in fact one of a series of laudatory reviews and summaries of François Véron Duverger de Forbonnais's (1722–1800) work. The great political economist also expressed his dissatisfaction with the physiocrats' new language: [François Véron Duverger de Forbonnais], 'Lettre de M. A.B.C.D. etc. aux auteurs du journal de la Gazette', *Journal de l'agriculture, du commerce et des finances*, August 1767, 58–9. For the attribution of the anonymous article to Forbonnais, see Charles and Théré, '*Jeux de mots*, Narrative and Economic Writing', 369. Later on, even Destutt de Tracy made similar remarks: Antoine-Louis-Claude Destutt de Tracy, *Traité de la volonté et de ses effets* (1815) (Paris: Vrin, 2015), 95.

[18] See, for example, Gabriel Bonnot de Mably, 'Du commerce des grains' (1775), in *Œuvres*, xiii. 296; Grimm et al., *Correspondance littéraire*, vii. 234 (February 1767) and 431 (October 1767); [Louis-François

from 1749, the personal physician of the Marquise de Pompadour (1721–1764), was 'the band's coryphaeus'.[19] A 'very speculative physician', to use Adam Smith's description, Quesnay came somewhat late in life – in his late fifties – to political economy. It was perhaps for this reason that he there adopted the approach and the methods of the natural sciences, which he had made his own in his earlier, highly successful career.[20] A juxtaposition between his studies on nature and society and certain of his economic theories had already been adumbrated in the final pages of his *Essai physique sur l'economie animale* (1736). Indeed, Quesnay's understanding of politics and economics was based on the application to society of his studies of the human body. It was a point grasped, among others, by Guillaume-François Le Trosne (1728–1780), a prominent physiocrat who noted that Quesnay's spirit of observation and the 'profound and stringent logic he had used in the art of curing illnesses' were now 'applied even more surely to seek the principles of political economy'.[21] Quesnay's metaphor that the circulation of wealth was to society what the circulation of blood was to the human body, which he outlined in his famous *Tableau économique* (1758), was just one of many biological analogies scattered throughout his works and, in part, those of his fellow physiocrats. It is interesting that none of this implied an explicitly organicist interpretation of society on Quesnay's part – not least because this would have clashed with his Cartesian and Malebranchian convictions.[22] But what is relevant, here, is that through his works and those of his followers the use of class was

Metra], *Correspondance littéraire secrete* (n.p.: 1775–1793), i. 303 (14 October 1775); Mercier, 'Mon bonnet de nuit', 501. Even Adam Smith, referred to the physiocrats as a 'sect': *An Inquiry into the Nature and Causes of the Wealth of Nations* (1776) (Oxford: Clarendon Press, 1979), ii. 678.

[19] The expression is in Petit de Bachaumont, Pidansat de Mairobert, and d'Angerville, *Mémoires secrets pour servir à l'histoire de la République des lettres en France*, ii. 833 (20 December 1767). The famous abbé Galiani (1728–1787) was one of the harshest opponents of the physiocratic theories. He went so far as to refer to Quesnay as the 'Antichrist': Ferdinando Galiani to Louise Tardieu d'Esclavelles Épinay, 28 April 1770, in Galiani and d'Esclavelles Épinay, *Correspondance* (Paris: Desjonquères, 1992–), ii. 155. On Quesnay's relationship with Madame de Pompadour and his life at court, see Vardi, *The Physiocrats and the World of the Enlightenment*, 40–6.

[20] Smith, *An Inquiry into the Nature and Causes of the Wealth of Nations*, ii. 674.

[21] Guillaume-François Le Trosne, *De l'ordre social* (Paris: Debure, 1777), 447. Also see Claude-Camille -François d'Albon, *Eloge historique de M. Quesnay* (Paris: Didot, 1775), 33–4, and Victor de Riqueti de Mirabeau, 'Eloge funèbre de M. François Quesnay', *Nouvelles éphémérides économiques*, 1775, i. 7–8. For a detailed discussion, see: Spencer H. Banzhaf, 'Productive Nature and the Net Product: Quesnay's Economies Animal and Political', *History of Political Economy*, 3 (2000), 517–51, and Peter Groenewegen, 'From Prominent Physician to Major Economist: Some Reflections on Quesnay's Switch to Economics in the 1750s', in Groenewegen (ed.), *Physicians and Political Economy: Six Studies of the Work of Doctor Economists* (London: Routledge, 2001), 93–115.

[22] This point is made by Karl Pribram, *A History of Economic Reasoning* (Baltimore: Johns Hopkins University Press, 1983), 107. However, it is difficult to entirely agree that the 'physiocratic conception of economics was a mechanistic one' (ibid.). On the influence of the ideas of Malebranche on

informed by the language of the natural sciences, acquiring a resonance that rendered it markedly different from the legal and fiscal meaning vested in it by Boisguilbert a century before. Resting on the assumption that the economy was a fact of nature, the new meaning was influenced by two fundamental preconceptions of the physiocratic school. On the one hand there was the notion that society was born out of the sheer physical need of men; on the other, the belief that to achieve this end nature had created an order in which private and collective interests were confounded – that is, society itself. Within such a frame of reference, the essential coherence of the opposing aims of free individuals was deemed to be a consequence of the natural and ever-growing division of labour which made men increasingly dependent, for their material needs, on the work and goods of others. When working for themselves and pursuing their own advantages, individuals were then also reinforcing the social tie by increasing the degree of interdependence.[23] How such views stood in relation to the Mandevillian paradigm is a matter for debate. The physiocrats' holistic approach, their constant references to the designs of the author of nature, or their views about luxury all contrasted with the Mandevillian vulgate about man and society. The point to grasp is that Quesnay and his followers firmly believed in an essential and primordial coincidence of private and common interest.[24]

In their attempt to create an all-embracing science of nature's dominion, the physiocrats took as their broadest object of enquiry society's self-sustaining economy, which they then divided into the largest possible functional groups. The underlying assumption was that understanding how the relationship among these worked was tantamount to understanding how the economy itself functioned. Accordingly, Quesnay imagined the circulation of wealth as a system involving different classes. A nation, he wrote in the *Tableau économique*, 'can be divided into three different classes: the productive class, the class of owners, and the sterile class'. The first one, cultivating the land, provided the nation with its annual revenue; the second included the king and all the landowners, while the last class was made up of all the 'citizens employed in services and works other than

Quesnay, see Catherine Larrère, 'Malebranche revisité: L'économie naturelle des physiocrates', *Dix-huitième siècle*, 26 (1994), 117–38.

[23] See the classic by Albert O. Hirschman, *The Passions and the Interests: Political Arguments for Capitalism before its Triumph* (Princeton: Princeton University Press, 1977), 96–100. Also see, the interesting discussion in Marcel Gauchet, 'De l'avènement de l'individu à la découverte de la société', in Gauchet, *La condition politique* (Paris: Gallimard, 2005), 405–31.

[24] Larrère, 'Malebranche revisité', 119.

farming'.[25] According to Quesnay, the wealth of a nation, what he called the 'net product', was always the yield of agriculture alone, for industry transformed and commerce distributed the goods of nature. In this scheme, Quesnay divided society into distinct parts which he then pieced together so as to reconstruct what he had initially divided. In doing so, he was perfectly aware that classes were his own fabrication and that, as such, they did not exist in the world he was observing. He was equally aware that the measure he had chosen to define the different parts of society depended on his own intellectual goal, namely, understanding the production and regeneration of the nation's revenue. In the definition laid out by Quesnay, a class was a group of individuals who played one and the same role in the production of wealth. A nation, conversely, was a group of classes that performed the different tasks that would be required to regenerate the wealth consumed. By the same token, and importantly, a nation was simply a self-sufficient economic system having as its sole purpose that of sustaining its members and meeting their material needs. In this scheme, society was naturally at peace with itself. Indeed, in their writings the physiocrats repeated time and again that the different classes shared one and the same interest. The 'common', 'general', or even 'national interest' was simply the increase in the production of wealth to its 'natural' levels, while the question of its fair distribution was usually neglected and the possibility of diverging interests among classes completely ignored – something that prompted the vehement protests of certain observers.[26] According to the abbé Baudeau (1730–1792) – who, for one detractor, was the 'most verbose and the most widely-read of the entire sect' – nothing was 'more important for the prosperity of developed societies than the clear, distinct, and always present awareness of this precious unity of interests, which is such that the fate of the class of owners depends on the fate of the sterile class and on the fate of the productive class'.[27] Pierre-Samuel Dupont de Nemours (1739–1817),

---

[25] François Quesnay, 'Analyse de la formule arithmétique du Tableau économique' (1766 – second edition), in Œuvres économiques complètes et autres textes (Paris: Institut national d'études démographiques, 2005), i. 546. On the physiocrats' idea of nation, see Georges Weulersse, La physiocratie à l'aube de la Révolution: 1781–1792 (Paris: EHESS, 1985), 212–9.

[26] See, for example, Gabriel Bonnot de Mably, 'Doutes proposés aux philosophes économistes sur l'ordre naturel et essentiel des sociétés politiques' (1768), in Œuvres, xi. 10, and Simon-Nicolas-Henri Linguet, Réponse aux docteurs modernes, ou Apologie pour l'auteur de la théorie des loix et des lettres sur cette théorie, avec la réfutation du système des philosophes économistes (Paris: n.p., 1771), i. 118–19.

[27] Nicolas Baudeau, Première introduction à la philosophie économique, ou Analyse des États policés (1767) (Paris: P. Geuthner, 1910), 168. The disparaging comment was by Jean François de La Harpe, Correspondance littéraire, adressée à S. A. I. Mgr le grand-duc, aujourd'hui empereur de Russie (Paris: Migneret, 1801–1807), iii. 302.

one of the most active advocates of the physiocratic cause, reiterated such an idea with yet greater conviction: 'A society is complete when it shows itself to be made of, and maintains itself as, three classes', the productive, the owning, and the sterile class. This distinction, which was 'necessary to classify and to understand human interests', was not one between men but between the work they did and their respective roles in the economy. Although Dupont de Nemours acknowledged that in relation to the distribution of wealth and the consumption of goods, classes and individuals might have different interests, he saw these as naturally subordinate to the 'primitive interest', the general interest of society, which was the greatest possible increase of production.[28] If the distribution of wealth among classes was iniquitous, it was either the fault of the rulers or a social necessity.

In their depiction of an essentially harmonious, smoothly functioning economy governed by natural and unchanging rules, Quesnay and the physiocrats were 'constructing a physiological-physics of social order'.[29] As both Joseph A. Schumpeter and, later on, Louis Dumont argued, the importance of Quesnay's break with previous economic thought lies precisely in his conception of the economy as an ordered whole formed of different parts working in accordance with the rules of nature. It was a holistic conception of society, one that did not abide by a discourse arising out of, nor developed within, the economic viewpoint. On the contrary, it was derived 'from the *projection on the economic plane of the general conception of the universe as an ordered whole*'.[30] This is a point that becomes particularly relevant when considering the way the physiocrats construed the relationship between polity and economy. In fact, given that the purpose of society was, in their judgement, that men might meet their material needs, increasing the nation's prosperity had to be the fundamental – or even the only – goal to pursue. However, Quesnay and the other physiocrats intended their science as a tool for understanding nature's self-rule – rather than a means to rule over nature – and for ridding man of all those positive norms that clashed with nature's order. As Quesnay wrote, with great emphasis: 'If the torch of reason were to enlighten the government,

[28] Pierre-Samuel Dupont de Nemours, 'Abrégé des principes de l'économie politique' (1772), in Eugène Daire (ed.), *Physiocrates* (Osnabrück: Otto Zeller, 1966), 376. On Dupont's ideas, see Martin Giraudeau, 'Performing Physiocracy: Pierre Samuel Dupont de Nemours and the Limits of Political Engineering', *Journal of Cultural Economy*, 3 (2010), 225–42.

[29] Serge Latouche, *L'invention de l'économie* (Paris: Albin Michel, 2005), 87.

[30] Louis Dumont, *From Mandeville to Marx: The Genesis and Triumph of Economic Ideology* (Chicago: Chicago University Press, 1977), 41. Italics in the text. Also see, Joseph A. Schumpeter, *History of Economic Analysis* (London: Allen & Unwin, 1954), 223–43.

all positive laws harmful to society and to the sovereign would vanish.'[31] Once the rules of nature were evident to all, they would simply replace the rule of men.[32] Indeed, Quesnay was adamant that the state should not be governed by the will of monarchs or their ministers but by immutable and self-evident natural rules – and here, clearly, the physiocrats were at odds with all other political economists of the day. As has been argued, the result of this economisation of politics would have been its abolition: 'It is by advocating the *absolute rationalisation* of politics, that the physiocrats, in fact, end up abolishing it.'[33] Indeed, the process would have implied a growing impotence of the monarch who, thanks to the *Tableau*, might properly and fully understand how the economy of his nation worked but could no longer intervene in it. From this angle, the society imagined by the physiocrats coincided with an economic system in which the only purpose of political authority was to oversee respect for natural laws.

Consistently with these views, and within such a frame of reference, conflict between individuals or classes, which needed one another, seemed impossible. Even the idea of an original social contract, that is, of a political foundation of society settling a primeval conflict, was rejected. Society was simply the outcome of the evolving state of nature and, as such, it required no historical explanation.[34] Crucially, the rejection of all the political and social antagonism so central to such reasonings also implied the denial of any idea of historical change as such, so much so that, as Pierre Rosanvallon has remarked, 'time is suspended for the physiocrats'.[35] The social order outlined in the works of Quesnay, Baudeau, and Dupont de Nemours, because it was natural, was also static and universal. In the words of a prominent physiocrat, Lemercier de la Rivière, what they sought was the 'unchanging order by which the Author of nature intended men to be governed in all places and in all times'.[36] Even the main idea behind the *Tableau*, the work around which the coterie's other writings for the most part revolved, was to offer a 'static image', to be grasped at a single glance, of how wealth circulated.[37] In it, the explanations of how the

---

[31] [François Quesnay], *Le droit naturel* (Paris: n.p., 1765), 34.

[32] Foucault refers to this as the 'Quesnay principle': Michel Foucault, *Du gouvernement des vivants* (Paris: EHESS, 2012), 15.

[33] Pierre Rosanvallon, *Le capitalisme utopique: Critique de l'idéologie économique* (Paris: Seuil, 1979), 51. Italics in the text.

[34] Dan Edelstein, *The Terror of Natural Right: Republicanism, the Cult of Nature, and the French Revolution* (Chicago: University of Chicago Press, 2009), 101–11.

[35] Rosanvallon, *Le capitalisme utopique*, 52.

[36] Paul-Pierre Lemercier de la Rivière, *L'ordre naturel et essentiel des sociétés politiques* (1767) (Paris: Fayard, 2001), 325.

[37] Dumont, *From Mandeville to Marx*, 41.

relationships between classes had come about simply fell out of the picture – literally. Once formed, and once nature prevailed, not only was knowing how a society had arisen a secondary matter, but all attempts to change it were always harmful. This is the key to understanding Quesnay's praise of Chinese despotism and Lemercier de la Rivière's own 'legal despotism'.[38] In fact, despotic rule was for the physiocrats the only way of suppressing politics – which they saw as a legacy of barbaric ages – and of allowing nature to follow its course. Suppressing politics was the way of safeguarding the unchanging and, in this sense, un-historical, natural order.[39] It was this unyielding denial of the importance of the past, history, and tradition in governing men that some opponents considered particularly dangerous. The authors of the *Correspondance littéraire*, commenting on Lemercier de la Rivière's *Ordre naturel et essentiel des sociétés politiques*, vehemently protested that passions, emotions, opinions, and also history had been wholly ignored: 'I do not believe that the author has mentioned one single historical event throughout his entire reverie. This fact alone shows what one ought to think of his work.'[40] It was a fault that belonged to most, if not all, texts of the physiocrats. Because of their cult of nature over and even against time, Tocqueville bitterly remarked that they had 'for the past a contempt that knows no limits'.[41] It was a reading that held some truth. Much later on, Furet made somewhat similar observations: in the works of the physiocrats, '[s]ociety becomes independent from its past, the idea of tradition is emptied of content, while the state is made to embody this reason, which is one with the public interest, royal absolutism being only absolute to the extent that its role is to implement the natural order'.[42] Inevitably, these assumptions influenced the physiocrats' definitions of class and nation, leading them to pay scant attention to the ways in which these evolved through time. But such a misconception was also the outcome of the specific kind of classification, a functional one, that they used to understand how the economy itself worked. In their view, a class invariably remained something of their own intellectual fabrication, and individuals would be inserted into it in an attempt to understand how society worked.[43]

---

[38] François Quesnay, 'Despotisme de la Chine' (1767), in *Œuvres*, ii. 1005–14; Lemercier de la Rivière, *L'ordre naturel et essentiel des sociétés politiques*, 188–97.

[39] Rosanvallon, *Le capitalisme utopique*, 52–4.

[40] Grimm et al., *Correspondance littéraire*, vii. 449 (October 1767).

[41] Tocqueville, *L'Ancien régime et la Révolution*, i. 210.

[42] François Furet, 'La Révolution de Turgot à Jules Ferry', in Furet, *La Révolution française* (Paris: Gallimard, 2007), 243.

[43] Other economists, writing at about the same time, were aware that it was they themselves who construed 'classes'. See, for example, Smith, *An Inquiry into the Nature and Causes of the Wealth of*

One author who did much to change the meaning of class, turning it into a concept that historians could use in their works, was Anne-Robert-Jacques Turgot.[44] Reliant in part on the ideas of the physiocrats, he was often held to be in cahoots with them. According to one detractor, he even 'chaired the gatherings' of the 'sect'.[45] In truth, Turgot was critical of many of their ideas and did his utmost to counter all rumours suggesting he belonged to the coterie.[46] One contention crucial to Turgot's views about nation and classes was that a developed economy produced more than was necessary for its own subsistence. In his influential 'Réflexions sur la formation et la distribution des richesses' (1769–1770), published in the physiocrats' *Éphémérides du citoyen*, he argued that such a surplus was exchanged on the market by the worker, who was the 'sole source of wealth', the one animating the entire economy, and who produced a greater wealth 'than his salary' earned him.[47] Looking at the economy, the first division Turgot identified was the one between two equally 'industrious classes'. The first, the 'productive class', drawing straight from nature a 'continuously renewed wealth', provided society with all its basic goods and raw materials; the 'stipendiary class', on the contrary, transformed the products of nature into those goods that were necessary to society. Interestingly, offering the outline of a conjectural history, Turgot went on to argue that although initially the worker always owned the land

Nations, ii. 664, and Antonio Genovesi, *Delle lezioni di commercio o sia di economia civile con elementi di commercio* (1765–1767) (Naples: Istituto italiano per gli studi filosofici, 2005), 301–14.

[44] On Turgot, see: Roberto Finzi, *Note su Turgot, la storia e l'economia* (Bologna: CLUEB, 1987); Claude Morilhat, *La prise de conscience du capitalisme: Economie et philosophie chez Turgot* (Paris: Klincksieck, 1988); Jean-Pierre Poirier, *Turgot: Laissez-faire et progrès social* (Paris: le Grand livre du mois, 1999). With an emphasis on his historical thought: Catherine Larrère, 'Histoire et nature chez Turgot', in Binoche and Tinland (eds.), *Sens du devenir et pensée de l'histoire au temps des Lumières*, 178–208; Giampiero Rossi, *Filosofia e storia in Anne Robert Jacques Turgot* (Bologna: Pendragon, 2009); Julie Boch, 'Turgot historien de l'esprit humain', in Boch, *Approches de la pensée des Lumières* (Rheims: Éditions et presses universitaires de Reims, 2012), 509–20.

[45] Petit de Bachaumont, Pidansat de Mairobert, and d'Angerville, *Mémoires secrets pour servir à l'histoire de la république des lettres en France depuis 1762 jusqu'à nos jours*, ix. 245.

[46] See, for example, Anne-Robert-Jacques Turgot to Pierre-Samuel Dupont de Nemours, 2 February 1770, in *Œuvres de Turgot et documents le concernant* (ed. Schelle) (Paris: Alcan, 1913–1923), iii. 374. On the differences between Turgot and the physiocrats, see Francine Markovits, *L'ordre des échanges: Philosophie de l'économie et économie du discours au XVIIIᵉ siècle en France* (Paris: Presses universitaires de France, 1986), 161–227. Also see, Pierre Henri Goutte and Gérard Klotz, 'Turgot: A Critic of Physiocracy? An Analysis of the Debates in *Éphémérides du citoyen* and in Correspondence with Dupont', *The European Journal of the History of Economic Thought*, 22 (2015), 500–33.

[47] Anne-Robert-Jacques Turgot, 'Réflexions sur la formation et la distribution des richesses', in *Œuvres* (ed. Daire), i. 10–11. The text, written in 1766, was first privately distributed in 1770 and became available as a book in 1788. See Giancarlo de Vivo and Gabriel Sabbagh, 'The First Translator in English of Turgot's *Réflexions sur la formation et la distribution des richesses*: Benjamin Vaughan', *History of Political Economy*, 47 (2015), 185–6.

he ploughed, things changed with the enclosure of plots and the birth of property in land.[48] Because fertile soil was scarce, all cultivable land soon had an owner. Workers who were landless would lose no time in trading their labour in exchange for a salary. Hence, the distinction was between those who worked the land and those who owned it. Turgot then proceeded to divide society into three classes: the producers who cultivated their own land, those 'who work[ed] for hire', and, finally, the class of owners. Not being tied to any duty, the latter could be employed by the state for its administration and all the tasks necessary for its existence – and it was called by him the 'disposable class'.[49] All this granted, and after arguing for further distinctions and divisions, Turgot then proposed that:

> 'The entire class employed in supplying the different needs of society, with an immense variety of works of industry, is, so to speak, subdivided into two orders. The first, that of the entrepreneurs, manufacturers, and masters, all owners of substantial amounts of capital which they impart value to by means of their advances; and the second order, composed of simple artisans, who have no other property but their physical strength and who advance only their daily labour and receive no profits but their wages.'[50]

The importance of Turgot's analysis of classes is twofold. On the one hand, he introduced a sharp dichotomy between two social groups that was far subtler than the one between rich and poor that pervaded the eighteenth-century literature. Indeed, Boisguilbert had already deplored the division of society between an idle and an industrious class, 'the one doing nothing and enjoying all pleasures, while the other, working from dawn to dusk, has barely the wherewithal' to survive. Later on, the famous barrister and journalist Simon-Nicolas-Henri Linguet (1736–1794) complained about the condition of waged workers, which, if anything, was even worse than that of slaves in the ancient world. Reasoning on the consequences that inequality might have for freedom, he concluded bitterly that the workers would always be slaves to the rich. Helvétius regretted the disproportion of wealth among citizens, remarking that when all riches were concentrated in the hands of the few, 'the nation is divided into two classes, of which the one abounds in superfluities and the other lacks the necessities'. Diderot used similar words. Voltaire remarked, with bitter irony, that it was 'impossible in our miserable world that men living in society should not

---

[48] Turgot, 'Réflexions sur la formation et la distribution des richesses', 11–12.
[49] Ibid., 14–15. Italics in text.   [50] Ibid., 39.

be divided into two classes; the rich who give orders and the poor who obey'. Raynal, for his part, noted that 'all nations seem divided into two irreconcilable parts' and that the rich and the poor formed 'two classes regrettably opposed to one another'.[51] Even more striking is the case of Rousseau, who inveighed against the political consequences of inequality his entire life, in the *Discours sur l'origine et les fondements de l'inégalité*, of course, but also in his *Émile*, the *Lettres de la montagne*, and the *Rêveries du promeneur solitaire* (1782).[52] These and other authors went beyond the traditional ethical denunciation of economic imbalances and formulated political and social arguments regarding the relationship between economic and political inequality.[53] However, Turgot took such reasonings a step further. The originality of his views lay in the fact that he deployed a strictly economic analysis – one devoid of all moral concerns – to highlight the deleterious consequences of a division of society into two classes. The true difference, he argued, was not between rich and poor, but between the owners of land or capital and the waged workers, who owned nothing except their own physical strength. Inequality of wealth was admittedly related to such a distinction, but the one was not entirely reducible to the other. First and foremost, in fact, Turgot saw inequality as stemming from the place a person occupied in the economy – a consideration with vast consequences for the history of political and economic ideas. This was a functional differentiation that could be explained through the workings and the needs of the economy as such.

---

[51] Pierre le Pesant de Boisguilbert, 'Dissertation sur la nature des richesses, de l'argent et des tributs' (1707), in Eugène Daire (ed.), *Économistes-financiers du XVIIIe siècle* (Osnabrück: Otto Zeller, 1966), 399; Simon-Nicolas-Henri Linguet, *Théorie des lois civiles, ou Principes fondamentaux de la société* (1767) (Paris: Fayard, 1984), 581–8; Helvétius, *De l'esprit*, 32; Denis Diderot, 'Homme', in Diderot and d'Alembert (eds.), *Encyclopédie*, viii. 278; Voltaire, 'Dictionnaire philosophique', xviii. 475; Raynal, *Histoire philosophique et politique de l'établissement et du commerce des Européens dans les deux Indes* (ed. 1780), ix. 207. As is well known, sections of the *Histoire philosophique* were written by Diderot. Yet this passage is not listed as such in Michèle Duchet, *Diderot et l'Histoire des deux Indes, ou L'écriture fragmentaire* (Paris: Nizet, 1978).

[52] Rousseau, 'Émile', 267; Rousseau, 'Lettres écrites de la montagne', 890; Jean-Jacques Rousseau, 'Rêveries du promeneur solitaire', in *Œuvres*, i. 1092–3. The *Rêveries*, written between 1776 and 1778, were published posthumously. On Rousseau's idea of social classes, see Hélène Desbrousses and Bernard Peloille, 'Rapports sociaux et luttes entre "classes" inégales chez Rousseau', *Cahiers pour l'analyse concrète*, 35 (1995), 39–46. On Rousseau's concerns over what he named 'moral or political inequality', see Raymond Polin, 'Le sens de l'égalité et de l'inégalité chez J.-J. Rousseau', in Journées d'étude sur le Contrat social (eds.), *Études sur le Contrat social de Jean-Jacques Rousseau* (Paris: Les Belles lettres, 1964), 143–64, and Jean Starobinski, 'Le discours sur l'origine et les fondements de l'inégalité', in Starobinski, *Jean-Jacques Rousseau: La transparence et l'obstacle suivi de Sept essais sur Rousseau* (Paris: Gallimard, 2003), 330–55.

[53] For an accessible overview, see Jonathan Israel, *A Revolution of the Mind* (Princeton: Princeton University Press, 2010), 92–123.

Arguably, the divisions Turgot discerned within society were then sharper than those identified by most thinkers, since their distinctions between rich and poor were, in a sense, a matter of degree. However, Turgot was far from being an advocate of the rights of the workers or the poorest ranks in society. To the contrary, as he made clear in a 1751 letter to Madame de Graffigny: 'The distribution of professions carries necessarily the inequity of conditions.' Inequality, in and of itself, was not seen as a problem. In effect, its 'usefulness and necessity might easily be proven' – or so claimed Turgot.[54]

Maintaining that insofar as it arose from the nature of things, inequality was inevitable and necessary – following, in this, the physiocrats – Turgot did nonetheless acknowledge the need to combat all privileges and monopolies because they interfered with the order of nature. It was in the general interest that the unfairness deriving from the subversion of the natural laws of economics be challenged. Aside from the causes occasioned by men, by dint of their ignorance and greed, Turgot recognised four natural reasons for inequality: the varying propensities to work, the fertility of the soil, the size of families, and, importantly, the different capacities of men to hoard money and turn it into capital – which, circulating, 'maintains movement and life in the political body and which is rightly compared to the circulation of blood within the animal body'.[55] All these causes interacted with the growing division of labour which, differentiating tasks and duties, carried the seeds of an increasing inequality among men because of the different distribution of wealth it caused.[56] While this implied, on the one hand, the existence of a close relationship between progress and inequality, Turgot assumed nonetheless that the process in question improved the overall condition of society and, moreover, increased social mobility by offering the members of the lower classes a chance to ameliorate their condition. In fact, Turgot was convinced that the division of labour created new opportunities for all those who could put to best use their skills and, by so doing, earmark capital to invest in the work of others.[57] Importantly for us, although Turgot did not claim that history and progress could be explained through economic changes alone, he did believe that the economy could only be understood by

[54] Anne-Robert-Jacques Turgot to Françoise d'Issembourg d'Happoncourt de Graffigny, 1751, in *Œuvres* (ed. Daire), ii. 785–6. Also see, Turgot, 'Réflexions sur la formation et la distribution des richesses', 7.

[55] Turgot, 'Réflexions sur la formation et la distribution des richesses', 45.

[56] Turgot, 'Second discours sur le progrès de l'Esprit humain', 598–9.

[57] On this, Sonenscher, *Before the Deluge*, 281–4.

looking at history. A major difference, when compared with the physio-crats and their essentially static image of the economy, lies precisely in this. Inequality among men and classes, which had been for Quesnay and his coterie the 'principle of conservation of society', was in Turgot's scheme 'the engine of the *evolution* of economy'.[58] As has been argued, from his viewpoint a nation's economy could only be understood by considering the 'type of society which historically preceded it and then asking oneself what alterations in its working were brought about when a new class of capitalist entrepreneurs entered upon the historical scene'.[59] Interestingly, it was precisely Turgot's capacity to offer a historical interpretation of the oppos-ition between classes that prompted Robert Nisbet to see in Turgot a precursor of Karl Marx (1818–1883).[60]

Ideas such as the ones expressed by Turgot, began to gain currency in the years following the publication of the *Réflexions*.[61] The abbé de Condillac, who was a friend and admirer, likewise divided society into two classes – and, regretted the abbé Baudeau, by doing so destroyed Quesnay's *Tableau*.[62] According to Condillac, '[t]here are, in general, only two classes of citizens: that of the owners, to whom all land and all production belong, and that of the waged workers, who, not having their own land nor production, survive through the wages to be paid for their work'. His definition of citizens included all those individuals useful to society and who repaid their debt to it through work or taxes. Importantly, Condillac brought together the idea of citizenship, understood as an active contribution to the common good, and the concept of class.[63] This conceptual linkage was destined to become

[58] Philippe Gilles and Jean-Pierre Berlan, 'Économie, histoire et genèse de l'économie politique: Quesnay, Turgot et Condorcet, Say, Sismondi', *Revue économique*, 42 (1991), 374–5. Italics in the text.

[59] Roland L. Meek, 'Introduction', in Anne-Robert-Jacques Turgot, *On Progress, Sociology and Economics* (Cambridge: Cambridge University Press, 1973), 20.

[60] Robert Nisbet, *History of the Idea of Progress* (New York: Basic Books, 1980), 185.

[61] On Turgot's impact on the history of economic thought, see Peter Groenewegen, *Eighteenth-Century Economics: Turgot, Beccaria and Smith and their Contemporaries* (London: Routledge, 2002), 331–62. Gilbert Faccarello has written of a 'Turgot school': Gilbert Faccarello, 'Le legs de Turgot: Aspects de l'économie politique sensualiste de Condorcet à Rœderer', in Gilbert Faccarello and Philippe Steiner (eds.), *La pensée économique pendant la Révolution française* (Grenoble: Presses universitaires de Grenoble, 1991), 67–107.

[62] Nicolas Baudeau, 'Suite des observations économiques à M. l'abbé de Condillac', *Nouvelles éphémérides économiques*, 1776, v. 140. On Condillac's 'language of economics', see Jeanine Gallais-Hamonno, 'Condillac et la langue de l'économie', in Jean Sgard (ed.), *Condillac et les problèmes du langage* (Geneva: Slatkine, 1982), 407–20.

[63] Étienne Bonnot de Condillac, 'Le commerce et le gouvernement considérés relativement l'un à l'autre' (1776), in *Œuvres philosophiques*, ii. 311–2. Condillac has variously been seen as a dissenting physiocrat or a follower of Turgot's economic views. For an assessment: Arnaud Orain, 'Condillac face à la physiocratie: Terre, valeur et répartition', *Revue économique*, 53 (2002), 1075–99.

prominent in public debates a few years later. Another author who shared many of Turgot's assumptions on the nature of class was Jacques Necker (1732–1804), the banker and minister of Louis XVI.[64] Intervening in the famous 'grain wars', in which, among others, the abbé Galiani, Mably, and Diderot became involved – and on which Voltaire made his usual barbed remarks – Necker argued that the division between two classes produced a profound chasm within France.[65] Tellingly, he identified the working class with 'the people', defining it as that 'part of the nation born without property, from parents of about the same condition and who, not having received any education, have but their natural faculties and no possessions other than their physical strength or some rudimentary and rough art'.[66] Because of their circumstances, he argued, the people/working class were 'condemned by the effects of the laws' to never obtain in exchange for their work and sacrifices anything more than the bare necessities.[67] Evidently, the interests of the two classes were profoundly at variance with one another, so that any advantage for the one could only be gained at the expense of the other. Adopting a moralistic tone absent from Turgot's drier analysis, Necker nonetheless followed the latter in advancing a historical inter-pretation of the gulf separating owners and waged workers. In fact, he wrote, 'there arises between these two classes a kind of obscure but terrible struggle' in which the 'strong, protected by the laws, oppress the weak', crushing those who lived off their own labour.[68] In such a struggle, since the owners passed down to their offspring their properties and wealth, these increased over time. So much so, indeed, that 'the disproportion between their condition and that of the greater mass of citizens must necessarily increase'.[69] Marx's remark that Necker 'already understood the oppos-

---

[64] On Necker, his life and ideas, see the classic by Jean Egret, *Necker: Ministre de Louis XVI, 1776–1790* (Paris: Honoré Champion, 1975). Also see, Henri Grange, *Les idées de Necker* (Paris: Klincksieck, 1974).

[65] Voltaire, 'Dictionnaire philosophique', xviii. 11. On the quarrel, see Cynthia A. Bouton, *The Flour War: Gender, Class, and Community in Late Ancien Régime French Society* (University Park: Pennsylvania State University Press, 1993), and Steven Kaplan, *Raisonner sur les blés: Essais sur les Lumières économiques* (Paris: Fayard, 2017).

[66] Jacques Necker, *Sur la législation et le commerce des grains* (1775) (Roubaix: EDIRES, 1986), 66. On the relationship between the concepts of 'people' and 'class' in eighteenth-century France, see Marie-France Piguet, 'A propos du rapport classe/peuple (1750–1830): Approche lexicale', *Cahiers pour l'analyse concrète*, 48 (2001), 13–31.

[67] Necker, *Sur la législation et le commerce des grains*, 67. On Necker's ideas about social inequality, see Henri Grange, 'Necker et l'inégalité sociale', in J.-M. Servet (ed.), *Idées économiques sous la Révolution, 1789–1794* (Lyons: Presses universitaires de Lyon, 1989), 407–19.

[68] Necker, *Sur la législation et le commerce des grains*, 38.

[69] Jacques Necker, *De l'administration des finances de la France* (n.p., 1785), iii. 67.

ition of the two classes as classes' may be an overstatement; but it is nonetheless the case that Necker discerned a struggle between two well-defined classes, one with a history of its own.[70]

Sieyès and the Third Estate/Nation

That Emmanuel-Joseph Sieyès deserves a central place in the history of the notion of class is incontrovertible, as is the complexity of the relationship he depicted between classes, orders, and the nation. In his reasonings, the abbé accepted a number of the ideas of the physiocrats while rejecting certain fundamental assumptions – above all the relationship they had posited between politics and economics; he deployed some of Turgot's ideas on classes but reached different conclusions regarding their actual relationship; he even adumbrated, in his writings, some of the intuitions of the champions of *industrialisme* though he never anticipated their concern with social injustice.[71] His was an eclectic perspective and, in adopting it, he contributed to a fundamental shift in the self-representation of the

[70] Karl Marx, *Theorien über den Mehrwert: 1. Die Anfänge der Theorie vom Mehrwert bis Adam Smith* (Stuttgart: Dietz Nachf, 1905), 74.

[71] On Sieyès, see: Glyndon Van Deusen, *Sieyès: His Life and his Nationalism* (New York: Columbia University Press, 1932); Paul Bastid, *Sieyès et sa pensée* (Paris: Hachette, 1939); Murray Forsyth, *Reason and Revolution: The Political Thought of the Abbé Sieyès* (Leicester: Leicester University Press, 1987); Jean-Denis Bredin, *Sieyès: La clé de la Révolution française* (Paris: le Grand livre du mois, 1988); Georges Benrekassa, 'Crise de l'Ancien régime, crise des idéologies: Une année dans la vie de Sieyès', *Annales: Histoire, sciences sociales*, 44 (1989), 25–46; William H. Sewell Jr., *A Rhetoric of Bourgeois Revolution: The Abbé Sieyès and* What is the Third Estate? (Durham, NC: Duke University Press, 1994); Pasquale Pasquino, *Sieyès et l'invention de la constitution en France* (Paris: O. Jacob, 1998); Jacques Guilhaumou, *Sieyès et l'ordre de la langue: L'invention de la politique moderne* (Paris: Éditions Kimé, 2002); Luca Scuccimarra, *La sciabola di Sieyès: Le giornate di Brumaio e la genesi del regime bonapartista* (Bologna: il Mulino, 2002); Jacques Guilhaumou, 'Sieyès et le point du peuple', in Hélène Desbrousses, Bernard Peloille, and Gérard Raulet (eds.), *Le peuple, figures et concepts: Entre identité et souveraineté* (Paris: de Guibert, 2003), 49–56; Michael Sonenscher, 'Introduction', in Emmanuel-Joseph Sieyès, *Political Writings* (Indianapolis: Hackett, 2003), vii–lxiv; Christine Fauré, 'L'abbé Sieyès, lecteur problématique des Lumières', *Dix-huitième siècle*, 37 (2005), 225–41; Pierre-Yves Quiviger, Vincent Denis, and Jean Salem (eds.), *Figures de Sieyès* (Paris: Publications de la Sorbonne, 2008); Pierre-Yves Quiviger, *Le principe d'immanence: Métaphysique et droit administratif chez Sieyès* (Paris: Honoré Champion, 2008); Luca Scuccimarra, 'Généalogie de la nation: Sieyès comme fondateur de la communauté politique', *Revue française d'histoire des idées politiques*, 33 (2011), 27–45; Erwan Sommerer, 'Le contractualisme révolutionnaire de Sieyès: Formation de la nation et prédétermination du pouvoir constituant', *Revue française d'histoire des idées politiques*, 33 (2011), 5–25; Erwan Sommerer, *Sieyès, le révolutionnaire et le conservateur* (Paris: Michalon, 2011); Stephanie Frank, 'The General Will beyond Rousseau: Sieyès' Theological Arguments for the Sovereignty of the Revolutionary National Assembly', *History of European Ideas*, 37 (2011), 337–43; Oliver W. Lembcke and Florian Weber, 'Introduction to Sieyès's political theory', in Emmanuel-Joseph Sieyès, *The Essential Political Writings* (Leiden: Brill, 2014), 1–42; Jacques Guilhaumou, *Cognition et ordre social chez Sieyès: Penser les possibles* (Paris: Kimé, 2018); Lucia Rubinelli, *Constituent Power: A History* (Cambridge: Cambridge University Press, 2020), 33–74. On *industrialisme*, see below.

French nation. Between 1771 and 1776, close study of the physiocrats' writings led the young Sieyès to pen a series of 'Lettres aux économistes sur leur système de politique et de morale' – which he meant to publish but never did – thoroughly scrutinising and criticising several of their key tenets.[72] Assuming that the source of all value lay in the land and that agriculture alone could produce wealth was, Sieyès reckoned, their principal error. Their description was that of an economy of circulation rather than production and, therefore, it could not shed light on the way the economy really worked. In contrast to their core beliefs, Sieyès made the lapidary claim that '*it is work that produces wealth*'.[73] In fact, should it not be obvious that it was 'not nature that reddens and softens the iron that the blacksmith exposes to the action of fire?'[74] All labour, regardless of its form and source, created wealth. This idea, which would be one of the pillars of Smith's *The Wealth of Nations*, published the following year, was in truth far from novel. Boisguilbert had already sought to separate wealth from property in land and goods in order to tie it to work and production. Cantillon dedicated an entire chapter of his *Essai sur la nature du commerce* to showing that the greater the number of workers in a state, the greater its wealth. Diderot made similar remarks in the *Encyclopédie*. For his part, the tax collector and scholar Jean-Joseph-Louis Graslin (1727–1790), attacking the physiocrats in his *Essai analytique sur la richesse et l'impôt* (1767), tried to convince his readers that work, rather than transforming the wealth produced by nature, created new wealth. Just like Sieyès, all of these authors, wittingly or unwittingly, were restating Locke's claim that land 'furnished only the most worthless materials', and that, if it were not for the work of farmers and ploughmen, it would produce nothing.[75] Although far

---

[72] Emmanuel-Joseph Sieyès, 'Lettres aux économistes sur leur système de politique et de morale', in *Des manuscrits de Sieyès* (Paris: Honoré Champion, 1999–2007), i. 171–84. He wrote the letters in 1775. On his intention to publish them, see Françoise Weil, 'Les *Lettres aux économistes sur leur système de politique et de morale*: Présentation du manuscrit', ibid., 169–70. On the importance of his reading of the physiocrats' writings, see Forsyth, *Reason and Revolution*, 48–55, and Catherine Larrère, 'Sieyès, lecteur des physiocrates: Droit naturel ou économie?', in Quiviger, Denis, and Salem (eds.), *Figures de Sieyès*, 195–211.

[73] Sieyès, 'Lettres aux économistes sur leur système de politique et de morale', 175, underlined by Sieyès. On Sieyès's economic thought, see Marcel Dorigny, 'La formation de la pensée économique de Sieyès d'après ses manuscrits (1770–1789)', *Annales historiques de la Révolution française*, 271 (1988), 217–34.

[74] Sieyès, 'Lettres aux économistes sur leur système de politique et de morale', 182.

[75] Boisguilbert, 'Dissertation sur la nature des richesses, de l'argent et des tributs', 394–5; Richard Cantillon, *Essai sur la nature du commerce en général* (written possibly between 1730 and 1734 but published in 1755) (Paris: Institut national d'études démographiques, 1997), 48–54; Denis Diderot, 'Homme (morale)', in Diderot and d'Alembert (eds.), *Encyclopédie*, viii. 279; Jean-Joseph-Louis Graslin, *Essai analytique sur la richesse et l'impôt* (1767) (Paris: L'Harmattan, 2008), 157–62;

from original, Sieyès used the assumption that work rather than nature produced wealth to formulate an idea of society that differed from that of the physiocrats and was more complex than that of their adversaries.

Some of the ideas that Sieyès set out in his works on the eve of, and during, the Revolution were already contained in the 'Lettres aux économistes'. As he noted later on, while 'clearing the dust' off his old papers and notes, he found the letters and still considered them an 'excellent thing'.[76] His point of departure was the notion, widespread in the second half of the century and later consecrated during the Revolution, that every 'man wishes to be happy' and that each should be free to pursue his own interests and aims. Uniting as a community was the means of increasing the possibilities of pursuing such aims since most goods required a combination of the work of many individuals. In line with these precepts, the abbé could argue that, on the broadest plane at least, 'the goal of each man becomes that of society at large'. The division of labour, augmenting the general wealth and strengthening the social bond, was the true foundation of society. To increase the common wealth, argued Sieyès, 'it is therefore necessary for society, independently of the power of nature that is productive of goods, [to have] a *vital force* that is co-productive of wealth, and it is necessary that the elements of this force, united by society, produce more than they would if they remained isolated. The sum of the work of all the citizens forms the vital force.'[77] These ideas, which others at the time certainly shared, would remain central to Sieyès's vision of society long afterwards.[78] He repeated them in his *Observations sur le rapport du comité de Constitution*, published in 1789. In the latter, after acknowledging the importance of Adam Smith's ideas on the division of labour and its effects on society, the abbé contended that it was to increase

---

John Locke, *Two Treatises on Government* (1690) (Cambridge: Cambridge University Press, 1992), 26.

[76] Emmanuel-Joseph Sieyès, 'Délinéaments politiques: Premier cahier', in *Des manuscrits de Sieyès*, i. 236. The fragment has no date.

[77] Sieyès, 'Lettres aux économistes sur leur système de politique et de morale', 175–6. Sieyès's own emphasis. That the aim of all societies was for its members to freely pursue their happiness was often repeated by Sieyès. See, for example, Emmanuel-Joseph Sieyès, *Préliminaire de la Constitution françoise* (Paris: Baudouin, 1789), 9, and Sieyès, *Qu'est-ce que le tiers-état?*, 168. On the idea of happiness in the eighteenth century, see the classic by Mauzi, *L'idée du bonheur dans la littérature et la pensée françaises au XVIII*e *siècle*, passim, and, during the Revolution, Cesare Vetter, 'Révolution française: Evidences lexicologiques, évidences lexicométriques et interprétations historiographiques', Cesare Vetter and Marco Marin (eds.), *La felicità è un'idea nuova in Europa: Contributo al lessico della Rivoluzione francese* (Trieste: EUT, 2005–2013), ii. 13–33.

[78] See Christophe Salvat, 'De division of labour à division du travail: Histoire d'une notion, d'un syntagme et de sa diffusion en France', in Jacques Guilhaumou and Marie-France Piguet (eds.), *Dictionnaire des usages socio-politiques, 1770–1815* (Paris: Honoré Champion, 2003), vii. 39–64.

one's own possessions and to assure the safety of property 'that man decides to unite with his fellows'. In so doing, reason also impelled him to use his energies in the best of ways to obtain 'a greater product with less trouble and less effort'. From this stemmed the 'division of labour, consequence and cause of the increase of wealth and the improvement of human industry'.[79] But one important consequence of the division of labour was 'the formation of different classes of individuals, since they start to distinguish themselves only when they start to be employed in different works'.[80] Obviously, Sieyès then saw classes as analytical divisions that the progress of the economy and the proliferation of tasks and professions made necessary. However, since the increasing division of labour would have meant the endless multiplication of classes, rendering it impossible to depict a well-ordered society, Sieyès resorted to a tripartite scheme in which classes carried out separate but complementary functions.[81] The 'nurturing class', the 'industrious class', and the 'political class' – the latter ensuring order and public services – were all 'relatively co-productive and directly productive, since they all add elementary values forming the venal value'.[82] The assumed complementarity of the different functions made of Sieyès's society a peaceful and harmonious union where classes worked together in view of a clear and common aim, namely, the creation and increase of wealth.[83]

While from Sieyès's standpoint the economic system, divided and yet necessarily integrated, was at peace with itself – in a manner recalling the physiocrats' views – the abbé saw nonetheless an irreconcilable political contrast threatening such harmony. In fact, although the division of labour produced a convergence of private and public interests, it remained the case that '[i]f a citizen withdraws his portion of activity, he renounces his rights. No man ought to enjoy the labour of another without exchange. General work is hence the foundation of society, and the social order is nothing but the best possible order of works.'[84] This tying of the

---

[79] Emmanuel-Joseph Sieyès, 'Observations sur le rapport du comité de Constitution' (1789), in *Écrits politiques* (Paris: Archives contemporaines, 1985). See also Sieyès, 'Lettres aux économistes sur leur système de politique et de morale', 176.

[80] Emmanuel-Joseph Sieyès, 'Notes et fragments inédits', in *Écrits politiques*, 63.

[81] Jacques Guilhaumou, 'Nation, individu et société chez Sieyès', *Genèses*, 26 (1997), 11–12.

[82] Sieyès, 'Notes et fragments inédits', 50–5.

[83] Dorigny, 'La formation de la pensée économique de Sieyès', 28. It was a notion already expressed by Condillac, who might have influenced Sieyès: Condillac, 'Le Commerce et le gouvernement considérés relativement l'un à l'autre', 258. On this, Reinhard Bach, *Rousseau et le discours de la Révolution*, Au piège des mots: *Les physiocrates, Sieyès, les idéologues* (Uzès: Inclinaison, 2011), 138–40.

[84] Sieyès, 'Lettres aux économistes sur leur système de politique et de morale', 176.

individual's economic role to his political rights represents a central aspect of Sieyès's thought, one that was to be of momentous importance in the ensuing history of the concepts of class and nation. In fact, if work and the division of labour were the foundations of society, then not taking part in the creation of wealth was tantamount to stepping outside of it. From such a viewpoint, a person's usefulness to the nation was the fundamental criterion for granting citizenship; conversely, his idleness or his unwilling-ness to contribute to the general well-being should determine his exclusion from society.[85] Centring his reasoning on work and on a person's useful-ness to society, Sieyès devised a principle of inclusion and exclusion through which he could imagine a nation at peace with itself, by the same token identifying the rights and duties of its citizens. Sketched out in his earlier writings, repeated in the *Essai sur les privilèges* (1788), and restated in his famous *Qu'est-ce que le tiers-état?*, such ideas, while undoubt-edly original, ought to be considered against the backdrop of eighteenth-century discussions on the moral worth of labour and the shift in the understanding of labour from a vile to a virtuous activity, one useful to the state – as Colbert had it – or to society – as the Encyclopaedists saw it.[86] Partly because of this, the abbé's association of the 'worker' with the 'citizen' as well as his ideas on the patriotic usefulness of work were destined to have a strong echo.[87] Interestingly, such an assumption even came to be shared by some of the abbé's opponents, such as the economist, André Morellet (1727–1819), who, in his polemic with Sieyès, highlighted the importance of the nobility's economic role in order to justify its privileges.[88] If with some ambiguities, the association between citizenship and labour was also meant to overcome the principle of the 'citizen proprietor' sustained by the physiocrats – consistently with their vision of wealth and land – but also shared by d'Holbach, Turgot, Condorcet, Germain Garnier (1754–1821), and many others.[89] On the contrary, that

[85] Annalisa Furia, 'Il *citoyen homme social* negli scritti prerivoluzionari di Sieyès, 1770–1780', *Il pensiero politico*, 38 (2005), 209.

[86] John Shovlin, 'The Cultural Politics of Luxury in Eighteenth-Century France', *French Historical Studies*, 23 (2000), 577–606; Annie Jacob, *Le travail, reflet des cultures: Du sauvage indolent au travailleur productif* (Paris: Presses universitaires de France, 1994), 59–108.

[87] Annie Jacob, 'Pas de citoyen qui ne soit un travailleur', *La revue du M.A.U.S.S.*, 2 (2001), 196–201.

[88] [André Morellet], *Lettres à la noblesse de Bretagne* (n.p., 1789), 32–3. See also André Morellet, footnote in Emmanuel-Joseph Sieyès, *Qu'est-ce que le tiers état? précédé de l'Essai sur les privilèges* (Paris: Coréard, 1822), 66 and 68. For a detailed discussion, see: Eugenio Di Rienzo, 'Morellet e Sieyès: Nobili, proprietari e organizzazione del potere nella Rivoluzione', *Studi storici*, 31 (1990), 457–80.

[89] Paul Henri Dietrich d'Holbach, 'Représentans', in Diderot and d'Alembert (eds.), *Encyclopédie*, xiv. 145; Anne-Robert-Jacques Turgot, 'Mémoire sur les municipalités à établir en France' (written in

political rights belonged to a citizen because he worked and not because he owned property was a fundamental part of Sieyès's theory. As he phrased it: 'Political rights, like civil rights, must belong to those endowed with the quality of citizenship. The ownership of legal entitlements of this kind must belong to all, regardless of the different amounts of real property making up each individual's fortune or the assets they enjoy.'[90] That the enjoyment of citizenship depended on a person's active contribution to the prosperity of society clearly shows the importance of the economy in Sieyès's views of politics. As Pasquale Pasquino and Michael Sonenscher have stressed, even his theory of representation was basically an extension of his understanding of the division of labour.[91] According to the abbé, in fact, since no citizen could produce everything he desired, he was forced to rely on others who took his place – that is, represented him – in creating the goods he needed. In this sense, wrote Sieyès, the division of labour was but the 'representative system establishing itself', shaping the progress of society.[92] And, in this sense too, it 'might truly be said that all work undertaken in society is *representative*'.[93]

While such a seemingly economistic interpretation of society remained a central aspect of Sieyès's thought from his earliest writings onwards, it would nonetheless be misleading to assume that his was a reduction of politics to the economy – as was largely the case with the physiocrats. On the contrary, the legitimacy of any political institution lay for the abbé not in its economic merits but in its political nature – an idea that had something of a Rousseauian timbre.[94] In point of fact, as Sieyès stated time and again, to be morally rightful and legitimate, any association of men had to be founded on the unanimous 'act of will' of its members, on a 'first convention' representing 'the will, which is free in its essence, as to the one source from which derive, directly or indirectly, all the laws that

1775 but published in 1787 as *Œuvres posthumes de M. Turgot, ou Mémoire de M. Turgot sur les administrations provinciales*), in *Œuvres* (ed. Schelle), iv. 584–5; Jean-Antoine-Nicolas de Condorcet, 'Déclaration des droits' (1789), in *Œuvres*, ix. 207; Germain Garnier, *La propriété dans ses rapports avec le droit politique* (Paris: Clavelin, 1792). On this, see Pierre Rosanvallon, *Le sacre du citoyen* (Paris: Gallimard, 1992), 45–54.

[90] Sieyès, *Qu'est-ce que le tiers-état?*, 70.

[91] Pasquino, *Sieyès et l'invention de la constitution en France*, 39–42; Sonenscher, 'Introduction', xxviii–xxix.

[92] Emmanuel-Joseph Sieyès, 'Base de l'ordre social' (possibly written in 1793), in *Des manuscrits de Sieyès*, i. 510. For the dating, see Sieyès's reference to the coup against the Girondins on page 514.

[93] Quoted in Sonenscher, 'Introduction', xxix, n. 43. Italics in the text.

[94] Bronisław Baczko, 'The Social Contract of the French: Sieyès and Rousseau', *The Journal of Modern History*, 60 (1988), 98–125. For a very different perspective, see Christine Fauré, 'Sieyès, Rousseau et la théorie du contrat', in Quiviger, Denis, and Salem (eds.), *Figures de Sieyès*, 213–25.

put man under true obligation'.[95] It was through this political commitment that men formed, wrote Sieyès, 'by this fact alone, a nation'.[96] Only
in this way might the tie between workers turn into a moral bond between
citizens. The community thus formed not only had the economic objective
of increasing the general wealth but, importantly, also had the political aim
of safeguarding the freedom and rights of the individual, first and foremost
that of engaging in an unconstrained pursuit of his interests. Between these
two objectives there was a tight relationship since the increase of wealth
encouraged by the division of labour made it easier to pursue individual
happiness. Unlike Smith – an author whom Sieyès admired – the abbé then
placed his emphasis on the political consequences of the division of labour;
unlike Rousseau – whose ideas have been linked to Sieyès's own – the abbé
considered social integration to be conducive to a greater individual
freedom.[97] Importantly, because Sieyès's social contract was the product
of a common act of will, each individual shared rights and duties with the
other members of a polity. That the nation was 'a body of associates living
under a *common* law and represented by the same *legislator*' was, therefore,
a contention crucial to such a scheme.[98] Individual or even class privileges
were seen as an aberration, not least because, argued the abbé, when
a person acquired a privilege 'his new interest is inevitably opposed to
the general interest'.[99] As he saw it, material needs and the exchange of
goods strengthened the social fabric only in the absence of boundaries
and privileges: 'Reciprocal needs are a cause of sociability only
between *equals*', he reasoned.[100] Of course, the full implications of
such reasoning emerged when considering the status of the nobility.
The latter he saw as an altogether different and separate nation. On
the one hand, its members lived under rules and norms shared by
them alone; on the other, they did not contribute to the general
welfare. This 'class of [the] privileged without [a] function', because
of the legal status it enjoyed and because of the '*idleness*' of its

---

[95] Emmanuel-Joseph Sieyès, *Vues sur les moyens d'exécution dont les représentants de la France pourront disposer en 1789* (n.p., 1789), 24.

[96] Sieyès, *Qu'est-ce que le tiers-état?*, 123.

[97] On the opposite views of Rousseau and Sieyès on the effects of integration on freedom, see Larrère, *L'invention de l'économie au XVIIIᵉ siècle*, 310–12. On the abbé's interest in and admiration for Smith's work, see Emmanuel-Joseph Sieyès, 'Cahiers "Smith"', in *Des manuscrits de Sieyès*, ii. 305–61. Sieyès believed that Smith was 'right, in general': ibid., 360. The manuscript text was possibly written after 1779–1780. For the dating, see Christine Fauré, 'Introduction', ibid., 34.

[98] Sieyès, *Qu'est-ce que le tiers-état?*, 40. Italics in the text.

[99] Sieyès, *Qu'est-ce que le tiers-état?*, 47.

[100] Emmanuel-Joseph Sieyès, 'Droits de l'homme' (persumably written in 1789), in *Des manuscrits de Sieyès*, i. 502. Italics in the text.

members, was an alien body, living as a parasite.[101] Shackling and weakening the nation and debasing its worthiest part, the nobility was no less of an enemy 'of the common order than the English are to the French in times of war'.[102] Although Sieyès conceded that by relinquishing their privileges noblemen could become part of the nation, this required an unconditional acceptance of and subjection to the will of the Third Estate. They had simply to cease to exist as a distinct class. It is partly for this reason that Tocqueville, one of Sieyès's harshest critics, saw in *Qu'est-ce que le tiers-état?* a veritable 'battle cry' against the nobility and 'an example of the violence and radicalism of opinions'.[103]

One of Sieyès's key arguments was that the members of the Third Estate, because they shared the same economic interest, made up 'a complete nation' and that only by asserting its political rights and expressing its free will, would it finally become 'the French nation'. However, such a goal could only be attained through the nation's representatives. In other words, national unity did not exist until the people had expressed their common will, and the latter, in its turn, could only be formed through the nation's representatives.[104] This was to distance Sieyès in no uncertain terms from Rousseau and his revolutionary followers, whom the abbé, in fact, bitterly criticised.[105] Although Sieyès's definition of the nation rested on the claim that all of its members were subject to the same laws and enjoyed the same rights, he nonetheless drew a distinction between those who had the right to choose their representatives and those who did not: between, that is, passive and active citizenship.[106] Excluded from such rights were children, women, foreigners, and 'all those who contribute nothing to sustain the public establishment'. According to Sieyès, the representatives of the French nation could only be chosen by those male

---

[101] Emmanuel-Joseph Sieyès, 'Essai sur les privilèges', in *Écrits politiques*, 109, footnote; Sieyès, *Qu'est-ce que le tiers-état*, 40; italics in the text. On this, Keith M. Baker, 'Sieyès', in François Furet and Mona Ozouf (eds.), *Dictionnaire critique de la Révolution française* (Paris: Flammarion, 1988), 339–40. On the parasitic nature of the nobility, Sieyès, *Qu'est-ce que le tiers-état*, 39, n. 1.

[102] Sieyès, *Qu'est-ce que le tiers-état?*, 63.

[103] Alexis de Tocqueville, 'Notes de lecture sur la pensée politique française à la veille de la Révolution', in *L'Ancien régime et la Révolution*, ii. 139.

[104] Emmanuel-Joseph Sieyès, 'Fragments politiques' (written, possibly, in 1793), in *Des manuscrits de Sieyès*, i. 463.

[105] Sieyès, 'Base de l'ordre social', 510. Famously, Rousseau denied that the nation's will could ever be represented: Rousseau, 'Du contrat social', 429.

[106] On this, see William H. Sewell Jr., 'Le citoyen/la citoyenne: Activity, Passivity, and the Revolutionary Concept of Citizenship', in Colin Lucas (ed.), *The French Revolution and the Creation of Modern Political Culture, vol. II: The Political Culture of the French Revolution* (Oxford: Pergamon, 1988), 106–13.

adults who were 'stockholders' (*actionnaires*) in public affairs and, therefore, were clearly aware of the fact that their interests and those of the
nation at large coincided.[107] Such a reading was founded on two principal
assumptions. On the one hand there was the idea that the people, 'dispersed' throughout the country, could not express their will nor decide
upon political matters.[108] On the other, like most eighteenth-century
political thinkers, Sieyès nurtured a deep distrust towards the people as
such, whom he believed were unaware of their true interests. In the words
of the abbé himself, 'the wretched, bowed under heavy labour, producers
of the pleasures of others who barely receive a subsistence for their suffering, needful bodies, in this immense crowd of two-legged implements,
without freedom or morality. . ., is that what you call men? One calls them
civilised! Is there one of them capable of gaining admission to society?'[109]
While denouncing the condition and the exploitation of the lower classes,
of those 'bought slaves', Sieyès dreaded nonetheless their impulsiveness in
political matters.[110] He was adamant that full active citizenship be granted
only to those 'whom nature or circumstances make into good citizens' and
denied to those whom 'nature and circumstances mark with the brand of
nonentity'.[111] From this angle, there was a coherence to what might seem,
prima facie, a paradox. The strength of numbers, on which Sieyès insisted
when campaigning for the rights of the Third Estate, those 'twenty-five
to twenty-six million souls' forming the nation, was also what he feared
the most.[112] It was a feeling he shared with many others sitting in the
National and the Constituent Assembly. Some, including the revolutionary
leader Louis Antoine de Saint-Just (1767–1794), in spite of radical views on
other issues, supported franchise limitations.[113] Having imagined a society
based on legal equality, many thought it was necessary to find a new

---

[107] Emmanuel-Joseph Sieyès, 'Préliminaire de la Constitution' (speech read at the Constitutional
Committee on 21 July 1789), in *Écrits politiques*, 199.

[108] Sieyès, 'Fragments politiques', 462–3.   [109] Sieyès, 'Notes et fragments inédits', 81.

[110] The expression is in Sieyès, 'Cahiers "Smith"', 323. See, on this, Jean-Denis Bredin,
'Emmanuel Sieyès et Jacques Necker', *Annales Benjamin Constant*, 23–24 (2000), 63–88.

[111] Sieyès, 'Notes et fragments inédits', 89.

[112] Sieyès, *Qu'est-ce que le tiers-état?*, 75. On Sieyès's insistence on the importance of numbers, see the
disparaging comments later made by the monarchist author Pierre Victor Malouet (1740–1814) in
his *Mémoires* (Paris: E. Plon, 1874), i. 266–7.

[113] Louis-Antoine-Léon Saint-Just, 'L'esprit de la Révolution' (1791), in *L'esprit de la Révolution, suivi de
Fragments sur les institutions républicaines* (Paris: 10–18, 2003), 50–2. For an overview,
Patrice Gueniffey, *Le nombre et la raison: La Révolution française et les élections* (Paris: EHESS,
1993), especially 31–76. On elite fear of the masses, also see, David Andress, '"A Ferocious and
Misled Multitude": Elite Perceptions of Popular Action from Rousseau to Robespierre', in
Malcolm Crook, William Doyle, and Alan Forrest (eds.), *Enlightenment and Revolution: Essays in
Honour of Norman Hampson* (Aldershot: Ashgate, 2004), 169–86.

principle to limit the strength of numbers while avoiding new divisions.[114] The solution proposed by Jacques-Guillaume Thouret (1746–1794) and voted by the Constitutional Assembly was the well-known payment of an annual sum equivalent to the value of three days' wages to be a voter.[115] It was a step on a path that would exclude the majority of the working population from active citizenship, stirring the bitter opposition of the intransigent leaders of the Revolution – the invectives of Maximilien Robespierre (1758–1794), Camille Desmoulins (1760–1794), and the abbé Grégoire (1750–1831) are only the best known.[116] However, it is important to point out that Sieyès would have seen no real contradiction between such a solution and his own views. In fact, the nation, once rid of the nobility, would be at peace with itself, and be composed of individuals all contributing to the general wealth through their labour. All would share the same objectives, and the part of the Third Estate enjoying active citizenship would have 'no other interest than that of the rest of the people'.[117] In truth, one of Sieyès's fundamental innovations was his identification of the Third Estate with the entire nation – an idea that has led some historians to consider him a forerunner of 'universal class' theory.[118] His scheme for political representation was based on the assumption that by working and increasing their own as well as society's wealth, the members of the Third Estate shared the same interest and that, thanks to this, the unity of the nation could be imagined. Although his ideas were successful in so far as they served to disseminate a cult of work, individual success, and legal equality – all values that might retrospectively be viewed as intrinsically bourgeois – they failed because the abbé neglected the crucial issue of the distribution of wealth. And such an oversight made it difficult, if not impossible, to maintain the fiction of the identity of the upper Third Estate with the entire French people.

---

[114] Immanuel Wallerstein, 'Citizens All? Citizens Some! The Making of the Citizen', *Comparative Studies in Society and History*, 45 (2003), 652.

[115] Jacques-Guillaume Thouret, 'Rapport sur les bases de la représentation proportionnelle', 29 September 1789, in Jêrome Mavidal (ed.), *Archives parlementaires: Première série* (Paris: Dupont, 1862–), ix. 204–5. See Melvin Edelstein, *The French Revolution and the Birth of Electoral Democracy* (Farnham: Ashgate, 2014), 43–6. Also see, Bastid, *Sieyès et sa pensée*, 86–7.

[116] Maximilien Robespierre, 'Sur le marc d'argent et sur le cens électoral' (speech delivered on 11 August 1791), in *Œuvres* (Paris: Phénix, 2000), vii. 618–23; Camille Desmoulins, *Révolutions de France et de Brabant* (Frankfurt: Keip, 1989), i. 108–9 (December 1789); Henri Grégoire, Debates at the Assemblée Nationale on 22 October 1789, in Mavidal (ed.), *Archives parlementaires*, ix. 479.

[117] Sieyès, *Qu'est-ce que le tiers-état?*, 68.

[118] Franco Venturi, *Jean Jaurès e altri storici della Rivoluzione francese* (Turin: G. Einaudi, 1948), 66–7; also see, Pasquino, *Sieyès et l'invention de la constitution en France*, 62.

Assuming a substantial unity of interests within the nation/Third Estate, Sieyès construed his concept of class as a distinction serving to explain the way a society and its economy worked. It was a mere intellectual fabrication. What were real were the differences between the orders; real differences because they entailed legal and political consequences. To those, the Third Estate had to put an end. Although it would be misleading to see in Sieyès an advocate of 'class struggle', as some scholars have in the past, it is undeniable that the abbé paved the way to the future development of the notion in several ways.[119] Crucially for us, he made clear that the opposition between Third Estate and nobility could no longer pivot on alleged historical rights. Formulating a sort of 'discourse of reason', he repeatedly downplayed in his writings the importance of tradition as a source of political legitimacy.[120] In 1851, in an illuminating essay on the abbé, Sainte-Beuve saw in him a new 'Descartes, a man who would gladly make tabula rasa of everything that has come before' to shape a wholly new society.[121] There was some truth to this. As Sieyès himself wrote in 1789, he was indignant and outraged

> at that mass of writers obsessed with asking the past what we should become in the future, who seek in miserable traditions, full of absurdities and lies, the laws that might restore public order; who endlessly persist in delving into every archive to collect and compile countless memoirs, searching for and revering the least scrap, however apocryphal, obscure or unintelligible it may be, and all in the hope of discovering what?[122]

Indeed, the abbé chastised 'philosophers and pamphleteers' alike for only 'being capable of reading the future in the past' and misinterpreting or ignoring altogether any chances that might be offered for the betterment of mankind.[123] The legitimacy of laws and political institutions, he argued, should no longer be sought in dusty archives or libraries: 'The archives of peoples have not been destroyed. They are to be found only in one sure and faithful repository. This is the repository of reason,' the surest means for

---

[119] It was a claim made some time ago by Roberto Zapperi, *Per la critica del concetto di rivoluzione borghese* (Bari: De Donato, 1974), 53–92. A firm criticism is in Erwan Sommerer, 'La "preuve par l'archive"? La place des manuscrits dans la pensée de Sieyès', *Recto/Verso*, 5 (2009), 7–8.

[120] The reference is to the distinction between the discourses of justice, reason, and will made in Keith M. Baker, 'On the Problem of the Ideological Origins of the French Revolution', in Baker, *Inventing the French Revolution*, 12–27.

[121] Charles-Augustin Sainte-Beuve, 'Sieyès' (1851), in *Causeries du lundi*, v. 156.

[122] Sieyès, *Vues sur les moyens d'exécution dont les représentants de la France pourront disposer en 1789*, 32.

[123] Emmanuel-Joseph Sieyès, 'Rapport de M. l'abbé Sieyès sur les délits de presse', 20 January 1790, in Mavidal (ed.), *Archives parlementaires*, xi. 260.

combating injustices and inequalities.[124] The abbé's was a strong and convinced endorsement of the progress of human reason. Consistently, he believed that the principles for improving society and the laws of what he called the 'social art' should not be sought in a nation's past or even in its origins. In fact, would anyone build a ship 'only with the theories used by the savages for the construction of their vessels?' All knowledge would be lost if one were to return to its origins, with deleterious consequences for society.[125] With this in mind, it made little sense to 'ask earlier barbarous centuries for laws that are suitable for civilised nations', losing oneself in 'ancient institutions and errors'. And so, he asked his readers, '[w]ould we, disdaining the modern products of an improved art, turn to the Otahitians or the ancient Germans for models to provide for the needs of life?'[126] In these invectives, the nobility, with its veneration of the past and tradition, was the abbé's main target.[127] In truth, to an eighteenth-century member of the ancient nobility, whose 'eyes are incessantly fixed upon the good old times', the contribution to the well-being of society of a yeoman, a tradesman, or a merchant would have been negligible. It was from the past that 'he contemplates his titles, his power. He exists in his ancestors.' On the contrary, he went on, the bourgeois, 'his eyes always fixed on the ignoble *present* and the indifferent *future*', sustained the nation by 'his own industry'.[128] In Sieyès's famous call for the Third Estate to examine without fear the past, to return to the age before the Frankish conquest and resist those 'families who wildly claim to descend from the race of the conquerors', was the clearest rejection of tradition as a source of legitimacy.[129]

From Sieyès to the Count de Saint-Simon: Rethinking the History of Classes

The influence of the abbé's writings can hardly be overestimated. Four editions of his *Qu'est-ce que le tiers état?* were published in 1789 alone, and by the end of the year some thirty thousand copies were being read and

[124] Sieyès, *Vues sur les moyens d'exécution dont les représentants de la France pourront disposer en 1789*, 34.
[125] Sieyès, 'Fragments politiques', 446.
[126] Sieyès, *Vues sur les moyens d'exécution dont les représentants de la France pourront disposer en 1789*, 1.
[127] Tocqueville, while agreeing with Sieyès on more than one point, accused him of failing to grasp that the dignity of the French nobility stemmed from its antiquity and that, through its antiquity, one had to understand its role in, and importance to, modern society: Tocqueville, 'Notes de lecture sur la pensée politique française à la veille de la Révolution', 141.
[128] [Sieyès], 'Essai sur les privilèges', 101; italics in the text.
[129] Sieyès, *Qu'est-ce que le tiers-état*, 43–4.

discussed throughout France and beyond.[130] An author of the *Correspondence littéraire* considered it 'one of the most vigorous works that have been published on current affairs'. The revolutionary leader Jacques-Pierre Brissot (1754–1793), commenting on the popularity of Sieyès's writings, was amazed by the 'intense reaction' they had produced in the public. Madame de Staël went as far as to tell the American ambassador, Gouverneur Morris (1752–1816), that the abbé's works would one day produce 'in politics a new era as that of Newton in physics'. Sieyès's friend the Count de Mirabeau even saw him as a prophet, a new 'Mohammed'.[131] In truth, several of the ideas in the pamphlets penned by the abbé were already circulating in 1789. Some of the advocates of the rights of the Third Estate accepted his notion that active citizenship ought to be viewed in terms of stake-holding.[132] Others contended that the 'Third Estate is not an order; it is the nation'.[133] But a few even anticipated some of the abbé's arguments. In 1788, Rabaut de Saint-Étienne, for example, remarked that if one were to remove the clergymen and nobles, 'the nation still remains since one can create a thousand noblemen as from tomorrow, as was done at the return from the Crusades. But if you take away the twenty-four million Frenchmen known by the name of "Third Estate", noblemen, and churchmen will remain, but [there will be] no nation.'[134] Yet while some of the abbé's arguments were not entirely new, his writings

---

[130] Louis Alceste Chapuys-Montlaville, 'Sieyès', in Emmanuel-Joseph Sieyès, *Qu'est-ce que le tiers état?* (Paris: Pagnerre, 1839), 18. On the diffusion of the text, see Roberto Zapperi, 'Introduction', in Emmanuel-Joseph Sieyès, *Qu'est-ce que le tiers état?* (Geneva: Droz, 1970), 84–107.

[131] Anonymous, review of Emmanuel-Joseph Sieyès, *Qu'est-ce que le tiers état?*, in Grimm et al., *Correspondance littéraire*, xv. 400 (February 1789); Jacques-Pierre Brissot de Warville, *Mémoires* (Paris: Ladvocat, 1830–1832), iii. 135; Brissot's *Mémoires* were published posthumously by his son; Gouverneur Morris, *A Diary of the French Revolution* (Boston: Mifflin, 1939), ii. 107 (25 January 1791); Étienne Dumont, *Souvenirs sur Mirabeau et sur les deux premières assemblées législatives* (Paris: Gosselin, 1832), 296.

[132] See, for example, [Charles-François Lebrun], *La voix du citoyen* (n.p., 1789), 19; Jean-Joseph Mounier, *Considérations sur les gouvernemens, et principalement sur celui qui convient à la France* (Paris: Baudouin, 1789), 22. On the point, Boyd C. Shafer, 'Bourgeois Nationalism in the Pamphlets on the Eve of the French Revolution', *The Journal of Modern History*, 10 (1938), 37.

[133] Anonymous, *De la différence qu'il y a entre États-généraux et les assemblées nationales, ou Principes radicaux de la constitution* (n.p., 1789), 16. Also see, Anonymous, *Le réveil du tiers état, c'est à dire de la nation* (n.p., 1789); [Jean-Claude-Antoine de Bourge], *Avis aux électeurs des assemblées du 21 avril 1789* (n.p., 1789), 5–6.

[134] [Jean-Paul Rabaut de Saint-Étienne], *Considérations très-importantes sur les intérêts du tiers état* (n.p., 1788), 30. Like Sieyès, Rabaut de Saint-Étienne also rejected the idea that history could be the source of political legitimacy: ibid., 13. A further two examples from 1788 of the identification of the Third Estate with the 'body of the nation' or the entire French people are: Anonymous, *Lettre à un plébéien au sujet de l'assemblée des États généraux* (n.p., September 1788), 43–4, and Louis-Alexandre de Launay d'Antraigues, *Mémoire sur les États-généraux, leurs droits, et la manière de les convoquer* (n. p., 1788), 246.

helped to crystallise and define them and thereby exerted a profound influence upon the reading public. Commenting on *Qu'est-ce que le tiers état?*, Tocqueville rightly remarked that it gave 'a colouring and a shape to the passions that existed in embryo or were developing in all hearts' at that time.[135]

The idea that the nation was essentially made up of those who contributed to the public wealth through their daily efforts and sacrifices was shared, among others, by Antoine Joseph Barnave (1761–1793), lawyer and member of the famous club of the Feuillants.[136] A liberal thinker and one of the many victims of the Revolution, he took Sieyès's ideas a step further. In a work completed during his imprisonment and only published in 1843 as the *Introduction à la Révolution française*, Barnave considered the rise of the Third Estate from a historical perspective, anticipating some of the arguments that became popular during the Restoration.[137] His point of departure was that the Revolution should not be understood as an isolated incident, 'detached from the states around us and the centuries preceding ours'.[138] Marshalling the rudiments of a conjectural history, he claimed that political power was originally founded on knowledge rather than property or force and, as such, it was the prerogative of an 'aristocracy based on knowledge', formed of priests, healers, and the elders. The progress of society created new needs and the desire to enjoy a more secure existence led to property in land. In turn, the passage from the pastoral stage to farming, coupled with ownership of the land, gave rise to a habit of labour and to a new form of property, what he termed 'industrial property'.[139] In time, '[j]ust as the possession of the land gave rise to aristocracy, so industrial property increased the power of the people'.[140] According to

[135] Tocqueville, 'Notes de lecture sur la pensée politique française à la veille de la Révolution', 139. Also see, the comments in Anne-Louise-Germaine de Staël, *Considérations sur la Révolution française* (1818 – posthumous) (Paris: Tallandier, 1983), 192.

[136] On Barnave, see Patrice Gueniffey, 'Terminer la Révolution: Barnave et la révision de la Constitution (Août 1791)', in François Furet and Mona Ozouf (eds.), *Terminer la Révolution: Mounier et Barnave dans la Révolution française* (Grenoble: Presses Universitaires de Grenoble, 1990), 147–70, and David Bates, 'Political Pathologies: Barnave and the Question of National Identity in Revolutionary France', *Canadian Journal of History*, 36 (2001), 427–52. With an emphasis on his historical thought and his *Introduction à la Révolution française*: Fernand Rude, 'Présentation', in Antoine Pierre Joseph Marie Barnave, *Introduction à la Révolution française* (Paris: Armand Colin, 1960), v–xvii; Emanuel Chill, 'Introduction: Barnave as Philosophical Historian', in Antoine Pierre Joseph Marie Barnave, *Power, Property, and History: Joseph Barnave's Introduction to the French Revolution and Other Writings* (New York: Harper, 1971), 1–74; Francesco Dendena, 'L'expérience de la défaite, la rencontre avec l'histoire: Barnave et ses écrits historiques', *La Révolution française*, 10 (2016), 1–17.

[137] To this we shall return in Chapters 8 and 9.

[138] Barnave, *Introduction à la Révolution française*, 1.   [139] Ibid., 6–10.   [140] Ibid., 9.

Barnave, it was through industrial property that the people, assembled in those great workshops, the towns, succeeded in limiting the power of the nobility. It was a process of emancipation that started in the Middle Ages throughout Europe. Barnave saw the existence of a crucial divide between the people – that is, all workers – and the nobility in their respective principles and ways of life, a divide that was mirrored in the opposing ways they had acquired their property. In fact, industrial property was the fruit of labour, while the lands of the aristocracy were originally the outcome of conquest or occupation. Despite its obvious limits, Barnave's was a remarkable explanation of the origins and causes of the Revolution, for it brought together economic, social, and political factors and established a close connection between forms of property and political power. Coupled with this, and equally remarkable, was his outline of the contrast between military and industrial society, one with important moral overtones.

Some of Sieyès's and Barnave's ideas, especially their belief that only those who worked might be truly virtuous citizens, would contribute to the future course of French liberal thought.[141] As early as 1793, the economist and politician the Count Pierre-Louis Roederer (1754–1835) disputed the assumption that property in land should be the foundation of citizenship. He condemned the division of France into two classes, the great land-owners and the 'class of citizens who are born without any other patrimony than their physical strength', a division that bestowed on the former all public authority and condemned the latter to marginality. A few years later, with the aim of ensuring that all workers rather than all owners as such enjoyed full citizenship, Roederer reiterated his conviction that the workers' skills and efforts were the true source of wealth.[142] Others concurred. In 1803, the liberal economist Jean-Baptiste Say (1767–1732), praising the beneficial effects of work on morals, made the case that all those who contributed to the economic growth of the nation deserved full political rights.[143] Although these arguments were partly directed at the physiocrats and their intellectual legacy, they were meant, more broadly, to

---

[141] Siep Stuurman, 'Productive Virtue: The Language of Citizenship and the Idea of Industrial Civilization', *The European Legacy*, 1 (1996), 329–35.

[142] Pierre-Louis Roederer, 'Cours d'organisation sociale' (1793), in *Œuvres* (Paris: Firmin-Didot, 1853–1859), viii. 144. Pierre-Louis Roederer, 'Mémoires sur quelques points d'économie publique' (read out in 1800), in *Œuvres*, viii. 42. On Roederer, see Kenneth Margerison, *P.-L. Roederer: Political Thought and Practice during the French Revolution* (Philadelphia: American philosophical society, 1983).

[143] See, for example, Jean-Baptiste Say, *Traité d'économie politique, ou Simple exposition de la manière dont se forment, se distribuent et se consomment les richesses* (Paris: Deterville, 1803), ii. 369–83. See, on

counter the argument that only landowners could be committed to the best interests of the nation, an idea widespread in the 1770s but still accepted by some during the Revolution and its immediate aftermath.[144]

These views were the cornerstone of the diverse theories that were to emerge under the label of *industrialisme*, most of them heralded by liberal thinkers.[145] Of course, not all liberals espoused the tenets of industrialism and some vehemently denied that work was the source of all wealth, or that workers had the intrinsic right to participate in the political sphere. Foremost among these perhaps was Benjamin Constant, who was adamant that only ownership of land should grant political rights.[146] And yet, interestingly, Constant may nonetheless have contributed to the forging of the industrialist doctrine, albeit involuntarily, by famously arguing that industrial had finally supplanted warring societies and that the future promised to be one of universal peace and prosperity. The character of modern nations, claimed Constant, was wholly incompatible with, and far superior to, that of ancient nations.[147] His accolade for industriousness and hard work dovetailed with some of the assumptions of industrialism. The liberal economist Charles Dunoyer (1786–1862) even believed that

this aspect of Say's thought, Richard Whatmore, 'The Political Economy of Jean-Baptiste Say's Republicanism', *History of Political Thought*, 19 (1998), 439–56. For an overview of Say's ideas, see Richard Whatmore, *Republicanism and the French Revolution: An Intellectual History of Jean-Baptiste Say's Political Economy* (Oxford: Oxford University Press, 2000). Also see, Michael James, 'Pierre-Louis Roederer, Jean-Baptiste Say, and the Concept of *Industrie*', *History of Political Economy*, 9 (1977), 455–75. Other *idéologues* also shared such views. See Thomas E. Kaiser, 'Politics and Political Economy in the Thought of the Ideologues', *History of Political Economy*, 12 (1980), 141–60. On the *idéologues*, see the classic by Sergio Moravia, *Il pensiero degli idéologues: Scienza e filosofia in Francia (1780–1815)* (Florence: La Nuova Italia, 1974).

[144] See, for example, Paul Henri Dietrich d'Holbach, *Système social* (1770) (Paris: Fayard, 1994), 477–8; André Morellet, *Mémoires* (1821) (Paris: Mercure de France, 2000), 331; Jean-Antoine-Nicolas de Condorcet, 'Réflexions sur le commerce des bleds' (1776), in *Œuvres*, xi. 168–70, and Jean-Antoine-Nicolas de Condorcet, 'Lettres d'un bourgeois de New-Haven à un citoyen de Virginie' (1787), in *Œuvres*, ix. 10–14. Condorcet changed his mind in 1789: Léon Cahen, *Condorcet et la Révolution française* (Geneva: Slatkine, 1970), 187–9. For an overview of the debate during the Revolution, see: Edgard Allix, 'La rivalité entre la propriété foncière et la fortune mobilière sous la Révolution', *Revue d'histoire économique et sociale*, 6 (1913), 297–348.

[145] For an overview of industrialism and its birth, see: Edgard Allix, 'J.-B. Say et les origines de l'industrialisme', *Revue d'économie politique*, 24 (1910), 303–13 and 341–63; Henri Gouhier, *La jeunesse d'Auguste Comte et la formation du positivisme: Vol. 3, Auguste Comte et Saint-Simon* (Paris: Vrin, 1970), 142–51; James, 'Pierre-Louis Roederer, Jean-Baptiste Say, and the Concept of *Industrie*', passim; Philippe Fontaine, 'The Concept of *Industrie* from the Physiocrats to J.-B. Say', *Contributions to Political Economy*, 12 (1993), 89–97; Robert Leroux, *Aux fondements de l'industrialisme: Comte, Dunoyer et la pensée libérale en France* (Paris: Hermann, 2015).

[146] Constant, *Principes de politique (1806)*, ii. 200–1. See also Benjamin Constant, 'Principes de politique' (1815), in *Écrits politiques*, 366–9. Also see the interesting remarks in Benjamin Constant, *Journaux intimes* (Paris: Gallimard, 2017), 281 (17 January 1805).

[147] Benjamin Constant, 'De l'esprit de conquête et de l'usurpation' (1814), in *Écrits politiques*, 129–32.

Constant's intuition had played a role in the shaping of industrialism itself, seeing in it the first recognition that modern nations were increasingly devoted to industry and trade rather than war and pillage.[148] In truth, Constant denied offering industrialism any support and criticised it for some of its most basic assumptions.[149] But what is relevant, here, is that the idea of an incessant and unremitting progress from a world based on conquest to one founded on the 'civilised calculation' of trade and industry was gaining currency.[150] In his unpublished manuscripts, Sieyès had already sketched a progress of civilisation from the warring to the industrial stage, a scheme that resembled, in some ways, Turgot's more famous theory.[151] Later on, Dunoyer came to advocate such views and so too did the lawyer and journalist Charles Comte (1782–1837). Auguste Comte (1798–1857) even made of them the lynchpin of his famous three-stage theory of progress.[152]

These ideas became crucial to Claude Henri de Rouvroy, Count de Saint-Simon (1760–1825).[153] Indeed, central to most of his works was the

---

[148] Also see, Charles Dunoyer, 'Esquisse historique des doctrines auxquelles on a donné le nom d'*Industrialisme*, c'est-à-dire, des doctrines qui fondent la société sur l'*Industrie*', *Revue encyclopédique*, 33 (1827), 370–1.

[149] Benjamin Constant, 'De M. Dunoyer et de quelques-uns de ses ouvrages (1826)', in *Écrits politiques*, 673–4. Constant was replying to the comments made by Dunoyer in his 'Du système de l'équilibre des puissance européennes', *Le censeur européen*, 1 (1817), i. 113, n. 1. On the relationship between Dunoyer and Constant, see Leonard P. Liggio, 'Charles Dunoyer and French Classical Liberalism', *Journal of Libertarian Studies*, 1 (1977), 153–78. On Constant and industrialism, see Michel Bourdeau and Béatrice Fink, 'De l'industrie à l'industrialisme: Benjamin Constant aux prises avec le saint-simonisme', *Œuvres et critique*, 33 (2008), 61–78.

[150] The expression is taken from Constant, 'De l'esprit de conquête et de l'usurpation', 130.

[151] Sieyès, 'Cahiers "Smith"', 325. Also see, Sieyès, 'Notes et fragments inédits', 73.

[152] On Charles Comte and Dunoyer's views about historical progress, see Leroux, *Aux fondements de l'industrialisme*, 96–113. On Auguste Comte's, see Laurent Clauzade, 'Auguste Comte et la naturalisation de l'esprit', *Methodos*, 2 (2002), 33–50.

[153] On Saint-Simon, his life and ideas and those of some of his followers, see: Georg G. Iggers, *The Cult of Authority: The Political Philosophy of the Saint-Simonians* (The Hague: Nijhoff, 1958); Domenico Fisichella, *Il potere nella società industriale: Saint-Simon e Comte* (Naples: Morano, 1965); Vittorio Martino, *Saint-Simon tra scienza e utopia* (Bari: Dedalo, 1978); Mirella Larizza Lolli, 'Introduzione', in Lolli (ed.), *Scienza, industria e società: Saint-Simon e i suoi primi seguaci* (Milan: Saggiatore, 1980), 7–119; Richard Martinus Emge, *Saint-Simon: Einführung in ein Leben und Werk, eine Schule, Sekte und Wirkungsgeschichte* (Munich: Oldenbourg, 1987); Pierre Musso, *Saint-Simon et le saint-simonisme* (Paris: Presses universitaires de France, 1999); Olivier Pétré-Grenouilleau, *Saint-Simon: L'utopie, ou La raison en actes* (Paris: Payot et Rivages, 2001); Jean-Luc Yacine, *La question sociale chez Saint-Simon* (Paris: L'Harmattan, 2002); Antoine Picon, *Les saint-simoniens: Raison, imaginaire et utopie* (Paris: Belin, 2002); Christophe Prochasson, *Saint-Simon, ou L'anti-Marx* (Paris: Perrin, 2004); Pierre Musso (ed.), *Actualité du saint-simonisme* (Paris: Presses universitaires de France, 2004); Nathalie Coilly and Philippe Régnier (eds.), *Le siècle des saint-simoniens: Du nouveau christianisme au canal de Suez* (Paris: Bibliothèque nationale de France, 2006); Pierre Musso, *Saint-Simon, l'industrialisme contre l'État* (La Tour-d'Aigues: Éditions de l'Aube, 2010).

notion that in a world in which 'gentility is nothing, and industry is everything', only those who actively contributed to the welfare of society deserved to rule the nation. Such a claim clearly echoed the one in *Qu'est-ce que le tiers état?* However, unlike Sieyès, Saint-Simon firmly placed such views within a historical framework.[154] As he saw it, history was in fact governed by the strict laws of progress: '[S]ociety marches slowly, in the shadow of the military constitution, which gradually changes, towards the industrial constitution, the destination of the civilised human species.'[155] Here, the centrality of work and industriousness merged with a faith in progress towards a more just, prosperous, and peaceful stage of European civilisation. It was a faith built on the works of Charles Comte, from whom Saint-Simon took the idea of a gradual shift from warring to industrial societies, and that germinated through his own reading of Condorcet's *Esquisse d'un tableau historique des progrès de l'esprit humain* – a work that, though 'sublime' in its intentions, had many faults that Saint-Simon sought to rectify.[156] Notably, it was from such a standpoint that the count offered his contribution to the development of the idea of class. One of his earlier definitions of the concept was in a fragment dated 1818 in which, after stating that the interests of the nobility and those of the Third Estate had always differed, Saint-Simon went on to argue that France had been torn apart by the struggle between two classes and that, in the long run, 'the class that has formed the last and which has always won over the other, must end up absorbing it and identifying itself with the whole'.[157] With even greater clarity, he restated this contention in another essay written in the same year: 'The *industrial class* is the only useful class', and since it 'becomes increasingly larger and grows at the expense of the others, it must end up becoming the *only class*' – a comment that, of course, presaged views of a class-less society.[158] Within the latter, bankers, workers, businessmen, scientists, artists, and anyone who contributed to the welfare

---

[154] The quote is from Claude-Henri de Saint-Simon, 'Du système industriel' (1821), in *Œuvres* (Paris: Presses universitaires de France, 2012), iii. 2440. See Keith M. Baker, 'Closing the French Revolution: Saint-Simon and Comte', in François Furet and Mona Ozouf (eds.), *The French Revolution and the Creation of Modern Political Culture, vol. III: The Transformation of Political Culture, 1789–1848* (Oxford: Pergamon, 1989), 328–9.

[155] Saint-Simon, 'Du système industriel', 2549.

[156] On the debt towards Charles Comte, see Claude-Henri de Saint-Simon, 'L'industrie' (1816–1818), in *Œuvres*, ii. 1637, n. For his criticism of Condorcet's ideas, Claude-Henri de Saint-Simon, 'La contestation avec M. Redern, II' (1811–1812), in *Œuvres*, i. 811–35.

[157] Claude-Henri de Saint-Simon, 'Les communes, ou Essais sur la politique pacifique' (1818), in *Œuvres*, ii. 1734–5.

[158] Saint-Simon, 'L'industrie', 1595. Italics in the text.

of society would be considered to be on an equal footing, for all were useful to one another.

Thus far, if one were to draw a parallel between Saint-Simon's industrial class and Sieyès's Third Estate, the similarity would be striking. In fact, according to both authors, a society at peace with itself was a society with only one class and, therefore, with only one economic and political interest – an assumption that Marx would later share. Moreover, for both, the fundamental division within French society was the one between idle noblemen and industrious commoners, a distinction which implied that the 'order' of the Third Estate coincided with the 'class' of the Third Estate embodying the nation. However, in another essay, also written in 1818, Saint-Simon introduced an important shift in his use of class. Reflecting on the Revolution, he regarded this as a product of eighteenth-century philosophy, which he considered to be, indeed, 'critical and revolutionary', but also abstract and misguidedly individualistic.[159] It had been driven by lawyers and professional politicians [*legistes*] who had unmasked the faults and vices of the Old Regime, proclaimed man's freedom and rights, destroyed old superstitions, and even 'changed the *mœurs* and habits' of the French.[160] Yet the *legistes* had now outlived their usefulness, replacing the nobility and acquiring many of its unjust privileges. Their rule, surely beneficial in many ways, had now been rendered obsolete by the rise of the new productive class. In an attempt to demonstrate how the political weight of the latter might be augmented, Saint-Simon stoutly denied the *legistes* any productive and economic role. They did not 'produce anything', weighing heavily as they did upon the *industrie*, 'which dresses, houses, and feeds them gratuitously'.[161] From such an angle, the Revolution had been but the clash between two 'idle and parasitic' classes, the nobility and the *legistes*. In this struggle, the nation, 'that is, the producers', had yet to take part.[162] In another pamphlet, written the following year, Saint-Simon reiterated the same arguments, insisting in no uncertain terms on the division between useful and worthless workers, represented, in a memorable analogy, by 'bees' and 'hornets' respectively.[163] In his famous *Du système industriel* (1821), Saint-Simon was even clearer:

---

[159] Claude-Henri de Saint-Simon, 'Esquisse d'une nouvelle encyclopédie, ou Introduction à la philosophie du XIXᵉ siècle' (1810), in *Œuvres*, i. 575.

[160] Saint-Simon, 'L'industrie', 1494.   [161] Ibid., 1616.

[162] Saint-Simon, 'Du système industriel', 2584.

[163] Claude-Henri de Saint-Simon, 'Sur la querelle des abeilles et des frélons, ou Sur la situation respective des producteurs et des consommateurs non producteurs' (1819), in *Œuvres*, iii. 1957–69. Others had already used the simile. See, for example, René-Louis de Voyer de Paulmy d'Argenson, 'Pensées sur la réformation de l'État' (written after 1735), in *Mémoires et Journal inédit,*

Throughout the ancient regime, society or, if you prefer, the nation, was divided into three great classes. The first... was formed of the clergy and the nobility. The second included the idle owners who were not nobles, and the men of arms of common origins; it also comprised all those citizens who were attached to the judicial order and all who practised professions deemed honourable. The third class was made up of all those who practised degrading professions..., in a word, all industry, those who guided productive works and those who executed them.[164]

Comparing Saint-Simon's views about society and its divisions with Sieyès's, the gulf separating the two emerges immediately. While in fact in the opposition between exploiters and exploited the two privileged orders were reduced to one single class – a grouping accepted by many of Saint-Simon's precursors, including Sieyès – the division of the members of the Third Estate into productive and unproductive workers precluded any simplistic identification of the Third 'order' with the industrious 'class' and so with the nation at large. Therefore, the possibility of an even partial coincidence of the concepts of order and class maintained by Sieyès – at least with regard to the Third Estate – was dismissed out of hand by Saint-Simon. As he saw things, in fact, in the aftermath of the revolutionary upheaval the nation was divided into 'two classes: the bourgeoisie, who have made the Revolution and who have led it pursuing their own interests', and 'the producers [*industriels*]', who now had to feed and maintain both 'the nobility and the bourgeoise'.[165] By narrowing down and further defining the class that truly embodied the nation, Saint-Simon sought to convince his readers that no contrast was possible within it. Somehow recalling the efforts made by Sieyès to prove the inner coherence of the Third Estate, Saint-Simon insisted that within the industrious class every member shared the same interest and this, in turn, coincided with that of society at large.[166] If *industrie* could be divided into classes, this was merely for the sake of intellectual clarity, simply referring as it did to the different roles of the workers themselves.

It should be noted that, in setting out the differentiations operative within society, Saint-Simon was partly following the distinctions drawn by Xavier Bichat (1771–1802), the 'immortal physiologist' whom he so greatly

---

v. 302. For his part, Destutt de Tracy referred to the sterile class as made up of 'hornets': *Traité de la volonté et de ses effets*, 96–7.

[164] Saint-Simon, 'Du système industriel', 2587.

[165] Claude-Henri de Saint-Simon, 'Catéchisme des industriels' (1823–1824), in *Œuvres*, iv. 2878–9.

[166] Saint-Simon, 'L'industrie', 1642.

admired.[167] Importantly, Bichat was not the only medical scholar held in esteem by the duke. Saint-Simon openly acknowledged his debt towards Félix Vicq d'Azyr (1748–1794), one of the fathers of comparative anatomy, and Pierre Jean Georges Cabanis (1757–1808), the physiologist, materialist philosopher, and prominent *idéologue*.[168] If one were to believe Saint-Simon's own account, it was thanks to a memorable discussion in July 1798 with the doctor and scholar Jean Burdin (b. 1770) that he convinced himself that the laws governing society were an extension of the laws of physics and biology.[169] Consistently, politics had to be interpreted by using the same methods as the natural sciences, above all those of physiology, 'the science not only of individual life, but also of life in general'.[170] Unsurprisingly, Saint-Simon's works abounded in organic metaphors. In his 1825 'De la physiologie appliquée à l'amélioration des institutions sociales', he claimed for example that 'the reunion of men constitutes a veritable being, the existence of which is more or less vigorous or wavering depending on whether its organs discharge their functions more or less regularly'.[171] *Industrie*, which Saint-Simon identified with the '*body of the nation*',[172] was, he wrote, a 'great body whose limbs are all connected and are, so to speak, all in agreement. The pleasure and the pain from which a part suffers extend to all others. Everywhere there is only one interest, only one need, only one life. But – he went on – if the feeling belongs to the entire body, it is only the head that thinks for the body. It is there that revolutions are conceived of, that the needs are declared, that the will is manifested.'[173] Were the nation to lose its producers, it would simply

---

[167] Saint-Simon, 'Du système industriel', 2483. Also see, Barbara Haines, 'The Inter-Relations Between Social, Biological, and Medical Thought, 1750–1850: Saint-Simon and Comte', *The British Journal for the History of Science*, 11 (1978), 19–35.

[168] See, on the *idéologues* and their intellectual world, Moravia, *Il pensiero degli idéologues*, passim and, on Cabanis in particular, ibid., 13–288.

[169] Claude-Henri de Saint-Simon, 'Mémoire sur la science de l'homme' (1813), in *Œuvres*, ii. 1079–90. See, on this, Mary Pickering, *Auguste Comte: An Intellectual Biography* (Cambridge: Cambridge University Press, 2006), i. 60–100.

[170] The expression is from a text by the physiologist and doctor, Etienne Marie Bailly (1789–1830), that Saint-Simon edited, completed, and published and with which he fully agreed: Claude-Henri de Saint-Simon, 'De la physiologie appliquée à l'amélioration des institutions sociales' (1825), in *Opinions littéraires, philosophiques et industrielles* (Paris: Hachette, 1977), 231. For authorship, see the comments by Juliette Grange, Pierre Musso, Philippe Régnier, and Frank Yonnet, in Saint-Simon, *Œuvres*, iv. 3252–3. Also see, Saint-Simon, 'Mémoire sur la science de l'homme', 1173. The idea that the study of society could be based on physiology was already adumbrated in an early work written between 1802 and 1803: Claude-Henri de Saint-Simon, 'Lettres d'un habitant de Genève à ses contemporains', in *Œuvres*, i. 118.

[171] Saint-Simon, 'De la physiologie appliquée à l'amélioration des institutions sociales', 228–9.

[172] Saint-Simon, 'Catéchisme des industriels', 2891; italics in the text.

[173] Saint-Simon, 'L'industrie', 1472, footnote.

turn into 'a soulless body'.[174] It is striking that the arguments and even the expressions used by the royalists to depict the king as the embodiment of the nation were now used to identify the nation with the 'industrious class', at once its head, body, and soul. Even the assumption that national character was best exemplified by that of its king had been overturned. According to Saint-Simon, the character of the French was now embodied in the men of industry, and it was their principles and values that the monarchy ought to embrace in ruling.[175]

Notwithstanding the recurrence of comparisons between social and moral phenomena and physiological and biological ones, Saint-Simon was far from merely assimilating the two – as has sometimes been claimed.[176] He called for a positivistic reading of society that would turn the study of men into a science on a par with the study of nature – a preoccupation rooted in eighteenth-century thought that would strongly influence nineteenth-century sociology.[177] It is a point confirmed by Saint-Simon's juxtapositions of organic and mechanistic similes, often within the same sentence. In a well-known passage of his 'De la physiologie appliquée à l'amélioration des institutions sociales', for example, he saw no contradiction in claiming that 'society is, and above all else, a veritable *organised machine* all parts of which contribute in a different way to the working of the ensemble'.[178] On the one hand, the idea of an 'organised machine' shows that Saint-Simon's supposedly organicist view of society is more complex than one might assume.[179] On the other, it confirms that up until the nineteenth century organic and mechanistic images were not mutually exclusive – as Hans Blumenberg has pointed out – and their coupling was

---

[174] Claude-Henri de Saint-Simon, 'L'organisateur: Premier extrait' (1819–1820), in *Œuvres*, iii. 2120.

[175] Saint-Simon, 'Catéchisme des industriels', 2926.

[176] See, for example, Frank E. Manuel, 'From Equality to Organicism', *Journal of the History of Ideas*, 17 (1956), 54–69, and Frank E. Manuel, *The Prophets of Paris* (Cambridge, Mass: Harvard University Press, 1962); Robert Carlisle, *The Proffered Crown: Saint-Simonianism and the Doctrine of Hope* (London: Johns Hopkins University Press, 1987); also see, Bernard Valade, *Introduction aux sciences sociales* (Paris: Presses universitaires de France, 1996), 232.

[177] On the continuity with eighteenth-century thought, see: Philippe Raynaud, 'L'utopie scientifique et le projet systématique: De d'Alembert à Saint-Simon', in Musso (ed.), *Actualité du saint-simonisme*, 35–46. Saint-Simon's influence on nineteenth-century sociology was already pointed out by Émile Durkheim, 'Saint-Simon, fondateur du positivisme et de la sociologie', *Revue philosophique*, 99 (1925), 321–41. Also see, on this, Steven M. Lukes, 'Saint-Simon', in Timothy Raison (ed.), *The Founding Fathers of Social Science* (Harmondsworth: Penguin, 1969), 27–34.

[178] Saint-Simon, 'De la physiologie appliquée à l'amélioration des institutions sociales', 228; emphasis added.

[179] Judith Schlanger, *Les métaphores de l'organisme* (Paris: L'Harmattan, 1995), 58–9.

used to indicate that society possessed an intelligible order that could be explained in terms of its own workings.[180]

While organic and mechanistic images allowed Saint-Simon to justify his *science de l'homme*, by stressing the existence of a given order within society, they inevitably failed to account for the social unrest and social change which were, in contrast, a fundamental part of his theory. Already in his *Lettres d'un habitant de Genève à ses compatriotes*, written between 1802 and 1803, the count saw the struggle between wealthy owners and indigent workers as inevitable – a struggle that he initially considered from a liberal and then a socialist perspective.[181] In part, Friedrich Engels's (1820–1895) recognition of the debt owed to Saint-Simon by nineteenth-century socialists stemmed from the importance that he had accorded to the 'struggle between the two classes forming society'.[182] The seeming contradiction between Saint-Simon's vision of a society at peace with itself, in which all members shared the same interests, and one lacerated by internecine struggle can only be explained by his rejection of the idea that social organisation was unchanging.[183] In fact, according to the reconstruction of his ideas offered by his disciples, above all Barthélémy-Prosper Enfantin (1796–1864), Saint-Simon had divided the course of human history into different epochs, which he then characterised as either 'organic' or 'critical' ages. The first were marked by 'unity and harmony in all spheres of human activity'; the latter by 'anarchy, confusion, and disorder'.[184] During organic ages, societies were at peace and the interests of the ruling elites were in tune with those of the rest of society. In the Feudal Age, for example, when war and religion were the pivots around which society revolved, the most important roles were those of men at arms and churchmen. In Saint-Simon's own words, 'until the invention of gunpowder, the ancient nobility held great political power since it offered society great services. It had to be at the head of the nation for it was the

---

[180] Hans Blumenberg, *Paradigmen zu einer Metaphorologie* (Frankfurt: Suhrkamp, 1999), 91–110. For a discussion, see Dominique Guillo, 'Biology-inspired Sociology of the Nineteenth Century: A Science of Social "Organization"', *Revue française de sociologie*, 43 (2002), 123–55.

[181] Saint-Simon, 'Lettres d'un habitant de Genève à ses contemporains', III.

[182] The expression is from Saint-Simon, 'Les communes', 1734. See Friedrich Engels, *Herrn Eugen Dührings Umwälzung der Wissenschaft (Anti-Dühring)* (1878) (Berlin: Deitz, 1988), 429.

[183] See Pierre Ansart, *Marx et l'anarchisme: Essai sur les sociologies de Saint-Simon, Proudhon, Marx* (Paris: Presses universitaires de France, 1969), 28–9.

[184] Barthélémy-Prosper Enfantin et al., *Doctrine de Saint-Simon: Première année, 1829* (Paris: au bureau de l'Organisateur, 1830), 75. On this, see François-André Isambert, 'Époques critiques et époques organiques: Une contribution de Buchez à l'élaboration de la théorie sociale des saint-simoniens', *Cahiers internationaux de sociologie*, 27 (1959), 131–52.

class that preserved national existence. Nobility was the most hard-working class there was in France.'[185] In the feudal as in other organic ages, class distinctions were wholly functional since all members of society shared the same interest. The most laudable quality in men was courage in combat, a quality that noblemen embodied to the full – or so it was assumed. However, something similar, all else being equal, could now be said of industrial societies. In these, argued Saint-Simon, the importance of industry for everyday life as well as the defence of the state was such that the interest of the *industriels* coincided with that of the nation at large. It was then logical they should rule over it. In organic ages, societies knew no real internal divisions, and if classes could be told apart from one another – as Saint-Simon did – it was only to better understand the way the economy-society worked. Much like noblemen in feudal societies, the *industriels* were fully representative of modern industrial nations and embodied their truest character. However, problems emerged in the passage from one organic phase to another, during so-called critical ages. In particular, the shift from feudal to industrial societies produced an antagonism between the ruling class, still belonging to the old system and justified by the old needs of society, and the class representing the new system. According to Saint-Simon, therefore, the divergence between traditional legal rights and new economic needs somehow turned the distinction between classes from a functional one to an opposition operative in history. In a sense, during critical ages classes thus became 'real' since they prompted historical changes. It was in line with such ideas, and surveying the history of France in the aftermath of the Revolution, that Saint-Simon could claim that:

> The descendants of the Gauls, that is, the industrial class [*les industriels*], have constituted the economic force. . ., but the government has remained in the hands of the Franks. It is the descendants of the Franks who administer the public wealth and the descendants of the Franks have maintained the direction they have received from their ancestors. Therefore, society presents today this extraordinary phenomenon: a nation that is essentially industrial with an essentially feudal government.[186]

One of Saint-Simon's most salient contributions to the shaping of the notion of class was his decision to accord it a central place in the understanding of history.[187] In his writings, when explaining the reasons for the French Revolution, classes were no longer the fabrication of scholars or

---

[185] Saint-Simon, 'Du système industriel', 2595.
[186] Saint-Simon, 'Catéchisme des industriels', 2891. Italics in the text.   [187] Piguet, *Classes*, 140–4.

observers, but something quite real since through their opposition, in the critical age unfolding before his eyes, Saint-Simon saw the cause of momentous changes. Above all, such a shift in the meaning of class was the product of Saint-Simon's juxtaposition – which he never conceived of as a simple identification – of the old economic meaning of class and the legal meaning of order. Class thereby came to be understood in relation to the discrepancy between legal rights and economic forces. And, as such, it became an important lens for viewing the past and, as we shall see shortly, a crucial tool for forging new historical narratives.

CHAPTER 8

A Bourgeois National Narrative
On Augustin Thierry's Réforme historique

The Nation's History and the Biography of Power

In the seventh of the fourteen letters that made up the *Organisateur*, a journal of liberal tendencies published between November 1819 and February 1820, Saint-Simon and Auguste Comte pondered the way historians tended to study the French past.[1] The conclusion they reached was trenchant. The prevailing method, the two contended, was misguided and the resulting works of little use or relevance to everyday lives or indeed to statesmen and politicians. Because they were so 'ill conceived', most histories not only failed to grasp the nature of the changes they portrayed but, moreover, often led to absurd utopias being mistaken for feasible projects.[2] There was a pressing need to transform what was still a branch of literature into a genuine science, capable of serving man's interests. As they saw it, one of the main faults of historical scholarship was that until the mid-eighteenth century it had been little else but 'a biography of power', in which nations featured only as the instruments of kings and their ministers. At best, one might find 'disseminated, here and there, a few sporadic notions on the civilisation of a people'.[3] Partly, Saint-Simon and Comte were restating concerns already voiced by Boulainvilliers, Voltaire, Montesquieu, and Mably among others. Indeed, the two conceded that much had already been done, but added that eighteenth-century scholars had offered more of a criticism of existing historiography than a new way of writing history. Proof lay in the fact that while the proper study of nations and civilisations required that ages be divided according to the great social,

---

[1] On the *Organisateur*, see Pickering, *Auguste Comte*, i. 164–6.

[2] Claude-Henri de Saint-Simon [and Auguste Comte], 'L'organisateur: Septième lettre', in *Œuvres*, iii. 2143. See, on the authorship of the letter, Pierre Laffitte, 'Matériaux pour servir à la biographie d'Auguste Comte: Considérations sur la période de sa vie qui s'étend de 1816 à 1822', *Revue occidentale*, 9 (1882, second semester), 40–7. Also see Gouhier, *La jeunesse d'Auguste Comte et la formation du positivisme*, 264.

[3] Saint-Simon [and Comte], 'L'organisateur: Septième lettre', 2146.

political, and cultural changes, 'the old division in terms of dynasties and realms has been retained by the best historians'. The histories penned by most eighteenth-century scholars were still 'the biography of sovereign families'.[4] The only way to hasten the radical reform of history writing, so much needed amidst the debris left by the Revolution, was to follow the path paved by Condorcet in his *Esquisse d'un tableau historique des progrès de l'esprit humain*, as some, like Volney and Pierre Claude François Daunou (1761–1840), the liberal statesman and historian, were doing already.[5] Such views were perfectly consistent with the claim, often made by Saint-Simon, that while the eighteenth century had been essentially critical, discarding old misguided systems of belief and preconceptions, the nineteenth century would lead to the creation of a new, truthful, and positivistic understanding of the world.[6] Comte would start to refine such views soon after, in the eighth and ninth letters to the *Organisateur*, laying the foundations of his famous three-stage theory of the development of mankind.[7]

Crucially, Saint-Simon and Comte's dissatisfaction with the eighteenth-century study of the past was shared by, and would have strong repercussions for, one of Saint-Simon's most famous disciples. As a young and brilliant student, Augustin Thierry moved to Paris from his home town of Blois to follow courses at the École normale, where he met and struck up a friendship with Villemain and Daunou.[8] It might well be the case that his

---

[4] Ibid., 2147.   [5] Ibid., 2149.

[6] See, for example, Saint-Simon, 'L'industrie', 1445–8, and Saint-Simon, 'L'organisateur: Prospectus de l'auteur', 2115–6. A similar claim was made, in those years, by the philosopher Victor Cousin (1792–1867) in his 'Discours prononcé à l'ouverture du cours, le 4 décembre 1817', in Cousin, *Du vrai, du beau et du bien* (Paris: Didier, 1853), 10.

[7] The claim to the authorship of the ninth and tenth letters was made by Comte in 1838: Comte, *Cours de philosophie positive: Leçons 46–51*, 23–5 ('Avertissement de l'auteur'). On this, see Pickering, *Auguste Comte*, i. 166–72 and, for differences and analogies between Comte and Saint-Simon's ideas about history, ibid., 172–8.

[8] On Augustin Thierry, his life and ideas, see: Robert Fossaert, 'La théorie des classes chez Guizot et Thierry', *La pensée*, 59 (1955), 59–69; Boris G. Reizov, *L'historiographie romantique française: 1815–1830* (Moscow: Éditions en langues étrangères, 1956), 104–89; Dietrich Gerhard, 'Guizot, Augustin Thierry und die Rolle des Tiers État in der französischen Geschichte', *Historische Zeitschrift*, 190 (1960), 290–310; Rulon N. Smithson, *Augustin Thierry: Social and Political Consciousness in the Evolution of a Historical Method* (Geneva: Droz, 1973); Charles Rearick, *Beyond the Enlightenment: Historians and Folklore in Nineteenth Century France* (Bloomington: Indiana University Press, 1974), 22–31 and 62–81; Lionel Gossman, 'Augustin Thierry and Liberal Historiography', *History and Theory: Beiheft 15*, 4 (1976); Anne Denieul Cormier, *Augustin Thierry: L'histoire autrement* (Paris: Publisud, 1996); Ceri Crossley, *French Historians and Romanticism: Thierry, Guizot, the Saint-Simonians, Quinet, Michelet* (London: Routledge, 1993), 45–70; Marcel Gauchet, 'Les "Lettres sur l'histoire de France" d'Augustin Thierry', in Nora (ed.), *Les lieux de mémoire*, i. 787–850; Paoladele Fiorentini, *Augustin Thierry: Storiografia e politica nella Francia della Restaurazione* (Catania: Edizioni del Prisma, 2003); Aude Déruelle, 'Introduction', in Augustin Thierry, *Lettres sur l'histoire de France* (Paris: Garnier, 2012), 13–53; Aurélien Aramini,

passion for the Middle Ages dates back to his years at the Collège de Blois, when, in 1810, he came across Chateaubriand's famous *Les martyres* (1809). According to his own recollection, he 'devoured' its pages and was struck by the vivid description of the 'dramatic contrast between the fighting savage and the civilised soldier'. The battle cry of the Frankish troops had an 'almost electrifying' impact on the young Thierry.[9] However, while he fondly recalled the stirring descriptions in the *Martyres*, Thierry's passion for history was in all likelihood crystallised much later. In fact, at the École he did not attend Guizot's courses on modern history. He was more interested in Rousseau and his *Émile* than in the study of the French past.[10] In effect, as he admitted, for some years he forgot the elation he had felt while reading the *Martyres*, and only after many 'trials and errors over the choice of a career' did he finally decide to devote himself 'entirely to history'.[11] It was in 1814, shortly after receiving from Saint-Simon a copy of his *Mémoire sur la science de l'homme* (1813), that Thierry agreed to work as his secretary.[12] The following three years would prove to be of crucial importance in his own as well as in Saint-Simon's intellectual life. The two co-authored the famous *De la réorganisation de la société européenne* (1814), wrote the *Opinion sur les mesures à prendre contre la coalition de 1815* (1815), and collaborated on several short articles and pamphlets.[13] Moreover, in those same years, through Saint-Simon, Thierry became acquainted with Dunoyer, Charles Comte, and Say.

The influence of Saint-Simon and his circle on the young Thierry was momentous and, importantly, it can certainly be discerned in the concept of nation outlined in his *Des nations et de leurs rapports mutuels*, a work published in early 1817. Thierry there made the claim that a nation was simply 'a part of humanity united by the pursuit of the same objective and

'L'archéologie linguistique du pouvoir et du peuple chez Augustin Thierry', *Revue d'histoire du XIXᵉ siècle*, 49 (2014), 179–93; Yann Potin and Aude Déruelle (eds.), *Augustin Thierry: L'histoire pour mémoire* (Rennes: Presses Universitaires de Rennes, 2018).

[9] Augustin Thierry, 'Préface' (1840), in Thierry, *Récits des temps mérovingiens précédés des Considérations sur l'histoire de France*, i. pp. xix–xxi. On the importance of Chateaubriand's works for the Romantic myth of the barbarian, see: Pierre Michel, *Les barbares, 1789–1848: Un mythe romantique* (Lyons: Presses Universitaires de Lyon, 1981), 83–102 and 423–48.

[10] Augustin Augustin-Thierry, *Augustin Thierry d'après sa correspondance et ses papiers de famille* (Paris: Plon-Nourrit, 1922), 17.

[11] Thierry, 'Préface', *Récits des temps mérovingiens précédés des Considérations sur l'histoire de France*, xxi.

[12] See Augustin-Thierry, *Augustin Thierry d'après sa correspondance et ses papiers de famille*, 24–5, and Gouhier, *La jeunesse d'Auguste Comte et la formation du positivisme*, 71–9.

[13] On Saint-Simon's collaboration with Thierry, see Pickering, *Auguste Comte*, i. 87–97, and Philippe Régnier, 'Thierry et Saint-Simon: Micro-histoire d'une collaboration', in Potin and Déruelle (eds.), *Augustin Thierry*, especially 31–5. On Thierry's acquaintances in those milieux see, Smithson, *Augustin Thierry*, 15–16.

by the will to pursue it'.[14] Any group of individuals united by a common aim, be it religious, cultural, or of self-defence, was therefore a nation. Historically, Thierry went on to argue, communities originally structured around aims that 'had something ideal, vague, metaphysical' about them felt only 'furious and blind hatred' towards one another.[15] This was a way of life, an attitude that shaped and was shaped by the fundamentally 'military character' of the peoples of the ancient world.[16] Borrowing and readapting some of Adam Ferguson's ideas, Thierry noted that, moved by a lust for action and adventure, seeking praise for bravery, in the ancient world men despised and avoided work, leaving it to women and slaves.[17] But then came 'knowledge, and following knowledge came needs; following needs came industry'. This was a slow but crucial turn that brought about a profound change in ways of life and character, since industry, 'calm and patient, toned down the heat of the blood that incessantly pushed men outwards'. Life became more contemplative since, argued Thierry, to produce and to create also meant 'acting on one's inner soul'.[18] Therefore, in the modern world work and industry were becoming the main factors uniting men, strengthening bonds that constantly expanded as local economies grew wider. Consistently – though far too optimistically – Thierry even claimed that the broadening of markets and their fusion would finally lead to a world consisting of one single nation, 'and that *nation* will be humanity'.[19] Sharing the views of the *industriels* and, more generally, of most liberal thinkers, Thierry assumed that the multiplication of needs and professions would encourage and foster a sentiment of 'brotherhood', since each individual would produce 'something that is missing to others, who produce all that is missing to him'. Thierry went on to claim that integration would stem from the growing division of labour, shaping a transnational community based on the common 'enjoyment of life' by its members.[20] Here he was by and large restating a notion

[14] Augustin Thierry, 'Des nations et de leurs rapports mutuels', in Claude-Henri de Saint-Simon, *L'industrie littéraire et scientifique liguée avec l'industrie commerciale et manufacturière* (Paris: Delaunay, 1817), i. part 2, 8.

[15] Thierry, 'Des nations et de leurs rapports mutuels', 11 and 26.

[16] Ibid., 27. In a footnote, on the same page, Thierry referred to Montesquieu's discussion of ancient Greek *mœurs*: Montesquieu, 'De l'Esprit des lois', 270–3 (book iv. ch. 8).

[17] Thierry, 'Des nations et de leurs rapports mutuels', 26. The reference to Ferguson is in footnote 1, on the same page. See Ferguson, *An Essay on the History of Civil Society*, 96–7.

[18] Thierry, 'Des nations et de leurs rapports mutuels', 27.   [19] Ibid., 12; italics in the text.

[20] Ibid., 42. On how such views reflected the thesis of the *industriels*, see Michael Drolet, 'Industry, Class and Society: A Historiographic Reinterpretation of Michel Chevalier', *English Historical Review*, 504 (2008), 1244–5.

already present in the writings of Quesnay, then in those by David Ricardo (1772–1823), Constant, and Say, and later expounded in greater detail by Richard Cobden (1804–1865) and John Stuart Mill (1806–1873).[21] Yet there is a particular point worthy of note. As Dunoyer remarked in a review of *Des nations*, an entire chapter was devoted to showing that the modern, industrious form of society was the most 'honourable'.[22] Importantly, Thierry understood honour as the measure of the usefulness of men to one another rather than of courage on the battlefield. Men of industry, moved by the desire to produce goods for other men, were worthier than soldiers, whose sole aim was that of killing, pillaging, and destroying. As he saw it, in modern societies men only fought one another 'by the strength of their minds', so much so that lasting glory may only stem from the advancement of science and knowledge or through hard work.[23] Only through such accomplishments could a person contribute to the greatness of his nation: 'Anyone today who wishes to really be free, to truly be a citizen, *works*', he wrote reasserting the guiding principle of *industrie*.[24]

Des nations was the last work Thierry produced during his partnership with Saint-Simon. Their relationship ended abruptly, in 1817. The reason is still not entirely known. For some, Thierry had grown tired of Saint-Simon's oppressive tutelage; for others, it was the increasingly abstract speculations of the latter that led the former to quit.[25] Be this as it may, Thierry soon started writing for the *Censeur européen*, an influential and successful journal founded by Charles Comte and Dunoyer with a view to defending the rights laid down in the *Charte*.[26] The new partnership

---

[21] See: François Quesnay, 'Remarques sur l'opinion de l'auteur de l'*Esprit des lois* concernant les colonies' (1766), in *Œuvres économiques completes et autres textes*, ii. 871–2; David Ricardo, *The Principles of Political Economy and Taxation* (1817) (London: J.M. Dent & Sons, 1995), 81; Constant, 'De l'esprit de conquête et de l'usurpation', 129–32; Jean-Baptiste Say, *Cours complet d'économie politique pratique* (Paris: Rapilly, 1828–1833), ii. 286–7; Richard Cobden, 'Russia' (1836), in *Political Writings* (London: Routledge, 1995), i. 188–91; John Stuart Mill, *Principles of Political Economy* (1848) (London: Routledge 1996), iii. 593–4.

[22] Charles Dunoyer, review of Augustin Thierry, *Des nations et de leurs rapports mutuels*, in *Le censeur européen*, 1 (1817), ii. 240–4.

[23] Thierry, 'Des nations et de leurs rapports mutuels', 122–6.

[24] Ibid., 97, in footnote; italics in the text.

[25] See Augustin-Thierry, *Augustin Thierry d'après sa correspondance et ses papiers de famille*, 36–9, and Anonymous, 'Notice sur Saint-Simon et sa doctrine, et sur quelques autres ouvrages qui en seraient le développement', in Alfred Péreire, *Autour de Saint-Simon, documents originaux* (Paris: Honoré Champion, 1912), 188–90.

[26] On *Le censeur* and *Le censeur européen*, see Éphraïm Harpaz, 'Le censeur: Histoire d'un journal libéral', *Revue des sciences humaines*, 92 (1958), 483–511, and Éphraïm Harpaz, '"Le censeur européen": Histoire d'un journal industrialiste', *Revue d'histoire économique et sociale*, 37/3 (1959), 185–218 and 328–57.

further reinforced Thierry's industrialist ideas. Two months after the first of his many articles in the *Censeur*, Thierry began publishing the four instalments of his *Vue des révolutions d'Angleterre* (1817–1819). It was a significant turn for the *Censeur* since, up until then at least, history had been rather marginal to it.[27] But it was an even greater change for Thierry, who, from then onwards, devoted himself wholly to the study of the past. He did so by drawing upon his eclectic intellectual formation, attempting to shed light on the past through an approach that was at once economic, social, and historical.[28]

The significance of the *Vue* is twofold. On the one hand, in fact, Thierry offered a key to the past based on his industrialist beliefs. On the other, and even more importantly, he set out to identify one single event that could make sense of the entire history of England. As he wrote much later on, in 1835, it was while reading Hume's *History of England* (1779) that he was suddenly struck by a single, straightforward idea: *'Everything there derives from a conquest: conquest is at the bottom of everything.'*[29] What his studies had gradually led him to believe was that the Norman Conquest was the key to the entire history of England. Its constitution, the way society was structured, and its most important political events ought to be seen against the backdrop of the subjugation of the Anglo-Saxons by the Normans. Importantly, Thierry believed that the relationship between the classes emerging from the Norman Conquest had remained essentially the same over the centuries. The division between nobility and commoners, and the relationship between crown and nobility, dated back, in their essence, to the eleventh century, when the Normans took possession of the English lands. Never ceasing to be an army and proud of their belligerent spirit, the Normans maintained a strict hierarchy and their capacity to wage war within and without the kingdom. In time, the heirs of their commanders became kings, those of their captains, barons, and those of the rank and file, knights. On the other side, the heirs of the conquered became subjects, and on them fell the burden of feeding and serving the conquerors.[30] Cast in such a mould, the history of England became the history of the struggle

---

[27] Shirley M. Gruner, 'Political Historiography in Restoration France', *History and Theory*, 8 (1969), 350.

[28] Augustin Thierry, 'Vue des révolutions d'Angleterre', *Le censeur européen*, 1 (1817), iv. 14–15.

[29] Augustin Thierry, 'Histoire de mes idées et de mes travaux historiques' (1834), in Thierry, *Dix ans d'études historiques* (Brussels: Hauman, 1835), iii; italics in the text. For some interesting thoughts on the analogies and differences between Thierry and Hume on this point, see: George C. Comninel, *Rethinking the French Revolution: Marxism and the Revisionist Challenge* (London: Verso, 1987), 60–3.

[30] Thierry, 'Vue des révolutions d'Angleterre', 20–1.

of two peoples living in the same state. But it was the history of those who had been subdued that Thierry found more fascinating. Eventually, he argued, these sought in hard work and in the growth of their wealth the means to win their emancipation: 'When the *subjects* started to appreciate the relationship between independence and wealth, fully grasping the interests by which they were tied together and the need of each for the liberty of all, they rallied together and became a nation.'[31] Their common condition, shaping a common interest, made of them a community. Over the centuries the ruling people had maintained their lust for war, while the subdued had developed their passion for industry and work. In the struggle between the two nations, their respective rallying cries were 'on the one hand, *idleness* and *power*, on the other, *industry* and *liberty*'.[32] According to Thierry, the opposition had turned into a struggle between two nations enshrining opposite values and ways of life. And here lay the key for understanding the whole of English history – or so he believed. In fact, he made the case that yet more recent events might be interpreted in the light of the Norman Conquest. Following this line of argument, Thierry viewed the Civil War as a 'great national reaction against' the Norman Conquest; Cromwell's (1599–1658) seizure of power as 'a new conquest treacherously made in the shadow of the national flag'; and in the Stuart Restoration a 'pact of alliance' between old and new conquerors. Indeed, in his later writings Thierry conceded the dangers of anachronism stemming from 'imposing on completely different ages wholly identical formulas'. However, not only did he maintain the notion of 'tightly tying the entire modern history of England to the Norman Conquest'.[33] Crucially for us, he would also shortly come to use such a principle to explain the history of France, even suggesting that the same might be done for all European nations.[34]

Thierry lost no time in turning to the study of the French past and, when he did so, he was immediately disappointed by the writings of his predecessors as much as by those of his contemporaries. Although the eighteenth century had held great hopes so far as the history of national cultures and *mœurs* was concerned, regrettably it had fallen short.[35] A new method leading to a narrative that described those masses upon whom the burdens of everyday life fell, rather than the royal lineage, was still lacking.

[31] Ibid., 45; italics in the text.   [32] Ibid., 67.
[33] Thierry, 'Histoire de mes idées et de mes travaux historiques', iv.
[34] Augustin Thierry, *Histoire de la conquête de l'Angleterre par les Normands* (Paris: Firmin Didot, 1825), i. p. i–iv.
[35] Thierry, 'Considérations sur l'histoire de France', 86–8.

Recalling his studies at the Collège de Blois, it struck him that his only history textbook had been the abbé Millot's *Abrégé de l'histoire de France à l'usage des élèves de l'École royale militaire* (1788), a work that taught the history of 'Pharamond, founder of the French monarchy', and the heroic deeds 'of Clovis the Great, one of the most illustrious sovereigns of the Merovingian dynasty'. Yet it said little of the French people, of their beliefs and passions, and of what they cherished, feared, and hated; in other words, nothing about their lives. Casting his mind back to his years as a pupil, Thierry despondently observed: '*French, throne, monarchy* were for me the beginning and the end, the foundation and the shape of our national history.'[36] He recognised that, in post-revolutionary France, 'Guizot, de Sismondi, and Barante' and other champions of a new approach to the past, one more focused on the people, had had their admirers. But he also remarked that 'Velly and Anquetil', with their works so preoccupied by the doings of kings and their ministers, still enjoyed the 'advantage of a much broader clientele'.[37] He expressed his bitter disappointment, and in no uncertain terms, in an 1820 letter to the *Courrier français*:

> The history of France, such as has been written by modern historians, is not the true history of the country, the national history, the history of the people. Such a history is still buried under the dust of contemporary chronicles.... The best part of our annals, the most serious, the most instructive is still to be written. We lack the history of citizens, the history of subjects, the history of the people.[38]

He would later consider this to be the manifesto of his proposed historical reform. Others, inside and outside France, would surely have concurred.[39]

In truth, Thierry's judgement might well be unfair towards those who in the eighteenth century had tried to produce the kind of history he yearned for – prominent among them Turgot, Voltaire, and Condorcet. However, it might be agreed that while several had criticised the old historiographical assumptions, calling for a history of the people, most had failed to write national narratives truly detached from the royal lineage. As Thierry

---

[36] Thierry, 'Préface', *Récits des temps mérovingiens précédés des Considérations sur l'histoire de France*, viii–xix; italics in the text.

[37] Thierry, 'Histoire de mes idées et de mes travaux', xxxi.

[38] Augustin Thierry, 'Première lettre sur l'histoire de France' (1820), in Thierry, *Dix ans d'études historiques*, 304.

[39] Augustin Thierry, 'Préface' (1834), in Thierry, *Dix ans d'études historiques*, xvi. Compare, for example, with the views expressed by Thomas Carlyle in his 'On History' (1830), in *Historical Essays* (Berkley: University of California Press, 2002), 5–6.

pointed out, there were several political and intellectual obstacles to a new, different way of making sense of the French past. One of these, as he ventured, was that since eighteenth-century authors relied heavily on the works of previous historians rather than on primary sources, their writings ended up perpetuating the classic canons of national dynastic histories.[40] Indeed, as we have seen, there is a kernel of truth to this. Since up until the early nineteenth century French history was largely written by authors who expanded and continued the works of their predecessors, little space was left for radical shifts in the way the past was portrayed.[41] So, in his 1805 *Histoire de France depuis les Gaulois*, Anquetil could still tell his readers that his was simply a collage of the histories of Duplex, Mézeray, Daniel, and Velly. When addressing a specific topic, it was sufficient for Anquetil to decide who presented it in the best way and take that story as the basis of his own.[42] Scant attention was paid to the critical use of sources or to careful archival research. One consequence of an excessive reliance on previous narrations, as Thierry contended, was that the explanations of the great episodes of French history remained essentially the same, centred, in other words and from his point of view, on the crown and the court. The people's customs, attitudes, interests, and beliefs continued to be mirrored in those of the king and his entourage. Offering the same reasons as to why events unfolded as they did simply meant endlessly reproducing the history of the nation as the biographies of its kings. To break this spell, reasoned Thierry, scholars had to start relying on the original manuscripts, books, and decrees stored in the libraries and the archives that the Revolution had made accessible to all. It can readily be seen that Thierry's version, for all its greater refinement, was largely a restating of the arguments already put forward by Boulainvilliers a century earlier in his letter to Mademoiselle Cousinot.[43]

Narration Complète *and the Politics of History*

In 1820 Thierry began his study of the vast collections of sources of Gallic and French history compiled by the eighteenth-century antiquaries and, in

---

[40] Augustin Thierry, 'Sur le besoin d'une histoire de France, et le principal défaut de celles qui existent' (1820), in Thierry, *Lettres sur l'histoire de France*, 5. Ten of the *Lettres* were first published in the *Courrier français* between July and October 1820. They were collected and published, with other essays, in 1827.

[41] See Chapter 2.

[42] Louis-Pierre Anquetil, *Histoire de France depuis les Gaulois jusqu'à la fin de la monarchie* (Paris: Garnery, 1805), i. pp. iv–v.

[43] On this, see Chapter 2.

particular, the *Rerum Gallicarum et Francicarum Scriptores* (1738–1904) –
his friend Alessandro Manzoni (1785–1873) referred to the run of nineteen
volumes so far published as Thierry's 'great accomplices'.[44] As the young
scholar persevered with his reading, his uneasiness turned into 'indigna-
tion' at the startling contrast between the images arising from the primary
sources and those in the 'dull' national narratives still so widespread in
France. It was unfortunate, he wrote, that many still held on to them as if
they were 'articles of faith'. He finally decided to embark on what would
become a life-long undertaking, pursuing his *réforme historique*. His aspiration was nothing less than to alter the way the nation's history was studied
and written, waging 'a war against those writers without erudition who
have not been able to see it, and to those writers without imagination who
have not been capable of portraying it'. As he conceived of it, this was
a struggle against Mézeray, Daniel, Velly, and their followers, as much as
a war against the 'philosophical school', with its 'calculated dryness' and its
'disdainful ignorance of national origins'.[45] But it was also a call for
bringing together two intellectual objectives that Thierry considered to
be inseparable. In his judgement, on the one hand historical scholarship
required researching and dissecting facts 'without any other purpose than
exactitude'; on the other, it entailed providing them with that 'life which
must never be wanting in displaying human things'.[46] Consistently, while
scrutinising and dissecting the French past through the lens of Saint-
Simonian positivism,[47] Thierry endeavoured to bring the past to life and
make his readers experience the same emotions stirred in him when first he
had read Chateaubriand's *Martyrs* and Walter Scott's (1771–1832) *Ivanhoe*
(1819).[48] It was thanks to the works of these two famed authors that,
according to Ernest Renan (1823–1892), Thierry acquired that 'profound
understanding of the eternal instincts of humanity' with which his works

---

[44] Alessandro Manzoni to Claude Fauriel, 17 October 1820, in Alessandro Manzoni and
Claude Fauriel, *Carteggio* (Milan: Centro nazionale studi Manzoniani, 2000), 267. Manzoni does
not explicitly mention the *Rerum Gallicarum*. That the reference is to the great collection started by
Dom Bouquet is a claim first made in Charles-Augustin Sainte-Beuve, 'M. Fauriel' (1845), in Sainte-
Beuve, *Portraits contemporains* (Paris: Presses de l'Université de Paris-Sorbonne, 2008), 1285, n. 104.

[45] Thierry, 'Histoire de mes idées et de mes travaux historiques', xiv–xv.

[46] Thierry, 'Considérations sur l'histoire de France', 191.

[47] See Jean Walch, 'Romantisme et positivisme: Une rupture épistémologique dans l'historiographie?',
Romantisme, 8 (1978), 162.

[48] On the importance of Chateaubriand and Scott for French Romantic historiography, see
Jean Molino, 'Qu'est-ce que le roman historique?', *Revue d'histoire littéraire de la France*, 75
(1975), 195–234. On the importance of Walter Scott's works for the understanding of the past in
France during the first half of the nineteenth century, see Louis Maigron's *Le roman historique à
l'époque romantique: Essai sur l'influence de Walter Scott* (Geneva: Slatkine, 1970), first published in
1912 but still highly instructive.

were so often imbued.[49] It is undeniable that the influence of the two fathers of literary Romanticism was momentous. Gripped by an 'unsettling fascination' with Chateaubriand, Thierry confessed to being taken aback by the vivid images of the past portrayed in his works. He later recognised his debt to the 'writer of genius who has opened and who dominates the new literary century'.[50] No less was his admiration for Scott, 'the greatest master of historical insight'.[51] His novels, so rich in detail, erudite, and yet so captivating, had offered 'a firmer and more penetrating glance at the history of his country than that of historians themselves'.[52] Thierry, in Stendhal's words a 'demi-Scott', could not but deplore the fact that the *mœurs* of the ancient French had never been presented in the picturesque manner of an *Ivanhoe* or a *Rob Roy* (1817).[53] The history of France needed a 'Walter Scott who might understand and express it', he wrote.[54] The merits of Scott's works and his contribution to the understanding of the past have been pointed out by many other observers.[55] Chateaubriand himself had extolled his *Life of Napoleon Bonaparte* (1827) as well as his historical novels for having brought 'back to life the Scottish past'.[56] But it was perhaps Alexandre Dumas père (1802–1870) who got to the nub of the matter in an article published in 1836. According to Dumas, Scott had managed to merge 'the study of men's hearts' with the 'science of the history of peoples' in such a way that, through his 'vivifying passion, his resurrecting genius', he had brought back 'an entire epoch, with its *mœurs*, interests, passions'. The path to follow was that between: 'History in the strict sense, which is but a tedious compilation of dates and facts

[49] Ernest Renan, 'M. Augustin Thierry' (1857), in *Œuvres complètes* (Paris: Calmann-Lévy, 1947–1961), ii. 90.
[50] Thierry, 'Préface', *Récits des temps mérovingiens précédés des Considérations sur l'histoire de France*, xxii. Thierry even acknowledged in person his debt to Chateaubriand. On this, see: François-René de Chateaubriand, *Mémoires d'outre-tombe* (1849–1850 – published posthumously) (Paris: Gallimard, 1951), ii. 510 and 574. Chateaubriand, in turn, went as far as to laud Thierry as the 'Homer' of history: Chateaubriand, 'Préface – Études historiques', 66. On the friendship between the two, see Augustin Augustin-Thierry, 'Lettres inédites de Chateaubriand et d'Augustin Thierry', *Revue des deux mondes*, 36 (1916), 53–76.
[51] Thierry, 'Histoire de mes idées et de mes travaux', xiv.
[52] Augustin Thierry, 'Sur l'histoire d'Ecosse, et sur le caractère national des Ecossais' (1824), in Thierry, *Dix ans d'études historiques*, 146.
[53] The expression is from Marie Henri Beyle Stendhal to Adolphe de Mareste, 22 December 1820, in *Correspondance*, iii. 324. Some interesting thoughts on Scott's influence on Thierry are in Ivan Jablonka's *L'histoire est une littérature contemporaine* (Paris: Seuil, 2014), 51–6.
[54] Augustin Thierry, 'Épisode de l'histoire de Bretagne' (1820), in Thierry, *Dix ans d'études historiques*, 342. See also Smithson, *Augustin Thierry*, 99–100.
[55] See Maigron's *Le roman historique à l'époque romantique*, especially 99–133.
[56] Chateaubriand, 'Préface – Études historiques', 64. For his comments on the *Life of Napoleon*, see Chateaubriand, *Mémoires d'outre-tombe*, i. 729–30, footnote.

chronologically tied to one another'; the 'historical novel which, unless it is written with Walter Scott's flair and science, is but a magic lantern without light, colour nor range'; and, finally, the 'original chronicles, a sure, profound and inexhaustible source but from which water gushes in so turbulent a fashion that it is almost impossible for untrained eyes to see the bottom through its waves'.[57] For his part, Thierry was aware of the underlying difficulties. Indeed, he was adamant that, on the one hand, the study of the past should be a science and that, on the other, history writing should adopt the canons of literature.[58] As he wrote in 1825, in his *Histoire de la conquête de l'Angleterre par les Normands*, in considering political events, *mœurs*, languages, and names he had tried to restore to each period 'its external aspect, its original features and, so to speak, its whole reality', giving it the 'certitude and fixity that are the distinguishing characteristics of the positive sciences'.[59] A few years later, in the 1830 edition of the *Conquête*, he stated the point with even greater clarity: '[E]very historical composition is a work of art as much as erudition; the form and style is a matter of no less importance than the search for and the critical examination of the facts.'[60] Indeed, Thierry wrote his works to instruct and inform but also to delight, amuse, and, above all, inspire his readers. He did so, while showing scrupulous respect for sources, by virtue of a somewhat poetical style that was characteristic of his works – and, for which, like Jules Michelet (1798–1874) and other Romantic historians, he would much later be criticised.[61]

In effect, one crucial task facing Thierry was that of combining a critical and careful interpretation of primary sources with his deeply felt need to write a history 'for everyone'.[62] Considering the two aims to be perfectly compatible, he was convinced that the solution was within his grasp. He believed in fact that the history of France was unappealing, 'cold and

---

[57] Alexandre Dumas, 'Introduction à nos feuilletons historiques', *La presse*, 15 July 1836, 1–2.

[58] See Smithson, *Augustin Thierry*, 298–301.

[59] Thierry, *Histoire de la conquête de l'Angleterre par les Normands*, i. p. xxvi–xxvii.

[60] Augustin Thierry, *Histoire de la conquête de l'Angleterre par les Normands* (Paris: Alexandre Mesnier, 1830), i. p. viii.

[61] See, for example, Henri Berr, *La synthèse en histoire* (Paris: Alcan, 1911), 238. Berr accused both Thierry and Michelet of being 'poets' whose works deformed history. These comments prompted an immediate reply from his friend Lucien Febvre: Lucien Febvre to Henri Berr, late July 1911, in Febvre, *De la 'Revue de synthèse' aux 'Annales': Lettres à Henri Berr, 1911–1954* (Paris: Fayard, 1997), 10. In his 1943–1944 lectures at the Collège de France, Febvre gave a detailed and compelling comparison of Thierry and Michelet's ideas: Lucien Febvre, *Michelet, créateur de l'Histoire de France: Cours au Collège de France, 1943–1944* (Paris: Vuibert, 2014), 115–54 and 221–33.

[62] Thierry, 'Considérations sur l'histoire de France', 208.

monotonous' for the simple reason that what had been told until then was 'false'. As he put it: '[I]t is truth that must restore to [the study of the past] the piquant and the interesting.'[63] And truth, Thierry went on, could only be attained through a 'complete narration'. Here was a seemingly straight-forward contention, fraught though with far-reaching implications. In point of fact, the cornerstone of his conception of history – and, come to that, of most French Romantic historiography – was the firm conviction that if historians were to pay the necessary attention to details, faithfully and carefully relating them in their works, not only would they make history more interesting and more accessible to the wider public but, furthermore, they would also give their readers the plain truth about the past. History writing could be objective if only the historian scrupulously portrayed every detail of a nation's *mœurs*, habits, faults, and beliefs. Thierry was persuaded that he had done as much while working on his *Histoire de la conquête de l'Angleterre*. Indeed, in the introduction he flattered himself that he had left 'little more to take' from the archives.[64] Meticulous work in archives and libraries was the prerequisite for a history that might stand as the perfect 'replica of the past', a narrative capable of withstanding thorough scrutiny because it was complete; because it left nothing out.[65] Its truthfulness would stem from its completeness. The bedrock of Thierry's historical theory was that the best kind of proof, 'the most capable of striking and convincing all minds, the one which allows the least mistrust and leaves the fewest doubts, is the complete narration'.[66] This consisted in the accurate recounting of episodes and events that were revealing of a people's cultural, political, and social life. By introducing the greatest possible number of details, duly and carefully sourced in footnotes open to the reader's scrutiny, a myriad of different fragments would fall into place so as to form a faithful representation of the past. The aim, in fact, was to arrive at a perfect reproduction of the past, as if the historian were faithfully reproducing on a canvas, in all its detail and intrinsic richness, the 'local colour', the *mœurs*, and the life of a people in a given epoch.[67] In several ways, we are faced here with a radical break from

---

[63] Augustin Thierry, 'Sur quelques erreurs de nos historiens modernes' (1820), in Thierry, *Dix ans d'études historiques*, 300–1.

[64] Thierry, *Histoire de la conquête de l'Angleterre par les Normands*, i. p. ix.

[65] Stephen Bann, 'Analyzing the Discourse of History', in Bann, *The Inventions of History: Essays on the Representation of the Past* (Manchester: Manchester University Press, 1990), 38–9.

[66] Augustin Thierry, 'Récits des temps mérovingiens' (1840), in Thierry, *Récits des temps mérovingiens précédés des Considérations sur l'histoire de France* i. 357.

[67] References to the historian as a painter of the past are disseminated throughout Thierry's works. See, for example, Thierry, 'Sur les histoires de France de Mézeray, Daniel et Anquetil', 33 and 36, and

previous history writing. In fact, the proposed shift entailed, on the one hand, that the historian examine, dissect, absorb, and exhaust all available primary sources and, on the other, it meant ascribing to detail an unprecedented and original place in historical scholarship. If grasping a people's *mœurs* and character was an aim shared by some of the most forward-thinking scholars of the eighteenth century, and while several would have insisted on the importance of grounding one's work on primary sources, many would have looked askance at the centrality accorded to details in Thierry's complete narration. Voltaire, for example, viewed the relationship between the meaning of detail and the broader context in an altogether different light.[68]

If a complete narration was the way to find the truth of the nation's past, it also served Thierry's second aim, that of producing a history accessible to the wider public. If, indeed, like other historians of his day, Thierry tried to broaden his readership by focusing on the people rather than on kings, court, and generals, differences with previous histories went beyond the subject matter. According to Lionel Gossman, Thierry's complete narration distanced itself from eighteenth-century scholarship also because it envisaged a new relationship between author and readers. By portraying 'the image of the whole in the account of each part', rather than engaging critically with the text, the reader would be enveloped 'in the seamless fabric of the past'. Against the kind of detachment pursued by eighteenth-century scholars addressing a like-minded public, Thierry's romanticised history by and large was on the contrary meant to inspire and move a wider readership. It was intended to arouse feelings of the kind that Scott's and Chateaubriand's works could elicit, offering a narrative that would not only interest and amuse the reader but would also envelop and involve him or her in a history he or she could be part of.[69] Such an aim would be attained not only by virtue of the events recounted, closer to the condition of early nineteenth-century bourgeois readers, but also because of the way in which they were recounted. In this, the overwhelming quantity of details marshalled was crucial. On the one hand, insisting on details would plunge the reader into the nation's past; on the other, and more importantly, it would help conceal the underlying thread, the narrative's deeper structure.

Thierry, 'Histoire de mes idées et de mes travaux historiques', xiv. On the notion of 'local colour' in Thierry's work, see Odile Parsis-Barubé, 'La notion de couleur locale dans l'œuvre d'Augustin Thierry', in Potin and Déruelle (eds.), *Augustin Thierry*, 63–77.

[68] On the complexity of Voltaire's stance on this, see Marc Hersant, '"Malheur au détail": Voltaire, l'historien pressé', *Écrire l'histoire: Histoire, littérature, esthétique*, 4 (2009), 15–24.

[69] On this point, François Hartog, *Évidence de l'histoire: Ce que voient les historiens* (Paris: Gallimard, 2005), 171–6.

Contrary to eighteenth-century historiography, the question of veracity would no longer be addressed by the reader's engaging with the text. In this new relationship between reader and author, the question of truthfulness would simply not arise.[70] By assuming that a work was based on sound research, carefully conducted by impartial professionals who had devoted their life to studying the past, the narrative's thread would elude questioning – at least by non-professional scholars. Through history writing of this sort the historian, as Gossman has contended, no longer preserved the 'detachment and freedom' of his reader from the narrative.[71]

Incontestably, the relationship that Thierry established between explanation and narration, as well as the opinion that a historian might properly distance himself from his subject as long as he reported each and every detail, is problematic at best.[72] The notion itself of a complete narration, of the possibility of exhausting all sources concerning an event, is also perplexing. All in all, the relationship between the narration and the past, as understood by Thierry, raises many theoretical questions that have been much debated.[73] Fascinating though these issues may be, what interests us here are the political assumptions and implications of his views or, rather, the relationship between power and knowledge implicit in Thierry's reasoning. Two specific aspects invite scrutiny. The first is that precisely because his narrative focused on details, describing them to the fullest extent possible, the canvas on which Thierry portrayed the events of French history would remain concealed from the reader, blinded by the excess of detail. Remaining as faithful as possible to the original sources meant protecting the truth from the dangers posed by what he referred to as 'the subtleties of logical argument'.[74] However, shielded from the reader's scrutiny, the structure underlying the narrative would then go unnoticed, languishing, in the main, unquestioned. As Roland Barthes has noted, Thierry's narrative strove to be the perfect mimesis of the past by pursuing a 'reality effect', where the narration itself, because of its

---

[70] On the question of 'vraisemblance' see Chapter 4.

[71] Gossman, 'Augustin Thierry and Liberal Historiography', 19.

[72] Gianna Pomata, 'Versions of Narrative: Overt and Covert Narrators in Nineteenth Century Historiography', *History Workshop*, 27 (1989), 1–17. Pomata discusses at length Thierry's views throughout.

[73] Needless to say, the works on this are legion. Hayden White, Frank Ankersmit, and Paul Ricœur's are only the most well known. A still useful overview is Lionel Gossman, *Between History and Literature* (Cambridge, Mass: Harvard University Press, 1990). Section II of Gossman's work is devoted to Michelet and Thierry.

[74] Augustin Thierry, 'Avertissement' (1827), in Thierry, *Lettres sur l'histoire de France*, xi. See Dominique Dupart, 'Augustin Thierry et le chant des sources', in Potin and Déruelle (eds.), *Augustin Thierry*, 55–61.

completeness, would render explanation redundant.[75] Thierry's claim that the aim of his work was to substitute for 'the reasoning about facts, the vision of the facts themselves', perfectly encapsulates the conception underlying his complete narration.[76] For our purposes, it is important to note that such a narrative was wholly consistent with nineteenth-century national history writing, since it helped mask the ways in which the unity of the narrative's actor – the nation – was construed. In a narrative so conceived, the complex combination of forgetting, remembering, and misremembering that the reshaping of a group's memory into a national memory necessarily requires could be more easily and more promptly ensconced. The second aspect, equally relevant, is that the greater professionalism of historical scholarship required by Thierry's approach – though this is true for nineteenth-century historical scholarship in general – did carry important consequences for the reader's intellectual freedom, as it did for the way he or she considered political affairs in the light of his or her understanding of the past.[77] As we have seen, the professionalisation of historical writing created an almost unbridgeable gap between reader and author, limiting the former's possibilities of engaging with the text and, therefore, curtailing his or her intellectual freedom. Historical debates increasingly came to be confined within the bounds of academia and professional scholarship, while the growing readership gradually became a passive recipient of knowledge dispensed from on high. This was one rather paradoxical effect of the nineteenth-century democratisation of historical knowledge. Yet here, in the changing relationship between author and reader, from the eighteenth to the early nineteenth century, lay a critical difference in the way politics and the knowledge of the past interacted – and a shift that deeply affected how the nation was perceived.[78] Perfectly in line with these changes, the kind of history writing called for by Thierry implied a shift from Voltaire and his readers to Lavisse and his readers, a move, that is, from histories written by and for elites to histories

---

[75] Roland Barthes, 'Le Discours de l'histoire', in Barthes, *Le bruissement de la langue* (Paris: Seuil, 1984), 166.

[76] Thierry, 'Considérations sur l'histoire de France', 313.

[77] On the political consequences of the professionalisation of historical scholarship, see Peter Novick, *That Noble Dream: The 'Objectivity Question' and the American Historical Profession* (Cambridge: Cambridge University Press, 1988), 21–46. On its effects on nineteenth-century nationalism, see Stefan Berger, Mark Donovan, and Kevin Passmore, 'Apologias for the Nation-State in Western Europe since 1800', in Berger, Donovan, and Passmore (eds.), *Writing National Histories: Western Europe since 1800* (London: Routledge, 1999), 4–9.

[78] On the relationship between the democratisation of nineteenth-century history writing and nationalism, see Monika Baár, 'Romantic Historiography in the Service of Nation Building', in Baár (ed.), *Historians and Nationalism: East-Central Europe in the Nineteenth Century* (Oxford: Oxford University Press, 2010), 46–74.

written by professionals and destined for schoolchildren and the wider public. It was an important step in educating the people in the nation's history, informing them of a past that, Thierry passionately and genuinely believed, they needed to learn, since it was a past that they had won by their own endeavours.

The self-contradictory outcome of Thierry's ideas, addressing a reader hitherto excluded from history, and yet, in doing so, curtailing that reader's own freedom, may have been the inevitable outcome of the initial premise, namely, that historical enquiry was infused with political passion and interest. 'Political passion', he declared unhesitatingly, 'can become a powerful spur to the spirit of research and discovery. If it closes off the intelligence on certain issues, it opens it up and invigorates it in relation to others; it suggests insights, intimations, sometimes bursts of genius to which disinterested study and pure zeal for truth would not have led.'[79] History and politics could explain – and, thus, even justify – each other. To be sure, the past had always been a crucial source of political legitimacy. However, what is striking about the 'century of history'[80] is that an allegedly scientific understanding of what historical scholarship should be was coupled with a clear awareness of its political role.[81] To an extent, this configuration might be imputed to the Revolution, an event that, turning history into a 'school of political theory', drastically altered the struggle over historical truth-claims.[82] In particular, the Revolution made it impossible for historians – and liberal historians especially – to be detached viewers of the past. On the one hand, in fact, many of those writing in the 1820s and 1830s had witnessed the revolutionary upheaval, so that it was difficult for them to form a dispassionate view. The remark made by Prosper de Barante (1782–1866), a historian whom Thierry knew personally and deeply admired, that 'we had seen so much history made, that we wished to rediscover in the past something we had seen or experienced' is somewhat revealing of the emotive implication of looking at those tragic

---

[79] Thierry, 'Considérations sur l'histoire de France', 72. On this point, see the still useful remarks by Renan, 'M. Augustin Thierry', 96–7.

[80] Monod, 'Du progrès des études historiques en France', 27. Some early nineteenth-century historians already saw theirs as the age of historical scholarship. See, for example Prosper de Barante, *Histoire des ducs de Bourgogne de la maison de Valois, 1364–1477* (Paris: Ladvocat, 1824–1826), i. p. xxxii.

[81] Thierry's own awareness of precisely this new relationship between history and politics was shared by Guizot: François Guizot, *Histoire des origines du gouvernement représentatif en Europe* (Paris: Didier, 1851), ii. 9–10. The book was based on a series of lectures delivered by Guizot between 1820 and 1822.

[82] Jean Walch, *Les maîtres de l'histoire: 1815–1850* (Geneva: Honoré Champion, 1986), 35; see also Loïc Rignol, 'Augustin Thierry et la politique de l'histoire: Genèse et principes d'un système de pensée', *Revue d'histoire du XIXᵉ siècle*, 25 (2002), 87–100.

and glorious events.[83] Moreover, several authors felt that the Revolution, the truly liberal revolution, had not yet ended. As we shall see shortly, it was certainly the case for Thierry, who considered 1789 as one single episode in the ongoing centuries-long class struggle of the bourgeoisie against their oppressors. If the Revolution was the (incomplete) culmination of the entire French past, its overwhelming presence forced the historian into an ambiguous position, one where the boundaries between past and present were continually shifting. Here, the role of historians, most of whom were deliberately looking to the past for arguments to support their beliefs, was inherently political.[84] From Thierry's viewpoint, in particular, history not only offered the answers that the French sought but, moreover, its study would further the cause of liberty, proving that the path of French history was one leading to freedom. As he wrote in 1834, recalling his nascent commitment to the study of the past:

> The renewal of the history of France, the need for which I had greatly stressed, presented itself to me under two faces: the one, scientific, the other political. I invoked at the same time a complete restoration of the altered or unknown truth, and a kind of rehabilitation for the middle and lower classes, for the ancestors of the Third Estate, forgotten by our modern historians.[85]

As he saw it, any historian who carefully and meticulously studied and dissected the sources of the French past would inevitably be a 'historiographer of French freedom'.[86] In this respect, as Guizot later pointed out, Thierry truly believed, 'without a doubt, to be offering to the new liberty an important service by reattaching it to the past, by reminding it of its cradle'.[87] He was discovering – though others might say inventing – its roots. Without them, Thierry thought, the struggle for freedom would be lost.

[83] Prosper de Barante, 'De l'histoire' (1828), in *Mélanges historiques et littéraires* (Paris: Ladvocat, 1835), ii. 43. On Thierry's admiration for Barante, see Thierry, 'Avertissement', in the *Lettres sur l'histoire de France*, viii. That the two were personal acquaintances is a claim made by Thierry's great-nephew: Augustin-Thierry, *Augustin Thierry d'après sa correspondance et ses papiers de famille*, 59.

[84] Thierry, 'Avertissement' (1827), in *Lettres sur l'histoire de France*, v–vii. On this, see Ceri Crossley, 'History as a Principle of Legitimation in France (1820–48)', in Berger, Donovan, and Passmore (eds.), *Writing National Histories*, 49–56; also see Stanley Mellon, *The Political Uses of History: A Study of Historians in the French Restoration* (Stanford: Stanford University Press, 1958).

[85] Thierry, 'Histoire de mes idées et de mes travaux historiques', xvi.

[86] Thierry, 'Première lettre sur l'histoire de France', 304.

[87] François Guizot, *Du gouvernement de la France depuis la Restauration, et du ministère actuel* (Paris: Ladvocat, 1820), 206. Guizot's views on the origins of the French nation are discussed in Chapter 9.

In the political and intellectual struggle succeeding the Revolution, a struggle Thierry was very much part of, the publication in 1814 of *De la monarchie française* by the Count de Montlosier (1755–1838), a politician, essayist, and former émigré, played a crucial role, inaugurating a seminal new phase in French historiography and in the debates over the nation's origins.[88] The crux of the count's thesis was that the Frankish invasion of Gaul at the fall of the Roman Empire had been followed by a gradual 'racial' mixing of conquerors and conquered, and by the elevation of all freemen to the rank of 'Franks'. The rest of the Gauls remained subject to the new ruling class. Over the centuries, out of the two groups emerged the nobility and the bourgeoisie. The latter, with the aid of royal authority, starting with the twelfth-century enfranchisement of the communes, slowly but steadily gained influence, finally seizing power during the Revolution – which, from Montlosier's standpoint, was an unjust usurpation of the nobility's ancient rights.[89] Because of the arguments put forward, and which at the time were often misinterpreted, *De la monarchie* became a rallying text for the conservatives, stirring at the same time new ideas among their opponents. Two lengthy and highly critical reviews, possibly by Charles Comte, were published in 1815 in the *Censeur*. For his part, in the *Revue encyclopédique*, Dunoyer rejected the conclusions reached by the count and remarked that, if anything and against his own intentions, Montlosier had extolled the 'vital force of *industrie*', recounting the slow, inexorable emancipation of the Third Estate.[90] Even Guizot accepted the idea that the history of France had started with the conquest of one people by another, but then he reached conclusions very different from Montlosier's, confirming, at the very least, that the thesis in *De la monarchie* was a double-edged sword.[91] Likewise, Thierry, who was profoundly impressed by Montlosier's book, accepted and even welcomed his division of French society into two separate races/nations.[92] But then he nonchalantly overturned Montlosier's conclusions: 'Let us grant it to those who claim it; and as for us, let us claim the opposite descent. We are the

---

[88] We shall return to Montlosier and his works in Chapter 9.

[89] On the debate stirred by *De la monarchie française*, see Fiorentini, *Augustin Thierry*, 68–78.

[90] G. F. [Charles Comte – uncertain attribution], review of François-Dominique de Montlosier, *De la monarchie française*, in *Le censeur*, 6 (1815), 192–244, and 7 (1815), 184–214; Dunoyer, 'Esquisse historique des doctrines auxquelles on a donné le nom industrialisme', 372. G. F. was an important contributor to the *Censeur*. That it might be Charles Comte is a claim made by Harpaz, '"Le censeur européen"', 186–7.

[91] Guizot, *Du gouvernement de la France depuis la Restauration*, iv–v.

[92] See Prosper de Barante, *Notice sur la vie et les ouvrages de M. le Comte de Montlosier* (Clermont-Ferrand: Thibaut-Landriot, 1842), 21.

sons of these serfs, of these tributaries, of these bourgeois that the conquerors devoured at will. We owe to them all that we are.'[93]

We shall return to Montlosier and his ideas in Chapter 9. Here, it is
worth noting that Thierry and the count did in fact have one motive in
common, namely, the impulse to write a new history, that of the nation, as
the history of the people.[94] In fact, Montlosier insisted it was time for the
French to discover their ancient customs which, he sardonically remarked,
had hitherto been to many 'as indifferent as those of the Iroquois and as
foreign as those of China'. Disappointingly, in most if not all history books
everything seemed to be centred on the king or on a small elite. Whenever
the nation was portrayed as a solid unit, with one single and clear intent or
interest, this, he deplored, 'always seemed to be that of a caste'.[95] Strikingly,
in much the same fashion Thierry castigated historians' stubborn refusal to
attribute any independent will to the masses: 'If new customs are established, it is some legislator who imagines them and imposes them; if a city
organises itself, it is always a prince who creates it. Always the people and
the citizens are stifled by the thoughts of a single man.'[96] In the *Histoire de
la conquête*, Thierry clarified that the essential object of his work was, and
that of other historians should be:

> [T]o consider the destiny of people, and not that of certain famous men; to
> tell the adventures of social life and not those of individual life. Human
> sympathy can attach itself to entire populations, as to beings endowed with
> feeling, whose existence, longer than our own, is filled with the same
> alternatives of sorrow and joy, hope and dejection. Considered from this
> standpoint, the history of the past acquires something of the interest which
> attaches itself to the present time; for the collective beings of which it speaks
> have not ceased to live and to feel: they are the same beings who still suffer
> and hope under our eyes.[97]

The centrality of the notions of empathy and identification, as well as the
importance of feelings in Thierry's national narrative, all feature

---

[93] Augustin Thierry, 'Sur l'antipathie de race qui divise la nation française' (1820), in Thierry, *Dix ans d'études historiques*, 279.

[94] See Philippe Boutry, 'Clovis romantique', in Michel Rouche (ed.), *Clovis: Histoire et mémoire. Le baptême de Clovis, son écho à travers l'histoire* (Paris: Presse de l'Université Paris-Sorbonne, 1997), 640–1.

[95] François-Dominique de Montlosier, *De la monarchie française, depuis son établissement jusqu'à nos jours, ou Recherches sur les anciennes institutions françaises et sur les causes qui ont amené la Révolution et ses diverses phases jusqu'à la déclaration d'empire* (Paris: H. Nicolle, 1814–1815), i. 107–8.

[96] Augustin Thierry, 'Sur l'affranchissement des communes' (1820), in Thierry, *Dix ans d'études historiques*, 326–7.

[97] Thierry, *Histoire de la conquête de l'Angleterre par les Normands*, iv. 124.

prominently in this passage. Crucially, these ideas stood opposed to the old, absolutist identification of king and nation. Consistently with such views, Thierry insisted time and again on the need to criticise the assumption that the royal lineage could represent and lend unity to the nation's history. It was almost with contempt that he remarked how, looking at the succession of the kings of France from Clovis to Louis XIV, it seemed that the monarch 'is always the same man, and that, by a kind of metempsychosis, the same soul, at every change of reign, has passed from one body to another'.[98] The final rejection of the notion of the king's immortal body could not be clearer. To support his views, Thierry also offered an explanation as to why the identification of the nation's history and the monarch's body had been upheld for so many centuries. The reasons for the misapprehension were to be sought in the short-sightedness of those historians who, not 'finding in themselves the principle which had to rally to the same interest the innumerable parts of the painting which they were trying to offer, . . .looked for one outside, in the seeming continuity of certain political existences, in the chimera of the non-interrupted transmission of an always identical power to the descendants of the same family'.[99] The bond uniting the French over the centuries into a coherent narrative had been mistakenly sought outside the nation itself – in the kings and their lineage. What historians needed, according to Thierry, was 'love for men as men, regardless of their fame or their social condition'.[100] Lacking such a passion, he argued, they failed to appreciate that what really united the French was not love of the same king, but simply inborn love for their kin, the love that now would give them their unity, shaping them into a single nation.

The Perennial Subject(s) of the Nation's History

One of Thierry's main assumptions – a crucial one since his attempt to change French historiography was founded upon it – was that while eighteenth-century scholars had confined themselves to criticising, albeit firmly and repeatedly, the old dynastic histories, the Revolution had radically changed things. It offered a new and previously unimaginable vantage point that made possible the recognition of a new character shaping the national narrative. In effect, on the one hand the Revolution

---

[98] Augustin Thierry, 'Sur le besoin d'une histoire de France, et le principal défaut de celles qui existent' (second, revised version, 1829), in Augustin Thierry, *Lettres sur l'histoire de France* (Paris: Sautelet, 1829), 10.

[99] Thierry, 'Première lettre sur l'histoire de France', 306–7.   [100] Ibid., 306.

had made it possible to dismiss the old identification of king and nation as nonsensical; on the other, it had also offered a substitute for the king; it had offered, that is, an actor capable of playing his role and giving a new meaning to the nation's past. From Thierry's perspective, the understanding of French history could only begin after the bourgeoisie had shown itself, in 1789, to embody the entire French nation.[101] Given such an assumption, it was unsurprising that the history of France had yet to be written: '[W]e still lack the history of the citizens, the history of the subjects, the history of the people.'[102] The revolution of method brought forth by modern-day historians, and in which he himself was the pioneer, Thierry saw as 'a consequence and a reflection of the social revolution': a shift moulded and shaped 'in its image'. As the one had ended the inequitable system of orders of the ancient regime, the other would soon end – or so Thierry thought – the struggle over the French past. In his own words: 'We shall never see again our history restlessly turn in a circle, being now Germanic and aristocratic, now Roman and monarchical following the current opinion, depending on whether the writer is a noble or a commoner. Its beginning, its principle and very end, are from now on fixed.' The new history would be written 'for all', and would embrace, include, and encompass all national traditions, usages, and *mœurs*. And yet, Thierry went on, it would place before those of all others the lives of 'the greatest number, those of the national mass', those of the descendants, 'by blood, by laws, by languages, by ideas', of the Gallo-Romans.[103]

The Revolution was then the prism through which Thierry, like many of the other liberal historians of Restoration France, gave to the entire course of French history its proper and true meaning. It offered a new lens that replaced the medium that had hitherto shaped the nation's unity – the king's body. The latter is a theme addressed in his illuminating contribution to *Les lieux de mémoire* by Marcel Gauchet, who has interpreted Thierry's approach to the study of the French past as an attempt to overturn the object of concern of historians, once the king and now the nation.[104] Claiming that Thierry pursued an 'extension of the historical object' entwined with and in response to an ongoing 'democratic process', Gauchet has argued that Thierry's conceptual overturning of the earlier object of concern led him to consider the nation as an entity whose unity, shaped through the centuries by the sovereign power, had finally been achieved thanks to the Revolution.[105]

---

[101] Ibid., 88–9.   [102] Ibid., 304.   [103] Ibid., 208.
[104] Gauchet, 'Les "Lettres sur l'histoire de France" d'Augustin Thierry', 808–11.
[105] Ibid., 809 and 819–35.

Therefore, the latter stood as 'the triumph of the abstract personification of the collective over the single individuality that continued to attach it to a concrete body'. Only after the Revolution did the nation, now 'disembodying itself, [acquire] its own subjective transcendence'. Going on to claim that the execution of Louis XVI ensured that 'the eternal body of the nation' would become fully personal, Gauchet has concluded that, 'no longer flesh', the nation was now 'only representable'.[106] Indeed, here Gauchet has surely grasped the significance of Thierry's epistemic turn, emphasising his rebuttal of the myth of the royal lineage embodying the nation's history. However, while this was a crucial shift in perspective, it was only one aspect of Thierry's *réforme historique*. Plausible as Gauchet's reading might be, it leaves untouched Thierry's search for 'the abstract personification' of the collective he refers to and which, though no longer clothed in 'flesh', still had to be defined in order to represent the nation's unity. From this angle, Thierry himself was aware that the rejection of the identification of king and nation created a conceptual void that had to be filled. The young Thierry had taken on a truly daunting task:

> I took it upon myself to write an history which, properly speaking, had no body; it was a matter of shaping one for it, of disentangling it, by means of abstraction, from everything that was not it, and it was necessary to give to a succession of insights and of general facts the movement and the interests of a narration.[107]

The need to shed light on the history of France required, at one and the same time, giving it a 'body' and finding the actor that truly was the nation. It required, in other words, a recourse to social groupings such as classes and races that, in effect, possessed a conceptual complexity that does not fully emerge in Gauchet's reasoning.

The underlying tendency, highlighted by Gauchet and leading towards a 'depersonalisation of history', was indeed a prominent feature in the works of many liberal historians – one that might easily be related to the 'historical fatalism' of François Mignet (1796–1884) and Adolphe Thiers (1797–1877) on which Chateaubriand bitterly commented and which, Michelet suggested, also informed Thierry's works.[108] Essentially, it was an outcome of the Revolution and had led to a decisive shift in the way

---

[106] Ibid., 824.

[107] Augustin Thierry, *Essai sur l'histoire de la formation et des progrès du tiers état* (Paris: Furne et C., 1853), xii.

[108] Chateaubriand, 'Préface – Études historiques', 74–5; Jules Michelet, 'Préface à l'histoire de France' (1868), in *Introduction à l'histoire universelle; Tableau de la France; Préface à l'Histoire de France* (Paris: Armand Colin, 1962), 167.

French society imagined and understood itself. First and foremost, it implied putting the masses, with their volitions and passions, at the very heart of political and historiographical debates. It was now to them, rather than to kings, ministers, generals, and solitary heroes, that historians had to look in order to understand and explain a nation's past. So, in their efforts to interpret the Revolution, Mignet, Thiers, and Guizot built their arguments on the assumption that it was the decisions of the people, more than those of a few politicians, that determined the course of history: 'A man is something of very small importance in a revolution that moves the masses', Mignet wrote in 1824.[109] The fact that in the unfolding of history a central place was now given to the people or the masses was also a consequence of the increasing concerns of historians to go beyond the surface of things. According to Guizot, 'as the historian's glance breaks through the facts, it meets with society itself, the nation, the country'; it meets, that is, with the people. The names of great personages, so crucial to previous historiography, were no longer the sole – nor, possibly, the main – key to unravelling the nation's past.[110] Thierry shared these views. For him too the revolutions, upheavals, and vicissitudes of history were the work of the people, the outcome of their strivings, and a consequence of their beliefs, more than of the volition of those kings and generals who, until then, had been the pivots on which national narratives had turned.[111]

However, if the course of history was now largely to be imputed to the action of the masses, understanding how a people's unity of intent was formed became an increasingly pressing need. It was necessary to grasp what a people's shared ideals, beliefs, and *mœurs* were, since there, many believed, was the true mainspring of history. Thanks to the lessons that might be drawn from the Revolution, several liberal historians thought they could give an answer and, importantly, some of the solutions were in line with the views on the nation expressed by Thierry in his *Des nations*. Following his industrialist beliefs, Thierry made the claim that tradesmen, lawyers, and shopkeepers – in other words, the true makers of the greatness and wealth of France – represented the nation. No longer the reflex of a shared loyalty towards the same monarch, the nation was now the

---

[109] Françoise-Auguste Mignet, *Histoire de la Révolution française* (Brussels: Aug. Wahlent et comp., 1824), 69. On Mignet's assumption, see the comments by Charles-Augustin Sainte-Beuve, review of Françoise-Auguste Mignet, *Histoire de la Révolution française* (1826), in *Œuvres* (Paris: Gallimard, 1956–1966), i. 15–6.

[110] François Guizot, *Essais sur l'histoire de France* (Paris: Brière, 1823), 68–9.

[111] Alice Gérard, 'Le grand homme et la conception de l'histoire au XIXe siècle', *Romantisme*, 100 (1998), 34–5.

product of the common interests and the shared efforts of its most industrious part. Throughout the centuries, the descendants of the Gallo-Romans had built France through their toil. At the same time, the division of labour had made them increasingly interdependent. Their shared efforts, the common memories of their struggles to rid themselves of their yoke, and their industriousness made of them a real community in which the unity of the nation could be reflected. In the main, Thierry was clearly following and expanding Sieyès's ideas. He even echoed his *Qu'est-ce que le tiers état?*, claiming that the Third Estate was not only a nation in and of itself but was 'a complete nation', then interpreting the history of France as the story of the emancipation of the bourgeoisie.[112]

Mindful of the difficulty of replacing the king's symbolic body with a new figure that might evoke the nation's unity, Thierry decided to offer his readers a simplified version of his views in the 'Histoire véritable de Jacques Bonhomme' (1820), the biography of a fictional peasant, from the creation of France to the Revolution.[113] The name had been used for centuries by the nobility, derisively, to refer to an ignorant, brutish, and simple-minded peasantry. But in Thierry's narrative this caricature is turned on its head, so that he becomes a symbol of hard work, sacrifice, freedom, and retribution. Jacques is a Gallo-Roman peasant living freely in southern France until he is enslaved by Germanic tribes from the north. Oppressed by those in power, belittled and having to work for them, Jacques repeatedly tries to throw off his yoke. However, whenever he is close to succeeding, he returns to his oppressed condition until finally he finds the strength to free himself and regain his lands. In the essay, Jacques and his oppressors embody industriousness and idleness respectively, defining two characters that remain unchanged throughout the story. And this makes the actions of the two actors perfectly intelligible, and even foreseeable by the reader.[114] Although in the final pages of his essay Thierry refers to the short story as a *plaisanterie*, as little more than a jest, the underlying rationale is certainly the same as that of his scholarly

[112] Thierry, 'Considérations sur l'histoire de France', 130–1. On this point, see Stephen Bann, 'L'histoire et le peuple héros: Augustin Thierry et Thomas Carlyle', in André Peyronie (ed.), *Révolution française, peuple et littératures* (Paris: Klincksieck, 1991), 19–24. Sieyès's ideas are discussed in Chapter 7.

[113] Augustin Thierry, 'Histoire véritable de Jacques Bonhomme' (1820), in Thierry, *Dix ans d'études historiques*, 282–91.

[114] On the notion of character in historical narratives, see Chapter 4. On the 'Histoire véritable de Jacques Bonhomme', see Ginzburg, 'Checking the Evidence', 85–6. Ginzburg has suggested that Michelet took inspiration from Thierry's story for the first section of his famous *La sorcière* (1862): ibid., 86.

works.[115] It was surely the case with his *Lettres sur l'histoire de France* (1827) and the *Essai sur l'histoire de la formation et des progrès du tiers état* (1853). In these, the Gallo-Romans symbolised the unity of all farmers, tradesmen, and guildsmen who, by means of their work, had made the wealth and greatness of France and who, nonetheless, were unjustly subjugated by their indolent masters, the descendants of the conquering Franks. Over the centuries, the domination over burghers and peasants, and the division of society into two distinct classes, continued generation after generation. The original conquest and the subjugation of the ancestors of the modern bourgeoisie, therefore, shaped the ensuing hostility between the oppressor and the oppressed, determining the course of French history. Indeed, Thierry knew that history only rarely sided with the vanquished, and such an awareness was becoming increasingly widespread. The great Genevan economist and historian Charles Simonde de Sismondi (1773–1842), a scholar whom Thierry profoundly admired, had made it clear a few years earlier, in his famous *Histoire des républiques italiennes du Moyen-âge* (1807–1809), when he noted that 'as long as Italy remained under the sway of the barbarians, there could be a history of the conquering nations but none of the conquered nation'.[116] For his part, Michelet would soon write of his deeply felt desire to 'make the silences of history speak', while Macaulay (1800–1859) drew attention to the 'noiseless revolutions' of those masses that had so often been neglected by historians.[117] But it was in the works of Thierry that the vanquished gained the central place. De Sismondi himself, criticising what he saw as an excessive fascination with the conquered, referred to Thierry as the 'genealogist of misfortune'.[118] Thomas Carlyle (1795–1881), for his part, had one of his favourite fictional mouthpieces Professor Sauerteig comment sarcastically on the *Histoire de la conquête de l'Angleterre*:

> M. Thierry has written an ingenious book, celebrating with considerable pathos the fate of the Saxons fallen under that fierce-hearted *Conquaestor*, Acquirer or Conqueror, as he is named. M. Thierry professes to have a turn for looking at that side of things: the fate of the Welsh too moves him; of the

---

[115] The expression is in Thierry, 'Histoire véritable de Jacques Bonhomme', 290.

[116] Jean Charles Léonard Simonde de Sismondi, *Histoire des républiques italiennes du moyen âge* (Zurich: Gessner, 1807–1809), i. 10. On Thierry's admiration for Sismondi, see the 'Avertissement', in the *Lettres sur l'histoire de France* (ed. 1827), viii.

[117] Jules Michelet, *Journal* (Paris: Gallimard, 1959–1976), i. 378 (30 January 1842); Thomas Babington Macaulay, 'On History' (1828), in *Reviews, Essays, and Poems* (London: Ward, Lock & Co., 1875), 90.

[118] Jean Charles Léonard Simonde de Sismondi, review of Augustin Thierry, *Histoire de la conquête de l'Angleterre par les Normands*, in *Revue encyclopédique*, 28 (1825), 86.

Celts generally, whom a fiercer race swept before them into the mountainous nooks of the West, whither they were not worth following. Noble deeds, according to M. Thierry, were done by these unsuccessful men, heroic sufferings undergone; which it is a pious duty to rescue from forgetfulness. True, surely! A tear at least is due to the unhappy.[119]

What should be noted, here, is that in Thierry's reading of French history, just as in Jacques's story, the crucial elements defining the two races/classes were the industriousness and civility of the Gallo-Romans and their descendants, as opposed to the idleness and fierceness of the Franks and their progeny. The legal and political relationship between the two groups did indeed change over the centuries, acquiring different forms, so that the initial divisions emerging out of the conquest slowly turned into legal and then economic distinctions.[120] But, crucially, these changes were played out on a firmly secured anthropological thread – or such was Thierry's assumption. The backdrop of the opposition remained essentially the same. The two groups embodied different values; different characters, each one purportedly embodying that of France.

This last aspect also helps us to highlight an important point of contention in Thierry's vision of French history, namely, the juxtaposition of the concepts of race and class. Both notions figured prominently in his writings, so much so that the idea of a struggle between two classes as the engine of history famously prompted Marx to think of Thierry as 'the father of the class struggle of French historiography'.[121] For his part, Camille Jullian, writing at the start of the twentieth century, underlined the impact of Thierry's idea on modern racialism. He deemed Thierry's to be 'a dreadful theory, with these words of Latin, German, Slav race'. Through these ideas, he went on, historians 'have harmed us very much'.[122] In truth, it is not difficult to show that Thierry's understanding of race lacked any sort of biological reference or implication.[123] This is clearly confirmed by Thierry's assumption that should political inequality disappear, then racial distinctions would be worthless – a statement that evidently clashes with or, rather, nullifies any racialist theory. From this

[119] Thomas Carlyle, 'Chartism' (1840), in *Selected Writings* (London: Penguin Classics, 2015), 174.
[120] Thierry, 'Sur l'antipathie de race qui divise la nation française', 279.
[121] Karl Marx to Friedrich Engels, 27 July 1854, in Marx and Engels, *Gesamtausgabe: Dritte Abteilung, Band 2 – Der Briefwechsel zwischen Marx und Engels, 1854–1860* (Berlin: Marx-Engels-Verlag G.M.B.H., 1930), 46. On this, Jean-Numa Ducange, 'Marx, le marxisme et le "père de la lutte des classes", Augustin Thierry', *Actuel Marx*, 58 (2015), 12–27.
[122] Camille Jullian, 'Augustin Thierry et le mouvement historique sous la Restauration', *Revue de synthèse historique*, 13 (1906), 138.
[123] This was noted, long ago, by Febvre, *Michelet, créateur de l'Histoire de France*, 141–54.

angle, Michelet's remark that Thierry was 'enslaved' to the notion of a 'permanence of races' is misleading.[124] Admittedly, the use he made of the word 'race' may strike a reader as ambiguous, but more relevant, and more problematic, is the relationship he construed between the ideas of race and class. An example may be found in the *Histoire de la conquête d'Angleterre* when, outlining the reasons for social and political strife in English history, he claimed that the 'race of invaders remained a privileged class from the moment it ceased to constitute a separate nation'.[125] Again, to the modern reader such use of the two words may seem an equivocal conceptual overlapping – and, for that reason, particularly dangerous, as Foucault noted.[126] However, this might be explained by considering that, for Thierry, both notions performed the same function, that of bringing together a group of individuals who would otherwise remain alien to one another. Importantly, both did so by implying the sharing by a group of people of the same values, ideals, and memories. This is made clear in the *Lettres sur l'histoire de France*, where Thierry argued that by the second half of the eleventh century the 'distinction between races had disappeared, though, in a way, it had been substituted by the differences of *mœurs*. Laws were at the time marked by the stamp of Germanic values. Contempt for the life and belongings of the weak and the love of domination and war formed the distinctive character of the lords and the members of the high clergy.' Against this, Thierry opposed the 'love for work and the unclear feeling of social equality' of the 'town's industrious inhabitants'.[127] Class and race were then notions that indicated two groups of individuals sharing the same political condition as a result of the conquest. But, importantly, their members were also united by the same values, ideals, memories, and character. Thierry's classes and races both defined, in other words, an ethnic group.

In Thierry's narrative the existence of a bond between the modern bourgeoisie and the ancient Gallo-Romans, shaped by a shared character passed down from one generation to another, was consistent with the claim that France owed what it at present was to the efforts of the Third Estate. The expansion of cities, the ever-growing exploitation of resources, the improvements in technology, and the flourishing of the arts – in other words, civilisation itself – were the fruit of the hard work of the Gallo-

---

[124] Michelet, 'Préface à l'histoire de France', 167.
[125] Thierry, *Histoire de la conquête de l'Angleterre par les Normands*, i. p. v–vi.
[126] Foucault, *Il faut défendre la société*, 208–12.
[127] Augustin Thierry, 'Sur la marche de la révolution communale – commune de Cambrai' (1827), in Thierry, *Lettres sur l'histoire de France* (ed. 1827), 233.

Romans first and the bourgeoisie latterly, an industrious class held back by an idle and violent nobility. The greatness of France, its wealth and its strength, were the achievement of the bourgeoisie alone, the nation's worthiest part. It was the bearer of the 'ancient Gallic civilisation' and the agent of progress, against the barbarism of the Frankish conquerors: '[T]here is a glory of the peasantry, that of industry and talent', Thierry wrote in 1827.[128] Coupled with these claims, and perfectly consistent with them, was the notion that the bourgeoisie was also the purveyor of freedom. From the twelfth century onwards, contended Thierry, thanks to their increasing economic importance, the cities gradually grew away from feudal tutelage, becoming the cradle 'of our modern freedom'.[129] The struggles to gain independence from the nobility Thierry saw as the 'forerunner of all those revolutions that have gradually raised the condition of the Third Estate', so that the 1789 upheavals were rooted in the 'communal revolution' of the Middle Ages.[130] On the one hand, this was a relentless and unremitting struggle, described by Thierry in almost messianic tones.[131] On the other, it was a rejection of the idea of Germanic freedom and the concomitant exaltation of the 'rejuvenating' barbarism of a Michelet.[132] Placed within such a frame, the Revolution itself, far from being a single episode disrupting the course of history, the outcome of an unforeseeable crisis, was on the contrary the result of a long process, lasting centuries.[133] Rather paradoxically, the new historiography born of the Revolution would strenuously assert the continuity of French history – and, thus, of the actor embodying it. It was on these premises that Thierry could insist on an empathic bond between the Gallo-Romans and the modern bourgeoisie, on their historical community over the centuries: 'We are the sons of these serfs, of these tributaries, of these bourgeois that the conquerors devoured at will; we owe them all that we are.'[134] This identification of the true, heroic, and industrious actor of the nation's

---

[128] Thierry, 'Sur le besoin d'une histoire de France, et le principal défaut de celles qui existent' (ed. 1820), 9.

[129] Walch, *Les maîtres de l'histoire*, 69–71.

[130] Thierry, 'Histoire de mes idées et de mes travaux historiques', v.

[131] See, for example, Thierry, *Essai sur l'histoire de la formation et des progrès du tiers état*, 67–8. On this, Isabelle Durand, 'Augustin Thierry et le Moyen Age romantique: Le mythe des origines', in Potin and Déruelle (eds.), *Augustin Thierry*, especially 164–8.

[132] See Jules Michelet, *Le peuple* (1846) (Paris: Flammarion, 1974), 72.

[133] See Jacques Neefs, 'Augustin Thierry: Le moment de la "véritable" histoire de France', *Romantisme*, 28–9 (1980), 290; see also Déruelle, 'Introduction', 40.

[134] Augustin Thierry, 'Commentaire sur l'*Esprit des lois* de Montesquieu', *Le censeur européen*, 2 (1818), vii. 251. On the empathic bond in Romantic historiography, see Giuseppe Nori, 'The Problematics of Sympathy and Romantic Historicism', *Studies in Romanticism*, 34 (1995), 3–28.

history with the reader was repeated throughout Thierry's works, helping to shape what might be considered a class memory made to coincide with that of France at large; or, from a different angle, an ethnic memory readapted into the nation's memory.

By construing the bourgeoisie as he did, imagining it represented the entire nation because of the values it embodied, for its ideals, character, and memories, Thierry offered his readers a coherent narrative detached from the king's body. Inherently political, it looked at the past in order to shape the future, fostering a project that envisaged an industrious and enlightened bourgeoisie ruling over state and society. Furthermore, by tying past and future into a meaningful teleology of freedom and progress, Thierry provided Sieyès's nation with what the abbé had neglected: a collective memory that could shape a national identity. It offered France the ethnic complex of myths and memories that, according to Anthony D. Smith, is necessary to ground the feeling of belonging to a community that transcends time, offering a solution to the question of where the collective 'we' comes from. On this point, it is not irrelevant that Thierry repeatedly criticised those men of the Revolution who propagated the idea that theirs was a radical break with the past.[135] To him, on the contrary, the notion of the continuity of the struggle of the Third Estate against the nobility, dating from the Middle Ages onwards, was crucial. It was a precondition for claiming the identity of the bourgeoisie with the Gallo-Romans who, he wrote, 'are the same men [as us]. Just as we can trace ourselves back to them by name and descent, so we could trace to them our ideas, hopes, and desires.' Once the nation's true history was made accessible to the wider public, a natural empathy between the reader and the previous generations of the bourgeoisie would necessarily ensue; between the modern French and the Gallo-Romans, argued Thierry. The reader would thus discover his true past: 'Our minds would be occupied far better with the destinies of the masses of men who have *lived and felt like us*.' It would be an empathy strengthened by telling the stories of its heroes whose qualities, clearly, the modern bourgeois also possessed: '[O]ur heroes have obscure names. We are the men of the cities, the men of the communes, the men of the glebe, the sons of the farmers threatened by the knights, the sons of those bourgeois who made Charles V tremble, the sons of the revolts and the Jacqueries.'[136] In the 1820s and 1830s, other liberal historians felt the need

---

[135] See Mellon, *The Political Uses of History*, 11.

[136] Augustin Thierry, 'Sur l'esprit national des Irlandais, à propos des *Mélodies irlandaises* de Thomas Moore' (1820), in Thierry, *Dix ans d'études historiques*, 123; emphasis added.

to restore to the bourgeoisie and to France its lost memory. Several did so on the assumption, as Guizot had it, that a nation, 'a society, to believe in itself, needs not to have been born yesterday'.[137] Like Thierry, they were adamant that only if France rediscovered its true past would it then also find its unity and peace. As we shall see in Chapter 9, it is surely revealing of the ambiguities of such a stance that many historians did so through the history of the race/class struggle, building on and reshaping some of the controversial arguments of the eighteenth-century debate on the origins of France.

[137] Guizot, *Du gouvernement de la France depuis la Restauration*, 206.

Debating the Nation's History:
Restoring to the Bourgeoisie its Lost Past

Burghers, Bourgeois, and Classes:
de Bréquigny, Le Gendre, d'Argenson, and Mably (Again)

In his *Considérations sur l'histoire de France*, Thierry discussed at length the ideas of the historian, antiquary, and member of the Académie Louis Feudrix de Bréquigny (1715–1795), lingering over his *Recherches sur les communes* and his *Recherches sur les bourgeoisies*.[1] The two works, originally introductions to the eleventh and twelfth books of the monumental *Ordonnances des rois de France*, were first published in 1769 and in 1777 respectively.[2] The core of Bréquigny's argument was that during the Middle Ages the communes were born out of the free association of townsmen against the tyranny of local lords. Growing stronger over time, they set their own rules which, accepted by the kings of France, turned into customary laws and legal rights curtailing the power of feudal lords.[3] According to Bréquigny, the 'founding act of the commune was the association of its inhabitants, united through oath, to defend themselves against the vexations of the lords oppressing them'.[4] Yet, he hastily added, 'such an association was only a revolt in so far as it was not authorised' by royal authority. In fact, the creation of a commune, a town with privileges attached to its citizens, required that the 'king sanction it by special concession'.[5] But from the reign of Louis VI (1081–1137) onwards, noted Bréquigny, it became common practice for the rulers of France to renew

---

[1] Thierry, 'Considérations sur l'histoire de France', 109–17. On Bréquigny, see: Ernest Dumont, *Notice sur la vie et les écrits de Louis-Georges-Oudart Feudrix de Bréquigny* (Rouen: P. Leprêtre, 1897); René Poupardin, 'Bréquigny', in Poupardin (ed.), *Catalogue des manuscrits des collections Duchesne et Bréquigny* (Paris: Leroux, 1905), xxi–xxiv; Carlrichard Brühl, 'Splendeur et misère de la diplomatique: Le cas de l'édition des diplômes royaux mérovingiens de Bréquigny à Pertz', *Comptes rendus des séances de l'Académie des inscriptions et belles-lettres*, 136 (1992), 251–9.
[2] Louis Feudrix de Bréquigny, 'Recherches sur les communes', in Leber (ed.), *Collection des meilleurs dissertations relatifs à l'histoire de France*, xx. 42–144, and Louis Feudrix de Bréquigny, 'Recherches sur les bourgeoisies', ibid., 145–211.
[3] Bréquigny, 'Recherches sur les communes', 72–86.   [4] Ibid., 87.   [5] Ibid., 87 and 95.

old or grant new privileges to towns and this, in turn, led to the creation of a class of privileged townsmen that finally formed the Third Estate. By granting its protection to the townsmen, the throne increased its authority over the nation, taming the ambitions of seditious lords. An alliance between the two was thus established. Importantly, although in Bréquigny's works the role of the crown remained crucial, so much so that one should be wary of any excessively liberal reading of his works – he was, ultimately, employed by the crown under Moreau's supervision – he allotted much more space to the nascent Third Estate than most scholars had done hitherto.[6] Indeed, the *Recherches sur les communes* and the *Recherches sur les bourgeoisies* essentially recounted the history of the communes and of the bourgeoisie. A laudatory undertone might even be discerned in the description of this 'intermediate class' between villeins and lords, open to all but serfs and the true agent of progress in the arts, industry, and commerce.[7] In fact, according to Bréquigny it was thanks to the hard-working bourgeoisie that the lands of France were now covered by 'luxuriant fields and rich and powerful towns'.[8]

In his assessment of Bréquigny's ideas, Thierry gave ample space to the discussion of merits as well as faults. On the one hand, he praised the abbé for having dealt 'for the first time' with the issue of municipal rights and for having sought the history of the Third Estate, 'the history of the new society'. On the other hand, he censured the learned antiquary for having failed to properly discuss the '*mœurs* and institutions of the time', ignoring 'the struggle between races', and overlooking the 'wonderful spectacle' offered by the lives of the Gallo-Romans and the Franks. Interestingly, according to Thierry, Bréquigny had paid excessive attention to secondary legal issues and had generally neglected the ways of life, character, and ideals of the ancestors of the modern French.[9] There may be some truth in such remarks, and this becomes clearer when considering the work of one of Bréquigny's predecessors who had, indeed, scrutinised the *mœurs* and ways of life of the members of the Third Estate. In 1712, the abbé Louis Le Gendre (1655–1733) published the *Mœurs et coutumes des François dans les différents temps de la monarchie*, which, in 1718, became part of his *Nouvelle*

---

[6] Gossman, for one, has suggested such a reading: Gossman, *Medievalism and the Ideologies of the Enlightenment*, 119–22. Gembicki, on the contrary, has emphasised the importance of Moreau's tutelage as regards Bréquigny's work. See Dieter Gembicki, 'La condition historienne à la fin de l'Ancien régime', in Gembicki, *Clio au XVIIIe siècle: Voltaire, Montesquieu et autres disciples* (Paris: L'Harmattan, 2008), 31–45.

[7] Bréquigny, 'Recherches sur les bourgeoisies', 154.   [8] Ibid., 209–10.

[9] Thierry, 'Considérations sur l'histoire de France', 114–6.

histoire de France.[10] In many ways, it was a remarkable work since it focused on the lives of the French people and touched upon a variety of subjects, including changes in legal customs, tournaments, taste in music, the arts, and architecture, and even the French passion for card games, gambling, and luxury.[11] Interestingly, and perhaps tellingly, when the *Nouvelle histoire* was published once again in 1755 it was preceded by Tacitus's *Germania*. This decision, the anonymous editor informed his readers, was due on the one hand to the fact that the continuity between the *mœurs* of the Franks and those of the French could easily be ascertained and, on the other, to Le Gendre and Tacitus sharing the same interest in a people's way of life.[12] In the early 1830s, Chateaubriand even went as far as to praise the abbé for having 'introduced, in the general study of history, the portraying of *mœurs* and customs, a felicitous innovation that opened a new path to history'.[13] Indeed, Le Gendre offered his readers a striking description of the rise of the townsmen to their present flourishing condition, seeing them as a historical agent worthy of the historian's attention. As he put it, following the end of what amounted to a condition of serfdom and thanks to Louis VII (1120–1180), the townsmen, now free, could decide their own future. Many engaged in trade and business while others devoted themselves to the arts or the sciences. Furthermore, they could now voice demands to the local lords, obtaining laws that would safeguard their freedom and the all-important right to be judged by their peers. All these changes were advantageous for the entire French nation since they encouraged and protected the initiative of men who, sure of their rights, could work to pursue their own interests. Soon, Le Gendre went on to argue, 'there were no uncultivated lands', the towns grew in size and wealth, and the French engaged in trade, an activity until then left to foreigners, occasioning great losses to the state. In time, towns became so powerful that, to make them contribute to state finances 'with less reluctance, their deputies were called to take part in General Assemblies'. Eventually, the increase of their wealth and political influence led to the creation of 'a *Third Estate*' that possessed 'as much as or even more power than the nobility and the clergy'. Here was the true agent of the economic, material

---

[10] On Le Gendre, see Charles Weiss, 'Legendre', in Michaud (ed.), *Biographie universelle ancienne et moderne*, xxiii. 558–9. Also see Phyllis K. Leffler, 'French Historians and the Challenge to Louis XIV's Absolutism', *French Historical Studies*, 14 (1985), especially 8–13.

[11] Leffler, 'French Historians and the Challenge to Louis XIV's Absolutism', 9–11.

[12] Anonymous, 'Préface', in Louis Le Gendre, *Mœurs et coutumes des François, dans les premiers temps de la monarchie* (Paris: Briasson, 1753), iii–vi.

[13] Chateaubriand, 'Préface – Études historiques', 33.

and cultural progress that had brought about the greatness of the French nation.[14]

According to Lenglet Du Fresnoy, Le Gendre's *Nouvelle histoire* 'was little read' – though, he added, 'regrettably so'. However, throughout the eighteenth century its many editions, as well those of the *Mœurs*, testify to the importance of the abbé's works.[15] Montesquieu, for one, knew Le Gendre's book and used it in the *Esprit* to discuss the ancient Franks. Fréron praised the *Mœurs* for having dealt with the ways of life of the ancient French with great 'precision' and for offering the reader 'an infinity of interesting things'. Among others, Velly and Hénault both profited from Le Gendre's books as a valuable source for their own.[16] More interesting were the comments made by Bricaire de La Dixmerie, who praised the abbé's works but also pointed out that Le Gendre 'was not always impartial' and went as far as to accuse him of being 'more of a panegyrist than a historian' when writing about Louis XIV.[17] It is an interesting contention for it contains a kernel of truth. In fact, although Le Gendre devoted several pages to the Third Estate, its history and *mœurs*, he did so despite his championing of the crown's cause. In fact, just like Bréquigny, Le Gendre was also writing under royal patronage. As a partial consequence, the image of the Third Estate conveyed by both authors was predicated upon its close alliance with the crown. Seeing Le Gendre and Bréquigny as two harbingers of the rights of the Third Estate and those of the bourgeoisie – as Thierry did, with reference to Bréquigny – would then be misleading. Remarkably, throughout the eighteenth century, many judged the Third Estate, as a class, to be indissolubly tied to the crown. At the close of the seventeenth century, Gabriel Daniel, albeit in passing, had made important remarks on the alliance between townsmen and the crown, tying the rights and the freedom of the former to the authority of the latter. The President Hénault discussed the alliance in the 1749 edition of his *Nouvel abrégé chronologique*, noting that Louis VI had rendered a number of French towns 'almost independent' in order to gain their

---

[14] Louis Le Gendre, *Mœurs et coutumes des François, dans les différens temps de la monarchie* (Paris: Collombat, 1712), 156–64. Quote is on page 163; italics in the text.

[15] Lenglet Du Fresnoy, *Méthode pour étudier l'histoire*, iv. 42. On circulation, see Grosperrin, *La représentation de l'histoire de France dans l'historiographie des Lumières*, i. 86–8.

[16] Montesquieu, 'Mes pensées', 1473–4 (§ 1953); the notes in the *Pensées* were then used in the *Esprit*: Montesquieu, 'De l'Esprit des lois', 812–3 (book xxviii. ch. 18); Élie Fréron, review of Louis Le Gendre, *Mœurs et coutumes des François, dans les premiers temps de la monarchie* (edition of 1753), in *Lettres sur quelques écrits de ce temps*, 8 (1753), 341.

[17] Bricaire de La Dixmerie, *Les deux âges du goût et du génie français sous Louis XIV et sous Louis XV*, 376.

support against the nobility. Voltaire adopted the same viewpoint.[18] The notion of an alliance between the Third Estate and the crown had effectively been a contention central to the works of Dubos, the supporters of the Romanist thesis, and the detractors of Boulainvilliers. Later, with a different intent and in a very different context, its importance would be reasserted in 1814, in the preamble to the *Charte*.[19] Although throughout the entire eighteenth century there had been, indeed, a growing interest in the enfranchisement of the communes, the issue was usually viewed in the main as an episode in the struggle between the crown and the nobility.[20] But it was within such a frame of reference and with the aim of defending the royal prerogatives, that the schema later used by Thierry, centred on the struggle of law-abiding and hard-working burghers against disreputable and idle noblemen, was initially formed.[21]

An interesting and original stance was adopted in a manuscript written in 1737 and with the suggestive title 'Jusques où la démocratie peut estre admise dans le gouvernement monarchique?' As the author made clear, this 'political treatise has been drafted in response to those of M. de Boulainvilliers on the ancient feudal government of France'.[22] The text soon started to circulate in manuscript form and was later published as the *Considérations sur le gouvernement ancien et présent de la France* (1764). Looking back at the origins of France, it partly repeated some of Le Gendre's and foreshadowed some of Bréquigny's reasonings but did so with the specific aim of defining a project of constitutional reform. Because it was a work written as a response to Boulainvilliers's theories, a series of analogies with Dubos's arguments on feudal rule inevitably stand out.[23] And yet the fact that its author, the Marquis d'Argenson, was a convinced

---

[18] Daniel, *Histoire de France* (ed. 1713), 1168–70; Charles-Jean-François Hénault, *Nouvel abrégé chronologique de l'histoire de France* (Paris: Prault père, 1749), 635–6; Voltaire, 'Essai sur les mœurs et l'esprit des nations', xii. 68–71.

[19] 'Charte constitutionnelle du 4 juin 1814', in Jacques Godechot (ed.), *Les constitutions de la France depuis 1789* (Paris: Garnier-Flammarion, 1979), 217–8.

[20] See Dieter Gembicki, 'Le renouveau des études sur les communes médiévales au XVIIIᵉ siècle', in Gembicki, *Clio au XVIIIᵉ siècle*, 23–30.

[21] See Salmon, 'Renaissance Jurists and "Enlightened" Magistrates', 396–7.

[22] René-Louis de Voyer de Paulmy d'Argenson, 'Jusques où la démocratie peut estre admise dans le gouvernement monarchique? Ce traitté de politique a esté composé à l'occasion de ceux de M. de Boulainvilliers, touchant l'ancien gouvernement féodal de France' (Paris: Bibliothèque de l'Arsenal, MS manuscrits français, 2334). On the differences between the 1737 manuscripts and the published versions, see Arthur Ongle, *The Marquis d'Argenson: A Study in Criticism* (Oxford: Fisher Unwin, 1893), 174–6.

[23] Carcassonne, *Montesquieu et le problème de la constitution française*, 81.

anti-absolutist marks the difference.[24] His was an alternative view to that of the count as much as the abbé's.[25] The kernel of d'Argenson's thesis was that the French constitution was built on a pact between the crown and the townsmen and that, to counter the debasing of the nation, that pact should be revived to fight back against the unjust privileges of the nobility. Crucially, the existence of the latter need not be understood as the outcome of the Frankish conquest, since, argued the marquis, the Gauls were never defeated by the Franks. In the *Considérations*, the conquest was essentially portrayed as the seizing of fortresses and military strongholds first, and of key positions in the administration and policy of the Gallic lands afterwards. Its inhabitants were never enslaved. Reverting to an idea held by many seventeenth-century scholars, the marquis even claimed it was 'known that the Romans were driven out of Gaul, rather than the Gauls conquered by the Franks'.[26] Feudalism, with all its flaws and injustices, only emerged later, as the consequence of a usurpation taking place under the rule of the last Carolingian kings. Seeing the alliance between king and towns as a lynchpin of the ancient constitution, d'Argenson went on to advocate its renewal through the creation of popular magistrates who, chosen from a list decided by the townsmen, would rule over each city and village.

Downplaying if not dismissing entirely the significance of the Frankish invasion, d'Argenson's system pursued a balancing of royal prerogatives and individual liberties through the cooperation of crown and municipal magistrates. Instrumental in such a scheme was the restraining of the feudal rights, which, he believed, not only were profoundly unfair, but also impeded economic and social progress.[27] Originally granted on merit, nobility had

---

[24] On d'Argenson's political thought, see: Sergio Cotta, 'Il problema politico del marchese d'Argenson', *Occidente*, 6 (1951), 192–222 and 295–310; Joseph Gallanar, 'Argenson's "Platonic Republics"', *Studies on Voltaire and the Eighteenth Century*, 56 (1967), 557–75; Nannerl O. Keohane, 'Democratic Monarchy: The Political Theory of the Marquis d'Argenson' (unpublished Ph.D. thesis – New Haven: Yale University, 1968); Neal Johnson, 'L'idéologie politique du Marquis d'Argenson, d'après ses œuvres inédites', in Roland Mortier and Hervé Hasquin (eds.), *Études sur le XVIIIᵉ siècle – Volume 11: Idéologies de la noblesse* (Brussels: Éditions de l'Université libre de Bruxelles, 1984), 21–8; Guy Thuillier, 'La réforme de l'administration selon le Marquis d'Argenson', *La revue administrative*, 44 (1991), 213–23; Péter Balázs, 'La monarchie républicaine du Marquis d'Argenson', *Studi francesi*, 53 (2009), 506–18.

[25] See Goulemot, *Le règne de l'histoire*, 341–2, and Péter Balázs, 'Philosophie et histoire dans l'œuvre du Marquis d'Argenson', *Dix-huitième siècle*, 42 (2010), 561–79. On the contrary, Elie Carcassonne insisted on the similarities between Dubos and d'Argenson's views: Carcassonne, *Montesquieu et le problème de la constitution française*, 45–50.

[26] D'Argenson, *Considérations sur le gouvernement ancien et présent de la France*, 122–3.

[27] D'Argenson, 'Pensées sur la réformation de l'État', 325–7.

gradually acquired a hereditary character, so that unwarranted privileges were now unjustly passed down from father to sons. As a result, nobility no longer performed its proper function, that is, rewarding those who served the state. Expounding his project in a later work, d'Argenson even considered the essential function of the monarchy to be that of impeding the rise of a hereditary nobility, in his view the greatest of evils. He was adamant that when 'the personal merits of a citizen enrich and win renown for his own race, and procure to his undeserving offspring a power that is dangerous to common liberty', the welfare of the state is in jeopardy.[28] Against the vestiges of feudal rule, this system 'so much praised by Monsieur de *Boulainvilliers*', d'Argenson boldly overturned the principle of hereditary nobility: '[T]there is', he declared, 'an aristocracy much nobler and more elevated, I believe: it is that *everyone be the son of his works*, and rule if he deserves'.[29] Although he accepted and even welcomed a separation of nobles and commoners, deeming it beneficial to the state, d'Argenson insisted nonetheless that the advantages of nobility as a legal status should be accessible to all who earned it. Men were always born commoners, and only their deeds made them noble. In accordance with these ideas, d'Argenson insisted that in order to reform the French state it was necessary that the privileges of the nobility be curtailed so that, a separate class, it would once again 'merge with the nation'.[30] As for the notion of there being a noble race, although d'Argenson conceded that some members of the high nobility might indeed have been the descendants of the barbaric leaders invading Europe at the fall of the Roman Empire, he insisted that this was of no political consequence. What counted was that the existence of a class enjoying undeserved privileges was detrimental to the nation at large.[31] It is worth noting that in several ways d'Argenson was following in the footsteps of his friend the abbé de Saint-Pierre, a scholar whom the marquis profoundly admired.[32] In 1734, in fact, the abbé had praised Louis XIV for taming the seditious ambitions of the kingdom's grandees and curbing their influence.[33] But like d'Argenson, the abbé was himself a critic of absolute rule and sought a reform of the monarchy to avoid the risk that France might fall prey to despotism.[34] Again, like d'Argenson he also insisted on the need to make of personal merit the

---

[28] Ibid., 265.   [29] Ibid., 305–6. Italics in the text.   [30] Ibid., 262.

[31] D'Argenson, *Considérations sur le gouvernement ancien et présent de la France*, 84.

[32] On d'Argenson's admiration, see his comment in the 'Pensées sur la réformation de l'État', on page 259.

[33] Charles-Irénée Castel de Saint-Pierre, 'Observations politiques sur le gouvernement des rois de France', in *Ouvrajes de politique*, ix. 278–80.

[34] See Thomas E. Kaiser, 'The abbé de Saint-Pierre, Public Opinion, and the Reconstitution of the French Monarchy', *The Journal of Modern History*, 55 (1983), 618–43, and Andrew Mansfield, *Ideas of*

sole criterion of social distinction and the principle to be followed when assigning offices.[35] But the two also shared a preoccupation with the condition of the lower classes. For his part, the abbé condemned the laziness of the wealthy and deemed it a duty of the state to assuage the sufferings of the poor – a rather original notion at that time.[36] The marquis was perhaps even more sympathetic. He admired the supposed egalitarianism and the sharing of property of the Jesuits' state in Paraguay, praised Rousseau for his *Discours sur l'origine et les fondements de l'inégalité*, and even lauded the work of the utopian thinker Étienne-Gabriel Morelly (1717–1778), the *Code de la nature* (1755), that 'excellent book, the book of books'.[37] As he wrote with much feeling, it was the 'inequality of wealth, which is daily increased by misery, that produces universal poverty, replacing abundance with famine. . . . All these unhappy people become a slave and fall into servitude under some rich man.'[38] But, d'Argenson asked his readers, what could be 'crueller than to see oneself oppressed' by someone who has no 'other talents than being born noble and rich?' To put an end to this wretched state of affairs, it would be 'necessary that the *lands be only owned by those who cultivate them*', according to their capacities. Not only would this be fairer, in the marquis's judgement, but it would moreover increase productivity tenfold, to the great advantage of the state.[39] Here was a vindication of the benefits of small properties and

---

Monarchical Reform: Fénelon, Jacobitism, and the Political Works of the Chevalier Ramsay (Manchester: Manchester University Press, 2015), 129–35.

[35] Simona Gregori, 'Éthique du travail, anoblissement et mérite chez l'abbé de Saint-Pierre', in Carole Dornier and Claudine Poulouin (eds.), *Les projets de l'abbé Castel de Saint-Pierre, 1658–1743: Pour le plus grand bonheur du plus grand nombre* (Caen: Presses universitaires de Caen, 2011), 81–90.

[36] On his censuring of the laziness of the wealthy, see Charles-Irénée Castel de Saint-Pierre, 'Avantages que doit produire l'agrandissement continuel de la ville capitale d'un État' (1733), in *Ouvrajes de politique*, iv. 144. That the state had the duty to take care of the poorest was a claim that the abbé repeated in many of his works. See, for example: Charles-Irénée Castel de Saint-Pierre, 'Observations concernant le ministère de l'Intérieur de l'État' (1734), in *Ouvrajes de politique*, vii. 252; Charles-Irénée Castel de Saint-Pierre, 'Agaton, archevêque très vertueux, très sage et très heureux' (1735), in *Ouvrajes de politique*, x. 364–8; Charles-Irénée Castel de Saint-Pierre, 'Pour multiplier les maîtres d'école et les sœurs grises' (1737), in *Ouvrajes de politique*, xiii. 366–7.

[37] René-Louis de Voyer de Paulmy d'Argenson, *Considérations sur le gouvernement ancien et présent de la France* (Amsterdam: n.p., 1784), 109–16, especially 113; the chapter on Paraguay was not included in the 1764 edition; René-Louis de Voyer de Paulmy d'Argenson, '*Discours sur l'inégalité des conditions des hommes*, par J.-J. Rousseau' (September 1755), in *Mémoires et journal inédit*, v. 123–4; René-Louis de Voyer de Paulmy d'Argenson, '*Code de la nature*, ou Le véritable *Esprit des lois*', in *Mémoires et journal inédit*, v. 137. The *Code* was published anonymously, and d'Argenson erroneously believed it was the work of François-Vincent Toussaint: ibid., 138.

[38] René-Louis de Voyer de Paulmy d'Argenson, *Journal et mémoires* (Paris: Veuve de J. Renouard, 1859–1867), vii. 90 (31 January 1751).

[39] D'Argenson, 'Pensées sur la réformation de l'État', 305 and 314; italics in the text.

praise of a work ethic and the capacity of men as much as a rejection of all privileges stemming from birth.

As might be expected, d'Argenson's idea of a 'monarchical democracy' was far from representative of the general opinion of the day. Even the abbé de Saint-Pierre, often himself labelled a utopian by his contemporaries, judged the marquis's ideas to be far too detached from reality.[40] However, it was a work much read and discussed, first of all within that remarkable forum of debate that was the Entresol Club – of which d'Argenson was a prominent member.[41] Even before its publication, it circulated widely in manuscript form. The abbé de Saint-Pierre knew the original text and commented on it. Fontenelle may well have read it too.[42] In 1764, the year of its publication, Rousseau quoted it in a footnote to his *Contrat social*, and as early as 1737 Voltaire, mistakenly seeing in it a celebration of enlightened monarchy, enthusiastically declared d'Argenson's manuscript to be the 'best work' he had 'read in over twenty years'.[43] To judge by the arguments set out in it, it might even be ventured that the marquis's work influenced Dupont de Nemours and Turgot's famous *Mémoires sur les municipalités*.[44] All this notwithstanding, and however influential the marquis's works may later have been, the history of the French burghers and of the bourgeoisie as a class was to be more profoundly affected by the work of another author. Enthusiastically hailed in 1790 as a 'masterpiece of patriotism, erudition, and philosophy', a work held in the 'hands of every citizen', and in which, for one observer, all Frenchmen could find 'the heritage of their fathers', Mably's *Observations sur l'histoire de France* was to become a foundational text of the republican discourse of the Revolution.[45]

---

[40] Charles-Irénée Castel de Saint-Pierre, 'Observations sur l'ouvrage politique manuscrit de M.' (Paris: Bibliothèque de l'Arsenal, MS manuscrits français, 2337), 4. The abbé's remarks were attached to a letter sent to d'Argenson on 8 April 1738. On the abbé as a utopian thinker see, for example: Saint-Simon, *Mémoires*, vi. 650 (1718); François-Marie Arouet Voltaire to Nicolas-Claude Thieriot, 29 December 1738, in *Correspondance* (Paris: Gallimard, 1977–1992), i. 1231; Grimm et al., *Correspondance littéraire*, iii. 474 (15 February 1758).

[41] See Nick Childs, *A Political Academy in Paris, 1724–1731: The Entresol and its Members* (Oxford: Voltaire Foundation, 2000), passim. A discussion of d'Argenson's *Considérations* is in ibid., 185–90.

[42] That Fontenelle had read it is suggested by the abbé de Saint-Pierre: Saint-Pierre, 'Observations sur l'ouvrage politique manuscrit de M.', 4.

[43] Rousseau, 'Du contrat social', 467; the quote is not to be found in the 1764 edition of the *Considérations* but is, instead, in the manuscript. François-Marie Arouet Voltaire to René-Louis de Voyer de Paulmy d'Argenson, 28 July 1739, in *Œuvres*, xxxv. 308. On the sincerity, or lack thereof, of Voltaire's comments, see Ongle, *The Marquis d'Argenson*, 253, n. 420.

[44] Turgot, 'Mémoire sur les municipalités à établir en France', 568–621. It is a suggestion made by Smith, *Nobility Reimagined*, 63. On Turgot and his influence on the notions of class and nation, see Chapter 7.

[45] François Marie de Kerversau, *Histoire de la Révolution de 1789* (Paris: Clavelin, 1790), i. 83. Mably's *Observations* were substantially revised and republished posthumously in 1788. See Wright,

Like several authors of his day, the abbé de Mably believed that the history of France amounted to little else but the lamentable story of the degeneration of its ancient constitution.[46] Trying to avoid the errors of the royalist as well as those of the nobility's interpretation of the French past, he espoused the idea of a Frankish conquest but insisted on the notion, already embraced by Montesquieu, that each and every Gaul had been free to decide whether to remain under Roman law or accept the laws of the conquerors. By simply declaring their resolve to abandon the Roman forms of rule and to live under the Salic or the Ripuarian Laws, the Gauls immediately started enjoying the rights of the Franks. Through this act of will, 'from subjects they became citizens, they acquired a place in the assemblies of the *Champs de Mars* and partook of the sovereignty and administration of the state'.[47] Mably's contention was that the Franks destroyed the imperial oppression and ruled only over those who resigned themselves to a condition of subjugation. Here was a drastic downplaying of the opposition between the two races – and, unsurprisingly, it earned Thierry's stern censure.[48] As for the reasons for the internecine divisions and conflicts within modern France, they had to be sought elsewhere. The deplorable predicament of the French, argued Mably, had been brought about by a series of events that had turned the benefits granted by the king upon merit into hereditary and undeserved privileges. It was to equality that the French nation had originally owed its inner cohesion. Distinctions and divisions were the outcome of revolutions that had led a few, impelled by their blind egoism, to take advantage of the weaker and 'form a separate class'.[49] The creation of the nobility, a class that was unknown to the Franks, was the result of turns that Mably dated back to the kingdom of Chlothar II (584–629) and that had finally led to the 'monstrous anarchy of feudal government'.[50] Before then, nobility had never been considered a quality passed on from father to sons, for it was 'not transmitted by blood'. The children of noblemen remained part of the 'common class of

A Classical Republican in Eighteenth-Century France, passim, and Baker, 'A Script for a French Revolution', 86–106. For convenience, other aspects of Mably's thought have been dealt with in Chapter 6.

[46] Wright, *A Classical Republican in Eighteenth-Century France*, 125–61; also see Furet and Ozouf, 'Deux légitimations historiques de la société française au XVIIIᵉ siècle', 165–83.

[47] Mably, 'Observations sur l'histoire de France', 151. For the baron's claim, see Montesquieu, 'Esprit des lois', 796–9 (book xxviii. ch. 4).

[48] Thierry, 'Considérations sur l'histoire de France', 91–105.

[49] Mably, 'Doutes proposés aux philosophes économistes sur l'ordre naturel et essentiel des sociétés politiques', 399.

[50] Mably, 'Observations sur l'histoire de France', 289.

citizens' until they had proven their valour and their dedication to the
nation.[51] Viewed from this angle, the debasing of France was largely
a consequence of the fact that while the composition of the classes of
commoners and nobles should have changed according to the merits of
each person, instead it remained essentially the same. Belonging to a class
had become a consequence of birth, so that the advantages enjoyed by the
nobles came to be detached from their real merits.

For the purposes of our own argument, it is noteworthy that Mably
contributed to introducing the notion of class, albeit with a still fluctuating
and uncertain meaning, in the debates over the origins of the French
constitution. In his *Doutes proposés aux philosophes économistes*, a work
written to counter Lemercier's views on the 'natural and essential order
of society', the abbé suggested in fact that the division between nobles and
commoners, though initially based on merit and honour, slowly became
inseparable from the unfair ambition of the nobility 'to live at the expense
of others without effort'.[52] Such a change was explained by Mably by the
fact that the Franks, after settling in Gaul, gradually lost their love of
freedom and their warring nature, lured by the luxuries and pleasures of
their newly sedentary existence. They exchanged, that is, their love
of honour for a passion for wealth.[53] Implied by Mably was the coupling
of the emergence of legal privileges with the increasing greed of the
nobility. In conjunction, these two factors would in the end engender
a clear-cut dichotomy between the interests of the wealthy second order on
the one hand, and those of the poor commoners and burghers on the other.
Confirmation lies in the fact that Mably used the word 'class' to indicate
a group united by a legal status – with a meaning close to that of 'order' – as
well as a group of individuals sharing an interest of an essentially economic
nature.[54] According to Mably, the divisions within the nation created by
privileges and unjust laws could only be overcome by extending political
power to all classes. To do so, it was necessary that group interests merge
into a single, coherent national interest. In the abbé's own words, since 'the
different orders that compose the nation have opposing interests, it is
necessary to draw them together and, by giving them a common interest,
to place them in a position to compromise with one another. The country

---

[51] Ibid., 181. Also see Guerci, 'Note sulla storiografia di Mably', 489–90.
[52] Mably, 'Doutes proposés aux philosophes économistes sur l'ordre naturel et essentiel des sociétés
politiques', 33. On the quarrel, see Wright, *A Classical Republican in Eighteenth-Century France*,
109–21, and Bach, *Rousseau et le discours de la Révolution*, 40–58.
[53] On Mably's views on the characters of the Gauls and the Franks, see Chapter 6.
[54] On the meaning of 'class' in the writings of the abbé, see Piguet, *Classe*, 26–30.

or the public good,' he went on, 'is a first bond uniting the citizens of a republic.'[55] If only citizens were permitted to debate their ideas and further their claims on equal terms with one another, they would learn to make reciprocal concessions. Although Mably's was not a call for a restoration of the ancient Frankish constitution, such views nonetheless took inspiration from his interpretation of their assemblies. In fact, the solution to the French predicament rested for him in a mixed government that, in this, resembled that of the Franks, a 'democratic rule with a moderate prince'.[56] Rejecting the idea of their ever having had an absolute ruler, Mably also claimed that the only distinction between the Franks and their king was a functional one, the latter acting more as a general and an administrator than as a monarch, and only wielding executive power through a council. The legislative authority was vested in the *Champs de Mars*, where all Franks, as well those Gauls who had joined them, took part in deciding the most important political matters. From the abbé's standpoint, this was a form of rule that, because it was moderate, might recompose divergent interests and pacify the nation, uniting classes and orders through a common and higher interest. Indeed, reconciling the divergent concerns of the different classes was tantamount to abolishing them as such or, rather, to abolishing nobility as a hereditary class. It is perhaps unsurprising, given the underlying implications of such an argument, that some observers saw in Mably an advocate of the rights of the people. The great German poet and scholar Heinrich Heine (1797–1856), for one, was led to believe that Mably had adopted 'everywhere in his history the democratic viewpoint', seeking justifications for the claims of the Third Estate lost in a 'never ending game of usurpations'.[57] However, in this regard it is worth remarking that rather than suppressing the rights of the nobility, the abbé sought to extend these to the Third Estate since the bedrock of his ideas was the Germanist thesis and the notion of an allegedly Frankish origin of the nation's constitution.[58] The Gallo-Romans, with their beliefs, values, and ways of life, were of seemingly little consequence to the abbé.

---

[55] Mably, 'Doutes proposés aux philosophes économistes sur l'ordre naturel et essentiel des sociétés politiques', 171.

[56] Mably, 'Observations sur l'histoire de France', 133.

[57] Heinrich Heine, 'Französische Zustände' (1832), in *Historisch-Kritische Gesamtausgabe der Werke* (Hamburg: Hoffmann & Campe, 1975–1997), xii/1. 468.

[58] Lucien Calvié, '*Liberté, libertés* et *liberté(s) germanique(s)*: Une question franco-allemande, avant et après 1789', *Mots*, 16 (1988), 15.

Classes and the French Constitution
in the Pre-revolutionary and the Early Revolutionary Years

The aftermath of the Maupeou coup, with the emergence of the *parti patriote*, witnessed an upsurge in books and pamphlets on the historical rights of the Third Estate.[59] Their number constantly increased over the ensuing years, reaching a peak at the time of the 1788–1789 debates following the Count de Brienne's (1730–1794) famous call for the crown's subjects to express their views on how the Estates General should be convoked.[60] Interestingly, in 1758 Mably correctly predicted that as soon as the 'nation will be wise enough to call for the convocation of the Estates General and sufficiently firm to obtain them. . ., a thousand pamphlets will appear to instruct the public as to its interests'.[61] Crucially, in these debates, the question of the place of history itself in assessing the legitimacy of the existing institutions was brought to the fore. Indeed, and for obvious reasons, a far greater weight was attributed to the past and to tradition by the champions of the first two orders. On their part, and for equally understandable motives, the advocates of the rights of the Third Estate often downplayed or denied altogether the importance of what had once been.[62] For one, Rabaut de Saint-Étienne flatly denied that 'our history is our code'. Others concurred. The essayists Philippe-Antoine Grouvelle (1758–1806) and Joseph-Antoine-Joachim Cérutti (1738–1792) both lamented that the French constitution had produced an incessant oscillation between barbaric anarchy and despotic rule and that, in effect, it amounted to little else than an inchoate congeries of Frankish, Roman, and Langobard rules. Others wondered whether 'in a century of philosophy' and given the many achievements of the 'science of legislation', men still ought to be led by the examples of centuries of 'ignorance and oppression'.[63] For his part, Mercier noted that 'the abbé Mably had no need to fight against M. Moreau', and that he had 'no need to recall the

---

[59] Echeverria, *The Maupeou Revolution*, 37–122, and Peter R. Campbell, 'La rhétorique patriotique et le monde parlementaire', in Lemaître (ed.), *Le monde parlementaire au XVIIIᵉ siècle*, 193–220.

[60] See the famous decree by the Conseil d'État du Roi, *Arrêt concernant la convocation des États généraux du Royaume du 5 Juillet 1788* (Paris: Nyon, 1788), 3–4 and 6–7.

[61] Gabriel Bonnot de Mably, 'Des droits et des devoirs du citoyen', in *Œuvres*, xi. 453.

[62] Carcassonne, *Montesquieu et le problème de la constitution française au XVIIIᵉ siècle*, 581–658.

[63] [Rabaut de Saint-Étienne], *Considérations très-importantes sur les intérêts du tiers état*, 13; [Philippe-Antoine Grouvelle], *De l'autorité de Montesquieu dans la révolution présente* (n.p., 1789), 114–5; Joseph-Antoine-Joachim Cérutti, *Vues générales sur la constitution françoise, ou Exposé des droits de l'homme, dans l'ordre naturel, social et monarchique* (Paris: Desenne, 1789), 17; P.-V. de Calonges, *Lettres aux notables, sur la forme et l'objet des États généraux* (London: chez les marchands de nouveautés, 1788), 17.

most ancient and most respectable monuments of our nation', for 'even if national freedom had never existed, nothing would impede the French from being freed today'.[64] Historical precedents were for Mercier of little relevance. The lawyer and politician Pierre-Louis de Lacretelle (1751–1824) sought to provoke his readers by expressing a wish for the destruction of the nation's monuments so that 'we would no longer be tempted to return to them, leading our reason astray'.[65] Obviously, denying historical scholarship any worth in appraising the legitimacy of the kingdom's institutions was tantamount to denying any importance to the idea of an ancient constitution, that is, a set of fixed rules and norms confirmed by tradition and influencing or even shaping the nation's history. It was a view that did not go unchallenged, even by the supporters of the Third Estate. For one, the magistrate and politician Jacques Duval d'Éprémesnil (1745–1794) censured those authors 'who are sufficiently foolish or sufficiently deceitful to claim that the French kingdom has no constitution'.[66] Even more interesting – and rather unusual – was the stance adopted by the Count d'Antraigues (1753–1812), in the early phases of the Revolution a supporter of the rights of the Third Estate. In a pamphlet published in 1788 he insisted, on the one hand, on the importance of the past in shedding light on the rights of the French nation. He expressed his admiration for the laws of 'our ancestors', as 'simple as their *mœurs*', on which Montesquieu had 'commented with great ingenuity', and he followed Mably's 'excellent work', the *Observations*, in portraying the laws of the ancient Franks.[67] On the other hand, the count wrote of the 'immutable law of nature' and emphasised the importance of the strength of numbers: 'The Third Estate is the people, and the people is the foundation of the state. It is the state itself. The other orders are but political divisions while the people are, by the immutable law of nature, everything.'[68]

[64] Louis-Sébastien Mercier, *Notions claires sur les gouvernemens* (Amsterdam: n.p., 1787), i. 149. See also Jean-Antoine-Nicolas de Condorcet, *Sur les fonctions des États-généraux et des autres assemblées nationales* (n.p., 1789), i. 134–5.
[65] Pierre-Louis de Lacretelle, *De la convocation de la prochaine tenue des États généraux en France* (n.p., 1788), 12.
[66] [Jacques Duval d'Éprémesnil – uncertain attribution], *Réflexions impartiales sur la grande question qui partage les esprits, concernant les droits du roi et de la nation assemblée en états généraux* (n.p., 1789), 5.
[67] D'Antraigues, *Mémoire sur les États-généraux, leurs droits, et la manière de les convoquer*, 16–17, 56–7, and 72. On the count's life and thought, see Roger Barny, *Le Comte d'Antraigues, un disciple aristocrate de J.-J. Rousseau: De la fascination au reniement, 1782–1797* (Oxford: Voltaire Foundation, 1991).
[68] D'Antraigues, *Mémoire sur les États-généraux, leurs droits, et la manière de les convoquer*, 246.

Importantly, in the works of the few learned scholars and the many pamphleteers and publicists who sought in the past the reasons for the claims of the Third Estate were merged – often incoherently – disparate elements of the Germanist and Romanist theses. As Furet noted some time ago, one remarkable aspect of the debates shaping the political discourses of the pre-revolutionary period and the early phases of the Revolution is that in many writings championing a greater role for the Third Estate the nation's history was held to begin with the Franks rather than the Gallo-Romans.[69] From this angle, the real alternative seemed at the time to have been between Boulainvilliers's and Mably's visions of the French past. In effect, although the ministerial party still resorted to Dubos's thesis, the belief that the foundations of the constitution lay in an original alliance between the Gallo-Roman burghers and the crown had lost much of its appeal. The importance of the enfranchisement did emerge in a few texts, and some authors even followed the arguments set out by Bréquigny.[70] Others, instead, to oppose the demands of the nobility and combat the claims of the royalists, revived a notion outlined in Hotman's *Francogallia* and other sixteenth-century works and wrote of a 'Gallic republic'.[71] However, the vast majority of the champions of the Third Estate founded their arguments on the Germanist thesis. It was an aim that they pursued by extending the rights of the nobility in such a way as to include the members of the Third Estate themselves. In many respects, it was a novel way of rethinking the old struggle between Franks and Gauls. Or, in some instances, erasing it altogether from the nation's past. Such was the case, for example, with a pamphlet published in 1788 by the Marquis de Casaux (1727–1796). In his *Le tiers état entièrement éclairé sur ses droits*, after identifying the Third Estate with the 'body of the French nation' at

[69] François Furet, 'Penser la Révolution française', in Furet, *La Révolution française*, 47–8. For a detailed account on the importance of historical arguments in the Pre-revolution, see Kenneth Margerison, 'History, Representative Institutions, and Political Rights in the French Pre-revolution (1787–1789)', *French Historical Studies*, 15 (1987), 68–98; also see Dale K. Van Kley, 'New Wine in Old Wineskins: Continuity and Rupture in the Pamphlet Debate of the French Prerevolution, 1787–1789', *French Historical Studies*, 17 (1991), 447–65.

[70] Joseph Honoré Remy, 'Communes', in Joseph-Nicolas Guyot (ed.), *Répertoire universel et raisonné de jurisprudence civile, criminelle, canonique et bénéficiale* (Paris: J. Dorez, 1775–1783), xiii. 301–17, especially 302–4.

[71] [Joseph-Michel Pellerin], *Mémoire historique sur la constitution des États de Bretagne, adressé aux gentilshommes bretons, à l'occasion de la question de droit public, actuellement agitée en cette province, si la noblesse a, par le droit constitutionnel de la province, celui d'assister en corps, et par individus aux assemblées des gens des trois états du pays et duché de Bretagne* (n.p., November 1788), 6. See François Hotman, *Francogallia* (Cambridge: Cambridge University Press, 1972), 146, and Michel de Castelnau, *Traitte des meurs et facons des anciens Gauloys* (Paris: Denys du Val, 1581), especially 20–2 and 95. The first edition of de Castelnau's work was published in Latin in 1559.

large, the marquis went on to make the rather unusual claim that its members represented 'essentially the first Franks who have founded the monarchy'. The 'irruption' of the Franks into the lands of the Gauls he saw as the beginning of the nation's history. He mentioned, glancingly, that the Gauls had been 'subjugated', but then claimed that both Franks and Gauls, 'merged together', had formed the *Champs de Mars* and the *Champs de Mai*, the precursors of the Estates General. The obvious inconsistency was left unexplained. Nor was there any attempt at describing the condition of the Gallo-Romans before the Franks crossed the Rhine. Furthermore, argued the marquis, the Franks saw themselves as being one and all equal since 'all distinctions would have been contrary to their character'. Therefore, they possessed no notion of nobility as a body separate from the rest of the nation. The divisions within modern France were the outcome of a usurpation that took place much later, with the creation of fiefs, under the Carolingian kings. Indeed, he noted, it was 'property in land that created nobility' rather than the title of nobleman granting possession.[72]

One common argument of this version of the Germanist thesis was that the Frankish conquest, if there had ever been one, did not have any lasting consequences and that, as one of the countless pamphleteers claimed, the nation's ancient constitution was essentially 'democratic'. The Franks had brought liberty to the Gauls.[73] Iniquity and oppression appeared much later on, partly as an outcome of the merging of the Gallo-Romans, a 'decadent people', and the Franks, a 'barbarous people'. Their union had deleterious effects, and finally led to division, violence, and 'hereditary economic privileges'.[74] The deep-seated divisions afflicting France were therefore not the outcome of a struggle between races but, rather, a consequence of injustice and class distinctions. It was now time to 'restore to the largest and most useful class . . .its imprescriptible rights, which are due to it by nature and by the ancient French constitution'.[75] It was an essentially egalitarian and republican argument rooted in a specific reading of the relationship between the *mœurs* of the Frankish tribes and their love for freedom and seen as the sole effective countermeasure to the distorting effects of class distinctions. In many respects, it recalled the arguments outlined long before by Mably – to whom the author of the pamphlet repeatedly referred.[76]

---

[72] Alexandre Charles de Casaux, *Le tiers état entièrement éclairé sur ses droits, ou supplément à l'avis important par le même auteur* (n.p., 1788), 5–6 and 9.

[73] [De Murat-Montferrand], *Qu'est-ce que la noblesse, et que sont ses privilèges?* (Amsterdam: n.p., 1789), 5–6.

[74] Ibid., 8.   [75] Ibid., 1.   [76] Ibid., footnotes on pages 4, 6, 11, and 14.

In truth, it is unsurprising that in works by authors who espoused
a version of the Germanist thesis sympathetic to the cause of the Third
Estate, references to Mably's views were common currency, many of his
arguments being revived, rethought, and recast in a new form.[77] Another
instance was a short pamphlet entitled the *Observations sur l'état passé,
présent et futur de la nation* (1789). Written after 'the most oppressed, but
the most learned' had 'declared themselves to be the nation', this pamphlet
recalled the centuries-long humiliations suffered by the Third Estate at the
hands of the privileged orders and under the yoke of absolute rule.[78] The
author asked his readers what had finally led the Third Estate to institute
the National Assembly. The unequivocal answer to that rhetorical question
involved a reference to the new awareness on the part of the French –
whom he identified with the Third Estate itself – of their rights. This turn
had been encouraged by the 'works of the writer philosophes' and Mably in
particular, the greatest of them all. In fact, the abbé had shown to all the
true role of Charlemagne, 'who recognised the inalienable rights of man'
and who 'persuaded the different orders' of the need to reconcile their
interests. It was under his rule that the French realised that 'a class of
citizens could not be happy if it oppressed the others'.[79] The lawyer and
representative of the Third Estate in the National Assembly Jean-Joseph
Mounier (1758–1806), himself an admirer of Mably, borrowed and
readapted many of the abbé's arguments. In his *Nouvelles observations sur
les États-généraux de France* (1789), he made the claim that at the inception
of the French monarchy all citizens, regardless of their Frankish or Gallic
origins, were able to participate in the polity. Although there were
distinctions of rank, 'these were not by birth', but based on their services
to the nation and an oath to the king. Moreover, noted Mounier, the
grandees and the prelates were not separate from other citizens, and 'their
families did not form a distinct class'.[80] Consistently with such views, he
concluded that in the assemblies all decisions were originally voted by
head and that the current vote by orders in the Estates General violated
the ancient laws. The authors of the *Testament du publiciste patriote*
(1789) repeated verbatim many of the passages contained in Mably's
Observations. They maintained that although the Franks wholly ignored

[77] On Mably's influence on the Pre-Revolution, see Schleich, *Aufklärung und Revolution*, 117–50.
[78] Mousnier, *Observations sur l'état passé, présent et futur de la nation; et De l'influence du publiciste Mably sur la Révolution* (Paris: Imprimerie nationale, n.d.), 5–7.
[79] Ibid., 11.
[80] Jean-Joseph Mounier, *Nouvelles observations sur les États-généraux de France* (n.p., 1789), 8–9.

the very meaning of slavery, in all political matters they considered 'Gallic blood lesser' than their own.[81] Over time and thanks to the mediation of the clergy, the Gauls became part of the 'body of the victorious nation'. They ceased living under the Roman and embraced the Salic Laws, now enjoying the prerogatives and rights of the Franks.[82] Within this new, cohesive society, divisions were established only on merit and service to the nation. Ennobling only concerned single citizens, not their families. Privileges were not hereditary, and the children of a noble 'remained in the class of commoners'. Indeed, the authors argued, citizens did belong to 'two different classes, but the families were all of the same order'. It was only later on that privileges became hereditary, giving birth to a new – and detestable – nobility that still endured. From then onwards, the families enjoying such honours 'formed a separate class'.[83]

To be sure, there was little originality in the arguments made by these pamphleteers. Following in Mably's footsteps, they all downplayed the role of the original conquest, argued for a gradual merging of Franks and Gauls, and insisted on the unjust transformation of rights granted upon merit into hereditary and undeserved privileges. What is interesting is instead the juxtaposition – curious to the modern reader – of ideas that belonged to Old Regime political thought, like the centrality of families, and concepts that are strikingly modern, such as the notion of individual rights. Of course, this confirms the sheer complexity of the political languages developing during this foundational phase. But it also highlights the vagueness of the idea of class, a term used, rather loosely, to indicate a sort of division within society and in some cases overlapping with the notion of order. In other pamphlets penned by the advocates of the Third Estate, the notion of class began to denote a group endowed with a unity of intent – necessary to conceive of it as a political and historical actor – and was predicated on the assumption that one class exploited the other – necessary to claim a moral right to seize political power. These ideas featured, for example, in the *États-généraux, ou Histoire des assemblées nationales en France* (1788) by the writer and lawyer Antoine-François Delandine (1756–1820). Rejecting the view that the ancient constitution established a division between Franks and Gauls, Delandine claimed that after the invasion of their lands, the Gauls were free to choose between different forms of rule.[84]

[81] [Jacob Vernes and Joseph-François-Marie Malherbe], *Testament du publiciste patriote, ou Précis des 'Observations de M. l'abbé de Mably sur l'histoire de France'* (The Hague: Bleuet fils aîné, 1789), 10–11.
[82] Ibid., 14.   [83] Ibid., 33–4.
[84] Antoine-François Delandine, *Des États-généraux, ou Histoire des assemblées nationales en France* (Paris: Cuchet, 1788), 9.

Distinctions of rank were not a consequence of the initial conquest but the outcome of rewards granted by the king to Gauls and Franks alike on the sole basis of merit.[85] As in Mably's works, this was an assessment that toned down the importance of conquest in the creation of the legal rights of the nobility. Yet departing from the abbé's theories, Delandine went on to claim that the Gallic form of rule was aristocratic in nature and that the 'druids and the nobles or the warriors' held all political authority. In contrast, the government of the Franks was monarchical, though 'regulated by the assemblies of the nation'. In the wake of the conquest, the Franks adopted the aristocratic form of government of the Gauls.[86] One interesting aspect of Delandine's argument was his claim that until there were nobles and serfs in France, that is to say, until there were 'two classes of men', the assemblies were 'never truly national, since the largest part of the nation did not take part in it and its wishes never contributed to the decisions taken'. Delandine lamented that under the Merovingian and Carolingian dynasties, workers, merchants, and artisans living in towns and villages were looked upon 'as useless to the glory of the state' and had no right to attend the assemblies. It was not until they were 'counted as men' that the kings encouraged the rise of the communes. Only then did the members of the lower classes become 'once again free men, if commoners', and able to take part in the 'assemblies of the nation, which henceforth deserve the proper title of "Estates General"'.[87]

The former Commissaire des guerres, Jean-Louis Mignonneau (1740?–1816?), followed the line of argument common to most champions of the Third Estate. In his *Considérations intéressantes sur les affaires présentes* (1788), he contended that, free at the time of Roman rule, the Gauls were equally free after the invasion of the Franks, who, having fought only against the Romans, had left them their freedom and possessions.[88] Originally and under the Merovingian dynasty, nobility was not a right stemming from conquest but a title granted by the crown to Franks and Gauls, who, therefore, were not a 'class or a caste separate from the nation'.[89] Birth, the author claimed trenchantly, 'was nothing', since rights conferred on merit could never be hereditary. The ancient constitution began to be debased at the end of the Merovingian dynasty, when the *Maires du Palais* took advantage of the weakness of the monarch and 'created a fixed hierarchy' that eventually gave birth 'to a class distinct

---

[85] Delandine, *Des États-généraux*, 19.   [86] Ibid., 10–13.   [87] Ibid., 33–4.
[88] [Jean-Louis Mignonneau], *Considérations intéressantes sur les affaires présentes* (London and Paris: Barrois, 1788), 37–9.
[89] Ibid., 53.

from the other classes of citizens'.[90] The crisis of the French monarchy was then a result of, and an incentive to, the rise of a privileged class, its members passing down their unjust entitlements from father to son. It was a consequence of the fact that 'the superior classes have affranchised themselves from most of the contributions', which now weighed entirely 'on the class of the people, which is yet the one suffering the most and the poorest'. This was largely imputable to the unjust division of the Estates General into three different orders, an unfair and damaging separation that went against 'the primitive constitution of the monarchy'.[91] For his part, Guy-Jean Baptiste Target (1733–1806), the well-known lawyer and member of the Society of Thirty, saluted as 'the Fontenelle of politics' during the Maupeou coup, insisted on the dangers of group and class interests running counter to the public good.[92] A convinced supporter of the 'union des ordres' and of the doubling of the representatives of the Third Estate, in a controversial pamphlet published in 1788 he offered an overview of the history of the Estates General, arguing that the source of all the perplexities faced by his fellow citizens lay in the division of orders. On the basis of a complex historical argumentation, Target tried to show that the principle of separate deliberation was a recent development and, on such an understanding, insisted that the convening of the Estates General should not abide by the rules used in 1614, since these were the expression of 'a degenerated constitution'.[93] Convening the Estates General on those principles would be contrary to tradition and would also entail an unfair representation of the Third Estate, the true bulk of the nation.[94] The union of orders, far from being a radical change of the French constitution, would involve reverting to 'following more faithfully the path of the ancient and national will'.[95] Although the increase in the number of the representatives of the Third Estate was intended by Target neither as an attack on the

[90] Ibid., 55.   [91] Ibid., 31.

[92] [Mathieu-François Pidanzat de Mairobert], *Journal historique de la révolution opérée dans la constitution de la monarchie françoise* (London: n.p., 1774–1776), ii. 69. On Target and the Society of Thirty, see Daniel L. Wick, *A Conspiracy of Well-Intentioned Men: The Society of Thirty and the French Revolution* (New York: Garland, 1987), and Kenneth Margerison, *Pamphlets and Public Opinion: The Campaign for a Union of Orders in the Early French Revolution* (West Lafayette: Purdue University Press, 1998), 51–70.

[93] Guy-Jean Baptiste Target, *Suite de l'écrit intitulé Les États-généraux convoqués par Louis XVI* (n.p., 1789), 28. On his campaigning for the 'union des ordres' and the doubling of the Third Estate, see Guy-Jean Baptiste Target, *Les États-généraux convoqués par Louis XVI* (n.p., 1788).

[94] Target, *Suite de l'écrit intitulé Les États-généraux convoqués par Louis XVI*, 7. The same point was repeated in other pamphlets as, for example, in [Baumier], *Protestation contre la forme des États-généraux de 1614* (n.p., 1788).

[95] Target, *Les États-généraux convoqués par Louis XVI*, 23–5.

ancient nobility nor as an opening towards democracy, it was indeed a call for a fairer balancing of power, necessary to lessen the risks of 'ministerial despotism and of the aristocracy of the higher classes'. Moreover, the union of orders would lessen the risk that personal and group identities would prevail over public and general interest – which, for Target, was the crux of the matter. In passing, it is worth noting that this did not concern the distinction made by Target between two classes – 'the owners and those who lived off their industry' – as owners were 'true' citizens since they were, allegedly, more readily attached to the interests of their country.[96]

Supporting the claims of the Third Estate, the anonymous *Esquisse de l'histoire de France par un philosophe impartial* (1788) did so through original arguments, seemingly bringing together certain of Bréquigny's and Mably's views. Acknowledging his debt to the latter and rhetorically asking his readers whether the Gauls had been conquered or freed by the Franks, the author went on to make the case for the existence of liberties enjoyed by the citizens of the towns since 'time immemorial'. He recognised that during the reigns of the Merovingian and Carolingian kings 'the nation comprised but two classes, freemen and slaves'. The first class was made up of the 'conquering race and of the small number of Gauls who escaped their yoke' and who retained their freedom and possessions. The members of such a class could bear arms, enjoyed special privileges, took part in national assemblies, and, together with the king, decided upon the laws of the nation.[97] The rest of the nation, continued the author, was made up of slaves whose only purpose was to feed their masters. Depicting the history of France as a constant fight between king and nobility, he dated to Charlemagne's death the birth of feudal rule and the beginning of a hideous anarchy.[98] Such a state of affairs started to change only with Louis VI, who 'first affranchised the communes', a decision hailed by the author as one of the most 'blissful' in French history. Although it was a reform that took place only in the estates of the monarch, in less than a century the same rights were recognised throughout France so that, finally, 'slavery was almost entirely abolished'.[99] With the increasing authority of the monarchy, the importance of the Third Estate grew enormously, and its weight was fully felt in the 1304 Estates General. And yet, if by then the lower classes had shaken off the yoke of the nobility, they were now facing the tyranny of the monarchy – a tyranny that, the

---

[96] Ibid., 26–7.

[97] Anonymous, 'Esquisse de l'histoire de France par un philosophe impartial', in Laurent-Pierre Bérenger, *Esprit de Mably et de Condillac* (Grenoble: Le Jay fils, 1789), ii. 350.

[98] Anonymous, 'Esquisse de l'histoire de France par un philosophe impartial', 352.   [99] Ibid., 355.

author insisted, could only be ended by restoring the strength of the Third
Estate in a permanent Estates General.

As is clear, in these historical vindications of the rights of the Third
Estate, the notion of class generally referred to uncertain divisions within
society. In some cases, it did denote distinctions between exploiters and
exploited; but usually it lacked the complexity it had, for example, in the
writings of a Turgot.[100] Moreover, in the texts we have considered, the idea
that such distinctions were the consequence of belonging to different races
was downplayed or even rejected altogether. Consequently, even the
identification of the Third Estate with the Gallo-Romans was usually
dismissed. This was a consequence of the attempts made by these authors
to present a more egalitarian image of the Frankish/Gallic assemblies.
Much tighter instead was the relationship they imagined between classes
and orders since the latter, as a legal sanctioning of privileges, grouped men
into parties with interests divergent from the general one – something that,
in turn, also determined the relationship of each party with the nation at
large. However, that legal distinctions favoured economic exploitation did
not automatically lead to the defining of two groups with two distinct sets
of values, *mœurs*, and character. It was only as the Revolution proceeded in
its course and as more radical ideas made headway that an equation
between class, order, and race was established more or less explicitly. The
final outcome would be felt in the writings of Thierry and in those of
Montlosier and Guizot – as we shall see shortly. Only then did class, order,
and race overlap, shaping opposite groups legally divided, with diverging
economic interests, and with different characters; embodying, that is,
opposite values.[101] Two distinct characters came to stand opposed to
each other: the one expressing idleness, the other industriousness; the
one a vice, the other a virtue; the one truly French, the other alien. The
attempts to reconcile nobility and bourgeoisie, made while vindicating
the rights of the Third Estate, were an important pacifying element in
the works considered above. It was lost in the turmoil of the revolutionary
upheaval. Writings like *Qu'est-ce que le tiers-état?*, with the incendiary
principle of exclusion they called for, equating one class-order-race with
the nation, took the assumptions implicit in the previous discourses of the
champions of the Third Estate a short – albeit fundamental – step
forward.[102] The radicalism the Revolution carried within itself, with its

---

[100] On this, see Chapter 7. [101] On this, see Part II of this book.
[102] Furet, 'Penser la Révolution française', 57–8. The crucial role played by Sieyès is discussed at length
in Chapter 7.

Saiges, Robespierres, and Saint-Justs, ultimately led to an ideological and political dichotomy in which two radically different peoples, with their clearly distinct histories and characters, two actors embodying radically different values, were opposed to one another.

In the Wake of the Revolution: Montlosier, Guizot, and Mignet

Amidst the debris of a devastated nation, divided by the Revolution, the Terror, and the civil war in the Vendée, the issue of the origins of France was revived once again by the Count François-Dominique de Montlosier.[103] Although his *De la monarchie française* had originally been commissioned by Napoleon to portray the continuity of monarchy, Consulate, and Empire and prove, in such a way, the legitimacy of his own rule, Montlosier's preoccupation with feudalism and his loathing for the abolition of hereditary ranks caused the emperor's rejection of the book.[104] It was published only in 1814 in three volumes, followed by a fourth in 1815. Montlosier has often been supposed to have rekindled Boulainvilliers's theories, a supposition lent credence by their common views on tradition and feudal rule.[105] In reality, Chateaubriand, who met Montlosier in London in the 1790s and who admired his passionate enthusiasm for the Middle Ages, was right to note that *De la monarchie* 'contained many new ideas' on feudalism and this is true even with reference to Boulainvilliers's own views.[106] Indeed, Montlosier shared with the latter his dread of and repugnance for absolute rule but departed significantly from his predecessor in a number of ways. A crucial divide lay

[103] On Montlosier, his life and ideas, see: Joseph Brugerette, *Le Comte de Montlosier et son temps (1755–1838)* (Aurillac: U.S.H.A., 1931); Robert Casanova, *Montlosier et le parti prêtre* (Paris: Laffont, 1970); Pierre Serna, 'Du noble radical à l'aristocrate tempéré, ou Le Comte de Montlosier et la naissance d'une famille de la droite française durant le Directoire', in Philippe Bourdin (ed.), *Les noblesses françaises dans l'Europe de la Révolution* (Rennes: Presses Universitaires de Rennes, 2010), 177–96; Marie-France Piguet, 'Les "Mémoires" de Montlosier: Ecriture de l'histoire, récit de soi et roman', in Olivier Ferret and Anne-Marie Mercier-Faivre (eds.), *Biographie et politique: Vie publique, vie privée de l'Ancien régime à la Restauration* (Lyons: Presses universitaires de Lyon, 2014), 199–214. Also see Montlosier's own *Souvenirs d'un émigré (1791–1798)* (Paris: Hachette, 1951).

[104] Paul-Laurent Ausson, 'Idéologie politique et lutte de classes dans le discours historiographique du "fatalisme historique" en France, sous la Restauration' (unpublished Ph.D. thesis – Paris: I.E.P.P., 1987), 291. On the importance of *De la monarchie française* in contemporary debates, see Gruner, 'Political Historiography in Restoration France', 346–50.

[105] See, for example, Agénor Bardoux, *Études sociales et politiques: Le Comte de Montlosier et le Gallicanisme* (Paris: Calmann-Lévy, 1881), 172, and, more recently, Crossley, *French Historians and Romanticism*, 7.

[106] Chateaubriand, *Mémoires d'outre-tombe*, i. 385–6 and ii. 129–32, and Chateaubriand, 'Préface – Études historiques', 56. Also see, Pierre Christophorov, 'Chateaubriand, Montlosier et le "Courier de Londres"', *Revue d'histoire littéraire de la France*, 61/1 (1961), 15–22.

in the different role that the two authors ascribed to the conquest in shaping the nation's past. In fact, in his works, Montlosier accorded the latter far less importance than Boulainvilliers had done, since he believed that, at the time of the Frankish invasion, the Gauls were already divided into freemen and slaves. It was a distinction deriving from the Roman way of life and not, as others believed, from the Frankish invasion. Far from creating a nation divided between two different peoples or two different races, the Franks simply merged with those free Gauls who chose to adopt the Salic Laws. Both 'francs' – that is, 'free men' – they merged into a single class.[107] It was simply 'false that the German nations, entering Gaul, enslaved its inhabitants'. On the contrary, following the invasion, Roman municipal organisation was abolished, slavery ended, and slaves turned into tributary workers. And equally misleading was the notion that 'from the first distinction of Franks and Gauls ensued that of nobles and bourgeois, of lords and commoners'. Montlosier even remarked that such a mistake, 'made by Boulainvilliers and so fully and correctly refuted by Dubos', had been more recently repeated by Madame de Staël, Guizot, and 'many other famous writers'.[108]

Indeed, in *De la monarchie*, the count wrote about and discussed in depth the initial opposition between Franks and Gauls, but he insisted that this soon changed and eventually lost importance since most free Gauls adopted the customs of the Franks, their mentality, and their *mœurs*.[109] All others remained serfs, even though promotion was always open to them should they be willing to adopt the Frankish ways of life. All freemen took part in public affairs and all enjoyed the right to vote, whether of Gallic or Frankish origin. In given cases, argued the count, even tributary artisans could rise to the higher class by virtue of their merits but, because of their new status, they would be forced to renounce all manual labour and accept the customs of the nobility. As a result, over the centuries, two different groups were formed. On the one hand were the members of the nobility who had made of the values of the Franks their own, whether or not they descended from them. On the other, were the serfs, bereft of any rights. This order of things was disrupted in the twelfth century when the king affranchised the communes and, for reasons of military and political convenience, granted the status of freemen to a large group of their tributaries even though these had adopted neither the *mœurs* of the

---

[107] Montlosier, *De la monarchie française, depuis son établissement jusqu'à nos jours*, i. 21–2.
[108] François-Dominique de Montlosier, *De la monarchie française au 1ᵉʳ janvier 1821* (Paris: Gide fils, 1821), 106–7.
[109] Montlosier, *De la monarchie française, depuis son établissement jusqu'à nos jours*, i. 151–2.

Franks nor, above all, their love for freedom and their martial character.[110] So, wrote the count, 'an immense class was elevated to the honour and the condition of the Franks, keeping its servile *mœurs*, habits, and professions'.[111] Turned into freemen but still artisans and workmen, this mass represented a new people within the nation. It was a crucial turn that, taken in complete disregard for its moral implications and its subversive impact, deeply affected the course of French history, with the 'rise, in the midst of the state, of a new state; in the midst of the ancient people, a new people; in the midst of the ancient laws and institutions, new *mœurs*, new institutions, new laws'. In effect, Montlosier's narrative portrayed the story of a 'double state, a double people, a double social order' that proceed 'parallel to one another, then fight and struggle furiously'.[112] Consequently, he interpreted the Revolution as the final and inevitable outcome of the twelfth-century affranchising of the communes, a tremendous upheaval completing a levelling of all conditions, shaping a society in which merit and qualities meant nothing. Now, in the wake of the Revolution, only wealth was hereditary, and wealth alone shaped distinctions, lamented Montlosier.

To these issues the count returned in the 1817 edition of *De la monarchie*, expounding on the idea of national character. As he saw it, the morals, the customs, and, more broadly, the mentality of the nobility had shaped for centuries the character of the entire nation, 'elevating France above all other nations of the world'. The qualities of the nobility, trickling down 'from each rank to the nearby ranks, progressively followed all the echelons of the social hierarchy, ending up embracing' the entire nation.[113] However, in time, the inverse course also manifested itself and the nobility came to be affected by the vile habits and the 'spirit of servitude' of the lower classes. The consequences, felt especially under Louis XIV, were political oppression and tyrannical rule. The mortification of the public spirit and the stifling of liberties poisoned public debate and harmed *mœurs*. The excessive refinement of manners was symptomatic of moral decadence. Luxury and petty concerns became all-important and the 'national *mœurs*, national character, national mind, took on the tinge of such futilities'. The need felt by many to 'ennoble such trivialities, the efforts to give them grandeur and importance, corrupted our *mœurs*' and, from this, 'came the multitude of small spirits and small talents' that,

---

[110] See Gruner 'Political Historiography in Restoration France', 347–8.

[111] Montlosier, *De la monarchie française, depuis son établissement jusqu'à nos jours*, i. 152.

[112] Ibid., i. 135–6.

[113] François-Dominique de Montlosier, *De la monarchie française, depuis le retour de la maison de Bourbon jusqu'au 1ᵉʳ avril 1815* (Paris: H. Nicolle, 1817), 364.

'under the name of philosophes, attacked our ancient edifice and covered France in ruins'.[114]

The opposition between the two groups, so central to Montlosier's thesis, clearly had momentous political implications. And yet that conflict affected the very foundations of politics for it was fought on the plane of values, ways of life, and world-views. In this struggle, the modern bourgeoisie and its beliefs had gained strength day by day: '[M]ovable property balanced itself out with real estate, money with land, towns with castles. Knowledge raised itself to compete with courage, intelligence with honour, commerce and industry with arms.'[115] It was the result of a slow but constant development starting in the twelfth century and reaching its height on the eve of the Revolution. It was no longer the case, argued Montlosier, that the members of the lower classes would rise to become part of the ruling class after accepting its values. What was now taking place was the political rise of the bourgeoisie as a class in itself, gaining an unprecedented authority without having renounced its ideals. It was a political and cultural fact entailing wider consequences and resulting in profound changes in the nation's character since this, maintained the count, always reflected that of its highest class. The Revolution itself was the result of the corruption of French *mœurs*, a process in which the values embodied by the nobility, courage, loyalty, respect for order and tradition, had been replaced by those of the commoners, finally extending to the whole nation. However, argued Montlosier, the process was neither complete nor irreversible. The Restoration had arrested the fall and the French were still likely to accord to the true virtues of nobility their rightful place. In a patriotic outburst, the count even praised the French contempt for wealth, which was particularly manifest in the Old Regime: '[I]t was almost with disgust that a Frenchman abandoned himself to those habits that are necessary to gain wealth: once prosperity was obtained, everybody aspired to separate themselves from their sources.'[116] In some ways, Montlosier's reasoning resembled those of the opponents of the *noblesse commerçante* and, more broadly, related to the perceived social usefulness of nobles and bourgeois for the nation and which had been so important during the Revolution and was still so in its aftermath.[117] The members of the Third

---

[114] Ibid., 115.

[115] Montlosier, *De la monarchie française, depuis son établissement jusqu'à nos jours*, i. 175.

[116] Montlosier, *De la monarchie française, depuis le retour de la maison de Bourbon jusqu'au premier avril 1815*, 377.

[117] On this, see Chapters 4 and 7.

Estate clearly saw themselves as industrious workers who furthered the cause of the country by increasing its wealth and power, while to their way of thinking the nobles were parasites indulging their own selfish pleasure; completely useless and even harmful to the nation. The nobles, on the contrary, saw themselves as the true repository of those moral values, first and foremost honour and courage, that were essential to the greatness of France, while they considered the bourgeoisie to be covetous and selfish. Here was a mingling of economic and, in a sense, anthropological concerns that the revolutionary outburst brought to the fore.

It would be misleading or at least simplistic to consider the one portrayed by Montlosier as a struggle between races turning over the centuries into an opposition between classes. In fact, by downplaying the role of the original conquest, Montlosier denied the distinction between Gauls and Franks any lasting political and social consequences. On the contrary, discerning in the affranchising of the communes the birth of a new people, the Third Estate, with interests separate from those of the nobility, the count took class distinctions to be the real divide within French society. The clash was between two groups, each one embodying a distinctive value, a specific character, and a clearly identifiable interest. On the one side were the nobles, who owed their freedom to their virtue and courage alone, and who selflessly dedicated themselves to defending their country. On the other were the commoners, free only thanks to their king, assiduously pursuing by means of their pitiful labours their trivial, private interests even against those of the nation. Crucially, the utter incompatibility of the interests and values embodied by the two groups created a gulf between them that made it impossible for the nobility to claim it represented the entire nation – and here lay another crucial difference with Boulainvilliers's thesis. Each class represented a set of values on which a given way of imagining France was built, and because it was the clash of two radically different sets of principles, it was depicted by Montlosier in terms of an equally radical struggle: as a 'civil war'.[118] The important aspect is that, in the way they were conceived, the two classes were cultural groups shaped by history, with their own traditions and customs, fighting each other for the right to represent France. They were, it might be argued, two distinct ethnic groups, each claiming to represent or embody the whole nation and its past.

---

[118] On Montlosier's notion of 'civil war', see Marie-France Piguet, '"Contre-révolution", "guerre civile", "lutte entre deux classes": Montlosier (1755–1838) penseur du conflit politique moderne', *Astérion: Philosophie, histoire des idées, pensée politique*, 6 (2009), 1–38.

One important response to Montlosier's writings was by François Guizot, who, after reviewing the count's book in 1818, published an influential pamphlet linking the social and political consequences of the Revolution to its historical causes.[119] In *Du gouvernement de la France depuis la Restauration* (1820), Guizot made the lapidary claim that:

> The Revolution was a war, a genuine war, as one between foreign people. For more than thirteen centuries, France had contained two: a victorious and a vanquished people. For more than thirteen centuries, the vanquished people had been fighting to shake off the yoke of the victorious people. Our history is the history of this struggle. In our days, a decisive battle has been waged. It is called the Revolution. . . . The result of the Revolution is beyond doubt. The ancient, vanquished people have become the victorious people.[120]

The pamphlet, which ran through three editions in less than three months, was later likened to a bomb hurled at the royalists during an electoral campaign.[121] Because of its radicalism, Bonald went as far as to compare its theories to the ideas of Louis Pierre Louvel (1783–1820), the murderer of the Duke de Berry (1778–1820). It was an opinion that chimed with those of other observers at that time.[122]

Responding to his critics in the third edition of the pamphlet, Guizot reiterated and elaborated on his original stance. Claiming that the French past could be interpreted as the history of a war between nobles and commoners, noted Guizot, was far from new. It had been a widely held assumption even before the Revolution, and one on which Boulainvilliers as much as the champions of the Third

---

[119] [François Guizot], review of François-Dominique de Montlosier, *De la monarchie française depuis la 2ème Restauration jusqu'à la fin de la session de 1816*, in *Archives philosophiques, politiques et littéraires*, 3 (1818), 385–409.

[120] Guizot, *Du gouvernement de la France depuis la Restauration*, 1–3.

[121] Charles H. Pouthas, *Guizot pendant la Restauration: Préparation de l'homme d'État (1814–1830)* (Paris: Plon-Nourrit, 1923), 265.

[122] Louis Gabriel Ambroise de Bonald, 'Sur les Francs et les Gaulois', *Le défenseur: Journal religieux, politique et littéraire*, 25 November 1820, 391. Also see Jean Cohen, *Du système des doctrinaires, ou Observations sur un écrit de M. Guizot intitulé 'Du gouvernement de la France depuis la Restauration, et du ministère actuel'* (Paris: A. Égron, 1820); Benjamin Laroche, *Lettres adressées l'une à tous les journalistes, l'autre à M. de Richelieu; précédées et suivies des considérations sur l'ouvrage de M. Guizot, intitulé: 'Du gouvernement de la France depuis la restauration'* (Paris: Les marchands de nouveautés, 1820). On Guizot's thought, the classic study is Pierre Rosanvallon's *Le moment Guizot*. Also see, on his life and ideas: Marina Valensise (ed.), *François Guizot et la culture politique de son temps* (Paris: Gallimard, 1991); Gabriel de Broglie, *Guizot* (Paris: Perrin, 2002); Robert Chamboredon (ed.), *François Guizot, 1787–1874: Passé-présent* (Paris: L'Harmattan, 2010); Michael Drolet, 'Carrying the Banner of the Bourgeoisie: Democracy, Self and the Philosophical Foundations to François Guizot's Historical and Political Thought', *History of Political Thought*, 32 (2011), 645–90; Laurent Theis, *Guizot: La traversée d'un siècle* (Paris: CNRS Éditions, 2014).

Estate would have agreed.[123] However, declared Guizot, because of the constant efforts of the enemies of 'constitutional equality' to advance their cause, he was compelled to unmask the nature of that universal law that 'elevates an ever greater number of families and individuals' to the rights of liberty and equality, and that 'in the infancy of societies force renders a privilege of the few'. Partly following Mably's own reasoning, Guizot insisted that, in the aftermath of the invasion of the Gallic lands, the 'political nation, the free and master nation' was composed of the Franks, the high clergy, and those 'rich and powerful Gauls' whom the Franks accepted as their equals. All of these took part in the national assemblies, while the commoners were excluded since they had no political existence of their own.[124] However, over the centuries, thanks to 'industry, commerce, and Christianity', the lower classes gained political influence as towns grew wealthier.[125] Over time, commoners and burghers bought or obtained municipal liberties from kings and lords. It was only through its relentless struggle against the nobility that the Third Estate came into existence as a political and social actor, 'a truly new nation', contended Guizot, 'since it was not part of the nation that has given its name to France'. Its existence did not date back to the conquest, but was instead the outcome of centuries of sacrifice, hard work, and struggle. The 'new nation' had finally turned against the French nobility in 1789, proving itself a 'truly conquering nation, for it conquered its own masters'.[126] However, according to Guizot, the Revolution was not the struggle of one class to replace another; nor was it simply the fight 'between wealthy and poor, between owners and proletarians'.[127] On the contrary, it was the culmination of the efforts of a class embodying the universal ideal of the equality of rights. Its aim was to replace 'all privileges, which belonged only to some, with right, which belonged to all'. From his viewpoint, the

---

[123] François Guizot, *Supplément aux deux premières éditions: Du gouvernement de la France depuis la restauration et du ministère actuel* (Paris: Ladvocat, 1820), 5–8.

[124] Ibid., 7–9.

[125] On the importance of religion in the works of Guizot, see Pierre-Yves Kirschleger, *La religion de Guizot* (Geneva: Labor et fides, 1999), and Laurent Theis, 'François Guizot, un protestant très politique', *Bulletin de la Société de l'histoire du protestantisme français*, 155 (October–November 2009), 831–40.

[126] Guizot, *Supplément aux deux premières éditions: Du gouvernement de la France depuis la restauration et du ministère actuel*, 11.

[127] Ibid., 17.

'new people' had eradicated the very notion of privilege so as to affirm that of a law common to all, establishing an equality of rights that would end social distinctions and, with them, the internecine divisions that were tearing France apart.[128]

That classes should have a crucial role in any understanding of society remained a lynchpin of Guizot's political and historical thought. In his famous *Histoire de la civilisation en France* (1829–1832), a work stemming from the lectures he gave at the Sorbonne, in Paris, between 1820 and 1822, he expanded on the point, explaining the relationship between class and the individual. Classes, he contended, influenced so deeply the life of a person that they could determine whether he would be a lord or a vassal, a wealthy owner or a poor factory worker. This 'natural, inevitable fact' ensured 'the perpetuity of social order, the progress of civilisation'. If it were not so, if 'society were, in each generation, entirely subordinated to the will of individuals', argued Guizot, then 'there would evidently be no ties between human generations'. Society would crumble into an unbearable chaos, and, he noted, 'nothing is more contrary to human nature'. However, if what he called the 'hereditariness of social situations' played a fundamental role in ensuring the stability and the existence itself of society, Guizot accorded equal importance to an individual's will and deeds in shaping his or her own destiny. A well-ordered society could only rest on the balance between the need for stability that the existence of classes made possible and the inviolable will to freedom of each person.[129] Viewed through such a lens, because they contributed to the solidity of society, classes shed a crucial light on a nation's history, and this in a twofold way. On the one hand, they brought into focus the existence of groups that transcended the lifespan of a single generation, making it possible to unfold a narrative distinct from, but related to, the national narrative. On the other, the notion of a fundamental struggle between classes, a struggle that in France had started with the affranchising of the communes, not only helped explain the turning points of history but, more importantly, highlighted the causes of a nation's moral and social progress. From Guizot's standpoint, in fact, class struggle, far from being a principle of immobility or of social disruption, 'was on the contrary a cause of progress', the wellspring for the development of that French civilisation of which the bourgeoisie had been the main agent. Importantly, Guizot

---

[128] Ibid., 19–20.
[129] François Guizot, *Histoire de la civilisation en France, depuis la chute de l'Empire Romain jusqu'en 1789* (Paris: Pichon et Didier, 1829–1832), iv. 343–4.

assumed that since the latter was the 'most active' class, then more than others it shaped the 'direction and the character' of French civilisation. It did so through its ever-increasing economic weight, at once a cause and a consequence of the dissemination of its values across society. Nowhere else had a class raised itself from the lower depths 'through a continuous movement and a work without respite', growing stronger at each generation, absorbing and encompassing 'everything it encountered' and gradually changing the nature of government and the social fabric itself. Nowhere else, contended Guizot, had a class become 'so dominant that one can say it is the nation itself'.[130]

Clearly, then, the class struggle depicted by Guizot was more complex than might be inferred from his references to 'a war between two different peoples'. In fact, one point he endeavoured to make clear in his works was that while in France the two main classes 'constantly fought and detested one another', nonetheless they had 'progressively moved closer, assimilated, extended'. If in the seventeenth and eighteenth centuries the 'social and moral separation of classes' still remained deep, no one could deny that 'there was a true French nation which was not a given class but which comprised them all'. All were animated by 'a common feeling, with a common social existence marked, finally, by a nationality'.[131] The two classes belonged to the same nation, and this made the struggle between them all the more 'despicable'. As Guizot had already remarked in an 1820 pamphlet, they 'bear the same name, speak the same language, and have lived thirteen centuries on the same land'. Despite divisions:

> [T]he course of time moves them closer to one another, mixes them, unites them by innumerable bonds and envelops them in a common destiny which makes us see a sole and same nation where there are still two distinct races, two social situations [that are] deeply different. Franks and Gauls, lords and peasants, nobles and commoners, all, well before the Revolution, both called themselves French and both recognised France as their country.[132]

Not only had the struggle between classes taken place within a single nation. In Guizot's account, it had been a clash pivoting around the claim made by each to embody the entire nation. For this reason, he understood classes to be much more than groups simply sharing an economic interest or role; they defined cultural divisions – a point that

[130] Ibid., v. 122–3.   [131] Guizot, *Histoire générale de la civilisation en Europe*, 30 (lecture 7).
[132] Guizot, *Du gouvernement de la France depuis la Restauration*, 2.

reflected his distance from Saint-Simonian industrialism.[133] It was the alleged industriousness of the bourgeoisie, and the love for freedom that seemingly accompanied it, that established the divide with the nobility. Its independence, its economic, political, and technical capacities, spoke to the values it embodied and which, in the late eighteenth century, had finally prevailed over the retrograde, illiberal, and violent ideals of the ancient nobility. The values of the bourgeoisie had conquered French society, shaping its civilisation and determining its progress.[134] In this respect, the reconciliation between classes referred to by Guizot simply amounted to the triumph of bourgeois ideals and values. It was on the history of this centuries-long revolution – recounting the story of the accomplishments of the Third Estate, rather than a discourse on its origins – that Guizot rested his political arguments, insisting (in line with Thierry) on the need to restore to the bourgeoisie its glorious and yet forgotten history and its lost memory; thereby recalling a successful past in order to legitimate its present rule.[135]

It is useful to point out, as Rosanvallon has done, that with his insistence on individual merit and capacities Guizot assumed the exist-ence of an aristocracy within the Third Estate itself, a group of people who bore a greater role in the shaping of French civilisation: '[J]udges, bailiffs, provosts, seneschals, and all the king's officers or the great lords', most of whom, of humble origins, 'contributed, more than others to the origins of the Third Estate and its conquest of social supremacy'.[136] Historically, Guizot saw in the enfranchisement of the communes a crucial step in the division of a higher from a lower class within the commoners. As he saw it, through their enfranchisement, the towns entered in a new guise into the complex system of laws and customs enshrined by the feudal world and, acquiring vassals of their own thanks to their new rights, they became suzerains, thus sharing part of the nation's sovereignty. However, divisions soon emerged within the towns themselves, between the higher ranks of the townsmen and 'the largest part of the population' whose 'degree of ignorance and brutality' was a constant source of unrest. According to Guizot, the populace were moved by 'a blind, democratic, wild, and ferocious spirit' against which the insecure and weaker upper classes sought compromise

---

[133] Gruner, 'Political Historiography in Restoration France', 361.
[134] See Maza, *The Myth of the French Bourgeoisie*, 150.
[135] Rosanvallon, *Le moment Guizot*, 194–204.
[136] Guizot, *Histoire de la civilisation en France, depuis la chute de l'Empire Romain jusqu'en 1789*, v. 238. Also see, on this, Rosanvallon, *Le moment Guizot*, 107–42.

with the nobility and the king.[137] Based exclusively on personal merit, this sort of aristocracy was the worthiest part of the nation and, as it had led the Third Estate in its struggle towards liberty, it should now rule France and further its moral, social, and economic prosperity. Importantly, the point to note here is that, beyond mere common economic interest, Guizot believed in a deeper, intimate unity of the different parts of the Third Estate, a unity based on the sharing of the same ideals and on a common past. Industriousness, love for freedom, and the memories of an unjust and unbearable oppression made of the bourgeoisie a single ethnic group. And this enabled Guizot to claim that the bourgeoisie, that is, the upper ranks of the Third Estate, could be identified with the nation at large, including what would later be its lower working class.

Guizot's distinction between a higher and a lower rank within the Third Estate, positing a division that seemingly left untarnished the nation's intimate unity, profoundly affected the way other liberal historians conceived of the French past. François Mignet's *Histoire de la Révolution française* (1824), a work inaugurating a string of books on the Revolution, is a case in point. Sharing with his friend Thierry the need to identify those collective actors that could explain the course of history, Mignet used the concept of class as a sociological tool, defining, through it, a group of people sharing the same social conditions and cultural attitudes.[138] Moreover, the distinction that Mignet, like Guizot, posited between an upper and a lower class within the Third Estate, although endowed with a strong 'hierarchical connotation', presupposed its cultural unity.[139] Both, in fact, had taken part in the material, intellectual, and social progress of France before 1789; both had combated the privileged classes during the Revolution; and both shared the same memories and believed in the same ideals – or so Mignet surmised.[140] But his views regarding the origins of France had been outlined in an earlier work, his *De la féodalité*, published in 1822. In it, Mignet engaged directly with the ideas of Boulainvilliers, Dubos, Montesquieu, Mably, and Montlosier. Although in several respects he sided with Mably and adopted many of his ideas, he criticised him

[137] Guizot, *Cours d'histoire moderne: Histoire générale de la civilisation en Europe*, 39–41.
[138] On Mignet's views regarding the study of history, see Yvonne Knibiehler, *Naissance des sciences humaines: Mignet et l'histoire philosophique au XIXe siècle* (Paris: Flammarion, 1973). Also see Reizov, *L'historiographie romantique française*, 353–86, and Walch, *Les maîtres de l'histoire*, 75–93. On Mignet's appreciation for Thierry, see his comments in the *Courrier français*, 4 May 1825, 3.
[139] Ausson, 'Idéologie politique et lutte de classes dans le discours historiographique du "fatalisme historique" en France', 274.
[140] Mignet, *Histoire de la Révolution française*, 10–11; also see Knibiehler, *Naissance des sciences humaines*, 136–40.

nonetheless for having failed to 'see the great social tendencies that decide events and that drive men' and for having neglected the fact that '[t]hings form a system; they develop following an almost inevitable order'.[141] Looking at its deep-rooted social and economic cause, Mignet argued that feudalism was not the outcome of the deeds of kings, nor a mere consequence of the Frankish conquest or the choice of the French people. On the contrary, it was the complex product of a series of overlapping and contrasting causes acting throughout the centuries. Among these were the changes in the *mœurs* of the Franks following the acquisition of lands in Gaul. In fact, while until then the Germanic tribes had always cherished their freedom, independence, and love for adventure above all else, they gradually turned into owners of vast estates and these, in turn, became the source of their power and prestige. Importantly, property in land was not an outcome of the original conquest but, rather, a consequence of the granting of fiefs. Looking on the other hand at the bourgeoisie and its rise to power, Mignet saw the enfranchisement of the communes as a crucial step in the history of France and the whole of Europe, a turn that had freed man and laid the ground for the development of the arts, letters, and trade. As he saw it, before then, the entire nation 'resided in the king and the nobility', who had held sway over the towns of France. The ancient 'class of free men' had gradually disappeared so that, with the rise of feudalism, there were in France but 'sovereigns and slaves'. According to Mignet, the origins of the enfranchisements of the communes lay in the insurrection of those who were subject to tallage and who, because of war and depopulation, in the twelfth century had less and yet were asked for more by their lords. Finally, they revolted, forcing the nobility and the kings to affranchise them, receiving rights that, in time, brought them even greater wealth and power.[142] This was an 'inevitable' turn, stemming from deep-seated and complex social and economic changes. The 'municipal system was a true surrender of sovereignty, and the communes [became] small republics'.[143] Gradually, the 'servile *mœurs*' of the townsmen vanished, new 'glorious peoples' were born, and the arts, the sciences, trade, and freedom dawned across Europe: 'Never has anything so great been witnessed throughout the world.'[144]

One important aspect to be emphasised is that in the works of Thierry, Guizot, Mignet, and the other liberal historians writing during the

---

[141] Françoise-Auguste Mignet, *De la féodalité, des institutions de St Louis, et de l'influence de la législation de ce prince* (Paris: L'Huillier, 1822), 210.
[142] Mignet, *De la féodalité*, 83–5.   [143] Ibid., 87.   [144] Ibid., 93.

Restoration, classes were thought to exercise a profound influence upon the lives of men and the course of history. They were no longer an intellectual fabrication conceived to impose an order upon the natural world, as most eighteenth-century scholars had construed them. A class now denoted a set of economic and social but also cultural constraints that influenced the existence of those who belonged to it – a definition that, interestingly, brings to mind Pierre Bourdieu's views on class and class distinctions.[145] A class was more than a group of people sharing the same economic condition, as it had been for a Boisguilbert; and it was more than a group with the same economic interest, as the *industrialistes* believed.[146] Here, from the Revolution to the Restoration, was a conceptual shift that dovetailed with the growing understanding of classes as historical actors, endowed with unity of intent and with ideals, values, memories, and a character of their own. Crucially for us, the unity of the bourgeoisie and the working classes imagined by the liberal thinkers became instrumental in conceiving of a united France. The nation's coherence was allegedly mirrored in the supposed unity of the Third Estate. Viewed from this angle, it might be ventured that the king's symbolic body which once represented France, giving it its imagined unity, had been replaced by the race/class of the Third Estate, culturally rooted in the Gallo-Roman ethnicity.

Of course, to the modern reader this identification of the bourgeoisie with the entire nation might seem to rest on unstable foundations. This was at least implied by Furet when, fleetingly referring to the thesis of Guizot, Mignet, and Thiers, he trenchantly noted that if history really were 'the science of class struggle', as their works largely argued, 'then why stop at the Third Estate?'[147] But the same point had already been made by one of Mignet's closest friends, Adolphe Thiers, in his influential ten-volume *Histoire de la Révolution française* (1823–1827).[148] Like Mignet, Thiers also believed that the oppression

---

[145] Pierre Bourdieu, *La distinction: Critique sociale du jugement* (Paris: Éditions de Minuit, 1979).

[146] On the changing meaning of class in the eighteenth and early nineteenth century, see Chapter 7.

[147] Furet, 'La Révolution de Turgot à Jules Ferry', 586.

[148] See Reizov, *L'historiographie romantique française*, 353–449. On Thiers, his life, and thought, see Georges Valance, *Thiers: Bourgeois et révolutionnaire* (Paris: Flammarion, 2007). On his approach to the study of the past, see Walch, *Les maîtres de l'histoire*, 137–92 and Robert Tombs, 'Thiers historien', *Cahiers de l'Association internationale des études françaises*, 47 (1995), 265–81. On the diffusion of the *Histoire de la Révolution française*, Anatole France's hyperbolic remark that it was the most widely read book in France, 'except for *The Three Musketeers*', hints at its significance: Anatole France, 'M. Thiers historien', in France, *La vie littéraire: Première série* (Paris: Calmann-Lévy, 1921), 239–40.

of the lower classes, coupled with their economic and social growth, made the Revolution inevitable, just as the seizing of power by the class with the greatest capacities was unavoidable.[149] His reasoning pivoted on the typically liberal claim that the Third Estate and its upper ranks, the bourgeoisie, represented the entire nation: 'The French people', wrote Thiers, 'have progressively liberated themselves through their own work, the first source of wealth and liberty. First farmers, then traders, and then manufacturers, they gained such an importance that soon they formed the entire nation.'[150] As he saw it, the existence of a divide between an upper bourgeoisie and a lower multitude within the Third Estate had become patent during the Revolution, wherein the latter played a role subordinate to the former. But the Revolution had also shown that this was a distinction of secondary importance when considering that the interests, values, and character of the upper part coincided with those of the nation at large. And yet, as Thiers himself admitted, the fact remained that once a class obtained power, proving its abilities and justifying its authority by its achievements, it inevitably risked being 'overwhelmed by those coming up behind them', as they came to see in the ruling class a new 'aristocracy'.[151] The truth is that if we exclude the possibility that in the decades following the Revolution class conflict was checked by armed repression alone – something difficult to believe, at least in the long run – then it might plausibly be argued that the values the bourgeoisie claimed to embody, such as the sacredness of work, the importance of personal merit, and the significance of social progress, gradually came to be more or less consciously shared by most French men and women, slowly ingrained in their ways of life. This is not to say that the identification of the nation's interests with those of a seemingly selfless bourgeoisie was particularly compelling; rather, that the notion of a 'Gallic' spirit of industriousness, ingenuity, and love for independence, belonging to the nation at large, came to be accepted by most French men and women. An important consequence was that the conflict between classes would then take place within a single nation, and not between two peoples with different values, histories, and memories – as many of the protagonists had interpreted the 1789 Revolution. Truly divided into different economic classes,

---

[149] See Yvonne Knibiehler, 'Une révolution "nécessaire": Thiers, Mignet et l'école fataliste', *Romantisme*, 10 (1980), 279–88, and Reizov, *L'historiographie romantique française*, 386.

[150] Adolphe Thiers, *Histoire de la Révolution française* (Paris: Lecointe et Durey, 1823–1827), i. 4.

[151] Thiers, *Histoire de la Révolution française*, ii. 7.

each with its political and social claims and interests, France would gradually come to be imagined as a single nation stemming from the same ethnic origin. Of course, such a belief would be the consequence of complex, slow, uncertain, and endless nationalising processes taking place in the second half of the nineteenth century and afterwards – but built up, in turn, on the foundations laid by the Sieyès, Thierrys, and Guizots during the intellectual struggles over the nation's origins.

CONCLUSION

About Renan
Deciding the Nation's Identity

Most if not all works on French nationhood and nationalism will refer, at some point or another, to the ideas of Ernest Renan. This book is no exception. However, rather than starting with his famous speech at the Sorbonne, *Qu'est-ce qu'une nation?* (1882), it might be more relevant to first consider his *Réforme intellectuelle et morale de la France* (1871), a lengthy essay published a few months after the fall of the Second Empire and the tragic ending of the Commune. In it, after censuring the aggressivity of the Germans, a great people now victim to a blind and ferocious nationalism, Renan offered his explanation for the defeat at Sedan and the miserable state of his country, seeking the causes within France itself:

> The war proved, to the point of obviousness, that we no longer possessed our old military abilities. This is not something that should surprise those who have formed a correct idea of the philosophy of our history. The France of the Middle Ages was a Germanic construction, built by a Germanic military aristocracy out of Gallo-Roman materials. The centuries-long task of France has consisted of expelling from its midst all the elements introduced by the Germanic invasion, up to the Revolution, which was the last convulsion in this endeavour. The military character of France came from its Germanic side; by violently ousting the Germanic elements and replacing them with a philosophical and egalitarian conception of society, France rejected, at a stroke, all that was military within it. It has remained a rich country, that considers war a foolish, rather unprofitable, enterprise.[1]

French decadence, as he perceived it, was a consequence of the increasingly prominent role of the southern, Latin, Catholic, and bourgeois forces, to the detriment of the northern, Germanic, and aristocratic elements within the French nation. Renan even went so far as to praise the merits of Protestantism and deplored the shortcomings of Catholicism, which he

---

[1] Ernst Renan, 'La réforme intellectuelle et morale de la France', in Renan, *Qu'est-ce qu'une nation? et autres écrits politiques* (Paris: Imprimerie nationale, 1996), 97.

saw as 'too hieratical to give a people its intellectual and moral nourishment'.[2] The *Réforme*, which, according to Georges Sorel (1847–1922), was 'Renan's most sincere work', offers several remarkable and thought-provoking insights.[3] A particular version of the 'two Frances thesis' emerges there, namely, the idea that the French nation has always been profoundly divided, torn by internecine conflicts and divisions that become manifest at moments of crisis and political or social unrest.[4] In many cases, and this was surely true during and right after the *anneé terrible*, a contrast was drawn between conservatives and Catholics on the one hand and liberals and atheists on the other: 'If there is a France of Voltaire, there is a France of Christ which will find itself and will win', wrote the journalist Louis Veuillot (1813–1883) in 1872.[5] Many have since restated the opposition in various different guises.[6]

For us, there are at least two noteworthy elements in Renan's *Réforme*. On the one hand, although the great historian was arguing from a conservative standpoint, he condemned Catholicism as a source of decadence – a stance that, obviously, at that time most conservatives would have rejected outright. On the other hand, and even more importantly, his whole reasoning had a solid and blatant ethnic foundation.[7] In fact, Renan associated Catholicism with the nation's Latin, Roman, and Mediterranean heritage: 'Our carelessness comes from the Midi' – so much so that, without it, 'we would be serious, active, Protestant, parliamentary'. It was his firm conviction that the 'racial background' of the French, like that of the British, was Germanic and that the leading cause of their debasement had been the rejection of their Germanic roots.[8] Given such

---

[2] Renan, 'La réforme intellectuelle et morale de la France', 142.

[3] The expression is in Georges Sorel to Édouard Berth, 24 June 1912, 'Lettres de Georges Sorel à Édouard Berth: Troisième partie, 1911–1917', *Cahiers Georges Sorel*, 5 (1987), 186.

[4] Though it is worth pointing out that, far from being a feature of a supposed French uniqueness, this holds true for many other countries, so much so that theories of 'two Germanies' or of 'two Italies', for example, are routinely discussed by historians and scholars alike.

[5] Louis Veuillot, *Paris pendant les deux sièges* (Paris: Librairie de Victor Palme, 1878), i. 16. Also see Charles Renouvier, 'L'éducation et la morale' (6 June 1872), *Critique philosophique*, i (1872), 279.

[6] See, for example, Paul Seippel, *Les deux Frances et leurs origines historiques* (Lausanne: Payot, 1905). In the immediate aftermath of the fall of Vichy, in his lectures on the relationship between conceptions of honour and the idea of nation, Lucien Febvre rekindled the dichotomy, giving it a new form: Lucien Febvre, *'Honneur et patrie'* (Paris: Perrin, 1996). For a general overview, see Émile Poulat, *Liberté, laïcité: La guerre des deux France et le principe de la modernité* (Paris: Éditions du Cerf, 1987). Also see Theodore Zeldin, 'Introduction: Were There Two Frances?', in Zeldin (ed.), *Conflicts in French Society: Anticlericalism, Education and Morals in the Nineteenth Century* (London: Allen & Unwin, 1970), 9–11.

[7] See Pierre Guiral, 'Les écrivains et la notion de décadence de 1870 à 1914', *Romantisme*, 42 (1983), 12–13.

[8] Renan, 'La réforme intellectuelle et morale de la France', 98–9.

arguments, it is unsurprising that the views expressed in the *Réforme* have been likened to those in Boulainvilliers's works.[9] In fact, Renan shifted his ground throughout his life, so much so that some scholars have even remarked on the seeming inconsistency and ambiguity underlying his views about nation and race.[10] It is in the comparison between the contentions in the *Réforme* and those in his *Qu-est ce que une nation?*, where Renan referred to the nation as a 'daily plebiscite' and which has often been seen as the epitome of the voluntaristic idea of nation, that a contrast seems to emerge.[11] In truth, the views expounded by Renan in his 1882 speech were more complex than is usually assumed since he there made the case that 'present-day consent' was as important as the 'possession of a rich legacy of memories'. The will to live together was inseparable from the desire to perpetuate the values enshrined in a shared heritage. And this because the nation's past, as Renan saw it, was sacred:

> The nation, like the individual, is the culmination of a long past of endeavours, sacrifices, and devotion. Of all cults, that of the ancestors is the most legitimate, for the ancestors have made us what we are. A heroic past, great men, glory (by which I understand genuine glory), this is the social capital upon which one bases a national idea.[12]

Indeed, the importance of sacrifice as the cement binding past, present, and future generations together would have been shared by Boulainvilliers as well as by most members of the second order throughout the seventeenth and eighteenth centuries. As is well known, pursuing a clearly political objective, Renan was here trying to assert a supposedly French over an allegedly German idea of nationhood to bolster his country's claims over Alsace and Lorraine. But the notion that to the former somehow corresponded a voluntaristic and to the latter an ethnocentric conception is misleading. In fact, Renan rejected the idea that a people's will, alone, could ever define a nation. Nor would he have thought of it as its main element. In truth, there is greater continuity between the *Réforme* and *Qu'est-ce qu'une nation?* than might at first appear. In both, Renan was advocating a view of the nation as a shared set of values, beliefs, memories,

---

[9] Laudyce Rétat, 'Les Gaulois et les substitutions d'origine dans la conscience historique de Renan', in Viallaneix and Erhard (eds.), *Nos ancêtres les Gaulois*, 341.

[10] Frédéric Darmau, 'Les ambiguïtés de Renan: Nation, Nationalisme, Internationalisme', *Raison présente*, 86 (1988), 27–35, and Robert D. Priest, 'Ernest Renan's Race Problem', *The Historical Journal*, 58 (2015), 303–30.

[11] Ernest Renan, 'Qu'est-ce qu'une nation?', in Renan, *Qu'est-ce qu'une nation? et autres écrits politiques*, 241.

[12] Ibid., 241.

and ways of life and as the bedrock on which the will of its people was formed. The decision of a people to be a nation was almost a given, something determined by their shared past, and Renan's choice of the word 'plebiscite' suggests a collective ritual more than a carefully weighed and wholly lucid decision.

The idea of a shift from a closed and almost racist conception, in the *Réforme*, to an open and civic one, in *Qu'est-ce qu'une nation?*, is then misleading. And this because Renan's idea of the nation was culturalist rather than naturalistic or voluntaristic. Importantly for us, the reasons why he might be misread are partly the same as those that have led scholars to misinterpret authors such as Boulainvilliers and Augustin Thierry, wrongly seen as exponents of pre-racialist or racist ideas. In effect, the latter two would have agreed with Renan that a nation is a cultural construction, built up over the centuries, and in which various groups, because of their devotion to the common good, might claim the right to rule. For most of the authors we have considered in this book, and evidently for the main ones, a nation was a cultural even before being a political entity. This was partly a consequence of the fact that, as historians or scholars strongly drawn to the study of the past, they were adamant that any claim to legitimacy had to be supported by historical evidence. In this, the growing attention paid to civic histories as distinct from political and diplomatic histories and the increasing mistrust for those royal genealogies that allegedly told the history of the nation had crucial consequences. In fact, from Boulainvilliers onwards, the greater importance now attributed to a people's *mœurs* and way of life meant that it was in these, rather than in legal treaties alone, that political legitimacy had to be sought. In this process, Montesquieu had a crucial role. His conviction that the legitimacy of any institution had to be assessed in relation to a nation's *mœurs* and character was destined to have a significant impact well beyond the frontiers of France. Seeking to found the legitimacy of a political claim upon ancient legal texts or capitularies was no longer enough – although it had still essentially been so in the seventeenth century. And while such a turn was surely prompted by social changes and political necessities there were also important intellectual concerns that need to be properly grasped. Indeed, the fact that developments in historical scholarship deeply affected the way nations represented themselves is still often neglected, especially in regard to the early modern period.

The latter point leads us to another crucial question, that is, the importance of *mœurs* in the shaping of what some scholars have considered a quintessentially French form of liberalism, one that differs from the Anglo-Saxon paradigm on account of its emphasis on the importance of civic participation in the nation's life. In a seminal essay published some time ago, Larry Siedentop made the case that nineteenth-century French liberal theorists avoided the mistake of considering the individual to be a monad, detached from his or her social milieu, and emphasised the importance of social context. In doing so, they also insisted that political values and ideas were deeply rooted in a nation's specific historical circumstances and that these limited and profoundly affected political options and possibilities. Finally, argued Siedentop, several nineteenth-century French liberal authors never considered freedom solely as a question of non-interference by the state in the individual's pursuit of happiness but always emphasised how the fulfilment of social and civic duties was a crucial aspect of citizenship. This strand of liberalism was concerned with the moral consequences of participation and was strongly alert to the need to educate men and women to citizenship.[13] More than others, it was the *Doctrinaires* who insisted on the need to properly grasp the significance of social structures and constraints and to investigate how these interacted with the development of a nation's *mœurs*. According to Siedentop, such a concern was based on the belief that law was 'less powerful than *mœurs*' and that, therefore, in these lay the key to the common as well as the individual good.[14] Clearly, here was a sort of liberalism that exhibited some elements so markedly republican as to be greatly at odds with Anglo-Saxon notions of freedom – of whatever kind they might be. Some of the arguments set out by Siedentop might be controversial, not least because of his use of 'liberalism' to designate discourses and views predating the 1840s and 1850s, but what interests us is that the specific French paradigm that he has defined was in fact deeply rooted in eighteenth-century thought and in the works of the writers taken into consideration in this book.[15] Montesquieu, for one, had done much to demonstrate the extent to which historical circumstances limited a nation's freedom or enhanced its political options, as well as to draw attention to the weight of the social and geographical context in which individuals pursued their aims. The

[13] Larry Siedentop, 'Two Liberal Traditions', in Raf Geenens and Helena Rosenblatt (eds.), *French Liberalism from Montesquieu to the Present Day* (Cambridge: Cambridge University Press, 2012), 15–35. The essay was originally published in Alan Ryan (ed.), *The Idea of Freedom: Essays in Honour of Isaiah Berlin* (Oxford: Oxford University Press, 1979).

[14] Siedentop, 'Two Liberal Traditions', 19.

[15] Arguably, it was only in the second quarter of the nineteenth century that the word 'liberalism' began to designate a distinct set of ideas and a political movement. See: Jörn Leonhard, *Liberalismus: Zur historischen Semantik eines europäischen Deutungsmusters* (Munich: Oldenbourg, 2001).

assumption that, at least in specific circumstances, *mœurs* were more
important than laws in explaining a nation's history was also
a contention central to the *Esprit des lois*. For his part, Boulainvilliers
staunchly defended the nobility's freedom and was determined to limit
the encroachments of royal authority. In doing so, he was articulating
a negative understanding of liberty, one close to Constant's definition of
modern freedom.[16] But with equal firmness he insisted on the nobility's
spirit of abnegation and its commitment to the security and greatness of
France, showing contempt for the notion itself of individual interest – and
to these ideas, in the second half of the century, the advocates of the *noblesse
militaire* would continue to cling. That the freedom and rights of the
nobility were a deserved reward for its devotion to the nation hints at the
complexity of the relationship between liberal and republican paradigms.
And, obviously, the fact that Boulainvilliers was denying to all non-nobles
any political existence of their own further complicates matters. As for
Thierry, the definition of the nation set out in *Des nations*, construed in
terms of a faith in the beneficial consequences for individual freedom of
economic integration, was indeed closer to those works that would later be
seen as supplying the intellectual foundations of liberalism. But then in his
more strictly historical works, later on, he would shift his focus to social
groups, their economic interests and, even more important, their shared
values and *mœurs*. Social forces and historical circumstances became paramount for Thierry, and the fact that Marx and Engels took much from his
later works should lead us to be wary of seeing in him a precursor of
liberalism. The same caution ought to apply in any discussion regarding
Boulainvilliers and Montesquieu – and partly for similar reasons.[17]

Many of the authors considered in this book ascribed great importance
to historical and cultural context for the understanding of politics, a feature
that Siedentop would see as distinctive of a specific French form of liberal
thought. The significance they attributed to historical circumstances was
such that their various understandings of freedom were somehow ethni-
cised. In fact, it was either on a 'Germanic' or a 'Gallic' idea of freedom that
they based most of their arguments. The fact that Montesquieu believed

[16] Of course, the classic definition of 'negative freedom' is in Isaiah Berlin, 'Two Concepts of Liberty',
in Berlin, *Four Essays on Liberty* (Oxford: Oxford University Press, 1969), 118–72. This had originally
been Berlin's inaugural lecture as Oxford's Chichele Professor of Social and Political Theory in 1958.
[17] Recently, Céline Spector has raised doubts as to whether Montesquieu should properly be considered a liberal at all: Céline Spector, 'Was Montesquieu Liberal? *The Spirit of the Laws* in the
History of Liberalism', in Geenens and Rosenblatt (eds.), *French Liberalism from Montesquieu to the
Present Day*, 57–72.

that some nations – especially non-European ones – would never enjoy freedom because of their past, character, and *mœurs* confirms the centrality of ethnicity to his views about politics. For his part, Boulainvilliers assumed the existence of a tight connection between the Franks, as an ethnic group, their love for freedom, and their loyalty to the nation. To an extent, Thierry replaced the Franks with the Gallo-Romans, making the case that their longing for independence was a reaction to centuries of injury and oppression at the hands of the Franks and their descendants. Treating ethnicity as the ground that would sustain their political theses, these authors all understood it to be a cultural and historical construction. Ethnicity was, in short, the product of a geographical setting, the outcome of kings' deeds and decisions and of those of their opponents, the consequence of complex social and cultural interactions, and, crucially, something that might slowly change over time. The latter point had momentous relevance so far as any claims to political legitimacy were concerned. Boulanvilliers, as well as many of the other advocates of the *thèse nobiliaire*, deplored for example the weakening of the Frankish warring character in the present-day nobility and considered this to be the root cause of French decadence – and then called for its moral regeneration. Only by restoring the ancient Frankish spirit and by regaining its lost authority could the nobility save the nation from dissolution and despotism, reasoned the count. In the opposite camp, throughout the latter part of the eighteenth century, many authors went to great lengths to show that the interests of the Third Estate coincided with those of the nation at large and that the efforts and labours of its members were the reason for French greatness. In doing so, they were clearly reclaiming for their own purposes an argument taken from the advocates of the *thèse nobiliaire*. Like the latter, they also believed that their character and *mœurs*, as a group, had become – or ought to become – those of the whole French nation. It was a key contention in their claims to political legitimacy. From this angle, it might be said that greater attention needs to be paid to the connection and interaction between feelings of nationhood and nationalism, class and group (self-)representations, and political, legal, and economic thought in the early modern period. After all, notions such as class and race were centred around a group's perceived character and *mœurs* and, because of this, could be used so very effectively in political arguments.

As we have seen, to support a group's claims to political legitimacy, references to sacrifice were often crucial. The arguments advanced by Roberto Esposito may prove enlightening in this regard. In his reworking of views expounded in Marcel Mauss's famous *Essai sur le don* (1925), Esposito has made the compelling case that a community is always structured around a series of gifts that create a complex social network based on feelings of gratitude and obligation in the receivers and of prestige in the donors. A gift creates a bond far stronger that the exchange of goods between individuals pursuing their own self-interest. Obviously, the greatest gift of all is the surrender of one's life for others and, for this reason, it is instrumental in shaping a strong feeling of community.[18] The belief that, on the battlefield, people offer their lives for the safety of their fellow countrymen and future generations creates a sense of community through a debt towards the dead. In a way, it is sacrifice that turns Anderson's imagined community into a real communion, a quasi-religious experience integrating men and women unknown to each other and commanding their loyalty. Reverting to late seventeenth- and eighteenth-century France, it might be said that the arguments set forth by the second order were consistent with such a logic, for the nobility portrayed itself as the heir of a warring race that had spilt its blood for the nation over the centuries. The reasonings of the champions of the Third Estate and the rising bourgeoisie were, instead, (even) more perplexing since in their camp claims to industriousness were indeed juxtaposed with claims over its readiness to take up arms and to fight for the nation. The proliferating attempts at self-ennoblement are revealing of a desire to appropriate a past of sacrifices and devotion to the nation. This might show that the idea that they had contributed to the material welfare of France through their toil, which was indeed an important and widespread argument, was not a solid enough grounding to their claims to an identity with the nation. The physiocrats' definition of nation, so devoid of all emotional elements, or the Mandevillian paradigm, seeing a community as the outcome of the pursuit of individual interest, could not sustain an entirely convincing political argument. There was almost an implicit understanding that self-interest might not serve to generate the social capital necessary for a community to believe in itself. It was in part to demonstrate their innate bravery and their devotion to the nation that many of the champions of the rights of the Third Estate, in the immediate pre-Revolution and during the Revolution itself, made the case that their ancestors, the Gauls, had been fierce and freedom-loving warriors. Although their progeny had turned into peaceful and industrious bourgeois, their valiant spirit had been kept alive, smouldering beneath the ashes, only to flare up again in times of need. They had once been capable and willing to give up their lives for the nation and, hence, would be ready to do so once again.

[18] Esposito, *Communitas*, passim.

This leads us to one last consideration, namely, the downplaying of what were, in a sense, the transnational elements underlying the discourses considered in the present book. The debate on the nation's origins involved in effect the Gauls, a people who had seemingly inhabited the Hexagon since time immemorial, as well as the Romans and the Franks. The question of the respective contributions of the Germanic and the Roman elements in forming the French past, character, and identity was key. Many of our authors offered explanations in which the different ethnic components interacted in complex ways, shaping what they believed was a coherent narrative. The history of France they saw as the superimposition of different layers, each one building upon, and being influenced by, those that had preceded it. Yet all the different ethnic components were usually present. The issue at stake was their respective weighting. The intellectual history of the second half of the nineteenth century tells a different story. If, as Arnaldo Momigliano has written about Italy, the 'eighteenth century truly is the century without Rome', the same might be said of nineteenth-century France, the century of the triumph of the Gauls.[19] At that time, the Gallo-Romans, as the fathers of the Third Estate and of France as such, were gradually replaced by the Gauls, while the Frankish conquest seemingly lost relevance as a constitutive element of the nation's identity. Arguably, this might have been a way of emphasising a purity of origin, an extirpation of what were increasingly perceived as foreign elements. The beginning of the French nation was no longer sought in the Middle Ages but in pre-Roman antiquity. Yet all this, importantly, was the outcome of a decision. In fact, the crucial point to grasp is that all processes of identity formation can be understood as the outcome of a collective decision, one made over time, either conscious or unconscious, in which scholars and intellectuals might have a greater or lesser role, over which elements contribute to an identity and which are to be omitted – that is, alternative local, regional, dynastic, imperial, religious, linguistic, ethnic elements – thus determining the principles of inclusion and exclusion; the 'us' and 'them'. Part of the process requires the veiling of the decision itself. It seems difficult to imagine that any society might function knowing that, rather than a natural fact or a historical necessity, it is the product of an arbitrary decision, one that might always be revoked. It seems difficult to imagine that any society might function if it realises that its form is simply one possibility among many others. Therefore,

---

[19] Arnaldo Momigliano, 'La nuova storia romana di G. B. Vico', in Momigliano, *Sesto contributo alla storia degli studi classici e del mondo antico* (Rome: Edizioni di Storia e Letteratura, 1980), i. 193.

concealing the arbitrary nature of its true origins is key. It is this kind of
reification that produces the bond, the trust, the social capital necessary for
a community to function. Yet this also destroys the very idea of alternative
societal possibilities.[20] It makes it impossible, that is, to conceive of other
forms of community and imagine new forms of a shared collective existence.
Unmasking the underlying mechanisms obscuring that decision is then
crucial in allowing men and women to participate in a new and different
choice; in giving them back their freedom. For this, knowledge and the study
of the past obviously play a key role. It might not be rash to venture that
Renan himself was hinting at this when he declared, in *Qu'est-ce qu'une
nation?*, that '[f]orgetting, I would even say historical error, is an essential
factor in the creation of a nation, and it is for this reason that the progress of
historical studies often poses a threat to nationality'.[21]

---

[20] Francesco Remotti, *L'ossessione identitaria* (Bari: Laterza, 2010).
[21] Renan, 'Qu'est-ce qu'une nation?', 227.

Bibliography

Primary Sources

Abbadie, Jacques, *L'art de se connaître soi-même* (Paris: Fayard, 2003).

Académie celtique, 'Liste des membres et associés correspondans', *Mémoires de l'Académie celtique*, 1 (1807), 1–20.

Académie Royale des inscriptions et médailles, 'Registre journal des assemblées et délibérations pendant l'année 1714' (Paris: Bibliothèque nationale de France, MS fonds français 9415).

Académie française, *Dictionnaire de l'Académie française* (Paris: Coignard, 1694).

Albon, Claude-Camille-François d', *Eloge historique de M. Quesnay* (Paris: Didot, 1775).

Alembert, Jean Baptiste le Rond d', *Œuvres* (Paris: Belin, 1821–1822).

Alembert, Jean Baptiste le Rond d', *Discours préliminaire de 'L'Encyclopédie' et articles de 'L'Encyclopédie'* (Paris: Honoré Champion, 2011).

Alès de Corbet, Pierre-Alexandre d' [Le vicomte D*****], *Origine de la noblesse françoise depuis l'établissement de la monarchie* (Paris: G. Desprez, 1766).

Algarotti, Francesco, *Saggi* (Bari: Laterza, 1963).

Amat de Graveson, Ignace Hyacinthe, 'Copie d'une lettre écrite à M. l'abbé de Camps', *Le nouveau Mercure*, August 1720, 48–9.

Anonymous, review of Pierre Audigier, *De l'origine des François et de leur empire*, in *Le journal des sçavans*, 29 March 1677, 73–7.

Anonymous, *Les soupirs de la France esclave, qui aspire après la liberté* (n.p., 1689).

Anonymous, review of [Bonaventure d'Argonne], *Sentimens critiques sur Les caractères de Monsieur de La Bruyère*, in *Mémoires pour l'histoire des sciences et des beaux-arts*, March–April 1701, 76–82.

Anonymous, review of Gottfried Wilhelm Leibniz, *De origine francorum disquisitio*, in *Journal de Trévoux, ou Mémoires pour servir à l'histoire des sciences et des arts*, January 1710, 1–28.

Anonymous, review of *Miscellanea Berolinensia ad incrementum scientiarum ex scriptis*, in *Le journal des sçavans*, 8 December 1710, 644–52.

Anonymous, *Tablettes de l'homme du monde, ou Analyse des sept qualités essentielles à former le beau caractère d'homme du monde accompli* (The Hague: A. Le Catholique, 1715).

Anonymous, review of Joseph Vaissette, *Dissertation sur l'origine des Français*, in *Le journal des sçavans*, 4 January 1723, 9–11.

Anonymous, 'Lettre à un ami sur le *Spectateur françois*, qui s'imprime en Hollande', *Bibliothèque françoise, ou Histoire littéraire de la France*, 4 (1724), 32–50.

Anonymous, review of [Charles Sevin Mis de Quincy], *Histoire militaire du règne de Louis le Grand*, in *Journal de Trévoux, ou Mémoires pour servir à l'histoire des sciences et des arts*, October 1724, 1796–806.

Anonymous, review of Jean-Baptiste Dubos, *Histoire critique de l'établissement de la monarchie française*, in *Le journal des sçavans*, May 1734, 272–87.

Anonymous, review of Jean-Baptiste Dubos, *Histoire critique de l'établissement de la monarchie française*, in *Bibliothèque raisonnée des ouvrages des savans de l'Europe*, October–December 1734, 388–405.

Anonymous, review of Jean-Baptiste Dubos, *Histoire critique de l'établissement de la monarchie française*, in *Journal littéraire*, 22 (1734), 130–55.

Anonymous, review of Claude-Marie Guyon, *Histoire des Amazones anciennes et modernes*, in *Journal de Trévoux, ou Mémoires pour servir à l'histoire des sciences et des arts*, April 1741, 678–98.

Anonymous, review of [Gabriel Bonnot de Mably], *Parallèle des Romains et des François par rapport au gouvernement*, in *Journal de Trévoux, ou Mémoires pour servir à l'histoire des sciences et des arts*, February 1741, 319–56.

Anonymous, review of Charles-Louis Secondat de Montesquieu, *De l'Esprit des lois*, in *Nouvelles ecclésiastiques*, 9 October 1749, 161–4 and 16 October 1749, 165–7.

Anonymous, review of Jacques Martin, *Histoire des Gaules, et des conquêtes des Gaulois, depuis leur origine jusqu'à la fondation de la monarchie françoise*, in *Le journal des sçavans*, June 1752, 348–56.

Anonymous, 'Préface', in Louis Le Gendre, *Mœurs et coutumes des François, dans les premiers temps de la monarchie* (Paris: Briasson, 1753), iii–xxxvi.

Anonymous, review of *Journal étrangère, ouvrage périodique*, in *Mercure de France*, February 1755, 83–5.

Anonymous, review of Gabriel-François Coyer, *La noblesse commerçante*, in *Journal de Trévoux, ou Mémoires pour servir à l'histoire des sciences et des arts*, March 1756, 726–50.

Anonymous, review of Adam Fitz-Adam, *Le monde, ou Feuilles périodiques sur les mœurs du tems*, and of [Roger Urbain], *Le traducteur, ou Traduction de diverses feuilles choisies, tirées des papiers périodiques Anglois*, in *Bibliothèque des sciences et des beaux-arts*, January–March 1757, 213–22.

Anonymous, 'Principes et observations économiques, par M. de Forbonnais: Second extrait', *Journal de l'agriculture, du commerce et des finances*, May 1767, 3–24.

Anonymous, review of Jean-Louis Castilhon, *Considérations sur les causes physiques et morales de la diversité du génie, des mœurs et du gouvernement des nations*, in *Journal encyclopédique*, 1 July 1769, 148–50.

Anonymous, review of Jean-Louis Castilhon, *Considérations sur les causes physiques et morales de la diversité du génie, des mœurs et du gouvernement des nations*, in *Journal encyclopédique*, 1 August 1770, 331–43.

Anonymous, 'An Essay on the National Sincerity of the French, in Opposition to the General Belief', *The London Magazine*, August 1771, 404–5.

Anonymous, 'Réflexions oubliées par quelques voyageurs', *Le nouveau Mercure*, 1775, ii. 91–7.

Anonymous, 'Nouvelles littéraires: France', *Journal encyclopédique*, 15 May 1780, 158–67.

Anonymous, *Valentine ou Lettres et mémoires interessants d'une famille anglaise* (Lausanne: n.p., 1786).

Anonymous, *Les vœux d'un patriote* (Amsterdam: n.p., 1788).

Anonymous, *Lettre à un plébéien au sujet de l'assemblée des États généraux* (n.p., September 1788).

Anonymous, review of Gabriel Bonnot de Mably, *Observations sur l'histoire de France*, in Grimm et al., *Correspondance littéraire*, xv. 358–61 (December 1788).

Anonymous, *De la différence qu'il y a entre États-généraux et les assemblées nationales, ou Principes radicaux de la constitution* (n.p., 1789).

Anonymous, 'Esquisse de l'histoire de France par un philosophe impartial', in Laurent-Pierre Bérenger, *Esprit de Mably et de Condillac* (Grenoble: Le Jay fils, 1789), ii. 347–88.

Anonymous, review of Emmanuel-Joseph Sieyès, *Qu'est-ce que le tiers état?*, in Grimm et al., *Correspondance littéraire*, xv. 400 (February 1789).

Anonymous, *Le réveil du tiers état, c'est à dire de la nation* (n.p., 1789).

Anonymous, *Réflexions d'un ami de la liberté ou Principes de M. l'abbé de Mably* (n.p., 1790).

Anonymous, 'Jean Le Laboureur', in Louis-Mayeul Chaudon, Antoine-François Delandine, and Louis-Marie Prudhomme (eds.), *Dictionnaire universel, historique, critique et bibliographique* (Paris: Mame frères, 1810–1812), 413–4.

Anonymous, 'Notice sur Saint-Simon et sa doctrine, et sur quelques autres ouvrages qui en seraient le développement', in Alfred Péreire, *Autour de Saint-Simon, documents originaux* (Paris: Honoré Champion, 1912), 175–203.

Anonymous, *Réflexions sur l'inviolabilité des rois et sur la prétendue souveraineté des peuples* (n.p., n.d.).

Anquetil, Louis-Pierre, *L'esprit de la Ligue, ou Histoire politique des troubles de France, pendant les XVIe et XVIIe siècles* (Paris: n.p., 1767).

Anquetil, Louis-Pierre, *Précis de l'histoire universelle, ou Tableau historique présentant les vicissitudes des nations* (Paris: Lesguilliez frères, 1799).

Anquetil, Louis-Pierre, *Histoire de France depuis les Gaulois jusqu'à la fin de la monarchie* (Paris: Garnery, 1805).

Antraigues, Louis-Alexandre de Launay d', *Mémoire sur les États-généraux, leurs droits, et la manière de les convoquer* (n.p., 1788).

Archives de la Chambre syndicale de la Librairie et Imprimerie de Paris, 'Registre des livres arrêtés dans les visites faites par les syndics et adjoints, 1742–1771' (Paris: Bibliothèque nationale de France, MS manuscrits français, 21932).

[Arcq, Philippe-Auguste de Sainte-Foix d'], *La noblesse militaire, ou Le patriote françois* ([Paris: Michel Lambert], 1756).

Argens, Jean-Baptiste de Boyer d', *Lettres juives* (Paris: Honoré Champion, 2013).

Argenson, René-Louis de Voyer de Paulmy d', 'Jusques où la démocratie peut estre admise dans le gouvernement monarchique? Ce traitté de politique a esté composé à l'occasion de ceux de M. de Boulainvilliers, touchant l'ancien gouvernement féodal de France' (Paris: Bibliothèque de l'Arsenal, MS manuscrits français, 2334).

[Argenson, René-Louis de Voyer de Paulmy d' – uncertain attribution], review of Gabriel-François Coyer, *La noblesse commerçante*, in *L'année littéraire*, 1756, i. 37–55.

Argenson, René-Louis de Voyer de Paulmy d', *Considérations sur le gouvernement ancien et présent de la France* (Amsterdam: Marc Michel Rey, 1764).

Argenson, René-Louis de Voyer de Paulmy d', *Considérations sur le gouvernement ancien et présent de la France* (Amsterdam: n.p., 1784).

Argenson, René-Louis de Voyer de Paulmy d', *Journal et mémoires* (Paris: Veuve de J. Renouard, 1859–1867).

Argenson, René-Louis de Voyer de Paulmy d', *Mémoires et journal inédit* (Nendeln: Kraus reprint, 1979).

Argenson, Antoine-René de Voyer de Paulmy d', and André-Guillaume Constant d'Orville, *Bibliothèque historique à l'usage des dames* (Paris: Moutard, 1779).

Audigier, Pierre, *De l'origine des François et de leur empire* (Paris: Barbin, 1676).

Baillet, Adrien, *Jugemens des savans sur les principaux ouvrages des auteurs* (Hildesheim: G. Olms, 1971).

Balzac, Honoré de, *Le cabinet des antiques* (Paris: Garnier, 1958).

Balzac, Jean-Louis Guez de, *Les entretiens* (Paris: Marcel Didier, 1972).

Barante, Prosper de, *Histoire des ducs de Bourgogne de la maison de Valois, 1364–1477* (Paris: Ladvocat, 1824–1826).

Barante, Prosper de, *Mélanges historiques et littéraires* (Paris: Ladvocat, 1835).

Barante, Prosper de, *Notice sur la vie et les ouvrages de M. le Comte de Montlosier* (Clermont-Ferrand: Thibaut-Landriot, 1842).

Barbier, Edmond-Jean-François, *Chronique de la régence et du règne de Louis XV (1718–1763), ou Journal de Barbier* (Paris: Charpentier, 1857–1866).

Baretti, Giuseppe, *Opere scelte* (Turin: UTET, 1975).

Barnave, Antoine Pierre Joseph Marie, *Introduction à la Révolution française* (Paris: Armand Colin, 1960).

Barral, Pierre, *Manuel des souverains* (n.p., 1754).

Baudeau, Nicolas, review of Claude François-Joseph d'Auxiron, *Principes de tout gouvernement, ou Examen des causes de la splendeur ou de la foiblesse de tout État considéré en lui-même, et indépendamment des mœurs*, in *Éphémérides du citoyen*, April 1767, 117–80.

Baudeau, Nicolas, 'Suite des observations économiques à M. l'abbé de Condillac', *Nouvelles éphémérides économiques*, 1776, v. 131–46.

Baudeau, Nicolas, *Première introduction à la philosophie économique, ou Analyse des États policés* (Paris: P. Geuthner, 1910).

Bauffremont de Sennecey, Henri de, 'Harangue de M. de Sennecey, président de la chambre de la noblesse, à la clôture des états et présentation des cahiers', in Jean Charlemagne Lalourcé and Jean-Jacques Duval d'Eprémesnil (eds.), *Recueil de pièces originales et authentiques, concernant la tenue des États généraux* (Paris: Barrois l'aîné, 1789), viii. 240–9.

Baumier, *Protestation contre la forme des États-généraux de 1614* (n.p., 1788).

Bayle, Pierre, *Pensées diverses sur la comète* (Paris: Nizet, 1984).

Bayle, Pierre et al., *Correspondance* (Oxford: Voltaire Foundation, 1999–).

Beaumarchais, Pierre-Augustin Caron de, *Œuvres* (Paris: Gallimard, 1988).

[Bedos], *Le négociant patriote, contenant un tableau qui réunit les avantages du commerce, la connoissance des spéculations de chaque nation* (Brussels: n.p., 1779).

Belleguise, Alexandre de, *Traité de la noblesse suivant les préjugez rendus par les commissaires deputez pour la vérification des titres de noblesse en Provence* (n.p., 1669).

Belloy, Pierre-Laurent Buirette de, *Le siège de Calais* (London: Modern Humanities Research Association, 2014).

Bergasse, Nicolas, *Observations sur les préjugés de la noblesse héréditaire* (n.p., 1789).

Bernard d'Héry, Pierre, 'Essai sur la vie et sur les ouvrages de l'abbé Prévost', in Antoine François Prévost, *Œuvres choisies* (Amsterdam: n.p., 1783–1785), i. 1–72.

[Bernier, François], 'Nouvelle division de la terre, par les différentes espèces ou races d'hommes qui l'habitent, envoyée par un fameux voyageur à M. l'abbé de la *** à peu près en ces termes', *Le journal des sçavans*, 24 April 1684, 133–140.

Bernier, François, 'Nouvelle division de la terre, par les différentes espèces ou races d'hommes qui l'habitent, de la beauté des femmes, etc.', *Mercure de France*, December 1722, 62–70.

Bertoux, Guillaume, *Anecdotes françoises, depuis l'établissement de la monarchie jusqu'au règne de Louis XV* (Paris: Vincent, 1767).

Bodin, Jean, *Les six livres de la république* (Paris: Fayard, 1986).

Boileau, Nicolas, *Œuvres* (Paris: Gallimard, 1966).

[Boisguilbert, Pierre le Pesant de], *Le détail de la France, la cause de la diminution de ses biens et la facilité du remède, en fournissant en un mois tout l'argent dont le Roi a besoin, et enrichissant tout le monde* (n.p., 1695).

Boisguilbert, Pierre le Pesant de, 'Dissertation sur la nature des richesses, de l'argent et des tributs', in Eugène Daire (ed.), *Économistes-financiers du XVIIIe siècle* (Geneva: Slatkine, 1971), 372–416.

[Bonald, Louis Gabriel Ambroise de], *Réflexions sur l'intérêt général de l'Europe, suivies de quelques considérations sur la noblesse* (Paris: Le Normant, 1815).

Bonald, Louis Gabriel Ambroise de, 'Sur les Francs et les Gaulois', *Le défenseur: Journal religieux, politique et littéraire*, 25 November 1820, 385–95.

Bonald, Louis Gabriel Ambroise de, *Œuvres* (Geneva: Slatkine, 1982).

Bossuet, Jacques-Bénigne, *Œuvres complètes* (Besançon: Outhenin-Chalandre fils, 1836).

Bossuet, Jacques-Bénigne, *Politique tirée des propres paroles de l'Ecriture sainte* (Geneva: Droz, 1967).

Bougainville, Jean-Pierre de, 'Eloge de Fréret', *Histoire de l'Académie royale des inscriptions et belles-lettres*, 23 (1756), 314–37.

Bouhier, Jean, *Correspondance littéraire du Président Bouhier* (Saint-Étienne: Université de Saint-Étienne, 1974–).

Boulainvilliers, Henri de, 'Abrégé de l'histoire universelle' (Paris: Bibliothèque nationale de France, MS fonds français, 6363).

Boulainvilliers, Henri de, 'Généalogie de la maison de Boulainvilliers' (Paris: Bibliothèque nationale de France, MS fonds français, 32948).

Boulainvilliers, Henri de, *État de la France* (London: Palmer, 1727).

Boulainvilliers, Henri de, *Histoire de l'ancien gouvernement de la France* (The Hague: aux dépens de la Compagnie, 1727).

Boulainvilliers, Henri de, *Mémoires présentez à Monseigneur le Duc d'Orléans* (The Hague: aux dépens de la Compagnie, 1727).

Boulainvilliers, Henri de, *La vie de Mahomet* (London: n.p., 1730).

Boulainvilliers, Henri de, *Essais sur la noblesse de France, contenant une dissertation sur son origine et abaissement* (Amsterdam: n.p., 1732).

Boulainvilliers, Henri de, *Lettres sur les anciens Parlemens de France que l'on nomme États-généraux* (London: T. Wood and S. Palmer, 1753).

Boulainvilliers, Henri de, 'Lettre à Mademoiselle Cousinot sur l'histoire et sa méthode', in Simon, *Un révolté du Grand siècle*, 71–83.

Boulainvilliers, Henri de, 'Préface critique au Journal de Saint Louis', in Simon, *Un révolté du Grand siècle*, 85–131.

Boulainvilliers, Henri de, *Astrologie mondiale, histoire du mouvement de l'apogée du soleil ou Pratique des règles d'astrologie pour juger des événements généraux* (Garches: Éditions du nouvel humanisme, 1949).

Boulainvilliers, Henri de, 'Dissertation sur la noblesse françoise', in Devyver, *Le sang épuré*, 501–48.

Boulainvilliers, Henri de, *Œuvres philosophiques* (The Hague: M. Nijhoff, 1973–1975).

Bouquet, Martin, *Recueil des historiens de la France* (Paris: Libraires Associés, 1739).

[Bouquet, Pierre], *Lettres provinciales, ou Examen impartial de l'origine, de la constitution et des révolutions de la monarchie française* (The Hague: Le Neutre, 1772).

[Bourge, Jean-Claude-Antoine de], *Avis aux électeurs des assemblées du 21 avril 1789* (n.p., 1789).

Bréquigny, Louis Feudrix de, 'Recherches sur les bourgeoisies', in Leber (ed.), *Collection des meilleurs dissertations relatifs à l'histoire de France*, xx. 145–211.

Bréquigny, Louis Feudrix de, 'Recherches sur les communes', in Leber (ed.), *Collection des meilleurs dissertations relatifs à l'histoire de France*, xx. 42–144.

Bricaire de la Dixmerie, Nicolas, *Les deux âges du goût et du génie français, sous Louis XIV et sous Louis XV* (Paris: Lacombe, 1769).

Brissot de Warville, Jacques-Pierre, *Mémoires* (Paris: Ladvocat, 1830–1832).

Brizard, Gabriel, 'Eloge historique de l'abbé Mably', in Mably, *Œuvres*, i. 1–120.

Buchet, Pierre-François, note in *Le nouveau Mercure*, October 1717, 20–1.

Buffon, Georges-Louis Leclerc, *Histoire naturelle, générale et particulière* (Paris: Imprimerie Royale, 1749–1789).

Bullet, Jean-Baptiste, *Mémoires sur la langue celtique* (Besançon: Daclin, 1754–1760).

Bullet, Jean-Baptiste, *Dissertations sur différens sujets de l'histoire de France* (Besançon: Charmet, 1759).

Bureaux de Pusy, Jean-Xavier, *Opinion de M. Bureaux de Pusy, député du bailliage d'Amont, dans la séance du mercredi 16 décembre 1789* (Paris: Imprimerie nationale, [1789]).

Burlamaqui, Jean-Jacques, *Principes du droit naturel* (Geneva: Barrillot, 1747).

Calonges, P.-V. de, *Lettres aux notables, sur la forme et l'objet des États généraux* (London: chez les marchands de nouveautés, 1788).

Camps, François de, 'Réponse de M. l'abbé de Camps, du 1 Mai 1720, à la réfutation du père Daniel', *Le nouveau Mercure*, June 1720, 3–45.

Camps, François de, 'De la noblesse de la race royale des François', *Le nouveau Mercure*, July 1720, 3–13.

Cantillon, Richard, *Essai sur la nature du commerce en général* (Paris: Institut national d'études démographiques, 1997).

[Caraccioli, Louis-Antoine], *L'Europe françoise* (Paris: Veuve Duchesne, 1776).

Carlyle, Thomas, *Historical Essays* (Berkley: University of California Press, 2002).

Carlyle, Thomas, *Selected Writings* (London: Penguin Classics, 2015).

Carra, Jean-Louis, *Discours contre la défense de Louis Capet, dernier roi des Français, par le citoyen Carra, député de Saône et Loire, prononcé à la séance du 3 janvier 1793* (Paris: Imprimerie nationale, 1793).

Casaux, Alexandre Charles de, *Le tiers-état entièrement éclairé sur ses droits, ou supplément à l'avis important par le même auteur* (n.p., 1788).

Caseneuve de Riez, Balthazar-Honoré de, *L'incomparable pieté des très-chrestiens rois de France* (Paris: Gilles Alliot, 1672–1674).

Castel de Saint-Pierre, Charles-Irénée, 'Observations sur l'ouvrage politique manuscrit de M.' (Paris: Bibliothèque de l'Arsenal, MS manuscrits français, 2337).

Castel de Saint-Pierre, Charles-Irénée, *Ouvrajes de politique* (Rotterdam: Beman, 1733–1740).

Castel, Louis Bertrand, *L'homme moral opposé à l'homme physique de M. R***: Lettres philosophiques, où l'on réfute le déisme du jour* (Toulouse: n.p., 1756).

Castelnau, Michel de, *Traitte des meurs et facons des anciens Gauloys* (Paris: Denys du Val, 1581).

Castiglione, Luigi Gonzaga di, *L'homme de lettres, bon citoyen* (Geneva: n.p., 1777).

Castilhon, Jean-Louis, *Considérations sur les causes physiques et morales de la diversité du génie, des mœurs et du gouvernement des nations* (Bouillon: aux dépens de la Société typographique, 1769).

Caylus, Anne Claude Philippe de, et al., *Correspondance inédite du Comte de Caylus, avec le P. Paciaudi, théatin (1757–1765), suivie de celles de l'abbé Barthélemy et de P. Mariette avec le même* (Paris: Imprimerie nationale, 1877).

Ceriziers, René de, *Les heureux commencements de la France chrétienne sous l'apôtre de nos rois S. Remy* (Paris: Angot, 1633).

Cérutti, Joseph-Antoine-Joachim, *Vues générales sur la constitution françoise, ou Exposé des droits de l'homme, dans l'ordre naturel, social et monarchique* (Paris: Desenne, 1789).

Chapelain, Jean, *Lettres* (Paris: Imprimerie nationale, 1880–1883).

Chapuys-Montlaville, Louis Alceste, 'Sieyès', in Emmanuel-Joseph Sieyès, *Qu'est-ce que le tiers état?* (Paris: Pagnerre, 1839), 1–30.

Chardin, Jean, *Voyages de Monsieur le Chevalier Chardin en Perse et autres lieux de l'Orient* (Amsterdam: J.-L. de Lorme, 1711).

Charron, Pierre, *De la sagesse* (Geneva: Slatkine, 1968).

Chassaignon, Jean-Marie, *Le tiers-état rétabli pour jamais dans tous ses droits, par la résurrection des bons rois et la mort éternelle des tyrans* (Langres: n.p., 1789).

Chateaubriand, François-René de, *De la monarchie selon la charte* (Brussels: A. Wahlen, 1816).

Chateaubriand, François-René de, *Œuvres complètes* (Paris: Pourrat Frères, 1836–1839).

Chateaubriand, François-René de, *Mémoires d'outre-tombe* (Paris: Gallimard, 1951).

Chiniac de La Bastide, Pierre, dedicatory letter to 'Monsieur le Dauphin', in Simon Pelloutier, *Histoire des Celtes, et particulièrement des Gaulois et des Germains* (Paris: Quillaud, 1771), i. n.p.

Cobden, Richard, *Political Writings* (London: Routledge, 1995).

Cohen, Jean, *Du système des doctrinaires, ou Observations sur un écrit de M. Guizot intitulé 'Du gouvernement de la France depuis la Restauration, et du ministère actuel'* (Paris: A. Égron, 1820).

[Comte, Charles – uncertain attribution], review of François-Dominique de Montlosier, *De la monarchie française*, in *Le censeur*, 6 (1815), 192–244, and 7 (1815), 184–214.

Comte, Auguste, *Cours de philosophie positive: Leçons 46–51* (Paris: Hermann, 2012).

Condillac, Étienne Bonnot de, *Cours d'études pour l'instruction du prince de Parme* (Deux-Ponts: n.p., 1782).

Condillac, Étienne Bonnot de, *Œuvres philosophiques* (Paris: Presses universitaires de France, 1947–1951).

Condorcet, Jean-Antoine-Nicolas de, *Sur les fonctions des États-généraux et des autres assemblées nationales* (n.p., 1789).

Condorcet, Jean-Antoine-Nicolas de, *Œuvres* (Paris: Firmin Didot, 1847–1849).

Conseil d'État du Roi, *Arrêt concernant la convocation des États généraux du Royaume du 5 Juillet 1788* (Paris: Nyon, 1788).

Constant, Benjamin, *Principes de politique (1806)* (Geneva: Droz, 1980).

Constant, Benjamin, *Écrits politiques* (Paris: Gallimard, 1997).

Constant, Benjamin, *Journaux intimes* (Paris: Gallimard, 2017).

Cordemoy, Géraud de, *Divers traitez de métaphysique, d'histoire et de politique* (Paris: Veuve de J.-B. Coignard, 1691).

Corneille, Pierre, *Théâtre complet* (Paris: Gallimard, 1957).

Coste, Pierre, *Défense de M. de La Bruyère et de ses Caractères contre les accusations et les objections de M. de Vigneul-Marville* (Amsterdam: Lombrail, 1702).

Cousin, Victor, *Du vrai, du beau et du bien* (Paris: Didier, 1853).

Coyer, Gabriel-François, *Dissertations pour être lues: La première, sur le vieux mot de patrie, la seconde, sur la nature du peuple* (The Hague: Pierre Gosse, 1755).

Coyer, Gabriel-François, *La noblesse commerçante* (Paris: Duchesne, 1765).

Coyer, Gabriel-François, *Plan d'éducation publique* (Paris: Duchesne, 1770).

Coyer, Gabriel-François, *Voyages d'Italie et de Hollande* (Paris: Veuve Duchesne, 1775).

Coyer, Gabriel-François, *Nouvelles observations sur l'Angleterre* (Paris: Veuve Duchesne, 1779).

Crébillon, Claude-Prosper Jolyot de, *Les égarements du cœur et de l'esprit* (Paris: Gallimard, 1990).

Croÿ-Solre, Emmanuel de, *Journal inédit (1718–1784)* (Paris: Flammarion, 1906–1921).

D'Origny, Pierre, 'Le Hérault de la noblesse de France', *Revue historique, nobiliaire et biographique*, 12 (1875), 322–56.

Damiens de Gomicourt, Augustin-Pierre, 'Dissertation historique et critique pour servir à l'histoire des premiers temps de la monarchie française', in Leber (ed.), *Collection des meilleurs dissertations relatifs à l'histoire de France*, v. 40–112.

Daniel, Gabriel, *Deux dissertations préliminaires pour une nouvelle histoire de France depuis l'établissement de la monarchie dans les Gaules* (Paris: Simon Benard, 1696).

Daniel, Gabriel, *Histoire de France, depuis l'établissement de la monarchie françoise dans les Gaules* (Paris: Simon Benard, 1696).

Daniel, Gabriel, *Histoire de France, depuis l'établissement de la monarchie françoise dans les Gaules* (Paris: J.-B. Delespine, 1713).

Daniel, Gabriel, *Histoire de la milice françoise* (Paris: Coignard, 1721).

Dantine, Maur, Ursin Durand, and Charles Clémencet, *L'art de vérifier les dates des faits historiques, des chartes, des chroniques, et autres anciens monumens depuis la naissance de Notre Seigneur* (Paris: Guillaume Desprez and Pierre-Guillaume Cavelier, 1750).

De Gournay, Jacques Claude Marie Vincent, *Mémoires et lettres* (Paris: Institut Coppet, 2017).

[De Pauw, Cornélius], *Défense des recherches philosophiques sur les Américains* (Berlin: George Jacques Decker, 1770).

De Staël, Anne-Louise-Germaine, *De la littérature considérée dans ses rapports avec les institutions sociales* (Geneva: Droz, 1959).

De Staël, Anne-Louise-Germaine, *Considérations sur la Révolution française* (Paris: Tallandier, 1983).

De Staël, Anne-Louise-Germaine, *De l'influence des passions sur le bonheur des individus et des nations, suivi de Réflexions sur le suicide* (Paris: Payot et Rivage, 2000).

Defoe, Daniel, *Robinson Crusoe* (London: Penguin, 2003).

Delandine, Antoine-François, *Des États-généraux, ou Histoire des assemblées nationales en France* (Paris: Cuchet, 1788).

Delort, Joseph, *Histoire de la détention des philosophes et des gens de lettres à la Bastille et à Vincennes* (Paris: Didot père et fils, 1829).

Denis, Paul (ed.), *Lettres autographes de la collection de Troussures* (Beauvais: Imprimerie départementale de l'Oise, 1912).

Desfontaines, Pierre-François Guyot and François Granet, *Observations sur les écrits modernes* (Paris: Chaubert, 1735–1743).

[Desfontaines, Pierre-François Guyot], review of Jean-George Le Franc de Pompignan, *Essai critique sur l'état présent de la République des lettres*, in *Jugemens sur quelques ouvrages nouveaux*, 1 (1744), ii. 121–30.

Desmaiseaux, Pierre (ed.), *Recueil de diverses pièces sur la philosophie, la religion naturelle, l'histoire, les mathématiques, etc.* (Amsterdam: H. Du Sauzet, 1740).

Desmoulins, Camille, *Révolutions de France et de Brabant* (Frankfurt: Keip, 1989).

Destutt de Tracy, Antoine-Louis-Claude, *Traité de la volonté et de ses effets* (Paris: Vrin, 2015).

Destutt de Tracy, Antoine-Louis-Claude, *Commentaire sur l'*Esprit des lois *de Montesquieu* (Paris: Vrin, 2016).

[Diderot, Denis – uncertain attribution], 'Artisan', in Diderot and d'Alembert (eds.), *Encyclopédie*, i. 745.

[Diderot, Denis – uncertain attribution], 'Artiste', in Diderot and d'Alembert (eds.), *Encyclopédie*, i. 745.

[Diderot, Denis – uncertain attribution], 'Manières, façons', in Diderot and d'Alembert (eds.), *Encyclopédie*, x. 36.

Diderot, Denis, 'Humaine, espèce', in Diderot and d'Alembert (eds.), *Encyclopédie*, viii. 344–8.

Diderot, Denis, *Œuvres complètes* (ed. Lewinter) (Paris: le Club français du livre, 1969–).

Diderot, Denis, *Œuvres complètes* (ed. Dieckmann et al.) (Paris: Hermann, 1975–2004).

Diderot, Denis and Jean Baptiste Le Rond d'Alembert (eds.), *Encyclopédie, ou Dictionnaire raisonné des sciences, des arts et des métiers* (Paris: Briasson, David l'aîné, Le Breton, Durand, 1751–1780).

Domat, Jean, *Œuvres complètes* (Paris: Firmin-Didot, 1828–1830).

Du Buat-Nançay, Louis-Gabriel, *Les origines ou L'ancien gouvernement de la France, de l'Allemagne et de l'Italie* (Paris: Didot, 1757).

Dubos, Jean-Baptiste, *Histoire critique de l'établissement de la monarchie française* (Paris: Osmont, 1734).

Dubos, Jean-Baptiste, *Réflexions critiques sur la poésie et la peinture* (Paris: Beaux-arts de Paris éditions, 2015).

[Ducalle], 'Les Gaulois et les Francs', *Revue rétrospective: Seconde série*, 1 (1835), 145–7.

[Duclos, Charles Pinot], *Confessions du Comte de **** (Amsterdam: n.p., 1741).

Duclos, Charles Pinot, 'Mémoire sur les épreuves par le duel et par les élémens, communément appellées Jugemens de Dieu par nos anciens François', *Mémoires de littérature tirés des registres de l'Académie royale des inscriptions et belles-lettres*, 15 (1743), 617–38.

Duclos, Charles Pinot, *Histoire de Louis XI* (Paris: Frères Guerin, 1745).

Duclos, Charles Pinot, 'Mémoire sur les Druides', *Histoire de l'Académie royale des inscriptions et belles-lettres*, 19 (1753), 483–94.

Duclos, Charles Pinot, *Histoire de Madame de Luz* (Saint-Brieuc: Presses universitaires de Bretagne, 1972).

Duclos, Charles Pinot, *Considérations sur les mœurs de ce siècle* (Paris: Honoré Champion, 2005).

Dufresny, Charles, *Amusements sérieux et comiques* (Paris: Bossard, 1921).

Dumarsais, César, *Des tropes ou des diférens sens dans lesquels on peut prendre un même mot dans une même langue* (Paris: Veuve de J.B. Brocas, 1730).

Dumas, Alexandre, 'Introduction à nos feuilletons historiques', *La presse*, 15 July 1836, 1–3.

Dumont, Étienne, *Souvenirs sur Mirabeau et sur les deux premières assemblées législatives* (Paris: Gosselin, 1832).

Dunoyer, Charles, 'Du système de l'équilibre des puissance européennes', *Le censeur européen*, 1 (1817), i. 93–142.

Dunoyer, Charles, review of Augustin Thierry, *Des nations et de leurs rapports mutuels*, in *Le censeur européen*, 1 (1817), ii. 222–46.

Dunoyer, Charles, 'Esquisse historique des doctrines auxquelles on a donné le nom d'*Industrialisme*, c'est-à-dire, des doctrines qui fondent la société sur l'*Industrie*', *Revue encyclopédique*, 33 (1827), 368–94.

Dupin, Claude-François-Étienne and . . . de Lagrange, *Pétition pour rendre à la France son véritable nom, par Dupin et Lagrange, républicains gaulois* (n.p., 1793).

Dupont de Nemours, Pierre-Samuel, 'Analyse du Tableau économique: Avis aux lecteurs', in François Quesnay, *Œuvres économiques et philosophiques* (Frankfurt: J. Baer, 1888), 440–3.

Dupont de Nemours, Pierre-Samuel, 'Abrégé des principes de l'économie politique', in Eugène Daire (ed.), *Physiocrates* (Geneva: Slatkine, 1971), 377–85.

[Duquesnoy, Adrien Cyprien], *L'ami des patriotes ou le Défenseur de la Révolution* (Paris: Demonville, 1790–1792).

Dutot, Nicolas, *Réflexions politiques sur les finances et le commerce* (The Hague: Frères Vaillant et N. Prevost, 1738).

Enfantin, Barthélémy-Prosper et al., *Doctrine de Saint-Simon: Première année, 1829* (Paris: au bureau de l'Organisateur, 1830).

[Éprémesnil, Jacques Duval d'– uncertain attribution], *Réflexions impartiales sur la grande question qui partage les esprits, concernant les droits du roi et de la nation assemblée en États généraux* (n.p., 1789).

Espiard de la Borde, François-Ignace d', *L'esprit des nations* (The Hague: Beauregard, 1752).

[Espiard de la Borde, François-Ignace d' – uncertain attribution], 'Lettre à l'auteur de ces feuilles au sujet d'un livre intitulé: *Considérations sur la diversité du génie des nations, etc.*', *Année littéraire*, 1770, i. 344–8.

Fabre d'Églantine, Philippe-François-Nazaire, *Rapport fait à la Convention nationale dans la séance du 3 du second mois de la seconde année de la République française, au nom de la Commission chargée de la confection du calendrier* (Paris: Imprimerie nationale, 1793).

Falconnet de la Bellonie, Camille, *La psycantropie, ou Nouvelle théorie de l'homme* (Avignon: Chambeau, 1748).

Faret, Nicolas, *L'honneste homme ou L'art de plaire à la court* (Geneva: Slatkine, 1970).

Feijóo, Benito Jerónimo, *Teatro crítico universal o Discursos varios en todo género de materias para desengaño de errores comunes* (Madrid: Castalia, 1986).

Fénelon, François de Salignac de La Mothe, *Les aventures de Télémaque* (Paris: Gallimard, 1995).

Fénelon, François de Salignac de La Mothe, *Lettre à l'Académie française* (Geneva: Droz, 1970).

Féraud, Jean-François, *Dictionnaire critique de la langue française* (Marseilles: Mossy, 1788).

Ferguson, Adam, *An Essay on the History of Civil Society* (Cambridge: Cambridge University Press, 1995).

Filangieri, Gaetano, *La scienza della legislazione* (Naples: Procaccini, 1995).

Fleury, André-Hercule de, *L'"Abrégé de l'histoire de France" écrit pour le jeune Louis XV* (Montigny-le-Bretonneux: Archives départementales des Yvelines, 2004).

Foncemagne, Étienne Lauréault de, 'Examen critique d'une opinion de M. le Comte de Boulainvilliers', *Mémoires de littérature tirés des registres de l'Académie royale des inscriptions et belles-lettres*, 10 (1736), 525–41.

Fontenelle, Bernard de, *Œuvres complètes* (Paris: Fayard, 1989–).

[Forbonnais, François Véron Duverger de], 'Lettre de M. A.B.C.D. etc. aux auteurs du journal de la Gazette', *Journal de l'agriculture, du commerce et des finances*, August, 1767, 57–101.

Fréret, Nicolas, 'Observations sur la religion des Gaulois et sur celle des Germains', *Mémoires de littérature, tirés des registres de l'Académie royale des inscriptions et belles lettres*, 24 (1756), 389–431.

Fréret, Nicolas, 'Sur l'usage des sacrifices humains, établi chez les différentes nations et particulièrement chez les Gaulois', *Mémoires de littérature tirés des registres de l'Académie royale des inscriptions et belles-lettres*, 18 (1753), 178–81.

Fréret, Nicolas, *Œuvres complètes* (Paris: Dandré, 1796).

Fréron, Élie, review of Louis Le Gendre, *Mœurs et coutumes des François, dans les premiers temps de la monarchie* (edition of 1753), in *Lettres sur quelques écrits de ce temps*, 1753, viii. 332–41.

Fréron, Élie, review of Philippe-Auguste de Sainte-Foix d'Arcq, *La noblesse militaire*, in *L'année littéraire*, 1756, ii. 31–50.

Fresneau, Pierre, *Petit abrégé chronologique et historique des rois de France, orné de leurs médaillons* (Paris: Veuve Hérissant, 1784).

Furetière, Antoine, *Dictionnaire universel* (The Hague and Rotterdam: Arnout & Reinier Leers, 1690).

Furetière, Antoine, *Dictionnaire universel* (The Hague and Rotterdam: Arnout & Reinier Leers, 1701).

Furetière, Antoine, *Dictionnaire universel* (The Hague: P. Husson, 1727).

Furetière, Antoine, *Le roman bourgeois* (Paris: Gallimard, 1981).

Galiani, Ferdinando and Louise Tardieu d'Esclavelles Épinay, *Correspondance* (Paris: Desjonquères, 1992–).

Galland, Antoine, *Le journal: La période parisienne* (Louvain: Peeters, 2011–).

Garat, Dominique-Joseph, review of Pierre Chabrit, *De la monarchie françoise, ou Ses loix*, in *Mercure de France*, 6 March 1784, 9–27.

Garnier, Charles-Georges-Thomas, 'Avertissement de l'éditeur', in Daniel Defoe, *La vie et les aventures surprenantes de Robinson Crusoé* (Amsterdam: n.p., 1787), i. 1–10.

Garnier, Germain, *La propriété dans ses rapports avec le droit politique* (Paris: Clavelin, 1792).

Garnier, Jean-Jacques, *De l'éducation civile* (Paris: Vente, 1765).

Garnier, Jean-Jacques, *Traité de l'origine du gouvernement français* (Paris: Vente, 1765).

Genovesi, Antonio, *Delle lezioni di commercio o sia di economia civile con elementi di commercio* (Naples: Istituto italiano per gli studi filosofici, 2005).

Gibbon, Edward, *The Decline and Fall of the Roman Empire* (London: David Campbell, 1993).

Gibert, Joseph-Balthasar, *Mémoires pour servir à l'histoire des Gaules et de la France* (Paris: Brunet fils, 1744).

Gimat de Bonneval, Jean-Baptiste, 'L'esprit de *L'Esprit des lois*', in Volpilhac-Auger (ed.), *Montesquieu*, 103–4.

Godechot, Jacques (ed.), *Les constitutions de la France depuis 1789* (Paris: Garnier-Flammarion, 1979).

Gosse, Pierre and Jean Néaulme, 'Avis des libraires', in *Boulainvilliers, Mémoires présentez à Monseigneur le Duc d'Orléans*, i. n.p.

Goujet, Claude-Pierre, *Supplément au Grand dictionnaire historique, généalogique, géographique de M. Louis Moreri* (Paris: Lemercier, 1735).

Gourcy, François-Antoine-Étienne de, *Quel fut l'état des personnes en France sous la seconde race de nos rois?* (Paris: Desaint, 1769).

Gourcy, François-Antoine-Étienne de, *Des droits et des devoirs du citoyen dans les circonstances présentes, avec un jugement impartial sur l'ouvrage de M. l'abbé de Mably* (n.p., 1789).

Grace, Thomas-François de, 'Avertissement de l'éditeur', in Samuel Pufendorf, *Introduction à l'histoire moderne, générale et politique de l'univers* (Paris: Merigot, 1753–1759), i. n.p.

Graffigny, Françoise d'Issembourg d'Happoncourt de, in *Correspondance* (Oxford: Voltaire Foundation, 1985–).

Graffigny, Françoise d'Issembourg d'Happoncourt de, *Lettres d'une Péruvienne* (Paris: Garnier, 2014).

Graslin, Jean-Joseph-Louis, *Essai analytique sur la richesse et l'impôt* (Paris: L'Harmattan, 2008).

Gravina, Gian Vincenzo, *Originum juris civilis libri tres* (Naples: Liguori, 2004).

Grégoire Henri, Debates at the Assemblée Nationale on 22 October 1789, in Mavidal (ed.), *Archives parlementaires*, ix. 476–83.

Griffet, Henri, *Traité des différentes sortes de preuves qui servent à établir la vérité de l'histoire* (Liège: J.F. Bassompierre, 1769).

Grimm, Friedrich Melchior et al., *Correspondance littéraire* (Paris: Garnier, 1877–1882).

Grimod de La Reynière, Alexandre-Balthazar-Laurent, *Réflexions philosophiques sur le plaisir, par un célibataire* (Neuchâtel: Veuve Duchesne, 1783).

Gros de Besplas, Joseph Marie Anne, *De l'utilité des voyages relativement aux sciences et aux mœurs* (Paris: Berthier, 1763).

Gros de Besplas, Joseph Marie Anne, *Des causes du bonheur public, ouvrage dédié à Monseigneur le Dauphin* (Paris: S. Jorry, 1768).

Grosley, Pierre-Jean, *De l'influence des loix sur les mœurs, mémoire présenté à la Société royale de Nancy* (Nancy: Hæner, 1757).

Grosley, Pierre-Jean, *Londres: Ouvrage d'un François, augmenté dans cette édition des notes d'un Anglois* (Neuchâtel: aux dépens de la Société typographique, 1770).

[Grouvelle, Philippe-Antoine], *De l'autorité de Montesquieu dans la révolution présente* (n.p., 1789).

Guénée, Antoine, *Lettres de quelques juifs portugais et allemands à M. de Voltaire, avec des réflexions critiques* (Paris: Prault, 1769).

Guillot de Marcilly, *Relation historique et théologique d'un voyage en Hollande et autres provinces des Pays-Bas* (Paris: J. Estienne, 1719).

[Guizot, François], review of François-Dominique de Montlosier, *De la monarchie française depuis la 2ème Restauration jusqu'à la fin de la session de 1816*, in *Archives philosophiques, politiques et littéraires*, 3 (1818), 385–409.

Guizot, François, *Du gouvernement de la France depuis la Restauration, et du ministère actuel* (Paris: Ladvocat, 1820).

Guizot, François, *Supplément aux deux premières éditions: Du gouvernement de la France depuis la restauration et du ministère actuel* (Paris: Ladvocat, 1820).

Guizot, François, *Essais sur l'histoire de France* (Paris: Brière, 1823).

Guizot, François, *Histoire générale de la civilisation en Europe* (Paris: Pichon et Didier, 1828).

Guizot, François, *Histoire de la civilisation en France, depuis la chute de l'Empire Romain jusqu'en 1789* (Paris: Pichon et Didier, 1829–1832).

Guizot, François, *Histoire des origines du gouvernement représentatif en Europe* (Paris: Didier, 1851).

Guyot, Guillaume Germain, *Histoire de France, représentée par figures accompagnées de discours* (Paris: David, 1787–1791).

Guyton De Morveau,Louis-Bernard, *Mémoire sur l'éducation publique* (n.p., 1764).

Heine, Heinrich, *Historisch-Kritische Gesamtausgabe der Werke* (Hamburg: Hoffmann & Campe, 1975–1997).

Helvétius, Claude-Adrien, *De l'esprit* (Paris: Fayard, 1988).

Helvétius, Claude-Adrien, *De l'homme* (Paris: Fayard, 1989).

[Hénault, Charles-Jean-François], *Nouvel abrégé chronologique de l'histoire de France* (Paris: Prault père, 1744).

Hénault, Charles-Jean-François, *Nouvel abrégé chronologique de l'histoire de France* (Paris: Prault père, 1749).

Hénault, Charles-Jean-François, *Histoire critique de l'établissement des Français dans les Gaules* (Paris: Buisson, 1801).

Hoffmann, Johann Wilhelm, 'Foedera quae imperatores Romani cum Francis ante tempora Clodovei fecerunt', *Bibliothèque germanique ou Histoire littéraire de l'Allemagne*, 42 (1738), 190–208.

Hoffmann, Johann Wilhelm and Jean-Baptiste Dubos, 'Lettres de Mrs. Hoffmann et Du Bos sur l'article précédent', *Bibliothèque germanique ou Histoire littéraire de l'Allemagne*, 42 (1738), 208–15.

Holbach, Paul Henri Dietrich d', *Système social* (Paris: Fayard, 1994).

Hotman, François, *Francogallia* (Cambridge: Cambridge University Press, 1972).

[Huet, Pierre-Daniel], *Les origines de la ville de Caen et des lieux circonvoisins* (Rouen: Maurry, 1702).

Hume, David, *Selected Essays* (Oxford: Oxford University Press, 1998).

Hume, David, *A Treatise of Human Nature* (Oxford: Clarendon Press, 2007).

Hume, David, *An Enquiry Concerning the Principles of Morals* (Oxford: Oxford University Press, 2009).

[Isoard de Lisle, Jean-Baptiste], 'Discours préliminaire', in Gabriel Bonnot de Mably, *Des droits et des devoirs du citoyen, édition augmentée d'un Discours préliminaire par l'auteur de La philosophie de la nature* (Paris: Louis, 1793), i. 1–32.

Jaucourt, Louis de [Louis de Neufville], *Histoire de la vie et des ouvrages de Leibnitz* (Amsterdam: François Changuion, 1734).

Jaucourt, Louis de, 'Caractère des nations', in Diderot and d'Alembert (eds.), *Encyclopédie*, ii. 666.

Jaucourt, Louis de, 'Germanie', in Diderot and d'Alembert (eds.), *Encyclopédie*, vii. 644–6.

Jaucourt, Louis de, 'Naissance', in Diderot and d'Alembert (eds.), *Encyclopédie*, xi. 8.

Jaucourt, Louis de, 'Nation', in Diderot and d'Alembert (eds.), *Encyclopédie*, xi. 36.

Jaucourt, Louis de, 'Patrie', in Diderot and d'Alembert (eds.), *Encyclopédie*, xii. 178–80.

Jaucourt, Louis de, 'Race', in Diderot and d'Alembert (eds.), *Encyclopédie*, xiii. 740.

Jaucourt, Louis de, 'Voyage', in Diderot and d'Alembert (eds.), *Encyclopédie*, xvii. 476–7.

[Jourdan, Jean-Baptiste], *Le guerrier philosophe, ou Mémoires de M. le Duc de *** (Amsterdam: aux dépens de la Compagnie, 1744).

Keralio, Louis-Félix Guinement, 'Géneral', in Louis-Félix Guinement Keralio, Jean-Girard Lacuée, and Joseph Servan (eds.), *Encyclopédie méthodique: Art militaire* (Paris: Panckoucke, 1784–1797), ii. 543–93.

Kerversau, François Marie de, *Histoire de la Révolution de 1789* (Paris: Clavelin, 1790).

Koch, Christophe-Guillaume, *Tables généalogiques des maisons souveraines de l'Europe* (Strasbourg: Jean-Frédéric Stein, 1780).

La Bléterie, Jean-Philippe-René de, 'Vie de Tacite, pour servir de préface à ses ouvrages', in Tacite, *Traduction de quelques ouvrages* (Paris: Duchesne, 1755), i. pp. v–cxxiv.

La Borde, Jean Benjamin de, *Tableaux topographiques, pittoresques, phys-iques, historiques, moraux, politiques, littéraires de la Suisse* (Paris: Lamy, 1780–1786).

La Bruyère, Jean, 'Préface: Discours de réception à l'Académie française', in Académie française (ed.), *Recueil des harangues prononcées par Messieurs de l'Académie françoise, dans leurs receptions, et en d'autres occasions differentes* (Amsterdam: aux dépens de la Compagnie, 1709), ii. 262–75.

La Bruyère, Jean de, *Les caractères de Théophraste traduits du grec avec Les caractères ou Les mœurs de ce siècle* (Paris: Honoré Champion, 1999).

La Chalotais, Louis-René de, *Essai d'éducation nationale ou plan d'études pour la jeunesse* (n.p., 1763).

La Framboisière, Nicolas Abraham de, *Œuvres* (Paris: n.p., 1624).

La Harpe, Jean François de, *Correspondance littéraire, adressée à S. A. I. Mgr le grand-duc, aujourd'hui empereur de Russie* (Paris: Migneret, 1801–1807).

La Mesnardière, Hippolyte Jules Pilet de, *La poétique* (Paris: Honoré Champion, 2015).

La Morlière, Jacques-Rochette de, *Angola: Histoire indienne* (Grenoble: Roissard, 1967).

La Mothe Le Vayer, François de, *Œuvres* (Paris: Billaine, 1669).

[La Porte, Joseph de], *Observations sur l'Esprit des loix, ou L'art de lire ce livre, de l'entendre et d'en juger* (Amsterdam: Pierre Mortier, 1751).

La Roque, Gilles-André de, *Le traité de la noblesse et des différentes espèces* (Paris: Mémoire et documents, 1994).

La Touche, Pierre de, *L'art de bien parler françois, qui comprend tout ce qui regarde la grammaire et les façons de parler douteuses* (Amsterdam: H. Desbordes, 1696).

La Touche, Pierre de, *L'art de bien parler françois, qui comprend tout ce qui regarde la grammaire et les façons de parler douteuses* (Amsterdam: Arkstee & Merkus, 1760).

La Tour d'Auvergne, Théophile Malo de, *Origines gauloises, celles des plus anciens peuples de l'Europe, puisées dans leur vraie source* (Paris: Quillau, 1796).

La Rochefoucauld, François de, *Œuvres complètes* (Paris: Gallimard, 1964).

Lacarry, Gilles, *Historia Coloniarum a Gallis in exteras nationes missarum, tum exterarum nationum Coloniae in Gallias deductae* (Clermont: Jacquard, 1677).

Lacombe de Prezel, Honoré, *Dictionnaire d'anecdotes, de traits singuliers et caractéristiques, historiettes, bons mots, naïvetés, saillies, réparties ingénieuses* (Paris: La Combe, 1766).

Lacretelle, Pierre-Louis de, *De la convocation de la prochaine tenue des États généraux en France* (n.p., 1788).

Lambert, Anne-Thérèse de Marguenat de Courcelles de, *Avis d'une mere à son fils et sa fille* (Paris: Ganeau, 1728).

Lamourette, Antoine-Adrien, *Lettre pastorale de M. L'évêque du département de Rhône et Loire, métropolitain du Sud-Est* (Lyons: Imprimerie d'Amable le Roy, 1791).

Lamy, François, *De la connaissance de soi-même* (Paris: Pralard, 1694–1698).

Langlès, Louis Mathieu, *Adresse de la Convention nationale au peuple français, décrétée dans la séance du 13 vendémiaire an III* (n.p., 1794).

Languet de Gergy, Jean-Joseph, 'Réponse de l'Archevêque de Sens', in Marivaux, *Journaux et œuvres diverses*, 452–5.

Lanjuinais, Joseph, *Le monarque accompli, ou Prodiges de bonté, de savoir et de sagesse qui font l'éloge de S. M. I. Joseph II* (Lausanne: J.P. Herbach, 1774).

Lanjuinais, Joseph, *Manuel des jeunes orateurs, ou Tableau historique et méthodique de l'éloquence* (Moudon: Société typographique, 1777).

Laroche, Benjamin, *Lettres adressées l'une à tous les journalistes, l'autre à M. de Richelieu; précédées et suivies des considérations sur l'ouvrage de M. Guizot, intitulé: 'Du gouvernement de la France depuis la restauration'* (Paris: Les marchands de nouveautés, 1820).

Lassay, Armand-Léon de Madaillan de Lesparre de, 'Réflexions de M. le Marquis de Lasse', *Mercure de France*, December 1754, 86–101.

Lavisse, Ernest, *La première année d'histoire de France* (Paris: Armand Colin, 1876).

Lavisse, Ernest, *Questions d'enseignement national* (Paris: Armand Colin, 1885).

Le Clerc, Jean, review of [Maximilien Misson], *Nouveau voyage d'Italie, fait en l'année 1688*, in *Bibliothèque universelle et historique*, September 1691, 158–60.

Le Clerc, Jean, *'Parrhasiana', ou Pensées diverses sur des matières de critique, d'histoire, de morale et de politique* (Amsterdam: Héritiers d'Antoine Schelte, 1699–1701).

Le Gendre, Louis, *Mœurs et coutumes des François, dans les différens temps de la monarchie* (Paris: Collombat, 1712).

[Le Laboureur, Jean], *Histoire de la pairie de France et du Parlement de Paris* (London: Harding, 1740).

Le Long, Jacques, *Bibliothèque historique de la France, contenant le catalogue de tous les ouvrages tant imprimez que manuscrits qui traitent de l'histoire de ce roïaume* (Paris: G. Martin, 1719).

Le Long, Jacques and Charles-Marie Fevret de Fontette, *Bibliothèque historique de France* (Paris: Herissant, 1768–1778).

Le Moyne, Pierre, *De l'histoire* (Paris: A. Billaine, 1670).

Le Noble, Eustache, *L'école du monde, ou Instruction d'un père à un fils, touchant la manière dont il faut vivre dans le monde, divisée en entretiens* (Paris: Martin Jouvenel, 1702).

[Le Paige, Louis-Adrien], *Lettre dans laquelle on examine s'il est vrai que la doctrine de l'État contenue dans les dernières remontrances du Parlement, au sujet du grand conseil, porte aucune atteinte à l'autorité souveraine du roi et à son caractère sacré de seul législateur dans son royaume* (n.p., n.d.).

Le Paige, Louis-Adrien, *Lettres historiques sur les fonctions essentielles du Parlement, sur le droit des pairs et sur les loix fondamentales du royaume* (Amsterdam: aux dépens de la Compagnie, 1753).

Le Roux, Philibert-Joseph, *Dictionnaire comique, satyrique, critique, burlesque, libre et proverbial* (Amsterdam: M.C. Le Cène, 1718).

Le Roy, Charles-Georges, 'Homme (morale)', in Diderot and d'Alembert (eds.), *Encyclopédie*, viii. 274–8.

Le Trosne, Guillaume-François, *De l'ordre social* (Paris: Debure, 1777).

Leber, Carl (ed.), *Collection des meilleurs dissertations relatifs à l'histoire de France* (Paris: J.-G. Dentu, 1826–1838).

Lebeuf, Jean, *Lettres* (Auxerre: G. Perriquet, 1866–1868).

[Lebrun, Charles-François], *La voix du citoyen* (n.p., 1789).

Leibniz, Gottfried Wilhelm, *Otium Hanoveranum, sive, Miscellanea, ex ore et schedis illustris viri, piæ memoriæ, Godofr. Gvileilmi Leibnitii* (Leipzig: Christiani Martini, 1718).

Leibniz, Gottfried Wilhelm, 'Essai sur l'origine des François', in Desmaiseaux (ed.), *Recueil de diverses pièces sur la philosophie, la religion naturelle, l'histoire, les mathématiques, etc.*, ii. 217–55.

Leibniz, Gottfried Wilhelm, 'Réponse aux objections du père de Tournemine contre la Dissertation sur l'origine des François', in Desmaiseaux (ed.), *Recueil de diverses pièces sur la philosophie, la religion naturelle, l'histoire, les mathématiques, etc.*, ii. 256–74.

Leibniz, Gottfried Wilhelm, *Opera Omnia* (Geneva: Fratres de Tournes, 1768).

Leibniz, Gottfried Wilhelm, *Opuscules et fragments inédits* (Paris: Alcan, 1903).

Leibniz, Gottfried Wilhelm, *Sämtliche Schriften und Briefe: Reihe 6, Philosophische Schriften* (Berlin: Akademie-Verlag, 1962).

Leibniz, Gottfried Wilhelm and Charles-Irénée Castel de Saint-Pierre, *Correspondance* (Paris: Paris II: Centre de philosophie du droit, 1995).

Lemercier de la Rivière, Paul-Pierre, *De l'instruction publique* (Paris: Didot l'ainé, 1775).

Lemercier de la Rivière, Paul-Pierre, *L'ordre naturel et essentiel des sociétés politiques* (Paris: Fayard, 2001).

Lemoine, Jacques J., *Discours qui a remporté le prix sur cette question proposée en 1808 par l'Académie des sciences, arts et belles-lettres de Dijon: La nation française mérite-t-elle le reproche de légèreté que lui font les nations étrangères?* (Paris: Giguet et Michaud, 1809).

Lemontey, Pierre Édouard, *Essai sur l'établissement monarchique de Louis XIV* (Paris: Déterville, 1818).

Lenglet Du Fresnoy, Nicolas, *Méthode pour étudier l'histoire* (Paris: Gandouin, 1729).

Lenglet Du Fresnoy, Nicolas [C. Gordon de Percel], *De l'usage des romans, où l'on fait voir leur utilité et leurs différens caractères* (Amsterdam: Veuve de Poilras, 1734).

Lenglet Du Fresnoy, Nicolas, *Tablettes chronologiques de l'histoire universelle sacrée et prophane depuis la création du monde jusqu'à l'an 1743* (Paris: De Bure l'aîné, 1744).

Lenoir, Alexandre, 'Discours préliminaire', *Mémoires de l'Académie celtique*, i (1807), 1–20.

Lessing, Gotthold Ephraim, *Werke und Briefe* (Frankfurt: Deutscher Klassiker, 1985–).

Levesque, Pierre-Charles, *Eloge historique de M. l'abbé de Mably* (Paris: Guillot, 1787).

Lézardière, Marie-Charlotte-Pauline Robert de, *Théorie des lois politiques de la monarchie française* (Paris: Comptoir des imprimeurs-unis, 1844).

Lézardière, Marie-Charlotte-Pauline Robert de, *Ecrits inédits* (Paris: Presses universitaires de France, 1927).

Lezay-Marnézia, Claude-François-Adrien, *Plan de lecture pour une jeune dame* (Paris: Prault, 1784).

Limiers, Henri-Philippe de, *Annales de la monarchie françoise, depuis son établissement jusques à présent* (Amsterdam: l'Honoré, 1724).

Linguet, Simon-Nicolas-Henri, *Réponse aux docteurs modernes, ou Apologie pour l'auteur de la théorie des loix et des lettres sur cette théorie, avec la réfutation du système des philosophes économistes* (Paris: n.p., 1771).

Linguet, Simon-Nicolas-Henri, *Mélanges de politique et de littérature* (Bouillon: n.p., 1778).

Linguet, Simon-Nicolas-Henri, *Théorie des lois civiles, ou Principes fondamentaux de la société* (Paris: Fayard, 1984).

Locke, John, *Two Treatises on Government* (Cambridge: Cambridge University Press, 1992).

Lombard, Daniel, *Comparaison des deux histoires de M. de Mézeray et du P. Daniel, en deux dissertations, avec une dissertation préliminaire sur l'utilité de l'histoire* (Amsterdam: aux dépens de la Compagnie, 1723).

Loyseau, Charles, *Traité des ordres et simples dignitez* (Châteaudun: Abel L'Angelier, 1610).

[Luynes, Louis-Joseph-Charles-Amable d'Albert de], *L'histoire, le cérémonial et les droits des États généraux du royaume de France* (n.p., 1789).

Mabillon, Jean, *Brèves réflexions sur quelques règles de l'histoire* (Paris: P.O.L., 1990).

Mably, Gabriel Bonnot de, *Œuvres* (Darmstadt: Scientia Verlag Aalen, 1977).

Mably, Gabriel Bonnot de, *Parallèle des Romains et des François par rapport au gouvernement* (Paris: Didot, 1740).

Macaulay, Thomas Babington, *Reviews, Essays, and Poems* (London: Ward, Lock & Co., 1875).

Machiavelli, Niccolò, *L'arte della guerra; Scritti politici minori* (Rome: Salerno Editrice, 2001).

Machiavelli, Niccolò, *Il principe* (Milan: Feltrinelli, 2004).

Maistre, Joseph de, *Œuvres complètes* (Geneva: Slatkine, 1979).

Malebranche, Nicolas, *Recherche de la vérité* (Paris: Galerie de la Sorbonne, 1991).

Mallet, Edmé-François, 'Caractère dans les personnages', in Diderot and d'Alembert (eds.), *Encyclopédie*, ii. 667–8.

Malouet, Pierre Victor, *Mémoires* (Paris: E. Plon, 1874).

Malte-Brun, Conrad, 'Mémoires de l'Académie celtique: Cahiers I – XIV', *Journal de l'Empire*, 26 April 1810, 3–4.

[Manson], *Examen impartial du Siège de Calais* (Calais: n.p., 1765).

Manzoni, Alessandro and Claude Fauriel, *Carteggio* (Milan: Centro nazionale studi Manzoniani, 2000).

Marais, Mathieu, *Journal et Mémoires (1715–1737)* (Paris: Firmin-Didot, 1863–1868).

Marat, Jean-Paul, *Œuvres politiques* (Brussels: Pôle Nord, 1989–1995).

Marivaux, Pierre de, *Journaux et œuvres diverses* (Paris: Garnier frères, 1969).

Marmontel, Jean-François, *Éléments de littérature* (Paris: Desjonquères, 2005).

Marolles, Michel de, *Histoire des rois de France* (Paris: Pierre le petit, 1663).

Martin, Henri, *Historie de France populaire depuis les temps les plus reculés jusqu'à nos jours* (Paris: Furne, 1867–1885).

Martin, Jacques, *La religion des Gaulois, tirée des plus pures sources de l'antiquité* (Paris: Saugrain Fils, 1727).

Martin, Jacques, *Histoire des Gaules, et des conquêtes des Gaulois, depuis leur origine jusqu'à la fondation de la monarchie françoise* (Paris: Imprimerie de Le Breton, 1752–1754).

Maupertuis, Pierre-Louis Moreau de, *Venus physique* (n.p., 1745).

Maupertuis, Pierre-Louis Moreau de, 'Relation d'un voyage fait dans la Laponie septentrionale, pour trouver un ancien monument', in Osmo Pekonen and Anouchka Vasak (eds.), *Maupertuis en Laponie: A la recherche de la figure de la Terre* (Paris: Hermann, 2014), 183–202.

Mavidal, Jêrome (ed.), *Archives parlementaires: Première série* (Paris: Dupont, 1862–).

Ménestrier, Claude-François, *Les diverses espèces de noblesse* (Paris: pour Thomas Amaulry, libraire à Lyon, 1681).

Ménestrier, Claude-François, *La source glorieuse du sang de l'auguste maison de Bourbon dans le coeur de saint Louis* (Paris: Michallet, 1687).

Ménestrier, Claude-François, *Les divers caractères des ouvrages historiques, avec le plan d'une nouvelle histoire de la ville de Lyon* (Paris: J. Collombat, 1694).

Mercier, Louis-Sébastien, *Eloge de René Descartes* (Geneva: Veuve Pierres, 1765).

Mercier, Louis-Sébastien, *Portraits des rois de France* (Neuchâtel: Imprimerie de la Société typographique, 1783).

Mercier, Louis-Sébastien, *Notions claires sur les gouvernemens* (Amsterdam: n.p., 1787).

Mercier, Louis Sébastien, *Tableau de Paris* (Paris: Mercure de France, 1994).

Mercier, Louis-Sébastien, *Mon bonnet de nuit, suivi de Du théâtre* (Paris: Mercure de France, 1999).

[Metra, Louis-François], *Correspondance littéraire secrete* (n.p.: 1775–1793).

Mézeray, François Eudes de, *Histoire de France depuis Pharamond jusqu'à maintenant* (Paris: Mathieu Guillemot, 1643–1651).

Michelet, Jules, *Journal* (Paris: Gallimard, 1959–1976).

Michelet, Jules, *Introduction à l'histoire universelle; Tableau de la France; Préface à l'Histoire de France* (Paris: Armand Colin, 1962).

Michelet, Jules, *Le peuple* (Paris: Flammarion, 1974).

Mignet, Françoise-Auguste, *De la féodalité, des institutions de St Louis, et de l'influence de la législation de ce prince* (Paris: L'Huillier, 1822).

Mignet, Françoise-Auguste, *Histoire de la Révolution française* (Brussels: Aug. Wahlent et comp., 1824).

[Mignonneau, Jean-Louis], *Considérations intéressantes sur les affaires présentes* (London and Paris: Barrois, 1788).

Mill, John Stuart, *Principles of Political Economy* (London: Routledge 1996).

Millot, Claude-François-Xavier, *Élémens de l'histoire de France, depuis Clovis jusqu'à Louis XV* (Paris: Durand neveu, 1770).

Millot, Claude-François-Xavier, 'Mémoires', *Nouvelle revue rétrospective*, 8 (January–June 1898), 73–120, 145–92, and 217–35.

Mirabeau, Honoré-Gabriel Riqueti de, *Œuvres* (Paris: Lecointe et Pougin, 1834–1835).

Mirabeau, Victor de Riqueti de, 'Eloge funèbre de M. François Quesnay', *Nouvelles éphémérides économiques*, 1775, i. 1–19.

Montaigne, Michel de, *Les essais* (Paris: Presses universitaires de France, 2004).

Montesquieu, Charles-Louis Secondat de, *Œuvres complètes* (ed. Caillois) (Paris: Gallimard, 1949–1951).

Montesquieu, Charles-Louis Secondat de, *Œuvres* (ed. Masson) (Paris: Nagel, 1950–1955).

Montesquieu, Charles-Louis Secondat de, *Œuvres complètes* (ed. Société Montesquieu) (Oxford: Société Montesquieu and Voltaire Foundation, 1998–).

Montfaucon, Bernard de, *Les monumens de la monarchie françoise* (Paris: Gandouin et Giffart, 1729–1733).

Montlosier, François-Dominique de, *De la monarchie française, depuis son établissement jusqu'à nos jours, ou Recherches sur les anciennes institutions françaises et sur les causes qui ont amené la Révolution et ses diverses phases jusqu'à la déclaration d'empire* (Paris: H. Nicolle, 1814–1815).

Montlosier, François-Dominique de, *De la monarchie française, depuis le retour de la maison de Bourbon jusqu'au 1er avril 1815* (Paris: H. Nicolle, 1817).

Montlosier, François-Dominique de, *De la monarchie française au 1er janvier 1821* (Paris: Gide fils, 1821).

Montlosier, François-Dominique de, *Souvenirs d'un émigré (1791–1798)* (Paris: Hachette, 1951).

Moreau, Jacob-Nicolas, 'De la monarchie en général et de son origine', *Le moniteur françois*, 1 (1760), 79–127.

Moreau, Jacob-Nicolas, 'Réponses aux objections contre le pouvoir paternel', *Le moniteur françois*, 1 (1760), 145–59.

Moreau, Jacob Nicolas, *Exposition et défense de notre constitution monarchique françoise, précédé de l'historique de toutes nos assemblées nationales, dans deux mémoires* (Paris: Moutard, 1789).

Moreau, Jacob-Nicholas, *Mes souvenirs* (Paris: Plon, 1898).

Moreau, Jacob-Nicolas, *Principes de morale, de politique et de droit public puisés dans l'histoire de notre monarchie, ou Discours sur l'histoire de France* (Paris: Imprimerie royale, 1777–1789).

[Morellet, André], *Lettres à la noblesse de Bretagne* (n.p., 1789).

Morellet, André, footnotes in Emmanuel-Joseph Sieyès, *Qu'est-ce que le tiers état? précédé de l'Essai sur les privilèges* (Paris: Coréard, 1822).

Morellet, André, *Mémoires* (Paris: Mercure de France, 2000).

Morris, Gouverneur, *A Diary of the French Revolution* (Boston: Mifflin, 1939).

Morvan de Bellegarde, Jean Baptiste, *Réflexions sur la politesse des mœurs, avec des maximes pour la société civile, suite des Réflexions sur le ridicule* (Paris: Guignard, 1698).

Mounier, Jean-Joseph, *Considérations sur les gouvernemens, et principalement sur celui qui convient à la France* (Paris: Baudouin, 1789).

Mounier, Jean-Joseph, *Nouvelles observations sur les États-généraux de France* (n.p., 1789).

Mousnier, *Observations sur l'état passé, présent et futur de la nation; et De l'influence du publiciste Mably sur la Révolution* (Paris: Imprimerie nationale, n.d.).

Muralt, Béat Louis de, *Lettres sur les Anglois et les François et sur les voiages* (Paris: Honoré Champion, 1933).

[Murat-Montferrand, de], *Qu'est-ce que la noblesse, et que sont ses privilèges?* (Amsterdam: n.p., 1789).

Necker, Jacques, *De l'administration des finances de la France* (n.p., 1785).

Necker, Jacques, *Sur la législation et le commerce des grains* (Roubaix: EDIRES, 1986).

Née de La Rochelle, Jean-Baptiste-François, *Le guide de l'histoire, à l'usage de la jeunesse, et des personnes qui veulent la lire avec fruit, ou L'écrire avec succès* (Paris: Bidault, 1803).

Oudin, Antoine and Lorenzo Ferretti, *Dictionnaire italien et françois* (Paris: n.p., 1681).

Pardessus, Jean-Marie, 'Notice sur les voyages d'antiquités celtiques et druidiques de M. É. Johanneau', *Mémoires de l'Académie celtique*, 1 (1807), 380–4.

Pascal, Blaise, *Pensées* (Paris: Gallimard, 2004).

Pecquet, Antoine, *L'esprit des maximes politiques, pour servir de suite à l'Esprit des lois, du Président de Montesquieu* (Paris: Prault, 1757).

Peignot, Gabriel, *Dictionnaire critique, littéraire, et bibliographique des principaux livres condamnés au feu, supprimés ou censurés* (Paris: Renouard, 1806).

[Pellerin, Joseph-Michel], *Mémoire historique sur la constitution des États de Bretagne, adressé aux gentilshommes bretons, à l'occasion de la question de droit public, actuellement agitée en cette province, si la noblesse a, par le droit constitutionnel de la province, celui d'assister en corps, et par individus aux assemblées des gens des trois états du pays et duché de Bretagne* (n.p., November 1788).

Pétigny, François Jules de, *Études sur l'histoire, les lois et les institutions de l'époque mérovingienne* (Paris: Brockhaus et Avenarius, 1843–1851).

[Petiot], *De l'opinion et des mœurs, ou De l'influence des lettres sur les mœurs* (Paris: Moureau, 1770).

Petit de Bachaumont, Louis, Mathieu-François Pidansat de Mairobert, and Mouffle d'Angerville, *Mémoires secrets pour servir à l'histoire de la république des lettres en France depuis 1762 jusqu'à nos jours* (London: Adamson, 1783–1789).

Pézron, Paul-Yves, *Antiquité de la nation et de la langue des Celtes, autrement appelés Gaulois* (Paris: Marchand, 1703).

Philippe de Prétot, Étienne-André, *Les amusemens du cœur et de l'esprit* (Paris: Veuve Pissot, 1748–1749).

[Pidanzat de Mairobert, Mathieu-François], *Journal historique de la révolution opérée dans la constitution de la monarchie françoise* (London: n.p., 1774–1776).

Piron, Alexis, *Œuvres complettes* (Paris: Imprimerie de M. Lambert, 1776).

[Plesse, Pierre Joseph], 'Lettre au P. B. J. sur le livre intitulé L'Esprit des lois', *Journal de Trévoux, ou Mémoires pour servir à l'histoire des sciences et des arts*, April 1749, 718–40.

[Poncelet, Polycarpe], *Principes généraux pour servir à l'éducation des enfans, particulièrement de la noblesse françoise* (Paris: P.G. Mercier, 1763).

Prévost, Antoine François et al., *Le pour et contre: Ouvrage périodique d'un goût nouveau* (Paris: Didot, 1733–1740).

Prévost, Antoine François, *Voyages du Capitaine Lade en différentes parties de l'Afrique, de l'Asie et de l'Amérique* (Paris: Didot, 1744).

Prévost, Antoine François, *Elémens de politesse et de bienséance, ou La civilité qui se pratique parmi les honnêtes gens; avec un nouveau Traité sur l'art de plaire dans la conversation* (Strasbourg: Armand König, 1766).

Priezac, Daniel de, *Discours politiques: Première partie* (Paris: P. Rocolet, 1652).

Proyart, Liévin-Bonaventure, *Œuvres* (Paris: Méquignon fils aîné, 1819).

Puget de Saint-Pierre, *Dictionnaire des notions primitives, ou Abrégé raisonné et universel des éléments de toutes les connaissances humaines* (Paris: J.-P. Costard, 1773).

[Quesnay, François], *Le droit naturel* (Paris: n.p., 1765).

Quesnay, François, *Physiocratie, ou Constitution naturelle du gouvernement le plus avantageux au genre humain* (Paris: Merlin, 1767–1768).

Quesnay, François, *Œuvres économiques complètes et autres textes* (Paris: Institut national d'études démographiques, 2005).

[Rabaut de Saint-Étienne, Jean-Paul], *Considérations très-importantes sur les intérêts du tiers état* (n.p., 1788).

Racine, Jean, *Œuvres* (Paris: Gallimard, 1950–1966).

Ramsay, Andrew Michael, *Essay philosophique sur le gouvernement civil, où l'on traite de la nécessité, de l'origine, des droits, des bornes et des différentes formes de la souveraineté selon les principes de feu M. François de Salignac de La Mothe-Fénelon* (London: n.p., 1721).

Rapin, René, *Instructions pour l'histoire* (Paris: Mabre-Cramoist, 1677).

Rapin, René, *Les réflexions sur la poétique et sur les ouvrages des poètes anciens et modernes (1684)* (Paris: Honoré Champion, 2011).

Raynal, Guillaume-Thomas, 'Nouvelles littéraires' (1747–1755), in Friedrich Melchior Grimm et al., *Correspondance littéraire*, i. 67–492.

Raynal, Guillaume-Thomas, *Histoire philosophique et politique des établissements et du commerce des Européens dans les deux Indes* (Geneva: Pellet, 1780).

[Reboul], *Essai sur les mœurs du temps* (Paris: Vincent, 1768).

Remi, Charles, *Considérations philosophiques sur les mœurs, les plaisirs et les préjugés de la capitale* (Paris: Leroy, 1787).

Rémond des Cours, Nicolas, *Les véritables devoirs de l'homme d'épée* (Amsterdam: Adrian Braakman, 1697).

Remy, Joseph Honoré, 'Communes', in Joseph-Nicolas Guyot (ed.), *Répertoire universel et raisonné de jurisprudence civile, criminelle, canonique et bénéficiale* (Paris: J. Dorez, 1775–1783), xiii. 301–17.

Renan, Ernest, *Œuvres complètes* (Paris: Calmann-Lévy, 1947–1961).

Renan, Ernst, *Qu'est-ce qu'une nation? et autres écrits politiques* (Paris: Imprimerie nationale, 1996).

Renouvier, Charles, 'L'éducation et la morale', *Critique philosophique*, 1 (1872), 273–80.

Ricardo, David, *The Principles of Political Economy and Taxation* (London: J.M. Dent & Sons, 1995).

Richelet, Pierre, *Dictionnaire françois* (Geneva: Widerhold, 1680).

Richelet, Pierre, *Dictionnaire françois* (Amsterdam: Jean Elzevir, 1709).

Robertson, William, *The History of the Reign of the Emperor Charles V: With a View of the Progress of Society in Europe, from the Subversion of the Roman Empire to the Beginning of the Sixteenth Century* (London: W. Strahan, 1769).

Robespierre, Maximilien, *Œuvres* (Paris: Phénix, 2000).

Robinet, Jean-Baptiste-René et al., *Dictionnaire universel des sciences, morale, économique, politique et diplomatique, ou Bibliothèque de l'homme d'État et du citoyen* (London: Libraires Associés, 1777–1783).

Roederer, Pierre-Louis, *Œuvres* (Paris: Firmin-Didot, 1853–1859).

Rolland d'Erceville, Barthélemy-Gabriel, *Lettre à M. l'abbé Velly, sur les tomes III et IV de son histoire de France: Au sujet de l'autorité des États, et du droit du Parlement de vérifier les édits, déclarations, etc.* (n.p., 1756).

Rolland, Jacques-Francis, *Nouveau vocabulaire* (Lyons: Rolland et Rivoire, 1809).

Rollin, Charles, *De la manière d'enseigner et d'étudier les belles-lettres* (Paris: Estienne, 1726–1728).

Roques, Pierre, *Les devoirs des sujets expliqués en quatre discours* (Basel: Thourneisen, 1737).

Rossel, *Histoire du patriotisme françois, ou Nouvelle historie de la France* (Paris: Lacombe, 1769).

Rousseau, Jean-Jacques, *Œuvres* (Paris: Gallimard, 1959–).

Sabatier de Castres, Antoine, *Dictionnaire de littérature, dans lequel on traite de tout ce qui a rapport à l'éloquence, à la poësie et aux belles-lettres, et dans lequel on enseigne la marche et les règles qu'on doit observer dans tous les ouvrages d'esprit* (Paris: Vincent, 1770).

Sabatier de Castres, Antoine, *Les trois siècles de notre littérature, ou Tableau de l'esprit de nos écrivains depuis François Ier jusqu'en 1772* (Amsterdam: Gueffier, 1772).

Sabbathier, François, *Les mœurs, coutumes et usages des anciens peuples* (Châlons-sur-Marne: Imprimerie de Bouchard, 1770).

Sade, Donatien Alphonse François de, *Œuvres* (Paris: Gallimard, 1990–1998).

Sainte-Beuve, Charles-Augustin, *Causeries du lundi* (Paris: Garnier frères, 1852–1876).

Sainte-Beuve, Charles-Augustin, *Œuvres* (Paris: Gallimard, 1956–1966).

Sainte-Beuve, Charles-Augustin, *Portraits contemporains* (Paris: Presses de l'Université de Paris-Sorbonne, 2008).

Saint-Foix, Germain-François Poullain de, *Essais historiques sur Paris* (Paris: Veuve Duchesne, 1766).

Saint-Just, Louis-Antoine-Léon, *L'esprit de la Révolution, suivi de Fragments sur les institutions républicaines* (Paris: 10–18, 2003).

Saint-Martin, Louis-Pierre de, *Les établissemens de Saint Louis, roi de France suivant le texte original, et rendus dans le langage actuel avec des notes; suivis du Panégyrique de S. Louis* (Paris: Nyon l'aîné, 1786).

Saint-Réal, César de, *De l'usage de l'histoire* (Paris: Barbin, 1671).

Saint-Simon, Claude-Henri de, *Opinions littéraires, philosophiques et industrielles* (Paris: Hachette, 1977).

Saint-Simon, Claude-Henri de, *Œuvres* (Paris: Presses universitaires de France, 2012).

Saint-Simon, Louis de Rouvroy de, *Écrits inédits* (Paris: Hachette, 1880–1893).

Saint-Simon, Louis de Rouvroy de, *Grimoires* (Paris: Klincksieck, 1975).

Saint-Simon, Louis de Rouvroy de, *Mémoires* (Paris: Gallimard, 1982–1985).

Savigny, Friedrich Carl von, *Geschichte des römischen Rechts im Mittelalter* (Heidelberg: Mohr and Zimmer, 1815–1831).

Say, Jean-Baptiste, *Traité d'économie politique, ou Simple exposition de la manière dont se forment, se distribuent et se consomment les richesses* (Paris: Deterville, 1803).

Say, Jean-Baptiste, *Cours complet d'économie politique pratique* (Paris: Rapilly, 1828–1833).

Ségur, Louis-Philippe de, *Œuvres complètes* (Paris: Eymery, 1824–1830).

Sénac de Meilhan, Gabriel, *Considérations sur l'esprit et les mœurs* (London: n.p., 1787).

[Servan, Joseph], *Le soldat citoyen, ou Vues patriotiques sur la manière la plus avantageuse de pourvoir à la défense du Royaume* (Dans le pays de la liberté [Neuchâtel]: n.p., 1780).

Sieyès, Emmanuel-Joseph, *Préliminaire de la Constitution françoise* (Paris: Baudouin, 1789).

Sieyès, Emmanuel-Joseph, *Vues sur les moyens d'exécution dont les représentants de la France pourront disposer en 1789* (n.p., 1789).

Sieyès, Emmanuel-Joseph, 'Rapport de M. l'abbé Sieyès sur les délits de presse', 20 January 1790, in Mavidal (ed.), *Archives parlementaires*, xi. 259–64.

Sieyès, Emmanuel-Joseph, *Écrits politiques* (Paris: Archives contemporaines, 1985).

Sieyès, Emmanuel-Joseph, *Qu'est-ce que le tiers-état?* (Paris: Flammarion, 1988).

Sieyès, Emmanuel-Joseph, *Des manuscrits de Sieyès* (Paris: Honoré Champion, 1999–2007).

[Sigrais, Bourdon de], *Considérations sur l'esprit militaire des Gaulois, pour servir d'éclaircissements préliminaires aux mêmes recherches sur les Français, et d'introductions à l'histoire de France* (Paris: Veuve Desaint, 1774).

Sismondi, Jean Charles Léonard, Simonde de, *Histoire des républiques italiennes du moyen âge* (Zurich: Gessner, 1807–1809).

Sismondi, Jean Charles Léonard Simonde de, review of Augustin Thierry, *Histoire de la conquête de l'Angleterre par les Normands*, in *Revue encyclopédique*, 28 (1825), 77–91.

Smith, Adam, *An Inquiry into the Nature and Causes of the Wealth of Nations* (Oxford: Clarendon Press, 1979).

Smith, Adam, *Lectures on Rhetoric and Belles Lettres* (Oxford: Clarendon Press, 1983).

Sobry, Jean-François, *Le mode françois, ou Discours sur les principaux usages de la nation française* (London: n.p., 1786).

Sorel, Charles, *Advertissement sur l'histoire de la monarchie françoise* (Paris: C. Morlot, 1628).

Stendhal, Marie Henri Beyle, *Correspondance générale* (Paris: Honoré Champion, 1997–1999).

[Sticotti, Antoine-Fabio], *Dictionnaire des gens du monde: Historique, littéraire, critique, moral, physique, militaire, politique, caractéristique et social* (Paris: J.-P. Costard, 1770).

Target, Guy-Jean Baptiste, *Les États-généraux convoqués par Louis XVI* (n.p., 1788).

Target, Guy-Jean Baptiste, *Suite de l'écrit intitulé Les États-généraux convoqués par Louis XVI* (n.p., 1789).

Tassin, René Prosper, *Histoire littéraire de la congrégation de Saint-Maur, ordre de Saint-Benoît* (Brussels: Humblot, 1770).

Thévenot, Jean, *Relation d'un voyage fait au Levant* (Paris: L. Bilaine, 1664).

Thierry, Augustin, 'Des nations et de leurs rapports mutuels', in Claude-Henri de Saint-Simon, *L'industrie littéraire et scientifique liguée avec l'industrie commerciale et manufacturière* (Paris: Delaunay, 1817), i. part 2, 5–134.

Thierry, Augustin, 'Vue des révolutions d'Angleterre', *Le censeur européen*, 1 (1817), iv. 1–73.

Thierry, Augustin, 'Commentaire sur l'*Esprit des lois* de Montesquieu', *Le censeur européen*, 2 (1818), vii. 191–260.

Thierry, Augustin, *Histoire de la conquête de l'Angleterre par les Normands* (Paris: Firmin Didot, 1825).

Thierry, Augustin, *Lettres sur l'histoire de France* (Paris: Sautelet, 1827).

Thierry, Augustin, *Histoire de la conquête de l'Angleterre par les Normands* (Paris: Alexandre Mesnier, 1830).

Thierry, Augustin, *Dix ans d'études historiques* (Brussels: Hauman, 1835).

Thierry, Augustin, *Récits des temps mérovingiens précédés des Considérations sur l'histoire de France* (Paris: Tessier, 1840).

Thierry, Augustin, *Essai sur l'histoire de la formation et des progrès du tiers état* (Paris: Furne et C., 1853).

Thiers, Adolphe, *Histoire de la Révolution française* (Paris: Lecointe et Durey, 1823–1827).

[Thiroux d'Arconville, Marie-Geneviève-Charlotte], *De l'amitié* (Amsterdam: Desaint & Saillant, 1761).

Thomas, Antoine Léonard, *Eloge de René Duguay-Trouin* (Paris: Bernard Brunet, 1761).

Thouret, Jacques-Guillaume, 'Rapport sur les bases de la représentation proportionnelle', 29 September 1789, in Mavidal (ed.), *Archives parlementaires*, ix. 202–6.

Tocqueville, Alexis de, *L'Ancien régime et la Révolution* (Paris: Gallimard, 1952–1953).

Tocqueville, Alexis de, *De la démocratie en Amérique* (Paris: Garnier-Flammarion, 1981).

Tournemine, René-Joseph de, 'Lettre à M. d'Argenson au sujet de l'emprisonnement de Nicolas Fréret' (Paris: Manuscrits de la bibliothèque interuniversitaire de la Sorbonne, MS 1638).

Tournemine, René-Joseph de, 'Réflexions sur la dissertation de M. Leibnits, touchant l'origine des François', *Journal de Trévoux, ou Mémoires pour servir à l'histoire des sciences et des arts*, January 1716, 10–22.

Toussaint, François-Vincent, *Les mœurs* (n.p., 1748).

[Trianon], 'Lettre d'un conseiller du Parlement de Rouen au sujet d'un écrit du Comte de Boulainvilliers', in Pierre-Nicolas Desmolets (ed.), *Continuation des Mémoires de littérature et d'histoire de M. de Sallengre* (Paris: Simart, 1726–1732), ix. 107–244 and 247–311.

Turgot, Anne-Robert-Jacques, *Œuvres de Turgot et documents le concernant* (ed. Schelle) (Paris: Alcan, 1913–1923).

Turgot, Anne-Robert-Jacques, *Œuvres* (ed. Daire) (Osnabrück: Zeller, 1966).

[Turlin], *Extrait des discours qui ont concouru pour le prix que l'académie des sciences, belles-lettres et arts de la ville de Lyon a adjugé à M. Turlin sur cette question: Les voyages peuvent-ils être considérés comme un moyen de perfectionner l'éducation?* (Lyons: Aimé de la Roche, 1788).

Vaissette, Joseph, 'Dissertation sur l'origine des Français', in Leber (ed.), *Collection des meilleurs dissertations relatifs à l'histoire de France*, i. 133–77.

Vauban, Sébastien Le Prestre de, *Les oisivetés de monsieur de Vauban* (Paris: Champ Vallon, 2007).

Velly, Paul-François, *Histoire de France depuis l'établissement de la monarchie jusqu'au règne de Louis XIV* (Paris: Desaint & Saillant, 1755–1786).

[Vernes, Jacob and Joseph-François-Marie Malherbe], *Testament du publiciste patriote, ou Précis des 'Observations de M. l'abbé de Mably sur l'histoire de France'* (The Hague: Bleuet fils aîné, 1789).

Vertot, René Aubert de, *Histoire de la conjuration du Portugal* (Amsterdam: H. Desbordes, 1689).

Vertot, René Aubert de, *Histoire des révolutions arrivées dans le gouvernement de la république romaine* (Paris: F. Barois, 1719).

Vertot, René Aubert de, 'Dissertation dans laquelle on tâche de démêler la véritable origine des Français, par un parallèle de leurs mœurs avec celles des Germains', in Leber (ed.), *Collection des meilleurs dissertations relatifs à l'histoire de France*, i. 43–96.

Viallon, Jean-Marie, *Clovis-le-Grand, premier roi chrétien, fondateur de la monarchie française* (Paris: Méquignon l'aîné, 1788).

Vico, Giambattista, *La scienza nuova (ed. 1730)* (Rome: Edizioni di storia e letteratura, 2013).

Villemain, Abel François, *Eloge de Montesquieu* (Paris: Didot, 1816).

Villemain, Abel François, *Cours de littérature française: Tableau du dix-huitième siècle* (Paris: Didier, 1838).

Volney, Constantin-François, *Voyage en Syrie et en Égypte* (Paris: Fayard, 1998).

Voltaire, François-Marie Arouet, 'François, ou Français', in Diderot and d'Alembert (eds.), *Encyclopédie*, vii. 284–7.

Voltaire, François-Marie Arouet, *Œuvres complètes* (Paris: Garnier, 1877–1885).

Vv. Aa., *Dictionnaire universel françois et latin, vulgairement appelé Dictionnaire de Trévoux* (Paris: Compagnie des libraires associés, 1704).

Secondary Sources

Acke, Daniel, 'La notion de caractère dans les *Journaux*', in Frank Salaün (ed.), *Marivaux subversif?* (Paris: Desjonquères, 2003), 209–19.

Adam, Ulrich, 'Nobility and Modern Monarchy – J. H. G. Justi and the French Debate on Commercial Nobility at the Beginning of the Seven Years War', *History of European Ideas*, 29 (2003), 141–57.

Adams, Leonard, *Coyer and the Enlightenment* (Oxford: Voltaire Foundation, 1974).

Adams, Percy Guy, *Travelers and Travel Liars, 1660–1800* (Berkeley: University of California Press, 1962).

Akagi, Shozo, '*Suite des Œuvres diverses de Mr de F***** de 1714: La première édition de l'*Origine des Fables* et de deux autres discours de Fontenelle', *Études de langue et littérature françaises*, 50 (1987), 18–31.

Alatri, Paolo, *Parlamenti e lotta politica nella Francia del Settecento* (Bari: Laterza, 1977).

Allix, Edgard, 'J.-B. Say et les origines de l'industrialisme', *Revue d'économie politique*, 24 (1910), 303–13 and 341–63.

Allix, Edgard, 'La rivalité entre la propriété foncière et la fortune mobilière sous la Révolution', *Revue d'histoire économique et sociale*, 6 (1913), 297–348.

Alocco-Bianco, Luciana, 'L'abbé de Mably et sa conception de l'histoire', in Centre aixois d'études et de recherches sur le XVIIIe siècle (ed.), *L'histoire au dix-huitième siècle* (Aix-en-Provence: La Calade, 1980), 223–32.

Althusser, Louis, *Montesquieu: La politique et l'histoire* (Paris: Presses universitaires de France, 2003).

Amalvi, Christian, *De l'art et de la manière d'accommoder les héros de l'histoire de France* (Paris: Albin Michel, 1988).

Anderson, Benedict, *Imagined Communities: Reflections on the Origins and Spread of Nationalism* (London: Verso, 1983).

Andress, David, '"A Ferocious and Misled Multitude": Elite Perceptions of Popular Action from Rousseau to Robespierre', in Malcolm Crook, William Doyle, and Alan Forrest (eds.), *Enlightenment and Revolution: Essays in Honour of Norman Hampson* (Aldershot: Ashgate, 2004), 169–86.

Andrew, Edward G., *Imperial Republics: Revolution, War, and Territorial Expansion from the English Civil War to the French Revolution* (Toronto: University of Toronto Press, 2011).

Andrivet, Patrick, *'Rome enfin que je hais'? Une étude sur les différentes vues de Montesquieu concernant les anciens Romains* (Orléans: Paradigme, 2012).

Annandale, Eric, 'Patriotism in de Belloy's Theatre: The Hidden Message', *Studies on Voltaire and the Eighteenth Century*, 304 (1992), 1225–8.

Ansart, Pierre, *Marx et l'anarchisme: Essai sur les sociologies de Saint-Simon, Proudhon, Marx* (Paris: Presses universitaires de France, 1969).

Apostolidès, Jean-Marie, 'The Problem of History in Seventeenth-Century France', *Diacritics*, 12 (1982), 59–68.

Apostolidès, Jean-Marie, *Le roi-machine: Spectacle et politique au temps de Louis XIV* (Paris: Éditions de Minuit, 1988).

Aramini, Aurélien, 'L'archéologie linguistique du pouvoir et du peuple chez Augustin Thierry', *Revue d'histoire du XIXᵉ siècle*, 49 (2014), 179–93.

Arendt, Hannah, 'Race-Thinking before Racism', *The Review of Politics*, 6 (1944), 36–73.

Ariès, Philippe, *Le temps de l'histoire* (Monaco: Éditions du Rocher, 1954).

Armenteros, Carolina, *The French Idea of History: Joseph de Maistre and his Heirs, 1794–1854* (Ithaca: Cornell University Press, 2011).

Armenteros, Carolina, 'Royalist Medievalism in the Age of Revolution: From Robert de Lézardière to Chateaubriand, 1792–1831', *RELIEF*, 8 (2014), 20–47.

Armstrong, John A., *Nations before Nationalism* (Chapel Hill: University of North Carolina Press, 1982).

Armstrong, John A., 'Definitions, Periodization, and Prospects of the longue durée', in Guibernau and Hutchinson (eds.), *History and National Destiny*, 9–18.

Aron, Raymond, *Les étapes de la pensée sociologique: Montesquieu, Comte, Marx, Tocqueville, Durkheim, Pareto, Weber* (Paris: Gallimard, 1967).

Aubert, Guillaume, '"The Blood of France": Race and Purity of Blood in the French Atlantic World', *William and Mary Quarterly*, 61 (2004), 439–78.

Aubert, Guillaume, 'Kinship, Blood, and the Emergence of the Racial Nation in the French Atlantic World, 1600–1789', in Christopher H. Johnson et al. (eds.), *Blood and Kinship: Matter for Metaphor from Ancient Rome to the Present* (New York: Berghahn Books, 2013), 175–95.

Auerbach, Erich, *Vier Untersuchungen zur Geschichte der französischen Bildung* (Bern: A. Francke Verlag, 1951).

Augustin-Thierry, Augustin, 'Lettres inédites de Chateaubriand et d'Augustin Thierry', *Revue des deux mondes*, 36 (1916), 53–76.

Augustin-Thierry, Augustin, *Augustin Thierry d'après sa correspondance et ses papiers de famille* (Paris: Plon-Nourrit, 1922).

Ausson, Paul-Laurent, 'Idéologie politique et lutte de classes dans le discours historiographique du "fatalisme historique" en France, sous la Restauration' (unpublished Ph.D. thesis – Paris: I.E.P.P., 1987).

Baár, Monika, 'Romantic Historiography in the Service of Nation Building', in Baár (ed.), *Historians and Nationalism: East-Central Europe in the Nineteenth Century* (Oxford: Oxford University Press, 2010), 46–74.

Bach, Reinhard, 'Les physiocrates et la science politique de leur temps', *Revue française d'histoire des idées politiques*, 20 (2004), 5–35.

Bach, Reinhard, *Rousseau et le discours de la Révolution, Au piège des mots: Les physiocrates, Sieyès, les idéologues* (Uzès: Inclinaison, 2011).

Baczko, Bronisław, *Rousseau: Solitude et communauté* (Paris: Mouton, 1974).

Baczko, Bronisław, 'Introduction', in Baczko (ed.), *Une éducation pour la démocratie: Textes et projets de l'époque révolutionnaire* (Paris: Garnier frères, 1982), 9–58.

Baczko, Bronisław, 'The Social Contract of the French: Sieyès and Rousseau', *The Journal of Modern History*, 60 (1988), 98–125.

Baczko, Bronisław, 'Le calendrier Républicain', in Nora (ed.), *Les lieux de mémoire*, i. 67–106.

Baecque, Antoine de, *Le corps de l'histoire: Métaphores et politique (1770–1800)* (Paris: Calmann-Lévy, 1993).

Baker, Keith M., 'Sieyès', in François Furet and Mona Ozouf (eds.), *Dictionnaire critique de la Révolution française* (Paris: Flammarion, 1988), 339–40.

Baker, Keith M., 'Closing the French Revolution: Saint-Simon and Comte', in François Furet and Mona Ozouf (eds.), *The French Revolution and the Creation of Modern Political Culture, vol. III: The Transformation of Political Culture, 1789–1848* (Oxford: Pergamon, 1989), 323–39.

Baker, Keith M., *Inventing the French Revolution* (Cambridge: Cambridge University Press, 1990).

Balázs, Péter, 'La monarchie républicaine du Marquis d'Argenson', *Studi francesi*, 53 (2009), 506–18.

Balázs, Péter, 'Philosophie et histoire dans l'œuvre du Marquis d'Argenson', *Dix-huitième siècle*, 42 (2010), 561–79.

Balcou, Jean, 'La Tour d'Auvergne, théoricien breton du mythe gaulois', in Viallaneix and Erhard (eds.), *Nos ancêtres les Gaulois*, 107–13.

Bann, Stephen, *The Inventions of History: Essays on the Representation of the Past* (Manchester: Manchester University Press, 1990).

Bann, Stephen, 'L'histoire et le peuple héros: Augustin Thierry et Thomas Carlyle', in André Peyronie (ed.), *Révolution française, peuple et littératures* (Paris: Klincksieck, 1991).

Banti, Alberto Mario, *La nazione del Risorgimento: Parentela, santità e onore alle origini dell'Italia unita* (Turin: Einaudi, 2000).

Banti, Alberto Mario, *L'onore della nazione: Identità sessuali e violenza nel nazionalismo europeo dal XVIII secolo alla Grande Guerra* (Turin: Einaudi, 2005).

Banti, Alberto Mario, 'Conclusions: Performative Effects and "Deep Images" in National Discourse', in Laurence Cole (ed.), *Different Paths to the Nation: Regional and National Identities in Central Europe and Italy, 1830–1870* (London: Palgrave, 2007), 220–9.

Banti, Alberto Mario, *Sublime madre nostra: La nazione italiana dal Risorgimento al fascismo* (Rome: Laterza, 2011).

Banzhaf, Spencer H., 'Productive Nature and the Net Product: Quesnay's Economies Animal and Political', *History of Political Economy*, 3 (2000), 517–51.

Bardoux, Agénor, *Études sociales et politiques: Le Comte de Montlosier et le Gallicanisme* (Paris: Calmann-Lévy, 1881).

Barling, Thomas J., 'Toussaint's *Les mœurs*', *French Studies*, 12 (1958), 14–20.

Barny, Roger, *Le Comte d'Antraigues, un disciple aristocrate de J.-J. Rousseau: De la fascination au reniement, 1782–1797* (Oxford: Voltaire Foundation, 1991).

Barrera, Guillaume, 'Introduction: *Essai sur les causes qui peuvent affecter les esprits et les caractères*', in *Œuvres* (ed. Société Montesquieu), ix. 205–17.

Barrera, Guillaume, *Les lois du monde: Enquête sur le dessein politique de Montesquieu* (Paris: Gallimard, 2009).

Barret-Kriegel, Blandine, *Les historiens et la monarchie: 1. Jean Mabillon* (Paris: Presses universitaires de France, 1988).

Barret-Kriegel, Blandine, *Les historiens et la monarchie: 2. La défaite de l'érudition* (Paris: Presses universitaires de France, 1988).

Barret-Kriegel, Blandine, *Les historiens et la monarchie: 3. Les académies de l'histoire* (Paris: Presses universitaires de France, 1988).

Barret-Kriegel, Blandine, 'Jean Mabillon et la science de l'histoire', in Mabillon, *Brèves réflexions sur quelques règles de l'histoire*, 7–101.

Barth, Fredrik (eds.), *Ethnic Groups and Boundaries: The Social Organization of Culture Difference* (Bergen: Universitetsforlaget, 1969).

Barthes, Roland, *Mythologies* (Paris: Seuil, 1957).

Barthes, Roland, *Essais critiques* (Paris: Seuil, 1981).

Barthes, Roland, *Le bruissement de la langue* (Paris: Seuil, 1984).

Barzun, Jacques, *The French Race: Theories of its Origins and their Social and Political Implications* (New York: Columbia University Press, 1932).

Bastid, Paul, *Sieyès et sa pensée* (Paris: Hachette, 1939).

Bates, David, 'Political Pathologies: Barnave and the Question of National Identity in Revolutionary France', *Canadian Journal of History*, 36 (2001), 427–52.

Battista, Anna Maria, *La 'Germania' di Tacito nella Francia illuminista* (Urbino: Quattro Venti, 1999).

Baum, Bruce David, *The Rise and Fall of the Caucasian Race: A Political History of Racial Identity* (New York: New York University Press, 2006).

Beales, Derek, 'Religion and Culture', in Tim Blanning (ed.), *The Short Oxford History of Europe: The Eighteenth Century, Europe 1660–1815* (Oxford: Oxford University Press, 2000), 131–77.

Beaune, Colette, *Naissance de la nation France* (Paris: Gallimard, 1985).

Behrent, Michael C., 'Liberal Dispositions: Recent Scholarship on French Liberalism', *Modern Intellectual History*, 13 (2016), 447–77.

Bell, David A., 'Lingua Populi, Lingua Dei: Language, Religion and the Origins of French Revolutionary Nationalism', *The American Historical Review*, 100 (1995), 1403–37.

Bell, David A., 'Recent Works on Early Modern French National Identity', *The Journal of Modern History*, 68 (1996), 84–113.

Bell, David A., *The Cult of the Nation: Inventing Nationalism, 1680–1800* (Cambridge, Mass: Harvard University Press, 2001).

Bell, David A., 'La nation et la loi à l'époque de la Révolution française', in Bernard Cottret (ed.), *Du patriotisme aux nationalismes (1700–1848), France, Grande-Bretagne, Amérique du Nord* (Paris: Éditions Créaphis, 2002), 89–100.

Bell, David A., 'Le caractère national et l'imaginaire républicain au XVIIIᵉ siècle', *Annales: Histoire, sciences sociales*, 57 (2002), 867–88.

Bell, David A., 'Nation et patrie, société et civilisation: Transformations du vocabulaire social français, 1700–1789', in Laurence Kaufmann and

Jean Guilhaumou (eds.), *L'invention de la société: Nominalisme politique et science sociale au XVIIIᵉ siècle* (Paris: EHESS, 2003), 99–112.

Bell, David A., 'Revolutionary France and the Origins of Nationalism: An Old Problem Revisited', in Lotte Jensen (ed.), *The Roots of Nationalism: National Identity Formation in Early Modern Europe, 1600–1815* (Amsterdam: Amsterdam University Press, 2016), 67–83.

Bell, David A. and Yair Mintzker (eds.), *Rethinking the Age of Revolutions: France and the Birth of the Modern World* (New York: Oxford University Press, 2018).

Beller, Manfred and Joep Leerssen (eds.), *Imagology: The Cultural Construction and Literary Representation of National Characters* (Amsterdam: Rodopi, 2007).

Belmessous, Saliha, 'Assimilation and Racialism in Seventeenth- and Eighteenth-Century French Colonial Policy', *American Historical Review*, 110 (2005), 322–49.

Belmont, Nicole, 'L'Académie celtique et George Sand: Les débuts des recherches folkloriques en France', *Romantisme*, 9 (1975), 29–38.

Belmont, Nicole, 'Introduction', in Belmont (ed.), *Aux sources de l'ethnologie française: L'Académie celtique* (Paris: Éditions du CTHS, 1995), 9–21.

Benharrech, Sarah, *Marivaux et la science du caractère* (Oxford: Voltaire Foundation, 2013).

Bénichou, Paul, *Morales du Grand siècle* (Paris: Gallimard, 1948).

Benítez, Miguel, 'Montesquieu, Fréret et les remarques tirées des entretiens avec Hoangh', in Montesquieu, *Œuvres* (ed. Société Montesquieu), xvi. 419–34.

Benítez, Miguel, 'Un spinozisme suspect: A propos du Dieu de Boulainvilliers', *Dix-huitième siècle*, 24 (1992), 17–28.

Benrekassa, Georges, 'Savoir politique et connaissance historique à l'aube des Lumières', *Studies on Voltaire and the Eighteenth Century*, 151 (1976), 261–85.

Benrekassa, Georges, *La politique et sa mémoire* (Paris: Payot, 1983).

Benrekassa, Georges, *Montesquieu: La liberté et l'histoire* (Paris: Librairie générale française, 1987).

Benrekassa, Georges, 'Crise de l'Ancien régime, crise des idéologies: Une année dans la vie de Sieyès', *Annales: Histoire, sciences sociales*, 44 (1989), 25–46.

Benrekassa, Georges, *Le langage des Lumières: Concepts et savoir de la langue* (Paris: Presses universitaires de France, 1995).

Berger, Stefan and Chris Lorenz (eds.), *The Contested Nation: Ethnicity, Class, Religion and Gender in National Histories* (Basingstoke: Palgrave Macmillan, 2008).

Berger, Stefan and Chris Lorenz, 'Introduction: National History Writing in Europe in a Global Age', in Berger and Lorenz (eds.), *The Contested Nation*, 1–23.

Berger, Stefan, Linas Eriksonas, and Andrew Mycock (eds.), *Narrating the Nation: Representations in History, Media, and the Arts* (New York: Berghahn, 2008).

Berger, Stefan, Mark Donovan, and Kevin Passmore (eds.), *Writing National Histories: Western Europe since 1800* (London: Routledge, 1999).

Berger, Stefan, Mark Donovan, and Kevin Passmore, 'Apologias for the Nation-State in Western Europe since 1800', in Berger, Donovan, and Passmore (eds.), *Writing National Histories*, 4–9.

Bergounioux, Louis-Alexandre, *L'esprit de polémique et les querelles savantes vers le milieu du XVIIe siècle: Marc Antoine Dominici (1605?–1650), un controversiste quercynois ami de Pascal* (Paris: Boivin, 1936).

Berlan, Françoise, 'Le mot "caractère" dans *Les caractères* de La Bruyère', *Champ du signe*, 1 (1991), 121–42.

Berlin, Isaiah, *Four Essays on Liberty* (Oxford: Oxford University Press, 1969).

Berr, Henri, *La synthèse en histoire* (Paris: Alcan, 1911).

Bertrand, Gilles, *Le Grand tour revisité: Pour une archéologie du tourisme. Le voyage des Français en Italie, milieu XVIIIe siècle – début XIXe siècle* (Rome: École française de Rome, 2008).

Beyssade, Jean-Marie, 'L'idée de tyrannie dans les *Mémoires* du Duc de Saint-Simon: L'ordre et les degrés de l'usurpation', *Cahiers de philosophie politique et juridique de l'Université de Caen*, 6 (1984), 127–46.

Bhabha, Homi (ed.), *Nation and Narration* (London: Routledge, 1990).

Bianchi, Lorenzo, 'Montesquieu et Fréret: Quelques notes', *Corpus: Revue de philosophie*, 29 (1995), 105–28.

Bianchi, Lorenzo and Rolando Minuti (eds.), *Montesquieu et les philosophies de l'histoire au XVIIIe siècle* (Naples: Liguori, 2013).

Bickart, Roger, *Les Parlements et la notion de souveraineté nationale au XVIIIe siècle* (Paris: Alcan, 1932).

Bindman, David, *Ape to Apollo: Aesthetics and the Idea of Race in the Eighteenth Century* (London: Reaktion, 2002).

Binoche, Bertrand, 'Montesquieu et la crise de la rationalité historique', *Revue germanique internationale*, 3 (1995), 31–53.

Binoche, Bertrand, *Introduction à* De l'Esprit des lois *de Montesquieu* (Paris: Publications de la Sorbonne, 2015).

Binoche, Bertrand and Franck Tinland (eds.), *Sens du devenir et pensée de l'histoire au temps des Lumières* (Seyssel: Champ Vallon, 2000).

Biondi, Carminella, '*Le siège de Calais* di Dormont de Belloy: Ragioni di un successo', in Corrado Rosso (ed.), *Intorno a Montesquieu* (Pisa: Goliardica, 1970), 5–20.

Biondi, Carminella, Mon frère, tu es mon esclave! *Teorie schiaviste e dibattiti antropologico-razziali nel Settecento francese* (Pisa: Goliardica, 1973).

Blanckaert, Claude, 'Les vicissitudes de l'angle facial et les débuts de la craniométrie (1765–1875)', *Revue de synthèse*, 108 (1987), 417–53.

Blanckaert, Claude, 'La science de l'homme entre humanité et inhumanité', in Blanckaert (ed.), *Des sciences contre l'homme, volume 1: Classer, hiérarchiser, exclure* (Paris: Autrement, 1993), 14–45.

Blanckaert, Claude, 'Contre la méthode: Unité de l'homme et classification dans l'anthropologie des Lumières', in Claude Calame and Mondher Kilani (eds.), *La fabrication de l'humain dans les cultures et en anthropologie* (Lausanne: Payot, 1999), 111–26.

Blanckaert, Claude, 'Les conditions d'émergence de la science des races au début du XIXe siècle', in Moussa (ed.), *L'idée de race dans les sciences humaines et la littérature*, 133–49.

Blanning, T. C. W., *The Culture of Power and the Power of Culture: Old Regime Europe, 1660–1789* (Oxford: Oxford University Press, 2002).

Blanquie, Christophe, *Saint-Simon, ou La politique des 'Mémoires'* (Paris: Garnier, 2014).

Blaufarb, Rafe, *The Great Demarcation: the French Revolution and the Invention of Modern Property* (Oxford: Oxford University Press, 2016).

Bloch, Marc, *La société féodale* (Paris: Albin Michel, 1989).

Bloch, Marc, *Apologie pour l'histoire, ou Le métier d'historien* (Paris: Armand Colin, 1997).

Blumenberg, Hans, *Paradigmen zu einer Metaphorologie* (Frankfurt: Suhrkamp, 1999).

Boch, Julie, *Approches de la pensée des Lumières* (Rheims: Éditions et presses universitaires de Reims, 2012).

Bonnel, Roland G., 'Le despotisme dans *Les lettres persanes*', *Studies on Voltaire and the Eighteenth Century*, 278 (1990), 79–103.

Borghero, Carlo, 'Sparta tra storia e utopia: Il significato e la funzione del mito di Sparta nel pensiero di Jean-Jacques Rousseau', in Giovanni Solinas (ed.), *Saggi sull'Illuminismo* (Cagliari: Pubblicazioni dell'Istituto di Filosofia, 1973), 253–318.

Borghero, Carlo, *La certezza e la storia: Cartesianesimo, pirronismo e conoscenza storica* (Milan: Franco Angeli, 1983).

Borghero, Carlo, 'Les philosophes face à l'histoire: Quelques discussions sur la connaissance historique aux XVIIe et XVIIIe siècles', in Chantal Grell and Jean-Michel Dufays (eds.), *Pratiques et concepts de l'histoire en Europe, XVIe–XVIIIe siècles* (Paris: Presses de l'Université Paris-Sorbonne, 1990), 73–83.

Borghero, Carlo, 'Méthode historique et philosophie chez Fréret', *Corpus: Revue de philosophie*, 29 (1995), 19–38.

Borghero, Carlo, 'Libertà e necessità: Clima ed "Esprit général" nell'*Esprit des lois*', in Domenico Felice (ed.), *Libertà, necessità e storia: Percorsi dell'Esprit des lois di Montesquieu* (Naples: Bibliopolis, 2003), 137–201.

Borghero, Carlo, 'La prova: Problemi comuni e prestiti disciplinari nel Settecento', in Carlo Borghero and Rosamaria Loretelli (eds.), *Le metamorfosi dei linguaggi nel Settecento* (Rome: Edizioni di storia e letteratura, 2011), 3–21.

Boulle, Pierre H., 'François Bernier and the Origins of the Modern Concept of Race', in Peabody and Stovall (eds.), *The Color of Liberty*, 11–27.

Boulle, Pierre H., *Race et esclavage dans la France de l'Ancien régime* (Paris: Perrin, 2007).

Bourdeau, Michel and Béatrice Fink, 'De l'industrie à l'industrialisme: Benjamin Constant aux prises avec le saint-simonisme', *Œuvres et critique*, 33 (2008), 61–78.

Bourdieu, Pierre, *La distinction: Critique sociale du jugement* (Paris: Éditions de Minuit, 1979).

Bourdieu, Pierre, 'Le Nord et le Midi: Contribution à une analyse de l'effet Montesquieu', *Actes de la recherche en sciences sociales*, 35 (1980), 21–5.

Bourdon, Étienne, *La forge gauloise de la nation: Ernest Lavisse et la fabrique des ancêtres* (Lyons: ENS éditions, 2017).

Bouton, Cynthia A., *The Flour War: Gender, Class, and Community in Late Ancien Régime French Society* (University Park, PA: Pennsylvania State University Press, 1993).

Boutry, Philippe, 'Clovis romantique', in Michel Rouche (ed.), *Clovis: Histoire et mémoire. Le baptême de Clovis, son écho à travers l'histoire* (Paris: Presse de l'Université Paris-Sorbonne, 1997), 637–47.

Brancourt, Jean-Pierre, *Le Duc de Saint-Simon et la monarchie* (Paris: Éditions Cujas, 1971).

Brancourt, Jean-Pierre, 'Un théoricien de la société au XVIIIe siècle: Le Chevalier d'Arcq', *Revue historique*, 250 (1973), 337–62.

Brass, Paul R., *Ethnicity and Nationalism: Theory and Comparison* (London: Sage, 1991).

Braude, Benjamin, 'The Sons of Noah and the Construction of Ethnic and Geographical Identities in the Medieval and Early Modern Periods', *The William and Mary Quarterly*, 54 (1997), 103–42.

Bravi, Massimiliano, 'Montesquieu, le invasioni barbariche e le ripercussioni del diritto germanico sulla storia giuridica della monarchia francese', in Domenico Felice (ed.), *Studi di storia della cultura:* Sibi suis amicisque (Bologna: CLUEB, 2012), 197–243.

Bredin, Jean-Denis, *Sieyès: La clé de la Révolution française* (Paris: le Grand livre du mois, 1988).

Brengues, Jacques, *Charles Duclos (1704–1772): Ou l'obsession de la vertu* (Saint-Brieuc: Presses universitaires de Bretagne, 1970).

Breuilly, John, *Nationalism and the State* (Manchester: Manchester University Press, 1982).

Breuilly, John, 'Risorgimento Nationalism in the Light of General Debates about Nationalism', *Nations and Nationalism*, 15 (2009), 439–45.

Breuilly, John (ed.), *Oxford Handbook of the History of Nationalism* (Oxford: Oxford University Press, 2013).

Brewer, Anthony, *Richard Cantillon: Pioneer of Economic Theory* (London: Routledge, 1992).

Brogi, Stefano, *Il cerchio dell'universo: Libertinismo, spinozismo e filosofia della natura in Boulainvilliers* (Florence: Olschki, 1993).

Broglie, Gabriel de, *Guizot* (Paris: Perrin, 2002).

Brown, Elizabeth A. R., 'Myths Chasing Myths: The Legend of the Trojan Origin of the French and its Dismantling', in Balázs Nagy and Marcell Sebők (eds.), *The Man of Many Devices, Who Wandered Full Many Ways: Festschrift in Honour of János M. Bak* (Budapest: Central European University Press, 1999), 613–33.

Brugerette, Joseph, *Le Comte de Montlosier et son temps (1755–1838)* (Aurillac: U.S. H.A., 1931).

Brühl, Carlrichard, 'Splendeur et misère de la diplomatique: Le cas de l'édition des diplômes royaux mérovingiens de Bréquigny à Pertz', *Comptes rendus des séances de l'Académie des inscriptions et belles-lettres*, 136 (1992), 251–9.

Brunner, Otto, Werner Conze, and Reinhart Koselleck (eds.), *Geschichtliche Grundbegriffe: Historisches Lexikon zur politisch-sozialen Sprache in Deutschland* (Stuttgart: Klett-Cotta, 1984–1992).

Bullard, Paddy and Alexis Tadié (eds.), *Ancients and Moderns in Europe: Comparative Perspectives* (Oxford: Voltaire Foundation, 2016).

Burguière, André, 'La mémoire familiale du bourgeois gentilhomme: Généalogies domestiques en France aux XVIIe et XVIIIe siècles', *Annales: Histoire, sciences sociales*, 46 (1991), 771–88.

Burguière, André, 'La généalogie', in Nora (ed.), *Les lieux de mémoire*, iii. 3879–907.

Burguière, André, 'L'historiographie des origines de la France: Genèse d'un imaginaire national', *Annales: Histoire, sciences sociales*, 58 (2003), 41–62.

Bury, Emmanuel, *Littérature et politesse: L'invention de l'honnête homme, 1580–1750* (Paris: Presses universitaires de France, 1996).

Butaud, Germain and Valérie Piétri, *Les enjeux de la généalogie (XIIe–XVIIIe siècle): Pouvoir et identité* (Paris: Autrement, 2006).

Buzon, Frédéric de, 'Leibniz, étymologie et origine des nations', *Revue française d'histoire des idées politiques*, 36 (2012), 383–400.

Cafmeyer, Géry de, 'Un manuscrit de Nicolas Fréret: *Mémoire sur le mot dunum* (1745)', in Daniel Droixhe and Chantal Grell (eds.), *La linguistique entre mythe et histoire* (Munster: Nodus Publikationen, 1993), 145–58.

Cahen, Léon, *Condorcet et la Révolution française* (Geneva: Slatkine, 1970).

Caillet, Maurice, 'Un ami des Lumières: Jean Castilhon', in Etienne Dennery (ed.), *Humanisme actif: Mélanges d'art et de littérature offerts à Julien Cain* (Paris: Herrmann, 1968), ii. 21–35.

Calvié, Lucien, '*Liberté, libertés* et *liberté(s) germanique(s)*: Une question franco-allemande, avant et après 1789', *Mots*, 16 (1988), 9–33.

Campbell, Peter R., 'La rhétorique patriotique et le monde parlementaire', in Lemaître (ed.), *Le monde parlementaire au XVIIIe siècle*, 193–220.

Campi, Alessandro, *La nazione* (Bologna: il Mulino, 2004).

Campi, Alessandro, Stefano De Luca, and Francesco Tuccari (eds.), *Nazione e nazionalismi: Teorie, interpretazioni, sfide attuali* (Rome: Historica, 2018).

Canova-Green, Marie-Claude and Alain Viala (eds.), *Racine et l'histoire* (Tübingen: G. Narr, 2004).

Caplan, Jay, *In the King's Wake: Post-Absolutist Culture in France* (Chicago: University of Chicago Press, 1999).

Carcassonne, Elie, 'Introduction', in Marie-Charlotte-Pauline Robert de Lézardière, *Ecrits inédits* (Paris: Presses universitaires de France, 1927), 1–38.

Carcassonne, Elie, *Montesquieu et le problème de la constitution française au XVIIIe siècle* (Geneva: Slatkine, 1978).

Carlisle, Robert, *The Proffered Crown: Saint-Simonianism and the Doctrine of Hope* (London: Johns Hopkins University Press, 1987).

Carmaux, Brigitte, 'Mlle de Lézardière: Une certaine idée de la monarchie française', *Annales de Bretagne et des pays de l'Ouest*, 102 (1995), 67–74.

Carr, David, *Narrative and History* (Bloomington: Indiana University Press, 1986).

Carrese, Paul, *Democracy in Moderation: Montesquieu, Tocqueville, and Sustainable Liberalism* (Cambridge: Cambridge University Press, 2016).

Carrithers, David, 'Montesquieu's Philosophy of History', *Journal of the History of Ideas*, 47 (1986), 61–80.

Casabianca, Denis de, *Montesquieu: De l'étude des sciences à l'Esprit des lois* (Paris: Honoré Champion, 2008).

Casadei, Thomas and Domenico Felice, 'Modi di sussistenza, leggi, costumi', in Domenico Felice (ed.), *Leggere Lo Spirito delle Leggi di Montesquieu* (Milan: Mimesis, 2010), i. 313–52.

Casanova, Robert, *Montlosier et le parti prêtre* (Paris: Laffont, 1970).

Ceccarelli, Alessandro, 'Il momento montesquieuiano di Louis Althusser', in Domenico Felice (ed.), *Montesquieu e i suoi interpreti* (Pisa: ETS, 2005), ii. 775–804.

Centre aixois d'études et de recherches sur le XVIIIᵉ siècle (ed.), *Images du peuple au dix-huitième siècle* (Paris: Armand Colin, 1973).

Chabod, Federico, *Storia dell'idea d'Europa* (Bari: Laterza, 1961).

Chabod, Federico *L'idea di nazione* (Bari: Laterza, 1961).

Chabod, Federico, *Alle origini della Rivoluzione francese* (Florence: Passigli, 1990).

Chamboredon, Robert (ed.), *François Guizot, 1787–1874: Passé-présent* (Paris: L'Harmattan, 2010).

Chapman, Sara E., *Private Ambition and Political Alliances: The Phélypeaux de Pontchartrain Family and Louis XIV's Government, 1650–1715* (Rochester, NY: University of Rochester Press, 2004).

Chappey, Jean-Luc, *La Société des observateurs de l'homme, 1799–1804: Des anthropologues au temps de Bonaparte* (Paris: Société des études robespierristes, 2002).

Charles, Loïc and Christine Théré, '*Jeux de mots*, Narrative and Economic Writing: The Rhetoric of Anti-physiocracy in French Economic Periodicals (1764–1769)', *The European Journal of the History of Economic Thought*, 22 (2015), 359–82.

Chartier, Roger, *Les origines culturelles de la Révolution française* (Paris: Seuil, 1990).

Chartier, Roger, *Au bord de la falaise: L'histoire entre certitudes et inquiétude* (Paris: Albin Michel, 2009).

Chaussinand-Nogaret, Guy, *Le citoyen des Lumières* (Brussels: Éditions complexe, 1994).

Cheminade, Christian, 'La querelle Fréret-Vertot (1714) et le débat sur les origines de la monarchie française', in Jacqueline Hoareau-Dodinau and Pascal Texier (eds.), *Mélanges Pierre Braun, anthropologies juridiques* (Limoges: Presses universitaires de Limoges, 1998), 161–8.

Childs, Nick, *A Political Academy in Paris, 1724–1731: The Entresol and its Members* (Oxford: Voltaire Foundation, 2000).

Chill, Emanuel, 'Introduction: Barnave as Philosophical Historian', in *Antoine Pierre Joseph Marie* Barnave, *Power, Property, and History: Joseph Barnave's*

Introduction to the French Revolution and Other Writings (New York: Harper, 1971), 1–74.

Chisick, Harvey, *The Limits of Reform in the Enlightenment: Attitudes to the Education of the Lower Classes in France, 1762–1789* (Princeton: Princeton University Press, 1981).

Christophorov, Pierre, 'Chateaubriand, Montlosier et le "Courier de Londres"', *Revue d'histoire littéraire de la France*, 61/1 (1961), 15–22.

Citron, Suzanne, *Quel imaginaire pour la France aujourd'hui?* (Talence: Presses universitaires de Bordeaux, 1991).

Citron, Suzanne, *La 'nationalisation' des mémoires* (Paris: Syros, 1993).

Citron, Suzanne, *Le mythe national: L'histoire de France revisitée* (Paris: Les Éditions de l'Atelier, 2008).

Citton, Yves, *Portrait de l'économiste en physiocrate: Critique littéraire de l'économie politique* (Paris: L'Harmattan, 2000).

Civardi, Jean-Marc, 'Introduction', in La Mesnardière, *La poétique*, 7–72.

Claiborne Isbell, John, 'Le contrat social selon Benjamin Constant et Mme de Staël, ou La liberté a-t-elle un sexe?', *Cahiers de l'Association internationale des études françaises*, 48 (1996), 439–56.

Clauzade, Laurent, 'Auguste Comte et la naturalisation de l'esprit', *Methodos*, 2 (2002), 33–50.

Clouatre, Dallas L., 'The Concept of Class in French Culture prior to the Revolution', *Journal of the History of Ideas*, 45 (1984), 219–44.

Coakley, John, '"Primordialism" in Nationalism Studies: Theory or Ideology?', *Nations and Nationalism*, 24 (2018), 327–47.

Cohler, Anne Marie, *Rousseau and Nationalism* (New York: Basic Books, 1970).

Coilly, Nathalie and Philippe Régnier (eds.), *Le siècle des saint-simoniens: Du nouveau christianisme au canal de Suez* (Paris: Bibliothèque nationale de France, 2006).

Coleman, Patrick, 'The Idea of Character in the *Encyclopédie*', *Eighteenth-Century Studies*, 13 (1979), 21–47.

Colonna d'Istria, Francesco, 'Introduction', in Baruch Spinoza, *Éthique* (Paris: Armand Colin, 1907), vii–xliii.

Comninel, George C., *Rethinking the French Revolution: Marxism and the Revisionist Challenge* (London: Verso, 1987).

Connor, Walker, 'The Timelessness of Nations', in Guibernau and Hutchinson (eds.), *History and National Destiny*, 35–47.

Connors, Logan J., 'Introduction', in Belloy, *Le siège de Calais*, 1–59.

Corada, Gian Carlo, 'La concezione della storia nel pensiero di Henry de Boulainviller', *A.C.M.E.: Annali della Facoltà di lettere e filosofia dell'Università degli Studi di Milano*, 28 (1975), 311–34.

Cornell, T. J., 'Ancient History and the Antiquarian Revisited: Some Thoughts on Reading Momigliano's *Classical Foundations*', in M. H. Crawford and C. R. Ligota (eds.), *Ancient History and the Antiquarian: Essays in Memory of Arnaldo Momigliano* (London: The Warburg Institute, 1995), 1–14.

Cotta, Sergio, 'Il problema politico del marchese d'Argenson', *Occidente*, 6 (1951), 192–222 and 295–310.

Cotta, Sergio, *Montesquieu e la scienza della società* (Turin: Ramella, 1953).

Cotta, Sergio, *Il pensiero politico di Montesquieu* (Rome: Laterza, 1995).

Coulet, Henri, *Marivaux romancier: Essai sur l'esprit et le cœur dans les romans de Marivaux* (Paris: Armand Colin, 1975).

Coulet, Henri, 'La notion de caractère dans l'œuvre de Beaumarchais', *Revue de l'Université de Moncton*, 1–3 (1978), 21–32.

Coulet, Henri, 'La notion de caractère dans l'œuvre de Duclos, moraliste et romancier', in Claire Blanche-Benveniste, André Chervel, and Maurice Gross (eds.), *Grammaire et histoire de la grammaire: Hommage à la mémoire de Jean Stéfanini* (Aix-en-Provence: Université de Provence, 1988), 157–68.

Courtois, Jean-Patrice, *Inflexions de la rationalité dans 'L'Esprit des lois'* (Paris: Presses universitaires de France, 1999).

Courtois, Jean-Patrice, 'Le physique et le moral dans la théorie du climat de Montesquieu', in Caroline Jacot-Grapa et al. (eds.), *Le travail des Lumières: Pour Georges Benrekassa* (Paris: Honoré Champion, 2002), 139–56.

Courtois, Jean-Patrice, 'Temps, corruption et histoire dans *L'Esprit des lois*', in Michel Porret and Catherine Volpilhac-Auger (eds.), *Le temps de Montesquieu* (Geneva: Droz, 2002), 305–18.

Courtois, Jean-Patrice, 'Le climat chez Montesquieu et Rousseau', in Emmanuel Le Roy Ladurie, Jacques Berchtold, and Jean-Paul Sermain (eds.), *L'événement climatique et ses représentations (XVIIe–XIXe)* (Paris: Desjonquères, 2007), 157–80.

Cox, Iris, *Montesquieu and the History of French Laws* (Oxford: Voltaire Foundation, 1983).

Crăiuțu, Aurelian, *Liberalism under Siege: The Political Thought of the French Doctrinaires* (Lanham: Lexington Books, 2003).

Crăiuțu, Aurelian, *A Virtue for Courageous Minds: Moderation in French Political Thought, 1748–1830* (Princeton: Princeton University Press, 2012).

Crépon, Marc, *Les géographies de l'esprit: Enquête sur la caractérisation des peuples de Leibniz à Hegel* (Paris: Payot, 1996).

Crévillon, Hervé and Diego Venturino (eds.), *Penser et vivre l'honneur à l'époque moderne* (Rennes: Presses universitaires de Rennes, 2011).

Creyghton, Camille, *Résurrections de Michelet: Politique et historiographie en France depuis 1870* (Paris: EHESS, 2019).

Croisille, Christian, 'Michelet et les Gaulois, ou Les séductions de la patrie celtique', in Viallaneix and Erhard (eds.), *Nos ancêtres les Gaulois*, 211–19.

Crossley, Ceri, 'History as a Principle of Legitimation in France (1820–48)', in Berger, Donovan, and Passmore (eds.), *Writing National Histories*, 49–56.

Crossley, Ceri, *French Historians and Romanticism: Thierry, Guizot, the Saint-Simonians, Quinet, Michelet* (London: Routledge, 1993).

Cuissard, Charles, 'Les Laureault de Boiscommun et Laureault de Foncemagne', *Annales de la Société historique et archéologique du Gâtinais*, 10 (1892), 345–67.

Curran, Andrew, 'Rethinking Race History: The Role of the Albino in the French Enlightenment Life Sciences', *History and Theory*, 48 (2009), 151–79.

D'Auria, Matthew, 'Risorgimento addio? Alcune riflessioni sulla "nazione italiana" di Alberto Mario Banti', *Rivista di politica*, 2 (2011), 17–30.

Dainotto, Roberto, *Europe (in Theory)* (Durham, NC: Duke University Press, 2007).

Danielou, C. F., 'La Rochefoucauld, ou L'impossible connaissance de soi', *Papers on French Seventeenth Century Literature*, 23 (1996), 635–49.

Dann, Otto and John Dinwiddy (eds.), *Nationalism in the Age of the French Revolution* (London: Hambledon Press, 1988).

Darmau, Frédéric, 'Les ambiguïtés de Renan: Nation, Nationalisme, Internationalisme', *Raison présente*, 86 (1988), 27–35.

Davies, Catherine Glyn, *Conscience as Consciousness: The Idea of Self-awareness in French Philosophical Writing from Descartes to Diderot* (Oxford: Voltaire Foundation, 1990).

Davies, Simon, *Paris and the Provinces in Eighteenth-Century Prose Fiction* (Oxford: Voltaire Foundation, 1982).

Davillé, Louis, *Leibniz historien: Essai sur l'activité et la méthode historique de Leibniz* (Paris: Alcan, 1909).

De Certeau, Michel, *L'écriture de l'histoire* (Paris: Gallimard, 1975).

De Francesco, Antonino, *La guerre de deux cents ans: Une histoire des histoires de la Révolution française* (Paris: Perrin, 2018).

De Mauro, Tullio, *Senso e significato: Studi di semantica teorica e storica* (Bari: Laterza, 1971).

De Vivo, Giancarlo and Gabriel Sabbagh, 'The First Translator in English of Turgot's *Réflexions sur la formation et la distribution des richesses*: Benjamin Vaughan', *History of Political Economy*, 47 (2015), 185–99.

Dedieu, Joseph, *Montesquieu* (Paris: Alcan, 1913).

Delpla, Isabelle and Philippe de Robert (eds.), *La raison corrosive: Études sur la pensée critique de Pierre Bayle* (Paris: Honoré Champion, 2003).

Dendena, Francesco, 'L'expérience de la défaite, la rencontre avec l'histoire: Barnave et ses écrits historiques', *La Révolution française*, 10 (2016), 1–17.

Denieul Cormier, Anne, *Augustin Thierry: L'histoire autrement* (Paris: Publisud, 1996).

Denton, Chad, *Decadence, Radicalism, and the Early Modern French Nobility: The Enlightened and Depraved* (Lanham: Lexington Books, 2017).

Depitre, Edgard, 'Le système et la querelle de la *noblesse commerçante* (1756–1759)', *Revue d'histoire économique et sociale*, 6 (1913), 137–76.

Derathé, Robert, 'La philosophie des Lumières en France: Raison et modération selon Montesquieu', *Revue internationale de philosophie*, 21 (1952), 275–93.

Derathé, Robert, 'Patriotisme et nationalisme au XVIIIᵉ siècle', *Annales de philosophie politique*, 8 (1969), 69–84.

Déruelle, Aude, 'Introduction', in Augustin Thierry, *Lettres sur l'histoire de France* (Paris: Garnier, 2012), 13–53.

Desbrousses, Hélène and Bernard Peloille, 'Rapports sociaux et luttes entre "classes" inégales chez Rousseau', *Cahiers pour l'analyse concrète*, 35 (1995), 79–127.

Descimon, Robert, 'Chercher de nouvelles voies pour interpréter les phénomènes nobiliaires dans la France moderne: La noblesse, "essence" ou rapport social?', *Revue d'histoire moderne et contemporaine*, 46 (1999), 5–21.

Desgraves, Louis, *Montesquieu: L'œuvre et la vie* (Bordeaux: L'esprit du temps, 1995).

Detienne, Marcel, *L'identité nationale, une énigme* (Paris: Gallimard, 2010).

Devyver, André, *Le sang épuré: Les préjugés de race chez les gentilshommes français de l'Ancien régime (1560–1720)* (Brussels: Éditions de l'Université de Bruxelles, 1973).

Dew, Nicholas, *Orientalism in Louis XIV's France* (Oxford: Oxford University Press, 2009).

Di Bartolomeo, Daniele, *Nelle vesti di Clio: L'uso politico della storia nella Rivoluzione francese (1787–1799)* (Rome: Viella, 2014).

Di Donato, Francesco, 'Le concept de représentation dans la doctrine juridico-politique de Louis-Adrien le Paige', in Centre d'études et de recherches d'histoire des idées et des institutions politiques (ed.), *Le concept de représentation dans la pensée politique* (Aix-en-Provence: Presses universitaires d'Aix-Marseille, 2003), 53–73.

Di Rienzo, Eugenio, 'Morellet e Sieyès: Nobili, proprietari e organizzazione del potere nella Rivoluzione', *Studi storici*, 31 (1990), 457–80.

Dijn, Annelien, *French Political Thought from Montesquieu to Tocqueville: Liberty in a Levelled Society?* (Cambridge: Cambridge University Press, 2008).

Dijn, Annelien, 'A Strange Liberalism: Freedom and Aristocracy in French Political Thought', in Stuart Jones and Julian Wright (eds.), *Pluralism and the Idea of the Republic in France* (New York: Palgrave, 2012), 66–84.

Dijn, Annelien, 'Was Montesquieu a Liberal Republican?', *The Review of Politics*, 76 (2014) 21–41.

Dorigny, Marcel, 'La formation de la pensée économique de Sieyès d'après ses manuscrits (1770–1789)', *Annales historiques de la Révolution française*, 271 (1988), 217–34.

Dorlin, Elsa, *La matrice de la race: Généalogie sexuelle et coloniale de la nation française* (Paris: la Découverte, 2006).

Dornier, Carole, 'Introduction', in Duclos, *Considérations sur les mœurs de ce siècle*, 7–64.

Doron, Claude-Olivier, 'Race and Genealogy: Buffon and the Formation of the Concept of "Race"', *Humana.Mente: Journal of Philosophical Studies*, 22 (2012), 75–109.

Doron, Claude-Olivier, *L'homme altéré: Races et dégénérescence, XVIIe–XIXe siècles* (Ceyzérieu: Champ Vallon, 2016).

Dosse, François, *Pierre Nora: Homo historicus* (Paris: Perrin, 2011).

Doyle, William, 'The Parlements of France and the Breakdown of the Old Regime, 1771–1788', *French Historical Studies*, 6 (1970), 415–58.

Droixhe, Daniel, *La linguistique et l'appel de l'histoire (1600–1800): Rationalisme et révolutions positivistes* (Geneva: Droz, 1978).

Drolet, Michael, 'Industry, Class and Society: A Historiographic Reinterpretation of Michel Chevalier', *English Historical Review*, 504 (2008), 1229–71.

Drolet, Michael, 'Carrying the Banner of the Bourgeoisie: Democracy, Self and the Philosophical Foundations to François Guizot's Historical and Political Thought', *History of Political Thought*, 32 (2011), 645–90.

Dubois, Claude-Gilbert, *Celtes et Gaulois au XVIe siècle: Le développement littéraire d'un mythe nationaliste* (Paris: Vrin, 1972).

Dubost, Jean-François, 'Les stéréotypes nationaux à l'époque moderne (vers 1500 – vers 1800)', *Mélanges de l'École française de Rome*, 11 (1999), 667–82.

Duby, Georges, *La société chevaleresque* (Paris: Flammarion, 1988).

Ducange, Jean-Numa, 'Marx, le marxisme et le "père de la lutte des classes", Augustin Thierry', *Actuel Marx*, 58 (2015), 12–27.

Duchet, Michèle, *Diderot et l'Histoire des deux Indes, ou L'écriture fragmentaire* (Paris: Nizet, 1978).

Duchet, Michèle, *Anthropologie et histoire au siècle des Lumières* (Paris: Albin Michel, 1995).

Dumont, Ernest, *Notice sur la vie et les écrits de Louis-Georges-Oudart Feudrix de Bréquigny* (Rouen: P. Leprêtre, 1897).

Dumont, Louis, *From Mandeville to Marx: The Genesis and Triumph of Economic Ideology* (Chicago: Chicago University Press, 1977).

Dumont, Louis, *Homo hierarchicus: Le système des castes et ses implications* (Paris: Gallimard, 1979).

Dunkley, John, 'Medieval Heroes in Enlightenment Disguises: Figures from Voltaire and Belloy', in Peter Damian-Grint (ed.), *Medievalism and* manière gothique *in Enlightenment France* (Oxford: Voltaire Foundation, 2006), 152–80.

Dupart, Dominique, 'Augustin Thierry et le chant des sources', in Potin and Déruelle (eds.), *Augustin Thierry*, 55–61.

Dupuy-Brègant, Hélène, 'Le roi dans la patrie', *Annales historiques de la Révolution française*, 284 (1991), 139–57.

Durand, Isabelle, 'Augustin Thierry et le Moyen Age romantique: Le mythe des origines', in Potin and Déruelle (eds.), *Augustin Thierry*, 159–69.

Duranton, Henri, '"Nos ancêtres les Gaulois": Genèse et avatars d'un cliché historique', *Cahiers d'histoire*, 16 (1969), 339–70.

Duranton, Henri, 'Le vase de Soissons et les historiens du XVIIIe siècle', *Revue de synthèse*, 79–80 (1975), 283–316.

Duranton, Henri, 'Les contraintes structurales de l'histoire de France: Le cas Pharamond', *Synthesis*, 4 (1977), 153–64.

Durdent, René-Jean, 'Brizard', in Michaud and Michaud (eds.), *Biographie universelle ancienne et moderne*, v. 632–3.

Durkheim, Émile, 'Saint-Simon, fondateur du positivisme et de la sociologie', *Revue philosophique*, 99 (1925), 321–41.

Durkheim, Émile, 'Montesquieu, sa part dans la fondation des sciences politiques et de la science des sociétés', *Revue d'histoire politique et constitutionnelle*, 1 (1937), 405–63.

Dziembowski, Edmond, *Un nouveau patriotisme français, 1750–1770: La France face à la puissance anglaise à l'époque de la guerre de Sept Ans* (Oxford: Voltaire Foundation, 1998).

Echeverria, Durand, *The Maupeou Revolution: A study in the History of Libertarianism* (Baton Rouge: Louisiana State University Press, 1985).

Edelstein, Dan, *The Terror of Natural Right: Republicanism, the Cult of Nature, and the French Revolution* (Chicago: University of Chicago Press, 2009).

Edelstein, Dan, *The Enlightenment: A Genealogy* (Chicago: University of Chicago Press, 2010).

Edelstein, Melvin, *The French Revolution and the Birth of Electoral Democracy* (Farnham: Ashgate, 2014).

Egret, Jean, *Louis XV et l'opposition parlementaire, 1715–1774* (Paris: Armand Colin, 1970).

Egret, Jean, *Necker: Ministre de Louis XVI, 1776–1790* (Paris: Honoré Champion, 1975).

Ehrard, Jean, *L'esprit des mots: Montesquieu en lui-même et parmi les siens* (Geneva: Droz, 1990).

Ehrard, Jean, *L'idée de nature en France dans la première moitié du XVIIIe siècle* (Paris: Albin Michel, 1994).

Ehrard, Jean, 'Rousseau et Montesquieu: Le mauvais fils réconcilié', *Annales de la société Jean-Jacques Rousseau*, 41 (1997), 57–77.

Ehrard, Jean, 'La notion de "loi(s) fondamentale(s)" dans l'œuvre et la pensée de Montesquieu', in Volpilhac-Auger (ed.), *Montesquieu en 2005*, 267–78.

Eisenstadt, Shmuel N. (ed.), *Multiple Modernities* (New Brunswick: Transaction, 2002).

Elden, Stuart, 'The War of Races and the Constitution of the State: Foucault's "Il faut défendre la société" and the Politics of Calculation', *Boundary 2* (2002), 125–51.

Elias, Norbert, *Die höfische Gesellschaft: Untersuchungen zur Soziologie des Königtums und der höfischen Aristokratie* (Neuwied: Luchterhand, 1969).

Elisabeth Fehrenbach, 'Nation', in Rolf Reichardt and Hans-Jürgen Lüsebrink (eds.), *Handbuch politisch-sozialer Grundbegriffe in Frankreich: 1680–1820* (Munich: R. Oldenbourg, 1986), vii. 75–107.

Ellis, Harold, 'Genealogy, History, and Aristocratic Reaction in Early Eighteenth-Century France: The Case of Henri de Boulainvilliers', *Journal of Modern History*, 58 (1986), 414–51.

Ellis, Harold, *Boulainvilliers and the French Monarchy* (Ithaca: Cornell University Press, 1988).

Emge, Richard Martinus, *Saint-Simon: Einführung in ein Leben und Werk, eine Schule, Sekte und Wirkungsgeschichte* (Munich: Oldenbourg, 1987).

Engels, Friedrich, *Herrn Eugen Dührings Umwälzung der Wissenschaft (Anti-Dühring)* (Berlin: Deitz, 1988).

Englund, Steven, 'The Ghost of Nation Past', *The Journal of Modern History*, 64 (1992), 299–320.

Eriksen, T. H., *Ethnicity and Nationalism: Anthropological Perspectives* (London: Pluto Press, 2010).

Esposito, Roberto, *Communitas* (Turin: Einaudi, 1998).

Fabiani, Jean-Louis, 'Disputes, polémiques et controverses dans les mondes intellectuels: Vers une sociologie historique des formes de débat agonistique', *Mil neuf cent: Revue d'histoire intellectuelle*, 25 (2007), 45–60.

Faccarello, Gilbert, 'Le legs de Turgot: Aspects de l'économie politique sensualiste de Condorcet à Rœderer', in Gilbert Faccarello and Philippe Steiner (eds.), *La pensée économique pendant la Révolution française* (Grenoble: Presses universitaires de Grenoble, 1991), 67–107.

Fatta, Corrado, *Esprit de Saint-Simon: 1. La mort de Vatel* (Paris: Corrêa, 1954).

Fauré, Christine, 'Mademoiselle de Lézardière entre Jeanne d'Arc et Montesquieu', in Marie-France Brive (ed.), *Les femmes et la Révolution française* (Toulouse: Presses universitaires du Mirail, 1989–1991), i. 183–90.

Fauré, Christine, 'Introduction', in Sieyès, *Des manuscrits de Sieyès*, ii. 15–57.

Fauré, Christine, 'L'abbé Sieyès, lecteur problématique des Lumières', *Dix-huitième siècle*, 37 (2005), 225–41.

Fauré, Christine, 'Sieyès, Rousseau et la théorie du contrat', in Quiviger, Denis, and Salem (eds.), *Figures de Sieyès*, 213–25.

Faÿ, Bernard, *La Franc-maçonnerie et la révolution intellectuelle du XVIIIᵉ siècle* (Paris: la Librairie française, 1961).

Febvre, Lucien, *'Honneur et patrie'* (Paris: Perrin, 1996).

Febvre, Lucien, *De la 'Revue de synthèse' aux 'Annales': Lettres à Henri Berr, 1911–1954* (Paris: Fayard, 1997).

Febvre, Lucien, *Michelet, créateur de l'Histoire de France: Cours au Collège de France, 1943–1944* (Paris: Vuibert, 2014).

Felice, Domenico, 'Francia, Spagna e Portogallo: Le monarchie europee "qui vont au despotisme" secondo Montesquieu', in Postigliola and Bottaro Palumbo (eds.), *L'Europe de Montesquieu*, 283–305.

Felice, Domenico, 'Introduzione', in Charles-Louis Secondat de Montesquieu, *Saggio sulle cause che possono agire sugli spiriti e sui caratteri* (Pisa: ETS, 2004), 1–33.

Felice, Domenico, 'Voltaire lettore e critico dell' "Esprit des lois"', in Felice (ed.), *Montesquieu e i suoi interpreti* (Pisa: ETS, 2005), i. 177–81.

Felice, Domenico, *Per una scienza universale dei sistemi politico-sociali: Dispotismo, autonomia della giustizia e carattere delle nazioni nell'Esprit des lois di Montesquieu* (Florence: Olschki, 2005).

Fink, Gonthier-Louis, 'De Bouhours à Herder: La théorie française des climats et sa réception Outre-Rhin', *Recherches germaniques*, 15 (1985), 3–62.

Finzi, Roberto, *Note su Turgot, la storia e l'economia* (Bologna: CLUEB, 1987).

Fiorentini, Paoladele, *Augustin Thierry: Storiografia e politica nella Francia della Restaurazione* (Catania: Edizioni del Prisma, 2003).

Fisichella, Domenico, *Il potere nella società industriale: Saint-Simon e Comte* (Naples: Morano, 1965).

Fontaine, Philippe, 'The Concept of *Industrie* from the Physiocrats to J.-B. Say', *Contributions to Political Economy*, 12 (1993), 89–97.

Fontana, Biancamaria, *Benjamin Constant and the Post-Revolutionary Mind* (New Haven: Yale University Press, 1991).

Fontana, Biancamaria, *Germaine de Staël: A Political Portrait* (Princeton: Princeton University Press, 2016).

Formel, François, *Alliances et généalogie à la cour du Grand Roi: Le souci généalogique chez Saint-Simon* (Paris: Éditions Contrepoint, 1983–1984).

Forsyth, Murray, *Reason and Revolution: The Political Thought of the Abbé Sieyès* (Leicester: Leicester University Press, 1987).

Fossaert, Robert, 'La théorie des classes chez Guizot et Thierry', *La pensée*, 59 (1955), 59–69.

Foucault, Michel, *Les mots et les choses: Une archéologie des sciences humaines* (Paris: Gallimard, 1966).

Foucault, Michel, *Histoire de la sexualité: 1 – La volonté de savoir* (Paris: Gallimard, 1976).

Foucault, Michel, *Dits et écrits: 1954–1988* (Paris: Gallimard, 1994).

Foucault, Michel, *Il faut défendre la société: Cours au Collège de France. 1976* (Paris: Seuil, 1997).

Foucault, Michel, *Du gouvernement des vivants* (Paris: EHESS, 2012).

Fox, Christopher, Roy Porter, and Robert Wokler (eds.), *Inventing Human Science: Eighteenth-Century Domains* (Berkeley: University of California Press, 1995).

Fox-Genovese, Elizabeth, *The Origins of Physiocracy: Economic Revolution and Social Order in Eighteenth-Century France* (Ithaca: Cornell University Press, 1976).

France, Anatole, *La vie littéraire: Première série* (Paris: Calmann-Lévy, 1921).

France, Peter, *Politeness and its Discontents: Problems in French Classical Culture* (Cambridge: Cambridge University Press, 1992).

Frank, Stephanie, 'The General Will beyond Rousseau: Sieyès' Theological Arguments for the Sovereignty of the Revolutionary National Assembly', *History of European Ideas*, 37 (2011), 337–43.

Friedmann, Georges, 'L'Encyclopédie et le travail humain', *Annales: Économies, sociétés, civilisations*, 8 (1953), 53–61.

Friedemann, Peter, *Die politische Philosophie des Gabriel Bonnot de Mably (1709–1785): Eine Studie zur Geschichte des republikanischen und des sozialen Freiheitsbegriffs* (Berlin: LIT, 2014).

Fritz, Gérard, *L'idée de peuple en France du XVIIe au XIXe siècle* (Strasbourg: Presses universitaires de Strasbourg, 1988).

Fumaroli, Marc, *La querelle des anciens et des modernes: XVIIe–XVIIIe siècles* (Paris: Gallimard, 2001).

Fumaroli, Marc, *Le sablier renversé: Des modernes aux anciens* (Paris: Gallimard, 2013).

Furet, François and Mona Ozouf, 'Deux légitimations historiques de la société française au XVIIIe siècle: Mably et Boulainvilliers', in Furet, *L'atelier de l'histoire* (Paris: Flammarion, 2007), 165–83.

Furet, François, *La Révolution française* (Paris: Gallimard, 2007).

Furia, Annalisa, 'Il *citoyen homme social* negli scritti prerivoluzionari di Sieyès, 1770–1780', *Il pensiero politico*, 38 (2005), 196–221.

Fustel de Coulanges, Numa Denis, *Histoire des institutions politiques de l'ancienne France* (Paris: Hachette, 1875–1889).

Gallais-Hamonno, Jeanine, 'Condillac et la langue de l'économie', in Jean Sgard (ed.), *Condillac et les problèmes du langage* (Geneva: Slatkine, 1982), 407–20.

Gallanar, Joseph, 'Argenson's "Platonic Republics"', *Studies on Voltaire and the Eighteenth Century*, 56 (1967), 557–75.

Galliani, Renato, *Rousseau, le luxe et l'idéologie nobiliaire: Étude socio-historique* (Oxford: Voltaire Foundation, 1989).

Gallie, W. B., 'Essentially Contested Concepts', *Proceedings of the Aristotelian Society*, 56 (1956), 167–98.

Gallo, Daniela, 'Pouvoirs de l'antiquité', in Jean-Claude Bonnet (ed.), *L'empire des muses: Napoléon, les arts et les lettres* (Paris: Belin, 2004), 317–29.

Ganofsky, Marine and Jean-Alexandre Perras (eds.), *Le siècle de la légèreté: Emergences d'un paradigme du XVIIIe siècle français* (Liverpool: Liverpool University Press, 2019).

Gargallo di Castel Lentini, Gioacchino, *Storia della storiografia moderna* (Rome: Bulzoni, 1985–).

Garin, Eugenio, 'La storia "critica" della filosofia nel Settecento', *Giornale critico della filosofia italiana*, 49 (1970), 37–69.

Gat, Azar, *Nations: The Long History and Deep Roots of Political Ethnicity and Nationalism* (Cambridge: Cambridge University Press, 2013).

Gauchet, Marcel, 'Les "Lettres sur l'histoire de France" d'Augustin Thierry', in Nora (ed.), *Les lieux de mémoire*, i. 787–850.

Gauchet, Marcel, *La condition politique* (Paris: Gallimard, 2005).

Gautier, Claude, 'À propos du "commencement" ou de l'"établissement": Quelques remarques sur l'histoire', in Louis Desgraves (ed.), *Actes du colloque international de Bordeaux pour le 250e anniversaire de L'Esprit des lois* (Bordeaux: Académie de Bordeaux, 1999), 353–69.

Gelléri, Gabor, 'Absences et présences de l'art du voyage dans la France du XVIIIe siècle', *Lumen: Selected Proceedings from the Canadian Society for Eighteenth-Century Studies*, 34 (2015), 55–69.

Gellner, Ernest, *Nations and Nationalism* (Oxford: Blackwell, 1983).

Gembicki, Dieter, *Histoire et politique à la fin de l'Ancien régime: Jacob-Nicolas Moreau (1717–1803)* (Paris: Nizet, 1979).

Gembicki, Dieter, 'Le Moyen Âge de Montesquieu', in Michel Porret and Catherine Volpilhac-Auger (eds.), *Le temps de Montesquieu* (Geneva: Droz, 2002), 363–76.

Gembicki, Dieter, *Clio au XVIIIe siècle: Voltaire, Montesquieu et autres disciples* (Paris: L'Harmattan, 2008).

Genette, Gérard, *Figures II* (Paris: Seuil, 1969).

Gérard, Alice, 'Le grand homme et la conception de l'histoire au XIXe siècle', *Romantisme*, 100 (1998), 31–48.

Gerber, Matthew, *Bastards: Politics, Family, and Law in Early Modern France* (Oxford: Oxford University Press, 2012).

Gerhard, Dietrich, 'Guizot, Augustin Thierry und die Rolle des Tiers État in der französischen Geschichte', *Historische Zeitschrift*, 190 (1960), 290–310.

Gerhardi, Gerhard, 'L'idéologie du sang chez Boulainvilliers et sa réception au 18ᵉ siècle', *Études sur le XVIIIᵉ siècle*, 11 (1984), 11–20.

Giesey, Ralph, *Cérémonial et puissance souveraine: France, XVᵉ–XVIIᵉ siècles* (Paris: Armand Colin, 1987).

Gildea, Robert, *The Past in French History* (New Haven: Yale University Press, 1996).

Gildea, Robert, *Children of the Revolution: The French, 1799–1914* (London: Penguin, 2009).

Gilles, Philippe and Jean-Pierre Berlan, 'Économie, histoire et genèse de l'économie politique: Quesnay, Turgot et Condorcet, Say, Sismondi', *Revue économique*, 42 (1991), 367–94.

Ginzburg, Carlo, 'Checking the Evidence: The Judge and the Historian', *Critical Inquiry*, 18 (1991), 79–92.

Girard, René, *La violence et le sacré* (Paris: B. Grasset, 1972).

Giraud, Yves, 'Le "Dictionnaire comique" de Le Roux', *Cahiers de l'association internationale des études françaises*, 35 (1983), 69–86.

Giraudeau, Martin, 'Performing Physiocracy: Pierre Samuel Dupont de Nemours and the Limits of Political Engineering', *Journal of Cultural Economy*, 3 (2010), 225–42.

Giuliani, Pierre, 'Le sang classique entre histoire et littérature: Hypothèses et propositions', *XVIIᵉ Siècle*, 239 (2008), 223–42.

Glacken, Clarence J., *Traces on the Rhodian Shore: Nature and Culture in Western Thought from Ancient Times to the End of the Eighteenth Century* (Berkeley: University of California Press, 1967).

Gliozzi, Giuliano, *Adamo e il Nuovo Mondo: La nascita dell'antropologia come ideologia coloniale, dalle genealogie bibliche alle teorie razziali, 1500–1700* (Florence: La Nuova Italia, 1977).

Gliozzi, Giuliano, 'Poligenismo e razzismo agli albori del secolo dei lumi', *Rivista di filosofia*, 70 (1979), 1–31.

Gliozzi, Giuliano, *Differenze e uguaglianza nella cultura europea moderna: Scritti, 1966–1991* (Naples: Vivarium, 1993).

Gobo, Giampietro, 'Class: Stories of Concepts. From Ordinary Language to Scientific Language', *Social Science Information*, 32 (1993), 467–89.

Godechot, Jacques, 'Nation, patrie et patriotisme en France au 18ᵉᵐᵉ siècle', *Annales historiques de la Révolution française*, 43 (1971), 481–501.

Goggi, Gianluigi, 'Les contributions de Diderot aux livres i–v', in Guillaume-Thomas Raynal, *Histoire philosophique et politique des établissements et du commerce des Européens dans les deux Indes* (Ferney-Voltaire: Centre international d'étude du XVIIIᵉ siècle, 2010–), i. 749–66.

Goldhammer, Jesse, *The Headless Republic: Sacrificial Violence in Modern French Thought* (Ithaca: Cornell University Press, 2005).

Goldzink, Jean, *La solitude de Montesquieu: Le chef-d'œuvre introuvable du libéralisme* (Paris: Fayard, 2011).

Gordon, Daniel, *Citizens Without Sovereignty: Equality and Sociability in French Thought, 1670–1789* (Princeton: Princeton University Press, 1994).

Gossiaux, Paul-Pierre, 'Anthropologie des Lumières ("Culture naturelle" et racisme rituel)', in Daniel Droixhe and Paul-Pierre Gossiaux (eds.), *L'homme des Lumières et la découverte de l'autre* (Brussels: Éditions de l'Université de Bruxelles, 1985), 49–69.

Gossman, Lionel, *Medievalism and the Ideologies of the Enlightenment: The World and Work of La Curne de Sainte-Palaye* (Baltimore: Johns Hopkins Press, 1968).

Gossman, Lionel, 'Augustin Thierry and Liberal Historiography', *History and Theory: Beiheft 15*, 4 (1976).

Gossman, Lionel, *Between History and Literature* (Cambridge, Mass: Harvard University Press, 1990).

Gouhier, Henri, *La jeunesse d'Auguste Comte et la formation du positivisme: Vol. 3, Auguste Comte et Saint-Simon* (Paris: Vrin, 1970).

Goulemot, Jean-Marie, 'De la représentation dans la pensée politique du Duc de Saint-Simon', *Procès: Cahiers d'analyse politique et juridique*, 11–12 (1983), 41–9.

Goulemot, Jean-Marie, 'Vision du devenir historique et formes de la révolution dans les *Lettres persanes*', *Dix-huitième siècle*, 21 (1989), 13–22.

Goutte, Pierre Henri and Gérard Klotz, 'Turgot: A Critic of Physiocracy? An Analysis of the Debates in *Éphémérides du citoyen* and in Correspondence with Dupont', *The European Journal of the History of Economic Thought*, 22 (2015), 500–33.

Grafton, Anthony, *What Was History? The Art of History in Early Modern Europe* (Cambridge: Cambridge University Press, 2007).

Grandière, Marcel, *L'idéal pédagogique en France au dix-huitième siècle* (Oxford: Voltaire Foundation, 1998).

Grange, Henri, *Les idées de Necker* (Paris: Klincksieck, 1974).

Grange, Henri, 'Necker et l'inégalité sociale', in J.-M. Servet (ed.), *Idées économiques sous la Révolution, 1789–1794* (Lyons: Presses universitaires de Lyon, 1989), 407–19.

Greenfeld, Liah, *Nationalism: Five Roads to Modernity* (Cambridge, Mass: Harvard University Press, 1992).

Gregori, Simona, 'Éthique du travail, anoblissement et mérite chez l'abbé de Saint-Pierre', in Carole Dornier and Claudine Poulouin (eds.), *Les projets de l'abbé Castel de Saint-Pierre, 1658–1743: Pour le plus grand bonheur du plus grand nombre* (Caen: Presses universitaires de Caen, 2011), 81–90.

Grell, Chantal, 'Les origines de Rome: Mythe et critique. Essai sur l'histoire aux XVIIe et XVIIIe siècles', *Histoire, économie et société*, 2 (1983), 255–80.

Grell, Chantal, *L'histoire entre érudition et philosophie: Étude sur la connaissance historique à l'âge des Lumières* (Paris: Presses universitaires de France, 1993).

Grell, Chantal, 'L'histoire de France et le mythe de la monarchie à la fin du XVIIe siècle', in Yves-Marie Bercé and Philippe Contamine (eds.), *Histoires de France, historiens de la France* (Paris: Honoré Champion, 1994), 165–88.

Grell, Chantal, 'Nicolas Fréret, la critique et l'histoire ancienne', in Grell and Volpilhac-Auger (eds.), *Nicolas Fréret*, 51–71.

Grell, Chantal, *Le dix-huitième siècle et l'antiquité en France: 1680–1789* (Oxford: Voltaire Foundation, 1995).

Grell, Chantal, 'Clovis: Du Grand siècle aux Lumières', *Bibliothèque de l'École des chartes*, 154 (1996), 173–218.

Grell, Chantal, 'Les philosophes et l'histoire en France au dix-huitième siècle', in Sonja Asal and Johannes Rohbeck (eds.), *Aufklärung und Aufklärungskritik in Frankreich: Selbstdeutungen des 18. Jahrhunderts im Spiegel der Zeitgenossen* (Berlin: Berliner Wissenschafts-Verlag, 2003), 145–66.

Grell, Chantal, 'L'éducation de l'enfant-roi', in Fleury, *L'Abrégé de l'histoire de France' écrit pour le jeune Louis XV*, 13–98.

Grell, Chantal, 'Les historiographes en France XVIe–XVIIIe siècles', in Grell (ed.), *Les historiographes en Europe de la fin du Moyen Âge à la Révolution* (Paris: Presses de l'Université Paris-Sorbonne, 2006), 127–56.

Grell, Chantal, 'Histoire et pouvoir dans la France du XVIIe siècle', in Chantal Grell and Benoît Pellistrandi (eds.), *Les cours d'Espagne et de France au XVIIe siècle* (Madrid: Casa de Velázquez, 2007).

Grell, Chantal and Catherine Volpilhac-Auger (eds.), *Nicolas Fréret: Légende et vérité* (Oxford: Voltaire Foundation, 1994).

Grell, Chantal and Christian Michel (eds.), *Primitivisme et mythe des origines dans la France des Lumières (1680–1820)* (Paris: Presses universitaires de la Sorbonne, 1989).

Griffin, Michael, 'Oliver Goldsmith and François-Ignace Espiard de la Borde: An Instance of Plagiarism', *The Review of English Studies*, 50 (1999), 59–63.

Groenewegen, Peter, 'From Prominent Physician to Major Economist: Some Reflections on Quesnay's Switch to Economics in the 1750s', in Groenewegen (ed.), *Physicians and Political Economy: Six Studies of the Work of Doctor Economists* (London: Routledge, 2001), 93–115.

Groenewegen, Peter, *Eighteenth-Century Economics: Turgot, Beccaria and Smith and their Contemporaries* (London: Routledge, 2002).

Grosperrin, Bernard, *La représentation de l'histoire de France dans l'historiographie des Lumières* (Lille: Atelier national de reproduction des thèses, 1982).

Groulx, Richard, *Michel Foucault, la politique comme guerre continuée: De la guerre des races au racisme d'État* (Paris: L'Harmattan, 2015).

Gruner, Shirley M., 'Political Historiography in Restoration France', *History and Theory*, 8 (1969), 346–65.

Gueniffey, Patrice, 'Terminer la Révolution: Barnave et la révision de la Constitution (Août 1791)', in François Furet and Mona Ozouf (eds.), *Terminer la Révolution: Mounier et Barnave dans la Révolution française* (Grenoble: Presses Universitaires de Grenoble, 1990), 147–70.

Gueniffey, Patrice, *Le nombre et la raison: La Révolution française et les élections* (Paris: EHESS, 1993).

Guerci, Luciano, 'Note sulla storiografia di Mably: Il problema dei Franchi nelle *Observations sur l'histoire de France*', in Istituto italiano per gli studi storici (ed.),

Saggi e ricerche sul Settecento (Naples: Istituto italiano per gli studi storici, 1963), 453–512.

Guerci, Luciano, *Libertà degli antichi e libertà dei moderni: Sparta, Atene e i philosophes nella Francia del Settecento* (Naples: Guida, 1979).

Guervin, M.-H., 'Deux amis: Nicolas Fréret (1688–1749), Henry de Boulainviller (1658–1722)', *XVIIe Siècle*, 7–8 (1950–1951), 197–204.

Guibernau, Montserrat and John Hutchinson (eds.), *History and National Destiny: Ethnosymbolism and its Critics* (Oxford: Blackwell, 2004).

Guilhaumou, Jacques, 'Nation, individu et société chez Sieyès', *Genèses*, 26 (1997), 4–24.

Guilhaumou, Jacques, *Sieyès et l'ordre de la langue: L'invention de la politique moderne* (Paris: Éditions Kimé, 2002).

Guilhaumou, Jacques, 'Sieyès et le point du peuple', in Hélène Desbrousses, Bernard Peloille, and Gérard Raulet (eds.), *Le peuple, figures et concepts: Entre identité et souveraineté* (Paris: de Guibert, 2003), 49–56.

Guilhaumou, Jacques, *Cognition et ordre social chez Sieyès: Penser les possibles* (Paris: Kimé, 2018).

Guillo, Dominique, 'Biology-inspired Sociology of the Nineteenth Century: A Science of Social "Organization"', *Revue française de sociologie*, 43 (2002), 123–55.

Guiomar, Jean-Yves, 'La Révolution française et les origines celtiques de la France', *Annales historiques de la Révolution française*, 64 (1992), 63–85.

Guion, Béatrice, 'Savoir comment écrire l'histoire de son temps: Les *Mémoires* de Saint-Simon et l'*ars historica* à l'âge classique', in Marc Hersant (ed.), *La guerre civile des langues:* Mémoires *de Saint-Simon, année 1710, 'Intrigue du mariage de M. le Duc de Berry'* (Paris: Garnier, 2011), 41–63.

Guiral, Pierre, 'Les écrivains et la notion de décadence de 1870 à 1914', *Romantisme*, 42 (1983), 9–22.

Gusdorf, Georges, *L'avènement des sciences humaines au siècle des lumières* (Paris: Payot, 1973).

Habermas, Jürgen, *Strukturwandel der Öffentlichkeit: Untersuchungen zu einer Kategorie der bürgerlichen Gesellschaft* (Berlin: Luchterhand, 1962).

Haddad, Élie, 'The Question of the Imprescriptibility of Nobility in Early Modern France', in Charles Lipp and Matthew Romaniello (eds.), *Contested Spaces of Nobility in Early Modern Europe* (London: Routledge, 2011), 147–66.

Haddad, Élie, 'De la terre au sang: L'héritage de la noblesse (XVIe–XVIIIe siècle)', in François Dubet (ed.), *Léguer, hériter* (Paris: la Découverte, 2016), 19–32.

Haines, Barbara, 'The Inter-Relations Between Social, Biological, and Medical Thought, 1750–1850: Saint-Simon and Comte', *The British Journal for the History of Science*, 11 (1978), 19–35.

Hanley, Sarah, 'Engendering the State: Family Formation and State Building in Early Modern France', *French Historical Studies*, 16 (1989), 4–27.

Hanrahan, James, *Voltaire and the Parlements of France* (Oxford: Voltaire Foundation, 2009).

Haran, Alexandre Y., *Le lys et le globe: Messianisme dynastique et rêve impérial en France à l'aube des temps modernes* (Seyssel: Champ Vallon, 2000).

Harpaz, Éphraïm, 'Mably et ses contemporains', *Revue des sciences humaines*, 82 (1955), 351–66.

Harpaz, Éphraïm, 'Le censeur: Histoire d'un journal libéral', *Revue des sciences humaines*, 92 (1958), 483–511.

Harpaz, Éphraïm, '"Le censeur européen": Histoire d'un journal industrialiste', *Revue d'histoire économique et sociale*, 37/3 (1959), 185–218 and 328–57.

Hartog, François, *Le XIXème siècle et l'histoire: Le cas Fustel de Coulanges* (Paris: Presses universitaires de France, 1988).

Hartog, François, 'Liberté des anciens, liberté des modernes: La Révolution française et l'antiquité', in Roger-Pol Droit (ed.), *Les Grecs, les Romains et nous: L'antiquité est-elle moderne?* (Paris: Le Monde, 1991), 119–38.

Hartog, François, 'Temps et histoire: "Comment écrire l'histoire de France?"', *Annales: Histoire, sciences sociales*, 50 (1995), 1219–36.

Hartog, François, *Évidence de l'histoire: Ce que voient les historiens* (Paris: Gallimard, 2005).

Hastings, Adrian, *The Construction of Nationhood: Ethnicity, Religion and Nationalism* (Cambridge: Cambridge University Press, 1999).

Hastings, Derek, *Nationalism in Modern Europe: Politics, Identity and Belonging since the French Revolution* (London: Bloomsbury Academic, 2017).

Hayman, John G., 'Notions on National Characters in the Eighteenth Century', *Huntington Library Quarterly*, 35 (1971), 1–17.

Hazard, Paul, *La crise de la conscience européenne (1680–1715)* (Paris: Boivin, 1935).

Hearn, Jonathan, 'Power, Culture, Identity, and the Work of Anthony Smith', *Nations and Nationalism*, 24 (2018), 286–91.

Herrero, Isabel and Lydia Vasquez, 'Types nationaux européens dans des œuvres de fiction françaises (1750–1789)', *Dix-huitième siècle*, 25 (1993), 115–27.

Hersant, Marc, '"Malheur au détail": Voltaire, l'historien pressé', *Écrire l'histoire: Histoire, littérature, esthétique*, 4 (2009), 15–24.

Hersant, Marc, *Saint-Simon* (Paris: Gallimard, 2016).

Hesse, Carla, 'French Women in Print, 1750–1800: An Essay in Historical Bibliography', in Haydn T. Mason (ed.), *The Darnton Debate: Books and Revolution in the Eighteenth Century* (Oxford: Voltaire Foundation, 1998), 65–82.

Hirschi, Caspar, *The Origins of Nationalism: An Alternative History from Ancient Rome to Early Modern Germany* (Cambridge: Cambridge University Press, 2012).

Hirschman, Albert O., *The Passions and the Interests: Political Arguments for Capitalism before its Triumph* (Princeton: Princeton University Press, 1977).

Hobsbawm, Eric, *Nations and Nationalism since 1780: Programme, Myth, Reality* (Cambridge: Cambridge University Press, 1990).

Hobsbawm, Eric and Terence Ranger, 'Introduction: Inventing Tradition', in Hobsbawm and Ranger (eds.), *The Invention of Tradition* (Cambridge: Cambridge University Press, 1983), 1–14.

Hodgen, Margaret T., *Early Anthropology in the Sixteenth and Seventeenth Centuries* (Philadelphia: University of Pennsylvania Press, 1964).

Hont, Istvan, *Jealousy of Trade: International Competition and the Nation State in Historical Perspective* (Cambridge, Mass: Harvard University Press, 2005).

Hont, Istvan, 'The Early Enlightenment Debate on Commerce and Luxury', in Mark Goldie and Robert Wokler (eds.), *The Cambridge History of Eighteenth-Century Political Thought* (Cambridge: Cambridge University Press, 2006), 379–418.

Hoquet, Thierry, 'Biologization of Race and Racialization of the Human: Bernier, Buffon, Linnaeus', in Nicolas Bancel, Thomas David, and Dominic Thomas (eds.), *The Invention of Race: Scientific and Popular Representations* (New York: Routledge, 2014), 17–32.

Hostiou, Jeanne-Marie and Alain Viala (eds.), *Le temps des querelles*, special issue of *Littératures classiques*, 81 (2013).

Hostiou, Jeanne-Marie and Alexis Tadié (eds.), *Querelles et création en Europe à l'époque moderne* (Paris: Garnier, 2019).

Hubert, Henri and Marcel Mauss, *Essai sur la nature et la fonction du sacrifice* (Paris: Presses universitaires de France, 2016).

Huchette, Jocelyn, 'La "gaieté française" ou la question du caractère national dans la définition du rire, de *L'Esprit des lois* à *De la littérature*', *Dix-huitième siècle*, 32 (2000), 97–109.

Huchette, Jocelyn, *La gaieté, caractère français?: Représenter la nation au siècle des Lumières (1715–1789)* (Paris: Classiques Garnier, 2015).

Hudson, Nicholas, 'From "Nation" to "Race": The Origin of Racial Classification in Eighteenth-Century Thought', *Eighteenth-Century Studies*, 29 (1996), 247–64.

Hulak, Florence, 'La guerre et la société: Le problème du "savoir historico-politique" chez Michel Foucault', *Philosophie*, 138 (2018), 61–75.

Hulliung, Mark, *Montesquieu and the Old Regime* (Berkeley: University of California Press, 1976).

Hundert, Edward M., *The Enlightenment's Fable: Bernard Mandeville and the Discovery of Society* (Cambridge: Cambridge University Press, 2005).

Hunt, Lynn, 'Discourses of *Patriarchalism* and anti-*Patriarchalism* in the French Revolution', in John Renwick (ed.), *Language and Rhetoric of the Revolution* (Edinburgh: Edinburgh University Press, 1990), 25–41.

Huppert, George, 'The Trojan Franks and Their Critics', *Studies in the Renaissance*, 12 (1965), 227–41.

Hutchinson, John, *Modern Nationalism* (London: Fontana Press, 1994).

Hyslop, Beatrice Fry, *French Nationalism in 1789, According to the General Cahiers* (New York: Octagon Books, 1968).

Iggers, Georg G., *The Cult of Authority: The Political Philosophy of the Saint-Simonians* (The Hague: Nijhoff, 1958).

Isambert, François-André, 'Époques critiques et époques organiques: Une contribution de Buchez à l'élaboration de la théorie sociale des saint-simoniens', *Cahiers internationaux de sociologie*, 27 (1959), 131–52.

Israel, Jonathan, *Radical Enlightenment: Philosophy and the Making of Modernity 1650–1750* (Oxford: Oxford University Press, 2001).

Israel, Jonathan, *A Revolution of the Mind* (Princeton: Princeton University Press, 2010).

Israel, Jonathan, *Democratic Enlightenment: Philosophy, Revolution, and Human Rights 1750–1790* (Oxford: Oxford University Press, 2011).

Israel, Jonathan, *Revolutionary Ideas: An Intellectual History of the French Revolution from the Rights of Man to Robespierre* (Princeton: Princeton University Press, 2014).

Israel, Jonathan, *The Enlightenment that Failed: Ideas, Revolution, and Democratic Defeat, 1748–1830* (Oxford: Oxford University Press, 2019).

Italiano, Federico, *Translation and Geography* (London: Routledge, 2016).

Jablonka, Ivan, *L'histoire est une littérature contemporaine* (Paris: Seuil, 2014).

Jacob, Annie, 'Pas de citoyen qui ne soit un travailleur', *La revue du M.A.U.S.S.*, 2 (2001), 196–201.

Jacob, Annie, *Le travail, reflet des cultures: Du sauvage indolent au travailleur productif* (Paris: Presses universitaires de France, 1994).

Jacouty, Jean-François, 'Une contribution à la pensée aristocratique des Lumières: La *Théorie des lois politiques de la monarchie française* de Pauline de Lézardière', *Revue française d'histoire des idées politiques*, 17 (2003), 3–47.

James, Michael, 'Pierre-Louis Roederer, Jean-Baptiste Say, and the Concept of *Industrie*', *History of Political Economy*, 9 (1977), 455–75.

Jaume, Lucien, *Hobbes et l'État représentatif moderne* (Paris: Presses universitaires de France, 1986).

Jaume, Lucien, *Le religieux et le politique dans la Révolution française: L'idée de régénération* (Paris: Presses universitaires de France, 2015).

Jean-Denis Bredin, 'Emmanuel Sieyès et Jacques Necker', *Annales Benjamin Constant*, 23–24 (2000), 63–88.

Jennings, Jeremy, 'Constant's Idea of Modern Liberty', in Helena Rosenblatt (ed.), *The Cambridge Companion to Constant* (Cambridge: Cambridge University Press, 2009), 69–91.

Jennings, Jeremy, *Revolution and the Republic: A History of Political Thought in France since the Eighteenth Century* (Oxford: Oxford University Press, 2011).

Johnson, Neal, 'L'idéologie politique du Marquis d'Argenson, d'après ses œuvres inédites', in Roland Mortier and Hervé Hasquin (eds.), *Études sur le XVIIIe siècle – Volume 11: Idéologies de la noblesse* (Brussels: Éditions de l'Université libre de Bruxelles, 1984), 21–8.

Jones, Colin, *The Great Nation: France from Louis XV to Napoleon* (London: Penguin, 2002).

Jouanna, Arlette, *L'idée de race en France au XVIe siècle et au début du XVIIe: 1498–1614* (Montpellier: Imprimerie de Recherche – Université Paul Valéry, 1981).

Joubert, Léo, 'Fréret', in Ferdinand Hoefer (ed.), *Nouvelle biographie générale, depuis les temps les plus reculés jusqu'à nos jours* (Paris: Firmin Didot, 1852–1866), xviii. 807–18.

Jouhaud, Christian, *Les pouvoirs de la littérature: Histoire d'un paradoxe* (Paris: Gallimard, 2000).

Jourdan, Annie, 'The Image of Gaul during the French Revolution: Between Charlemagne and Ossian', in Terence Brown (ed.), *Celticism* (Amsterdam: Rodopi, 1996), 183–206.

Joutard, Philippe, 'Une passion française: L'histoire', in André Burguière and Jacques Revel (eds.), *Histoire de la France: Choix culturels et mémoire* (Paris: Seuil, 2000).

Jullian, Camille, 'Introduction', in Charles-Louis Secondat de Montesquieu, *Considérations sur les causes de la grandeur des Romains et de leur décadence* (Paris: Hachette, 1896), v–xxxviii.

Jullian, Camille, 'Augustin Thierry et le mouvement historique sous la Restauration', *Revue de synthèse historique*, 13 (1906), 125–42.

Kaiser, Thomas E., 'Politics and Political Economy in the Thought of the Ideologues', *History of Political Economy*, 12 (1980), 141–60.

Kaiser, Thomas E., 'The abbé de Saint-Pierre, Public Opinion, and the Reconstitution of the French Monarchy', *The Journal of Modern History*, 55 (1983), 618–43.

Kaiser, Thomas E., 'The abbé Dubos and the Historical Defence of Monarchy in Early Eighteenth-Century France', *Studies on Voltaire and the Eighteenth Century*, 267 (1989), 77–102.

Kaiser, Thomas E., 'Rhetoric in the Service of the King: The abbé Dubos and the Concept of Public Judgment', *Eighteenth-Century Studies*, 23 (1989–1990), 182–99.

Kantorowicz, Ernst H., *The King's Two Bodies: A study in Medieval Political Theology* (Princeton: Princeton University Press, 1997).

Kaplan, Steven, *Raisonner sur les blés: Essais sur les Lumières économiques* (Paris: Fayard, 2017).

Kaplan, Steven and Sophus Reinert (eds.), *The Economic Turn: Recasting Political Economy in Enlightenment Europe* (London: Anthem Press, 2019).

Kappler, Émile, *Bibliographie critique de l'œuvre imprimée de Pierre Jurieu, 1637–1713* (Paris: Honoré Champion, 2002).

Keither, Chimène I., *The Paradoxes of Nationalism: The French Revolution and its Meaning for Contemporary Nation Building* (Albany: State University of New York Press, 2007).

Kelley, Donald R., *Foundations of Modern Historical Scholarship: Language, Law, and History in the French Renaissance* (New York: Columbia University Press, 1970).

Kelley, Donald R., *François Hotman: A Revolutionary's Ordeal* (Princeton: Princeton University Press, 1973).

Keohane, Nannerl O., 'Democratic Monarchy: The Political Theory of the Marquis d'Argenson' (unpublished Ph.D. thesis – New Haven: Yale University, 1968).

Kidd, Colin, *Subverting Scotland's Past: Scottish Whig Historians and the Creation of an Anglo-British Identity, 1689–c. 1830* (Cambridge: Cambridge University Press, 1993).

Kidd, Colin, *The Forging of Races: Race and Scripture in the Protestant Atlantic World, 1600–2000* (Cambridge: Cambridge University Press, 2006).

Kinneging, Andreas A. M., *Aristocracy, Antiquity, and History: Classicism in Political Thought* (New Brunswick: Transaction, 1997).

Kirschleger, Pierre-Yves, *La religion de Guizot* (Geneva: Labor et fides, 1999).

Kisaki, Kiyoji, 'Controversy on the *Noblesse commerçante* between abbé Coyer and Chevalier d'Arcq', *The University of Kyoto Economic Review*, 49 (1979), 48–79.

Knibiehler, Yvonne, 'Une révolution "nécessaire": Thiers, Mignet et l'école fataliste', *Romantisme*, 10 (1980), 279–88.

Knibiehler, Yvonne, *Naissance des sciences humaines: Mignet et l'histoire philosophique au XIXe siècle* (Paris: Flammarion, 1973).

Koller, Armin Hajman, *The Abbé du Bos: His Advocacy of the Theory of Climate. A Precursor of Johann Gottfried Herder* (Champaign, Ill: Garrard Press, 1937).

Körner, Axel, 'The Risorgimento's Literary Canon and the Aesthetics of Reception: Some Methodological Considerations', *Nations and Nationalism*, 15 (2009), 410–18.

Koselleck, Reinhart, *Kritik und Krise: Eine Studie zur Pathogenese der bürgerlichen Welt* (Freiburg: Alber, 1959).

Kra, Pauline, 'Rousseau et la politique du caractère national', in Thiéry (ed.), *Jean-Jacques Rousseau, politique et nation*, 813–22.

Kra, Pauline, 'The Concept of National Character in Eighteenth-Century France', *Cromohs*, 7 (2002), 1–6.

Kremer, Nathalie, *Vraisemblance et représentation au XVIIIe siècle* (Paris: Honoré Champion, 2011).

Kulessa, Rotraud von (ed.), *Démocratisation et diversification: Les littératures d'éducation au siècle des Lumières* (Paris: Garnier, 2015).

Labatut, Jean Pierre, 'Patriotisme et noblesse sous le règne de Louis XIV', *Revue d'histoire moderne et contemporaine*, 29 (1982), 622–34.

Laffitte, Pierre, 'Matériaux pour servir à la biographie d'Auguste Comte: Considérations sur la période de sa vie qui s'étend de 1816 à 1822', *Revue occidentale*, 9 (1882, second semester), 40–7.

Landucci, Sergio, *I filosofi e i selvaggi: 1580–1780* (Turin: Einaudi, 2014).

Larizza Lolli, Mirella, 'Introduzione', in Lolli (ed.), *Scienza, industria e società: Saint-Simon e i suoi primi seguaci* (Milan: Saggiatore, 1980), 7–119.

Larrère, Catherine, 'Galiani, lecteur de Montesquieu', in Jean-Louis Jam (ed.), *Éclectisme et cohérences des Lumières* (Paris: Nizet, 1992), 97–109.

Larrère, Catherine, *L'invention de l'économie au XVIIIe siècle: Du droit naturel à la physiocratie* (Paris: Presses universitaires de France, 1992).

Larrère, Catherine, 'Malebranche revisité: L'économie naturelle des physiocrates', *Dix-huitième siècle*, 26 (1994), 117–38.

Larrère, Catherine, 'Montesquieu et les sauvages', *Les colloques ethnologiques de Bordeaux*, 1 (1994), 59–68.

Larrère, Catherine, 'Histoire et nature chez Turgot', in Binoche and Tinland (eds.), *Sens du devenir et pensée de l'histoire au temps des Lumières*, 178–208.

Larrère, Catherine, 'Montesquieu: L'éclipse de la souveraineté', in Gian Mario Cazzaniga and Yves Charles Zarka (eds.), *Penser la souveraineté à l'époque moderne et contemporaine* (Paris: Vrin, 2002), i. 199–214.

Larrère, Catherine, 'Droit et mœurs chez Montesquieu', in Céline Spector and Thierry Hoquet (eds.), *Lectures de l'*Esprit des lois (Pessac: Presses universitaires de Bordeaux, 2004), 233–46.

Larrère, Catherine, 'Le législateur chez Montesquieu', *Il pensiero politico*, 40 (2007), 301–12.

Larrère, Catherine, 'Sieyès, lecteur des physiocrates: Droit naturel ou économie?', in Quiviger, Denis, and Salem (eds.), *Figures de Sieyès*, 195–211.

Larrère, Catherine, 'Montesquieu et l'espace', in Thierry Paquot and Chris Younès (eds.), *Espace et lieu dans la pensée occidentale: De Platon à Nietzsche* (Paris: la Découverte, 2012), 147–69.

Latouche, Serge, *L'invention de l'économie* (Paris: Albin Michel, 2005).

Lavabre, Marie-Claire, 'Usages du passé, usages de la mémoire', *Revue française de science politique*, 44 (1994), 480–93.

Lawrence, Paul, *Nationalism: History and Theory* (Harlow: Pearson, 2005).

Le Roux, Nicolas, 'Introduction: Aux âmes bien nées ... Les obligations du sang', in Nicolas Le Roux and Martin Wrede (eds.), *Noblesse oblige: Identités et engagements aristocratiques à l'époque moderne* (Rennes: Presses universitaires de Rennes, 2017), 7–23.

Le Roy Ladurie, Emmanuel, *Saint-Simon, ou Le système de la Cour* (Paris: Fayard, 1997).

Leerssen, Joep, 'L'effet de typique', in Alain Montandon (ed.), *Mœurs et images: Études d'imagologie européenne* (Clermont-Ferrand: Université Blaise Pascal, 1997), 129–34.

Leerssen, Joep, 'The Rhetoric of National Character: A Programmatic Survey', *Poetics Today*, 21 (2000), 267–92.

Leerssen, Joep, *National Thought in Europe: A Cultural History* (Amsterdam: Amsterdam University Press, 2006).

Leerssen, Joep, 'Nation and Ethnicity', in Berger and Lorenz (eds.), *The Contested Nation*, 75–103.

Leerssen, Joep, 'Setting the Scene for National History', in Stefan Berger and Chris Lorenz (eds.), *Nationalizing the Past: Historians as Nation Builders in Modern Europe* (Basingstoke: Palgrave Macmillan, 2010), 71–85.

Leerssen, Joep (ed.), *Encyclopaedia of Romantic Nationalism in Europe* (Amsterdam: Amsterdam University Press, 2018).

Leffler, Phyllis K., 'French Historians and the Challenge to Louis XIV's Absolutism', *French Historical Studies*, 14 (1985), 1–22.

Leffler, Phyllis K., 'The "Histoire raisonnée", 1660–1720: A Pre-Enlightenment Genre', *Journal of the History of Ideas*, 37 (1976), 219–40.

Lehuërou, Julien Marie, *Histoire des institutions mérovingiennes et du gouvernement des Mérovingiens* (Paris: Joubert, 1842).

Lemaire, André, *Les lois fondamentales de la monarchie française d'après les théoriciens de l'Ancien régime* (Geneva: Slatkine, 1975).

Lemaître, Alain J. (ed.), *Le monde parlementaire au XVIIIᵉ siècle: L'invention d'un discours politique* (Rennes: Presses universitaires de Rennes, 2010).

Lembcke, Oliver W. and Florian Weber, 'Introduction to Sieyès's Political Theory', in Emmanuel-Joseph Sieyès, *The Essential Political Writings* (Leiden: Brill, 2014), 1–42.

Lenarda, Antonio, 'La concezione del dispotismo cinese in Montesquieu', *Annali dell'Istituto di filosofia dell'Università di Firenze*, 1 (1979), 261–90.

Leonhard, Jörn, *Liberalismus: Zur historischen Semantik eines europäischen Deutungsmusters* (Munich: Oldenbourg, 2001).

Leroux, Robert, *Aux fondements de l'industrialisme: Comte, Dunoyer et la pensée libérale en France* (Paris: Hermann, 2015).

Lester, Paul, 'L'anthropologie et la paléontologie humaine', in Maurice Daumas (ed.), *Histoire de la science* (Paris: Gallimard, 1957), 1337–406.

Levine, Joseph M., *The Battle of the Books: History and Literature in the Augustan Age* (Ithaca: Cornell University Press, 1991).

Lévi-Strauss, Claude, *La pensée sauvage* (Paris: Plon, 1962).

Lézardière, Eutrope-Charles-Athanase-Benjamin Robert de, 'Avertissement', in Lézardière, *Théorie des lois politiques de la monarchie française*, i. pp. v–x.

Liggio, Leonard P., 'Charles Dunoyer and French Classical Liberalism', *Journal of Libertarian Studies*, 1 (1977), 153–78.

Lilti, Antoine, 'Querelles et controverses: Les formes du désaccord intellectuel à l'époque moderne', *Mil neuf cent: Revue d'histoire intellectuelle*, 25 (2007), 13–28.

Lilti, Antoine, *Figures publiques: L'invention de la célébrité, 1750–1850* (Paris: Fayard, 2014).

Lilti, Antoine, *L'héritage des Lumières: Ambivalences de la modernité* (Paris: EHESS, 2019).

Linton, Marisa, *The Politics of Virtue in Enlightenment France* (Basingstoke: Palgrave, 2001).

Lockwood, Richard, 'Subject and Ceremony: Racine's Royalist Rhetoric', *MLN*, 100 (1985), 789–802.

Lombard, Alfred, *L'abbé Du Bos: Un initiateur de la pensée moderne* (Paris: Hachette, 1913).

Losfeld, Christophe, *Politesse, morale et construction sociale: Pour une histoire des traités de comportements (1670–1788)* (Paris: Honoré Champion, 2011).

Losurdo, Domenico, *Controstoria del liberalismo* (Rome: Laterza, 2005).

Lukács, György, *Die Zerstörung der Vernunft: Der Weg des Irrationalismus von Schelling zu Hitler* (Berlin: Aufbau, 1955).

Lukes, Steven M., 'Saint-Simon', in Timothy Raison (ed.), *The Founding Fathers of Social Science* (Harmondsworth: Penguin, 1969), 27–34.

Mackrell, John Q. C., *The Attack upon Feudalism in Eighteenth-Century France* (London: Routledge and Kegan Paul, 1973).

Magendie, Maurice, 'Introduction', in Faret, *L'honneste homme, ou L'art de plaire à la court*, i–lii.

Maigron, Louis, *Le roman historique à l'époque romantique: Essai sur l'influence de Walter Scott* (Geneva: Slatkine, 1970).

Maire, Catherine, *De la cause de Dieu à la cause de la nation: Le jansénisme au XVIIIème siècle* (Paris: Gallimard, 1998).

Maire, Catherine, 'Louis-Adrien Le Paige entre Saint-Simon et Montesquieu', *Cahiers Saint-Simon*, 27 (1999), 37–47.

Malik, Kenan, *The Meaning of Race: Race, History and Culture in Western Society* (Basingstoke: Macmillan, 1996).

Manent, Pierre, *La cité de l'homme* (Paris: Fayard, 1994).

Mansfield, Andrew, 'Fénelon's Cuckoo: Andrew Michael Ramsay and Archbishop Fénelon', in Doohwan Ahn, Christoph Schmitt-Maaß, and Stefanie Stockhorst (eds.), *Fénelon in the Enlightenment: Traditions, Adaptations, and Variations* (Amsterdam: Rodopi 2014), 73–93.

Mansfield, Andrew, *Ideas of Monarchical Reform: Fénelon, Jacobitism, and the Political Works of the Chevalier Ramsay* (Manchester: Manchester University Press, 2015).

Mansfield, Andrew, 'The Burgundy Circle's Plans to Undermine Louis XIV's "Absolute" State through Polysynody and the High Nobility', *Intellectual History Review*, 27 (2016), 223–45.

Manuel, Frank E., 'From Equality to Organicism', *Journal of the History of Ideas*, 17 (1956), 54–69.

Manuel, Frank E., *The Prophets of Paris* (Cambridge, Mass: Harvard University Press, 1962).

Marande, Max de, 'Un Don Juan du Grand siècle et de la Régence: Le Marquis de Lassay', *Revue de France*, July–August 1936, 468–93.

Marchal, Roger, *Madame de Lambert et son milieu* (Oxford: Voltaire Foundation, 1991).

Margerison, Kenneth, *P.-L. Roederer: Political Thought and Practice during the French Revolution* (Philadelphia: American philosophical society, 1983).

Margerison, Kenneth, 'History, Representative Institutions, and Political Rights in the French Pre-revolution (1787–1789)', *French Historical Studies*, 15 (1987), 68–98.

Margerison, Kenneth, *Pamphlets and Public Opinion: The Campaign for a Union of Orders in the Early French Revolution* (West Lafayette: Purdue University Press, 1998).

Marin, Louis, 'De l' *Utopia* de More à la Scandza de Cassiodore-Jordanès', *Annales: Économies, sociétés, civilisations*, 26 (1971), 306–27.

Marin, Louis, *Le récit est un piège* (Paris: Éditions de Minuit, 1973).

Marin, Louis, *Le portrait du Roi* (Paris: Éditions de Minuit, 1981).

Markovits, Francine, *L'ordre des échanges: Philosophie de l'économie et économie du discours au XVIIIe siècle en France* (Paris: Presses universitaires de France, 1986).

Marks, John, 'Foucault, Franks, Gauls. *Il faut défendre la société*: The 1976 Lectures at the Collège de France', *Theory, Culture and Society*, 17 (2000), 127–47.

Marraud, Mathieu, 'Dérogeance et commerce: Violence des constructions socio-politiques sous l'Ancien régime', *Genèses*, 95 (2014), 2–26.

Martin, Christophe (ed.), *Fictions de l'origine (1650–1800)* (Paris: Desjonquères, 2012).

Martin, Xavier, 'L'image du Gaulois (et celle de la femme) dans le miroir du français révolutionnaire', *Revue d'histoire du droit*, 77 (1999), 463–89.

Martino, Vittorio, *Saint-Simon tra scienza e utopia* (Bari: Dedalo, 1978).

Marx, Karl, *Theorien über den Mehrwert: 1. Die Anfänge der Theorie vom Mehrwert bis Adam Smith* (Stuttgart: Dietz Nachf, 1905).

Marx, Karl and Friedrich Engels, *Gesamtausgabe: Dritte Abteilung, Band 2 – Der Briefwechsel zwischen Marx und Engels, 1854–1860* (Berlin: Marx-Engels-Verlag G.M.B.H., 1930).

Mas, Raymond, 'Recherches sur les Gaulois et sentiment national en France au XVIIIe siècle', in Chantal Grell and Jean-Michel Dufays (eds.), *Pratiques et concepts de l'histoire en Europe: XVIe–XVIIIe siècles* (Paris: Presses de l'Université de Paris-Sorbonne, 1990), 161–221.

Mas, Raymond, 'Dom Jacques Martin, historien des Gaulois (1684–1751)', in Viallaneix and Erhard (eds.), *Nos ancêtres les Gaulois*, 41–50.

Mason, Sheila and Catherine Volpilach-Auger, 'Introduction: Réflexions sur le caractère de quelques princes et sur quelques événements de leur vie', in Montesquieu, *Œuvres* (ed. Société Montesquieu), ix. 45–9.

Matytsin, Anton M., *The Specter of Skepticism in the Age of Enlightenment* (Baltimore: Johns Hopkins University Press, 2016).

Maury, Alfred, *L'ancienne Académie des inscriptions et belles-lettres* (Paris: Didier et Cie, 1864).

Mauzi, Robert, *L'idée du bonheur dans la littérature et la pensée françaises au XVIIIe siècle* (Geneva: Slatkine, 1979).

Maza, Sarah, 'Stories in History: Cultural Narratives in Recent Works in European History', *The American Historical Review*, 101 (1996), 1493–515.

Maza, Sarah, 'Luxury, Morality, and Social Change: Why There Was No Middle-Class Consciousness in Prerevolutionary France', *The Journal of Modern History*, 69 (1997), 199–229.

Maza, Sarah, *The Myth of the French Bourgeoisie* (Cambridge, Mass: Harvard University Press, 2003).

Maza, Sarah, 'Bourgeoisie', in William Doyle (ed.), *The Oxford Handbook of the Ancien Régime* (Oxford: Oxford University Press, 2011), 127–40.

Mazzolini, Renato Giuseppe, 'Dallo "spirito nerveo" allo "spirito delle leggi": Un commento alle osservazioni di Montesquieu su una lingua di pecora', in Giles Barber and C. P. Courtney (eds.), *Enlightenment Essays in Memory of Robert Shackleton* (Oxford: Voltaire Foundation, 1988), 205–21.

McKenna, Antony, '*Les Soupirs de la France esclave, qui aspire après la liberté*: La question de l'attribution', in Pierre Bonnet (ed.), *Littérature de contestation: Pamphlets et polémiques du règne de Louis XIV aux Lumières* (Paris: Éditions le Manuscrit, 2011), 229–68.

McKenna, Antony, *Études sur Pierre Bayle* (Paris: Honoré Champion, 2015).

Meek, Roland L., 'Introduction', in Anne-Robert-Jacques Turgot, *On Progress, Sociology and Economics* (Cambridge: Cambridge University Press, 1973), 1–33.

Meinecke, Friedrich, 'Montesquieu, Boulainvilliers, Dubos', *Historische Zeitschrift*, 145 (1932), 53–69.

Meinecke, Friedrich, *Die Entstehung des Historismus* (Munich: Oldenbourg, 1965).

Mellon, Stanley, *The Political Uses of History: A Study of Historians in the French Restoration* (Stanford: Stanford University Press, 1958).

Menant, Sylvain, 'La genèse des Mémoires de Saint-Simon et l'historiographie des Lumières', in Marc Hersant et al. (eds.), *Histoire, histoires: Nouvelles approches de Saint-Simon et des récits des XVIIe–XVIIIe siècles* (Arras: Artois presses université, 2011), 19–26.

Mercer, Ben, 'The Moral Rearmament of France: Pierre Nora, Memory, and the Crises of Republicanism', *French Politics, Culture and Society*, 31 (Summer 2013), 102–16.

Mercier, Roger, 'La théorie des climats des "Réflexions critiques" à "L'Esprit des Lois"', *Revue d'histoire littéraire de la France*, 53 (1953), 17–37 and 159–75.

Mergey, Anthony, *L'État des physiocrates: Autorité et décentralisation* (Aix-en-Provence: Presses universitaires d'Aix-Marseille, 2010).

Méricam-Bourdet, Myrtille, *Voltaire et l'écriture de l'histoire: Un enjeu politique* (Oxford: Voltaire Foundation, 2012).

Merle, Alexandra and Alicia Oïffer-Bomsel (eds.), *Tacite et le tacitisme en Europe à l'époque moderne* (Paris: Honoré Champion, 2017).

Merrick, Jeffrey, *The Desacralization of the French Monarchy in the Eighteenth Century* (Baton Rouge: Louisiana State University Press, 1990).

Merrick, Jeffrey, 'Fathers and Kings: Patriarchalism and Absolutism in Eighteenth-Century French Politics', *Studies on Voltaire and the Eighteenth Century*, 308 (1993), 281–330.

Meyssonnier, Simone, *La balance et l'horloge: La genèse de la pensée libérale en France au XVIIIe siècle* (Montreuil: Éditions de la passion, 1989).

Michaud, Joseph and Louis-Gabriel Michaud (eds.), *Biographie universelle ancienne et moderne* (Paris: Michaud Frères, 1811–1828).

Michel, Pierre, *Les barbares, 1789–1848: Un mythe romantique* (Lyons: Presses Universitaires de Lyon, 1981).

Mills, Charles W., *The Racial Contract* (Ithaca: Cornell University Press, 1997).

Minuti, Rolando, *Oriente barbarico e storiografia settecentesca: Rappresentazioni della storia dei Tartari nella cultura francese del XVIII secolo* (Venice: Marsilio, 1994).

Minuti, Rolando 'L'abate Coyer e "le vieux mot de patrie": A proposito del tema della patria nella cultura francese settecentesca', *Giornale di storia costituzionale*, 8 (2004), 229–38.

Minuti, Rolando, 'La geografia del dispotismo nelle *Lettres persanes* di Montesquieu', in Lea Campos Boralevi and Sara Lagi (eds.), *Viaggio e politica* (Florence: Firenze University Press, 2009), 135–47.

Minuti, Rolando, *Studies on Montesquieu – Mapping Political Diversity* (Cham: Springer, 2018).

Moeglin, Jean-Marie, *Les bourgeois de Calais: Essai sur un mythe historique* (Paris: Albin Michel, 2002).

Molino, Jean, 'Qu'est-ce que le roman historique?', *Revue d'histoire littéraire de la France*, 75 (1975), 195–234.

Momigliano, Arnaldo, 'Ancient History and the Antiquarian', *Journal of the Warburg and Courtauld Institutes*, 13 (1950), 285–315.

Momigliano, Arnaldo, 'Gibbon's Contribution to Historical Method', *Historia: Zeitschrift für Alte Geschichte*, 4 (1954), 450–63.

Momigliano, Arnaldo, *Sesto contributo alla storia degli studi classici e del mondo antico* (Rome: Edizioni di Storia e Letteratura, 1980).

Monnier, Raymonde, *Républicanisme, patriotisme et Révolution française* (Paris: L'Harmattan, 2005).

Monod, Gabriel, 'Du progrès des études historiques en France depuis le XVIe siècle', *Revue historique*, 1 (1876), 5–38.

Monod, Jean-Claude, 'Structure, spatialisation et archéologie, ou: "L'époque de l'histoire" peut-elle finir?', in Jocelyn Benoist and Fabio Merlini (eds.), *Historicité et spatialité* (Paris: Vrin, 2001), 55–76.

Montandon, Alain (ed.), *L'Europe des politesses et le caractère des nations: Regards croisés* (Paris: Anthropos, 1997).

Montoya, Alicia C., *Medievalist Enlightenment: From Charles Perrault to Jean-Jacques Rousseau* (Cambridge: D.S. Brewer, 2013).

Montoya, Alicia C., 'Montesquieu's Aristocratic Medievalism', in Bianchi and Minuti (eds.), *Montesquieu et les philosophies de l'histoire au XVIIIe siècle*, 31–45.

Moravia, Sergio, *Il pensiero degli idéologues: Scienza e filosofia in Francia (1780–1815)* (Florence: La Nuova Italia, 1974).

Moravia, Sergio, *La scienza dell'uomo nel Settecento* (Bari: Laterza, 2000).

Moreau, Isabelle, 'L'araignée dans sa toile: Mise en images de l'âme du monde de François Bernier et Pierre Bayle à l'*Encyclopédie*', in Moreau (ed.), *Les Lumières en mouvement: La circulation des idées au XVIIIe siècle* (Lyons: ENS éditions, 2009), 199–228.

Morilhat, Claude, *La prise de conscience du capitalisme: Economie et philosophie chez Turgot* (Paris: Klincksieck, 1988).

Moro, Roberto, *Il tempo dei signori: Mentalità, ideologia, dottrine della nobiltà francese di antico regime* (Rome: Savelli, 1981).

Mortier, Roland, *Diderot en Allemagne (1750–1850)* (Geneva: Slatkine, 1986).

Mosse, George L., *Toward the Final Solution: A History of European Racism* (New York: Howard Fertig, 1997).

Motley, Mark, *Becoming a French Aristocrat: The Education of the Court Nobility, 1580–1715* (Princeton: Princeton University Press, 1990).

Motsch, Andreas, *Lafitau et l'émergence du discours ethnographique* (Paris: Presses de l'Université de Paris-Sorbonne, 2001).

Moussa, Sarga (ed.), *L'idée de race dans les sciences humaines et la littérature (XVIIIe–XIXe siècles)* (Paris: L'Harmattan, 2003).

Muceni, Elena, 'Mandeville and France: The Reception of the Fable of the Bees in France and its Influence on the French Enlightenment', *French Studies*, 69 (2015), 449–61.

Mullet, Isabelle, 'Fontenelle et l'histoire: Du fixisme des passions aux progrès de l'esprit humain', *Dix-huitième siècle*, 44 (2012), 335–47.

Munslow, Alun, *Narrative and History* (Basingstoke: Palgrave, 2007).

Musso, Pierre, *Saint-Simon et le saint-simonisme* (Paris: Presses universitaires de France, 1999).

Musso, Pierre (ed.), *Actualité du saint-simonisme* (Paris: Presses universitaires de France, 2004).

Musso, Pierre, *Saint-Simon, l'industrialisme contre l'État* (La Tour-d'Aigues: Éditions de l'Aube, 2010).

Nairn, Tom, *The Break-up of Britain: Crisis and Neo-nationalism* (London: Verso, 1981).

Nassiet, Michel, 'Idée d'une excellente noblesse', in Vauban, *Les oisivetés de monsieur de Vauban*, 237–40.

Nassiet, Michel, 'L'honneur au XVIe siècle: Un capital collectif', in Drévillon and Venturino (eds.), *Penser et vivre l'honneur à l'époque moderne*, 71–90.

Nassiet, Michel, *La violence, une histoire sociale* (Paris: Champ Vallon, 2011).

Naves, Raymond, 'Un adversaire de la théorie des climats au XVIIe siècle: Adrien Baillet', *Revue d'histoire littéraire de la France*, 43 (1936), 430–3.

Neal, Andrew W., 'Cutting Off the King's Head: Foucault's *Society Must Be Defended* and the Problem of Sovereignty', *Alternatives: Global, Local, Political*, 29 (2004), 373–98.

Neefs, Jacques, 'Augustin Thierry: Le moment de la "véritable" histoire de France', *Romantisme*, 28–9 (1980), 289–303.

Nelson, William Max, 'Making Men: Enlightenment Ideas of Racial Engineering', *The American Historical Review*, 115 (2010), 1364–94.

Nicolet, Claude, *La fabrique d'une nation: La France entre Rome et les Germains* (Paris: Perrin, 2003).

Nisbet, Robert, *History of the Idea of Progress* (New York: Basic Books, 1980).

Nora, Pierre (ed.), *Les lieux de mémoire* (Paris: Gallimard, 1997).

Nora, Pierre, 'Entre mémoire et histoire: La problématique des lieux', in Nora (ed.), *Les lieux de mémoire*, i. 23–43.

Nora, Pierre, 'L'"Histoire de France" de Lavisse', in Nora (ed.), *Les lieux de mémoire*, i. 851–90.

Nora, Pierre, *Présent, nation, mémoire* (Paris: Gallimard, 2011).

Nori, Giuseppe, 'The Problematics of Sympathy and Romantic Historicism', *Studies in Romanticism*, 34 (1995), 3–28.

Novick, Peter, *That Noble Dream: The 'Objectivity Question' and the American Historical Profession* (Cambridge: Cambridge University Press, 1988).

O'Leary, Brendan, 'On the nature of Nationalism: An Appraisal of Ernest Gellner's Writings on Nationalism', *British Journal of Political Science*, 27 (1997), 191–222.

O'Neal, John C., 'Pour une mappemonde de l'âme: Les effets du climat sur la culture d'une nation dans *L'Esprit des lois* de Montesquieu', in Jean Dagen et al. (eds.), *Morales et politique* (Paris: Honoré Champion, 2005), 247–69.

Oexle, Otto Gerhard, Werner Conze, and Rudolf Walther, 'Stand, Klasse', in Brunner, Conze, and Koselleck (eds.), *Geschichtliche Grundbegriffe*, vi. 155–284.

Ongle, Arthur, *The Marquis d'Argenson: A Study in Criticism* (Oxford: Fisher Unwin, 1893).

Orain, Arnaud, 'Condillac face à la physiocratie: Terre, valeur et répartition', *Revue économique*, 53 (2002), 1075–99.

Osterhammel, Jürgen, *Die Entzauberung Asiens: Europa und die asiatischen Reiche im 18. Jahrhundert* (Munich: C.H. Beck, 1998).

Outram, Dorinda, *The Enlightenment* (Cambridge: Cambridge University Press, 2005).

Özkirimli, Umut, *Theories of Nationalism: A Critical Introduction* (Basingstoke: Palgrave Macmillan, 2017).

Ozouf, Mona, 'L'invention de l'ethnographie française: Le questionnaire de l'Académie celtique', *Annales: Histoire, sciences sociales*, 36 (1981), 210–30.

Ozouf, Mona *L'école de la France: Essais sur la Révolution, l'utopie et l'enseignement* (Paris: Gallimard, 1984).

Ozouf, Mona, '"Public Opinion" at the End of the Old Regime', *The Journal of Modern History – Supplement: Rethinking French Politics in 1788*, 60 (1988), S1–S21.

Ozouf, Mona, 'La Révolution française et la formation de l'homme nouveau', in Ozouf, *L'homme régénéré: Essais sur la Révolution française* (Paris: Gallimard, 1989).

Pagden, Anthony, *The Enlightenment and Why it Still Matters* (Oxford: Oxford University Press, 2013).

Pageaux, Daniel-Henri, 'De l'imagerie culturelle à l'imaginaire', in Pierre Brunel and Yves Chevrel (eds.), *Précis de littérature comparée* (Paris: Presses universitaires de France, 1989), 133–61.

Palonen, Kari, *Quentin Skinner: History, Politics, Rhetoric* (Cambridge: Polity Press, 2003).

Parkin, Robert, *Louis Dumont and Hierarchical Opposition* (New York: Berghahn, 2003).

Parsis-Barubé, Odile, 'La notion de couleur locale dans l'œuvre d'Augustin Thierry', in Potin and Déruelle (eds.), *Augustin Thierry*, 63–77.

Pasquino, Pasquale, *Sieyès et l'invention de la constitution en France* (Paris: O. Jacob, 1998).

Peabody, Sue, *'There Are No Slaves in France': The Political Culture of Race and Slavery in the Ancien Régime* (Oxford: Oxford University Press, 1996).

Peabody, Sue and Tyler Stovall (eds.), *The Color of Liberty: Histories of Race in France* (Durham, NC: Duke University Press, 2003).

Peabody, Sue and Tyler Stovall, 'Introduction: Race, France, Histories', in Peabody and Stovall (eds.), *The Color of Liberty*, 1–7.

Penke, Olga, 'L'abbé Millot et l'historiographie des Lumières françaises', *Acta Romanica Szegediensis*, 7 (1982), 339–87.

Pereira, Jacques, *Montesquieu et la Chine* (Paris: L'Harmattan, 2008).

Perinetti, Dario, 'Philosophical Reflection on History', in Knud Haakonssen (ed.), *The Cambridge History of Eighteenth-Century Philosophy* (Cambridge: Cambridge University Press, 2006), 1107–40.

Pétré-Grenouilleau, Olivier, *Saint-Simon: L'utopie, ou La raison en actes* (Paris: Payot et Rivages, 2001).

Philonenko, Alexis, *Jean-Jacques Rousseau et la pensée du malheur* (Paris: Vrin, 1984).

Pickering, Mary, *Auguste Comte: An Intellectual Biography* (Cambridge: Cambridge University Press, 2006).

Picon, Antoine, *Les saint-simoniens: Raison, imaginaire et utopie* (Paris: Belin, 2002).

Piguet, Marie-France, 'Réduire en classes / être divisés en ordres: Les sources françaises du mot "classe" au 18eme siècle', *Mots*, 17 (1988), 43–69.

Piguet, Marie-France, *Classe: Histoire et genèse du concept des physiocrates aux historiens de la Restauration* (Lyons: Presses universitaires de Lyon, 1996).

Piguet, Marie-France, 'Quesnay, le langage et le "langage de la science économique"', *Histoire, épistémologie, langage*, 21 (1999), 123–47.

Piguet, Marie-France, 'A propos du rapport classe/peuple (1750–1830): Approche lexicale', *Cahiers pour l'analyse concrète*, 48 (2001), 13–31.

Piguet, Marie-France, '"Contre-révolution", "guerre civile", "lutte entre deux classes": Montlosier (1755–1838) penseur du conflit politique moderne', *Astérion: Philosophie, histoire des idées, pensée politique*, 6 (2009), 1–38.

Piguet, Marie-France, 'Noblesse *commerçante* / Nation *commerçante*: Genèse d'un adjectif', in Loïc Charles, Frédéric Lefebvre, and Christine Théré (eds.), *Le cercle de Vincent de Gournay: Savoirs économiques et pratiques administratives en France au milieu du XVIIIe siècle* (Paris: INED, 2011), 161–78.

Piguet, Marie-France, 'Les "Mémoires" de Montlosier: Ecriture de l'histoire, récit de soi et roman', in Olivier Ferret and Anne-Marie Mercier-Faivre (eds.), *Biographie et politique: Vie publique, vie privée de l'Ancien régime à la Restauration* (Lyons: Presses universitaires de Lyon, 2014), 199–214.

Pinna, Mario, *La teoria dei climi: Una falsa dottrina che non muta da Ippocrate a Hegel* (Rome: Società Geografica Italiana, 1988).

Piqué, Nicolas, *De la tradition à l'histoire: Éléments pour une généalogie du concept d'histoire à partir des controverses religieuses en France, 1669–1704* (Paris: Honoré Champion, 2009).

Piva, Franco, 'Crise du roman, roman de la crise: Aspects du roman français à la fin du XVIIe siècle', in Dipartimento di lingue e letterature straniere moderne dell'Università di Pavia (ed.), *Perspectives de la recherche sur le genre narratif français du XVIIe siècle* (Geneva: Slatkine, 2000), 281–303.

Platania, Marco, *Montesquieu e la virtù: Rappresentazioni della Francia di Ancien Régime e dei governi repubblicani* (Turin: UTET, 2007).

Plötner, Bärbel, 'Langue, littérature et identité nationales et régionales. Jacob Grimm entre l'Allemagne et la France: Le cas breton', in Michel Espagne and Michel Werner (eds.), *Philologiques 3: Qu'est-ce que c'est une littérature nationale?* (Paris: Éditions de la Maison des sciences de l'homme, 1994), 212–34.

Pocock, J. G. A., *Virtue, Commerce, and History: Essays on Political Thought and History* (Cambridge: Cambridge University Press, 1985).

Pocock, J. G. A., *Barbarism and Religion. Volume 1: The Enlightenments of Edward Gibbon, 1737–1764* (Cambridge: Cambridge University Press, 1999).

Pocock, J. G. A., *Barbarism and Religion. Volume 2: Narratives of Civil Government* (Cambridge: Cambridge University Press, 1999).

Pocock, J. G. A., 'Quentin Skinner: The History of Politics and the Politics of History', *Common Knowledge*, 10 (2004), 532–50.

Pocock, J. G. A., *Political Thought and History: Essays on Theory and Method* (Cambridge: Cambridge University Press, 2009).

Poirier, Jean-Pierre, *Turgot: Laissez-faire et progrès social* (Paris: le Grand livre du mois, 1999).

Poliakov, Léon, *Le mythe aryen: Essai sur les sources du racisme et des nationalismes* (Paris: Calmann-Lévy, 1971).

Polin, Raymond, 'Le sens de l'égalité et de l'inégalité chez J.-J. Rousseau', in Journées d'étude sur le Contrat social (eds.), *Études sur le Contrat social de Jean-Jacques Rousseau* (Paris: Les Belles lettres, 1964), 143–64.

Pomata, Gianna, 'Versions of Narrative: Overt and Covert Narrators in Nineteenth Century Historiography', *History Workshop*, 27 (1989), 1–17.

Pomeau, René, 'Voyages et Lumières dans la littérature française du dix-huitième siècle', *Studies on Voltaire and the Eighteenth Century*, 57 (1967), 1269–89.

Pomian, Krzysztof, *L'ordre du temps* (Paris: Gallimard, 1984).

Pomian, Krzysztof, 'Francs et Gaulois', in Nora (ed.), *Les lieux de mémoire*, ii. 2245–300.

Popkin, Richard H., *The High Road to Pyrrhonism* (San Diego: Austin Hill Press, 1980).

Postigliola, Alberto and Maria Grazia Bottaro Palumbo (eds.), *L'Europe de Montesquieu* (Naples: Liguori, 1995).

Potin, Yann and Aude Déruelle (eds.), *Augustin Thierry: L'histoire pour mémoire* (Rennes: Presses Universitaires de Rennes, 2018).

Poulat, Émile, *Liberté, laïcité: La guerre des deux France et le principe de la modernité* (Paris: Éditions du Cerf, 1987).

Poulet, Georges, *Les métamorphoses du cercle* (Paris: Plon, 1961).

Poulouin, Claudine, *Le temps des origines: L'Eden, le Déluge et 'les temps reculés' de Pascal à L'Encyclopédie* (Paris: Honoré Champion, 1998).

Poupardin, René, 'Bréquigny', in Poupardin (ed.), *Catalogue des manuscrits des collections Duchesne et Bréquigny* (Paris: Leroux, 1905), xxi–xxiv.

Pouthas, Charles H., *Guizot pendant la Restauration: Préparation de l'homme d'État (1814–1830)* (Paris: Plon-Nourrit, 1923).

Pribram, Karl, *A History of Economic Reasoning* (Baltimore: Johns Hopkins University Press, 1983).

Priest, Robert D., 'Ernest Renan's Race Problem', *The Historical Journal*, 58 (2015), 303–30.

Prochasson, Christophe, *Saint-Simon, ou L'anti-Marx* (Paris: Perrin, 2004).

Proietti, Fausto, *Il tema del comune nel dibattito politico francese (1807–1830)* (Florence: Centro editoriale toscano, 2002).

Quérard, Joseph-Marie, *La France littéraire ou Dictionnaire bibliographique des savants, historiens et gens de lettres de la France* (Paris: Firmin Didot père et fils, 1827–1839).

Quiviger, Pierre-Yves, *Le principe d'immanence: Métaphysique et droit administratif chez Sieyès* (Paris: Honoré Champion, 2008).

Quiviger, Pierre-Yves, Vincent Denis, and Jean Salem (eds.), *Figures de Sieyès* (Paris: Publications de la Sorbonne, 2008).

Racault, Jean-Michel, *Nulle part et ses environs: Voyage aux confins de l'utopie littéraire classique (1657–1802)* (Paris: Presses de l'Université de Paris-Sorbonne, 2003).

Radica, Gabrielle, 'Trois interprétations de la notion de "lois fondamentales" au XVIIIe siècle', in Moreau (ed.), *Les Lumières en mouvement*, 229–53.

Raedts, Peter, 'Representations of the Middle Ages in Enlightenment Historiography', *The Medieval History Journal*, 5 (2002), 1–20.

Rahe, Paul A., *Montesquieu and the Logic of Liberty: War, Religion, Commerce, Climate, Terrain, Technology, Uneasiness of Mind, the Spirit of Political Vigilance, and the Foundation of the Modern Republic* (New Haven: Yale University Press, 2009).

Rahe, Paul A., 'Was Montesquieu a Philosopher of History?', in Bianchi and Minuti (eds.), *Montesquieu et les philosophies de l'histoire au XVIIIe siècle*, 71–86.

Ranum, Orest, 'Courtesy, Absolutism, and the Rise of the French State, 1630–1660', *Journal of Modern History*, 52 (1980), 426–51.

Ranum, Orest, *Artisans of Glory: Writers and Historical Thought in Seventeenth-Century France* (Chapel Hill: University of North Caroline Press, 1980).

Raskolnikoff, Mouza, *Des anciens et des modernes* (Paris: Publications de la Sorbonne, 1990).

Raskolnikoff, Mouza, *Histoire romaine et critique historique dans l'Europe des Lumières* (Rome: École française de Rome, 1992).

Rasmussen, Dennis C., *The Pragmatic Enlightenment: Recovering the Liberalism of Hume, Smith, Montesquieu, and Voltaire* (Cambridge: Cambridge University Press, 2014).

Raynaud, Philippe, 'L'utopie scientifique et le projet systématique: De d'Alembert à Saint-Simon', in Musso (ed.), *Actualité du saint-simonisme*, 35–46.

Raynaud, Philippe, *La politesse des Lumières: Les lois, les mœurs, les manières* (Paris: Gallimard, 2013).

Rearick, Charles, *Beyond the Enlightenment: Historians and Folklore in Nineteenth Century France* (Bloomington: Indiana University Press, 1974).

Rechniewski, Elizabeth, 'References to "national character" in the *Encyclopédie*', *Studies on Voltaire and the Eighteenth Century*, 2003:12 (2003), 221–37.

Reese, Helen Reese, *La Mesnardière's Poëtique (1639): Sources and Dramatic Theories* (Baltimore: Johns Hopkins University Press, 1937).

Régnier, Philippe, 'Thierry et Saint-Simon: Micro-histoire d'une collaboration', in Potin and Déruelle (eds.), *Augustin Thierry*, 23–38.

Reizov, Boris G., *L'historiographie romantique française: 1815–1830* (Moscow: Éditions en langues étrangères, 1956).

Rémond, René, 'La fille aînée de l'Eglise', in Nora (ed.), *Les lieux de mémoire*, iii. 4321–51.

Remotti, Francesco, *L'ossessione identitaria* (Bari: Laterza, 2010).

Rétat, Laudyce, 'Les Gaulois et les substitutions d'origine dans la conscience historique de Renan', in Viallaneix and Erhard (eds.), *Nos ancêtres les Gaulois*, 339–45.

Rey, Alain, *Des pensées et des mots* (Paris: Hermann, 2013).

Riall, Lucy, 'Nation, "Deep Images" and the Problem of Emotions', *Nations and Nationalism*, 15 (2009), 402–9.

Ribard, Dinah, 'Livres, pouvoir et théorie: Comptabilité et noblesse en France à la fin du XVIIe siècle', *Revue de synthèse*, 128 (2007), 97–122.

Ribard, Dinah, 'Travail intellectuel et violence politique: Théoriser la noblesse à la fin du XVIIe siècle', in Vincent Azoulay and Patrick Boucheron (eds.), *Le mot qui tue: Une histoire des violences intellectuelles de l'antiquité à nos jours* (Seyssel: Champ Vallon, 2009), 353–68.

Richard de Ruffey, Gilles-Germain, *Histoire secrète de l'Académie de Dijon (de 1741 à 1770)* (Paris: Hachette, 1909).

Richter, Melvin, 'An Introduction to Montesquieu's "An Essay on the Causes that May Affect Men's Minds and Characters"', *Political Theory*, 4 (1976), 132–8.

Richter, Melvin, 'Montesquieu and the Concept of Civil Society', *The European Legacy*, 3 (1998), 33–41.

Ricœur, Paul, *La mémoire, l'histoire, l'oubli* (Paris: Seuil, 2000).

Rigney, Ann, 'Narrative Representation and National Identity: On the "Frenchness" of the Revolution', *Yearbook of European Studies*, 2 (1989), 53–69.

Rigney, Ann, *Imperfect Histories: The Elusive Past and the Legacy of Romantic Historicism* (Ithaca: Cornell University Press, 2001).

Rignol, Loïc, 'Augustin Thierry et la politique de l'histoire: Genèse et principes d'un système de pensée', *Revue d'histoire du XIXe siècle*, 25 (2002), 87–100.

Roberto, Umberto, 'Montesquieu, i germani e l'identità politica europea', in Felice (ed.), *Libertà, necessità e storia*, 277–322.

Roberts, Warren, *Morality and Social Class in Eighteenth-Century French Literature and Painting* (Toronto: University of Toronto Press, 1974).

Roche, Daniel, *La culture des apparences: Une histoire du vêtement, XVIIe–XVIIIe siècle* (Paris: Fayard, 1989).

Roche, Daniel, *Humeurs vagabondes: De la circulation des hommes et de l'utilité des voyages* (Paris: Fayard, 2003).

Rochette, Raoul, 'Fréret', in Michaud and Michaud (eds.), *Biographie universelle ancienne et moderne*, xvi. 28–37.

Rogister, John, 'Louis-Adrien Lepaige and the Attack on *De l'Esprit* and the *Encyclopédie* in 1759', *The English Historical Review*, 92 (1977), 522–39.

Rogister, John, *Louis XV and the 'Parlement' of Paris, 1737–1755* (Cambridge: Cambridge University Press, 1995).

Rogister, John, 'The Frankish Tradition and New Perceptions of the Monarchy: Louis XV – The New Pharamond?', *History and Anthropology*, 15 (2004), 207–17.

Romani, Roberto, *National Character and Public Spirit in Britain and France, 1750–1914* (Cambridge: Cambridge University Press, 2002).

Rosanvallon, Pierre, *Le capitalisme utopique: Critique de l'idéologie économique* (Paris: Seuil, 1979).

Rosanvallon, Pierre, *Le sacre du citoyen* (Paris: Gallimard, 1992).

Rosanvallon, Pierre, *Le peuple introuvable: Histoire de la représentation démocratique en France* (Paris: Gallimard, 1998).

Rosellini, Michèle, 'Écrire l'histoire de France au service de la patrie: Le projet singulier de Charles Sorel', *Dix-septième siècle*, 246 (2010), 69–95.

Roshwald, Aviel, *The Endurance of Nationalism: Ancient Roots and Modern Dilemmas* (Cambridge: Cambridge University Press, 2006).

Rossi, Giampiero, *Filosofia e storia in Anne Robert Jacques Turgot* (Bologna: Pendragon, 2009).

Rotta, Salvatore, *Il pensiero politico francese da Bayle a Montesquieu* (Pisa: Pacini, 1974).

Rotta, Salvatore, 'Quattro temi dell'*Esprit des lois*', *Miscellanea storica ligure*, 20 (1988), 1347–407.

Roux, Jean-Paul, *Le sang: Mythes, symboles et réalités* (Paris: Fayard, 1988).

Roza, Stéphanie, 'L'abbé de Mably, entre modérantisme et radicalité', *Tangence*, 106 (2014), 29–50.

Rubiés, Joan-Pau, 'Oriental Despotism and European Orientalism: Botero to Montesquieu', *Journal of Early Modern History*, 9 (2005), 109–80.

Rubiés, Joan-Pau, 'Race, Climate and Civilization in the Works of François Bernier', in Marie Fourcade and Ines G. Zupanov (eds.), *L'Inde des Lumières: Discours, histoire, savoirs (XVIIᵉ–XIXᵉ siècle)* (Paris: Purusartha, 2013), 13–38.

Rubinelli, Lucia, *Constituent Power: A History* (Cambridge: Cambridge University Press, 2020).

Rude, Fernand, 'Présentation', in Barnave, *Introduction à la Révolution française*, v–xvii.

Rustighi, Lorenzo, 'Pour une théologie politique du contemporain: La perspective de Boulainvilliers', *Dix-huitième siècle*, 48 (2016), 369–85.

Sahlins, Peter, *Boundaries: The Making of France and Spain in the Pyrenees* (Berkeley: University of California Press, 1989).

Sahlins, Peter, *Unnaturally French: Foreign Citizens in the Old Regime and After* (Ithaca: Cornell University Press, 2004).

Said, Edward, *Orientalism* (New York: Pantheon Books, 1978).

Saint-Victor, Jacques de, *Les racines de la liberté: Le débat français oublié, 1689–1789* (Paris: Perrin, 2007).

Sala-Molins, Louis, *Les misères des Lumières: Sous la raison, l'outrage* (Paris: R. Laffont, 1992).

Salaün, Franck, *L'ordre des mœurs: Essai sur la place du matérialisme dans la société française du XVIIIᵉ siècle (1734–1784)* (Paris: Éditions Kimé, 1996).

Salmon, J. H. M., 'Renaissance Jurists and "Enlightened" Magistrates: Perspectives on Feudalism in Eighteenth-Century France', *French History*, 8 (1994), 387–402.

Salvat, Christophe, 'De division of labour à division du travail: Histoire d'une notion, d'un syntagme et de sa diffusion en France', in Jacques Guilhaumou and Marie-France Piguet (eds.), *Dictionnaire des usages socio-politiques, 1770–1815* (Paris: Honoré Champion, 2003), vii. 39–64.

Samuel, Ana J., 'The Design of Montesquieu's *The Spirit of the Laws*: The Triumph of Freedom over Determinism', *American Political Science Review*, 103 (2009), 305–21.

Schaich, Michael, 'Introduction', in Schaich (ed.), *Monarchy and Religion: The Transformation of Royal Culture in Eighteenth-Century Europe* (Oxford: Oxford University Press, 2007), 1–11.

Schalk, Ellery, *From Valor to Pedigree: Ideas of Nobility in France in the Sixteenth and Seventeenth Centuries* (Princeton: Princeton University Press, 1986).

Schaub, Diana J., 'The Regime and Montesquieu's Principles of Education', in David W. Carrithers and Patrick Coleman (eds.), *Montesquieu and the Spirit of Modernity* (Oxford: Voltaire Foundation, 2002), 77–100.

Schemann, Ludwig, *Gobineaus Rassenwerk: Aktenstücke und Betrachtungen zur Geschichte und Kritik des* Essai sur l'inégalité des races humaines (Stuttgart: F. Frommann, 1910).

Schlanger, Judith, *L'enjeu et le débat: Les passés intellectuels* (Paris: Denoël-Gonthier, 1979).

Schlanger, Judith, *Les métaphores de l'organisme* (Paris: L'Harmattan, 1995).

Schleich, Thomas, *Aufklärung und Revolution: Die Wirkungsgeschichte Gabriel Bonnot de Mablys in Frankreich (1740–1914)* (Stuttgart: Klett-Cotta, 1981).

Schleich, Thomas, 'Presupposti, forme e conseguenze della risonanza politica di Mably nel periodo della Rivoluzione francese', *Rivista di storia della filosofia*, 39 (1984), 687–719.

Schumpeter, Joseph A., *History of Economic Analysis* (London: Allen & Unwin, 1954).

Schwarz, Robert M., 'Le paysan comme héro: Rousseau, Restif de la Bretonne et la représentation des vertus rustiques', in Jean-Jacques Clère, Françoise Fortunet, and Philippe Jobert (eds.), *Le bonheur est une idée neuve: Hommage à Jean Bart* (Dijon: Centre Georges Chevrier, 2000), 385–408.

Scuccimarra, Luca, *La sciabola di Sieyès: Le giornate di Brumaio e la genesi del regime bonapartista* (Bologna: il Mulino, 2002).

Scuccimarra, Luca, 'Généalogie de la nation: Sieyès comme fondateur de la communauté politique', *Revue française d'histoire des idées politiques*, 33 (2011), 27–45.

Seguin, Maria Susana, 'Boulainvilliers, de l'inédit au clandestin', *La lettre clandestine*, 11 (2002), 21–32.

Seippel, Paul, *Les deux Frances et leurs origines historiques* (Lausanne: Payot, 1905).

Senarclens, Vanessa de, *Montesquieu, historien de Rome: Un tournant pour la réflexion sur le statut de l'histoire au XVIIIᵉ siècle* (Geneva: Droz, 2003).

Senn, Henry, 'Folklore Beginnings in France: The Académie Celtique, 1804–1813', *Journal of the Folklore Institute*, 18 (1981), 23–33.

Serna, Pierre, 'Du noble radical à l'aristocrate tempéré, ou Le Comte de Montlosier et la naissance d'une famille de la droite française durant le Directoire', in Philippe Bourdin (ed.), *Les noblesses françaises dans l'Europe de la Révolution* (Rennes: Presses Universitaires de Rennes, 2010), 177–96.

Sewell, William H. Jr., *Work and Revolution in France: The Language of Labor from the Old Regime to 1848* (Cambridge: Cambridge University Press, 1980).

Sewell, William H. Jr., 'Le citoyen/la citoyenne: Activity, Passivity, and the Revolutionary Concept of Citizenship', in Colin Lucas (ed.), *The French Revolution and the Creation of Modern Political Culture, vol. II: The Political Culture of the French Revolution* (Oxford: Pergamon, 1988), 106–13.

Sewell, William H. Jr., *A Rhetoric of Bourgeois Revolution: The Abbé Sieyès and What is the Third Estate?* (Durham, NC: Duke University Press, 1994).

Shackleton, Robert, 'The Evolution of Montesquieu's Theory of Climate', *Revue internationale de philosophie*, 9 (1955), 317–29.

Shackleton, Robert, *Montesquieu: A Critical Biography* (Oxford: Oxford University Press, 1961).

Shafer, Boyd C., 'Bourgeois Nationalism in the Pamphlets on the Eve of the French Revolution', *The Journal of Modern History*, 10 (1938), 31–50.

Shennan, J. H., 'The Political Vocabulary of the Parlement of Paris in the Eighteenth Century', in Società italiana di storia del diritto (ed.), *Diritto e potere nella storia europea: Atti in onore di Bruno Paradisi* (Florence: Olschki, 1982), 951–64.

Shklar, Judith N., *Montesquieu* (Oxford: Oxford University Press, 1987).

Shovlin, John, 'The Cultural Politics of Luxury in Eighteenth-Century France', *French Historical Studies*, 23 (2000), 577–606.

Shovlin, John, *The Political Economy of Virtue: Luxury, Patriotism and the Origins of the French Revolution* (Ithaca: Cornell University Press, 2006).

Siedentop, Larry, 'Two Liberal Traditions', in Raf Geenens and Helena Rosenblatt (eds.), *French Liberalism from Montesquieu to the Present Day* (Cambridge: Cambridge University Press, 2012), 15–35.

Simon, Renée, *A la recherche d'un homme et d'un auteur: Essai de bibliographie des ouvrages du Comte de Boulainviller* (Paris: Boivin, 1941).

Simon, Renée, *Henry de Boulainviller: Historien, politique, philosophe, astrologue, 1658–1722* (Paris: Boivin, 1942).

Simon, Renée, *Un révolté du Grand siècle: Henry de Boulainviller* (Garche: Éditions du nouvel humanisme, 1948).

Simon, Renée, *Nicolas Fréret: Académicien* (Geneva: Institut et musée Voltaire, 1961).

Singer, Brian C. J., *Society, Theory, and the French Revolution: Studies in the Revolutionary Imaginary* (New York: St. Martin's Press, 1986).

Singer, Brian C. J., *Montesquieu and the Discovery of the Social* (Basingstoke: Palgrave Macmillan, 2013).

Skinner, Quentin, *Visions of Politics. 1: Regarding Method* (Cambridge: Cambridge University Press, 2002).

Skornicki, Arnault, *L'économiste, la cour et la patrie: L'économie politique dans la France des Lumières* (Paris: CNRS Éditions, 2011).

Slimani, Ahmed, *La modernité du concept de nation au XVIIIe siècle* (Aix-en-Provence: Presses universitaires d'Aix-Marseille, 2004).

Smeed, J.W., *The Theophrastan 'Character': The History of a Literary Genre* (Oxford: Clarendon Press, 1985).

Smith, Anthony D., *The Ethnic Origins of Nations* (Oxford: Blackwell, 1986).

Smith, Anthony D., *National Identity* (Reno: University of Nevada Press, 1991).

Smith, Anthony D., *Myths and Memories of the Nation* (Oxford: Oxford University Press, 1999).

Smith, Anthony D., *The Nation in History: Historiographical Debates about Ethnicity and Nationalism* (Cambridge: Polity Press, 2000).

Smith, Anthony D., *The Cultural Foundations of Nations: Hierarchy, Covenant and Republic* (Malden: Blackwell, 2008).

Smith, Anthony D., *Ethno-symbolism and Nationalism: A Cultural Approach* (London: Routledge, 2009).

Smith, Anthony D., *Nationalism: Theory, Ideology, History* (Cambridge: Polity Press, 2010).

Smith, Anthony D., *The Nation Made Real: Art and National Identity in Western Europe, 1600–1850* (Oxford: Oxford University Press, 2013).

Smith, Jay M., *The Culture of Merit: Nobility, Royal Service, and the Making of Absolute Monarchy in France: 1600–1789* (Ann Arbor: University of Michigan Press, 1996).

Smith, Jay M., 'Social Categories, the Language of Patriotism, and the Origins of the French Revolution: The Debate over *noblesse commerçante*', *The Journal of Modern History*, 72 (2000), 339–74.

Smith, Jay M., *Nobility Reimagined: The Patriotic Nation in Eighteenth-Century France* (Ithaca: Cornell University Press, 2005).

Smith, Justin E. H., *Nature, Human Nature, and Human Difference: Race in Early Modern Philosophy* (Princeton: Princeton University Press, 2015).

Smithson, Rulon N., *Augustin Thierry: Social and Political Consciousness in the Evolution of a Historical Method* (Geneva: Droz, 1973).

Société des Amis de Jacob Spon (eds.), *Camille Jullian, l'histoire de la Gaule et le nationalisme français* (Lyons: Presses Universitaires de Lyon, 1991).

Soll, Jacob, 'Healing the Body Politic: French Royal Doctors, History, and the Birth of a Nation. 1560–1634', *Renaissance Quarterly*, 55 (2002), 1259–86.

Soll, Jacob, 'Empirical History and the Transformation of Political Criticism in France from Bodin to Bayle', *Journal of the History of Ideas*, 64 (2003), 297–316.

Sommer, Antje and Werner Conze, 'Rasse', in Brunner, Conze, and Koselleck (eds.), *Geschichtliche Grundbegriffe*, v. 135–78.

Sommerer, Erwan, 'La "preuve par l'archive"? La place des manuscrits dans la pensée de Sieyès', *Recto/Verso*, 5 (2009), 1–11.

Sommerer, Erwan, 'Le contractualisme révolutionnaire de Sieyès: Formation de la nation et prédétermination du pouvoir constituant', *Revue française d'histoire des idées politiques*, 33 (2011), 5–25.

Sommerer, Erwan, *Sieyès, le révolutionnaire et le conservateur* (Paris: Michalon, 2011).

Sonenscher, Michael, *Work and Wages: Natural Law, Politics and the Eighteenth-Century French Trades* (Cambridge: Cambridge University Press, 1989).

Sonenscher, Michael, 'Physiocracy as Theodicy', *History of Political Thought*, 23 (2002), 326–39.

Sonenscher, Michael, 'Introduction', in Emmanuel-Joseph Sieyès, *Political Writings* (Indianapolis: Hackett, 2003), vii–lxiv.

Sonenscher, Michael, *Before the Deluge: Public Debt, Inequality and the Intellectual Origins of the French Revolution* (Princeton: Princeton University Press, 2007).

Sonenscher, Michael, *Sans-culottes: An Eighteenth-Century Emblem in the French Revolution* (Princeton: Princeton University Press, 2008).

Sorel, Georges and Édouard Berth, 'Lettres de Georges Sorel à Édouard Berth: Troisième partie, 1911–1917', *Cahiers Georges Sorel*, 5 (1987), 143–204.

Spavin, Richard, *Les climats du pouvoir: Rhétorique et politique chez Bodin, Montesquieu et Rousseau* (Oxford: Voltaire Foundation, 2018).

Spector, Céline, *Montesquieu, les 'Lettres persanes': De l'anthropologie à la politique* (Paris: Presses universitaires de France, 1997).

Spector, Céline, 'Montesquieu et l'histoire: Théorie et pratique de la modération', in Binoche and Tinland (eds.), *Sens du devenir et pensée de l'histoire au temps des Lumières*, 53–75.

Spector, Céline, *Le vocabulaire de Montesquieu* (Paris: Ellipses, 2001).

Spector, Céline, *Montesquieu: Pouvoirs, richesses et sociétés* (Paris: Presses universitaires de France, 2004).

Spector, Céline, 'Quelle justice? Quelle rationalité? La mesure du droit dans *L'Esprit des lois*', in Volpilhac-Auger (ed.), *Montesquieu en 2005*, 219–42.

Spector, Céline, '"Il faut éclairer l'histoire par les lois et les lois par l'histoire": Statut de la romanité et rationalité des coutumes dans l'*Esprit des lois* de Montesquieu', in Mikhail Xifaras (ed.), *Généalogie des savoirs juridiques: Le carrefour des Lumières* (Brussels: Bruylant, 2007), 15–41.

Spector, Céline, *Montesquieu: Liberté, droit et histoire* (Paris: Michalon, 2010).

Spector, Céline, 'Was Montesquieu Liberal? *The Spirit of the Laws* in the History of Liberalism', in Geenens and Rosenblatt (eds.), *French Liberalism from Montesquieu to the Present Day*, 57–72.

Spector, Céline, 'L'équivoque du concept de "mœurs": La lecture althussérienne de Montesquieu', in Francesco Toto, Laetitia Simonetta, and Giorgio Bottini (eds.), *Entre nature et histoire: Mœurs et coutumes dans la philosophie moderne* (Paris: Classiques Garnier, 2017), 191–203.

Spencer, Stephen, *Race and Ethnicity: Culture, Identity and Representation* (London: Routledge, 2006).

Spencer, Philip and Howard Wollman, 'Blood and Sacrifice: Politics versus Culture in the Construction of Nationalism', in Kevin J. Brehony and Naz Rassool (eds.), *Nationalisms Old and New* (Basingstoke: Macmillan Press, 1999), 87–124.

Spitz, Jean-Fabien, 'Droit et vertu chez Mably', *Corpus: Revue de philosophie*, 14–15 (1990), 61–95.

Starobinski, Jean, *L'œil vivant* (Paris: Gallimard, 1961).

Starobinski, Jean, 'Le mythe au XVIIIᵉ siècle', *Critique: Revue générale des publications français et étrangères*, 366 (1977), 975–97.

Starobinski, Jean, *Le remède dans le mal: Critique et légitimation de l'artifice à l'âge des Lumières* (Paris: Gallimard, 1989).

Starobinski, Jean, *Montesquieu* (Paris: Seuil, 1994).

Starobinski, Jean, *Jean-Jacques Rousseau: La transparence et l'obstacle suivi de Sept essais sur Rousseau* (Paris: Gallimard, 2003).

Staszak, Jean-François and Marie-Dominique Couzinet, ' À quoi sert la 'théorie des climats'? Éléments d'une histoire du déterminisme environnemental', *Corpus: Revue de philosophie*, 34 (1998), 9–43.

Stefanovska, Malina, *Saint-Simon, un historien dans les marges* (Paris: Honoré Champion, 1998).

Stoler, Ann Laura, *Race and the Education of Desire: Foucault's History of Sexuality and the Colonial Order of Things* (Durham, NC: Duke University Press, 1995).

Strenski, Ivan, *Contesting Sacrifice: Religion, Nationalism, and Social Thought in France* (Chicago: University of Chicago Press, 2002).

Stuurman, Siep, 'Productive Virtue: The Language of Citizenship and the Idea of Industrial Civilization', *The European Legacy*, 1 (1996), 329–35.

Stuurman, Siep, 'François Bernier and the Invention of Racial Classification', *History Workshop Journal*, 50 (2000), 1–21.

Su Rasmussen, Kim, 'Foucault's Genealogy of Racism', *Theory, Culture and Society*, 28 (2011), 34–51.

Sullivan, Vickie B., *Montesquieu and the Despotic Ideas of Europe: An interpretation of* The Spirit of the Laws (Chicago: University of Chicago Press, 2017).

Sutcliffe, Frank E., 'The Abbé Coyer and the Chevalier d'Arc', *Bulletin of the John Rylands Library*, 65 (1982), 235–45.

Swann, Julian, *Politics and the Parlement of Paris under Louis XV, 1754–1774* (Cambridge: Cambridge University Press, 1995).

Swann, Julian, 'Repenser les parlements au XVIIIᵉ siècle: Du concept de "l'opposition parlementaire" à celui de "culture juridique des conflits politiques"', in Lemaître (ed.), *Le monde parlementaire au XVIIIᵉ siècle*, 17–38.

Swedberg, Richard, 'Auguste Rodin's *The Burghers of Calais*: The Career of a Sculpture and its Appeal to Civic Heroism', *Theory, Culture and Society*, 22 (2005), 45–67.

Tadié, Alexis (ed.), *Theories of Quarrels*, special issue of *Paragraph*, 40 (2017).

Taine, Hippolyte, *L'Ancien régime* (Paris: Éditions Complexe, 1991).

Tatin-Gourier, Jean-Jacques, 'Les recherches de Fréret sur l'origine de la nation française', in Grell and Volpilhac-Auger (eds.), *Nicolas Fréret*, 73–87.

Teysseire, Daniel, 'De l'usage historico-politique de *race* entre 1680 et 1820 et de sa transformation', *Mots*, 33 (1992), 43–52.

Theis, Laurent, 'François Guizot, un protestant très politique', *Bulletin de la Société de l'histoire du protestantisme français*, 155 (October–November 2009), 831–40.

Theis, Laurent, *Guizot: La traversée d'un siècle* (Paris: CNRS Éditions, 2014).

Théré, Christine and Loïc Charles, 'The Writing Workshop of François Quesnay and the Making of Physiocracy', *History of Political Economy*, 40 (2008), 1–42.

Thiéry, Robert (ed.), *Jean-Jacques Rousseau, politique et nation* (Paris: Honoré Champion, 2001).

Thiesse, Anne-Marie, *La création des identités nationales: Europe XVIIIᵉ–XXᵉ siècle* (Paris: Seuil, 1999).

Thiesse, Anne-Marie, 'Modernising the Past: The Life of the Gauls under the French Republic', in Lotte Jensen, Joep Leerssen, and Marita Mathijsen (eds.), *Free Access to the Past: Romanticism, Cultural Heritage and the Nation* (Leiden: Brill, 2010), 41–51.

Tholozan, Olivier, *Henri de Boulainvilliers: L'anti-absolutisme aristocratique légitimé par l'histoire* (Aix-en Provence: Presses universitaires d'Aix-Marseille, 1999).

Thom, Martin, *Republics, Nations and Tribes* (London: Verso, 1995).

Thomson, Ann, 'Issues at Stake in Eighteenth-Century Racial Classification', *Cromohs*, 8 (2003), 1–20.

Thuillier, Guy, 'La réforme de l'administration selon le Marquis d'Argenson', *La revue administrative*, 44 (1991), 213–23.

Todorov, Tzvetan, *Nous et les autres: La réflexion française sur la diversité humaine* (Paris: Seuil, 1989).

Todorov, Tzvetan, *Les morales de l'histoire* (Paris: Grasset, 1991).

Tombs, Robert, 'Thiers historien', *Cahiers de l'Association internationale des études françaises*, 47 (1995), 265–81.

Trevor-Roper, Hugh, *History and the Enlightenment* (New Haven: Yale University Press, 2010).

Tuccari, Francesco, *La nazione* (Rome: Laterza, 2000).

Tyvaert, Michel, 'L'image du roi: Légitimité et moralité royales dans les histoires de France au XVIIᵉ siècle', *Revue d'histoire moderne et contemporaine*, 21 (1974), 521–46.

Valade, Bernard, *Introduction aux sciences sociales* (Paris: Presses universitaires de France, 1996).

Valance, Georges, *Thiers: Bourgeois et révolutionnaire* (Paris: Flammarion, 2007).

Valensise, Marina, 'Le sacre du roi: Stratégie symbolique et doctrine politique de la monarchie française', *Annales: Histoire, sciences sociales*, 41 (1986), 543–77.

Valensise, Marina (ed.), *François Guizot et la culture politique de son temps* (Paris: Gallimard, 1991).

Van Delft, Louis, *Littérature et anthropologie: Nature humaine et caractère à l'âge classique* (Paris: Presses universitaires de France, 1993).

Van Deusen, Glyndon, *Sieyes: His Life and his Nationalism* (New York: Columbia University Press, 1932).

Van Gennep, Arnold, *Textes inédits sur le folklore français contemporain* (Paris: Maisonneuve et Larose, 1975).

Van Kley, Dale K., 'New Wine in Old Wineskins: Continuity and Rupture in the Pamphlet Debate of the French Prerevolution, 1787–1789', *French Historical Studies*, 17 (1991), 447–65.

Van Kley, Dale K., *The Religious Origins of the French Revolution: From Calvin to the Civil Constitution, 1560–1791* (New Haven: Yale University Press, 1996).

Van Hal, Toon, 'Sprachen, die Geschichte schreiben: Zu Leibniz' sprachhistorischem Forschungsprogramm und dessen Nachwirkung', in Wenchao Li (ed.), *Einheit der Vernunft und Vielfalt der Sprachen – Beiträge zu Leibnizens Sprachforschung und Zeichentheorie* (Stuttgart: Franz Steiner Verlag, 2014), 177–206.

Vardi, Liana, *The Physiocrats and the World of the Enlightenment* (Cambridge: Cambridge University Press, 2012).

Venturi, Franco, *Jean Jaurès e altri storici della Rivoluzione francese* (Turin: G. Einaudi, 1948).

Venturino, Diego, 'Metodologia della ricerca e determinismo astrologico nella concezione storica di Henry de Boulainvilliers', *Rivista storica italiana*, 95 (1983), 389–418.

Venturino, Diego, 'Feudalismo e monarchia nel pensiero di Henri de Boulainvilliers', *Annali della fondazione Luigi Einaudi*, 18 (1984), 215–41.

Venturino, Diego, 'Parlement e génie nel linguaggio storico di Henry de Boulainvilliers', in Caterina Cicala (ed.), *Lo storico e il suo lessico* (Naples: Società degli Storici Italiani, 1985), 85–92.

Venturino, Diego, 'Un prophète "philosophe"? Une *Vie de Mahomet* à l'aube des Lumières', *Dix-huitième siècle*, 24 (1992), 321–31.

Venturino, Diego, *Le ragioni della tradizione: Nobiltà e mondo moderno in Boulainvilliers (1658–1722)* (Turin: Le lettere, 1993).

Venturino, Diego, 'Boulainvilliers et Montesquieu, ou De la modération nobiliaire', in Postigliola and Bottaro Palumbo (eds.), *L'Europe de Montesquieu*, 103–12.

Venturino, Diego, 'Histoire et politique: Quelques réflexions autour de l'*Histoire du Parlement de Paris*', in Ulla Kölving and Christiane Mervaud (eds.), *Voltaire et ses combats* (Oxford: Voltaire Foundation, 1997), ii. 1371–8.

Venturino, Diego, 'Race et histoire: Le paradigme nobiliaire de la distinction sociale au début du XVIIIe siècle', in Moussa (ed.), *L'idée de race dans les sciences humaines et la littérature*, 19–38.

Venturino, Diego, 'Ni dieu ni roi: Avatars de l'honneur dans la France moderne', in Drévillon and Venturino (eds.), *Penser et vivre l'honneur à l'époque moderne*, 91–107.

Vergne, Arnaud, *La notion de constitution d'après les cours et assemblées à la fin de l'Ancien régime, 1750–1789* (Paris: De Boccard, 2006).

Verjus, Anne, 'Du patriarchalisme au paternalisme: Les modèles familiaux de l'autorité politique dans les républiques de France et d'Amérique', in Pierre Serna (ed.), *Républiques sœurs: Le Directoire et la révolution atlantique* (Rennes: Presses universitaires de Rennes, 2009), 35–51.

Vernière, Paul, *Spinoza et la pensée française avant la Révolution* (Paris: Presses universitaires de France, 1954).

Vetter, Cesare, 'Révolution française: Evidences lexicologiques, évidences lexicométriques et interprétations historiographiques', in Cesare Vetter and Marco Marin (eds.), *La felicità è un'idea nuova in Europa: Contributo al lessico della Rivoluzione francese* (Trieste: EUT, 2005–2013), ii. 13–33.

Veuillot, Louis, *Paris pendant les deux sièges* (Paris: Librairie de Victor Palme, 1878).

Viallaneix, Paul and Jean Erhard (eds.), *Nos ancêtres les Gaulois* (Clermont-Ferrand: Publications de la Faculté des lettres de Clermont II, 1982).

Viselli, Santé A., '*Les Soupirs de la France esclave* (1689) et la pensée pré-révolutionnaire', *Romance Quarterly*, 37 (1990), 279–92.

Vivanti, Corrado, 'Les *Recherches de la France* d'Étienne Pasquier: L'invention des Gaulois', in Nora (ed.), *Les lieux de mémoire*, i. 759–86.

Viola, Paolo, *Il trono vuoto: La transizione della sovranità nella Rivoluzione francese* (Turin: Einaudi, 1989).

Voegelin, Eric, *From Enlightenment to Revolution* (Durham, NC: Duke University Press, 1975).

Volpilhac, Catherine, 'Les Gaulois à l'Académie des inscriptions et belles-lettres de 1701 à 1793', in Viallaneix and Erhard (eds.), *Nos ancêtres les Gaulois*, 77–83.

Volpilhac-Auger, Catherine, *Tacite et Montesquieu* (Oxford: Voltaire Foundation, 1985).

Volpilhac-Auger, Catherine, *Tacite en France de Montesquieu à Chateaubriand* (Oxford: Voltaire Foundation, 1993).

Volpilhac-Auger, Catherine, '*Mon siège est fait*, ou La méthode historique de l'abbé de Vertot', *Cromohs*, 2 (1997), 1–14.

Volpilhac-Auger, Catherine, 'La dissertation *Sur la différence des génies*: Essai de reconstitution', *Revue Montesquieu*, 4 (2000), 226–37.

Volpilhac-Auger, Catherine (ed.), *Montesquieu: Mémoire de la critique* (Paris: Presses de l'Université de Paris-Sorbonne, 2003).

Volpilhac-Auger, Catherine (ed.), *Montesquieu en 2005* (Oxford: Voltaire Foundation, 2005).

Vovelle, Michel and Daniel Roche, 'Bourgeois, rentiers, propriétaires: Éléments pour la définition d'une catégorie sociale à la fin du XVIIIe siècle', *Actes du 77e congrès des sociétés savantes*, 84 (1959), 419–52.

Vyverberg, Henry, *Human Nature, Cultural Diversity, and the French Enlightenment* (Oxford: Oxford University Press, 1989).

Wade, Ira O., *The Clandestine Organization and Diffusion of Philosophic Ideas in France* (Princeton: Princeton University Press, 1938).

Wade, Ira O., *The Intellectual Development of Voltaire* (Princeton: Princeton University Press, 1969).

Wade, Ira O., *The Structure and Form of the French Enlightenment* (Princeton: Princeton University Press, 1977).

Walch, Jean, 'Romantisme et positivisme: Une rupture épistémologique dans l'historiographie?', *Romantisme*, 8 (1978), 161–72.

Walch, Jean, *Les maîtres de l'histoire: 1815–1850* (Geneva: Honoré Champion, 1986).

Walckenaer, Charles-Athanase, *Rapport à l'Académie des inscriptions et belles-lettres au sujet des manuscrits inédits de Fréret* (Paris: Imprimerie nationale, 1850).

Wallerstein, Immanuel, 'Citizens All? Citizens Some! The Making of the Citizen', *Comparative Studies in Society and History*, 45 (2003), 650–79.

Weber, Eugen, *Peasants into Frenchmen: The Modernization of Rural France, 1870–1914* (Stanford: Stanford University Press, 1976).

Weber, Eugen, *My France: Politics, Culture, Myth* (Cambridge, Mass: Harvard University Press, 1991).

Weil, Françoise, 'Les *Lettres aux économistes sur leur système de politique et de morale*: Présentation du manuscrit', in Sieyès, *Des manuscrits de Sieyès*, i. 169–70.

Weiss, Charles, 'Legendre', in Michaud and Michaud (eds.), *Biographie universelle ancienne et moderne*, xxiii. 558–9.

Weiss, Charles, 'Millot', in Michaud and Michaud (eds.), *Biographie universelle ancienne et moderne*, xxix. 50–3.

Weiss, Charles, 'Tournemine', in Michaud and Michaud (eds.), *Biographie universelle ancienne et moderne*, xlvi. 369–71.

Welch, Ellen R., *A Taste for the Foreign: Worldly Knowledge and Literary Pleasure in Early Modern French Fiction* (Newark: University of Delaware Press, 2011).

Weulersse, Georges, *Le mouvement physiocratique en France (de 1756 à 1770)* (Paris: Alcan, 1910).

Weulersse, Georges, *La physiocratie à l'aube de la Révolution: 1781–1792* (Paris: EHESS, 1985).

Whatmore, Richard, 'The Political Economy of Jean-Baptiste Say's Republicanism', *History of Political Thought*, 19 (1998), 439–56.

Whatmore, Richard, *Republicanism and the French Revolution: An Intellectual History of Jean-Baptiste Say's Political Economy* (Oxford: Oxford University Press, 2000).

Whelan, Ruth, *The Anatomy of Superstition: A Study of the Historical Theory and Practice of Pierre Bayle* (Oxford: Oxford Foundation, 1989).

White, Hayden, *The Content of the Form: Narrative Discourse and Historical Representation* (Baltimore: Johns Hopkins University Press, 1990).

Wick, Daniel L., *A Conspiracy of Well-Intentioned Men: The Society of Thirty and the French Revolution* (New York: Garland, 1987).

Willaime, Jean-Paul, 'De la sacralisation de la France: *Lieux de mémoire* et imaginaire national', *Archives des sciences sociales des religions*, 66 (1988), 125–45.

Wokler, Robert, 'Anthropology and Conjectural History in the Enlightenment', in Fox, Porter, and Wokler (eds.), *Inventing Human Science*, 31–52.

Wolff, Larry and Marco Cipolloni (eds.), *The Anthropology of the Enlightenment* (Stanford: Stanford University Press, 2007).

Wolfzettel, Friedrich, *Le discours du voyageur: Pour une histoire littéraire du récit de voyage en France, du Moyen Age au XVIIIe siècle* (Paris: Presses universitaires de France, 1996).

Wood, Ian, *The Modern Origins of the Early Middle Ages* (Oxford: Oxford University Press, 2013).

Wright, Johnson K., *A Classical Republican in Eighteenth-Century France: The Political Thought of Mably* (Stanford: Stanford University Press, 1997).

Wright, Johnson K., 'The Idea of a Republican Constitution in Old Régime France', in Martin van Gelderen and Quentin Skinner (eds.), *Republicanism: A Shared European Heritage* (Cambridge: Cambridge University Press, 2002), i. 289–306.

Wyngaard, Amy S., *From Savage to Citizen: The Invention of the Peasant in the French Enlightenment* (Newark: University of Delaware Press, 2004).

Yacine, Jean-Luc, *La question sociale chez Saint-Simon* (Paris: L'Harmattan, 2002).

Yardeni, Myriam, *Enquêtes sur l'identité de la 'nation France': De la Renaissance aux Lumières* (Seyssel: Champ Vallon, 2005).

Yvernault, Virginie, 'La trilogie, une œuvre révolutionnaire?', in Sophie Lefay (ed.), *Nouveaux regards sur la trilogie de Beaumarchais* (Paris: Garnier, 2015), 25–37.

Zaccone Sina, Maria G., 'L'interpretazione della *Genesi* in Henry de Boulainvilliers. Fonti: Jean Le Clerc e Thomas Burnet', *Rivista di filosofia neo-scolastica*, 72 (1980), 494–532.

Zanola, Maria Teresa, *Arts et métiers au XVIIIe siècle: Études de terminologie diachronique* (Paris: L'Harmattan, 2014).

Zapperi, Roberto, 'Introduction', in Emmanuel-Joseph Sieyès, *Qu'est-ce que le tiers état?* (Geneva: Droz, 1970), 7–117.

Zapperi, Roberto, *Per la critica del concetto di rivoluzione borghese* (Bari: De Donato, 1974).

Zeldin, Theodore, 'Introduction: Were There Two Frances?', in Zeldin (ed.), *Conflicts in French Society: Anticlericalism, Education and Morals in the Nineteenth Century* (London: Allen & Unwin, 1970), 9–11.

Zoberman, Pierre, 'Représentation de l'homme, représentation du roi', in Gilles Declercq and Michèle Rosellini (eds.), *Jean Racine: 1699–1999* (Paris: Presses universitaires de France, 2003), 211–29.

Index